NANCY M. HOLLOWAY, RN, MSN, CCRN, CEN

Michelle Williams

Michelle Williams

MEDICAL SURGICAL CARE PLANS

NANCY M. HOLLOWAY, RN, MSN, CCRN, CEN

Springhouse Corporation
Springhouse, Pennsylvania

Staff For This Volume

CLINICAL STAFF

Clinical Director
Barbara McVan, RN

Clinical Editor
Diane Schweisguth, RN, BSN, CCRN, CEN

Consulting Editor
Ruth E. Malone, RN, CEN
Staff Nurse, Emergency Department
Children's Hospital Medical Center
Oakland, Calif.

Consultant
Patricia C. Hanson, RN
President
Healthcare Management Services
Eagan, Minn.

Consultant
Diane Sadler Benson, RN, MEd, MS
Nurse Specialist/Educator in Private Practice
Eureka, Calif.

PUBLICATION STAFF

Executive Director, Editorial
Stanley Loeb

Executive Director, Creative Services
Jean Robinson

Design
John Hubbard (art director), Stephanie Peters (associate art director), Elaine K. Ezrow

Editing
Susan L. Taddei (senior acquisitions editor), Diana Potter, David Prout

Copy Editing
David Moreau (manager), Edith McMahon (supervisor), Nick Anastasio, Keith de Pinho, Diane Labus, Doris Weinstock, Debra Young

Art Production
Robert Perry (manager), Mark Marcin, Loretta Caruso, Anna Brindisi, Donald Knauss, Robert Wieder, Christina McKinley

Typography
David Kosten (manager), Diane Paluba (assistant manager), Nancy Wirs, Brenda Mayer, Joyce Rossi Biletz, Robin Rantz

Manufacturing
Deborah Meiris (manager), T.A. Landis

Project Coordination
Aline S. Miller (supervisor), Bernadette M. Glenn, Elizabeth B. Kiselev

Authorization to photocopy items for internal or personal use, or the internal or personal use of specific clients, is granted by Springhouse Corporation for users registered with the Copyright Clearance Center (CCC) Transactional Reporting Service, provided that the base fee of $00.00 per copy, plus $.75 per page, is paid directly to CCC, 27 Congress St., Salem, Mass. 01970. For those organizations that have been granted a photocopy license by CCC, a separate system of payment has been arranged. The fee code for users of the Transactional Reporting Service is 0874341280/88 $00.00 + $.75.

© 1988 by Springhouse Corporation. All rights reserved. No part of this book may be used or reproduced in any manner whatsoever without written permission except for brief quotations embodied in critical articles and reviews. Printed in the United States of America. For information write Springhouse Corporation, 1111 Bethlehem Pike, Springhouse, Pa. 19477.

MSURG-010488

Library of Congress Cataloging-in-Publication Data
Holloway, Nancy Meyer, 1947-
   Medical/surgical care plans. Nancy M. Holloway.
    p. cm.
   Includes bibliographies and indexes.
   ISBN 0-87434-128-0
   1. Nursing care plans.   2. Nursing.
  3. Surgical nursing.
  4. Diagnosis related groups.   I. Title.
  [DNLM: 1. Diagnostic Related Groups.
  2. Nursing Assessment.
  3. Patient Care Planning.   WY 100 H745m]
RT49.H64 1988
610.73—dc19
DNLM/DLC
for Library of Congress   88-1118
                                  CIP

Contents

Contributors and Consultants

CONSULTING EDITOR

Ruth E. Malone, RN, CEN
Staff Nurse, Emergency Department
Children's Hospital Medical Center
Oakland, Calif.

Contributors

Ruth Brewer, RN, MN, PhD
Professor of Nursing
McNeese State University
College of Nursing
Lake Charles, La.
(Inflammatory Bowel Disease)

Suzanne Clark, RN, MA, MSN
Project Coordinator, Psychosocial
Aspects of Cancer
Neuropsychiatric Institute, Jonsson
Cancer Center
University of California, Los Angeles
(Ineffective Individual Coping, Congestive
Heart Failure)

John M. Clochesy, RN, CS, MS
Clinical Nurse Specialist
Veterans Administration Medical Center
Los Angeles
(Myasthenia Gravis)

Beth Colvin, RNC, MSN
Gynecologic Oncology
Clinical Nurse Specialist
Vanderbilt University Medical Center
Nashville, Tenn.
(Radioactive Implant for Cervical Cancer)

Michelle J. Conant, RN, CS, MSN
Psychiatric Nursing Program Manager
Somerset Medical Center
Somerville, N.J.
(Anorexia Nervosa and Bulimia)

Kathleen A. Dobkin, RN, ET, BSN
Enterostomal Therapy Coordinator
Emory Clinic and Egleston Hospital
Atlanta
(Ileal Conduit Urinary Diversion)

Dorothy B. Doughty, RN, ET, MN
Program Director, Enterostomal Therapy
Nursing Education Program
Emory University
Atlanta
(Colostomy)

**Phyllis R. Easterling, RN, MS,
EdD Candidate**
Department Chairperson,
Medical-Surgical Nursing
Samuel Merritt College of Nursing
Oakland, Calif.
(Retinal Detachment, Skin Grafts,
Urolithiasis)

Mary Gray, RN, RNP, BSN, MNSc
Associate Professor, College of Nursing
Baccalaureate and Graduate Programs
Clinical Nurse Specialist, Medical Nursing
Coordinator for Nursing Practice Standards
University of Arkansas for Medical Sciences
Little Rock, Ark.
(Low Back Pain—Conservative Medical
Management, Total Joint Replacement in
the Lower Extremity)

Patricia C. Hanson, RN
President
Healthcare Management Services
Eagan, Minn.
(Delivering Quality Care in a Cost-
Conscious Environment, DRG
Information, Nursing Discharge Criteria)

Barbara S. Henzel, RN, CGC, BSN
Clinical Nurse Supervisor,
GI Endoscopy Suite
Hospital of the University of Pennsylvania
Philadelphia
(Esophagitis and Gastroenteritis)

Patricia A. Hinton-Walker, RN, PhD
Associate Dean and Professor
Emory University, Nell Hodgson Woodruff
School of Nursing
Atlanta
(Knowledge Deficit, Pain)

Lauren Marie Isacson, RNC
Inservice Instructor
Jersey Shore Medical Center
Neptune, N.J.
(Peritoneal Dialysis)

Larry E. Lancaster, RN, MSN, EdD
Associate Professor and Chairman,
Department of Adult Health
Vanderbilt University, School of Nursing
Nashville, Tenn.
(Chronic Renal Failure)

**Claudia Beverly Leath, RN, RNP,
MSN**
Associate Professor
University of Arkansas for Medical
Sciences, College of Nursing
Little Rock, Ark.
(Low Back Pain—Conservative Medical
Management, Total Joint Replacement in
the Lower Extremity)

Jean Lertola, RN, C, MA
Assistant Professor
Castleton State College
Castleton, Vt.
(Acute Myocardial Infarction)

Ruth E. Malone, RN, CEN
Staff Nurse, Emergency Department
Children's Hospital Medical Center
Oakland, Calif.
(Acquired Immune Deficiency Syndrome,
Cerebrovascular Accident, Death and
Dying, Diabetes Mellitus, Fluid and
Electrolyte Imbalances, Fractured Femur,
Grief/Grieving)

Barbara J. Martin, RN, MS
Unit Leader
Rush–Presbyterian–St. Luke's
Medical Center
Chicago
(Permanent Pacemaker Insertion)

Celestine B. Mason, RN, BSN, MA
Associate Professor
Pacific Lutheran University
Tacoma, Wash.
(Alzheimer's Disease, Multiple Sclerosis,
Thrombophlebitis)

Jean Eiko Masunaga, RN, MS
Nursing Supervisor, Emergency
Department
Kaiser Permanente Medical Center
Hayward, Calif.
(Hysterectomy)

Ellen J. Moir, RN, BSN, MSN
Practitioner-Teacher, Operating Room
and Surgical Nursing
Rush University College of Nursing
Chicago
(Cholecystectomy, Surgical Intervention)

Molly J. Moran, RN, OCN, MS
Hematology Clinical Nurse Specialist
The Ohio State University Hospitals
Columbus, Ohio
(Anemia, Total Parenteral Nutrition)

Scarlott K. Mueller, RN, BSN, MPH
Head Nurse, Oncology Research Unit
Clinical Associate–School of Nursing
Duke University Medical Center
Durham, N.C.
(Grief/Grieving, Prostatectomy)

Elizabeth Poulson, RN, MA, MS
Practitioner-Teacher
Rush–Presbyterian–St. Luke's
Medical Center
Chicago
(Permanent Pacemaker Insertion)

Carla Powell, RN, CNSN
Coordinator, Nutrition Support Service
The Ohio State University Hospitals
Columbus, Ohio
(Total Parenteral Nutrition)

**Katherine Purgatorio-Howard, RN,
MSN**
Instructor of Nursing
Ann May School of Nursing
Jersey Shore Medical Center
Neptune, N.J.
(Angina Pectoris, Leukemia)

Julia D. Quiring, RN, PhD
Graduate Program Director
Rush University
Chicago
(Geriatric Considerations)

Ellene Rifas, RN, MSN, EdD
Director, Department of Education
American River Hospital
Carmichael, Calif.
(Asthma, Chronic Obstructive Pulmonary
Disease, Pneumonia)

Dennis Ross, RN, CNOR, MAE, MSN
Associate Professor of Nursing
Castleton State College
Castleton, Vt.
(Osteomyelitis)

Cecilia E. Shaw, RN, COCN, BSN
Oncology Clinical Instructor
St. Francis Hospital
Tulsa, Okla.
(Lymphoma)

Suzy Temple, RN, MSN
Assistant Professor
Mississippi College School of Nursing
Clinton, Miss.
(Lung Cancer)

M. Susan Theodoropoulos, RN, MSN
Assistant Professor
University of Tennessee at Knoxville
College of Nursing
(Amputation)

Charlene Thomas, RN, MSN
Practitioner-Teacher
Rush–Presbyterian–St. Luke's
Medical Center
Chicago
(Permanent Pacemaker Insertion)

Barbara Tueller, RN, CCRN, MS
Faculty, Department of Medical-Surgical
Nursing
Samuel Merritt College of Nursing
Oakland, Calif.
(Acquired Immune Deficiency Syndrome)

Susan A. Van De Velde-Coke, RN, MA, MBA
Director of Nursing, Medical/Surgical
Health Sciences Centre
Department of Nursing
Winnipeg, Manitoba, Canada
(Duodenal Ulcer)

Patricia Harvey Webb, RN, MS
Assistant Professor
Department of Medical-Surgical Nursing
Samuel Merritt College of Nursing
Oakland, Calif.
(Fluid and Electrolyte Imbalances,
Laminectomy, Glaucoma)

Alice Whittaker, RN, CCRN, MS
Director, Nursing Planning
University Medical Center
Tucson, Ariz.
(Ineffective Family Coping)

Patricia R. Wilson, RN, BSN
Graduate Teaching Assistant
University of South Carolina/Richmond
Memorial Hospital
College of Nursing
Columbia, S.C.
(Radical Neck Dissection)

Consultants

Diane Sadler Benson, RN, MEd, MS
Nurse Specialist/Educator
In Private Practice
Eureka, Calif.

Marion B. Dolan, RN
President, C.E.O.
Heritage Home Health
Bristol, N.H.

David Greenberg, RN, BSc
Clinical Coordinator
Immunology Clinic
Peralta Hospital
Oakland, Calif.

Lola Kallman, RN
Nursing Coordinator
Eating Disorders Unit
Eden Hospital
Castro Valley, Calif.

Acknowledgments

Publishing a book is never a sole creative endeavor; many individuals contributed to this book's final version. Special recognition is given to the following professionals:

Ruth Malone, consulting editor and contributor, whose ability to share the vision was a source of delight and inspiration for me and a joy for us both.

Camden Rutter, administrative assistant, whose skill at manuscript preparation and organization contributed immeasurably to smooth, efficient project management.

Diane Benson, clinical reviewer, who supported the idea for this book from its beginning and whose perceptive questions strengthened the manuscript content.

Special appreciation is extended to Susan Taddei, senior acquisitions editor at Springhouse Publishing Company. Her creative input to this book's genesis, unflagging enthusiasm for our mission, and valuable editorial guidance during this arduous undertaking were critical to its success.

Dedication
This book is dedicated to Michael and Jason Holloway, for their love and support, and to the memory of my brother, Carl Hans Meyer.

Preface

This book is essential. Why? Because it integrates three major trends in nursing: care planning, nursing diagnosis, and diagnosis-related groups (DRGs). The purpose of this book is to provide an organized and comprehensive—yet concise—data bank for the clinical nurse to use daily in planning quality, "hands-on" nursing care.

Focusing on the adult medical-surgical inpatient, this book for the first time:

• distinguishes clearly between nursing's collaborative functions (those shared with medicine) and its independent functions (those uniquely nursing's)
• offers the less-experienced bedside nurse, nursing student, and nursing educator comprehensive, realistic clinical plans
• offers the experienced bedside nurse condensed plans concise enough to be used easily in today's hectic, cost-conscious practice environment.

Key Features
• 74 clinical care plans covering a wide variety of medical-surgical conditions organized by body system, principal medical diagnosis, and general conditions nurses encounter daily
• care plans developed by 43 clinical experts throughout North America
• nursing discharge criteria developed by a nationally recognized expert in discharge planning
• the latest clinically relevant information on DRGs
• common assessment findings organized according to Gordon's Functional Health Patterns and by body systems
• patient problems, including both collaborative problems (areas of responsibility shared with medicine) and nursing diagnoses (areas of independent nursing responsibility)—a dual focus, unique among care-planning books, providing a complete picture of patient care
• plans blending standardized and individualized aspects of care
• use of North American Nursing Diagnosis Association (NANDA) terminology in labeling nursing diagnoses
• goal-directed, action-oriented approach to planning care
• problems and interventions ranked according to priority
• specific outcome criteria identified
• discharge teaching and documentation checklists
• an emphasis on providing quality care in the age of cost containment.

Under the DRG system, the nurse can have the greatest impact on maintaining quality care while reducing health care costs for those patients who have the most common diagnoses, the longest mean length of stay, or the greatest likelihood of exceeding the average length of stay. This book contains clinical care plans for major disorders encountered in the medical-surgical setting, including the most common DRGs and selected DRGs with geometric mean lengths of stay of 10 days or longer.

Why Are Care Plans Important?
Care plans are important for numerous reasons. Clinically, they offer a way to plan for and communicate appropriate patient care. Legally, they offer a framework for establishing the standard of care in a given situation. Financially, they can offer a way to validate the appropriateness of care given and to justify staffing levels and patient-care charges.

If Care Plans Are So Important, Why Don't More Nurses Use Them?

Most nurses are first exposed to care plans as students. They rapidly learn that writing care plans can be frustrating and time-consuming. As graduates, many nurses view care plans as irrelevant or too cumbersome to use.

Even among nurses who would like to use written care plans, however, the concepts of nursing diagnosis and DRGs are so recent that many don't know how to integrate them into care plans. Overwhelmed, they may turn to previously published books for guidance, only to encounter frustration there, too. You'll hear them say, for instance:

> "These care plans won't work for me—they're too general. I'd have to rewrite everything for a *real* patient."

> "This is great information on nursing diagnosis, but I can't figure out quickly which ones go with which medical disorder!"

> "This information's too theoretical—it doesn't fit the 'real world'."

And yet, it's obvious that nurses would welcome the guidance that could be provided by clinically relevant care plans. If you listen closely to their questions about patient care, you hear concerns like these:

• Problems nurses face on admission:

> "When I obtain a patient's history, what risk factors should I be alert for?"

> "What's really important to note when doing a physical assessment? I haven't got time to check everything!"

> "What laboratory tests and diagnostic procedures should I anticipate? What do they usually show?"

> "What are the complications that can occur with this disorder?"

• Problems nurses face in providing care:

> "What nursing diagnoses should I consider for this type of patient?"

> "How do I know if they're actually present in my patient?"

> "What are the nursing priorities for this patient?"

> "Once I've identified a problem, what should I do about it?"

> "Why are certain interventions important?"

> "How do I know when a problem's resolved?"

• Problems nurses face in discharge planning:

> "How long is this patient likely to be in the hospital?"

> "From a nursing standpoint, how do I know when a patient's ready for discharge?"

> "What discharge teaching's realistic to do?"

The Solution: This Book

In responding to questions like these, this book provides answers that are practical and clinically relevant because they are targeted to the needs of the "hands-on" nurse clinician.

Standardized vs. Individualized Care

The most common and important question nurses raise about written care plans is: "How can I write care plans? Who's got the time?" Their concern about time is valid because most nurses practice in a hectic, complex environment that allows little time for thoughtful care planning.

To cope with this problem, some nurses have turned to published standard care plans. Nurses like standard care plans because they decrease the repetition involved in writing individual care plans, help inexperienced staff learn about patient care, and remind experienced staff about aspects of care they may have overlooked. But standard care plans have some disadvantages, too. They may be misused as the *only* care plan—promoting standardized rather than individualized care—or they may be ignored altogether.

Major differences of opinion exist in nursing concerning standardized vs. individualized care plans. Opponents of standardization argue that it equals depersonalization in delivering care. Advocates argue that standardization is efficient because it limits care-planning time without sacrificing quality and that it fosters quality assurance. This disagreement cannot be resolved easily; however, this book combines the advantages of standard care plans with unusual features that help to overcome their disadvantages:

• The plans blend standardized and individualized aspects of care. Standardization works better in some areas of care planning than it does in others: problems, priorities, and interventions can usually be standardized, but outcome criteria, timing of interventions, and discharge criteria require a significant amount of individualization. This book takes both sets of factors into account.
• Space is provided at the end of each problem to append "additional individualized interventions."

These unusual features challenge the nurse to think creatively. Because the resulting plan is pertinent and individualized, its clinical usefulness is assured. *These* care plans won't be dismissed—they'll be used every day.

The most important point to remember in the debate over standardized vs. individualized care plans is this: *it is not a care plan that causes depersonalized care; it is the nurse's attitude.* The nurse who appreciates patients as individuals will use a standardized care plan as a basis from which to work creatively, staying attuned to individual patient responses while applying the art and science of nursing.

Because of its unusual focus, this book helps bridge the chasms that separate the different factions in nursing. In doing so, it helps resolve three major issues nurses struggle with: medical vs. nursing care, standardized vs. individualized care, and cost containment vs. quality care. It takes the philosophical position that these stances need not be adversarial: that, in fact, one can provide care that blends interdependence and independence, standardization and individualization, and cost containment and quality. By being selective and tailoring the strategy to the appropriate circumstances, the nurse can benefit from the best aspects of all these approaches to patient care. More important, so can the patient.

Ultimately, any care plan is only as good (and as beneficial to the patient) as the nurse who puts it into action by providing the care. Conscientious nurses find care plans a resource for learning new information quickly, refreshing their knowledge, and focusing their energy on the most important problems their patients may encounter. The nurses who contributed care plans to this book had the "front-line" nurse in mind. Recognizing that most "front-line" nurse clinicians welcome assistance in dealing with these problems caringly, efficiently, and expertly, they have provided that assistance in this unique book.

Section I

Three professional challenges are covered here: distinguishing nursing from medical care, balancing standardized and individualized care, and reconciling cost-containment with quality care.

Delivering Quality Care in a Cost-Conscious Environment

The advent of Medicare's prospective payment system (PPS) in 1983 dramatically altered the U.S. health care system in ways that nurses are only now beginning to understand. Faced with new restrictions and regulations affecting delivery of care, nurses are confronted by twin challenges: sicker patients and shorter hospitalizations. Nurses also play a key role in maintaining a hospital's financial viability in this competitive, market-driven health care environment. So, to maintain quality patient care under PPS, they must become increasingly sophisticated and innovative.

Evolution of PPS

Before 1983, charges for hospital care were based on a retrospective method of payment. Hospital charges reflected what the market would bear and often were arbitrary, unrelated to the actual costs of delivering services. Nursing, for the most part, was a nonbillable direct service that was "bundled" under room and board charges in the hospital bill. But since 1983, third-party payers have demanded more explicit accounting for all services and appropriate charges for every area of health care delivery. In response, hospitals have begun to "unbundle" all units of service, including nursing.

Medicare, as one of the nation's primary insurers, was the first to change its reimbursement method. PPS was a desperate attempt to conserve the rapidly dwindling dollars available in the Medicare trust fund set up in the 1960s to ensure that America's elderly would have access to health care.

Under PPS, diagnosis-related groups (DRGs) were developed to identify clinically homogeneous groups of diagnoses that use similar tests, treatments, and services and therefore could be reimbursed at similar rates. These groups also could be used to predict resource consumption. This federal system is now mandatory for Medicare recipients at all acute-care hospitals.

At present, 475 DRGs are grouped into 23 Major Diagnostic Categories (MDCs) based on anatomical organ systems such as the respiratory system. The predetermined rate of reimbursement for each DRG is based on numerous factors, including the principal diagnosis, the patient's age, the presence of complications or comorbidities, and the occurrence of an operating room procedure. All these factors are taken into account upon patient discharge to determine which of the 475 DRGs will be assigned.

The DRG system is incongruous in many ways. For example, although it takes the patient's age into account (some DRGs pay more for a patient who is over age 17), it does not consider the severity of the patient's illness. Thus, a patient who is severely ill and needs more services and a longer length of stay has hospitalization paid for at the same rate as a patient with the same illness and assigned DRG who is not severely ill. DRGs are, in effect, an averaging system: a hospital will lose money on some cases whose cost of care will be more than the amount paid for the assigned DRG, and make money on cases whose costs are less than the DRG payment. Many patients who would have been hospitalized in the past, however, now receive treatment in outpatient settings; since only patients who meet strict criteria may be admitted to acute-care facilities, hospitals have, overall, sicker patients to care for than in the past. Thus, patient care must be managed as efficiently as possible for a hospital to maintain financial viability.

How DRGs are assigned

After discharge, a patient is assigned a DRG based on the following factors:
• principal diagnosis—the diagnosis that is determined to have necessitated admission to the hospital
• secondary diagnosis—all secondary conditions that exist at the time of admission or that develop during hospitalization, and affect the treatment or length of stay (LOS)
• operative procedures—any surgical procedures performed for definitive treatment rather than for diagnostic or exploratory purposes
• age—for some conditions, a different reimbursement rate applies for patients under and over age 17
• discharge status—for example, discharged home or transferred to another hospital

---

TEN FREQUENTLY OCCURRING DRGs

127 Heart Failure and Shock
89 Simple Pneumonia and Pleurisy
182 Esophagitis, Gastroenteritis, Digestive Disorders
140 Angina Pectoris
14 Cerebrovascular Disorders
96 Bronchitis and Asthma
138 Cardiac Arrhythmia*
296 Nutritional and Metabolic Disorders
88 Chronic Obstructive Pulmonary Disease
209 Major Joint Procedures
121 Circulation Disorders and Acute Myocardial Infarction

*Because patients with this disorder as the primary diagnosis are usually treated in a critical-care unit, a care plan for this disorder is not included in this book.

• complications—any conditions arising during hospitalization that may prolong LOS at least 1 day in 75% of patients (diabetes is an example)
• comorbidity—a preexisting condition that will increase LOS at least 1 day in 75% of cases.

All these factors need to be considered and the presence or absence of each factor determined to identify the correct DRG.

How DRGs are used
Once the correct DRG has been determined, further statistical measures affecting reimbursement can be identified:
• geometric mean LOS—each DRG has an assigned geometric mean LOS. The terms "geometric mean LOS" or "mean LOS" in this book refer to specific DRG statistical data for *groups* of patients. The unqualified term "LOS" is a general abbreviation referring to an *individual* patient's length of stay. The geometric mean LOS usually is thought of as the average LOS for all patients within a specified DRG; however, this is a misconception. Actually, the geometric mean LOS is a statistical measure used in cost accounting for the sole purpose of determining when a patient becomes a "day outlier," a status discussed in the third box, below.

The geometric mean LOS is an average derived from 1986 data that indicated the mean LOS for patients with specific diagnoses or procedures at the time the DRG system was developed. This fact has four important implications:

☐ The geometric mean LOS should be understood as an indicator of when most patients within each DRG *were* discharged in 1986. It was never intended as a guide to determine when a specific patient *should* be discharged.

☐ Current hospital stays are significantly shorter than the geometric mean LOS. Since 1983, when PPS began, the actual LOS across the country for nearly every DRG has decreased dramatically as doctors have learned to treat in outpatient facilities, in their offices, and within a much shorter length of time in the hospital.

☐ The geometric mean LOS has nothing to do with the LOS after which a hospital loses money on a case. That point can be determined only after studying each case.

☐ In most cases, a hospital begins losing money before the geometric mean LOS is reached because actual costs of caring for the patient usually exceed reimbursement before this point. This is partially because hospital costs have continued to increase as actual LOS has continued to decrease.
• relative weight—a statistical term used in DRG reimbursement that determines the actual dollars a particular hospital is paid for a given DRG. Among other factors, it is based on categorizing the hospital as acute or chronic, teaching or nonteaching, urban or rural. The

weight assigned each DRG has been reevaluated and revised at regular intervals. Because relative weights vary greatly from hospital to hospital and area to area, and because of their periodic revision, they are not specified in the care plans in this book.
• outlier—a case that uses more than the assigned resources. Two types of outliers exist: day outliers and cost outliers. A day outlier is a case that remains hospitalized, on average, 17 days or more beyond the geometric mean LOS. Although hospitals receive an additional payment for cases that reach day outlier status, payment is never enough to cover the costs or charges incurred during an extended LOS.

Day outliers were predicted to be 5% of all Medicare discharges when PPS was begun. The latest data suggest only 1.5% of discharges are reaching outlier status. In nearly every instance, day outliers are those patients that have multisystem failure and are severely ill. Preventing a patient from becoming a day outlier is rarely under the control of the nurse.

A cost outlier is a case that does not exceed the allowed number of days but does exceed the expected cost. Cost outliers are even rarer than day outliers. This book does not include information on cost outliers.

Keys to success under DRGs
Several major factors affect financial success under DRGs:
• accurate coding of all medical record data upon patient discharge. This is achieved by choosing the diagnosis that was chiefly responsible for the admission and taking into account all of the factors that will place the diagnosis in the highest-paying category, for example, complications and comorbidities. Medical record professionals, responsible for coding, depend on the documentation in the medical record when assigning the DRG.
• effective and efficient management of the "products" of hospitals—that is, hours of nursing care, laboratory tests, medications, supplies, and other services. The more efficiently care is delivered, the greater the hospital's profit.
• an appropriate "case mix" (a hospital's mixture of patients), defined by severity of illness and by assigned DRGs. A hospital must maintain a mixture of patients with various DRGs to plan and manage resource allocation within defined reimbursement parameters.
• utilization of the appropriate site of care and LOS. Care will be reimbursed only if it is provided in the appropriate setting; for example, hospitals will not be reimbursed for care that could have been appropriately provided in an outpatient setting. LOS also must be appropriate. Patients must not be discharged before they are medically stable, yet the hospital must ensure that unnecessary costs will not be incurred.
• prevention of complications. Because development of complications increases the likelihood that care costs will exceed reimbursement, their prevention is a key factor in maintaining fiscal control.

• early discharge planning. Discharge planning must be considered before admission (when possible), upon admission, or as soon after as practicable, to minimize LOS and prevent readmissions.

The nurse's role in a PPS
The increasing impact of government regulations and third-party payers on the health care delivery system presents the nurse with challenges and opportunities. The nurse is instrumental in assuring both the quality of care and the hospital's financial success under any PPS. Some of the ways the nurse can maintain quality care and yet dramatically affect a hospital's reimbursement include:
• care planning. The nurse must be able to prioritize and deliver care that realistically correlates with the projected LOS—which means establishing and following an explicit plan of care. Care planning provides an essential means of determining goals and desired outcomes of care delivery. Only by this means can care be managed effectively and efficiently. This book is designed to help the nurse provide quality care in the age of cost containment.
• early discharge planning. Besides developing and using care plans, the nurse must become involved in the discharge planning process from the moment of patient admission, whenever possible. By beginning the process early, the nurse can help ensure appropriate posthospital care. For example, the nurse can emphasize patient and family education, maximize self-care abilities, and arrange for continued care by other professionals when indicated, such as home care nursing or nursing home placement.
• patient education. Patient and family education is a key element in preventing readmissions. The patient's perception of quality care is also enhanced by the nurse's promoting self-care and teaching about posthospital management of health problems.
• documentation. Accurate documentation promotes communication among caregivers that maximizes the benefits of hospitalization while minimizing LOS. Also, documentation is crucial for assigning appropriate reimbursement for services.
• quality assurance. This mandatory element should include both specific nursing standards and monitoring of adherence to those standards.

The nurse also needs to become aware of the impact of the new economics on the professional status of nursing. This is an opportune time to advance the function and image of nursing as an independent health care practice that can be judged not only on its benefits for patients but also on its contribution to hospitals' economic viability. Nursing services now can be costed out and charged for separately, based on their use by patients.

Advent of retrospective review
Besides DRGs, other changes occurring in health care are increasing the pressure to deliver care in the most efficient manner possible. Particularly important is the advent of health maintenance organizations (HMOs) and other competitive medical plans.

The nurse should be aware of the complexity of reimbursement methods now used in health care. Most third-party payers (not just Medicare) are using some form of prospective payment mechanism to reimburse hospitals. For example, many HMOs currently pay hospitals on a negotiated rate not unlike DRGs. Also, all third-party payers are negotiating discounted rates for services provided in acute-care facilities in return for guaranteeing that their subscribers will use those specific facilities for their acute-care needs. Such arrangements are important for hospitals because they ensure a constant volume of patients. With LOSs much shorter than they were before PPS, hospitals must count on a stable census to ensure maximum efficiency and a constant cash flow.

For patients, the hospital incentives in every PPS mean shorter stays and potential decreases in hospital services. Some patients who have been accustomed to remaining in the hospital until they perceive themselves as ready for discharge believe that they are being discharged prematurely; nurses, doctors, and other health care providers have expressed the same concern. Because of these perceptions of premature patient discharges and underutilization of necessary services, state peer review organizations (PROs) have been mandated to increase review of care provided in acute-care facilities.

This mandate has led PROs to establish explicit review criteria specific to the provision of medical care. Within the DRG system, however, information is evolving that could be useful to nurses and may become mandatory—specifically, the screening criteria being developed and used by the Health Care Financing Administration (HCFA) and state PROs. The PROs are using generic and disease-specific criteria retrospectively to identify the appropriateness of admission and discharge and the quality of care.

Although PROs are reviewing only Medicare cases now, in the near future all hospital admissions, outpatient procedures, home care services, and care in doctors' offices and long-term settings will be reviewed in much the same manner.

The nursing challenge
Today, the nurse faces greater challenges than ever: sicker patients, more complex care, and shorter patient stays. This book offers the nurse the expertise of professional colleagues who understand the complexities of those challenges and who offer powerful help in meeting them.

Nursing Diagnosis

The American Nurses Association Social Policy Statement (1980) defines nursing as "the diagnosis and treatment of human responses to actual or potential health problems." Gordon (1987) defines a nursing diagnosis as "an actual or potential health problem amenable to nursing intervention." Although nurses have been diagnosing patient problems for years, the term "nursing diagnosis" is relatively new.

Past diagnostic efforts have been hampered by the lack of a common language for labeling nursing problems. To remove this barrier, the National Conference Group on the Classification of Nursing Diagnoses began identifying and classifying health problems that nurses treat. That organization, formed at the first National Conference on Classification of Nursing Diagnoses in 1973, is now the North American Nursing Diagnosis Association (NANDA).

This book identifies nursing diagnoses using the terminology recommended by NANDA whenever possible. The NANDA list represents those diagnoses that the organization has accepted for study and clinical testing. The current list appears in the Appendix.

Two major issues relate to the NANDA diagnoses: clinical usefulness of the terminology and the renaming of medical diagnoses.

• Because the nursing diagnosis movement is evolving, nurses have encountered significant difficulty in using the list. Gordon (1986) has reported that some authors have criticized the categories' complexity, esoteric language, lack of specificity, and differing levels of abstraction. Others have described the terminology as wordy, vague, confusing, and inconsistent (Iyer et al., 1986).

These responses highlight an important problem: some NANDA diagnostic labels are not yet useful. Because the clinical experts who wrote the care plans in this book found some of the NANDA diagnoses functional and others not, the editor has made the following decisions reflected in the care plans:

□ Some of the NANDA diagnosis labels contain a general classification and a specific diagnosis (Gordon, 1986). In these situations, we have dropped the categorical labels and used the most precise term.
□ We used alternate terminology for one diagnosis because of its wordiness. In place of "Alteration in nutrition: less than body requirements," we used "nutritional deficit."
□ Because people do not speak in the language of nursing diagnoses (for example, "airway clearance, ineffective"), we have modified the wording slightly to reflect usual conversational sequences and phrasing.

• A serious problem has provoked substantial controversy and major differences of opinion within the nursing diagnosis community: the renaming of medical diagnoses. Many nurses believe that several of the accepted nursing diagnoses rename medical diagnoses; examples are decreased cardiac output, decreased tissue perfusion, and impaired tissue integrity. In part, this controversy stems from the continued difficulty nurses face in articulating the dimensions of their practice and, particularly, in differentiating it from medical practice.

Because the editor believes that renaming problems already defined by other disciplines simply perpetuates the confusion between nursing and medicine, these diagnoses have not been used as identified nursing diagnoses. Instead, when they are used, they are clearly identified as collaborative problems requiring both nursing and medical interventions.

References

American Nurses Association, Congress for Nursing Practice. *Nursing: A Social Policy Statement.* Kansas City, Mo.: American Nurses Association, 1980.

Gordon, Marjory. "Nursing Diagnosis and the Diagnostic Process," *American Journal of Nursing* 76(6):1298-1300, 1986.

Gordon, Marjory. *Nursing Diagnosis: Process and Application,* 2nd ed. New York: McGraw-Hill Book Co., 1987.

Gordon, Marjory. "Structure of Diagnostic Categories," in *Classification of Nursing Diagnoses: Proceedings of the Sixth NANDA Conference.* Edited by Hurley, M. St. Louis: C.V. Mosby Co., 1986.

Health Care Financing Administration. "Changes to the In-Patient Hospital Prospective Payment System and Fiscal Year 1988 Rates; Final Rule." *Federal Register* 52:33,034, September 1, 1987.

Health Systems International. *Diagnosis Related Groups,* 4th revision. New Haven, Conn.: Health Systems International, 1987.

Iyer, Patricia, et al. *Nursing Process and Nursing Diagnosis.* Philadelphia: W.B. Saunders Co., 1986.

Kritek, Phyllis. "Development of a Taxonomic Structure for Nursing Diagnoses: A Review and Update," in *Classification of Nursing Diagnoses: Proceedings of the Sixth NANDA Conference.* Edited by Hurley, M. St. Louis: C.V. Mosby Co., 1986.

McLane, Audrey, ed. *Classification of Nursing Diagnoses: Proceedings of the Seventh NANDA Conference.* St. Louis: C.V. Mosby Co., 1987.

Prospecive Payment: Laws, Regulations, Guidelines and Decisions. Owings Mills, Md.: National Health Publishing, 1984.

Using the Care Plans

These care plans are designed to give the practicing nurse a maximal amount of clinically relevant information within a minimal number of pages. This book is intended not as a substitute for the broad clinical knowledge base found in more exhaustive nursing references, but as a guide for providing quality "hands-on" nursing care to patients in the medical-surgical inpatient setting.

Every care plan is subdivided into sections, each presenting the nurse with a different type of information. Becoming familiar with the basic format will enhance their practical value for the clinical nurse.

DRG information
Immediately after the name of the clinical plan, abbreviated *DRG information* related to the disorder appears. Included are:
• relevant DRG number(s). Some clinical disorders always have the same DRG; an example is myasthenia gravis. Others, such as circulatory disorders, are subdivided into several DRGs. Where appropriate in the care plans, relevant DRGs are indicated.
• an indication of whether the DRG is medical or surgical
• mean geometric LOS for each DRG
• comments, if any, designed to provide a perspective on the DRG.

Ideally, each care plan would include a current usual LOS for the patient's particular disorder, to guide patient and family teaching and to provide a benchmark against which the nurse could assess the patient's progress toward discharge. Unfortunately, such information is not available. However, this book provides the best substitute: the mean LOS, previously defined. The mean LOS gives you an idea of the average LOS for patients with this diagnosis. You could use this information to anticipate when teaching and discharge planning should be well under way and when maximum hospital benefit usually has been reached. Do not use the mean LOS as a target for discharge; doing so will almost certainly ensure that the hospital loses money. Instead, plan for a LOS shorter than the mean LOS, when possible, yet appropriate for the patient's needs.

Introduction
In *Definition and Time Focus*, the disease process, surgical procedure, or patient problem that forms the focus of the care plan is briefly defined and discussed. The time frame of the care plan (for example, during the initial diagnostic period, as opposed to during exacerbations) is delineated.

Listed next in *Etiology/Precipitating Factors* are factors that directly or indirectly contribute to the condition's development, grouped according to pathophysiologic mechanism when possible.

Focused assessment guidelines
Focused assessment guidelines is further subdivided into Nursing History, Physical Findings, Diagnostic Studies, and Potential Complications.

Patient assessment is assumed to be one of the primary skills of the clinical nurse professional, so this section does not review assessment technique. Instead, the assessment guidelines delineate specific findings common to most patients with the identified condition. The intent is to give the clinician a picture of the typical patient presentation in a given condition. Classic or definitive findings are underlined.

The first assessment section, *Nursing History (Functional health pattern findings)*, presents subjective and historical data common to the identified condition and organized under the Functional Health Patterns framework articulated by Marjory Gordon. The health patterns (see *Functional Health Patterns*) represent 11 categories within the holistic wellness/illness system. Each of the health patterns provides useful parameters for assessment of any given patient. Since the emphasis is on definitive or common findings, only those patterns with data relevant to the condition are included. If the patient presenting with a specified condition does not typically give information pertinent to a particular health patterns category, that pattern is not listed.

The second assessment section, *Physical Findings*, presents typical objective findings in a patient who presents with the identified condition. The physical findings are organized in the body systems format familiar to most nurses.

Diagnostic Studies, the next section of the care plan, provides the nurse with information regarding laboratory and diagnostic tests usually performed for the diagnosis and treatment of a patient with the specified condition. Not all the tests listed may be performed on a particular patient; what actually is ordered depends on individual factors. However, the astute nurse is aware of the significance of studies and tests that may pertain to the patient's condition and, when indicated, offers collaborative input to the doctor regarding selection of such studies.

Finally, *Potential Complications* are listed for the identified condition. The complications listed are those most common for patients with the condition. Nurses must be aware of associated complications to take preventive action on the patient's behalf.

FUNCTIONAL HEALTH PATTERNS

1. Health Perception–Health Management Pattern
- perceived pattern of health and well-being
- general level of health care behavior (how health is managed)
- health status related to future planning

2. Nutritional-Metabolic Pattern
- food and fluid consumption relative to metabolic need
- pattern, types, quantity, preferences of food and fluids
- skin lesions and healing ability
- indicators of nutritional status (such as skin, hair, and nail condition)

3. Elimination Pattern
- patterns of excretory function
- routines and devices used

4. Activity-Exercise Pattern
- exercise, activity, leisure, recreation
- activities of daily living
- sports
- factors interfering with activity

5. Sleep-Rest Pattern
- pattern of sleep, rest, and relaxation
- perception of quantity and quality of rest
- energy level
- sleep aids and problems

6. Cognitive-Perceptual Pattern
- adequacy of sensory modes
- pain perception and management
- cognitive functional ability

7. Self-Perception–Self-Concept Pattern
- attitudes about self
- perception of abilities
- body image, identity, and general emotional pattern
- pattern of body posture and speech

8. Role-Relationship Pattern
- role engagements—family, work, social
- perception of responsibilities

9. Sexuality-Reproductive Pattern
- satisfaction or disturbances in sexuality
- reproductive stage
- reproductive pattern

10. Coping-Stress Tolerance Pattern
- general coping pattern and effectiveness
- perceived ability to manage situations
- reserve capacity and resources

11. Value-Belief Pattern
- values, goals or beliefs that guide choices
- conflicts related to health status

Adapted from: Gordon, Marjory. *Nursing Diagnosis: Process and Application*, 2nd ed. New York: McGraw-Hill Book Co., 1987.

Collaborative problems and nursing diagnoses

This section contains the main body of the care plan: the major problems specific to the condition. They are the predictable patient health responses usually caused by the pathophysiology of the disorder.

Problems may be actual or potential. An actual problem is one that usually is present and presents identifiable signs and symptoms. A potential problem is one the patient is at high risk of developing; although signs and symptoms are not present, risk factors are.

Because nursing practice is based on both medical and nursing diagnoses, patient problems are identified as either *Nursing Diagnoses* or *Collaborative Problems*, represented by two distinctive logos. Care plans that focus only on nursing diagnoses are shown with a circle in a box, which symbolizes independent action. Disease-related care plans are shown with two boxes joined together forming a plus sign, which symbolizes collaboration.

Collaborative problems are those that fall within the domain of both medicine and nursing; their etiologies are amenable primarily to medical interventions. The nurse does not treat them independently but may initiate monitoring for them. Nursing diagnoses are those problems that fall within nursing's expertise. They are

responses that the nurse can identify and treat independently; etiologies are primarily amenable to independent nursing interventions.

Some problems identified here as nursing diagnoses have the potential to become collaborative problems; for example, the nurse may have primary responsibility for airway clearance, but if complications necessitate endotracheal intubation, the problem becomes a collaborative one. The intent in this book is not to split hairs over functional terminology but to increase nursing awareness of the diagnostic activities that are currently a part of nursing practice.

In most plans, the patient problems are presented in order of descending importance. Exceptions may be found in some surgical-procedure care plans, where preoperative problems are presented first to provide logical continuity.

After problem identification, the *Nursing Priority* in dealing with the problem is specified. The nursing priority indicates the focus for the nursing interventions that follow. *Interventions* and *Rationales* are presented in a two-column format, interventions on the left and corresponding rationales on the right. Interventions are based on clinical experience and the nursing literature; thus, they represent a blend of clinical practice and theory-based interventions.

Interventions usually are ranked in order of decreasing priority; those considered clinically essential are italicized. Interventions may be interdependent or independent in nature: for interdependent functions, initiation is the responsibility of another health care provider, typically a doctor. However, whether performed under direct or indirect supervision or under protocol, they always require the application of nursing judgment. Independent functions do not require initiation by another health care provider; they are initiated by the nurse under his or her professional license.

Note that both types of problems—collaborative and nursing diagnoses—can contain both types of interventions—interdependent and independent. Usually, a collaborative problem will have mostly interdependent interventions, with a few independent ones; a nursing diagnosis will have mostly independent interventions but may contain a few interdependent ones. The rationales, although purposely brief, incorporate relevant physiologic mechanisms whenever possible, along with other helpful data.

Nurses have long recognized that patients respond best to care that takes personal characteristics and preferences into consideration. Space is provided at the end of each problem section for notation of additional individualized interventions.

Each problem is followed by specific *Outcome criteria*, defined as ideal expected patient responses to the interventions. These criteria, based on the clinical expertise of the nurses who contributed to this book, focus on specific, measurable patient responses that provide the nurse with guidance in evaluating the results of care provided. Outcome criteria are grouped according to recommended time periods for achievement. These criteria are intended only as a guide; individual variation is to be expected, and professional judgment must be used, because outcomes obviously depend on many factors.

Discharge planning

The final section of the care plan includes three guides for the nurse to use in planning for discharge and in documenting care.

Nursing Discharge Criteria, the first subsection, provides specific guidelines for assessing the patient's readiness for discharge. These guidelines were developed by a discharge planning expert and are consistent with the criteria used by most state PROs.

The discharge criteria listed in this section help alert the nurse to factors that must be considered before the doctor decides to discharge the patient. Again, these criteria are intended only as a guide. Some patients may not meet all criteria by the time of discharge; if not, the nurse needs to do special planning to prevent a lapse in needed care.

The *Patient/Family Discharge Teaching Checklist* gives the nurse a tool to identify needed patient and family teaching related to the specified condition. Such teaching can be, and usually is, done by various health professionals other than the nurse: dietitians, doctors, clinical specialists, social workers, and others will be responsible for patient education during hospitalization. The nurse, however, is responsible for reviewing documentation (nurses notes, progress notes, teaching record, discharge planning form, flow sheets) and for assessing patient understanding to ensure that, before discharge, all appropriate teaching has been accomplished and satisfactorily documented.

Finally, the *Documentation Checklist* provides the nurse with a summary of items that should be documented in the patient record. As has been previously noted, recent changes in health care payment systems make thorough documentation more essential than ever. Accurate documentation also helps protect the nurse in the event of case-related litigation, although now, as always, the best way to avoid legal problems is to maintain high standards of care, impeccable professionalism, and warm, caring relationships with patients.

Concluding each care plan is a list of *Associated Care Plans* found elsewhere in this book and *References,* which may be helpful to the nurse seeking further information.

In using these care plans in clinical practice, the nurse may benefit from reading through the applicable care plan first. Thereafter, the care plan should be referred to on a shift-by-shift basis, with problems addressed and interventions documented in the nurse's notes. Before the patient is discharged, the nurse should review the appropriate sections and evaluate all teaching and documentation, using the checklists as a guide. The nurse may wish to place a copy of the *Patient/Family Discharge Teaching Checklist* in the front of the patient's chart so that other health care providers may refer to it and check off any patient education they provide.

Organization of the book

The comprehensive clinical care plan contains the depth of detail appropriate for education and reference, but nurses familiar with the care appropriate for a particular condition may prefer an abbreviated version. To provide a clinically workable care planning system, this book includes an innovative feature: a special section containing condensed care plans (arranged alphabetically) for selected conditions nurses encounter most frequently.

This book contains two types of care plans: those pertaining to a specific medical diagnosis or surgical procedure, which constitute the main portion of the book, and those referred to as "general" care plans, which are presented in a separate section. The general care plans provide the nurse with detailed interventions for dealing with common patient problems (for example, pain, knowledge deficit, grief and grieving) that may be encountered in caring for any patient. They are designed to be used with the diagnosis- or procedure-based clinical plans.

Section II

Comprehensive care plans, arranged by body system, incorporate functional health patterns, nursing diagnoses, collaborative problems, patient-family teaching, documentation checklists, discharge criteria, and DRGs.

Death and Dying

Introduction

DEFINITION AND TIME FOCUS

Death, according to Dr. Elisabeth Kübler-Ross, is "the key to the door of life." Awareness of death's inevitability, and the unflinching contemplation of our own fears and feelings about it, can lead to a heightened appreciation for life and a more courageous and thoughtful response to the challenges life provides. Nurses deal with death on a day-to-day basis and thus have an opportunity to make a profoundly meaningful contribution to dying patients and their families.

More than any other professional, the nurse has close and continuing contact with patients, direct experience with those who die, and concern for meeting their emotional and physiologic needs. So she is in the best position to help dying patients and their families cope with this ultimate loss. Death remains the "great unknown," but the patient and his loved ones have the right to continue sharing life until the end; the nurse can facilitate this process. This care plan focuses on the needs of the dying patient and the bereaved family in the hospital setting.

ETIOLOGY/PRECIPITATING FACTORS

Death may be the result of:
• disease (or, occasionally, complications of the treatment of disease)
• injury or accident
• aging or debilitation
• suicide or homicide.

Focused assessment guidelines

NURSING HISTORY (Functional health pattern findings)

Note: Because etiologic factors vary so widely in dying persons, no typical findings exist. Thus, this section presents an assessment guide to assist the nurse in planning care for the patient who is admitted with a diagnosis suggesting impending death. However, no such guide is appropriate for all patients. The answers to the following questions may help the nurse intervene effectively on behalf of the dying and their families, but the nurse must use professional judgment in deciding what, when, and how much to ask a patient.

Health perception–health management pattern

• Is the patient aware of the prognosis? If so, for how long? If not, whose decision was it not to tell the patient?
• If not aware of the prognosis, what does the patient believe is the reason for hospitalization?

• What measures were taken to help support or improve the patient's physical or emotional condition before this hospitalization? Does the patient believe they have helped? If so, how?
• What are the patient's expectations about this hospital admission and the proposed treatment?

Nutritional-metabolic pattern

• Does the patient have any particular dietary preferences or intolerances?
• Has the patient been anorexic, vomiting, or dysphagic?

Elimination pattern

• What is the patient's present elimination status and pattern?
• Are any elimination aids currently used?

Activity-exercise pattern

• What is the patient's current activity level and tolerance?

Sleep-rest pattern

• What are the patient's present sleeping habits?
• Does the patient feel he has been getting enough sleep? If not, why not?

Cognitive-perceptual pattern

• Does the patient have pain? If so, how severe is it?
• Is the patient's pain (if present) controlled? If so, by what?

Self-perception–self-concept pattern

• What events or achievements in life have brought the patient the most satisfaction?
• What does the patient want most to accomplish before dying?

Role-relationship pattern

• Who are the patient's significant others?
• Among these, are there any with whom the patient has long-standing, unresolved conflicts or other "unfinished business"?
• Has the patient been able to talk about death and dying with significant others?
• How are significant others handling the situation?

Coping-stress tolerance pattern

• If the patient is aware of the prognosis, how is he coping?
• What resources are available to help the patient cope?

Value-belief pattern
• What is the patient's religious or spiritual orientation?
• What does the patient believe about death?

PHYSICAL FINDINGS
Physical findings in dying patients vary widely, depending on the cause of impending death; see care plans related to the specific patient's disease or condition.

DIAGNOSTIC STUDIES
See care plans related to the patient's specific disease or condition.

POTENTIAL COMPLICATIONS
• ineffective coping

Nursing diagnosis: *Fear related to potential pain, loss, emotional upheaval, and the unknowns of the dying process*

NURSING PRIORITY: Promote identification and confrontation of specific realistic fears.

Interventions

1. *Examine personal fears and feelings about death.* Before involvement with the dying patient and the family, identify previous experiences with death, and be aware of personal emotions, religious or spiritual beliefs, and fears. If talking about death is too uncomfortable, refer the patient and family to another professional with the necessary skills.

2. *Assess the patient's coping style and stage of acceptance.* Assess previous experience with death. Observe patient behaviors, and confer with the family and other caregivers as needed.

3. Use role modeling to facilitate expression of feelings, as appropriate: "If I were facing what you face right now, I think I might feel scared (or 'angry' or 'depressed')."

4. *Support coping mechanisms.* Avoid forcing the patient to confront emotional issues.

5. As indicated by the patient's responsiveness to role modeling, help the patient identify specific fears and prioritize them. Acknowledge the unknowns.

Rationales

1. A caregiver's personal feelings about death and experiences with it affect ability to promote healthy emotional responses. Nurses who have not faced the issues of death are less able to empathize with the patient and family. Appropriate referral allows emotional needs to be addressed.

2. Each person responds differently to the threat of death. When threatened, most people initially revert to familiar coping mechanisms, and caregivers must be aware of these in establishing therapeutic communication. Assessment of the stage of acceptance helps guide interventions. Previous experiences with death do much to shape behavioral responses and may contribute significantly to the patient's overall ability or inability to achieve acceptance.

3. Patients may need "permission" to discuss fears. Opening discussion by focusing on the caregiver's feelings allows the patient the option of responding with an expression of personal feelings (if ready) and reassures the patient that such feelings are normal and acceptable.

4. Each patient moves through various stages, at various times, in coping with this ultimate threat to individuality. Forcing issues is counterproductive and may damage the therapeutic relationship. Respect for the individual promotes trust.

5. Identification of specific fears helps reduce the sense of overwhelming threat. Pain, loss of control, and being a burden to others are common fears of dying patients; identifying them or other fear-causing factors allows a patient to begin making specific plans to cope with them and to deal with actual problems that may arise. Acknowledging unknowns reassures the patient that the caregiver recognizes the enormity of the questions faced.

(continued)

Interventions *continued*

6. *Identify the patient's support system and resource base.* Coordinate involvement of patient, family, and other members of the health care team in making plans to deal with anticipated problems and needs.

7. *Provide appropriate referrals* as needed, such as to a psychiatric liaison nurse, social worker, hospice, chaplain, or to support groups related to the specific disorder.

8. Provide companionship when possible.

9. If the patient is confronting imminent unexpected death (for example, as a result of trauma), provide brief, clear explanations and offer to call a clergyman. Provide a support person to be with the family, and—if at all possible—allow a family member to see the patient before death.

10. Additional individualized interventions: _____

_____
_____

Outcome criteria
According to individual readiness, the patient will:
• identify specific fears

Rationales *continued*

6. Coordination of resources and support for the patient is essential in reducing the sense of isolation, which contributes to fear.

7. The patient and family may be unaware of resources available to them. Even if referrals are not used, knowledge of their availability can be comforting.

8. Simply sitting quietly beside the patient communicates concern and decreases the sense of isolation.

9. Even in the emergency care setting, patients have the right to caring communication, which may help reduce fear. Survivors of near-death experiences report hearing conversation and being aware of activity around them even when they appeared unresponsive. Surviving spouses of victims of sudden death list their need to see their spouse during resuscitation or before death as the concern that produced the most anguish for them.

10. Rationale: _____

_____
_____

• express feelings, as desired
• use appropriate resources.

Nursing diagnosis: *Powerlessness related to inevitability of death, lack of control over body functions, and/or dependence on others for care*

NURSING PRIORITY: Increase the patient's sense of personal power while promoting acceptance of realities of condition.

Interventions

1. *Encourage personal decision making whenever possible.* Allow maximum flexibility for scheduling activities, treatments, or visitors. Include the dying patient in making care-related decisions, as appropriate.

2. *Recognize and support courageous attitudes.*

3. *Accept personal powerlessness* to alter the fact that the patient is dying.

Rationales

1. Hospitalized patients must relinquish many freedoms, regardless of the reason for their hospitalization. Allowing as many choices as possible promotes a sense of control and increases the patient's coping ability. "Taking over" by caregivers diminishes the patient's self-esteem and should be avoided unless absolutely necessary.

2. Regardless of external circumstances, individuals maintain the freedom to choose their attitude and approach to life—and death. Acknowledgment of courageous attitudes reinforces feelings of self-worth.

3. Health care professionals often find it difficult to be unable to "make it better" for their patients. Realistic self-assessment is essential to prevent caregiver "burnout" and maintain the potential for effective intervention in areas that can be altered.

Interventions *continued*

4. *Help the patient identify inner strengths.* Ask the patient to recall past losses: How were they dealt with? What was learned from them?

5. *Encourage the patient to establish realistic goals* for the remainder of life.

6. *Assist the patient, as needed, to put affairs in order*—for example, funeral and memorial planning, writing a will, settling economic affairs, and making arrangements for survivors.

7. Additional individualized interventions: _____
_____
_____

Outcome criteria
According to individual readiness, the patient will:
• participate in decisions related to care
• verbalize inner strengths

Rationales *continued*

4. Recalling other losses may help the patient build on previously learned coping skills. Losses throughout life may have uniquely prepared the individual with qualities that can be utilized in facing death.

5. Establishing goals provides a focus for energy and reduces any sense of helplessness. Realistic evaluation of capabilities helps in the process of acceptance.

6. Putting affairs in order increases the patient's sense of control and may help soften the anticipated effects of the death on loved ones.

7. Rationale: _____
_____
_____

• set realistic goals
• initiate activity to put affairs in order.

Nursing diagnosis: *Disturbed self-concept: personal identity, related to imminent threat of loss of self*

NURSING PRIORITY: Help the patient maintain and enrich personal identity throughout the remainder of life.

Interventions

1. *Use active listening skills,* paying special attention to nonverbal or symbolic communication. Use reflective statements and open-ended observations to offer an opportunity for discussion of difficult issues. Accept and respect the patient's right to use denial or avoidance behavior. Whatever the patient's response, try to communicate the attempt to understand.

2. *Be honest with the patient* in answering questions, but do not force discussion of issues the patient has not introduced or has not responded to in discussion.

3. Encourage reminiscence and review of life experiences.

4. Promote creative expression. Encourage family and friends to provide materials the patient can use for drawing, painting, writing or other creative pursuits. Or obtain materials from the Occupational Therapy department.

Rationales

1. Patients facing their own mortality often use nonverbal or symbolic communication to describe their experience and to test others' willingness to talk about it. Rushed or distracted behavior from caregivers may distance the dying patient and contribute to feelings of alienation. Active listening and sharing show concern and respect for the patient as a unique individual. The patient may choose to use denial or avoidance to the end, and the right to make this choice should be respected as a reflection of the patient's unique selfhood.

2. Honesty, even when truths are painful, reflects respect for the patient as an individual. But the patient has the right to choose which issues he or she wishes to discuss.

3. Life experiences have helped to shape the patient's unique identity. Reminiscence helps the patient remain connected to important "core" experiences and provides the caregiver with additional information that may aid in understanding the patient's behavior and responding to it.

4. Creative activity gives voice to individual expression, helping the patient maintain a sense of uniqueness. Also, drawings, paintings, or other original work by the patient may provide clues to his or her state of acceptance.

(continued)

Interventions *continued*

5. Explore the option of preparing audio- or videotaped messages or mementos for family and friends to share after the patient's death (or earlier, if the patient wishes).

6. Use touch generously when providing care, unless it makes the patient uncomfortable. Encourage family affection, including holding, rocking, even lying next to the patient.

7. Additional individualized interventions: _____
_____
_____

Outcome criteria
According to individual readiness, the patient will:
• maintain preferred coping behaviors
• recall and review life experiences

Rationales *continued*

5. Some patients may feel more comfortable expressing feelings in this way. The process of recording helps achieve acceptance of impending death. Such mementos may offer the patient comfort in sensing that some individual identity will endure. These records may also be valued by families in preserving the memory of the loved one.

6. Illness and hospitalization may reduce the frequency of physical contact with others, which normally helps provide body image self-definition. Encouraging family affection helps maintain physical contact. Also, touch provides comfort and communicates genuine caring more effectively than almost any other single measure.

7. Rationale: _____
_____
_____

• participate in creative activity (as able)
• touch family members freely.

Nursing diagnosis: *Potential spiritual distress related to confrontation with the unknown*

NURSING PRIORITY: Help the patient savor the remaining period of life and identify meaning in impending death.

Interventions

1. *Support the patient's personal spiritual beliefs*, even if they seem unusual or unfamiliar.

2. *Recognize that facing death and dealing with separation are developmental tasks for all humans.* Promote a focus on growth and learning, rather than on disease or injury.

3. Acknowledge what dying patients have to teach others, and express this to the patient and family, when appropriate.

Rationales

1. Spiritual beliefs are extremely varied and usually provide comfort based on specific personal meaningfulness to the patient. Attempting to alter such beliefs or supplant them with others shows lack of respect for choices made by the patient and may precipitate undue conflict and distress.

2. Because our culture places such emphasis on youth, we lack the societal integration of death as part of life that many primitive cultures take for granted. To help a patient accept impending death, caregivers must acknowledge it as a stage of development and validate its importance. Non-disease–related interventions (discussed throughout this plan) help redirect coping efforts toward positive life closure.

3. Nurses can learn much from dying patients that may help in caring for others who follow. In such ways, dying patients may touch the lives of others they will never meet. Recognition of the lessons a dying person may pass on to others in this way can help the patient find meaning in death and a sense of connectedness with life.

Interventions *continued*

4. Provide privacy according to the patient's wish.

5. Offer to call the spiritual adviser of the patient's choice—for example, clergy, counselor, or friend. Obtain and provide religious tests and other inspirational readings if requested.

6. Explore the possibility of organ donation, if appropriate, with the patient and family. Be familiar with your hospital's and region's policy and procedure for arranging harvest of organs. Consider the underlying disease before discussing donation of specific organs.

7. Address the patient while providing care, even if the patient has apparently become unresponsive or comatose. Encourage family members to continue talking to the patient.

8. Worry less about saying the "wrong thing" than about being afraid to communicate caring. In this way, set an example family members may follow.

9. Maintain a positive attitude. Promote activities that provide even a few moments of enjoyment. Avoid pat generalizations that attempt to provide explanations for the patient's suffering.

10. Additional individualized interventions: _____
_____
_____

Outcome criteria
Throughout the remainder of life, the patient will:
• maintain personally meaningful spiritual and religious practices
• find pleasure in some activities.

Rationales *continued*

4. The hospital environment may allow patients minimal time to be alone. A patient struggling with spiritual issues may need uninterrupted time for prayer or meditation.

5. A spiritual adviser may provide guidance or perform rituals viewed as essential by the patient. Religious readings may be satisfying to a patient with a traditional religious orientation, although others may find comfort in nonreligious literature that has special personal significance.

6. Patients and families can find meaning and consolation in knowing others may benefit from organ donation. Many transplant programs now have broad interlinking systems for identification of donors and harvest and transplantation of donated organs. Underlying disease may make some organs unsatisfactory for donation, but others (such as skin) are typically usable and do not always require immediate transplantation.

7. Survivors of near-death experiences and persons who recover from deep or prolonged coma often report remembering conversation around them while they were apparently unconscious.

8. Nurses, because of prolonged close contact with dying patients and interaction with their families, are uniquely suited to help facilitate dialogue about dying between the patient and family. In many cases, patients and families are afraid to raise the subject with each other directly, out of concern that they may cause emotional upset. No cultural prescriptions exist to guide families, but the nurse may be able to act as a liaison to help communication, thereby reducing guilt and anxiety and further preparing the patient and family for separation.

9. The caregiver's positive attitude may help the patient maintain hope and find pleasure in living even while facing death. Small pleasures may be extremely meaningful when the patient's world view is narrowed by illness. Generalizations or attempts to provide simplistic explanations (for example, "It may be a blessing") indicate shallow appreciation for the patient's situation and may be interpreted as dismissal of real concerns.

10. Rationale: _____
_____
_____

Nursing diagnosis: *Potential pain related to underlying disease or injury*

NURSING PRIORITY: Relieve pain while allowing the patient to remain as alert as possible.

Interventions

1. *See the "Pain" care plan,* page 64.

2. *Assess the patient's level of discomfort frequently* and urge calling for medication before the pain becomes severe.

3. To the extent possible, include the patient in decisions regarding pain medications.

4. *When possible, control pain with oral medication* (Brompton's cocktail or an equivalent narcotic mixture) rather than with intramuscular injections.

5. *Recognize that the usual "safe dose" levels may not apply for the terminally ill patient.* Consult the doctor if the ordered dosage no longer seems effective.

6. If abdominal distention causes pain, consider using return-flow enemas.

7. Additional individualized interventions: _____
_____
_____

Rationales

1. This care plan provides interventions useful for any patient in pain.

2. A patient's level of discomfort has a significant impact on the emotional adjustment to limited life expectancy: Patients with poorly controlled pain tend to have more difficulty achieving acceptance. Medication given early in the pain cycle is most effective.

3. Ability to control pain allows the patient to use limited energy for other, more rewarding, purposes.

4. Repeated intramuscular injections, particularly in the debilitated patient, traumatize skin and gradually become less effective as areas of scarring develop and inhibit absorption. Also, use of oral medication increases the patient's sense of control over pain.

5. A patient maintained on narcotic analgesics for an extended period may develop significant tolerance and require amounts of medication considerably larger than the usual dosage to achieve comparable effects.

6. Lack of activity and resultant slowing of peristalsis may cause painful abdominal distention. Gentle return-flow enemas may reduce discomfort.

7. Rationale: _____
_____
_____

Outcome criteria

Throughout the period of hospitalization, the patient will:
• participate in decisions regarding pain control (to the extent possible)
• verbalize the effectiveness of pain-control measures.

Nursing diagnosis: *Potential fluid volume deficit related to anorexia and dehydration associated with imminent death*

NURSING PRIORITY: Promote patient comfort during the dying process.

Interventions

1. *Avoid vigorous fluid replacement for terminally ill patients.*

2. Offer frequent mouth care, ice chips, or hard candy, as indicated by the patient's condition.

Rationales

1. Dehydration is a normal part of the dying process in terminal illnesses. I.V. fluid replacement may unnecessarily prolong the process.

2. These measures may help reduce discomfort related to mouth dryness and minimal oral intake.

Interventions *continued*

3. Provide careful skin care. Use soap sparingly and lotion generously if dry skin is present. Turn the patient carefully to prevent shearing.

4. Additional individualized interventions: _____
_____
_____

Rationales *continued*

3. Dehydration and debilitation contribute to poor skin turgor and increased risk of skin breakdown. Soap dries skin, increasing irritation. Gentle massage with lotion and careful turning demonstrate care and help prevent complications.

4. Rationale: _____
_____
_____

Outcome criterion
During the final phase of the dying process, the patient will:
• experience minimum discomfort related to dehydration.

Nursing diagnosis: *Alteration in family processes related to imminent death of family member*

NURSING PRIORITY: Minimize disruption in family integrity by facilitating healthy coping, mutual support, and communication with the dying person.

Interventions

1. *See the "Ineffective Family Coping" care plan, page 47.*

2. *Assess the family's level of acceptance and coping* by observing behaviors and interactions of individuals with the patient and by providing time for private discussions with family members, as needed. Be alert to differences among individual family members and clues to the family's previous experience with death, if any.

3. *Liberalize visiting policies,* as needed. Allow private time for the family to be with the patient. Encourage family members to participate in care, remaining alert for signs of possible anxiety or discomfort.

4. *When possible, facilitate family dialogue,* remaining cognizant of established family roles and expectations. Offer to introduce topics, as needed; strive to promote face-to-face communication when possible.

Rationales

1. This care plan provides guidelines for helping families at risk for crisis.

2. Effective intervention must be appropriately correlated with the stage of acceptance. Each member of the family may respond differently to the threat of loss. Previous family deaths may affect members' ability to cope in mutually supportive ways.

3. Family integrity is more likely to be maintained when members are able to continue their usual level of contact with one another. Helping with patient care reduces the family's sense of helplessness and provides special comfort to the patient. However, this should not substitute for the nurse's cultivation of close involvement with the patient and family: The nurse must avoid giving the impression of dismissing or neglecting the patient.

4. Discussing issues surrounding death is difficult for most families and may be compounded by unresolved conflicts, guilt, or role demands. The nurse may be able to act as a liaison to open up communication about sensitive issues. Family stability is related to long-standing family patterns of behavior, so interventions that are at odds with these will be unsuccessful. Direct communication promotes maximum understanding and helps minimize later guilt over things left unsaid.

(continued)

Interventions *continued*

5. Be aware of cultural attitudes that may affect family response.

6. *Help the family identify and mobilize external resources,* such as friends, clergy, counselors, and sourses of financial support. Provide referrals to a psychiatric clinician or social worker or for pastoral care, as needed.

7. Encourage family members to keep up their own physical and emotional strength. Emphasize the importance of adequate rest, food, and exercise. Suggest that family members take turns at the bedside if they are reluctant to leave the patient unattended.

8. Additional individualized interventions: _____
_____
_____

Outcome criteria
Throughout the period of hospitalization, the family will:
• participate in care
• share concerns with patient and each other
• appear well rested most of the time.

Rationales *continued*

5. Different cultures view death in different ways. Some observe specific rituals for the occasion; others emphasize withdrawal from others. Being aware of such differences helps the nurse plan interventions to support the family's cultural resource base.

6. A family coping with death, especially if the dying process is prolonged, often requires added support to deal with stresses. Other professionals may offer such assistance as spiritual or psychological counseling, temporary housing placement, and guidance in identifying programs to help with the financial burden of care.

7. Maintenance of physical and emotional well-being is essential if family members are to continue providing support for the patient and each other. "Break times" help the family maintain contact with external resources and reduce the emotional strain of constant attendance to the dying person's needs.

8. Rationale: _____
_____
_____

Throughout the period of hospitalization, the patient will:
• exhibit minimal anxiety over family's well-being.

Nursing diagnosis: *Family coping: potential for growth, related to bereavement and mourning*

NURSING PRIORITY: Facilitate the initiation of healthy grieving after death occurs.

Interventions

1. See the "Grief/Grieving" care plan, page 41.

2. If not already acquainted with the family, introduce yourself, identify your relationship as the patient's caregiver, and express sympathy.

3. *Allow family members to see and touch the body.* If death was sudden and unexpected, prepare them for the appearance of the body in advance, explaining that all measures were tried in an attempt to restore life. Ensure that the body is respectfully covered but not inaccessible; do not clean up all indications of emergency intervention before allowing the family into the room.

Rationales

1. This care plan contains general interventions helpful in caring for bereaved families.

2. If the family arrives after the patient has died, or if the family does not know caregivers from previous contact, such an introduction serves to reassure them that the patient died with concerned caregivers at hand.

3. Seeing and touching the body of the loved one helps the family accept the reality of death. If death was sudden and resuscitation efforts altered the body's appearance, advance preparation for viewing the body may help reduce distress for the family. Gross blood or other secretions should be cleaned up before the family enters, but putting away all supplies and cleaning the room before the family sees the body may create doubts that "everything possible was done" for the patient.

Interventions *continued*

4. *Use direct, simple sentences,* avoiding use of euphemisms, to describe the death. Provide comforting observations when possible—such as, "He died quietly and appeared to have no pain" or "She told me last night about the good times you used to have, and she seemed very happy."

5. *Acknowledge the family's loss* by gently reorienting them to the reality of death: "It must be hard to accept that he's really dead." Avoid overly sentimental responses.

6. Avoid recommending or encouraging sedation of a family member unless severely dysfunctional behavior is present.

7. *Offer to call a friend, member of the clergy, or counselor of choice to help with immediate arrangements.* If the family does not designate such a person, offer the services of the hospital chaplain, a liaison nurse, or another in-house professional skilled in dealing with grief.

8. Prepare the family for the work of grieving. Emphasize the normality of a wide range of emotional responses (such as anger, guilt, sadness, frustration, resentment, fear, and depression) and behaviors (such as crying, laughing, withdrawal, and confusion) in response to loss of a loved one.

9. Listen patiently to retellings of the story of the death, especially if it was unexpected. Avoid responses that might be interpreted as judgmental.

10. Reemphasize the need for health-promoting self-care behaviors during the grieving period.

11. *Ensure that significant others will be available to be with survivors* after they leave the hospital.

12. If possible, provide a follow-up call to surviving family members 1 to 3 months after bereavement. Keeping a callback calendar on the unit can help in organizing this task.

Rationales *continued*

4. Most family members are too anxious at this time to comprehend complex explanations. Euphemisms such as "passed on" may offend some family members and can interfere with reality orientation. Sharing selected, specific observations with family members may help minimize guilt and promote healthy grieving.

5. Shock and disbelief are normal initial responses to sudden death and, to a certain degree, even to expected death. Gentle reorientation aids in the process of integrating death into reality. Overly sentimental responses may be inappropriate to the family's actual relationship with the deceased.

6. Sedation may delay initiation of the normal grieving process.

7. During the initial stages of the grieving process, decision making becomes difficult, and disorganization and disorientation are common. Providing an advocacy person helps reduce the family's distress while they are making necessary arrangements, such as for disposition of the body.

8. Family members are sometimes unprepared for the various feelings experienced in the grieving process; some may feel they are "going crazy" when unexpected feelings occur. Understanding that such emotional disorganization is a normal and healthy response to loss can help the family deal with these feelings.

9. Retelling of events by survivors is an essential part of reality acceptance and coping. Judgmental responses may provoke severe guilt reactions in family members.

10. Grieving places additional stress on survivors, who are at increased risk for developing physical illness during mourning. Health-promoting behavior, such as exercise, can help release emotional energy and reduce the effects of stress.

11. The grieving process is facilitated by sharing feelings with others. Few instances of loneliness are as profound as that of a bereaved person, newly alone.

12. Follow-up from caregivers to survivors is the final step in care of the dying patient and provides the family with added assurance that their loved one was "special" and received care accordingly. This call also provides an opportunity to identify dysfunctional grieving and make appropriate referrals, if needed.

(continued)

Interventions *continued*

13. Additional individualized interventions: _____
_____
_____

Outcome criteria
Before survivors leave the hospital, they will:
• view and touch the body, if desired
• express initial grief or disbelief

Rationales *continued*

13. Rationale: _____
_____
_____

• make contact with advocacy groups or support persons.

One to three months after death, family members will:
• cope effectively, with adequate support.

Discharge planning
NURSING DISCHARGE CRITERIA
If the patient is discharged home before death, documentation shows evidence of:
• referral to a hospice or to a home health care agency
• adequate support system for family members.

PATIENT/FAMILY DISCHARGE TEACHING CHECKLIST
If the patient is discharged home before death, document patient and family understanding of:
___ support and resources available
___ what to do when death is imminent
___ what to do after death occurs
___ what to expect in normal mourning/grieving.

DOCUMENTATION CHECKLIST
If patient is discharged home before death, using outcome criteria as a guide, document:
___ fears
___ feelings expressed
___ goals
___ preferred coping behaviors
___ spiritual or religious practices
___ pain-control measures
___ family members' behaviors
___ patient/family teaching
___ discharge planning.
If death occurs in the hospital, document:
___ time and circumstances of death
___ disposition of body and effects
___ family support measures implemented.

ASSOCIATED CARE PLANS
(See also the patient care plan for the specific disease or disorder.)
Geriatric Considerations
Grief/Grieving
Ineffective Family Coping
Ineffective Individual Coping
Pain

REFERENCES
Fanslow, Julia. "Needs of Grieving Spouses in Sudden Death Situations: A Pilot Study," *Journal of Emergency Nursing* 9:4 (1)213-16, July/August 1983.
Frankl, Viktor E. *Man's Search for Meaning*. New York: Washington Square Press, 1969.
Hoff, Lee Ann. *People in Crisis: Understanding and Helping*, 2nd ed. Menlo Park, Calif.: Addison-Wesley Publishing Co., 1984.
Hudak, Carolyn M., and Gallo, Barbara M. *Critical Care Nursing: A Holistic Approach*, 4th ed. Philadelphia: J.B. Lippincott Co., 1985.
Jung, Carl G. *Modern Man in Search of a Soul*. New York: Harcourt, Brace and Co., 1934.
Kneisl, Carol R., and Ames, Sue Ann. *Adult Health Nursing: A Biopsychosocial Approach*. Menlo Park, Calif.: Addison-Wesley Publishing Co., 1986.
Kübler-Ross, Elisabeth, ed. *Death: The Final Stage of Growth*. Englewood Cliffs, N.J.: Prentice-Hall, 1975.
Kübler-Ross, Elisabeth. *Living with Death and Dying*. New York: Macmillan Publishing Co., 1982.
Tatelbaum, Judy. *The Courage to Grieve: Creative Living, Recovery, and Growth Through Grief*. New York: Harper & Row Publishers, 1980.

Fluid and Electrolyte Imbalances

Introduction

DEFINITION AND TIME FOCUS

Fluid and electrolyte imbalances are complex, interrelated manifestations of altered homeostasis to which almost any patient with an acute illness or injury may be susceptible. Assessment and treatment of these disorders require not only an awareness of specific factors that affect fluid and electrolyte balance but also an understanding of the net effect of their interaction. At times, a delicate "balancing act" is required to avoid precipitating more serious imbalances through the treatment of existing disorders.

Body fluid is made up of two subtypes: intracellular fluid (ICF), constituting approximately 70% of total body water, and extracellular fluid (ECF), accounting for the other 30%. The ECF is further subdivided as follows: interstitial fluid, which lies outside both the cells and the vascular system, and plasma, which makes up the liquid portion of blood.

Electrolytes are present in both ICF and ECF in varying concentrations. Potassium and phosphate are found predominantly in ICF; sodium and chloride are the primary electrolytes in ECF. Although the serum concentration is usually used to measure electrolyte values, this provides only an approximate indication of overall solute status.

Fluid and electrolytes within the body are in constant flux as body processes occur. Water is lost through such processes as respiration and evaporation from the skin, and electrolytes move continuously into and out of the cells and are excreted with water through various mechanisms. Processes involved in the movement of fluid and electrolytes include diffusion, osmosis, active transport, and the effects of hydrostatic pressure, filtration pressure across the capillary membrane, and osmotic pressure.

Homeostasis, the balanced state maintained by the body's constant adaptation to changing conditions, results from the coordinated functioning of lungs, kidneys, regulatory hormones, and the cardiovascular system.

Fluid and electrolyte disorders may be classified into four types: hypovolemia (for example, shock caused by hemorrhage), hypervolemia (for example, congestive heart failure), hyperosmolar states (for example, diabetic ketoacidosis or hypernatremia), and hypoosmolar states (for example, water intoxication). These are not always clearly distinct from one another; in fact, some overlapping almost always occurs because these classifications represent dynamic states.

Comprehensive discussion of fluid and electrolyte balance is beyond the scope of this care plan. Instead, this plan presents an overview of primary considerations in caring for the hospitalized patient who is at risk for developing fluid and electrolyte disorders.

ETIOLOGY/PRECIPITATING FACTORS

• conditions causing an excess of fluid or electrolytes: excessive intake, impaired excretion, or retention because of severe injury to tissues
• conditions causing a deficit of fluid or electrolytes: inadequate intake, excessive excretion, or biochemical destruction
• conditions increasing use of fluid or electrolytes: increased metabolism from fever, activity, or hormonal imbalances
• conditions causing accumulation of fluid or electrolytes in body tissues or cavities—such as hepatic disease or myxedema
• conditions causing interference with homeostatic regulation—for example, renal disease, liver disease, pancreatic disease, central nervous system (CNS) disorders, or hormonal disturbances

Focused assessment guidelines

Note: Because of the wide variation in findings expected with different fluid and electrolyte imbalances, the "Nursing History (Functional health pattern findings)" and "Physical Findings" sections of this care plan have been omitted. Specific findings for each type of imbalance are delineated in the problem covering it.

DIAGNOSTIC STUDIES

Because laboratory and diagnostic findings vary widely in fluid and electrolyte imbalances, specific findings for each type of imbalance are discussed in the problem covering it. The following laboratory tests, followed by normal values, are commonly ordered for fluid and electrolyte imbalances:
• serum hemoglobin levels—12 to 18 g/dl
• serum hematocrit levels—38% to 54%
• serum electrolyte levels—sodium, 136 to 142 mEq/liter; potassium, 3.5 to 5 mEq/liter; calcium, 8.5 to 10.8 mg/dl; and chloride, 96 to 106 mEq/liter
• serum osmolality—285 to 295 mOsm/kg
• blood urea nitrogen (BUN) levels—8 to 20 mg/dl
• serum creatinine levels—1 to 1.4 mg/dl
• urine specific gravity—1.010 to 1.025

POTENTIAL COMPLICATIONS

• cardiac arrest
• respiratory arrest
• shock
• coma
• renal failure
• circulatory overload
• heart failure
• cerebral edema

CLUES TO ELECTROLYTE IMBALANCES

Signs and Symptoms	Hyper-kalemia	Hypo-kalemia	Hyper-calcemia	Hypo-calcemia	Hyper-magnesemia	Hypo-magnesemia
CARDIOVASCULAR						
Dysrhythmias	▲	▲				
Irregular heart rate	▲	▲	▲	▲	▲	▲
P waves	▲[1]	▲[2]				
PR prolongation	▲	▲			▲	
QRS prolongation	▲				▲	
Q-T interval			▲[3]	▲[4]		
ST depression	▲					
T waves	▲[2]	▲[5]			▲[6]	
U waves		▲				
GASTROINTESTINAL						
Constipation			▲			
Cramps	▲					
Diarrhea	▲			▲		
Ileus		▲				
Nausea	▲	▲	▲	▲		
Vomiting		▲	▲	▲		
GENITOURINARY						
Renal calculi			▲			
MUSCULOSKELETAL						
Deep bone pain			▲			
Flank pain			▲			
Pathologic fracture			▲			
NEUROLOGIC						
Convulsions				▲		▲
Hyperactive reflexes	▲					▲
Hypoactive reflexes		▲	▲		▲	
Irritability				▲		
Lethargy, coma			▲			
Muscle cramps						▲
Paresthesia	▲[7]	▲				
Tetany				▲		▲
Twitching	▲					▲
PULMONARY						
Hypoventilation		▲			▲	

(1) lost; (2) peaked; (3) shortened; (4) prolonged; (5) flattened; (6) increased; (7) a late symptom of hypercalcemia

Collaborative problem: *Potential hypovolemia (ECF volume deficit) related to excessive losses of sodium and water in relatively equal proportions or to inadequate replacement of sodium and water*

NURSING PRIORITY: Restore fluid volume.

Interventions

1. *Assess for conditions increasing the risk of hypovolemia,* such as kidney disease, gastrointestinal disease, trauma, hemorrhage, severe burns, draining fistula, systemic infection, diuretic therapy, hyperthermia, peritonitis, confusion, depression, coma, diarrhea, fever, vomiting, or inability to swallow.

In any patient with one or more of these conditions, monitor intake and output carefully every shift, assess weight daily using consistent technique, and monitor vital signs at least every 4 hours.

2. *Assess for signs and symptoms of hypovolemia* and report findings to the doctor immediately; anticipate fluid replacement needs.
• Cardiovascular findings may include tachycardia, orthostatic hypotension, weak and thready pulse, or narrow pulse pressure.
• Gastrointestinal findings may include dry mucous membranes, a furrowed and coated tongue, or excessive thirst.
• Integumentary findings may include poor skin turgor, pallor, and cool clammy skin.
• Other findings include weakness, anorexia, fatigue, restlessness, tachypnea, decreased level of consciousness, and oliguria or anuria (urine output <20 ml/hour).

3. Evaluate laboratory findings for indications of hypovolemia, as follows, and report findings to the doctor:
• urinalysis—increased specific gravity, increased osmolality
• serum osmolality level—increased
• hematocrit level—usually increased from hemoconcentration; may be decreased if bleeding is cause of hypovolemia
• BUN and serum creatinine levels—increased
• serum electrolyte levels—findings may vary; because serum electrolyte values represent concentrations rather than absolute amounts of electrolytes, values may be normal or elevated, giving a misleading impression of total body stores
• arterial blood gas (ABG) measurements—findings vary according to the cause of volume loss
• 12-lead EKG—findings vary with the cause and presence of associated electrolyte imbalances.

Rationales

1. Early assessment and prophylactic intervention for patients at risk may prevent an actual deficit from occurring. Any condition in which large amounts of fluid are lost predisposes the patient to hypovolemia. Hypovolemia may also occur gradually, in which case early findings may be subtle and go unrecognized. Careful clinical observation is essential for patients who are confused or who otherwise may be unable to recognize their need for fluids.

2. Signs and symptoms of severe hypovolemia correlate with those of shock. Although fluid loss initially affects the extracellular space, deficits eventually result in intracellular dehydration as well, as fluid and electrolytes move out of the cells in response to the changed osmolality. Blood volume is reduced, and osmotic pressure increases. In response, hypothalamic osmoreceptors stimulate the thirst center and also trigger release of antidiuretic hormone (ADH). The adrenal gland also releases aldosterone, which, like ADH, causes renal water retention. Blood volume loss is sensed by baroreceptors in the aortic arch and carotid sinus. These baroreceptors cause the compensatory tachycardia and peripheral vasoconstriction. Postural hypotension results when blood volume and cardiac output are sufficient to maintain blood pressure when the patient is supine but insufficient to maintain pressure when the patient is in an upright position and gravity reduces central venous return.

3. Laboratory findings in early hypovolemia may reflect minor abnormalities. Urine specific gravity and osmolality are increased as the kidneys attempt to retain fluid in response to ADH and aldosterone release. Serum osmolality reflects serum concentration and indicates overall fluid volume loss. BUN and creatinine levels increase in response to the reduced glomerular filtration rate. Generally, electrolytes will be lost in proportion to volume loss; conditions in which this is not true are discussed in the problems dealing with imbalances of hypoosmolality and hyperosmolality.

Disorders that cause volume deficit commonly cause associated acid-base imbalances. For example, loss of acidic gastric fluids may result in metabolic alkalosis, whereas decreased oxygen transport caused by hemorrhage can trigger metabolic acidosis.

EKG changes typically occur late in the course of hypovolemia and thus are of questionable value in assessing for the condition.

(continued)

Interventions *continued*

4. Estimate the patient's average daily fluid loss in consultation with the doctor (most adults need about 2,000 to 3,000 ml/day).

5. *Estimate the degree of preexisting fluid deficit* in consultation with the doctor by observing the following signs and symptoms:
• for mild deficits (about 20% of blood volume)—tachycardia; normal or slightly decreased blood pressure; positive postural vital signs (a systolic blood pressure decrease of >20 mm Hg or a pulse increase of >20 beats/minute); cool, pale skin; capillary filling >3 seconds; urine output 30 to 50 ml/hour; patient alert and oriented
• for moderate deficits (about 30% of blood volume)—rapid and thready pulse; supine hypotension; cool truncal skin; oliguria (urine output <30 ml/hour); marked thirst; patient restless, confused, or agitated
• for severe deficits (>40% of blood volume)—a very rapid, weak pulse; systolic blood pressure <80 mm Hg; mottled, cyanotic, cold skin; urine output <20 ml/hour; patient disoriented or unresponsive.

6. *Use discretionary judgment in selecting appropriate therapy.* Obtain appropriate orders from the doctor if indicated.

• For a mild deficit, offer small amounts of ice chips or preferred oral fluids frequently. Chill the fluids if the patient's mouth or throat is sore.

• Enlist the patient's and family's cooperation in reaching the target intake level: Stress its importance, and teach how to keep a tally of intake.

• For a moderate to severe deficit, or when oral intake is contraindicated, initiate I.V. access, per protocol or as ordered. Depending on the degree of deficit, use the largest needle possible (typically 16- to 18-gauge). If active bleeding is present, use a 14-gauge needle.

7. Monitor EKGs for the characteristic changes of hypokalemia or hyperkalemia or hypocalcemia or hypercalcemia (see *Clues to Electrolyte Imbalances*, page 22.)

8. Exercise caution when treating hypovolemia in a patient with renal or cardiac failure. Observe closely for indications of fluid overload (see the following problem for details).

Rationales *continued*

4. The fluid replacement plan is based on the patient's steady-state fluid maintenance level and therapeutic needs. The average daily fluid loss for a 200-lb healthy adult is 1,500 ml in urine, 200 ml in feces, and 1,300 ml in insensible fluid loss (via perspiration and respiration).

5. The degree of fluid deficit affects the amount and route of replacement.

6. Mild fluid volume deficit usually can be managed by nursing measures. Selection of the type and amount of therapeutic replacement for moderate to severe deficits requires medical judgment.

• Small amounts are less likely to provoke nausea and vomiting. Offering fluids of the preferred type and temperature increases their appeal.

• The patient is more likely to comply with fluid prescription by understanding its significance. Tracking fluid intake and output is a simple method of involving the patient in self-care and may increase self-esteem and active participation in recovery.

• In moderate to severe deficit, or when oral intake is contraindicated, I.V. replacement is necessary. I.V. access is more easily established before severe deficit and accompanying vascular collapse occur. The size of the needle lumen determines the rate of flow. A 14-gauge needle allows for more rapid replacement of large volumes of blood when necessary.

7. Altered electrolyte levels that may accompany fluid deficit can precipitate serious dysrhythmias. Potassium and calcium play crucial roles in maintaing normal cellular transmembrane electrical balance.

8. Too-rapid fluid replacement in a patient with impaired renal or cardiac function may precipitate pulmonary edema and acute heart failure.

Interventions *continued*

9. Provide appropriate patient/family teaching to correlate with interventions.

10. Additional individualized interventions: _____
_____
_____

Outcome criteria
Throughout the period of hospitalization, the patient will have:
• approximately equal fluid intake and output
• constant weight within a 4-lb fluctuation

Rationales *continued*

9. The patient and family who understand the rationales for interventions, as well as their key features, is most likely to support and participate appropriately in them.

10. Rationale: _____
_____
_____

• vital signs within normal limits for this patient
• urine output > 60 ml/hour (except in renal failure)
• warm and dry skin.

Collaborative problem: *Potential hypervolemia (ECF volume excess) related to excessive intake of sodium and water in relatively equal proportions or to inadequate excretion of sodium and water*

NURSING PRIORITY: Decrease fluid volume.

Interventions

1. *Assess for conditions increasing the risk of hypervolemia,* such as renal failure, cardiac failure, liver disease (portal obstruction), cerebral injury, steroid therapy, noncompliance with diuretic therapy, excessive or rapid infusion of saline solution, or conditions causing hyperaldosteronism.
   In any patient with one or more of these conditions, monitor intake and output carefully on at least a shift-to-shift basis, assess weight daily using consistent technique, and monitor vital signs at least every 4 hours.

2. *Assess for signs and symptoms of hypervolemia* and report findings to the doctor; anticipate initiation of diuretic therapy.
• Cardiovascular findings may include such early signs as bounding pulse, normal to high systolic blood pressure, and neck vein distension as well as tachycardia, S_3 and S_4 heart sounds, edema (peripheral or periorbital), and ascites.
• Pulmonary findings may include shallow respirations (an early sign), tachypnea, crackles, cough, orthopnea, dyspnea, diminished breath sounds (pleural effusion), and frothy sputum.
• Other findings may include taut, shiny skin and altered level of consciousness (a late sign).

3. Evaluate laboratory findings for indications of hypervolemia, as follows, and report findings to the doctor:
• urinalysis—decreased specific gravity
• serum osmolality level—usually decreased, depending on renal function
• hematocrit level—decreased

Rationales

1. Early assessment and prophylactic intervention for patients at risk may prevent an excess from occurring. Any condition in which excretion is impaired predisposes the patient to developing circulatory overload. Careful monitoring of total intake and output is essential for early detection of imbalance.

2. Signs and symptoms of hypervolemia correlate with those of congestive heart failure or pulmonary edema. Blood volume is increased, and the heart must work harder to handle the added load. Blood backs up into the pulmonary microcirculation, and the increased pressure on engorged pulmonary capillaries causes leakage into interstitial spaces, with swelling and obstruction of alveoli. Increased vascular volume increases capillary pressure, resulting in edema (usually peripheral in early stages), followed by development of periorbital edema or ascites if portal hypertension is present.

3. Laboratory findings in early hypervolemia may reflect minor abnormalities. Specific gravity reflects urine concentration, which is low because of either an increased glomerular filtration rate (if renal function is intact) or the loss of tubular capacity for adjusting urine concentration (if renal function is impaired). The serum osmolality level reflects serum concentration

(continued)

Interventions *continued*

- BUN and creatinine levels—usually decreased; may be increased if renal impairment is cause of excess
- serum electrolyte levels—findings vary, depending on cause of hypervolemia
- ABG measurements—findings vary, depending on the cause of the imbalance
- 12-lead EKG—findings vary with the cause and presence of associated electrolyte imbalance
- chest X-ray—enlarged heart, pleural effusion, patchy densities.

4. Consult with the doctor regarding therapeutic interventions. These vary, depending on the cause and severity of volume excess, but usually include fluid restriction and diuretic therapy. Provide appropriate patient/family teaching to correlate with interventions.

5. Additional individualized interventions: _____
_____
_____

Outcome criteria

Throughout the period of hospitalization, the patient will have:
- approximately equal fluid intake and output
- consistent weight

Rationales *continued*

and is an indicator of overall fluid volume status. The hematocrit level decreases because of hemodilution. BUN and creatinine levels may be increased, if renal failure is present, or may decrease in response to increased glomerular filtration. Because serum electrolyte values represent concentrations rather than absolute amounts, values may be decreased disproportionately. Disorders causing hypervolemia commonly cause associated acid-base imbalance. For example, heart failure that results in pulmonary edema may result in respiratory or metabolic acidosis from retention of CO_2 and from anaerobic metabolism. EKG changes are generally not of diagnostic value in assessing for hypervolemia. Cardiac hypertrophy, visible on X-ray, reflects the presence of heart failure and muscle enlargement in response to an increased work load. Effusion or densities may indicate areas of atelectasis.

4. Treatment of hypervolemia should address the underlying cause. Hypervolemia from cardiac failure may require digitalis therapy; renal failure may necessitate dialysis. Fluid restriction and diuretic therapy reduce volume load but will provide only temporary relief unless the specific pathophysiologic abnormality is compensated for or corrected.

5. Rationale: _____
_____
_____

- vital signs within normal limits for this patient
- urine output > 60 ml/hour (except in renal failure)
- warm and dry skin.

Collaborative problem: *Potential hyperosmolar imbalance related to extracellular solute excess or water deficit*

NURSING PRIORITY: Restore water-solute balance.

Interventions

1. *Assess for conditions increasing the risk of hyperosmolar imbalance,* such as diabetes mellitus, diabetes insipidus (impaired ADH), renal disease, excessive protein intake, inability to swallow, coma, profuse watery diarrhea, prolonged vomiting, gastric suction, hyperthermia, cerebral injury (causing impairment of thirst mechanism), hyperventilation (water loss through breathing), profuse diaphoresis, and excessive administration of hypertonic solutions, glucose, or sodium bicarbonate.
   In any patient with one or more of these conditions, monitor intake and output carefully on at least a shift-to-shift basis, assess weight daily using consistent technique, and monitor vital signs at least every 4 hours.

Rationales

1. Early assessment and prophylactic intervention for patients at risk may prevent an imbalance from occurring. In hyperosmolar states, actual fluid volume may be normal and the solute level elevated (for example, in diabetes mellitus), or the solute level may be normal with reduced water volume (for example, in diabetes insipidus). In either case, the result is an abnormally concentrated fluid state—hyperosmolality.

Interventions *continued*

2. *Assess for signs and symptoms of hyperosmolar imbalance,* such as elevated temperature; neurologic disorders (tremors, restlessness, apprehension, seizures, and coma); a dry, furrowed tongue; muscle rigidity; poor skin turgor; and soft sunken eyeballs (a late sign). Although most patients have concentrated urine, polyuria and dilute urine output may be an initial sign in diabetes mellitus or diabetes insipidus.

3. Evaluate laboratory findings for indications of hyperosmolar imbalance, as follows, and report findings to the doctor:
• urinalysis—in diabetes insipidus, low specific gravity, low osmolality; in other conditions, urine concentrated, with high specific gravity; possible glycosuria if diabetes mellitus is underlying cause
• hemoglobin level—elevated
• serum sodium level—usually elevated above 150 mEq/liter
• serum potassium level—may be elevated
• serum glucose level—elevated in diabetes mellitus
• BUN level—may be decreased
• serum osmolality level—increased
• ABG levels—findings vary, depending on the cause.

4. Consult with the doctor about therapeutic interventions. These vary, depending on the cause and severity of the hyperosmolar disorder, but usually include water replacement, isotonic I.V. hydration (usually dextrose 5% in water unless diabetes mellitus is present), monitoring for dysrhythmias, and appropriate patient teaching.

5. Observe the patient carefully during rehydration for signs of water intoxication (see the following problem).

6. Additional individualized interventions: _____
_____
_____

Outcome criteria
Throughout the period of hospitalization, the patient will have:
• approximately equal fluid intake and output
• consistent weight

Rationales *continued*

2. Signs and symptoms of hyperosmolar states correlate with those of dehydration. As the ECF becomes more concentrated, fluid leaves the cells to dilute the ECF, causing the cells to shrink. In the brain, this causes particularly deleterious effects on cerebral function; if the imbalance is not corrected, death may result from impairment of basic central nervous system functions. If the condition stems from diabetes mellitus or solute excess, the kidneys will initially increase output to handle the excess solute load. But, as dehydration progresses (depending on the patient's clinical state), the kidneys may begin to try to compensate by concentrating urine to conserve remaining water.

3. Laboratory findings may show considerable variation, depending on the cause and level of imbalance. The tests listed are only a few of many that may be significant in determining the underlying condition.

In diabetes insipidus, inadequate ADH levels cause excessive output of dilute urine and excessive diaphoresis, leading to water deficit. In diabetes mellitus, the kidneys attempt to dilute the solute load caused by increased blood glucose levels, and this results in increased water loss. Also, water leaves the cells to dilute the ECF.

Elevated hemoglobin level reflects hemoconcentration; elevated serum sodium level reflects dehydration, water loss in excess of sodium excretion, or sodium retention, which may occur as ADH and aldosterone are released. Serum potassium level may be misleadingly elevated as potassium leaves the cells along with fluid.

Hyperosmolar disturbances commonly cause associated acid-base imbalances; for example, hyperglycemia in diabetes mellitus may precipitate metabolic acidosis from incomplete glucose metabolism and accumulation of protein by-products.

4. Treatment of the dehydration that results from hyperosmolar states must address the underlying cause. Hyperosmolarity caused by mild solute excess may be treated with oral hydration, whereas a patient with hyperosmolar hyperglycemia may need insulin and hypotonic I.V. fluids. Diabetes insipidus from vasopressin deficiency may be corrected by vasopressin replacement. Altered potassium levels from hyperosmolar states may interfere with normal transmembrane electrical conductivity, producing dysrhythmias.

5. Overvigorous fluid replacement, especially if hypotonic fluids are used, may precipitate water intoxication.

6. Rationale: _____
_____
_____

• vital signs within normal limits for this patient
• urine output >60 ml/hour (except in renal failure)
• warm and dry skin.

Collaborative problem: *Potential hypoosmolar imbalance related to extracellular solute deficit or water excess*

NURSING PRIORITY: Restore water-solute balance.

Interventions

1. *Assess for conditions increasing the risk of hypoosmolar imbalance,* such as renal disease, cerebral injury, syndrome of inappropriate antidiuretic hormone, alcoholism, psychotropic therapy that causes dry mouth or impaired water excretion, and compulsive behavior patterns causing excessive water ingestion. Also, excessive I.V. hydration with hypotonic or isotonic solutions, diuretic therapy, a very low-sodium diet, vomiting with intake limited to ice chips, excessive use of tap-water enemas, gastric suction, severe burns, and altered aldosterone secretion from any cause put a patient at increased risk.

   In any patient with one or more of these conditions, monitor intake and output carefully every shift, assess weight daily using consistent technique, and monitor vital signs at least every 4 hours.

2. *Assess for signs and symptoms of hypoosmolar imbalance.*
• Cardiovascular findings may include a full bounding pulse, peripheral or periorbital edema, normal or elevated blood pressure, and increased pulse pressure.
• Neurologic findings may include cerebral edema, confusion, apprehension, irritability, restlessness, headache, decreased reflexes, seizures, hallucinations, hemiplegia, and coma.
• Pulmonary findings may include crackles, tachypnea, and shortness of breath.
• Other findings may include abdominal cramps, diarrhea, muscle weakness or twitching, poor skin turgor, "finger printing" over the sternum, polyuria, and oliguria (if renal disease is present or as hyponatremia worsens).

3. Evaluate laboratory findings for indications of hypoosmolar imbalance, as follows, and report findings to the doctor:
• urinalysis—decreased specific gravity
• urine sodium level—reduced
• hemoglobin and hematocrit levels—usually below normal
• serum sodium level—usually below 135 mEq/L
• serum potassium level—usually low
• serum osmolality level—decreased
• BUN level—decreased due to overhydration
• ABG measurements—results vary, depending on cause and level of imbalance.

Rationales

1. Early assessment and prophylactic intervention for patients at risk may prevent an actual hypoosmolar state from occurring. Whether actual fluid volume is normal and the solute level reduced or (more commonly) the solute level is normal with excess water, the net result is an abnormally dilute ECF.

2. Hypoosmolar states cause generalized edema, as in simple hypervolemia. Cerebral function also is markedly affected, because the cells swell in response to the hypotonicity of the ECF, and the signs and symptoms reflect this phenomenon. When ECF becomes less concentrated, fluid enters the cells to equalize the concentration on both sides of the cell membrane. The resulting cellular edema causes cerebral edema and rapid deterioration in level of consciousness if the condition is not corrected promptly.

3. Laboratory findings vary, depending on the cause and level of the imbalance. Usually, increased water causes initial inhibition of ADH, and the kidneys attempt to excrete the excess. However, as hyponatremia progresses, the adrenal glands may try to conserve sodium by releasing aldosterone, thereby reducing urinary output and worsening the water excess. Urine sodium levels are thought to be a better early indicator of sodium imbalances than serum sodium levels. Hemoglobin and hematocrit levels may be reduced from hemodilution. As ECF becomes more dilute, serum sodium concentration decreases. As with the other fluid and solute imbalances discussed in this care plan, hypoosmolar states may precipitate acid-base abnormalities.

Interventions continued

4. *Consult with the doctor regarding therapeutic interventions.* These vary, depending on the cause, but usually include:
• water restriction
• treatment of the underlying cause
• monitoring for dysrhythmias
• appropriate patient teaching.

5. Additional individualized interventions: _____
_____
_____

Outcome criteria
Throughout the period of hospitalization, the patient will have:
• approximately equal fluid intake and output
• consistent weight

Rationales continued

4. Treatment of the edema from hypoosmolar states must address the underlying cause. If severe cerebral edema is present, osmotic diuretics such as mannitol may be indicated as an emergency measure. Monitoring the patient for dysrhythmias related to altered potassium levels is essential because such alterations interfere with normal transmembrane electrical conductivity.

5. Rationale: _____
_____
_____

• vital signs within normal limits for this patient
• urine output >60 ml/hour (except in renal failure)
• warm and dry skin.

Discharge planning
NURSING DISCHARGE CRITERIA
Upon discharge, documentation shows evidence of:
• no signs or symptoms of dehydration
• no signs or symptoms of fluid overload
• electrolyte values within normal limits
• verbalized understanding of fluid and dietary recommendations
• any criteria appropriate to the underlying condition(s).

PATIENT/FAMILY DISCHARGE TEACHING CHECKLIST
Document evidence that patient/family demonstrates understanding of:
___ underlying condition: implications for fluid and electrolyte status
___ fluid and dietary recommendations
___ signs and symptoms indicating possible fluid or electrolyte imbalance
___ precautionary measures to prevent fluid or electrolyte imbalance
___ importance of monitoring weight and other parameters at home
___ all discharge medications' purpose, dosage, administration schedule, and side effects requiring medical attention
___ factors increasing fluid requirements
___ date, time, and location of follow-up appointments
___ how to contact doctor.

DOCUMENTATION CHECKLIST
Using outome criteria as a guideline, document:
___ clinical status on admission
___ significant changes in status
___ laboratory test findings
___ intake and output
___ therapeutic intervention and response
___ patient/family teaching
___ discharge planning.

ASSOCIATED CARE PLANS
Chronic Renal Failure
Congestive Heart Failure
Diabetes
Knowledge Deficit
Surgical Intervention

REFERENCES
Carpenito, L. *Nursing Diagnosis: Application to Clinical Practice.* Philadelphia: J.B. Lippincott Co., 1983.
Felver, L. "Understanding the Electrolyte Maze," *American Journal of Nursing* 1591-95, September 1980.
Gordon, Marjory. *Manual of Nursing Diagnosis.* New York: McGraw-Hill Book Co., 1982.
Holloway, Nancy M. *Nursing the Critically Ill Adult.* Menlo Park, Calif.: Addison-Wesley Publishing Co., 1988.
Kneisl, Carol R., and Ames, Sue Ann. *Adult Health Nursing: A Biopsychosocial Approach.* Menlo Park, Calif.: Addison-Wesley Publishing Co., 1986.
Luckmann, Joan, and Sorenson, Karen. *Medical-Surgical Nursing: A Psychophysiologic Approach,* 3rd ed. Philadelphia: W.B. Saunders Co., 1987.
Masiak, M.J., et al. *Fluids and Electrolytes Through the Life Cycle.* East Norwalk, Conn.: Appleton-Century-Crofts, 1985.
Ulrich, W.P., et al. *Nursing Care Planning Guides.* Philadelphia: W.B. Saunders Co., 1986.

Geriatric Considerations

Introduction

DEFINITION AND TIME FOCUS
The geriatric patient is defined as the person age 75 or older who is admitted to an acute care hospital setting. This care plan focuses on care needs specific to aging and on the sudden impact of a hospitalization experience.

ETIOLOGY/PRECIPITATING FACTORS
The geriatric person is prone to health problems because of the following changes associated with aging:
• increased susceptibility to infection
• decreased muscle strength and generalized debility
• escalated potential for chronic disease because of genetic flaws that appear only with advancing age
• psychosocial isolation
• limited income and earning ability.

Focused assessment guidelines

NURSING HISTORY (Functional health pattern findings)

Health perception–health management pattern
• may report a variety of presenting problems, depending on underlying disease

Nutritional-metabolic pattern
• may report decreased appetite resulting from trauma or disease state and impact of hospitalization
• when stable, likely to prefer usual dietary pattern of frequent small meals
• may report use of dentures or problems with dentition

Elimination pattern
• may report constipation
• may report regular use of laxatives or enemas
• may report urinary incontinence or retention related to prostatic hypertrophy (males), relaxation of perineal support (females), immobility, or environmental changes

Activity-exercise pattern
• may identify stiffness resulting from bed rest and decreased activity
• may be afraid of falling because of general weakness

Sleep-rest pattern
• may report shorter sleep cycles and early morning awakening

Cognitive-perceptual pattern
• may report difficulty remembering or comprehending events that led to hospitalization
• may report discomfort from forced hospital confinement and limited physical activity
• may report visual or sensory deficits

Self-perception–self-concept pattern
• may report lack of self-confidence in maintaining independent activities
• may communicate sense of despair because of inability to provide personal self-care (if ability is curtailed by disease or health problem)

Role-relationship pattern
• may report social isolation with hospitalization or may experience isolation in usual home setting
• may express fear of uselessness and of becoming a family burden with increased care needs arising from health problem

Coping-stress tolerance pattern
• may evidence anticipatory grief over loss of personal independence caused by chronic nature of disease
• may become dependent and give up interest in living because of helplessness precipitated by illness

Value-belief pattern
• may mourn loss of meaningful religious practices such as church attendance
• may become angry at God and direct anger toward others or self, reflecting depression
• may see no meaning or purpose in existence

PHYSICAL FINDINGS
Note: General physiologic differences associated with aging are noted here. Specific physical findings related to particular disease and illness are not discussed.

Gastrointestinal
• decreased saliva and ptyalin secretion
• decreased esophageal nerve function
• decreased gastric and intestinal motility
• decreased hydrochloric acid
• delayed gastric emptying
• decreased fat and calcium absorption

Cardiovascular
• increased systolic pressure
• increased pulse rate
• orthostatic hypotension
• arterial insufficiency
• narrowing of vessels
• decreased blood flow to organs
• thickening of capillary walls

Neurologic
• decreased sense of smell, taste, vision, touch, hearing
• decreased deep-tendon reflexes
• reduced nerve conduction time
• generally slower responses
• reduced speed of fine motor movements
• alteration in sleep patterns (3- to 4-hour sleep periods)

Integumentary
- increased wrinkles
- loss of skin turgor (elasticity)
- thinning skin (from reduced subcutaneous fat)
- reduced sebaceous and sweat gland function
- skin dryness
- changes in nail thickness
- brown or black wartlike areas of skin (seborrheic keratosis)
- red-purple overgrowth of dilated blood vessels (cherry angioma)

Musculoskeletal
- decreased bone mass, possible osteoporosis
- decrease in height
- flexed posture
- calcified cartilage and ligaments
- decreased muscle tone and strength
- gait changes
- decreased range of motion (may be from calcium salt deposits around joints)

Respiratory
- decreased lung tissue compliance (elasticity)
- calcification of vertebral cartilage, with reduced rib mobility and chest expansion
- decreased vital capacity
- decreased coughing efficiency

Genitourinary
- in male, enlarged prostate
- decrease in number of renal nephrons
- decrease in urine concentration ability
- increased nocturia
- in female, reduced vaginal lubrication

Endocrine
- thyroid—increased nodularity
- parathyroid—decreased hormone release
- pancreas—delayed insulin release from beta cells
- adrenals—decreased aldosterone and ketosteroid levels

Eye
- decreased light permeability of lens and cornea (cataracts)
- decreased speed of adaptation to darkness
- decreased accommodation
- increased astigmatism
- less efficient intraocular fluid absorption (can lead to glaucoma)
- white lipid deposit at edge of iris (arcus senilis)
- drying of conjunctivae
- increased nystagmus on lateral gaze

Ear
- loss of pure tones
- high-frequency loss
- impacted cerumen

Nose
- increase in coarse hairs

Mouth and throat
- decreased saliva
- increased dryness
- loss of teeth
- receding gums
- atrophy of taste buds
- slowed gag reflex

DIAGNOSTIC STUDIES
Tests ordered depend on the particular disease process or on presenting pathophysiology or symptomatology.

POTENTIAL COMPLICATIONS
- mental confusion
- contractures
- bowel impaction
- falls and fractures
- urinary retention and cystitis
- pulmonary emboli
- depression
- hopelessness
- loneliness
- grief

Nursing diagnosis: *Potential altered thought processes: slowed or diminished responsiveness* related to cerebral degeneration

NURSING PRIORITY: Allow ample time for all behaviors and responses.

Interventions

1. *Assess mental status:* Note orientation, remote and recent memory, ability to interpret and abstract, and general rapidity of response.

Rationales

1. Mental status may be altered because of cerebral degeneration or other factors, such as medications, but must be assessed on an individual basis. Many elderly patients retain full alertness.

(continued)

---

*non-NANDA diagnosis

Interventions *continued*

2. *Depending on deficits identified, institute appropriate measures:*

• Allow increased response time when speaking with an older person.
• Give information concisely and slowly.

• Allow ample time for activities of daily living (ADLs) and care-related procedures.
• Do not shout at the patient or use baby talk when communicating.

3. Once hospital activities are established, maintain a routine as standard as possible.

4. Additional individualized interventions: _____
_____
_____

Outcome criteria
Throughout the period of hospitalization, the patient will:
• perform self-care activities (to the degree possible) without evidence of feeling rushed

Rationales *continued*

2. Compensation for any deficits allow older persons to maintain dignity and active participation in daily activities.
• Thought processing is slower in older adults.

• Concise, slowed speech helps prevent information overload and decreases the risk of misunderstanding.
• Slower thinking is accompanied by slower performance of tasks.
• Slowed responses do not of themselves imply a hearing deficit. Shouting may increase the patient's anxiety, further impairing performance of tasks. Use of "baby talk" is demeaning and may cause erosion of self-esteem—already compromised by disability and dependence on others for care.

3. Change adaptation may be slower in older persons. Routines provide security and reassurance. Major environmental alterations, particularly when accompanied by physiologic changes, may precipitate depression, confusion, or psychosis.

4. Rationale: _____
_____
_____

• appear relaxed
• adapt to hospital routine without agitation.

Nursing diagnosis: *Potential altered thought processes: confusion related to diminished perception of sensory data*

NURSING PRIORITIES: (a) Promote increased clarity of sensory-perceptual stimuli, and (b) decrease agitation related to confusion.

Interventions

1. *When confusion is evidenced, attempt to identify the cause,* such as hearing, visual ability, or mental status (see previous diagnosis). Be aware of other factors that can cause confusion, such as metabolic alterations, hypoxemia, electrolyte imbalances, or medications.

2. *Before speaking, alert the patient by touch;* speak only when clearly in the patient's line of vision.

3. *Speak in a low tone.* (If the patient's hearing is greatly impaired and no hearing aid is available, place a stethoscope into the patient's ears, then speak into the bell.)

Rationales

1. Confusion may be related to misunderstanding because of deafness or to disorientation related to visual impairment. Confusion may also be a symptom of more serious problems. Assuming confusion is the normal mental state of a patient may leave problems unresolved that have physical or physiologic causes.

2. If information is not heard clearly it may be misperceived, increasing confusion. Older persons may compensate for hearing deficits by partial lipreading.

3. Loss of high-frequency hearing ability usually occurs first.

Interventions *continued*

4. Provide the patient's own glasses for reading, as needed.

5. Allow extra time for adjustment to changes in light levels. Turn on lights slowly if there are several in the room.

6. *Provide adequate illumination* during daytime and at night.

7. *Use restraints only as necessary* to prevent injury when the patient is unattended. Explain the reasons for using restraints to both patient and family.

8. Provide environmental cues to orient the patient: for example, a clock, a calendar, or pictures of loved ones.

9. Encourage the use of audio- or videotaped messages from family members if disorientation persists.

10. Additional individualized interventions: _____
_____
_____

Rationales *continued*

4. Distance accommodation decreases with aging.

5. Light accommodation also decreases with aging.

6. Sundowning is a condition in which the elderly tend to become confused at the end of the day, when fading light causes loss of visual cues. Often marked by wandering, it is reduced when the available lighting provides clear visualization of persons, objects, and surroundings.

7. Confusion may contribute to falls and accidents, but restraints should not be used as a substitute for adequate care and supervision. Use of restraints may be damaging to the patient's self-esteem and promote dependence on others for meeting basic needs.

8. Confusion and disorientation are reduced by familiar objects in the immediate environment.

9. Taped messages provide the comfort of familiar voices (or voices and faces) when the family is not able to visit and may decrease agitation and restlessness associated with disorientation.

10. Rationale: _____
_____
_____

Outcome criteria
Within 2 days of admission, the patient will:
• maintain orientation at or above the usual level

• participate appropriately in care activities without agitation.

Collaborative problem: *Potential renal impairment related to physiologic degeneration of functioning nephron units and filtering glomeruli*

NURSING PRIORITY: Compensate for decreased renal function.

Interventions

1. *Monitor all medications for toxic side effects.*

2. Administer narcotics and sedatives judiciously.

3. Collaborate with the doctor to adjust fluid intake.

Rationales

1. Altered and erratic renal functioning caused by aging changes may affect the excretion rate, causing toxicity at lower doses.

2. Normal doses of these drugs may create an overdose for the older person because of the cumulative effect of reduced renal function.

3. Impaired renal function may precipitate congestive heart failure (CHF). In addition, the aging heart is less efficient, further contributing to the risk of CHF.

(continued)

Interventions *continued*

4. Monitor for signs of fluid overload, such as neck vein distention, increased central venous pressure readings, crackles, dependent edema, increased pulse rate, and rapid weight gain.

5. Additional individualized interventions: _____

_____

_____

Rationales *continued*

4. Impaired renal function may precipitate fluid retention.

5. Rationale: _____

_____

_____

Outcome criteria
Throughout the period of hospitalization, the patient will show:
• no medication-induced confusion or stupor
• no toxic side effects from medications

• no medication overdose from cumulative effect of reduced renal function
• no signs or symptoms of fluid overload.

Nursing diagnosis: *Potential nutritional deficit related to taste bud atrophy, poor dentition, decreased saliva and ptyalin secretion, economic limitations, and/or poor dietary habits*

NURSING PRIORITY: Promote optimal nutritional intake.

Interventions

1. *With the dietitian, assess the patient's dietary habits and history.* Note the adequacy of protein, calorie, vitamin, and mineral intake. Assess the levels of saturated fat and sodium in the usual diet. Note special dietary preferences.

2. *Plan, with the patient and dietitian, for meeting therapeutic dietary needs during hospitalization,* providing foods according to the patient's usual pattern if the diet is nutritionally adequate. If the diet isn't adequate, teach the patient about dietary recommendations.

3. Ensure that the diet plan is compatible with dental capability. Arrange for a dental consultation if poor dentition is a factor.

4. Encourage liberal seasoning of food with herbs and spices, observing dietary limitations required for underlying conditions.

5. *Assess for environmental, physical, and emotional factors that may contribute to poor nutritional intake at home.* Examples include:
• inadequate income
• lack of transportation for shopping
• lack of space or equipment for food preparation or storage
• lack of energy for preparing food
• loneliness and depression.

Rationales

1. Nutritional deficits place the patient at increased risk for infection, skin breakdown, and other complications. A high intake of saturated fats and salt may contribute to coronary artery disease and hypertension—two factors associated with significant mortality in the elderly. Preferences must be considered, however, because older patients may be reluctant to alter established dietary patterns.

2. Including the patient in diet planning promotes a sense of being in control and may increase the likelihood of compliance. Usual foods are more likely to be eaten. Maintaining usual patterns whenever possible helps provide a sense of security—particularly important to the elderly person in an unfamiliar environment.

3. Chewing difficulty inhibits adequate nutritional intake.

4. Since taste bud sensitivity diminishes with age, bland foods may be left uneaten.

5. Elderly patients are often reluctant to verbalize reasons for poor nutrition unless questioned specifically.

Interventions *continued*

6. Before discharge, make appropriate referrals to alleviate or eliminate any identified problems. Consider Meals on Wheels, increased family contact, volunteer drivers or companions, social services assistance, home care services, or other available resources.

7. Additional individualized interventions: _____

_____

Rationales *continued*

6. Careful predischarge assessment, problem solving, and referral are essential to prevent exacerbation of nutritional problems after discharge.

7. Rationale: _____

_____

Outcome criteria

Within 1 day of admission, the patient will:
• verbalize dietary habits and preferences
• identify factors interfering with adequate nutritional intake
• express satisfaction with meals.

By the time of discharge, the patient will:
• list dietary recommendations and specific foods to avoid or increase in diet
• identify resources and referrals for assistance with meals, shopping, or financial needs (if appropriate).

Nursing diagnosis: *Potential impaired physical mobility related to general weakness, calcification around joints, arthritis, and/or debilitation from underlying disease*

NURSING PRIORITY: Maintain healthy skin, optimal activity pattern, and bowel functions.

Interventions

1. Skin care
• Omit soap in providing hygiene.

• Apply oil to dry skin areas.

• Maintain the patient's usual bathing pattern—for example, every other day.

• *Inspect the patient's skin twice daily for tissue breakdown.*

2. Activity
• *Take the patient's history to identify ADLs and any special exercises.*

• Institute active and passive exercise, or both, as soon as medical protocol permits.

• Maintain all parts of the patient's body in functional anatomic alignment.
• If the patient is on bed rest, turn from back to side according to nursing protocol or at least every 2 hours during the day and every 4 hours at night.
• Encourage deep-breathing exercises hourly while the patient is awake. Each shift, assess lung sounds. Report decreased breath sounds, crackles, or other abnormal findings promptly.

Rationales

1. Skin care
• Soap is drying, and older persons have fewer sebaceous glands.
• Oil may prevent increasing dryness, which can lead to tissue breakdown.
• Increasing the frequency of baths may reduce normal skin flora, thus reducing the skin's function as a barrier to infection. Frequent bathing also causes increased skin irritation and dryness.
• Pressure on bony prominences may produce decubitus ulcers because body tissue is less elastic and older adults have less fatty tissue.

2. Activity
• Maintaining normal activity and exercise patterns is essential for optimal physiologic function. Special exercises may be required to maintain the tone of particular muscle groups.
• Exercise helps prevent thrombophlebitis, contractures, foot drop, and external rotation of the legs—complications associated with impaired mobility.
• Functional alignment prevents contractures and external rotation.
• Physical movement reduces the risk of hypostatic pneumonia and decubiti.

• Decreased elasticity in lung tissue, commonly associated with aging, places these patients at increased risk for stasis of pulmonary secretions and resultant pulmonary infection. In the elderly, pneumonia is associated with higher mortality.

(continued)

Interventions *continued*

3. Bowel function

• *Identify the patient's typical bowel care regimen.* If the patient is dependent on enemas or laxatives, discuss more appropriate alternatives.

• Add bran, prune juice, or other acceptable roughage to meals, as the patient's medical condition allows.

• Administer and document the use of stool softeners or laxatives, as ordered.

• Provide bedpan or commode assistance, following the patient's schedule as closely as possible.

4. Additional individualized interventions: _____
_____
_____

Rationales *continued*

3. Bowel function

• Individualized care is essential for normal bowel function and a sense of emotional well-being.

• Decreased physical mobility contributes to constipation. Adding roughage to the diet stimulates peristalsis.

• If unable to assume a normal anatomic position on the toilet, the older person may need some medicinal assistance with bowel elimination.

• Maintaining routine timing facilitates bowel evacuation.

4. Rationale: _____
_____
_____

Outcome criteria

Throughout the period of hospitalization, the patient will:
• show no evidence of reddened skin areas
• show no new dry skin areas
• show no pruritus
• show no skin lesions or infections

• have no crackles, fever, or other evidence of hypostatic pneumonia
• establish regular bowel elimination
• have stool normal in amount, color, and consistency according to bowel pattern history.

Nursing diagnosis: *Sleep pattern disturbance related to reduction in exercise, stress arising from concern with illness, anticipation of personal losses, unfamiliarity of surroundings, and/or discomfort associated with illness*

NURSING PRIORITY: Minimize sleep disturbance during hospitalization.

Interventions

1. *Provide frequent rest and sleep periods.*

2. *Assess for and document factors that may cause sleep disruption. Treat causes appropriately*—for example, if pain causes wakefulness, administer analgesics before bedtime or provide other comfort measures. Group procedures to avoid interrupting sleep cycles.

3. Adapt the hospital environment to simulate the patient's home setting whenever possible.

4. Provide as quiet an environment as possible (for example, turn off the radio or television if this reflects the usual home situation).

Rationales

1. Older persons have less stage IV sleep and frequently awaken spontaneously. Shorter, more frequent sleep and rest periods are, in many cases, more appropriate than one long sleep period.

2. Sleep deprivation may result in confusion, irritability, short-term memory loss, or other neuropsychiatric manifestations.

3. Moving the bed into a position similar to that at home or modifying other room details (such as the position of the radio or television) facilitates a sense of security and familiarity and promotes environmental comfort, inducing rest and sleep.

4. Similarity of environmental sounds enhances relaxation.

Interventions continued

5. "Shorten" the night by arranging activities around late bedtime and "checking in" early in the morning with food and conversation.

6. Additional individualized interventions: _____
_____
_____

Outcome criteria
Within 2 days of admission, the patient will:
• appear rested
• verbalize "I slept well."

Rationales continued

5. Because older people sleep for shorter periods, their actual night's sleep often spans only 4 to 5 hours.

6. Rationale: _____
_____
_____

Nursing diagnosis: *Disturbed self-concept: self-esteem related to dependent patient role, anxiety over loss of physical or mental competence, powerlessness to alter the aging process, societal emphasis on youth, and/or sense of purposelessness*

NURSING PRIORITY: Promote a positive self-image while providing opportunities to demonstrate competence.

Interventions

1. *Whenever possible, offer choices and include the patient in decision making related to care.*

2. *Involve the patient in self-care activities* as much as possible, paying special attention to grooming and hygiene needs.

3. *Affirm positive qualities* (for example, "You have a good sense of humor"). Help the patient identify and use coping behaviors learned in dealing with earlier losses successfully.

4. Move the conversation away from constant repetition of bodily problems.

5. Review life activities that reflect accomplishments.

6. *Allow time for verbalization of feelings,* such as sadness and powerlessness. Avoid overoptimistic responses.

7. Encourage realistic goal setting.

8. Facilitate behavior that considers others.

9. Provide diversionary activity appropriate to the patient's abilities, allowing opportunities for creative expression whenever possible. Refer the patient to the occupational therapist, as indicated.

Rationales

1. Participating in decision making increases the patient's sense of personal competence and promotes independence.

2. "Taking over" by caregivers devalues the patient's abilities and may lead to dependence and depression. A neat, clean personal appearance contributes to feelings of self-worth.

3. Expressing appreciation of positive attributes helps reinforce associated behaviors. Examining coping skills learned from previous life experiences may help the patient build strengths in dealing with the current situation.

4. Repetition of negative thoughts only reinforces their impact.

5. Achievements and recognition bolster a sense of societal usefulness.

6. Aging entails dealing with multiple losses, and feelings of sadness are a part of normal coping. Active listening and acceptance show respect for the patient as an individual and promote a sense of self-worth.

7. Goal achievement fosters feelings of self-mastery.

8. Focusing on others' needs reduces dependence and increases feelings of usefulness.

9. Emotional well-being is enhanced by diversionary activities. Creative activities allow another avenue for expression of feelings and demonstration of unique abilities. The occupational therapist can help the patient select diversionary activities appropriate to functional capabilities.

(continued)

Interventions *continued*

10. Additional individualized interventions: _____

_____

Rationales *continued*

10. Rationale: _____

_____

Outcome criteria

Throughout the period of hospitalization, the patient will:
• participate in decision making

• participate in self-care to the extent possible
• set realistic goals and pursue them
• initiate involvement with others.

Nursing diagnosis: *Social isolation related to decreased physical capacity, effects of illness, fear of burdening others, death or disability of peers, and/or sense of personal uselessness*

NURSING PRIORITY: Promote social interaction and provide opportunities for positive feedback from others.

Interventions

1. *Assess personal social resources and their availability* to the patient—family, friends, other caregivers—as well as their willingness and ability to participate in care.

2. *Involve significant others in care planning and, when possible, in provision of care.* Ask family members to identify specific needs or preferences the patient may have.

3. *Encourage generous use of touch* in care provision and as affectionate gestures, unless the patient appears uncomfortable with physical contact.

4. Encourage family members to help the patient maintain previously established roles and functions in the family as much as possible.

5. Ensure telephone access. Discuss bedside telephone costs with the family or social worker, explaining the critical need for the patient to maintain communication with family and friends.

6. Initiate a Social Services referral, as needed, to arrange transportation for visitors—such as a senior citizens' van or church group transportation.

7. Present socialization concerns and problems to other members of the hospital staff, including the chaplain, dietitian, and housekeepers.

Rationales

1. Social isolation may be a result of numerous factors. In many cases, elderly patients are hesitant to verbalize needs because of pride and independence; tactful intervention by the nurse may help link the patient with untapped social contacts.

2. Involvement of loved ones in care helps reduce isolation related to unfamiliar surroundings and prevents a sense of abandonment, which can occur in hospitalized elderly patients. Participation in care while the patient is hospitalized also allows significant others to practice care techniques and ask questions in a "safe" setting. Family members are most attuned to the patient's idiosyncratic needs or preferences.

3. Older adults have diminished sensory capacities. Touch reduces "skin hunger" (the desire for human tactile contact) and communicates caring, helping to lessen feelings of isolation.

4. Maintaining roles—for example, as wise counselor or confidante—helps the older person maintain a sense of belonging and decreases feelings of uselessness.

5. For many elderly patients with impaired mobility, the telephone provides an essential link to the "outside world." Also, elderly friends may be unable to visit, so the telephone may be their only means of offering support to the patient.

6. The patient and family may be unaware of available transportation resources.

7. Interaction with all members of the hospital staff may serve as a temporary replacement for the patient's normal social contacts.

Interventions *continued*

8. Additional individualized interventions: _____

_____

_____

Rationales *continued*

8. Rationale: _____

_____

_____

Outcome criteria

Within 3 days of admission, the patient will:
• maintain social contacts
• make no comments reflecting loneliness.

Within 3 days of the patient's admission, family members will:
• approach nurses freely with care suggestions and questions.

Nursing diagnosis: *Spiritual distress related to inability to maintain usual religious and spiritual practices (if any) and/or loss of sense of life's meaning and purpose*

NURSING PRIORITY: Provide for participation in meaningful religious and spiritual practices, if desired.

Interventions

1. Identify the patient's normal preference and pattern for religious activities, if appropriate. Encourage participation in formal services if available. Arrange for visits by clergy as permitted, or suggest that the family provide a tape of the religious service. See the "Death and Dying" care plan, page 10.

2. Read (or get a volunteer to read) from appropriate religious books if an older patient wishes to read but cannot do so.

3. Provide privacy for personal prayer time, when desired.

4. Keep religious articles such as rosary beads conveniently available.

5. Additional individualized interventions: _____

_____

_____

Rationales

1. Maintenance of usual spiritual support increases coping ability. The "Death and Dying" care plan contains other specific interventions for patients experiencing spiritual distress.

2. Maintaining continuity in religious experience provides special comfort.

3. Encouraging expressions of trust and faith in God or a supreme being provides solace and a sense of providential care during crises.

4. Religious articles may provide reassurance and serve as a reminder of spiritual resources.

5. Rationale: _____

_____

_____

Outcome criteria

Throughout the period of hospitalization, the patient will:
• verbalize appreciation for assistance in providing for spiritual needs (if appropriate)

• show a tranquil facial expression
• express an ability to endure crisis (if appropriate).

Discharge planning
NURSING DISCHARGE CRITERIA

Upon discharge, documentation shows evidence of:
• meeting of discharge criteria for the specific disease or condition necessitating hospitalization

• appropriate referrals made for home care asistance, as needed, or for care facility placement, if indicated
• special attention to age-related needs during hospitalization, such as hearing aid or eye glasses.

PATIENT/FAMILY DISCHARGE TEACHING CHECKLIST

Document evidence that the patient/family demonstrates understanding of:
__ details specific to the patient's disease or condition
__ care needs arising from illness
__ dietary needs
__ feeding assistance needs
__ mental status changes: thought processing, insight, judgment, confusion
__ continence needs (toileting)
__ mobility and transfer needs
__ hygiene needs
__ speech changes
__ social and emotional needs to reduce loneliness, isolation
__ need for relationships with family and friends
__ family and friends' access to care facility, if placement planned
__ resources available for older persons
__ how to contact doctor.

DOCUMENTATION CHECKLIST

Using outcome criteria as a guide, document:
__ clinical status on admission
__ significant changes in status
__ patient/family teaching
__ discharge planning
__ other data pertinent to specific disease or condition.

ASSOCIATED CARE PLANS

(See also the care plan for the patient's specific disease or condition.)
Death and Dying
Fluid and Electrolyte Imbalances
Grief/Grieving
Ineffective Family Coping
Ineffective Individual Coping
Knowledge Deficit
Pain

REFERENCES

Aiken, Lewis. *Later Life,* 2nd ed. New York: Holt, Rinehart & Winston, 1982.

Carnevali, Doris L., and Patrick, Maxine. *Nursing Management for the Elderly.* Philadelphia: J.B. Lippincott Co., 1979.

Ebersole, P., and Hess, P. *Toward Healthy Aging,* 2nd ed. St. Louis: C.V. Mosby Co., 1985.

Forbes, J., and Fitzsimmons, V. *The Older Adult.* St. Louis: C.V. Mosby Co., 1981.

Helping Geriatric Patients. Nursing Photobook Series. Springhouse, Pa.: Springhouse Corp., 1983.

Steffl, Benita, *Handbook of Gerontological Nursing.* New York: Van Nostrand Reinhold Co., 1984.

Thompson, J., and Bower, A. *Clinical Manual of Health Assessment.* St. Louis: C.V. Mosby Co., 1984.

Wolanin, M., and Phillips, L. *Confusion.* St. Louis: C.V. Mosby Co., 1981.

Yurick, Ann, et al. *The Aged Person and the Nursing Process,* 2nd ed. East Norwalk, Conn.: Appleton-Century Crofts, 1984.

Grief and Grieving

Introduction

DEFINITION AND TIME FOCUS

Grief is the normal response to an actual or potential loss. It is a natural, necessary, and dynamic process. Anticipatory grief is the process of grieving before an actual loss. Dysfunctional grieving is the ineffective, pathologic, delayed, or exaggerated response to an actual or potential loss. Theoretical phases of the grieving process have been outlined by various authors (see the table below). As in all theoretical models, the phases are overlapping. The process may or may not be sequential and the patient or family may fluctuate between phases during the process.

THE GRIEVING PROCESS

LINDEMAN (1944)
Shock/disbelief—Acute mourning—Reentry into daily life—Decreased image of deceased

ENGEL (1964)
Denial—Developing awareness—Restitution

KÜBLER-ROSS (1969)
Denial—Anger—Bargaining—Depression—Acceptance

RANDO (1981)
Avoidance—Confrontations—Reestablishment

This clinical plan focuses on the patient and family members coping with impending or actual losses during hospitalization.

ETIOLOGY/PRECIPITATING FACTORS
• loss of body image or some aspect of self (such as social role; body part by amputation or mastectomy)
• loss of loved one or significant other through separation, divorce, or death
• loss of material objects (such as income, belongings, and pets)
• loss through a maturational or developmental process (such as aging or weaning an infant from its mother's breast)

Focused assessment guidelines

NURSING HISTORY (Functional health pattern findings)

Health perception–health management pattern
• loss may be real or imagined

Nutritional-metabolic pattern
• may report nausea and vomiting, weight loss, or anorexia
• may report increased food, drug, or alcohol intake as means of self-gratification

Elimination pattern
• may report *gastrointestinal upset,* diarrhea, or constipation

Activity-exercise pattern
• may report shortness of breath
• may report feelings of *exhaustion,* weakness, inability to maintain organized activity patterns, or restlessness

Sleep-rest pattern
• may report *insomnia* caused by disruption of normal sleep pattern or frequent crying episodes

Cognitive-perceptual pattern
• may describe feelings of *guilt*
• may report feelings of *sorrow,* emptyness, or "heaviness"

Self-perception–self-concept pattern
• may express feelings of worthlessness
• may report decreased ability to fulfill personal life expectations

Role-relationship pattern
• may report episodes of withdrawal or social isolation (especially with dysfunctional grieving)

Sexuality-reproductive pattern
• may report loss of sexual desire or hypersexuality
• if female, may report menstrual irregularity

Coping-stress tolerance pattern
• may have difficulty expressing feelings about the loss
• may rationalize or intellectualize the loss to make it less painful, especially during bargaining phase
• may be tearful and describe frequent episodes of crying, usually during shock and denial and depression phases
• may be hostile during the anger phase in an attempt to resist the impact of the loss
• may avoid discussing the loss (especially with dysfunctional grieving)
• may report previous experiences with depression

Value-belief pattern
• may express need for increased spiritual or pastoral support
• may report increased use of prayer or meditation
• may report doubts in religious belief system

PHYSICAL FINDINGS

Loss is a body stressor that can trigger physiologic as well as psychological stress and can decrease the ability of the body's immune system to resist infection and illness.

Cardiovascular
- palpitations
- hypertension
- dysrhythmias

Pulmonary
- increased respirations
- deep sighing

Gastrointestinal
- vomiting
- diarrhea or constipation

Neurologic
- irritability
- anxiety
- agitation
- paresthesias

Integumentary
- diaphoresis
- cold, clammy skin
- flushed skin

Musculoskeletal
- decreased muscle tone
- weakness

DIAGNOSTIC STUDIES

Physical debilitation and illness resulting from the grieving process may require studies, but these will vary widely, depending on the signs and symptoms exhibited. For example, palpitations and pulse irregularities may indicate the need for an EKG to rule out significant cardiac problems.

POTENTIAL COMPLICATIONS
- crisis state
- major depression with suicidal or homicidal potential
- physical deterioration
- dysfunctional grieving

Nursing diagnosis: *Grief and grieving related to impending or actual physical or functional loss*

NURSING PRIORITY: Facilitate a healthy grieving process.

Interventions

1. Provide the person with accurate information before any procedure or treatment that may affect appearance, physical or sexual functioning, or role changes.

2. Assess and document the person's response to information about disease process, implications, and treatment. Include responses to past experiences with loss.

3. Discuss meaning of the loss with the person.

4. Discuss changes in social roles or relationships that may result from the loss.

5. Provide time to be with the patient and family.

6. *Assess and document the current phase of grief* the person is experiencing. Recognize that fluctuations in the grief process may occur.

Rationales

1. Accurate information prevents misconceptions and may decrease fears related to the loss.

2. Past experiences and values influence the current loss experience.

3. Establishing the significance of the loss enhances the person's ability to identify and release feelings related to the loss.

4. Physical or functional loss may result in social changes associated with income, career, and relationships. Discussion of these changes helps to identify the impact of the loss and alternatives for adjustments in life-style.

5. The nurse's availability and presence with patient and family encourage the necessary review and processing of the loss. Feelings of loneliness or social isolation may also be decreased, reassuring the person that caregivers perceive the loss as significant.

6. Identifying unresolved issues fosters restitution of the grieving process.

Interventions *continued*

7. *Support and facilitate the expression of feelings* associated with anger, guilt, sorrow, and sadness during any phase of the grieving process. Listen nonjudgmentally. Recognize and accept the feelings of anger that may be directed toward the health care team.

8. Encourage the release of emotion through crying. Hold the person's hand and use touch liberally, if accepted by the person.

9. *Assess for and promote positive coping mechanisms,* for example, building and sharing close relationships, creative activities, exercise, and open expression of feelings related to loss and readjustment. See the "Death and Dying" care plan, page 10.

10. Provide spiritual support as requested by the person throughout the grieving process, or suggest resources.

11. Encourage participation in daily self-care activities.

12. Provide positive reinforcement and realistic hope about the patient's progress.

13. Allow the person to make decisions whenever possible.

14. Assess and assist activation of available personal support systems.

15. Additional individualized interventions: _____
_____
_____

Rationales *continued*

7. Expressing feelings openly may enable the person to move more easily through the phases of the grieving process. Nonjudgmental listening enables the person to express feelings without fear of rejection.

8. The nurse's encouragement reassures the person (and family, if indicated) that crying is a normal response to loss. Hand holding and use of touch provide reassurance and help the person relax.

9. Coping with loss is a developmental task. Losses increase in occurrence and intensity throughout the life cycle. Adaptive coping methods are derived from previous losses. The "Death and Dying" care plan contains general interventions helpful to those coping with loss.

10. Spiritual support assists with fostering a sense of meaning, hope, love, and satisfaction with life.

11. Self-care promotes feelings of self-control and independence, increasing self-esteem.

12. Reinforcement and reassurance build self-confidence.

13. Decision making enables the person to maintain control.

14. The person may need gentle guidance to identify resources. Sharing feelings with closest friends and/or family aids in adjustment to loss.

15. Rationale: _____
_____
_____

Outcome criteria

By the time of discharge, the person will:
• identify the meaning of the loss
• communicate feelings of anger, guilt, sorrow
• identify strategies to cope with the loss

• identify role and relationship changes
• identify and utilize spiritual support and resources
• perform self-care
• make decisions about care.

Nursing diagnosis: *Potential for dysfunctional grieving related to unresolved feelings about physical or functional loss*

NURSING PRIORITY: Identify dysfunctional grieving and make appropriate referrals.

Interventions

1. *Assess and document the responses of the person to the grief experience.* Identify feelings of unresolved guilt or anger. Recognize avoidance of discussing the loss. Be alert to possible use of alcohol or recreational drugs as an escape mechanism.

Rationales

1. Accurate assessment allows understanding of the dynamics of the grieving process. Unresolved guilt and anger are common symptoms of pathologic grief and may result in major depression. Avoidance of the loss may indicate delayed grief. Drug or alcohol abuse contributes to dysfunctional resolution of loss.

(continued)

ASSESSMENT OF SUICIDE POTENTIAL

The alert nurse is aware of suicide risk factors and specifically assesses patients at risk by asking direct questions:

MAJOR RISK FACTORS	**QUESTIONS**
Intent Contrary to popular myth, asking patients directly about suicide does not precipitate attempts. Patients tend to answer truthfully and are often relieved that someone has acknowledged their distress.	"Are you thinking about killing yourself?" or "Are you considering suicide?"
Plan Patients who verbalize clearly defined, detailed plans for suicide are at greater risk than those who vaguely want to die.	"Do you have a plan to do it?"
Lethality of method Highly lethal methods (such as firearms, hanging, jumping from a height) greatly increase risk.	"How would you do it?"
Availability of means Patients who have the means readily available are at higher risk.	"Do you have a gun at home?"
Personal/family history A majority of people who succeed at suicide have made previous attempts. If previous attempts used highly lethal means or were unsuccessful only by accident (that is, if the plan did not allow for rescue), risk is increased. Those who have lost loved ones to suicide are at greater risk.	"Have you tried to kill yourself before?" "How? What happened?" "Has anyone in your family committed suicide?"
Future goals If the patient is unable to envision or articulate future goals or plans, suicide potential is increased.	"Where do you see yourself next month? In 1 year? In 5 years?"

These factors associated with serious suicide risk also should be assessed by questioning the person, his family, or other health care providers.

ADDITIONAL RISK FACTORS

Resources
Lack of social and personal resources to deal with external or internal crises, or a perception by the patient that such resources are unavailable, increases the likelihood of suicide.

Recent loss or life changes
Loss or the threat of loss increases suicide risk. Even other kinds of change (a promotion, a household move, or changes in roles or responsibilities) can increase stress and overwhelm the individual's coping abilities.

Physical illness
Physical illness may increase suicide risk, particularly if the illness involves major life changes or a threat to essentials of self-image.

Alcohol or drug abuse
Substance abuse may increase impulsive behavior and contribute to depression, thus increasing suicide risk. Additionally, alcohol or drugs may increase lethality by potentiating other drugs or decreasing overall level of awareness.

Sudden behavior change
Abrupt changes in behavior, of any kind, may signal suicidal intent.

Isolation
Physical or emotional isolation from others greatly increases suicide risk.

Age, sex, marital status
Older males have a higher rate of successful suicide, possibly because they tend to choose more lethal means. Risk of suicide may be increased for separated, widowed, or divorced persons. These parameters, however, are less reliable predictors than those above.

Interventions *continued*

2. Assess and document the person's daily activity level and ability to perform roles.

3. Assess the physical well-being of the person and initiate a medical referral as indicated. Teach the importance of maintaining physical health.

4. Monitor and document the administration of tranquilizers, antidepressants, or sedatives.

Rationales *continued*

2. Withdrawal and social isolation commonly occur with chronic grieving.

3. Grieving requires emotional and physical energy. Prolonged grieving may result in physical illness and debilitation. Somatic symptoms may mask a depression resulting from a delayed or absent grief process.

4. Tranquilizers, antidepressants, and sedatives may occasionally be helpful; however, overmedication may result in prolonging the grieving process.

Interventions *continued*

5. *Observe the person for signs and symptoms of potential suicide or homicide:* increased agitation, insomnia, self-incrimination, and feelings of worthlessness, helplessness, and hopelessness.

6. *Assess suicide risk* (see *Assessment of Suicide Potential*), by talking with the person. Consult with the patient's doctor regarding referral or intervention.

7. Utilize other resource persons such as social workers, chaplains, or psychiatrists, as indicated or requested by patient and family.

8. *Provide follow-up referral* for the person after discharge.

9. Additional individualized interventions: _____
_____
_____

Rationales *continued*

5. Anxiety and depression may be exaggerated during chronic grieving states.

6. Frank discussion of suicide potential with the person helps identify and define stressors, may relieve anxiety, and will not precipitate a suicide attempt.

7. Interdisciplinary referral helps identify available financial, social, spiritual, and community resources. Psychiatric intervention focuses on understanding of the unhealthy responses and the reactivation of a healthy grieving process.

8. Follow-up visits by nurses, chaplains, social workers, and so forth, should be based on individual needs. During early grieving, weekly visits are likely to be most helpful. Support groups may also be helpful.

9. Rationale: _____
_____
_____

Outcome criteria
By the time of discharge, the person will:
• acknowledge the loss
• discuss the experience realistically
• utilize healthy coping strategies

• understand and accept own and other's responses
• express and accept own feelings
• identify resources within the family and community
• verify the absence of suicidal or homicidal potential.

Discharge planning

NURSING DISCHARGE CRITERIA
Upon discharge, documentation shows evidence of:
• acknowledgment of the loss and its meaning
• demonstration of positive coping behaviors
• identification of social and community support systems
• no display of suicidal or homicidal potential.

PATIENT/FAMILY DISCHARGE TEACHING CHECKLIST
Document evidence that patient/family demonstrates understanding of:
___ normal grief responses
___ phases of the grieving process
___ information concerning role changes and physical loss
___ importance of maintaining physical health and well-being of patient and family
___ information about the patient's illness and medical treatment
___ need to be understanding and accepting of others during grieving process
___ community resources including support groups and interagency referral.

DOCUMENTATION CHECKLIST
Using outcome criteria as a guide, document:
___ past experiences and responses to loss
___ current perception and meaning of loss
___ changes in role-relationship, body image, and self-esteem
___ positive or maladaptive coping behaviors
___ support systems
___ level of activity and participation in self-care
___ medication with tranquilizers, antidepressants, or sedatives
___ signs and symptoms of suicidal or homicidal potential
___ interdisciplinary referrals
___ patient teaching
___ discharge planning.

ASSOCIATED CARE PLANS
Death and Dying
Ineffective Family Coping
Ineffective Individual Coping

REFERENCES

Brown, Marie S. *Nursing and the Concept of Loss.* New York: John Wiley & Sons, 1980.

Clark, Mary D. "Healthy and Unhealthy Grief Behaviors," *Occupational Health Nursing* 32(12):633-35, December 1984.

Hoff, Lee A. *People in Crisis: Understanding and Helping*, 2nd ed. Menlo Park, Calif.: Addison-Wesley Publishing Co., 1984.

McIntire, Sue N., and Cioppa, Ann L. *Cancer Nursing: A Developmental Approach.* New York: John Wiley & Sons, 1984.

McNally, Joan C., et al. *Guidelines for Cancer Nursing Practice.* Orlando, Fla.: Grune & Stratton, 1985.

Martocchio, Benita. "Grief and Bereavement: Healing Through Hurt, Loss Through Death," *Nursing Clinics of North America* 20(2):327-41, June 1985.

Rando, Therese A. *Grief, Dying and Death: Clinical Interventions for Caregivers.* Champaign, Ill.: Research Press Co., 1984.

Schoenberg, Bernard, et al. *Anticipatory Grief.* New York: Columbia University Press, 1974.

Ineffective Family Coping

Introduction
DEFINITION AND TIME FOCUS
A patient's hospitalization can precipitate a crisis within the family because their usual coping and support mechanisms may be overwhelmed. This clinical plan focuses on the family's ability to manage the stressors that affect them during the patient's hospitalization.

ETIOLOGY/PRECIPITATING FACTORS
• illness or injury of family member
• disruption of usual family activities and routines
• previously existing family disunity
• loss of control by patient or family
• role changes within the family
• unfamiliar hospital environment, restricted visitation of loved one(s)
• loss of income, costs of medical care
• poverty

Focused assessment guidelines
NURSING HISTORY (Functional health pattern findings for family system)

Nutritional-metabolic pattern
• *may neglect dietary intake* while family member is hospitalized

Sleep-rest pattern
• *may not get adequate sleep or rest* while family member is hospitalized

Cognitive-perceptual pattern
• may have inaccurate understanding of the patient's condition
• may not request clarification of information about the patient's situation
• *may pay attention to only some aspects* of the information given
• may lack skills or education to understand complex medical information

Self-perception–self-concept pattern
• *may report feeling unable to cope* with current situation
• *may verbalize anxiety, fear, or anger*
• may express unresolved feelings of guilt or hostility

• may lack awareness of each other's feelings or perceptions
• may appear uncomfortable with each other's emotional reactions

Role-relationship pattern
• may not interact with each other
• may have difficulty communicating feelings and perceptions to each other
• may experience difficulty reaching decisions
• may have rigidly established roles within family structure
• may be unable to provide emotional support for each other

Coping-stress tolerance pattern
• *may use inappropriate coping methods* in the present situation
• may have used non-growth–promoting methods to handle past crises (denial, depression, violence, or substance abuse)
• may not identify all coping strategies available within the family system
• may exhibit regression or increased dependence by relying on others to solve problems

Value-belief pattern
• may have value conflicts between family members
• may have unrealistic beliefs about health, disease, or roles and abilities of other family members

PHYSICAL FINDINGS
Not applicable

POTENTIAL COMPLICATIONS
• transfer of anxiety from family to patient
• high anxiety levels among family members
• unrealistic expectations of patient—for example, expecting full recovery of neurologic function in brain-damaged person
• unrealistic expectations of other family members—for example, expecting formerly uncommunicative member to become emotionally supportive in crisis
• inattention to family member's physical and psychosocial needs
• inadequate preparation for the patient's discharge or death
• disintegration of family unit

Nursing diagnosis: *Ineffective family coping related to illness and hospitalization of family member*

NURSING PRIORITY: Help the family identify, develop, and use healthy coping skills.

Interventions

1. *Assess the origins of the crisis and the family members' response to it.* Identify factors contributing to vulnerability in a crisis state. Observe nonverbal behaviors, such as eye contact and body posture. Document the etiology of the crisis and the family's response to it.

2. *Demonstrate interest and concern* for the patient's family members. Acknowledge the family's feelings about the situation, for example, "This must be very difficult for you."

3. *Take measures to minimize the family members' level of anxiety:* provide a quiet, private place for discussion. Avoid elaborate information or unnecessary questions. Remain available to the family. Document the family's initial emotional status and response to nursing interventions.

4. *Provide accurate, timely information* about the patient's treatment and care. Give explanations in lay terms; encourage questions. Reinforce information given by the doctor. Document the information given to the family.

5. Clarify family members' perceptions of the information given to them. Document the family's level of understanding.

6. *Soften the stress associated with the hospital environment.* Individualize visitation privileges. Orient the family to hospital facilities. Arrange for a quiet place for the family to meet with the doctor. Provide pillows and blankets for family members spending the night at the hospital.

7. *Assist family members to care for their own physical and psychosocial needs.* Encourage adequate rest periods. Reinforce the need for adequate dietary intake.

Rationales

1. Consider situational factors (such as illness or death), transitional states (developmental turning points or life cycle phase), and sociocultural factors. Families in which several of these factors are present are at higher risk for crisis development. Nonverbal behaviors, such as clenched fists or lack of eye contact, provide valuable clues about the family's emotional state.

2. Approaching the family with a warm and respectful attitude lays the groundwork for developing a trusting relationship between family and nurse.

3. In states of heightened anxiety, the ability to think clearly, handle new information, and make appropriate decisions is impaired. Minimizing distractions reduces anxiety and helps family members regain control of their thinking processes.

4. Family members must be well informed to develop an accurate perception of the patient's illness or injury. Medical jargon may increase anxiety in some individuals. Clear, simple explanations will be understood best. Encouraging questions dispels possible discomfort over not knowing answers, while suggesting topics dispels possible discomfort over not knowing what to ask. Anxiety and misunderstanding can be minimized by giving explanations in lay terms and by reinforcing or clarifying information given by the doctor. Family members who understand their own problems as well as the patient's can recognize their needs and identify appropriate solutions.

5. Do not assume that what was said was what the family heard. Asking for feedback and clarification allows the nurse to determine the family members' actual level of understanding.

6. Manipulating the hospital environment decreases the family's physical distress in adjusting to the patient's hospitalization.

7. Development of problem-solving skills and effective coping strategies is impaired when family members are physically exhausted, malnourished, or stressed by unmet emotional or other psychosocial needs.

Interventions *continued*

8. *Encourage family members to express their feelings* about the impact of the patient's illness. Ask open-ended questions. Listen carefully to each person. Support communication among family members. Observe how feelings are expressed and how family members behave. Document the family's response and behavior. Identify, when possible, the family member who is the primary health and illness resource for the family, and include that person in all teaching. Also, make sure that person has an adequate support system.

9. *Promote awareness of family strengths* by identifying areas in which the members work well together. Document identified family strengths and weaknesses. Direct nursing interventions toward encouraging family strengths; for example, support family efforts to learn care techniques or to bring in special items from home, as permitted.

10. Facilitate communication when dysfunctional family processes are present. Encourage verbalization and recognition of feelings. Provide referrals to other professionals (mental health liaison nurse, social worker, clinical specialist, clinical psychologist, or clergy) when family problems lie outside the role of the staff nurse.

11. *Focus on immediate, concrete problems.*

12. *Help the family develop a realistic appraisal of the situation and an action plan.* Explore coping skills and support systems available to the family. Help them identify available resources, such as friends, other family members, self-help groups related to the diagnosis, home health care nurses, or homemaking assistance. Ensure that the plan is appropriate to the family's functional level, dependence needs, and life-style.

13. Encourage independent decision making by family members.

14. With the patient and family, follow up and evaluate the action plan's implementation.

Rationales *continued*

8. Awareness of feelings and the ability to express them clearly and appropriately are important elements of healthy coping behaviors. Help-seeking behaviors are aided by intrafamily communication and realistic discussion of how the patient's illness may affect family functioning. By using open-ended questions, the nurse can guide the family's communication process. Listening to the family and helping them clarify their feelings and perceptions will help the nurse identify areas where additional support is needed. Most families have one member who is the informed "health liaison person" who may act as caregiver, teacher, and interpreter. Acknowledgment of this role facilitates therapeutic intervention.

9. Acknowledging family strengths, such as closeness, open communication, or willingness to help each other, helps the family identify their own resources for coping with the crisis.

10. The nurse's role is to listen, support, and clarify, not to solve the family's problems. The nurse helps the family to identify available resources and to make informed decisions on using them.

11. A primary nursing focus is to decrease the family members' anxiety, so they can pull their thinking together and make use of problem-solving skills. In many cases, anxiety can be decreased by attending to easily removed stressors; for example, refer an out-of-town family to the social services department to arrange for housing while the patient is hospitalized.

12. In establishing an action plan, family members need to match their own needs and the patient's with available resources. By providing such information, the nurse helps the family develop a plan to meet their needs.

13. The nurse who makes decisions for the family fosters dependence in family members.

14. Evaluation of the action plan reinforces successful strategies and may suggest additional or alternate interventions. Evaluation done with the family is an excellent way to provide positive feedback and acknowledge their new coping skills.

(continued)

Interventions *continued*

15. Avoid imposing personal values or codes of behavior on family members.

16. Additional individualized interventions: _____
_____
_____

Rationales *continued*

15. In order to intervene effectively with families in crisis, the nurse must develop an awareness of personal value systems and beliefs related to cultural norms. This allows the nurse to view the family's problems without imposing his or her personal values on the family system.

16. Rationale: _____
_____
_____

Outcome criteria
Within 2 days of admission, family members will:
• verbalize feelings to the nurse
• recognize their physical needs for food and rest.

By the time of the patient's discharge, family members will:
• verbalize feelings appropriately to each other
• participate actively in caring for the ill family member

• utilize healthy coping mechanisms
• demonstrate listening and supportive behaviors to each other
• identify resources within and outside the family
• develop a plan or strategy to provide necessary care and support for the ill family member after discharge.

Discharge planning
NURSING DISCHARGE CRITERIA
Upon discharge, documentation shows evidence of:
• identification of the impact of the patient's illness on family function
• plan for dealing with changes within the family
• identification of internal and external resources available to them
• initial contact with selected external resources.

PATIENT/FAMILY DISCHARGE TEACHING CHECKLIST
Document evidence that the patient/family demonstrates understanding of:
___ extent and implication of the patient's illness and limitations
___ changes in family roles and function, such as new responsibilities each member must assume to facilitate care of the patient at home
___ resources and referrals available to family.

DOCUMENTATION CHECKLIST
Using outcome criteria as a guide, document:
___ family's initial emotional status
___ precipitating factors in crisis and meaning of crisis to family members
___ changes in emotional status related to nursing interventions
___ treatment and care information given to family members
___ family's level of understanding of information provided
___ family members' ability to express feelings
___ identified family strengths and weaknesses
___ referrals to community resources.

ASSOCIATED CARE PLANS
Death and Dying
Grief/Grieving
Ineffective Individual Coping
Knowledge Deficit

REFERENCES
Bayuk, L.L. "Nursing Families in Crisis: Protecting Yourself," *Washington State Journal of Nursing* 54(2):17-20, Summer/Autumn 1983.
Carpenito, L. *Nursing Diagnosis: Application to Clinical Practice,* 2nd ed. Philadelphia: J.B. Lippincott, 1983.
Hoff, Lee A. *People in Crisis: Understanding and Helping,* 2nd ed. Menlo Park, Calif.: Addison-Wesley Publishing Co., 1984.
Miller, S., and Winstead-Fry, P. *Family Systems Theory in Nursing Practice.* Reston, Va.: Reston Publishing Co., 1982.
Molter, N.C. "Needs of Relatives of Critically Ill Patients: A Descriptive Study," *Heart & Lung* 8:332-39, March/April 1979.
Warmbrod, L.L.S. "Supporting Families of Critically Ill Patients," *Critical Care Nurse* 3(5):49-52 September/October 1983.

Ineffective Individual Coping

Introduction

DEFINITION AND TIME FOCUS
Ineffective coping is the inability to use adapative behaviors in response to a perceived threat, with a resulting disruption in physiologic and psychological balance. The patient is unable to problem-solve to find a solution to the situation that is causing feelings of insecurity and uncertainty. This clinical plan focuses on the patient who is hospitalized on a medical-surgical unit for an acute illness or an exacerbation of a chronic condition, and whose usual coping mechanisms are not effective in helping to maintain psychological equilibrium.

ETIOLOGY/PRECIPITATING FACTORS
• stimuli likely to cause ineffective coping in illness
  □ pain and incapacitation
  □ lack of sleep
  □ stressful hospital environment and treatment procedures
  □ loss of control over what is happening to him/her
  □ loss of hope
  □ lack of meaningful contact with significant others
  □ uncertain future
• conditions necessary for a stimulus to cause ineffective coping
  □ perception of a harmful stimulus, or cues that indicate a harmful stimulus is imminent
  □ perception that the harmful stimulus threatens the individual's goals or values
  □ perception that the patient's resources are not equal to coping with the threat

Focused assessment guidelines

NURSING HISTORY (Functional health pattern findings)

Health perception—health management pattern
• commonly *perceives illness and hospitalization as a loss of control* that threatens fulfillment of usual roles or threatens life itself
• may report *drastically reduced ability to problem-solve effectively*
  □ may select course of action without weighing alternatives
  □ may become overwhelmed by alternatives and unable to select a course of action
• may not be following treatment plan

Nutritional-metabolic pattern
• may report anorexia, nausea, or vomiting
• may report loss of weight from anorexia
• may report frequent overeating to deal with stress

Elimination pattern
• may report experiencing diarrhea or constipation from dietary changes or stress

Activity-exercise pattern
• may report occasional hyperactivity and inability to rest
• may report occasional withdrawal, listlessness,

Sleep-rest pattern
• may report sleep disturbance
  □ may have increased the usual amount of time spent sleeping
  □ may have difficulty falling asleep
  □ may report falling asleep but awakening early, then being unable to return to sleep (early-morning insomnia)
  □ may report frequent awakening during the night

Cognitive-perceptual pattern
• may show *diminished ability to view the world objectively*
• may display *decreased ability to take in information*
• typically expresses lack of information necessary to make decisions
• may report experiencing delusions (rare)

Self-perception—self-concept pattern
• may feel the *threat is greater than available internal resources* to combat it
• may feel *unable to control events* affecting the current situation

Role-relationship pattern
• may report or show *decreased ability to communicate needs*
• may report often feeling isolated and unable to experience caring from others
• may report occasional inability to control impulsive behavior; may become suicidal or hostile and aggressive

Sexuality-reproductive pattern
• may report loss of libido, impotence, or orgasmic dysfunction

Coping-stress tolerance pattern
• may report experiencing physiologic responses related to sympathetic nervous system stimulation, such as tachycardia
• may report increased number of infections related to alteration in the immune system
• may have denied symptoms and delayed seeking treatment
• may display variety of negative coping behaviors, depending on individual and environmental factors
  □ anger and hostility
  □ anxiety and hyperactivity
  □ depression and withdrawal
  □ suicidal ideation

• may behave in a manner that alienates caregivers and removes a source of support
• may have a history of ineffective coping mechanisms, such as drug or alcohol abuse, nicotine addiction, or overeating

Value-belief patterns
• may have experienced a loss of faith related to feelings of hopelessness and abandonment

PHYSICAL FINDINGS
General appearance
• *anxious facial expression*
• flat affect
• poor eye contact

Cardiovascular
• elevated blood pressure
• *increased heart rate*
• occasionally, increased ventricular dysrhythmias

Pulmonary
• increased rate and depth of respirations

Gastrointestinal
• vomiting
• diarrhea
• if stress ulcer develops, GI bleeding

Neurologic
• occasional dilated pupils (sympathetic nervous system response)
• restlessness
• lethargy

Integumentary
• occasionally, diaphoresis

Musculoskeletal
• *increased muscle tension* and pain

DIAGNOSTIC STUDIES
In the clinical setting, laboratory tests are not normally done to identify ineffective coping. However, it is important to remember that physiologic responses to stress can mimic disease.
• arterial blood gas measurements may reveal respiratory alkalosis from an increased rate and depth of respiration (hyperventilation)
• white blood cell (WBC) count may be increased
• mental status examination:
  □ appearance may yield clues about how a person perceives self (patients coping ineffectively may not care about their appearance)
  □ behavior (facial expression, posture, body movements, tone of voice) is indicator of person's ability to express self effectively, an important coping skill;

behavior may vary, depending on patient's expressive style; relationship of patient with caregivers is also important to assess: is patient controlling, passive, aggressive, suspicious, uncooperative?; may demonstrate inability to problem-solve
  □ feelings are assessed to determine what emotions the patient expresses and whether they are appropriate to the situation; wide variety of feelings possible, ranging from anxiety to anger to depression and typically including feelings of isolation and hopelessness
  □ perceptions indicate patient's view of the situation; threatening perceptions are based on previous experience, values, and beliefs along with perception of inadequate resources in relation to the magnitude of the threat. What coping mechanisms were used in the past? Which were useful? Which are potentially harmful—for example, smoking, alcohol use, or drug use?
• suicide assessment—a patient who is feeling hopeless and helpless needs to be asked if he or she is contemplating suicide; this question does not cause a patient to think about suicide but, rather, provides an opportunity to talk about these disturbing feelings. Factors known to be associated with high risk include:
  □ high level of anxiety or panic
  □ severe depression
  □ minimal ability to perform activities of daily living
  □ few or no sources of support or significant others
  □ continued abuse of alcohol, or drugs, or both
  □ negative view of previous psychiatric help (if applicable)
  □ one or more previous suicide attempts
  □ marked hostility
  □ frequent or constant thoughts of suicide
  □ suicide plan that is specific in terms of method, timing, and so forth
  □ possession of means to carry out the plan, such as physical capacity, weapons, and so forth
(See also *Assessment of Suicide Potential*, page 44, in the Grief/Grieving care plan.)

POTENTIAL COMPLICATIONS
• physiologic
  □ increased risk of falls and accidents
  □ ventricular dysrhythmias
  □ increased susceptibility to infections
  □ sudden death (possible)
• psychological
  □ suicide or homicide
  □ major depression
  □ psychosis
  □ disintegration of family unit

Nursing diagnosis: *Ineffective individual coping related to perception of a harmful stimulus*

NURSING PRIORITY 1: Establish rapport and trust.

Interventions

1. *Form a positive relationship with the patient.*
• Convey a sense of caring and concern for what happens to the patient.
• Use appropriate eye contact.
• Convey feelings of comfort and relaxation by approaching the patient calmly, including the patient in all bedside conversations, and speaking in a well-modulated tone.
• Identify personal reactions to the patient's coping style that could interfere with formation of a helping relationship. Avoid judging patients.

Rationales

1. Patients report that feelings of being uncared for interfere with their recovery and contribute to feelings of hopelessness. An ineffective relationship with caregivers uses up energy that could be better used for healing. Conversely, patients who feel positive about their nurses say this gives them an energy that helps with the healing process, decreases isolation, and increases coping ability.

People express anxiety, pain, and needs for privacy and intimacy in a variety of ways, depending on their cultural and personal biases. For example, if the patient who feels comfortable expressing pain openly is cared for by a nurse who believes that pain should be tolerated in silence, an ineffective nurse-patient relationship may result. Recognizing one's own cultural and personal biases is the first step in avoiding prejudicial responses.

NURSING PRIORITY 2: Accurately identify threat and coping resources.

Interventions

1. *Rule out organic causes* for such behavioral changes as decreased alertness, impaired memory, confusion, restlessness, or depression.

2. *Provide factual information* about the illness and treatment plan. Reinforce information the patient has received from the doctor. Be prepared to repeat information in clear, concise language.

3. *With the patient, identify the source of the threat.*

4. *Help the patient be specific* about what he perceives as threatening.

5. With the patient, *identify modifiable components* of the threat.

Rationales

1. Behavioral changes that appear to be signs of ineffective coping may actually represent such physiologic changes as hypoxia, electrolyte changes, or drug toxicity. Assuming that all behavioral responses are related to psychological mechanisms may delay needed medical treatment.

2. For the problem-solving process to begin, the patient must have accurate information. Patients who are coping ineffectively have a decreased ability to hear and assimilate information.

3. Whether or not a stimulus is perceived as threatening depends on values, beliefs, and the perception of available resources. An obvious, identifiable threat (such as a diagnosis of cancer) may not be the primary threat perceived by the patient. Conversely, what seems routine to the nurse may be frightening to the patient.

4. Patients often have misconceptions about what is happening to them. If they can specify their fears, specific actions can be planned. The nurse can provide information that helps the patient consider his fears less threatening.

5. People coping ineffectively are often unable to separate their situation into manageable parts; rather, the problem is viewed as overwhelming and unmanageable. If the problem can be viewed in component parts, anxiety may be reduced and effective coping behaviors instituted.

(continued)

Interventions *continued*

6. *Help the patient identify existing personal strengths and external resources*, such as family, friends, and economic means.

7. Identify external resources and make appropriate referrals—for example, for social services, spiritual counseling, or psychiatric interventions.

NURSING PRIORITY 3: Intervene to optimize coping skills.

Interventions

1. *Keep pain at a tolerable level.*

2. *Ensure adequate nutrition and sleep.*

3. *Control environmental stimuli* that use up adaptive energy and decrease the amount available for psychological equilibrium: provide privacy for all invasive procedures and for nursing and self-care activities; eliminate conversation around the bedside that does not include the patient; and decrease environmental noise.

4. *Offer alternative strategies to counteract the effects of the threat*—for example, guided imagery, relaxation techniques, or back rubs.

5. *Give the patient choices* related to the individual's own care and situation whenever possible.

6. *Provide opportunities for loved ones to interact with the patient in meaningful ways.*

NURSING PRIORITY 4: Evaluate the effectiveness of interventions.

Interventions

1. *Assess responses to nursing interventions, and collaborate with the doctor to determine if pharmacologic intervention would be helpful.*

2. Additional individualized interventions:_____
_____
_____

Outcome criteria
Within 2 days of identification of ineffective coping, the patient will:
• express an accurate understanding of the current situation and treatment plan

Rationales *continued*

6. People in crisis are often unable to identify the strengths that they do have. They need assistance in assessing available resources and identifying ways to activate them.

7. Expansion of the patient's base of support helps decrease the perceived magnitude of the specific threat.

Rationales

1. Pain is a common source of fear. Uncontrolled pain increases anxiety and decreases the amount of energy available for coping.

2. Inadequate diet and lack of sleep are stressors themselves and, as such, decrease the amount of energy available for coping and adaptation.

3. Every stimulus in the environment can be a potential source of threat. Stimuli not normally viewed as threatening may, in combination, create more stress and decrease coping ability.

4. The relaxation response is the physiologic opposite of anxiety. Relaxation techniques may help the patient cope with stress and regain control.

5. Maintaining some ability to control one's life helps to combat feelings of helplessness.

6. A positive response from loved ones encourages a more positive response to treatment and decreases the sense of isolation.

Rationales

1. Antianxiety medications may be helpful in decreasing potentially harmful physiologic and psychological effects of anxiety.

2. Rationale: _____
_____
_____

• state any pain is within tolerable limits
• participate in developing a plan of care
• utilize support offered by caregivers.

Discharge planning

NURSING DISCHARGE CRITERIA

Upon discharge, documentation shows evidence of:
• perception of increased ability to cope with the situation
• ability to name resources appropriate to the situation
• increased ability to problem-solve the current situation by defining the problem and reasonable alternative solutions.

PATIENT/FAMILY DISCHARGE TEACHING CHECKLIST

Document evidence that the patient/family demonstrates understanding of:
__ diagnosis, treatment plan, and prognosis
__ expected physiologic responses during recovery
__ community resources appropriate to perceived problems
__ appropriate alternative coping strategies
__ how to contact the doctor.

DOCUMENTATION CHECKLIST

Using outcome criteria as a guide, document:
__ coping status on admission
__ significant changes in appearance, affect, behavior, and perception
__ psychological responses to hospitalization and interventions
__ significant physiologic stress responses
__ sleep patterns
__ nutritional intake
__ pain control
__ response to caregivers
__ response to intervention designed to increase coping skills
__ suicide risk
__ referrals made
__ patient and family teaching
__ discharge planning.

ASSOCIATED CARE PLANS

Death and Dying
Grief/Grieving
Ineffective Family Coping
Knowledge Deficit
Pain

REFERENCES

Beglinger, J.E. "Coping Tasks in Critical Care," *Dimensions of Critical Care Nursing* 2(2): 80-89, March/April 1983.

Drew, N. "Exclusion and Confirmation: A Phenomenology of Patient's Experience with Caregivers," *Image: Journal of Nursing Scholarship* 18(2) 39-43, Summer 1986.

Hatton, Corrine, et al. *Suicide: Assessment and Intervention*, 2nd ed. New York: Appleton & Lange, 1983.

Janis, I.L. "Coping Patterns Among Patients with Life-Threatening Diseases," *Issues in Mental Health Nursing* 7(14): 461-76, 1985.

Kim, M.J., and Moritz, D.A., eds. *Classification of Nursing Diagnoses: Proceedings of the Third and Fourth National Conferences*. New York: McGraw-Hill Book Co., 1982.

Lazarus, R. *Psychological Stress and the Coping Process*. New York: McGraw-Hill Book Co., 1966.

Locke, S.E. "Stress, Adaptation and Immunity: Studies in Humans," *General Hospital Psychiatry* 4:49-58, April 1982.

Lown, B., et al. "Psychophysiologic Factors in Sudden Cardiac Death," *American Journal of Psychiatry* 137(11):1325-34, 1980.

Moos, Rudolf H., and Tsu, V.S. "The Crisis of Physical Illness: An Overview," in *Coping with Physical Illness*. Edited by Moos, Rudolph. New York: Plenum Pubs., 1977.

Perry S., and Viederman, M. "Management of Emotional Reactions to Acute Medical Illness," *Medical Clinics of North America* 65(1):3-14, 1981.

Slaby, Andrew E., and Glicksman, Arvin S. *Adapting to Life-Threatening Illness*. New York: Praeger Pubs., 1985.

Snyder, J.C., and Wilson, M.F. "Elements of a Psychological Assessment," *American Journal of Nursing* 77:235-39, February 1977.

Spielberger, C. *Understanding Stress and Anxiety*. New York: Harper and Row, 1979.

Knowledge Deficit

Introduction

DEFINITION AND TIME FOCUS

A knowledge deficit is present when a person expresses or displays a lack of knowledge or psychomotor skills needed for health recovery or maintenance.

This clinical plan focuses on the patient and family who require health-related teaching at any stage of hospitalization.

ETIOLOGY/PRECIPITATING FACTORS
• unfamiliar diagnostic procedure
• new diagnosis
• alteration in preexisting health problem
• unfamiliar or altered treatment plan
• complex treatment regimen
• denial
• anxiety

Focused assessment guidelines

NURSING HISTORY (Functional health pattern findings)

Health perception–health management pattern
• may have delayed seeking needed medical attention
• may express lack of knowledge about disease or condition
• may express lack of confidence in ability to manage condition
• may express misconception about health status
• may not comply with recommended health practices
• may not participate in self-care
• may abuse health care system by seeking treatment for a problem that could have been solved by self or another resource

Nutritional-metabolic pattern
• may express concerns about effects of disease or condition on nutrition and eating habits
• may express difficulty staying on dietary regimen

Activity-exercise pattern
• may express concerns about life-changing limitation of activity caused by disease or condition

Cognitive-perceptual pattern
• may express concern about understanding details of disease or condition
• may have questions regarding rationale for procedures or treatments
• may have concerns regarding specific details of diagnostic or therapeutic procedures

• may describe sensory deficits (such as impaired seeing or hearing)
• may describe lack of psychomotor skills needed to maintain treatment regimen at home
• may report confusion or changes in thought processes caused by disease or condition
• may misinterpret information

Self-perception–self-concept pattern
• may express concerns about inability to maintain treatment regimen
• may report anxiety about changes in body image caused by disease or condition

Role-relationship pattern
• may describe self as needing significant other present or available during procedures
• may express concerns about job, income, or family responsibilities related to disease or condition
• may express concerns about family's response to lifestyle changes related to disease or condition

Sexuality-reproductive pattern
• may report concern about impact of disease or condition on sexual activity
• may express concern about impact of changes in sexual activity on spouse or partner

Coping-stress tolerance pattern
• may report anxiety
• may be experiencing denial of disease or condition
• may report depression from life-style changes caused by disease or condition
• may express concerns about coping behaviors and motivation needed to maintain treatment regimen

Value-belief pattern
• may express disbelief over current experience

PHYSICAL FINDINGS
• may not perform a necessary health procedure correctly
• may display physical signs of anxiety, such as restlessness, tremulousness, or talkativeness
• may display sensory deficits (for example, blindness or impaired hearing)

DIAGNOSTIC STUDIES
Not applicable.

POTENTIAL COMPLICATION
• exacerbation of disease

Nursing diagnosis: *Potential knowledge deficit related to lack of readiness to learn**

NURSING PRIORITY: Determine readiness to learn.

Interventions

1. *Assess the impact of the person's disease or condition on life-style.*

2. *Determine the person's stage of adaptation* to the disease or condition: shock and disbelief; developing awareness; or resolution and reorganization. Dovetail teaching objectives and content with psychological issues during each phase.

3. *Assess the person's physical readiness to learn:* Is he or she physiologically stable? Rested? Pain-free?

4. *Determine the person's motivation (emotional readiness) to learn.* For example, are appropriate questions asked about status or care? Is the person preoccupied, distracted, or emotionally labile?

5. Determine the general pattern of health maintenance; for example, has the person sought regular medical check-ups, followed previous health recommendations, eaten a balanced diet, and exercised regularly?

6. *Assess the person's current knowledge* of the disease or condition and its implications for the future; the likelihood of complications; and the likelihood of cure or disease control. Specifically, ask about the doctor's explanations, the person's past experiences, and information received from family, friends, and the media.

7. *Determine learning needs.* Consider expressed needs; predictable disease- or condition-related concerns and responses; and activities necessary to monitor health status, prevent disease, implement prescribed therapy, and prevent complications or recurrence.

8. *Estimate learning capacity.* Assess the person's age; language spoken; ability to read, write, and reason; and educational, religious, and cultural background.

Rationales

1. The degree of impact determines the extent of teaching necessary. Areas of impact provide foci around which learning experiences should be structured.

2. Different psychological work occurs in each of these phases. Attempting to provide teaching inappropriate for a particular phase results in increased learner anxiety or irritation and inability to absorb information.

3. Teaching is most effective when the person is ready to learn. Readiness to learn is a complex state that depends on physical as well as psychological factors. Determining readiness to learn requires weighing the interaction of numerous variables. Learning requires energy that will not be available if the person is unstable, tired, or in pain.

4. Motivation is the crucial variable in learning. It may be absent initially because of anxiety, preoccupation with other needs, or other emotional causes. Prolonged absence of interest in learning about the condition may be a clue to an underlying emotional disorder requiring treatment before the patient assumes independent self-care responsibility. Motivation may be developed through teaching by linking relevant learning to the person's particular concerns.

5. The general pattern can provide clues to overall acceptance of responsibility for self-care and the likelihood of receptivity to teaching.

6. Adults learn best when teaching builds on previous knowledge or experience. Assessing recall of the doctor's explanations as well as the patient's past experiences and information provides an opportunity for assessing the accuracy and completeness of knowledge and attitudes toward illness.

7. Learning needs determine appropriate content. Learning occurs most rapidly when it is relevant to current needs and past experiences. Predictable concerns and responses and necessary self-care activities help the nurse identify learning needs of which the patient or family may not yet be aware.

8. Sociocultural factors influence the speed and degree of learning. Awareness of the person's age, background, and general ability to think logically and express thoughts aids in presenting material at the appropriate intellectual level.

(continued)

*Note: Because of the importance of knowledge deficit as a patient/family problem and the large number of possible interventions, the problem here is subdivided by etiology.

Interventions *continued*

9. Additional individualized interventions: _____
_____
_____

Outcome criteria
Before the initiation of teaching, the patient will:
• show a stable physiologic condition
• discuss knowledge of the disease or condition

Rationales *continued*

9. Rationale: _____
_____

• identify primary perceived teaching needs
• display motivation to learn.

Nursing diagnosis: *Potential knowledge deficit related to a teaching program that is inappropriate for the patient's needs*

NURSING PRIORITY: Plan an individualized teaching strategy.

Interventions

1. *Work with the patient and family to set realistic, mutually agreed-upon learning goals.* Set both short-term and long-term goals.

2. *Determine what content to teach* by assessing what is essential from the person's viewpoint. Base content on comprehensive objectives. Prioritize content by dividing it into "need to know" and "nice to know" categories.

3. *Sequence content appropriately.* In general, teach first:
• information related to expressed concerns

• nonthreatening information

• high-priority information—specific teaching without which the patient's condition may be seriously jeopardized.

4. *Select appropriate teaching methods,* such as individual bedside instruction, group instruction, lectures, discussions, or demonstrations (see *Teaching Strategies*).

5. Be creative in choosing appropriate teaching materials, such as booklets, instruction sheets, posters, films, videotapes, models, dolls, slides, and audiotapes. In choosing, consider advantages, availability, and the person's learning style.

Rationales

1. Goals determine content. Goal-directed learning is more efficient than fragmented, unfocused learning. Active participation in goal setting increases the likelihood that the patient and family will understand goals and support them.

2. Because the person's attention span may be limited and the patient's hospitalization may be short, content must be prioritized. Content largely determines the choice of teaching method.

3. Sequencing allows the person to build upon current knowledge and experience.
• Learning is strongest when it occurs in response to perceived needs. Dealing with initial concerns displays sensitivity to the person, helps establish rapport and trust, and frees the patient's energy to focus on further learning.
• Illness and the need to learn may themselves threaten the patient and family. Presenting "neutral" information first allows the person time to adapt to the learner role and facilitates a smoother transition to dealing with more threatening or emotionally charged information.
• Presenting essential information early in the teaching period helps ensure that all the critical information will have been covered by the time of discharge.

4. Teaching methods vary according to content. Matching content with appropriate methods enhances the opportunity for learning to occur.

5. The more senses involved in learning, the more likely it is that retention will occur. Printed materials provide consistency, reinforce verbally presented information, and provide a source to which the patient can refer as needed. Slides, audiotapes, films, and videotapes can vividly present the sights and sounds of an experience—for example, by showing the personnel and equipment of a diagnostic procedure room from the patient's-eye view. Films and videotapes ensure consis-

Interventions *continued*

Rationales *continued*

tency of presentation but should be supplemented by one-on-one follow-up discussion. Models (for example, of a pacemaker) help the person picture more vividly how something works. Dolls may be useful adjuncts for teaching children.

6. Determine how best to teach this content to this person at this time. Consider the advantages and disadvantages of the various teaching methods, the appropriateness and availability of educational materials, and the person's personality.

6. In many cases, several combinations of content, teaching methods, and educational materials can achieve a desired goal. Selecting the combination most appropriate to this person makes learning "come alive."

(continued)

TEACHING STRATEGIES

Method	Characteristics	Most appropriate for	Disadvantages
Individual bedside instruction	One-on-one interaction between teacher and learner Immediate feedback Informal	Acute phase Sensitive topics "Private" person Emotionally labile person Persons with language difficulties Persons with limited education	Time-consuming
Group session	Small or large number of people Informal Interchange of ideas	General content teaching Persons with similar readiness-to-learn levels	Lack of individualization
Lecture	Highly structured Efficient	Large amount of factual content Rehabilitation program	Lack of opportunity for teacher-learner interaction Possible failure to engage learner's interest (Disadvantages may be overcome by alternating lectures with interactive learning opportunities, such as question-and-answer periods or skill demonstrations.)
Discussion	Interchange of ideas More informal than lecture More opportunity to adapt content and evaluate learner comprehension	Acute phase Sensitive topics When attitudinal change is desired Highly verbal patients	Time-consuming May be uncomfortable for some patients because of their cultural norms against expression
Demonstration/return demonstration	Observation and supervised practice Immediate feedback	Teaching psychomotor skills	Does not lend itself to demonstrating abstract concepts

Interventions *continued*

7. Decide who should teach what. Consider the primary nurse, a nurse with special related expertise, other health care professionals, and visitors from community or self-help groups.

8. Decide when and where to teach.

9. Plan evaluation strategies, such as observation, questions, and return demonstration of skills, based on goals and objectives.

10. Communicate the teaching strategy to other health-care professionals involved in the patient's care.

11. Additional individualized interventions: _____
_____
_____

Rationales *continued*

7. Depending on the content and the learner's preferences, different teachers may be necessary or appropriate and may be useful in reinforcing learning. Peer-group lay teachers, for example, may provide especially relevant tips based on personal experience with the patient's disease or condition; health professionals provide a broader range of general health care education.

8. Choosing appropriate times to teach capitalizes on learning readiness. Appropriate sequencing (see Intervention 3 above) builds upon previously presented material and enhances integration of learning. An environment free of distractions increases attentiveness.

9. Evaluation often is interwoven with presentation of teaching. Clear evaluation methods determined in advance help ensure measurability of goals and increase the likelihood that the nurse will recognize spontaneous opportunities for evaluation and respond appropriately to them.

10. Communication enhances consistency of information provided by caregivers, allows for appropriate reinforcement, and minimizes unnecessary repetition.

11. Rationale: _____
_____
_____

Outcome criteria
Throughout the period of hospitalization, the patient will:
• identify priority learning needs
• participate in goal setting.

Nursing diagnosis: *Potential knowledge deficit related to inadequate or ineffective implementation of teaching plan*

NURSING PRIORITY: Implement an individualized teaching plan that maximizes learning, retention, and compliance.

Interventions

1. *Present yourself as enthusiastic, knowledgeable, and approachable.*

2. *Present manageable amounts of information* at any one time.

3. *Provide simple explanations*, using easy-to-understand terminology.

Rationales

1. Enthusiasm is contagious. Presenting yourself as knowledgeable increases credibility, and maintaining approachability allows the person to capitalize on your expertise.

2. Too much information causes confusion. The person may lose sight of key points.

3. Medical or nursing "jargon" distances patients and family members. Intricate explanations may confuse or overwhelm them.

Interventions *continued*

4. *Use review and repetition judiciously,* considering individual factors. (Stress, physiologic changes, and medications can contribute to a short attention span and poor retention.)

5. Before planned teaching, assess for the presence of physiologic needs and intense emotions. Meet any physiologic needs, and encourage expression of strong emotions.

6. Incorporate teaching into other nursing activities. Be alert for serendipitous opportunities for teaching; for example, use treatment of insulin reaction in a new diabetic to help the patient and family learn to identify symptoms.

7. Provide opportunities for immediate application of learning. For example, when teaching pulse taking, show the person what to do, then have him count your radial pulse while you take your carotid pulse for comparison.

8. *Ask for feedback:* Were the words understandable? Was the presentation too fast, too slow, too much, too little? Adjust terminology, pace, and amount of information accordingly.

9. Be alert for signs of pain, fatigue, confusion, or boredom—for example, fidgeting, yawning, lack of eye contact, grimacing, or agitation.

10. Promote a positive outlook: solicit feelings, and convey confidence in the person's ability to learn.

11. Encourage active participation. Use interactive teaching methods.

12. Document teaching sessions. Communicate progress to appropriate caregivers.

13. Additional individualized interventions: _____
_____
_____

Outcome criteria
Throughout the period of hospitalization, the patient will:
• express satisfaction with the level, amount, timing, and quality of teaching presented

Rationales *continued*

4. Review and repetition aid recall and increase retention.

5. Unmet physiologic needs (such as thirst or the urge to void) and strong emotions interfere with the ability to concentrate on learning.

6. The hectic pace of most units may allow little time for extended, "sit-down" teaching sessions. Incorporating teaching into other activities increases the likelihood that it will be accomplished and contributes to an atmosphere of naturalness and informality. Activity-related teaching also provides opportunities to reinforce learning (for example, teaching stoma care whenever the stoma is visible).

7. Immediate application improves retention.

8. The person may be reluctant to volunteer lack of understanding. Soliciting feedback demonstrates respect for the learner and permits adjustments before the person becomes lost, overwhelmed, or bored.

9. These nonverbal signs may provide clues to the need for modification or conclusion of the current teaching session.

10. The person may initially feel overwhelmed and insecure about his or her ability to learn because of the magnitude, urgency, or unfamiliarity of necessary adaptations to illness.

11. Adults learn best when actively involved. Active participation also facilitates changes needed to allow recovery from or adaptation to the patient's disease or condition.

12. Documentation provides a teaching record for legal purposes; communication enhances the continuity of teaching among caregivers.

13. Rationale: _____
_____
_____

• indicate an interest in learning during care activities
• provide relevant feedback to persons doing the teaching.

Nursing diagnosis: *Potential knowledge deficit related to lack of modification of teaching as needed*

NURSING PRIORITIES: (a) Evaluate learning and (b) modify teaching when appropriate.

Interventions

1. During and after teaching, *determine what learning has occurred:* for example, observe the person, ask questions, or ask for a skill demonstration.

2. With the person, compare learning against previously identified goals.

3. Modify the teaching plan as indicated by unmet goals or new learning needs.

4. Refer the patient, family, or both to health care agencies and community agencies, as appropriate, before discharge.

5. If the patient is noncompliant, evaluate why. See the "Noncompliance" problem in the "Congestive Heart Failure" care plan, page 210.

6. Additional individualized interventions: _____

_____

Rationales

1. Determination of learning accomplishment permits resolution of some teaching needs and provides guidance for meeting others.

2. Comparison indicates whether or not goals have been attained and whether or not they should be reevaluated for appropriateness.

3. Frequent evaluation and modification of the teaching plan ensures that the teaching is tailored to individual learning capabilities and ongoing learning needs.

4. Needs not met by the time of discharge require further follow-up.

5. Patients have the right to control their own lives, including the right to reject treatment or teaching. In many cases, patients have valid reasons for noncompliance—for example, the need to focus energy on meeting basic needs for food, clothing, and shelter may preclude participation in time-consuming self-care behaviors. The "Noncompliance" problem in the "Congestive Heart Failure" care plan contains further details about assessment of noncompliant behavior and appropriate interventions.

6. Rationale: _____

Outcome criteria

By the time of discharge, the patient will:
• demonstrate learning through appropriate methods
• evidence minimal anxiety related to self-care

• express satisfaction with the learning level achieved
• express a realistic appraisal of additional learning needs and identify appropriate teaching resources.

Discharge planning
NURSING DISCHARGE CRITERIA

Upon discharge, documentation shows evidence of:
• verbalization of signs and symptoms of disease or condition
• sharing of thoughts and feelings regarding procedures and life-style changes
• verbalization of understanding of treatment regimen for disease or condition
• demonstration of psychomotor skills necessary for recovery or for maintaining normal activities of daily living
• identification of community resources that can assist with life changes related to patient's diagnosis and treatment.

PATIENT/FAMILY DISCHARGE TEACHING CHECKLIST

Document evidence that the patient/family demonstrates understanding of:
__ disease or condition information necessary for life-style adjustment
__ all discharge medications' purpose, dosage, administration schedule, and side effects requiring medical attention
__ signs and symptoms requiring medical attention
__ dietary regimen or modifications, if appropriate
__ community resources for adjustment to life-style changes
__ date, time, and location of follow-up appointments
__ how to contact the doctor.

DOCUMENTATION CHECKLIST

Using outcome criteria as a guide, document:
___ assessment of readiness for learning
___ identification of factors that could inhibit learning
___ identification of learning goals
___ response of patient and family to teaching plan
___ problems encountered in teaching
___ evaluation of learning.

ASSOCIATED CARE PLANS

(See also the care plan for the
patient's specific disease or condition.)
Ineffective Family Coping
Ineffective Individual Coping
Pain

REFERENCES

Alfaro, Rosalinda A. *Application of Nursing Process: A Step-by-Step Guide to Care Planning.* Philadelphia: J.B. Lippincott Co., 1986.

Carpenito, L. *Nursing Diagnosis: Application to Clinical Practice.* Philadelphia: J.B. Lippincott Co., 1983.

Gordon, Marjory. *Nursing Diagnosis: Process and Application,* 2nd ed. New York: McGraw-Hill Book Co., 1982.

Hochbaum, Godfrey M. "Patient Counseling vs. Patient Teaching," *Topics in Clinical Nursing* 2:1-7, July 1980.

Scalzi, Cynthia, and Burke, Lora. "Education of the Patient and Family," in *Cardiac Nursing.* Edited by Underhill, Sandra, et al. Philadelphia: J.B. Lippincott Co., 1982.

Pain

Introduction
DEFINITION AND TIME FOCUS
Pain is a subjective, highly unpleasant state involving a neurologic or emotional response to a noxious stimulus. Pain is probably the single most frequently encountered patient problem in nursing practice, yet it is unique for each patient. Effective nursing intervention to help patients deal with pain requires astute assessment skills, knowledge about the pain phenomenon, a repertoire of pain control techniques, and the compassion and skilled judgment to apply them appropriately. This clinical plan focuses on care of the patient with acute or chronic pain.

ETIOLOGY/PRECIPITATING FACTORS
• existing medical conditions or disease processes, congenital malformations, or inflammatory processes
• invasive diagnostic procedures, such as lumbar puncture
• trauma or surgery
• chronic immobility, overactivity, or pressure to parts of the body
• psychogenic origins, such as hostility or a threat to the integrity of the body

Focused assessment guidelines
NURSING HISTORY (Functional health pattern findings)

Health perception—health management pattern
• typically *verbalizes presence of sharp, well-localized pain or describes poorly localized pain as vague discomfort, pressure, or a burning sensation*
• may complain about lack of energy

Nutritional-metabolic pattern
• may report changes in nutritional habits or status, typically anorexia, as a result of pain
• may report nausea and vomiting in response to severe or chronic pain

Elimination pattern
• may report pain on elimination
• may report delaying urination or defecation to avoid pain

Activity-exercise pattern
• may report immobility as a method of coping with pain
• may express inability to conduct normal activities because of pain
• may report *fatigue*

Sleep-rest pattern
• may report *inability to sleep or rest* because of pain

Cognitive-perceptual pattern
• may report concern that others do not believe pain exists
• may describe *inability to concentrate*

Self-perception—self-concept pattern
• may report a diminished sense of self-worth
• may report depression
• may express concern about being dependent

Role-relationship pattern
• may report concern about response of other to pain
• may report limited interactions with others because of pain
• may describe self as dependent on others because of pain

Sexuality-reproductive pattern
• may express concern about inability to maintain sexual relationship because of chronic pain

Coping-stress tolerance pattern
• may report *tension and increased stress*
• may express *inability to tolerate any amount of stress* in normal activities of daily living (ADLs)
• may report feelings of increased frustration because of inability to obtain relief from pain
• may report certain ways of coping with pain
• may express concern about being dependent on chemical substances for pain relief

Value-belief pattern
• may express belief in need for suffering as punishment for wrongdoing or "bad" deeds
• may express reluctance to take medication for pain relief because of religion, belief system, or fear of addiction

PHYSICAL FINDINGS
Cardiovascular
• *hypertension*
• *tachycardia*
• hypotension (uncommon)
• bradycardia (uncommon)

Pulmonary
• *tachypnea*
• shortness of breath
• gasping

Neurologic
• *inability to concentrate*
• *restlessness*
• *irritability*
• disorientation
• crying
• moaning

Integumentary
• *diaphoresis*

Musculoskeletal
• *tense body posture*
• *muscle spasms, tremors*
• *guarded positioning, tenderness*
• *grimacing*
• pacing
• writhing
• unnatural stillness (less common)

DIAGNOSTIC STUDIES
Laboratory and diagnostic findings vary with the cause of pain. See care plans for specific disorders for details.

POTENTIAL COMPLICATIONS
• exhaustion
• intractable pain
• suicide

Nursing diagnosis: *Acute or chronic pain related to tissue damage, pressure, ischemia, distention, spasm, or other pathologic mechanism*

NURSING PRIORITY: Prevent or minimize pain.

Interventions

1. *Obtain a pain history:* location, character, intensity, frequency, duration, associated signs and symptoms, and relief measures used.

2. *Assess for nonverbal indicators of pain,* such as restlessness, tension, writhing, grimacing, diaphoresis, guarded positioning, tachypnea, tachycardia, and hypertension (typically), or bradycardia and hypotension (rarely). Also, be alert for "clock watching" for the next analgesic dose.

3. *Repeatedly reassess the pain* to prevent misjudging its severity, distancing oneself ("tuning out"), or stereotyping the patient as a "pain personality." Seek emotional support from co-workers if stressed by inability to relieve pain or by the necessity of inflicting pain.

4. *Provide anticipatory guidance* for impending painful experiences, such as drawing of arterial blood gas samples. Describe the location and character of the pain as typically experienced. Clarify what the patient should and should not do in response to the pain, such as, "It's okay to squeeze your husband's hand with your other hand, but hold this arm still for me."

5. *Provide support, clarification, and positive reinforcement* during and after painful procedures or episodes. For example, say, "You're doing really well keeping your arm still. We're almost done now." Or, afterward, "I know it was tough for you to hold still, but you really helped. Thank you." Keep explanations as simple as possible, and avoid constant chatter during the painful episode. Speak quietly and calmly.

Rationales

1. Identifying characteristics of the pain helps determine relief measures.

2. The patient may not verbalize pain, but observations of facial expressions, positioning, body tension, and other physical signs can help the nurse assess the severity of pain and its relationship to activity and position. Tachypnea, tachycardia, and hypertension result from sympathetic nervous system stimulation; bradycardia and hypotension result from a vasovagal response to pain. The main reason for "clock-watching" behavior is inadequate pain relief.

3. Nurses who cannot relieve pain or who must inflict it may resort to distancing as a defense mechanism. The first step in successful pain relief intervention is compassionate, understanding assessment. Co-workers may help provide objectivity and support.

4. Anxiety, lack of knowledge, and fear of the unknown commonly increase pain. Explanation decreases anxiety and helps the patient prepare for and cope with pain.

5. Providing encouragement and praise helps reinforce the patient's ability to cope with future pain and increases the patient's sense of control. Providing explanations in very simple terms promotes maximum understanding (pain and anxiety may reduce comprehension of verbal stimuli). Constant chatter may be irritating and may aggravate discomfort. A quiet, calm tone is reassuring.

(continued)

Interventions *continued*

6. *Reduce factors that may increase pain*, such as anxiety that reports of pain will not be believed, isolation, fear of being overwhelmed by pain, and fatigue. Accept the patient's description of pain. Convey the sense that the patient is not alone, and state the goal to prevent or "stay on top of" any pain. Encourage the patient to obtain sufficient rest. Control environmental factors, such as noise, temperature, and lighting, when possible.

7. *Work with the patient to identify ways to control pain.* Explore various pain-control methods. Use positive terms and the power of suggestion.

8. Position the patient to decrease pain. Avoid pressure or tension on the painful area (for example, avoid pulling on sutures). If the painful area is on an extremity, elevate the limb. Encourage the patient to assume a position of comfort but to change it at least hourly. If the patient is immobile, change his or her position at least hourly.

9. Apply heat or cold to the affected area (unless contraindicated).

10. Massage the painful area, or encourage the patient to massage it, unless contraindicated.

11. Encourage contralateral stimulation if the painful area cannot be massaged.

12. Teach the patient relaxation techniques, such as rhythmic breathing and autogenic training. If the patient has difficulty establishing rhythmic breathing, establish eye contact and say, "Focus on me. Now breathe as I do . . ." while demonstrating the technique.

13. Encourage the patient to try dietary measures for pain control. If not contraindicated by the underlying condition, the following suggestions may be helpful: drinking small amounts of wine or other alcoholic beverages at bedtime, reducing intake of caffeine and acidic foods, and taking tryptophan supplements.

Rationales *continued*

6. Listening to the patient respectfully and implying an alliance against pain help reduce anxiety. Explicitly stating the goals of pain prevention or aggressive management promotes a sense of control. Feeling well-rested increases tolerance of pain and the ability to cope with it. Environmental factors may exacerbate the pain: constant, irritating noise, for example, may cause increased muscle tension and irritability.

7. Involving the patient in pain-control strategies promotes a sense of control. Trying a variety of pain-control measures allows for individual responses and provides a multifaceted approach, which is more likely to be successful than a single strategy. Using positive terms interrupts the cycle of negativity that can develop—in which pain worsens negativity and negativity worsens pain. Capitalizing on the power of suggestion creates an expectation that interventions will be successful. It may also help trigger release of endorphins, opiate-like analgesic substances that the body releases in response to certain stimuli.

8. The measures cited avoid adding other sources of possible pain to an already painful area. Position changes are necessary to increase the blood supply to damaged tissues and to prevent the complications of decreased mobility, such as atelectasis and thrombophlebitis. Because the act of changing position may temporarily increase pain, the nurse may need to remind the patient gently but persistently not to overlook this important measure.

9. Heat increases the blood supply to the area and may relax painful muscle spasms. Cold reduces swelling. It also decreases neurotransmission along small-diameter type A peripheral fibers, which carry sharp or acute pain sensations, and type C peripheral fibers, which carry dull or chronic pain sensations.

10. Massage provides cutaneous stimulation. Stimulation of sensory fibers for touch limits pain impulse transmission along ascending pain pathways to the brain, according to the gate control theory.

11. Stimulating the opposite side of the body may trigger endorphin release.

12. Relaxation techniques help decrease tension, help the patient focus on relaxing certain body parts, and promote endorphin release. Endorphins also potentiate narcotic analgesia.

13. Alcohol decreases neurotransmission as does tryptophan, a precursor of serotonin. Serotonin stimulates release of enkephalins, which inhibit pain impulse transmission. Caffeine and acidity increase production of norepinephrine, which enhances transmission of pain stimuli.

Interventions *continued*

14. Encourage the patient to use distraction as a pain control method. Examples include talking, singing, and listening to music.

15. Encourage patients to try such pain-control techniques as transcutaneous electrical nerve stimulation (TENS) or acupuncture, when appropriate.

16. Encourage the patient with chronic or intractable pain to explore behavioral methods, such as hypnosis, biofeedback, and guided imagery.

17. When the above methods are inappropriate or do not control pain, encourage the patient to request medication before the pain becomes severe.

18. *Administer and document prescribed analgesics* as ordered, while monitoring for side effects and exercising nursing judgment. Options include:
• high-potency narcotics, such as morphine or meperidine (Demerol)

• mild narcotics (such as codeine or oxycodone [Percodan]) or narcotic agonists/antagonists (such as butorphanol [Stadol], nalbuphine [Nubain], or pentazocine [Talwin])

• nonnarcotic analgesics, such as aspirin and acetaminophen

• analgesic adjuncts, such as diazepam (Valium), promethazine (Phenergan), or hydroxyzine (Vistaril).

Rationales *continued*

14. Distraction helps control pain by reducing monotony, refocusing attention, and promoting endorphin release. Distraction is particularly helpful for brief periods of sharp, intense pain.

15. TENS is a technique that uses electrodes placed near a painful area and a generator box to transmit an electrical impulse (a tapping or massaging sensation). Acupuncture is an invasive technique in which needles are inserted into specific sites. Both may stimulate the production of endorphins and enkephalins or stimulate large-fiber impulse transmission to block pain impulses from small fibers (gate control theory). Both techniques may be helpful with chronic pain; TENS also is suitable for acute postoperative pain.

16. Hypnosis alters the patient's perception of pain and is useful for pain of a psychogenic nature or intractable pain. Biofeedback helps pain by self-control of physiologic states. Guided imagery involves structured use of imagination to recall pleasurable sensations or to visualize relief. Because these techniques require motivation and discipline, they are more appropriate for chronic pain.

17. Giving explicit permission to request medication early reduces stoicism and unnecessary suffering.

18. Analgesics are more effective when given before pain is severe.

• Appropriate for severe pain, narcotics alter pain perception in the central nervous system. Side effects include drowsiness, respiratory depression, vasodilation, nausea and vomiting, constipation, tolerance, dependence, and addiction.

• Appropriate for moderate pain, narcotic agonists/antagonists have different effects, depending on whether or not the patient is on narcotics. If so, these medications antagonize the narcotics and may decrease pain relief and provoke withdrawal symptoms. If not, these medications act like narcotics. Compared to narcotics, they are less likely to cause respiratory depression but more likely to cause unpleasant psychological reactions. Pentazocine is also addictive.

• Nonnarcotic analgesics are appropriate for mild pain. Aspirin and acetaminophen block synthesis of prostaglandins—inflammatory mediators generated by tissue damage that sensitize pain receptors.

• Analgesic adjuncts increase the analgesic's effects and promote pain relief by decreasing anxiety and causing relaxation and sedation. The most common side effect is oversedation.

(continued)

Interventions *continued*

19. Exert particular caution with central (epidural or intrathecal) narcotic administration.

• Double-check the dosage.
• Reduce or delete the parenteral dose, as ordered.

• Use preservative-free morphine or meperidine.

• Maintain the catheter as prescribed by unit protocol.

20. Teach the patient to use patient-controlled (inhalation or I.V.) analgesia devices, if prescribed. Set the dosage and timing controls as ordered.

21. *Evaluate and document evidence of response to pain-relief measures* hourly and as needed.

22. If chronic pain is present, collaborate with the patient, family, and doctor to determine the appropriate analgesic for long-term use. Teach the patient and a family member the procedure for administering pain medication after discharge, including signs of overmedication.

23. Additional individualized interventions: _____
_____
_____

Rationales *continued*

19. These techniques are used for long-term pain control in cancer and postoperative patients. They allow potent pain control without the side effects of systemic analgesics by delivering small doses of analgesic agents, such as morphine or meperidine, close to endogenous endorphin receptor sites.
• Narcotic doses delivered via this route can be lethal.
• Central narcotic administration is so potent that continuation of normal parenteral dosage will result in narcotic overdose.
• The preservative in most commercial preparations causes meningeal irritation.
• Specific catheter care varies but includes maintenance of catheter patency and observation for catheter displacement.

20. These devices promote the patient's sense of control because analgesia may be obtained promptly when needed. The controls prevent overmedication.

21. Monitoring the effectiveness of pain relief determines the appropriateness of methods used.

22. The "usual dose" of pain medication is only a guideline; optimal pain relief requires individualizing the medication and the dose.

23. Rationale: _____
_____
_____

Outcome criteria
Within 1 hour of pain onset, the patient will:
• be free of signs and symptoms of pain

• verbalize pain relief
• experience minimal interference with ADLs.

Nursing diagnosis: *Alteration in comfort: constipation, nausea, vomiting, stomatitis, or injury related to use of narcotic analgesics*

NURSING PRIORITY: Minimize discomfort from side effects of narcotic analgesics.

Interventions

1. Constipation

• Encourage bowel evacuation as soon as the urge to defecate occurs.

• Encourage intake of at least 2 liters of fluids daily and a high-fiber, well-balanced diet.

Rationales

1. Constipation may be avoided or relieved in various ways:
• Bowel evacuation can be delayed by voluntary inhibition of the urge to defecate, leading to constipation. Learning to defecate as soon as the urge occurs avoids this problem.
• A diet high in fiber increases peristalsis; fluids promote optimal stool consistency.

Interventions *continued*

• Encourage moderate exercise, unless contraindicated, with emphasis on increasing abdominal muscle tone.

• Administer and document medications for increasing bowel elimination, as ordered.

• Evaluate and document the frequency of elimination and consistency of stool.

2. Nausea and vomiting

• Instruct the patient that nausea may decrease after a few doses.

• Eliminate noxious sights and smells from the environment.

• Encourage the patient to move and change position slowly.

• Encourage the patient to deep-breathe and voluntarily swallow.

• Consult with the doctor to obtain a possible change in narcotic analgesic.

• Administer and document an antiemetic, as ordered, using nursing judgment.

• Evaluate and document the effects of antiemetics in relieving nausea and vomiting.

3. Oral mucous membrane breakdown

• Encourage or provide mouth care at frequent intervals, after meals and as needed.

• Encourage the patient to breathe through the nose, if possible.

• Encourage fluid intake of at least 2 liters per day.

• Instruct the patient not to use mouthwashes or other products that contain alcohol.

4. Injury

• Orient the patient to time and place, verbally and with touch, and explain the call system.

• Instruct the patient to request assistance when getting out of bed.

• Secure the side rails and keep the bed at its lowest level.

• Instruct the patient and family regarding the hazards of sedation when driving, smoking in bed, and so forth.

5. Additional individualized interventions: _____

_____

_____

Rationales *continued*

• Voluntary contraction of abdominal wall muscles helps expel feces.

• Stool softeners retard reabsorption of water and coat the intestinal lining. Laxatives stimulate peristalsis or add bulk.

• Monitoring of elimination patterns determines the effectiveness of, and need for, continued use of laxatives.

2. Both behavioral and physiologic methods may be successful in controlling nausea.

• Information helps reduce anxiety, which can increase nausea.

• Noxious stimuli can stimulate the vomiting center.

• Movement may stimulate the vomiting center in the medulla.

• Deep-breathing and swallowing decrease the strength of the vomiting reflex.

• The patient may have less nausea and vomiting in response to another narcotic.

• Antiemetics decrease stimulation of the vomiting center and usually potentiate narcotic effects.

• Monitoring the response to medication determines its effectiveness and the need for continued antiemetics.

3. Measures to protect the oral mucous membrane work in several different ways.

• Narcotic-induced mouth dryness may cause discomfort and contribute to mucous membrane breakdown (stomatitis). Cleanliness and moisture maintain the integrity of the mucous membrane.

• Dryness of the mucous membrane may cause breakdown.

• Adequate hydration reduces discomfort and helps maintain the integrity of the mucous membrane.

• Alcohol and similar products have a drying effect on the oral mucous membrane.

4. Consistent attention to these measures helps prevent injury.

• Information provides support and relieves anxiety.

• Assistance with ambulation will help prevent falls.

• These measures prevent injuries and avert the possibility of the patient's falling out of bed.

• Information about specific hazards helps prevent accidents and injury.

5. Rationale: _____

_____

_____

Outcome criteria

After medication for pain, the patient will:
• have normal bowel elimination
• experience no nausea and vomiting

• have healthy mucous membranes
• experience no injury.

Discharge planning

NURSING DISCHARGE CRITERIA

Upon discharge, documentation shows evidence of:
• ability to utilize noninvasive pain-relief techniques
• ability to verbalize purpose, dosage, administration schedule, and side effects of medication for pain relief
• ability to verbalize symptoms and severity of pain that may indicate need for medical intervention
• ability to identify the expected course of pain related to type of disease or condition.

PATIENT/FAMILY DISCHARGE TEACHING CHECKLIST

Document evidence that the patient/family demonstrates understanding of:
___ expected course and severity of pain related to disease or condition
___ noninvasive pain-relief measures, including importance of family support for these measures
___ all discharge medications' purpose, dosage, administration schedule, and side effects requiring medical attention (usual discharge medications are oral analgesics)
___ symptoms and severity of pain warranting medical care
___ dates, times, and location of follow-up appointments
___ how to contact the doctor.

DOCUMENTATION CHECKLIST

Using outcome criteria as a guide, document:
___ clinical assessment of factors decreasing pain tolerance
___ pain patterns
___ other symptoms associated with pain
___ patient and family response to pain
___ analgesics administered for pain relief
___ noninvasive pain-relief measures used
___ responses to pain-relief measures
___ patient/family teaching
___ discharge planning.

ASSOCIATED CARE PLANS

Death and Dying
Grief/Grieving
Ineffective Family Coping
Ineffective Individual Coping

REFERENCES

Alfaro, Rosalinda A. *Application of Nursing Process: A Step-by-Step Guide to Care Planning*. Philadelphia: J.B. Lippincott Co., 1986.

Booker, Jack E. "Pain: It's All In Your Patient's Head (Or Is It?)," *Nursing* 12:31, March 1982.

Carpenito, L. *Nursing Diagnosis: Application to Clinical Practice*. Philadelphia: J.B. Lippincott Co., 1983.

Fortin, Jacqueline. *A Reformulation and Methodologic Approach to the Diagnosis of Chronic Pain: Proceedings of the Fifth National Conference*. St. Louis: C.V. Mosby Co., 1984.

Gordon, Marjory. *Nursing Diagnosis: Process and Application*, 2nd ed. New York: McGraw-Hill Book Co., 1987.

Guyton, Arthur C. *Textbook of Medical Physiology*, 7th ed. Philadelphia: W.B. Saunders Co., 1986.

Heidrich, George, and Perry, Samuel. "Helping the Patient in Pain," *American Journal of Nursing* 82(12): 1828-33, December 1982.

Holloway, N., and Gregory, C. "Pain," in *Nursing the Critically Ill Adult*, 3rd ed. Edited by Holloway, Nancy M. Menlo Park, Calif: Addison-Wesley Publishing Co., 1988.

Luckmann, Joan, and Sorensen, Karen. "Theories and Types of Pain," in *Medical-Surgical Nursing: A Psychophysiologic Approach*, 3rd ed. Luckmann, J., and Sorenson, K., eds. Philadelphia: W.B. Saunders Co., 1987.

Mason, Elizabeth J. *How to Write Meaningful Nursing Standards*, 2nd ed. New York: John Wiley & Sons, 1984.

Meyer, Theresa M. "Relieving Pain Through Electricity," *Nursing* 12:57-59, September 1982.

Rudy, Ellen B. *Advanced Neurological and Neurosurgical Nursing*. St. Louis: C.V. Mosby Co., 1984.

Sandroff, Ronni. "When You Must Inflict Pain on a Patient," *RN* 47:35-39, January 1984.

Ulrich, Susan, et al. *Nursing Care Planning Guides: A Nursing Diagnosis Approach*. Philadelphia: W.B. Saunders Co., 1986.

West, B. Anne. "Understanding Endorphins: Our Natural Pain Relief System," *Nursing* 11(2):50-53, February 1981.

Surgical Intervention

Introduction

DEFINITION AND TIME FOCUS

Surgical intervention is an important mode of medical therapy used for various diagnostic, curative, restorative, palliative, or cosmetic reasons. This clinical plan focuses on care of the patient admitted to the hospital for any type of surgical intervention.

ETIOLOGY/PRECIPITATING FACTORS

Precipitating factors are not applicable in this general clinical plan because of the wide variety of disorders treated with surgical intervention. Precipitating factors related to particular types of surgery are presented in the care plans for specific clinical disorders.

Focused assessment guidelines

Focused assessment guidelines also are not applicable in this general clinical plan because of the wide variety of disorders treated with surgical interventions. Focused assessment guidelines related to particular types of surgery are presented in the care plans for specific clinical disorders.

DIAGNOSTIC STUDIES

The following laboratory tests are standard preoperative studies:
- urinalysis
- complete blood count (CBC)
- prothrombin time and partial thromboplastin time
- electrolyte panel
- blood urea nitrogen and creatinine levels
- blood typing and cross-matching.

The following are standard preoperative diagnostic procedures:
- chest X-ray
- 12-lead EKG.

POTENTIAL COMPLICATIONS

- shock
- atelectasis
- pulmonary embolism
- thrombophlebitis
- wound infection, dehiscence, and evisceration
- paralytic ileus
- acute renal failure

Nursing diagnosis: *Knowledge deficit: perioperative routines, related to lack of familiarity with hospital procedures*

NURSING PRIORITY: Prepare the patient for perioperative routines.

Interventions

1. *See the "Knowledge Deficit" care plan,* page 56.

2. *Instruct the patient in the various aspects of perioperative routines,* such as time for surgery, food or fluid restrictions, type of anesthesia, the environments of the operating and recovery rooms and surgical intensive care unit, type of wound and dressing, tubes, drains, and postoperative respiratory care. Include demonstrations and return demonstrations of coughing, deep breathing, spirometry, splinting the incision, and leg exercises.

3. Additional individualized interventions: _____
_____
_____

Outcome criteria

Before surgery, the patient will:
- verbalize understanding of perioperative routines

Rationales

1. Generalized interventions regarding patient teaching are included in the "Knowledge Deficit" care plan.

2. Patients will be more likely to remember and comply with postoperative procedures if they understand the rationale for them, have been instructed preoperatively, and have practiced activities where appropriate.

3. Rationale: _____
_____
_____

- demonstrate ability to cough, deep-breathe, use the incentive spirometer, and perform leg exercises.

Collaborative problem: *Potential postoperative shock related to hemorrhage or hypovolemia*

NURSING PRIORITY: Detect shock.

Interventions

1. *Monitor and document vital signs* on admission to the nursing unit and every 4 hours. If vital signs have changed significantly from recovery room findings, monitor every 30 to 60 minutes until stable. Report abnormalities.

2. *Assess the surgical dressing on* admission to the nursing division, every hour for 4 hours, then every 4 hours. Mark any drainage and note on the dressing the date and time it occurred. Document and report excessive drainage.

3. *Assess the amount and character of drainage* from wound drainage tubes when assessing the surgical dressing. Report bright-red blood drainage.

4. *Reinforce the surgical dressing as needed.* Do not change the original surgical dressing unless specifically ordered to do so.

5. *Assess the surgical area for swelling or hematoma.* Document and report abnormalities.

6. *Monitor for changes in mental status.* Be alert for restlessness and a sense of impending doom. Document and report such signs.

7. *Assess and maintain I.V. patency.* Maintain I.V. fluids at the ordered rate.

8. *Monitor urine output* every hour for 4 hours, then every 4 hours, during the immediate postoperative period. Report urine output of <60 ml/hour. Measure urine specific gravity if urine output is <60 ml/hour. Administer I.V. fluids and diuretics as ordered, to maintain urine output >60 ml/hour and specific gravity at 1.010 to 1.025.

9. Monitor hematocrit and hemoglobin levels, as ordered.

10. *Monitor intake and output* every 8 hours with an accumulated total every 24 hours for at least 3 to 4 days postoperatively.

Rationales

1. Hypotension and tachycardia may indicate hemorrhage.

2. Hemorrhage usually occurs within the first several hours postoperatively. Frequent assessments allow for prompt detection of hemorrhage. Marking the extent of drainage permits objective serial measurements of the amount.

3. Bright-red blood from drainage tubes may indicate hemorrhage.

4. Changing the surgical dressing may disrupt the wound edge and precipitate bleeding.

5. Swelling or hematoma may indicate internal bleeding.

6. Changes in mental status may reflect cerebral hypoxia, indicating decreased cerebral perfusion from hemorrhage or hypovolemia.

7. A patent I.V. is essential to fluid replacement. Fluids will be ordered according to the surgeon's preference. At times, fluid replacement is the only treatment necessary for hypovolemic shock.

8. Urine output decreases if the patient is bleeding or is hypovolemic. The kidneys retain fluid to maintain intravascular pressure. Urine specific gravity will reveal concentrated urine as the body attempts to conserve fluid. Additionally, blood flow to the kidneys is reduced if the patient is in shock, thereby decreasing the glomerular filtration rate and urine output. I.V. fluids and diuretics help maintain the glomerular filtration rate to prevent acute tubular necrosis.

9. Hematocrit and hemoglobin levels do not drop immediately with excessive blood loss, because plasma is lost along with red blood cells. If bleeding persists, the blood remaining in the vessels will become more dilute as kidneys conserve water and as fluid shifts from interstitial to intravascular spaces; then hematocrit and hemoglobin levels will drop.

10. For the first 48 hours after surgery, intake may exceed output because of loss of fluids (from hemorrhage, vomiting, or diaphoresis) and increased secretion of antidiuretic hormone and aldosterone.

Interventions continued	**Rationales** continued
11. Additional individualized interventions: _____	11. Rationale: _____

Outcome criteria

Within 12 hours postoperatively, the patient will:
• have vital signs within normal limits
• display minimal bloody drainage on dressing and in wound drains

• maintain a urine output >60 ml/hour.
Within 2 days postoperatively, the patient will:
• display balanced intake and output.

Nursing diagnosis: *Pain related to surgical tissue trauma and reflex muscle spasm*

NURSING PRIORITY: Relieve pain.

Interventions	**Rationales**
1. *See the "Pain" care plan,* page 64.	1. The "Pain" care plan contains detailed information on pain assessment and management.
2. Additional individualized interventions: _____	2. Rationale: _____

Outcome criteria

Within 1 hour of a complaint of pain, the patient will:
• verbalize adequacy of pain relief measures
• appear relaxed.

Collaborative problem: *Potential postoperative atelectasis related to immobility and ciliary depression from anesthesia*

NURSING PRIORITY: Prevent atelectasis.

Interventions	**Rationales**
1. *Assess vital signs* every 4 hours. Note the characteristics of respirations. Monitor the amount and characteristics of sputum. Document and report abnormalities.	1. Elevated temperature may indicate atelectasis, which can lead to pneumonia. Respirations may be shallow after anesthesia.
2. *Auscultate breath sounds* every 4 hours on the first postoperative day, then once per shift. Document and report abnormalities.	2. Breath sounds may be diminished postoperatively because air exchange is decreased in atelectatic areas.
3. *Instruct and coach the patient in diaphragmatic breathing.*	3. Diaphragmatic breathing increases lung expansion by allowing the diaphragm to descend fully.
4. *Assist the patient in using the incentive spirometer*—10 breaths every hour when awake, every 2 hours at night. In the first 24 hours, coach the patient on its use; then, once the patient is alert, encourage independent use and assess its effectiveness.	4. Use of the incentive spirometer promotes sustained maximal inspiration, which inflates alveoli as fully as possible.
5. *Turn the patient* every 2 hours unless contraindicated.	5. Position changes provide for better ventilation of all lobes of the lungs and promote drainage of secretions.

(continued)

Interventions *continued*

6. *Help the patient progressively increase ambulation.*

7. Encourage adequate fluid intake.

8. Additional individualized interventions: _____
_____
_____

Rationales *continued*

6. Ambulation promotes adequate ventilation by stimulating an increased respiratory rate.

7. Respiratory secretions will be thinner and more easily expectorated if the patient is well hydrated.

8. Rationale: _____
_____
_____

Outcome criteria

Throughout the postoperative period, the patient will:
• display respiratory rate of 12 to 20 breaths/minute

• have nonlabored, deep respirations
• manifest audible, clear breath sounds in all lobes.

Collaborative problem: *Potential postoperative thromboembolic phenomena related to immobility, dehydration, and possible fat particle escape or aggregation*

NURSING PRIORITY: Prevent thromboembolism.

Interventions

1. *Instruct and coach the patient to do leg exercises hourly while awake:* dorsiplantar flexion, ankle rotation, flexing and extending knees, and quadriceps setting.

2. *Assess b.i.d. for signs of thromboembolic phenomena:*

• *thrombophlebitis* (redness, swelling, increased warmth along the path of the vein, possibly a positive Homans' sign, and pain)
• *pulmonary thromboembolism* (sharp, stabbing chest pain, worsening on deep inspiration or coughing; hemoptysis; pleural friction rub; and tachypnea)
• *fat embolism* (dyspnea, restlessness, and petechiae).
If any of these signs or symptoms is present, alert the doctor promptly.

3. Encourage early ambulation postoperatively.

4. Avoid using the knee gatch or placing pillows under the patient's knees.

5. Encourage adequate fluid intake (in the initial postoperative period, I.V. fluids will be administered).

6. Apply antiembolism stockings, if ordered. Remove them b.i.d. for 1 hour.

Rationales

1. Leg exercises promote blood flow in the legs. Muscle contractions compress the veins and help prevent venous stasis, a major cause of clot formation.

2. Systematic observations aid in prompt detection of thromboembolic phenomena.
• Vessel wall inflammation and clot formation produce signs and symptoms of thrombophlebitis.

• Pulmonary thromboembolism occurs when a clot detaches from a vessel and lodges in the lungs.

• Fat embolism is a risk after fractures or surgery on long bones (such as femur fractures) or flat ones (such as sternum-splitting incisions). It is thought to result from the escape of fat particles from bone marrow or from an aggregation of fat particles in the bloodstream. Prompt treatment reduces the risk of clot extension, pulmonary infarction, or pulmonary arrest.

3. Ambulation promotes blood flow in the legs.

4. Pressure on the popliteal blood vessels can slow blood circulation to and from the legs. Appropriate positioning also decreases venous stasis.

5. Adequate fluid intake prevents dehydration, which leads to increased blood viscosity—another major contributor to clot formation.

6. Antiembolism stockings compress the leg veins and prevent venous stasis. Stockings should be removed periodically to allow for thrombophlebitis assessment and skin inspection.

Interventions *continued*

7. Before discharge, teach the patient and family about guidelines for resuming normal activity after discharge.

8. Additional individualized interventions: _____
_____
_____

Rationales *continued*

7. Patients and families often have specific questions or concerns about the type and progression of allowable activity after discharge. Providing guidelines promotes the resumption of activity at an appropriate pace, which in turn lessens immobility-related complications and promotes a sense of well-being.

8. Rationale: _____
_____
_____

Outcome criteria

Throughout the postoperative period, the patient will:
• show no signs of thromboembolic phenomena.

By the time of discharge, the patient will:
• be able to identify an appropriate postdischarge activity schedule.

Nursing diagnosis: *Potential for postoperative injury related to possible changes in mental status due to anesthesia and analgesia*

NURSING PRIORITY: Prevent injury.

Interventions

1. *Assess the patient's level of consciousness,* orientation, and ability to follow directions every 30 to 60 minutes in the first 8 to 10 hours postoperatively.

2. *Position the patient in a side-lying position when drowsy.*

3. *Keep side rails up* in the initial postoperative period, until the patient is awake and alert.

4. Keep the call cord within the patient's reach.

5. Keep the bed in the low position.

6. *Monitor postural vital signs and assist the patient with initial postoperative activity.*
• Observe for a pulse rate increase of 20 to 30 beats/minute, a systolic blood pressure decrease of 20 to 30 mm Hg, and dizziness or an unsteady gait. If present, reposition the patient slowly.
• Observe for a pulse rate increase >30 beats/minute, a systolic blood pressure decrease >30 mm Hg, a decreased level of consciousness, diaphoresis, and cyanosis. If present, discontinue activity and alert the doctor.

7. Additional individualized interventions: _____
_____
_____

Rationales

1. A greater risk of injury exists if the patient is drowsy or disoriented. Frequent observation allows prompt detection of injury risk factors, if present.

2. In a side-lying position, the patient has less risk of aspirating secretions or vomitus.

3. Side rails help prevent falls.

4. If the call cord is within reach, the patient is more likely to ask the nurse for assistance.

5. The low bed position is safer for the patient.

6. When first ambulating, the patient may feel dizzy or have an unsteady gait from orthostatic hypotension. This occurs because immobility compromises the ability of peripheral vessels to constrict when the patient assumes an upright position. Orthostatic hypotension can also occur if the patient is hypovolemic, producing the more alarming signs listed and requiring medical evaluation and I.V. fluid replacement.

7. Rationale: _____
_____
_____

Outcome criterion

Within 36 hours postoperatively, the patient will:
• be free from injury

• seek appropriate assistance with activity from the nurse.

Nursing diagnosis: *Postoperative impairment of skin integrity related to surgical intervention*

NURSING PRIORITY: Promote wound healing.

Interventions

1. *Assess the surgical wound once a shift for:*

• *evidence of normal healing*—such as approximation of wound margins and absence of purulent or foul-smelling drainage

• *signs of dehiscence*—such as poorly approximated wound edges and serous drainage from a previously nondraining wound (if dehiscence occurs, cover with a dry sterile dressing and notify the doctor immediately)

• *signs of evisceration*—such as disruption of the surgical wound with protrusion of the viscera (if evisceration occurs, cover the viscerated organs with sterile saline-soaked gauze and notify the doctor immediately).

2. *Monitor temperature* every 4 hours. Document and report elevations.

3. *Maintain a clean, dry incision.* Perform wound care as ordered.

4. *Use strict aseptic technique* when performing wound care. Instruct the patient and family in hand washing technique; aseptic technique; and wound care, including dressing change and application, irrigations and cleansing procedures, proper disposal of soiled dressings, and bathing by shower (not tub until the wound is healed).

5. Instruct the patient and family regarding signs and symptoms of infection: elevated temperature, abdominal pain, and purulent or foul-smelling wound drainage.

6. Encourage adequate nutritional intake every shift. Document intake every shift.

7. Additional individualized interventions: _____

_____

_____

Rationales

1. Regular assessment promotes early detection of suboptimal healing.

• The normally healing wound is well approximated and without evidence of infection. (The surgical wound may be reddened in the first 3 postoperative days, however, from the normal inflammatory response.)

• Wound dehiscence most commonly occurs 3 to 11 days postoperatively. Application of a sterile dressing reduces the risk of infection.

• Eviscerated organs must be kept moist and surgical intervention must be prompt because blood supply to tissues is compromised when organs protrude.

2. A low-grade temperature present in the first 3 postoperative days is associated with the normal inflammatory response. Fever that persists may signify infection.

3. A clean, dry incision is at less risk for infection. Moisture can harbor microorganisms.

4. Aseptic technique prevents cross-contamination and transmission of bacterial infections to the surgical wound.

5. Educating the patient and family promotes their sense of control and minimizes anxiety and fear during preparation for discharge home.

6. Sufficient intake of protein, calories, vitamins, and minerals is essential to promote tissue healing.

7. Rationale:_____

_____

_____

Outcome criteria

Within 3 days postoperatively, the patient will:
• be afebrile
• show no signs of infection.

Within 7 days postoperatively, the patient will:
• have a clean, dry, and well-approximated surgical wound.

Nursing diagnosis: *Potential postoperative urinary retention related to neuroendocrine response to stress, anesthesia, and recumbent position*

NURSING PRIORITY: Prevent urinary retention.

Interventions

1. *Assess for signs of urinary retention.* Include subjective complaints of urgency as well as objective signs, such as bladder distention, urine overflow, and marked discrepancy between the fluid intake amount and the time of the last voiding.

2. *Initiate interventions to promote voiding* as soon as the patient begins to sense bladder pressure.

3. Provide noninvasive measures to promote voiding, such as normal position for voiding, ambulation to the bathroom if possible, running water, relaxation, a warm bedpan if needed, pouring warm water over the perineum, and privacy.

4. Provide a nonthreatening supportive atmosphere: use conscious positive suggestion; reassure the patient that voiding usually occurs eventually; do not threaten catheterization.

5. If the patient complains of bladder discomfort or has not voided by 8 hours after surgery, obtain an order for catheterization with a straight catheter.

6. If the patient requires catheterization, drain the bladder of < 1,000 ml at a time. If urine output reaches 1,000 ml, clamp the catheter, wait 1 hour, then drain the rest of the urine from the bladder.

7. After catheterization, assess for dysuria, hematuria, pyuria, burning, frequency, and urgency of urination as well as for suprapubic discomfort. Assess and document the amount, appearance, odor, and clarity of urine. Report any signs of urinary infection.

8. Additional individualized interventions: _____
_____
_____

Rationales

1. The distended bladder can be palpated above the level of the symphysis pubis. Overflow incontinence occurs when intravesical pressure exceeds the restraining ability of the sphincter and enough urine flows out to decrease the intravesical pressure to a level at which the sphincter can control the flow of urine. A reduction of several hundred milliliters between fluid intake and output, with the passage of several hours since the last voiding, implies urinary retention.

2. Prompt treatment of potential voiding problems may reduce anxiety, which can further impair the ability to void.

3. These measures are designed to promote relaxation of the urinary sphincter and facilitate voiding. Successful use of noninvasive measures prevents unnecessary catheterization and related psychological strain and urethral trauma.

4. Conscious positive suggestion and reassurance promote relaxation and set up expectations for success with spontaneous voiding.

5. Straight catheterization poses less risk of infection than indwelling catheterization; an indwelling catheter can provide a pathway for bacteria to ascend into the bladder.

6. Draining > 1,000 ml from the bladder releases pressure on the pelvic vessels. The sudden release of pressure allows subsequent pooling of blood in these vessels. Rapid withdrawal of this blood from the central circulating volume may cause shock.

7. Urinary retention (stasis) and the introduction of a urethral catheter increase the risk for lower urinary tract infection.

8. Rationale: _____
_____
_____

Outcome criterion

Within 1 day postoperatively, the patient will:
• void adequate amounts (at least 200 ml at a time) of clear urine.

Collaborative problem: *Potential postoperative paralytic ileus, abdominal pain, or constipation related to immobility, anesthesia, and analgesia*

NURSING PRIORITIES: (a) Detect paralytic ileus and (b) prevent constipation.

Interventions

1. *Assess the abdomen* b.i.d. for bowel sounds and distention. Assess for the presence of flatus or stool. Question the patient about abdominal fullness.

2. If paralytic ileus occurs, implement measures, as ordered, such as instructing the patient not to eat or drink anything, connecting a nasogastric tube to low intermittent suction, using a rectal tube to expel flatus, and administering I.V. fluids.

3. Implement comfort measures if paralytic ileus occurs: provide frequent mouth care, tape and position the nasogastric (NG) tube carefully, and administer analgesics as needed.

4. *Provide a diet appropriate to peristaltic activity.* Ensure that peristalsis has returned before progressing from NPO status to liberal fluids and solid food.

5. *Encourage fluid intake of at least 2 liters per day* unless contraindicated by preexisting status (for example, congestive heart failure) or surgery. Provide fluids that the patient prefers.

6. *Encourage frequent position changes and ambulation,* as tolerated by the patient.

7. Provide privacy for the patient during defecation. Assist with ambulation to the bathroom if necessary.

8. Consult with the doctor concerning use of laxatives, suppositories, or enemas.

9. Additional individualized interventions: _____
_____
_____

Rationales

1. Bowel sounds will be hypoactive initially but should become normoactive within the first 2 days postoperatively. The presence of flatus or stool signals the return of peristalsis. Abdominal distention and absence of bowel sounds, flatus, and stools may indicate paralytic ileus.

2. These measures help prevent abdominal distention while promoting return of peristalsis. Administration of I.V. fluids maintains fluid and electrolyte balance while the patient is NPO.

3. Maintaining patient comfort is important to prevent further anxiety.

4. If peristalsis has not returned, feeding the patient will cause distention.

5. Sufficient fluid intake is required for proper stool consistency. Providing well-liked fluids promotes hydration.

6. Activity promotes peristalsis.

7. Providing privacy eliminates possible embarrassment.

8. A laxative, suppository, or enema may be needed to promote bowel evacuation. These supplements should be used judiciously to avoid bowel dependence or possible damage to healing tissues.

9. Rationale: _____
_____
_____

Outcome criteria

Within 2 days postoperatively, the patient will:
• have normal bowel sounds.

Within 4 days postoperatively, the patient will:
• have soft, formed bowel movements
• not strain at stool.

Within 7 days postoperatively, the patient will:
• establish a regular bowel elimination pattern.

Nursing diagnosis: *Altered comfort: nausea or vomiting related to GI distention, rapid position changes, and/or cortical stimulation of the vomiting center or chemoreceptor trigger zone*

NURSING PRIORITY: Prevent or relieve nausea or vomiting.

Interventions	Rationales
1. *Prevent GI overdistention:* maintain patency of the NG tube, if present; advance the patient's diet only as tolerated.	1. Overdistention of the GI tract, particularly the duodenum, triggers the vomiting reflex.
2. *Limit unpleasant sights, smells, and psychic stimuli,* such as intense anxiety and pain.	2. These factors cause cortical stimulation of the chemoreceptor trigger zone in the medulla, which causes vomiting.
3. Caution the patient to change position slowly.	3. Rapid position changes also stimulate the trigger zone.
4. *As soon as possible, advance the patient from narcotics to other analgesics* (as ordered), and then to nonpharmacologic pain-control measures.	4. Medications, especially narcotics, may excite the chemoreceptor trigger zone.
5. *Administer antiemetics,* as ordered.	5. Agents to depress the vomiting center or trigger zone responsiveness may be necessary when the measures described in Interventions 1 to 4 above are inappropriate or ineffective.
6. Additional individualized interventions: _____ _____	6. Rationale: _____ _____

Outcome criteria
Within 1 hour of onset of nausea or vomiting, the patient will:
• verbalize relief of nausea
• be free of vomiting.

Discharge planning
NURSING DISCHARGE CRITERIA
Upon discharge, documentation shows evidence of:
• return to preoperative level of consciousness
• absence of fever
• absence of pulmonary and cardiovascular complications
• stable vital signs
• healing wound with no signs of infection
• hemoglobin and white blood cell counts within normal parameters
• I.V. lines discontinued for at least 24 hours before discharge
• ability to tolerate oral nutritional intake
• ability to perform wound care independently
• ability to void and have bowel movements same as before surgery
• ability to ambulate and perform activities of daily living same as before surgery
• knowledge of activity restrictions
• ability to control pain using oral medications
• adequate home support, or referral to home care or a nursing home if indicated by lack of home support system or by self-care inability.

PATIENT/FAMILY DISCHARGE TEACHING CHECKLIST
Document evidence that patient/family demonstrates understanding of:
___ plan for resumption of normal activity
___ wound care
___ signs and symptoms of wound infection or other surgical complications
___ all discharge medications' purpose, dosage, administration, and side effects requiring medical attention (postoperative patients may be discharged with oral analgesics)
___ when and how to contact doctor
___ date, time, and location of follow-up appointment with doctor
___ community resources appropriate for surgical intervention performed.

DOCUMENTATION CHECKLIST
Using outcome criteria as a guide, document:
__ clinical status on admission
__ significant changes in preoperative status
__ preoperative teaching and its effectiveness
__ preoperative checklist (includes documentation regarding operative consent, urinalysis, CBC, 12–lead EKG, chest X-ray, surgical skin preparation, voiding on call from operating room, and removal of nail polish, jewelry, dentures, glasses, hearing aids, and prostheses)
__ clinical status on admission from recovery room
__ amount and character of wound drainage (on dressing and through drains)
__ patency of tubes (I.V., NG, Foley, drains)
__ pulmonary hygiene measures
__ pain-relief measures
__ activity tolerance
__ nutritional intake
__ elimination status (urinary and bowel)
__ pertinent laboratory test findings
__ patient/family teaching
__ discharge planning.

ASSOCIATED CARE PLANS
Fluid and Electrolyte Imbalances
Grief/Grieving
Ineffective Individual Coping
Knowledge Deficit
Pain

REFERENCES
Carpenito, L.J. *Nursing Diagnosis: Application to Clinical Practice.* Philadelphia: J.B. Lippincott Co., 1983.
Guyton, Arthur C. *Textbook of Medical Physiology*, 7th ed. Philadelphia: W.B. Saunders Co., 1986.
Kneisl, Carol R., and Ames, Sue A. *Adult Health Nursing: A Biopsychological Approach.* Menlo Park, Calif.: Addison-Wesley Publishing Co., 1986.
Long, B.C., and Phipps, W.J. *Essentials of Medical-Surgical Nursing: A Nursing Process Approach.* St. Louis: C.V. Mosby Co., 1985.
McConnell, E.A., and Zimmerman, M.F. *Care of Patients with Urologic Problems.* Philadelphia: J.B. Lippincott Co., 1982.
Patrick, Maxine L., et al. *Medical-Surgical Nursing: Pathophysiological Concepts.* Philadelphia: J.B. Lippincott Co., 1986.
Perry, A.G., and Potter, P.A. *Clinical Nursing Skills and Techniques.* St. Louis: C.V. Mosby Co., 1986.

Alzheimer's Disease

DRG information
DRG 12 [Medical DRG] Degenerative Nervous System
Disorders.
　　Mean LOS = 6.9 days

Additional DRG information: Patients are rarely admitted with only Alzheimer's disease (AD); usually, another disorder, such as pneumonia or dehydration, is
the primary diagnosis. Because AD as a comorbidity
would probably increase the other disorders' LOS and
relative weight (depending on the primary diagnosis), a
patient with AD is more likely to be assigned that DRG
number than DRG 12.

Introduction
DEFINITION AND TIME FOCUS
AD is chronic, irreversible neuronal degeneration of the
central nervous system, leading to severe disorders of
cognition in the absence of other neurologic manifestations. Senile plaques and neurofibrillary tangles characterize the insidious, relentless progression of
structural brain atrophy. This clinical plan focuses on
the AD patient admitted at any of the progressively deteriorating stages of the disease process.

ETIOLOGY/PRECIPITATING FACTORS
Etiology is obscure, but ongoing research suggests the
following theories:
• neurochemical deficiency of neurotransmitters acetylcholine and somatostatin (important for cognition and
memory)
• neurometabolic disorder, causing diminished cellular
protein synthesis
• genetic and environmental factors, with autosomal
dominant transmission in certain families with AD
• aluminum deposits in senile plaques (a conglomeration
of protein) and neurofibrillary tangles (twisted nerve fibers) abundant in the hippocampus of the brain, a cortical area considered necessary for memory
• slow viruses (those that invade the host but remain
dormant in the body for years before symptoms develop)
whose effects sometimes resemble those of AD
• immune system dysfunctions implicated in the degenerative disease process

Focused assessment guidelines
NURSING HISTORY (Functional health pattern findings)

Health perception–health management pattern
• *may perceive memory loss as related to normal aging process*
• *may disguise confusion and disorientation* by using
learned social skills and fabrication
• significant others may describe patient's mental decline

Nutritional-metabolic pattern
• family may report patient's *anorexia* from patient's forgetting to eat or not recognizing the signs of hunger
• family may report patient weight loss
• may report fatigue and malaise
• may report dysphagia (in later stages of AD)

Elimination pattern
• family may report *constipation* related to forgetfulness
and disorientation
• family may report urinary and fecal incontinence (in
later stages of AD)

Activity-exercise pattern
• family may describe *activity limited to familiar environment* as confusion and disorientation increase
• family may describe *compromise of activities of daily
living* as dependence increases because of inability to
sequence actions
• may demonstrate incompetence in performing complex
tasks, such as shopping, telephoning, and banking
• may have jeopardized personal safety through loss of
locomotion or wandering behavior

Sleep-rest pattern
• *nocturnal restlessness with insomnia*
• altered sleep-wake cycle
• arousal more difficult as disease progresses

Cognitive-perceptual pattern
• according to cognitive impairment assessment guide
(Murray and Huelskoetter, 1983):
　□ judgment: ability to make reasonable decisions becomes impossible
　□ orientation: ability to orient self in environment
becomes impaired
　□ memory: immediate, recent, and remote memory
loss, including episodic (events) and semantic
(knowledge) memory, occurs
　□ affect: tendency for emotional expression to be incongruent and inconsistent
　□ cognition: progressive reduction in intellectual con-
ceptualization, concentration, and abstract thinking
faculties occurs
• language impairment may include expressive and receptive aphasia

Self-perception–self-concept pattern
• may demonstrate varied attempts to sustain internal
"locus of control," sense of dignity, and self-esteem

Role-relationship pattern
• *altered family dynamics* as role reversals occur with increased dysfunction
• social withdrawal (isolationism)

Sexuality-reproductive pattern
• may reject intimate contact

Coping-stress tolerance pattern
• may demonstrate defense mechanisms of *rationalization, denial, and projection*
• may demonstrate behavioral responses of *apathy, depression, and helplessness*
• may exhibit primary emotional lability fluctuating among irritability, anger, fear, agitation
• may exhibit signs of disintegration of ego preservation—hallucinations, illusions, and suicidal ideology

Value-belief pattern
• confusion within value system may be related to defective mental faculties

PHYSICAL FINDINGS
Neurologic
• *confusion*
• *disorientation*
• *memory loss*
• *language disintegration*
• irritability
• cognitive dysfunction
• labile affect

Integumentary
• poor skin turgor (or other signs of dehydration)

Musculoskeletal
• decreased activity tolerance
• lack of coordination
• immobility
• limited range of motion

Genitourinary
• *urinary retention*
• *urinary incontinence*

Gastrointestinal
• *fecal incontinence*

DIAGNOSTIC STUDIES
• *hematologic measurements of neurotransmitters and neurotransmitter metabolites—may be low, implicating a biochemical deficiency* as etiologic factor
• complete blood count, VDRL test, blood chemistries, endocrine studies performed for differential diagnosis of reversible cognitive impairment
• vitamin B$_{12}$ levels—may be low, indicating nutritional deficit
• positron emission tomography—may reflect diminished brain metabolism
• *computed tomography scan—may indicate cortical atrophy and widening of the ventricles*
• *lumbar puncture for cerebrospinal fluid examination—may show presence of abnormal protein levels* (common in AD patients)
• skull X-rays—may reflect cerebral atrophy associated with AD
• *EEG—may show decreased electrical activity contributing to AD dysfunction*
• magnetic resonance imaging—performed to rule out reversible cognitive impairment
• language ability tests—performed for differential diagnosis of AD
• vision and hearing tests—establish sensory deficits (versus cognitive impairment) as the cause of selected AD symptoms
• 12-lead EKG—may indicate coronary insufficiency contributing to the symptoms of AD

POTENTIAL COMPLICATIONS
• total decay of mental faculties
• pneumonia
• injury

Collaborative problem: *Impaired cognitive function related to degenerative loss of cerebral tissue*

NURSING PRIORITIES: (a) Provide a safe, structured environment, (b) promote an optimum level of functioning, and (c) establish effective communication patterns.

Interventions

1. *Assess the present level of cognitive functioning.* Prepare the patient for psychological testing.

2. Assign a room close to the nursing station for frequent observation.

3. *Minimize hazards in the environment.*

Rationales

1. Information gleaned from patient and family provides a guide for planning care. Psychological testing will provide information necessary to structure a therapeutic regimen.

2. New surroundings foster confusion; the patient may wander aimlessly.

3. Confusion and faulty judgment contribute to accidental injury.

Interventions *continued*

4. *Maintain consistency in nursing routines.*

5. *Promote self-care independence* within the scope of the patient's abilities; assist when necessary. Identify specific individual needs in the care plan.

6. *Establish a therapeutic relationship.* Approach the patient in a calm, reassuring, affirming manner.

7. Give simple, specific directions for accomplishing tasks, using eye contact and unobtrusive guidance.

8. Orient the patient to reality frequently and repetitively.

9. *Administer medications,* as ordered. Document.

10. Use aids to improve language skills. Use verbal repetition and offer pictures to improve recall.

11. Minimize communication barriers. Be aware that anxiety, cultural influences, spiritual beliefs, and language difficulties may contribute to paranoia and withdrawal.

12. *Encourage social interaction* with individuals and groups by including the patient in unit activities when possible, allowing maximum flexibility in visiting hours, and providing occupational therapy referral.

13. Prevent excessive stimulation.

14. *Be attentive and consistent* in verbal and nonverbal responses to the patient.

15. *Encourage reminiscence* in patient dialogue.

16. *Prepare an identity card,* a bracelet, or a name tag for the patient. Include name, address, phone number, medical problem, and so forth.

Rationales *continued*

4. Assigning the same nurse, serving meals on time, scheduling rest periods, and so forth provide the decompensating patient with structure in an unfamiliar environment.

5. Self-esteem is preserved when the patient can provide self-care. As the disease progresses, complete physical care by the nurse (bathing, dressing, toileting) becomes necessary. Identifying needs in the care plan promotes consistency.

6. Trust must be established to achieve any goal because of the patient's suspicions and increasing paranoia.

7. The effects of memory loss and a short attention span can be minimized with clear directions and some guidance from the nurse.

8. Although disorientation seems to prevail, repetitive reorientation may reduce the patient's anxiety.

9. Praxilene for improving memory and bethanechol for increasing neurotransmission are under study. Anti-anxiety drugs may be helpful.

10. Both methods may assist the patient with word recall.

11. Knowing and understanding the patient's ecosystem facilitates open communication.

12. Continued social interaction reinforces reality and contributes to a sense of self-worth and identity.

13. Moderate stimulation is necessary and important for orientation, but excessive stimulation increases confusion.

14. Nurse-patient dialogue must reflect trust and understanding. Consistency between verbal and nonverbal responses to the patient reduces cognitive dissonance.

15. Remembering past events assists the patient in maintaining self-identity. Distant memory may be retained even when recent memory is impaired.

16. During wandering episodes, identification information facilitates the patient's prompt return.

(continued)

Interventions *continued*

17. Additional individualized interventions:_____

_____

_____

Rationales *continued*

17. Rationale:_____

_____

_____

Outcome criteria
Within 1 week of admission, the patient will:
• be free from injury
• perform self-care as much as possible

• communicate needs clearly
• wear some means of identification.

Nursing diagnosis: *Nutritional deficit related to memory loss and inadequate food intake*

NURSING PRIORITY: Stabilize and improve nutritional status.

Interventions

1. *Assess present nutritional status:* weigh the patient and record customary dietary intake on admission. See the "Total Parenteral Nutrition" care plan, page 265, for more information on nutritional assessment.

2. *Offer a balanced diet* consisting of small meals at regular intervals and nutritional snacks in between.

3. *Prepare the tray in advance with appropriate portions of food arranged conveniently so that the patient may eat unassisted* (precut the meat, provide a spoon, open containers, and so forth).

4. Provide time and privacy for meals.

5. *Monitor and record daily weights and the amount and type of food intake.* Adjust the dietary plan accordingly.

6. Provide dietary information to the home caregiver.

7. Additional individualized interventions: _____

_____

_____

Rationales

1. Assessing the patient's present nutritional status provides necessary information in determining actual deficits; an appropriate dietary regimen may then be implemented.

2. Regularly scheduled times for meals are important in maintaining a structured environment for the patient. Small quantities may be more appealing and provide the patient with a sense of achievement when all the food is consumed.

3. Coordination difficulties may develop, impairing use of utensils. Prepreparation of food servings avoids the humiliation of being unable to provide self-care and decreases frustration.

4. If the patient has difficulty chewing or swallowing, more time will be needed to finish eating. Lack of coordination may result in socially unacceptable eating habits.

5. Evaluation of weight and intake provides guidelines for modification of the dietary plan.

6. The patient will probably continue to need assistance in menu selection, cooking, and eating after discharge. The person shopping, cooking, and offering meals to the patient may need to be instructed on individual dietary needs.

7. Rationale: _____

_____

_____

Outcome criterion
Within 1 week of admission, the patient will:
• gain a predetermined number of pounds, or maintain a stable weight.

Nursing diagnosis: *Potential for injury related to wandering behavior, aphasia, agnosia, and/or hyperorality*

NURSING PRIORITY: Prevent injury while maximizing independence.

Interventions

1. *Consider use of a bell* to alert caregivers when the patient is wandering.

2. *Ensure that the patient is dressed appropriately* for the temperature. Provide shoes that fit well; avoid loose slippers.

3. *Avoid using restraints.*

4. *Recommend safety measures* to the family for home care:
• safely storing knives, medications, matches, firearms, and cleaning solutions and other toxic household chemicals
• using night lights

• storing small objects safely

• using bells on the patient's person and secure door locks
• using consistency in placement of objects

• alerting neighbors to the patient's condition.

5. Encourage a regular exercise program as tolerated by the patient.

6. *Observe for nonverbal cues to potential injury*, such as grimacing, rubbing, panting, or protecting the injured area. Also note repetitive words or seemingly inappropriate statements. Alert the family to cues observed.

7. Additional individualized interventions: _____
_____
_____

Rationales

1. Wandering behavior and restlessness characterize later stages of AD. Unattended, the patient may become lost even in familiar settings.

2. The patient may be unable to make appropriate choices about dress and may have reduced ability to identify or verbalize discomfort. Loose slippers may be lost or may contribute to injuries from falls.

3. Restraints increase the patient's agitation and paranoia and may contribute to injury.

4. The home environment may contribute to injuries if the family is not prepared.
• The patient may be unable to recognize familiar objects (agnosia) and so may inadvertently cause self-injury or harm to others by using them inappropriately.
• Night lights may decrease falls and help with ongoing reorientation to the environment.
• AD patients may be prone to hyperorality and may put small objects in their mouths, swallowing or choking on nonfood items they no longer recognize.
• Door locks and bells may help prevent wandering behavior or alert the family to it.
• Consistency may help expedite environmental reorientation.
• If neighbors are aware of the patient's illness, they can alert the family to wandering or other unsafe behavior they witness.

5. Regular exercise decreases restlessness and agitation, promotes muscle tone, and contributes to a sense of well-being. Overactivity, however, may contribute to fatigue and confusion.

6. The patient may be unable to identify or express discomfort but may reveal illness or injury through nonverbal cues. Because aphasia may make expressions of discomfort convoluted, such words as "cold" or "hurt," especially if repetitive, may require investigating.

7. Rationale: _____
_____
_____

Outcome criteria

Through the period of hospitalization, the patient will:
• be appropriately dressed for the temperature
• wander only when attended
• perform daily exercise

• avoid injury.
By the time of discharge, the family will:
• list five safety measures for the home environment.

Nursing diagnosis: *Constipation related to memory loss about toileting behaviors and to inadequate diet*

NURSING PRIORITY: Establish an effective elimination pattern.

Interventions

1. *Identify the bathroom clearly*—signs or color codes may be helpful.

2. *Prompt the patient, at regular intervals, to use toileting facilities.*

3. *Encourage a therapeutic diet with ample fluid and fiber intake during waking hours.*

4. *Observe the patient for nonverbal clues* signaling the need for elimination.

5. Administer elimination aids (stool softener, laxative, or cathartic), as ordered. Document.

6. *Monitor and document the frequency of elimination.*

7. Additional individualized interventions: _____
_____
_____

Rationales

1. An AD patient may develop constipation because of not knowing where the bathroom is.

2. When memory fails, the patient may neglect toileting. Reminders, with assistance at regular intervals, promote a regular elimination program and help prevent accidents.

3. Proper diet promotes effective elimination. Ample fluids help prevent constipation.

4. The patient may exhibit restlessness, picking at clothing, or clutching the genitals but may be unable to verbalize the need to eliminate.

5. Aids may be necessary to facilitate regular elimination.

6. Noting the frequency of elimination helps to identify a regular bowel pattern and minimize problems.

7. Rationale: _____
_____
_____

Outcome criteria
Within 1 week of admission, the patient will:
• demonstrate knowledge of bathroom location
• regularly eliminate soft, formed stools.

Nursing diagnosis: *Altered family processes related to progressive mental deterioration of the family member with AD*

NURSING PRIORITY: Facilitate necessary role transitions while maintaining family integrity.

Interventions

1. *Involve the family in all teaching.* Use teaching as an opportunity to assess family roles, resources, and coping behavior. See the "Ineffective Family Coping" general care plan, page 47.

2. *Offer support, understanding, and reassurance* to the family. Support efforts to provide care for the patient in the home setting. Encourage family members to give each other "vacations" from providing care.

Rationales

1. Because AD patients require long-term care, the family must be taught how to cope effectively with this chronic progressive disease. If the patient develops a childlike dependence after holding a strong provider role, others must assume new roles to maintain family stability. Assessment of family status provides a baseline for determining the best approach and needed interventions.

2. Caring for the AD patient is frequently a frustrating and thankless task, involving endless repetition and, often, emotional confrontations that may leave family members drained. However, maintenance of a stable

Interventions *continued*

3. Involve a social worker or discharge planner in decisions regarding home care or nursing home placement. If appropriate, encourage family members to verbalize feelings regarding the decision to place the patient in a nursing home.

4. Provide information about community resources, such as home care, financial and legal assistance, and an Alzheimer's support group. Encourage utilization of all available resources.

5. Additional individualized interventions: _____

_____

_____

Outcome criteria
Throughout the period of hospitalization, the family will:
• become involved in teaching and care provision.

Rationales *continued*

home environment and the presence of familiar caregivers help provide the patient with a sense of worth, reduce isolation, and may minimize disorientation. Frequent breaks from caregiving help increase family cohesiveness and prevent burnout.

3. Patient needs may become unmanageable in the home setting. The social worker or discharge planner may offer special expertise in answering questions about long-term care. Family members may feel guilt, relief, anguish, and conflicting emotions and will need support if this decision becomes necessary.

4. Community support may help lessen the family's burden and promote healthy family adaptation to change. The AD patient is likely to appear in the emergency department when the family becomes overwhelmed. A social service referral may decrease such inappropriate use of resources and help avert family crises.

5. Rationale: _____

_____

_____

By the time of discharge, the family will:
• arrange a plan for care and mutual support
• identify resources for community support.

Discharge planning
NURSING DISCHARGE CRITERIA
(See also specific nursing discharge criteria for primary diagnosis if other than AD.)
Upon discharge, documentation shows evidence of:
• vital signs stable and within normal limits for this patient
• adequate nutritional intake
• regular bowel and bladder elimination
• adequate home support system or referral to home care or a nursing home if indicated by inadequate home support.

PATIENT/FAMILY DISCHARGE TEACHING CHECKLIST
Document evidence that patient/family demonstrates understanding of:
__ diagnosis and disease process, for example, literature from the John Douglas French Foundation for Alzheimer's Disease (Los Angeles) and the *American Journal of Alzheimer's Care and Related Disorders*
__ preparatory plans for adequate supervision and behavior management
__ approaches recommended to minimize environmental hazards
__ instructions for promotion of self-care independence
__ recommended procedure for reorientation to home environment

__ identification bracelet or other medical alert device
__ for all discharge medications: purpose, dosage, administration schedule, and side effects requiring medical attention (Discharge medications may include antianxiety agents.)
__ techniques for continued improvement in language skills
__ specific suggestions for meeting nutritional and elimination needs
__ knowledge of available community resources
__ need for restoration of family equilibrium as roles change and patient dependence increases
__ awareness of probability of total patient regression
__ how to contact doctor.

DOCUMENTATION CHECKLIST
Using outcome criteria as a guide, document:
__ clinical status on admission, including level of cognitive function
__ planned approach to maintain patient safety, security, and orientation
__ laboratory data and diagnostic findings
__ any change in the patient's behavioral response
__ level of communication and social interaction
__ dietary and elimination patterns
__ patient/family teaching
__ discharge planning.

ASSOCIATED CARE PLANS
Fluid and Electrolyte Imbalances
Geriatric Considerations
Grief/Grieving
Ineffective Family Coping
Ineffective Individual Coping
Knowledge Deficit

REFERENCES
Alfaro, Rosalinda A. *Application of Nursing Process: A Step-by-Step Guide to Care Planning.* Philadelphia: J.B. Lippincott Co., 1986.

Carnevali, Doris L., and Patrick, Maxine, eds. *Nursing Management for the Elderly,* 2nd ed. Philadelphia: J.B. Lippincott Co., 1986.

Chiverton, Patricia, and Goldenberg, Beth. "A Guide for Effective Coping for the Alzheimer Family," *Medical Times* 8:84-88, October 1986.

Cox, Kim G. "Milieu Therapy: The Person with Alzheimer's Disease," *Geriatric Nursing* 6(3):152-54, May/June 1985.

Gordon, Marjory. *Nursing Diagnosis: Process and Application.* New York: McGraw-Hill Book Co., 1982.

"High Notes. News from the John Douglas French Foundation for Alzheimer's Disease," vol. 1, no. 1, Winter 1986.

Iyer, Patricia W., et al. *Nursing Process and Nursing Diagnosis.* Philadelphia: W.B. Saunders Co., 1986.

Murray, Ruth B., and Huelskoetter, M. Marilyn. *Psychiatric and Mental Health Nursing: Giving Emotional Care.* New York: Appleton & Lange, 1987.

Nee, Linda E. "Studying the Family," *Geriatric Nursing* 6(3):154-56, May/June 1985.

Ninos, Mary, and Makohon, Rennie. "Functional Assessment of the Patient," *Geriatric Nursing* 6(3):139-42, May/June 1985.

Patrick, Maxine, et al. *Medical-Surgical Nursing: Pathophysiological Concepts.* Philadelphia: J.B. Lippincott Co., 1986.

Reisberg, Barry. "Dementia: A Systemic Approach to Identify Reversible Causes," *Geriatrics* 41(4):30-46, April 1986.

Schafer, Susan C. "Modifying the Environment," *Geriatric Nursing* 6(3):157-59, May/June 1985.

Schneider, Edward, and Emr, Marion. "Alzheimer's Disease: Research Highlights," *Geriatric Nursing* 6(3):136-38, May/June 1985.

Tariot, Pierre, et al. "How Memory Fails: A Theoretical Model," *Geriatric Nursing* 6(3):144-47, May/June 1985.

Cerebrovascular Accident

DRG information

DRG 14 [Medical DRG] Specific Cerebrovascular
  Disorders. Except TIA.
  Mean LOS = 7.5 days
  Principal Diagnoses for DRG 14:
  nonruptured cerebral aneurysm
  aphasia
  intracerebral hemorrhage
  intracranial hemorrhage
  subarachnoid hemorrhage
  occlusion of cerebral arteries

Introduction

DEFINITION AND TIME FOCUS

A cerebrovascular accident (CVA), commonly called a
stroke, can take the form of any of several pathophysiologic events that disrupt cerebral circulation. The resulting cerebral ischemia can cause widely varied
symptoms or functional deficits, the most classic being
hemiplegia.

The most common causes of CVA are thrombosis,
embolism, and hemorrhage. Rarely, CVA may be related
to arterial spasm or to compression of cerebral blood
vessels from tumor growth or other causes. The consistent factor in all CVAs, regardless of etiology, is brain
injury resulting from circulatory disruption.

Deficits resulting from CVA may be either temporary
or permanent, depending on the portion of the brain
and the vessels involved, the extent of injury, the patient's preexisting physical and emotional health, and
the presence of other diseases or injuries.

This clinical plan focuses on the care of the noncriti-
cal patient who is admitted to a medical-surgical unit
for diagnosis and nonsurgical treatment of a CVA. Surgical interventions for CVA—such as carotid endarter-
ectomy, extracranial-intracranial bypass, and
craniotomy—are not discussed in this care plan.

ETIOLOGY/PRECIPITATING FACTORS

• factors causing occlusion of blood supply to cerebral
tissue:
  □ cerebral thrombosis, such as from atherosclerosis,
  inflammation related to infection or other disease
  process, mechanical constriction as in increased intracranial pressure, prolonged vasoconstriction, systemic hypotension, and hematologic disorders that
  increase clotting tendencies
  □ cerebral embolism, such as from cardiac disease,
  plaques or clots from elsewhere in circulatory system, substances (such as air, fat, or tumor particles)
  that enter bloodstream, and clotting disorders

• factors contributing to intracerebral bleeding:
  □ hemorrhage, hypertension, ruptured aneurysm,
  trauma, ruptured arteriovenous malformations,
  bleeding related to tumor growth, bleeding disorder
  associated with a disease state (for example, leukemia, anemia, sickle cell disease, hemophilia) or with
  anticoagulant therapy, and edema
• factors causing cerebral ischemia:
  □ arterial spasm, systemic hypoxemia, and compression of cerebral blood vessels
• factors that are known to increase an individual's risk
of CVA:
  □ hypertension, heart disease, diabetes, hypercholesterolemia, use of oral contraceptives, obesity, family
  history of CVA, and congenital anomalies

Focused assessment guidelines

NURSING HISTORY (Functional health pattern findings)

Health perception–health management pattern
• *symptoms may have developed over several days (thrombosis), minutes to hours (hemorrhage), or a few minutes
(embolus)*
• may have had *recent episodes of sudden weakness, vertigo, numbness or tingling sensation of face, speech or vision disturbances that resolved spontaneously (transient
ischemic attacks, or TIAs) or left minor deficits (reversible
ischemic neurologic deficits)*
• if young female, may be taking oral contraceptives or
may smoke cigarettes
• if older adult, likely to be under treatment for
hypertension, heart disease, diabetes, or other chronic
condition
• may be noncompliant with antihypertensive regimen
or may have not seen doctor for many years

Nutritional-metabolic pattern
• may report difficulty swallowing
• may report nausea and vomiting, associated
with hemorrhage

Elimination pattern
• may report incontinence of urine or stool

Activity-exercise pattern
• may be unable to move one side of body *(hemiparesis)*
• may be afraid of falling, related to TIA

Cognitive-perceptual pattern
• may be unable to understand explanations of what has
happened or to respond to questions

• may complain of dizziness, drowsiness, headache, burning or aching pain in extremities, and stiff neck
• may complain of slowed mentation and clumsiness

Sleep-rest pattern
• symptoms—most commonly from thrombosis—may have developed during sleep or shortly after awakening

Self-perception–self-concept pattern
• may show *no awareness of affected side of body*

Role-relationship pattern
• family may note *emotional lability,* behavioral changes in patient

PHYSICAL FINDINGS
General appearance
• *facial droop*
• *lateralized weakness or flaccidity* on side opposite brain lesion

Cardiovascular
• hypertension

Pulmonary
• respirations may be increased or decreased, depending on site of CVA

Neurologic
• seizures
• *altered level of consciousness*
• nuchal rigidity
• *memory impairment*
• *confusion*
• retinal hemorrhage
• *hemianesthesia*
• *hemianopia* (visual deficit in one eye)
• apraxia (inability to perform purposeful acts)
• *aphasia*
• agnosia (inability to recognize familiar objects)
• disorientation
• unequal pupil size

Integumentary
• flushing

Musculoskeletal
• *flaccidity*
• *paralysis*
• *sensory deficits*

DIAGNOSTIC STUDIES
Initially, the priority in obtaining diagnostic studies is determined by whether the CVA is from hemorrhagic or nonhemorrhagic causes (treatment is significantly different for each). Laboratory data may show no significant abnormalities unless other conditions are present.
• complete blood count—performed for baseline; may reveal blood loss if CVA was caused by significant hemorrhage
• chemistry panel—obtained for baseline; assesses renal function and electrolyte levels, which may be significant in patients requiring fluid restriction; rules out hypoglycemia and hyperglycemia as contributors to altered mental state
• prothrombin time (PT), partial thromboplastin time (PTT)—performed for baseline because patient with CVA caused by occlusion may be started on anticoagulants as part of treatment regimen
• urinalysis—baseline study of renal adequacy rules out preexisting urinary tract infection (important because these patients are often catheterized)
• *computed tomography (CT) scan* of head—may be performed with or without contrast medium; *differentiates infarction from hemorrhage and reveals extent of bleeding and brain compression,* if present; contrast medium aids in visualizing cerebral vessels
• *cerebral angiography—visualizes cerebral blood vessels and reveals site of bleeding or blockage*
• positron emission tomography scan—computer interpretation of gamma ray emissions provides information on cerebral blood flow, volume, and metabolism
• brain scan—cerebral infarction indicated by areas of radioisotope uptake
• EEG—reveals areas of abnormal brain activity and may be helpful in diagnosis; however, a normal EEG does not rule out a pathologic condition
• lumbar puncture—bloody cerebrospinal fluid may indicate intracerebral hemorrhage; used less frequently since CT scan became available
• skull and cervical spine X-rays—may be ordered to rule out fractures, especially if patient suffered a fall with CVA

POTENTIAL COMPLICATIONS
• brain stem failure, cardiopulmonary arrest
• brain compression
• brain infarction
• mycotic aneurysm
• brain abscess
• encephalitis
• pulmonary embolism
• dysrhythmias
• congestive heart failure
• thrombophlebitis
• pneumonia
• dysfunctional limb contractures
• decubitus ulcers

Nursing diagnosis: *Potential ineffective airway clearance related to hemiplegic effects of CVA*

NURSING PRIORITIES: (a) Maintain a patent airway and (b) prevent pulmonary complications.

Interventions

1. Position the patient with head turned to the side, supporting the trunk with pillows as needed. Elevate the head of the bed slightly. Never leave a CVA patient supine while unattended. Provide a call button within easy reach of the unaffected arm, or provide alternative means of signaling for help, as needed.

2. Provide supplemental oxygen, as ordered.

3. If hemiplegia is present, position the patient on the affected side for shorter periods (1 to 1½ hours) than on the unaffected side (2 hours). Avoid positioning a hemiplegic arm over the abdomen.

4. Encourage coughing (except in the patient with a hemorrhagic CVA) and deep breathing every 2 hours while awake. Suction accumulated secretions as necessary.

5. Assess lung sounds at least every 4 hours while awake. Also note the adequacy of respiratory effort, the rate and characteristics of respirations, and skin color. Investigate restlessness promptly, especially in the aphasic patient. Report any abnormalities.

6. Assist with or observe the patient's eating, as needed. Place small bites of food in the unaffected side of the mouth. (Semisolid foods are usually handled better than liquids.)

7. Additional individualized interventions: _____
_____
_____

Rationales

1. Hemiplegia, aphasia, or dysphagia may render the patient unable to clear the airway or call for help. Elevating the head helps minimize cerebral edema, which can contribute to decreased alertness. If left supine while unattended, the CVA patient may aspirate; additionally, the supine position increases the risk of airway obstruction from the tongue, especially if the patient is obtunded. Providing the means to call for help is essential when the airway is potentially compromised.

2. The brain uses 20% of the oxygen normally available to the body. When CVA causes cerebral ischemia, supplemental oxygen may help prevent brain tissue death.

3. Lying on the affected side may cause pooling of secretions, which are ineffectively cleared because of hemiplegia. The weight of a hemiplegic arm over the abdomen may further reduce the adequacy of thoracic expansion.

4. Accumulation of secretions may cause airway obstruction or predispose the patient to atelectasis or pneumonia. (Respiratory infection is one of the primary causes of death for CVA patients.) Coughing should be avoided by the patient with hemorrhagic CVA to prevent increasing intracranial pressure, which can precipitate further bleeding.

5. Many CVA patients have preexisting hypertension or heart disease, which may predispose them to development of congestive heart failure. Abnormal lung sounds (crackles, rhonchi) may be the first indicators of complications related to hypoventilation. Increased respiratory effort, tachypnea, ashen or cyanotic color, or restlessness may indicate hypoxemia. Early detection and reporting facilitates prompt treatment.

6. Hemiplegia and associated dysphagia predispose the patient to aspiration. The patient may be better able to initiate swallowing if food is placed on the unaffected side. Small bites decrease the risk of choking from aspiration.

7. Rationale: _____
_____
_____

Outcome criteria

Within 2 days of admission, the patient will:
• cough and perform deep-breathing exercises every 2 hours.

Throughout the period of hospitalization, the patient will:
• have a clear airway

• have clear lung sounds or pulmonary problems promptly identified and treated
• take food and fluids (as ordered) without aspirating or choking.

Collaborative problem: *Potential extension of cerebrovascular injury related to continued occlusion or further intracerebral bleeding*

NURSING PRIORITY: Prevent or minimize further cerebrovascular disturbances.

Interventions

1. *Assess neurologic status* at least every 4 hours while awake, checking level of consciousness, orientation, grips, leg strength, pupillary response, and vital signs. *Promptly report any abnormalities or changes,* especially decreasing alertness, progressing weakness, restlessness, unequal pupil size, widening pulse pressure, flexor or extensor posturing, seizures, severe headache, vertigo, syncope, or epistaxis.

2. If CVA is occlusive:
• Administer anticoagulants, as ordered. Monitor appropriate laboratory findings (PT and PTT), and check current results before giving each dose. Observe carefully for (and advise the patient or family to report) melena, petechiae, epistaxis, hematuria, ecchymosis, oozing from wounds, or any unusual bleeding. Observe for and report headache, irritability, weakness, or any signs of intracranial bleeding.

• Administer antiplatelet aggregation medications, as ordered. Observe for gastric irritation.

• Administer medications to control blood pressure, as ordered. Be alert for signs of decreased cerebral perfusion (as noted in Intervention 1 above); immediately report any that occur. Check blood pressure at least every 4 hours while the patient is awake.

3. If CVA is hemorrhagic:
• Maintain the patient on complete bed rest for the first 24 hours to 1 week, as ordered. Minimize stress and external stimulation as much as possible. Administer stool softeners and/or laxatives, as ordered.

• Administer medications to control blood pressure, as ordered. Be alert for signs of neurologic deterioration and immediately report any that occur.

• Administer I.V. aminocaproic acid, as ordered. Observe for and report hypotension, bradycardia, or signs of thrombus formation, such as calf pain, sudden chest pain, or shortness of breath.

Rationales

1. When blood flow to the brain is decreased and insufficient oxygen is present, cerebral vasodilation and edema occur as the body attempts to compensate for the deficiency. Increasing cerebral edema causes increased intracranial pressure and may have fatal consequences if not treated promptly. Hemorrhage into enclosed intracranial space may also increase pressure. A decline in neurologic signs indicates progressive injury.

2. For an occlusive CVA:
• Use of anticoagulants, although still somewhat controversial, has been shown to inhibit stroke progression and possibly reduce the number of reoccurrences of thromboembolic events. Heparin inactivates thrombin, thus preventing fibrin clots. Therapeutic PTT should be 2 to 2½ times normal value. Warfarin interferes with vitamin K production, thus decreasing synthesis of several clotting factors. Therapeutic PT should be 1½ to 2½ times normal value. Anticoagulants predispose the patient to systemic bleeding and may also precipitate intracranial bleeding.

• Drugs such as aspirin and dipyridamole inhibit platelet aggregation and thus reduce the risk of embolus formation. Undesirable side effects include GI upset and bleeding, so these drugs should not be used if the patient has preexisting GI problems.

• Many CVA patients have preexisting hypertension, and their cerebral circulation has accommodated to higher pressures over time. Sudden lowering of blood pressure may cause further ischemia.

3. For a hemorrhagic CVA:
• Minimizing activity and stimulation helps decrease the risk of further intracerebral hemorrhage. Stool softeners or laxatives prevent straining at stool, which can precipitate bleeding.

• Patients with hemorrhagic CVA often have significant vasospasm; lowering blood pressure too much, or too rapidly, may cause cerebral ischemia.

• Normally, a fibrin clot breaks down spontaneously about 7 days after a hemorrhagic episode. Aminocaproic acid inhibits breakdown of the fibrin clot by preventing activation of plasminogen. Because the drug acts systemically to prevent fibrinolysis, thrombus formation and embolic complications may occur elsewhere in the body.

Interventions *continued*

• Monitor the patient to maintain optimal fluid status, observing fluid restrictions as ordered. Administer osmotic diuretics, as ordered. Monitor intake and output carefully.

Rationales *continued*

• Fluid overload may cause fatal increases in intracranial pressure and/or recurrent hemorrhage. Osmotic diuretics such as mannitol reduce cerebral edema by drawing fluid into the intravascular system and stimulating diuresis. Mannitol also reduces the volume of circulating cerebrospinal fluid. Patients with other preexisting conditions, such as cardiac or renal disease, may poorly tolerate the temporarily increased intravascular volume from mannitol. Careful patient monitoring, including an accurate intake and output record, is essential to prevent such complications.

4. Additional individualized interventions: _____

_____

_____

4. Rationale: _____

_____

_____

Outcome criteria

Within 2 days of admission, the patient with occlusive CVA will:
• show no further decrease in level of consciousness
• show stable or improving neurologic signs.

Within 1 to 3 days of admission, the patient with hemorrhagic CVA will:
• maintain bed rest

• show no further decrease in level of consciousness
• show stable or improving neurologic signs.

Throughout the period of hospitalization, all CVA patients will:
• maintain fluid balance
• maintain normal electrolyte values.

Nursing diagnosis: *Impaired physical mobility related to impaired cerebral function*

NURSING PRIORITY: Minimize effects of immobility and prevent associated complications.

Interventions

1. *Maintain the patient's body in a position of functional alignment while at rest,* using a footboard, handroll, or trochanter roll, as necessary. Support the affected arm when the patient is out of bed.

2. *Provide passive (and active, as permitted) range-of-motion exercise* to all extremities at least four times a day, beginning immediately upon admission. Increase activity levels as permitted and tolerated, depending on the CVA's cause. Collaborate with the physical therapist to plan a rehabilitation schedule with the patient and family.

3. *When permitted, encourage the patient to perform as much self-care as possible.*

4. Provide antiembolism stockings, as ordered. Assess for signs of thromboembolic complications. Report immediately any chest pain, shortness of breath, calf pain, or redness or swelling in an extremity.

Rationales

1. Maintenance of a functional position prevents contractures and deformities that further complicate the recovery process. The weight of an unsupported arm may cause shoulder dislocation, joint inflammation, or both.

2. Even passive exercise helps maintain muscle tone and establish new impulse pathways and neuron regeneration. Adjacent brain cells may take up the function of damaged cells, new nerve cell fibers may "sprout" collaterally, or alternate nerve pathways may function to resume activity. Learning and repetition appear to be key factors in the development of new neuronal connections. Establishing a schedule helps the patient set goals, maintain a sense of control, and measure progress.

3. Independence in self-care helps maintain self-respect and may increase motivation and decrease boredom.

4. Antiembolism stockings promote venous return, thus decreasing the risk of thrombus formation related to immobility and venous stasis. The signs and symptoms noted may indicate pulmonary embolus or thrombophlebitis.

(continued)

Interventions continued

5. *Turn the patient from side to side* at least every 2 hours. Keep bedding clean and dry. Massage bony prominences. Be alert to fragile, thin, or excoriated skin, which may shear against turning sheets. Provide special mattresses or foam or other padding. Report any red or broken skin areas immediately.

6. Maintain adequate elimination. If the patient is catheterized, begin bladder retraining as soon as possible, according to an established protocol or medical order. If the patient is not catheterized, offer a bedpan every 2 hours. Observe urine and report cloudiness, excessive sediment, or pyuria. Provide stool softeners and laxatives, as ordered, and monitor the frequency and characteristics of bowel movements. Provide reassurance that bowel and bladder control usually returns as rehabilitation progresses.

7. Additional individualized intervention: _____

_____

_____

Outcome criteria
Within 24 hours of admission, the patient will:
• begin passive range-of-motion exercises
• have clean and dry skin
• have a patent urinary catheter or use a bedpan every 2 hours with minimal incontinence.

Throughout the period of hospitalization, the patient will:
• maintain functional alignment

Rationales continued

5. Impeccable skin care is necessary to prevent skin breakdown in the immobilized patient. Moisture promotes bacterial growth and increases skin friability. Turning and massage help prevent pressure areas and promote circulation. Older patients are likely to have delicate skin, particularly if debilitated. The older CVA patient may have been "down" for some time before help arrived, so skin may be excoriated from urine, pressure, and dehydration effects. Special mattresses and padding help redistribute pressure. Prompt intervention helps prevent development of serious skin problems that can interfere with the recovery process.

6. When neurosensory pathways are disturbed by injury, the patient may have limited or altered sphincter control related to either actual brain damage or CVA-related memory/inhibitory lapses. Incontinence and urinary stasis predispose the patient to infection. Bladder and bowel retraining reestablish patterns and bolster the patient's confidence in resuming activities as permitted. Reassurance that incontinence is usually temporary helps decrease anxiety, embarrassment, and a sense of helplessness.

7. Rationale: _____

_____

_____

• perform as much self-care as possible
• maintain intact skin
• maintain adequate bowel and bladder elimination, with no signs of infection
• show no thromboembolic complications.

Nursing diagnosis: *Potential sensory-perceptual alteration and impaired verbal communication related to cerebral injury*

NURSING PRIORITY: Minimize effects of deficits in perception and communication, and prevent related complications.

Interventions

1. Establish closeness by using a calm and reassuring manner, eye contact, and touch. Call the patient by a preferred name. Approach the patient's unaffected side.

2. *Assess communication ability.* Explain to the patient that the CVA may have affected speech. Ask simple questions that evaluate ability to repeat words, interpret, follow directions, and express feelings. Allow ample time for responses.

Rationales

1. Sensory-perceptual and communication deficits may contribute to profound isolation for the patient who has suffered a CVA. Use of nonverbal communication establishes contact and helps decrease anxiety. The patient may be unable to see or feel on the affected side of the body.

2. Identification of speech problems (expressive vs. receptive aphasia, for example) is the first step in planning rehabilitation. A patient with receptive aphasia may still be able to process information, but interpretation of stimuli and formation of responses is slowed.

Interventions continued

3. *Speak slowly and clearly,* using short sentences. Do not shout at the patient. Use simple explanations and gestures. Always include the patient in conversation when others are present in the room. Avoid answering for the patient. Never use baby talk. *Provide alternative means of communication (for example, a word board or pencil and paper) if needed.*

4. *If significant speech deficits are present, arrange referral to a speech therapist* for more comprehensive evaluation and for rehabilitation services.

5. *Reassure the patient that functional recovery is possible* with patience and consistent rehabilitation efforts. Help with practice and repetition of verbal and physical exercises. Involve family members in practice. If inappropriate profanity occurs because of CVA, counsel the family.

6. *Protect the patient from injury to the affected side.* Give regular reminders to look at the affected side and touch affected extremities.

7. If visual field deficits are present, remind the patient that frequent head-turning will widen the visual field. Always ensure that food and objects at bedside are placed well within the patient's visual field.

8. Additional individualized interventions: _____
_____
_____

Outcome criteria
Within 1 hour of admission, the patient will:
• establish some form of verbal or non-verbal communication (unless comatose).

Rationales continued

3. Rapid or complex explanations may cause neurosensory overload and contribute to patient frustration. Hearing is usually not impaired, and shouting may add to the patient's distress over deficits. Answering for the patient, "talking around" the patient, and using baby talk are demeaning and contribute to the patient's sense of helplessness. Alternate means of communication may be needed while the patient relearns verbal skills.

4. A speech therapist can provide expertise in pinpointing and treating specific speech problems.

5. A patient with severe deficits may despair of ever resuming normal activities, but maintaining hope is essential for the fullest possible recovery. Over time, the brain can develop new pathways for functions: repetition aids this process. Family support helps maintain morale. Family members may be shocked by inappropriate profanity; advise them that this is common in patients whose speech has been affected by CVA.

6. Hemiplegia may be accompanied by full or partial hemianesthesia; the patient may thus be unaware of actual or impending injury. Relearning awareness and acceptance of the affected side, by engaging in activities using that side, is a necessary step toward functional recovery.

7. Visual field deficits may prevent the patient from receiving warnings or other cues to prevent injury. Accidents or insufficient nutritional intake may result if visual field defects are not considered in arranging the bedside tray.

8. Rationale: _____
_____
_____

Within 2 days of admission, the patient will:
• look at and touch the affected side of the body.

Nursing diagnosis: *Potential alteration in family processes related to emotional lability associated with cerebral injury*

NURSING PRIORITY: Provide support for the patient and family and minimize distress related to emotional outbursts.

Interventions

1. *Maintain an attitude of acceptance and understanding.* Do not exacerbate emotional outbursts by reacting personally to them. Encourage normal expression of feelings related to lost abilities.

Rationales

1. A patient who has suffered a CVA typically exhibits excessive or inappropriate emotions as a result of brain injury. The profound alteration such deficits as aphasia cause in the patient's relationship with his surround-

(continued)

Interventions *continued*

Rationales *continued*

ings can also precipitate widely varied emotional reactions ranging from rage to grief; expression of such feelings is part of the coping process. These patients are often unable to control their emotional responses, and excessive reactivity on the part of family members or caregivers may add to their isolation and distress.

2. Explain to the family that some emotional lability is commonly associated with cerebral injury but that such behavior usually decreases over time. Help the family provide the patient with gentle guidance in relearning appropriate emotional, as well as physical, responses. Encourage affection, patience, and use of humor.

2. Family members may be confused and distressed by unexpected emotional outbursts, and it may reassure them to know that physiologic factors are at least partially responsible. The family may help the patient reestablish appropriate responses by supportive, gentle reminders of them. Family understanding and patience, with humor at appropriate moments, may defuse potentially volatile emotional outbursts.

3. Additional individualized interventions: _____
_____
_____

3. Rationale: _____
_____
_____

Outcome criteria
Throughout hospitalization, the patient will:
• express appropriate grieving responses (within limits of deficits).

Throughout the patient's period of hospitalization, the family will:
• understand emotional implications of CVA.

Nursing diagnosis: *Knowledge deficit related to the rehabilitation process and ongoing home care*

NURSING PRIORITY: Provide thorough patient and family teaching.

Interventions

1. See the "Knowledge Deficit" care plan, page 56.

Rationales

1. This care plan provides general information for use in patient and family teaching.

2. *Instruct the patient and family about all medications to be taken at home,* including antihypertensives, anticoagulants, and antiplatelet aggregation medication.

2. Thorough understanding helps minimize the risk of inadvertent errors and/or noncompliance. Pharmacologic control may decrease the risk of CVA recurrence.

3. If the patient is to be discharged home on anticoagulant therapy, provide thorough instructions about:

3. Because anticoagulant use may cause life-threatening bleeding, it is critical that both patient and family understand the regimen completely.

• medications' action, dosage, and schedule

• Anticoagulants should be taken on a regular schedule in the dosage determined by the doctor.

• the need for frequent follow-up laboratory testing to determine dosage requirements

• Tests determine the need for dosage adjustments.

• signs of bleeding problems (melena, petechiae, easy bruising, hematuria, epistaxis) and the need to report them

• Untoward bleeding may indicate the need for a dosage adjustment, a therapeutic antidote, or both.

• measures to control bleeding

• Uncontrolled hemorrhage can be fatal.

• dietary considerations

• Vitamin K intake affects dosage requirements.

• avoidance of aspirin and other over-the-counter medications

• Aspirin and other over-the-counter medications may potentiate anticoagulants' effects.

Interventions *continued*

• avoidance of trauma

• the importance of wearing a Medic Alert tag and of notifying other health professionals (for example, the dentist, or eye doctor) of anticoagulant therapy.

4. *Teach the importance of life-style modifications* to minimize the risk of CVA recurrence; these include blood pressure control, weight control, smoking cessation, control of diabetes (if present), dietary modifications, and stress reduction.

5. *Teach the patient and family to recognize and report symptoms associated with TIAs:* vertigo, vision disturbances, sudden weakness or falls without loss of consciousness ("drop attacks"), paresthesias of face or extremities, speech disturbances, and lateralized temporary weakness.

6. *Teach the patient and family about rehabilitation plans and arrange home care follow-up or in-home assistance,* as needed. Teaching should also address specific individualized information on activity, safety, and positioning recommendations; use of mobility aids (slings, braces, or walkers); airway maintenance and feeding considerations; a bowel and bladder control program; signs and symptoms of complications (decreasing neurologic status, infection, bleeding, or thromboembolic events); food and fluid intake recommendations; skin care; communication techniques; and coping with emotional lability.

7. Discuss with the family the advisability of learning cardiopulmonary resuscitation (CPR) techniques.

8. Additional individualized interventions: _____
_____
_____

Rationales *continued*

• Even minimal trauma may cause serious injury in the patient whose clotting status is altered by anticoagulants.

• Other health care providers must be aware of the patient's medication regimen so that their interventions can be altered accordingly to prevent injury.

4. The risk factors listed may directly or indirectly contribute to CVA recurrence.

5. TIAs may be precursors of CVA recurrence; prompt reporting allows for preventive intervention, such as medication adjustment for better blood pressure control.

6. The rehabilitation level at discharge varies from patient to patient and may also depend on the availability of home care resources. Most CVA patients require some assistance at home after discharge, either from motivated and well-taught family members or from professional caregivers. Because of the impact of DRGs, a CVA patient may be discharged from the hospital at an early stage of the rehabilitation process. Discharge planning should always address ongoing rehabilitation.

7. Many risk factors for stroke—such as hypertension and atherosclerosis—also are risk factors for myocardial infarction and cardiac arrest. Cardiac arrest also can cause further stroke from ischemia.

8. Rationale: _____
_____
_____

Outcome criteria

Within 24 hours of admission, the patient will:
• express understanding of what has happened (unless aphasic).

By the time of discharge, the patient or family will:
• name risk factors associated with potential recurrence of CVA
• list and discuss all medications for use at home
• list four signs of bleeding (if patient is on anticoagulants)
• list signs of TIA and CVA
• demonstrate understanding of the activity regimen and perform activities

• appropriately use mobility aids, if needed
• name measures to protect the affected side
• verbalize understanding of the bowel and bladder control program
• express understanding of food and fluid intake recommendations
• tolerate frustration over speech deficits and use alternate measures to communicate
• understand the plan for ongoing rehabilitation.

Discharge planning

NURSING DISCHARGE CRITERIA

Upon discharge, documentation shows evidence of:
• absence of fever and pulmonary or cardiovascular complications*
• stable vital signs*
• absence of signs and symptoms indicating progression of neurologic deficit*
• prothrombin level within acceptable parameters*
• absence of skin breakdown and contractures
• ability to tolerate activity within expected parameters
• ability to transfer and ambulate
• ability to perform activities of daily living
• ability to compensate for neurologic deficit, such as paralysis, spasticity, or speech impairment
• ability to control bowel and bladder functions
• ability to tolerate nutritional intake*
• physical and occupational therapy program with maximum hospital benefit attained*
• referral to home care if indicated by patient's progress toward maximum rehabilitation potential and by capabilities of home support system, or, if home support is inadequate or patient's condition indicates a need for continued rehabilitation that can only be performed in a setting other than the home:
    □ referral to rehabilitation facility or nursing home for continued rehabilitation
    □ referral form reflecting patient's progress, potential, and goals and containing all other appropriate information necessary to provide continuity of care.

PATIENT/FAMILY DISCHARGE TEACHING CHECKLIST

Document evidence that patient/family demonstrates understanding of:
___ injury or disease process and implications
___ all discharge medications' purpose, dosage, administration schedule, and side effects requiring medical attention (discharge medications may include anticoagulants, antiplatelet aggregation medications, and antihypertensives)
___ need for follow-up laboratory test (if indicated)
___ signs of cerebral impairment
___ signs of infection
___ signs of thromboembolic or other complications
___ activity and positioning recommendations, mobility aids
___ food and fluid intake recommendations
___ bowel and bladder control program
___ risk factors
___ safety measures
___ use of Medic Alert tag
___ advisability of CPR classes for family
___ skin care
___ communication measures
___ verbal practice exercises

___ expected emotional lability and coping methods
___ community resources
___ when and how to access emergency medical system
___ date, time, and location of follow-up appointment
___ home care arrangements.

DOCUMENTATION CHECKLIST

Using outcome criteria as a guide, document:
___ clinical status on admission
___ significant changes in status
___ neurologic assessments
___ pertinent laboratory and diagnostic test findings
___ medication therapy
___ activity and positioning
___ food intake
___ fluid intake and output
___ bowel and bladder control measures
___ communication measures
___ patient/family teaching
___ discharge planning.

ASSOCIATED CARE PLANS

Fluid and Electrolyte Imbalances
Geriatric Considerations
Grief/Grieving
Ineffective Family Coping
Ineffective Individual Coping
Knowledge Deficit
Thrombophlebitis

REFERENCES

Emergencies. Nurse's Reference Library: Springhouse, Pa.: Springhouse Corp., 1985.

Luckmann, Joan, and Sorensen, Karen. *Medical-Surgical Nursing: A Psycholphysiologic Approach*, 3rd ed. Philadelphia: W.B. Saunders Co., 1987.

Rudy, Ellen B. *Advanced Neurological and Neurosurgical Nursing.* St. Louis: C.V. Mosby Co., 1984.

*Factors that must be met by the time of discharge. All other factors must be addressed in the medical record but may not be within normal parameters upon discharge since maximum return of function may not be achieved by discharge.

Laminectomy

DRG information
DRG 214 [Surgical DRG] Back and Neck Procedures.
  With Complication or Comorbidity (CC).
  Mean LOS = 13.1 days
DRG 215 [Surgical DRG] Back and Neck Procedures.
  Without CC.
  Mean LOS = 9.3 days

Introduction
DEFINITION AND TIME FOCUS
Laminectomy is a major spinal surgery in which one or more vertebral laminae are removed to expose the spinal cord and nearby structures. Most commonly, it is performed to facilitate removal of part or all of a disk (nucleus pulposus) that has herniated and is pressing on a spinal nerve root. Almost all herniated disks occur in the lumbar spine, 90% to 95% occurring at the level of L4 or L5 to S1.

A laminectomy also may be performed for spinal cord compression from a fracture, dislocation, hematoma, or abscess; spinal nerve surgery; or removal of a spinal cord tumor or vascular malformation. Less often, it may be performed to treat intractable pain by sectioning posterior nerve roots or interrupting spinothalamic tracts.

Lumbar laminectomy is more common than cervical laminectomy. A posterior surgical approach is used most often for lumbar laminectomy, an anterior approach for cervical laminectomy.

If the spine is unstable, a spinal fusion may be done at the same time, typically using iliac crest bone fragments. Recovery takes longer with fusion because the bone graft heals slowly.

This clinical plan focuses on the patient undergoing lumbar laminectomy for lumbar disk herniation that has not responded to conservative medical management. Spinal fusion is not discussed.

ETIOLOGY/PRECIPITATING FACTORS
For herniated disk:
• disk degeneration
• trauma, for example, accidents, strain, or repeated minor stresses
• poor body mechanics (causing low back strain)
• congenital predisposition

Focused assessment guidelines
NURSING HISTORY (Functional health pattern findings)

Health perception–health management pattern
• *typically reports pain in the lumbosacral area accompanied by varying degrees of sensory and motor deficit*

• *may report dull pain in the buttocks followed by unilateral or bilateral leg pain that may extend to the foot, depending on the level of disk herniation*
• *may report numbness and tingling in toes and feet*
• *may report pain usually increased with activities that cause increased intraspinal pressure* (such as sitting, sneezing, coughing, straining, and lifting)
• may have natural deformity of the lumbar spine
• may be obese
• may have a history of chronic low back pain
• may have a history of employment involving straining, lifting, or twisting
• if between ages of 20 and 45 and male, at increased risk

Nutritional-metabolic pattern
• may have a dietary history consistent with obesity (high-calorie, high-fat)

Activity-exercise pattern
• may report altered mobility because of asymmetrical gait
• may report lack of physical activity because of pain

Sleep-rest pattern
• may report sleep disturbances related to chronic low back pain, aggravated by sleeping on stomach

Role-relationship pattern
• may report self as most concerned about ability to return to work, especially if work involves lifting

PHYSICAL FINDINGS
General appearance
• anxious or pained facial expression

Cardiovascular
• radiating pain elicited by compression of the jugular veins with the patient in a standing position (Naffziger's test) indicates lumbar disk disease

Gastrointestinal
• constipation (related to inactivity or pressure on spinal nerve roots)

Genitourinary
• urinary retention (related to pressure on spinal nerve roots)

Neurologic
• *increased pain in affected leg with straight-leg raising* (Lasègue's sign)
• sensory and motor deficit in affected leg and foot
• presence of Kernig's sign—pain with extension of knee when both hip and knee are at 90-degree flexion

• pain with deep palpation over affected area
• decreased or absent Achilles and patellar reflexes
• deformity of lumbar spine

Musculoskeletal
• *muscle spasms*
• *muscle weakness or atrophy* in affected leg and foot
• *asymmetrical gait*
• decreased ability to bend forward
• restricted lateral movement
• leaning away from affected side during standing or ambulation
• absence of normal lumbar lordosis and presence of lumbar scoliosis with reflex muscle spasms
• tense posture

DIAGNOSTIC STUDIES
• cerebrospinal fluid (CSF)—protein may be elevated 70 to 100 mg/dl

• hemoglobin and hematocrit—measurement obtained as a prerequisite for surgery and as a baseline for comparison with postoperative values to detect bleeding
• *computed tomography scan—may show disk protrusion or prolapse*
• spine X-ray—may show narrowed vertebral interspaces at the level of disk degeneration, with flattening of the lumbar curve
• magnetic resonance imaging (MRI)—may reveal disk pressure on the spinal cord or nerve root
• myelogram—may confirm presence of a herniated disk and indicate the precise level of herniation
• electromyelogram—may indicate neural and muscle damage as well as the level and site of injury

POTENTIAL COMPLICATIONS
• unrelieved acute pain
• muscle weakness and atrophy
• paralysis
• altered bowel or bladder function

Nursing diagnosis: *Preoperative knowledge deficit related to impending surgery*

NURSING PRIORITY: Prepare the patient to cope with the surgical experience.

Interventions

1. *Provide specific preoperative teaching* for the patient who will have a lumbar laminectomy. Also provide general preoperative teaching (see the "Surgical Intervention" care plan, page 71, for details).

2. Provide information about the postoperative routine:
• frequent taking of vital signs and neurovascular observations of the extremities
• turning by logrolling during the first 48 hours
• positioning with pillows to maintain proper body alignment
• coughing and deep breathing with the back firmly against the mattress or with a pillow held against the chest for splinting purposes
• using a urinal or bedpan while flat in bed
• wearing antiembolism stockings and doing ankle and foot exercises
• beginning progressive activity 24 to 48 hours after surgery, depending on the doctor's preference
• avoiding flexing, hyperextending, turning, or twisting the lumbar spine
• using the correct method for moving from the lying to the standing position (for example, maintaining spinal alignment and using arm and leg muscles to change position)
• exercising as ordered to strengthen arm, leg, and abdominal muscles
• using a trapeze as ordered by the doctor.

Rationales

1. The patient having a laminectomy usually has undergone a long period, or intermittent periods, of conservative treatment. The surgery is preceded by chronic pain, a decrease in physical activity, and possible absence from work. The patient may view the surgery with relief but also with anxiety about the results. Information about the specific procedure will help to allay anxieties about having spinal surgery.

2. The patient's understanding of the postoperative routine helps avoid complications, such as increased pressure on the operative site or twisting of the spinal column. Perfect alignment of the body should be maintained in all positions to prevent trauma to the surgical site and to decrease discomfort. Other potential complications, such as pneumonia or atelectasis and thromboembolism, also may be prevented by proper postoperative care.

Interventions *continued*

3. Provide instruction about sources of postoperative pain. Explain that preoperative numbness or pain in the affected leg(s) will remain for some time after the surgery because of nerve irritation and postoperative edema. Also explain that muscle spasms may occur.

4. Provide information about comfort measures:

• open communication with the staff about the patient's pain (characteristics and tolerance) and anxiety

• availability of analgesics

• avoidance of injections in painful areas

• positioning

5. Additional individualized interventions: _____
_____
_____

Rationales *continued*

3. This knowledge helps allay the patient's anxiety or fear that the surgery has not been successful when numbness or tingling is experienced or when weakness makes moving the extremities difficult postoperatively.
 Muscle spasms that typically occur on the 3rd or 4th postoperative day are accompanied by severe pain.

4. The patient should know that measures are available for his postoperative comfort.
• Pain tolerance is different for each patient. Anxiety regarding injury from movement potentiates postoperative discomfort.
• Medicating as needed and encouraging the patient to request medication before the pain becomes severe help maintain comfort.
• Intramuscular injections should be given in the unaffected buttock or in the deltoid muscle if there is pain in both buttocks.
• Proper body alignment increases patient comfort.

5. Rationale: _____
_____
_____

Outcome criteria
By the day of surgery, the patient will:
• verbalize understanding of preoperative instruction
• list five measures to prevent postoperative complications.

Collaborative problem: *Potential sensory and motor deficits related to the surgical procedure, edema, and/or hematoma at the operative site*

NURSING PRIORITY: Prevent or minimize neurovascular impairment.

Interventions

1. Document the lower extremities' neurovascular status every 2 hours or as needed for 24 to 48 hours: skin color and temperature, sensation and motion, edema, peripheral pulses, capillary refill, ability to flex and extend the foot and toes, muscle strength, numbness or tingling in the extremities, and tone and strength in the quadriceps muscles.

2. *If signs and symptoms of neurovascular damage occur, notify the doctor immediately.*

3. *Implement measures to prevent neurovascular damage* in the lower extremities:
• Maintain proper body alignment by logrolling (every 2 hours for the first 24 to 48 hours) and positioning with pillows.
• Use a firm mattress and a bedboard.

Rationales

1. Postoperative deficits may result from pressure on the spinal cord or spinal nerve roots caused by surgical trauma or hematoma. Early detection of altered function facilitates prompt intervention.

2. Prompt intervention may help minimize neurovascular damage.

3. These measures will assist in reducing stress and pressure on the surgical site until healing has taken place.

(continued)

Interventions *continued*

4. *Implement measures to prevent hematoma development:* maintain patency of the wound drainage system if present; see the "Alteration in comfort" nursing diagnosis in this section for details.

5. Administer corticosteroids, if ordered, and document.

6. Implement measures to minimize neurovascular damage if initial signs and symptoms of impairment occur.
• Assess for and correct improper body alignment.
• If footdrop is present, initiate passive range-of-motion exercises every 1 to 2 hours.
• Stabilize the foot with ancillary equipment, such as a footboard, sandbags, pillows, foam boots, or foot positioners.

7. Prepare the patient for surgical intervention if evacuation of a hematoma at the surgical site is indicated. See the "Surgical Intervention" care plan, page 71.

8. Additional individualized interventions: _____

_____

_____

Outcome criteria
Within 48 hours postoperatively, the patient will:
• have normal circulatory, motor, and sensory function in the lower extremities (same as before hospitalization or improved)

Rationales *continued*

4. Maintaining drainage decreases pressure on the surgical site. Hematoma development may precipitate serious neurovascular complications.

5. Corticosteroids decrease inflammation in the surgical area.

6. These measures help prevent further damage from uneven or excessive pressure on the operative site. Permanent disability may be prevented by careful attention to the occurrence and prompt treatment of motor and sensory deficits.

7. Prompt evacuation of a hematoma may minimize damage. Adequate preparation of the patient for surgical intervention helps allay anxieties. The "Surgical Intervention" care plan provides further details.

8. Rationale: _____

_____

_____

• have no signs and symptoms of hematoma
• maintain correct body alignment.

Collaborative problem: *Potential cerebrospinal fistula associated with incomplete closure of the dura at the surgical site*

NURSING PRIORITY: Detect any CSF leakage promptly.

Interventions

1. *Observe the patient carefully every 2 to 4 hours for CSF drainage on the dressing:* a clear halo or a watery pink ring around bloody or serosanguineous drainage.

2. *Test the dressing with Dextrostix or Tes-Tape to determine if glucose is present.*

3. *Determine if the patient has a headache.*

4. *Document any CSF drainage, and notify the doctor immediately if it occurs.*

Rationales

1. An abnormal opening between the subarachnoid space and the incision causes CSF to drain. Drainage on the dressing is a major sign of the presence of a fistula, usually a late postoperative complication occurring about a week after surgery. Early detection of CSF leakage facilitates prompt intervention and treatment.

2. Glucose is a CSF component whose presence indicates a fistula. Glucose is not normally present in serous wound drainage.

3. Headache is a common symptom associated with CSF loss.

4. Untreated, CSF leakage may be fatal.

Interventions *continued*

5. Implement measures to reduce stress on the surgical site. See the "Alteration in comfort" nursing diagnosis in this section.

6. Change the dressing when damp, using strict aseptic technique. Assess for infection at the incision site.

7. Administer antibiotics, as ordered, and document.

8. Monitor temperature every 4 hours for 48 to 72 hours postoperatively. Monitor the white blood cell (WBC) count daily, as ordered.

9. *Assess for signs and symptoms of meningitis:* headache, fever, chills, nuchal rigidity, photophobia, and positive Kernig's and Brudzinski's signs.

10. If a fistula occurs and does not heal spontaneously, prepare the patient for surgical closure. See the "Surgical Intervention" care plan, page 71.

11. Additional individualized interventions: _____
_____
_____

Rationales *continued*

5. Decreasing stress on the surgical site promotes healing of the dura, which is incised during the surgical procedure. The "Alteration in comfort" problem contains specific details about stress reduction measures.

6. Microorganisms can ascend through the fistula, multiply in the CSF, and infect the central nervous system. Changing a damp dressing immediately, using aseptic technique, helps prevent infection at the site and reduces the risk of meningitis.

7. Antibiotics combat specific causative microorganisms.

8. The temperature may be elevated to 102° F. (38.9° C.) for the first few postoperative days because of the body's normal response to tissue injury and inflammation. Temperature elevation from infection would normally be accompanied by an increased WBC count.

9. Meningitis is a common complication resulting from contamination of CSF. Undetected, it may be fatal within a short time.

10. Adequate preparation before surgical closure of the dura helps allay patient anxiety.

11. Rationale: _____
_____
_____

Outcome criteria
Throughout the postoperative period the patient will have:
• no CSF drainage from a lower back incision
• no signs or symptoms of meningitis.

Nursing diagnosis: *Alteration in comfort related to immobility, pain, muscle spasm, and paresthesias secondary to surgical trauma and postoperative edema*

NURSING PRIORITY: Relieve discomfort or pain.

Interventions

1. *Assess the patient for discomfort or pain*—specifically, muscle spasm and pain in the lower back and hips, and pain, numbness, or tingling in the affected leg or legs—every 2 to 4 hours.

2. Assess for associated signs and symptoms: rubbing the lower back and hips, guarding the affected extremity, and showing reluctance to move.

Rationales

1. Preoperative numbness and pain in the lower back and affected leg(s) will remain for some time after surgery. (Some patients experience pain and muscle spasm throughout the hospital stay). Postoperative pain and muscle spasm are usually caused by nerve root and muscle irritation from edema and surgical trauma. Muscle spasms tend to occur on the 3rd to 4th postoperative day.

2. The patient may not report pain, but nonverbal indicators may reveal its presence. Some people do not like to request pain medication.

(continued)

Interventions continued

3. *Administer muscle relaxants or anti-inflammatory agents,* as ordered, and document their effects.

4. *Administer analgesics judiciously,* as ordered, and document. Assess for pain relief 30 minutes after medication is administered, and document.

5. Implement measures to reduce discomfort:
• proper positioning to maintain body alignment with the spine straight
• using a firm mattress or a bedboard under the mattress
• avoiding the prone position
• logrolling for the first 48 hours postoperatively to avoid twisting, flexing, or hyperextending the spine
• elevating the head of the bed with the patient's knees slightly flexed or positioned as ordered
• turning the patient every 2 hours
• using a bed cradle over areas of paresthesia
• placing personal items within the patient's reach
• teaching the patient to avoid coughing, sneezing, or straining at stool.

6. *Maintain the patient on bed rest* for 24 to 48 hours or as ordered.

7. Use a trapeze bar if prescribed.

8. When increased activity is ordered, instruct the patient about getting out of bed using arm and abdominal muscles; limiting activity to lying flat in bed, sitting in a straight-backed chair for short intervals, or ambulation; and avoiding slumping or limping.

9. Consult with the doctor for antitussives, decongestants, laxatives, or stool softeners, as needed.

10. Additional individualized interventions: _____
_____
_____

Rationales continued

3. These drugs decrease pain and discomfort. Muscle relaxants (such as diazepam or methocarbamol) decrease muscle spasms; anti-inflammatory agents (such as dexamethasone) reduce edema and inflammation at the operative site.

4. Pain medication is more effective when given before the onset of severe pain. Because the patient is accustomed to chronic back pain, he or she may wait until the pain is severe to request medication, when it may provide less than optimal relief.

5. These measures help alleviate discomfort by reducing stress and strain on the surgical site and by reducing pressure on the spinal nerve roots.

6. Bed rest promotes the healing process.

7. This will assist the patient in moving.

8. Activity must be increased gradually and proper body alignment must be maintained at all times to prevent muscle spasm and spinal trauma. Although slumping and limping may be comfortable at first, they cause fatigue.

9. Use of these medications, as indicated, prevents pressure and associated stress to the surgical site.

10. Rationale: _____
_____
_____

Outcome criteria
Within 1 day of surgery, the patient will:
• verbalize decreased pain, numbness, and tingling
• show relaxed facial expression and body posture.

Within 2 days of surgery, the patient will:
• increase participation in activities (as allowed).

Within 3 days, of surgery, the patient will:
• tolerate prescribed activity.

By the time of discharge, the patient will:
• use correct body mechanics, ambulating well.

Collaborative problem: *Potential paralytic ileus related to anesthesia, medications, retroperitoneal bleeding, and/or injury to the spinal nerve roots*

NURSING PRIORITY: Prevent or promptly detect paralytic ileus.

Interventions

1. *Perform a complete abdominal assessment* every 4 hours for at least the first 48 hours postoperatively, then as needed. Auscultate for bowel sounds and inspect, palpate, and percuss for abdominal distention. Measure abdominal girth if distention is present.

2. Assess for associated signs of ileus, such as nausea, vomiting, and increased back pain.

3. *Document assessment findings and notify the doctor of abdominal distention or absent bowel sounds.* See the "Surgical Intervention" care plan, page 71, for further management.

4. Allow the patient to sit for bowel movements, condition permitting. Otherwise, logroll the patient onto a fracture bedpan.

5. Additional individualized interventions: _____
_____
_____

Rationales

1. Transient paralytic ileus is a common complication after laminectomy. Parasympathetic nervous system and sympathetic nervous system (SNS) innervation of the bowels originates in the lumbosacral spine. SNS stimulation contributes to loss of peristalsis and to decreased contraction of the internal sphincters, resulting in paralytic ileus. Normal bowel sounds (5 to 30/minute) and a soft, tympanic, nondistended abdomen indicate normal bowel functioning.

2. If ileus is present, attempts to take fluids orally will cause nausea and vomiting. Back pain may be increased from increased pressure on the surgical site.

3. These may indicate ileus has developed. Immediate intervention is required. The "Surgical Intervention" care plan provides further details.

4. The sitting position facilitates the patient's ability to expel flatus and stool while allowing for correct spinal alignment.

5. Rationale: _____
_____
_____

Outcome criteria
Within 2 days of surgery, the patient will:
• have bowel sounds
• expel flatus.

By the time of discharge, the patient will:
• have normal bowel sounds.

Collaborative problem: *Potential hypovolemia related to blood loss during the surgical procedure, vascular injury, hemorrhage at the incision site, or retroperitoneal hemorrhage*

NURSING PRIORITY: Prevent or minimize bleeding.

Interventions

1. Implement standard postoperative care related to potential hypovolemia: monitor vital signs, clinical status, hemoglobin and hematocrit values, and surgical drainage. See the "Surgical Intervention" care plan, page 71, for details.

2. Assess for flank pain, tenderness, and paresthesias every 2 to 4 hours for the first 72 hours, then every 8 hours. Compare findings to previous assessments.

3. Notify the doctor of any unusual bleeding or a change in status.

Rationales

1. The "Surgical Intervention" care plan contains detailed general measures applicable to any postoperative patient. This care plan provides additional measures specific to laminectomy.

2. These symptoms may indicate retroperitoneal hemorrhage.

3. Prompt intervention is essential to prevent shock.

(continued)

Interventions continued

4. Additional individualized interventions: _____

_____

_____

Rationales continued

4. Rationale: _____

_____

_____

Outcome criteria

Within 4 hours of surgery, the patient will have:
• no unusual bleeding or change in status.

Within 24 hours of surgery, the patient will have:
• stable vital signs, no signs of bleeding, and normal hemoglobin and hematocrit values.

Nursing diagnosis: *Urinary retention related to supine positioning, pain, anxiety, anesthesia, decreased activity, and/or injury to the spinal nerve roots innervating the bladder*

NURSING PRIORITY: Prevent or minimize urinary retention.

Interventions

1. *Assess for signs and symptoms of urinary retention,* such as absence of voiding within 8 hours of surgery, frequent voiding of small amounts (50 ml or less), complaints of bladder fullness or urgency, and suprapubic distention.

2. Implement standard postoperative care related to intake and output monitoring, measures to facilitate voiding, and catheterization. See "Surgical Intervention" care plan, page 71, for details.

3. Additional individualized interventions: _____

_____

_____

Rationales

1. Transient voiding problems are common after lumbar laminectomy caused by temporary loss of bladder tone from cord edema. Autonomic innervation of the bladder smooth muscle is from the thoracolumbar sympathetic outflow and the sacral parasympathetic outflow. The micturition center is located in the lumbosacral area.

2. These measures are the same for any postoperative patient. They are explained further in the "Surgical Intervention" care plan.

3. Rationale: _____

_____

_____

Outcome criteria

Within 3 hours of surgery, the patient will have:
• adequate urine output
• no complaints of urgency, fullness, or suprapubic discomfort
• no suprapubic distention.

• Within 2 days of surgery, the patient will:
• show balanced intake and output
• void sufficiently at normal intervals.

Nursing diagnosis: *Knowledge deficit related to posthospitalization care*

NURSING PRIORITY: Increase knowledge about home care.

Interventions

1. Provide information on signs and symptoms to report to the doctor:
• change in movement, sensation, color, pain, or temperature in the extremity or extremities
• increased pain at the operative site
• difficulty standing erect
• persistent or severe headache
• drainage from the incision site
• elevated temperature
• loss of bowel or bladder function.

Rationales

1. Knowing what to observe for and report will help minimize postoperative complications.

Interventions *continued*

2. Provide information regarding what postsurgical activity restrictions to observe at home and when it is safe to resume activities:
• restricted driving and riding in cars
• avoidance of pulling, bending, pushing, lifting, twisting, or stair climbing
• avoidance of tub bathing
• avoidance of sexual activity
• avoidance of sitting for prolonged periods of time
• avoidance of heavy work for 6 to 12 weeks after surgery.

3. Provide information about comfort measures, including:
• lying with knees bent
• using stronger muscles, such as arm and leg muscles, to change positions
• shifting weight from one foot to the other when standing for long periods of time
• sitting with knees higher than hips
• using good posture when sitting or standing
• sitting forward with knees crossed and with abdominal muscles tightened to flatten the back (if sitting for long periods of time)
• sleeping in the side-lying position
• sleeping on the back only if the knees are supported with a pillow
• using a heating pad as needed
• using prescribed muscle relaxants or analgesics
• avoiding fatigue and chilling.

4. Provide information about recommended alterations in life-style to reduce back strain:
• sleeping on a firm mattress or a bedboard
• sitting on firm, straight-backed chairs
• using proper body mechanics (for example, bending at the knees rather than at the waist and carrying objects close to the body)
• maintaining good posture
• wearing supportive shoes with moderate heel height
• avoiding lifting heavy objects
• using thoracic and abdominal muscles when lifting objects
• scheduling adequate rest periods
• reducing or stopping any activity that precipitates or aggravates discomfort
• reducing weight after a prescribed, progressive exercise program.

5. Additional individualized interventions: _____
_____
_____

Outcome criteria
By the time of discharge, the patient will:
• list signs and symptoms of complications to report to the doctor
• verbalize understanding of recommended follow-up care at home

Rationales *continued*

2. Patients may hesitate to ask questions about home activities. Providing information about activities that place stress on the spinal column and operative site, before discharge, may prevent postoperative complications.

3. Muscle spasms and pain may persist for a period of time after surgery. Reducing pain, spasms, and stress on the lumbosacral spine will increase comfort.

4. Disk herniation can recur in the same area or at other levels of the lumbosacral spinal cord, particularly if degenerative changes are already present. Reducing back strain lessens the potential for disk herniation.

5. Rationale: _____
_____
_____

• list five ways to help prevent recurrent disk herniation.

Discharge planning
NURSING DISCHARGE CRITERIA
Upon discharge, documentation shows evidence of:
• stable vital signs
• absence of fever
• absence of signs and symptoms of infection
• absence of cardiovascular or pulmonary complications—for example, atelectasis, thrombophlebitis
• white blood cell count and hemoglobin and hematocrit values within normal parameters
• decreasing pain, muscle spasm, numbness, and tingling in lower extremities
• ability to control pain using oral medications
• absence of bowel and bladder dysfunction
• wound drainage within expected parameters
• ability to perform wound care independently or with minimal assistance, using appropriate technique
• ability to tolerate adequate nutritional intake
• knowledge of activity restrictions
• ability to perform activities of daily living and to transfer and ambulate independently or with minimal assistance
• completion of initial physical therapy assessment/instructions
• adequate home support system or referral to home care if indicated by inadequate home support system or inability to perform self-care.

PATIENT/FAMILY DISCHARGE TEACHING CHECKLIST
Document evidence that patient/family demonstrates understanding of:
___ all discharge medications' purpose, dosage, administration schedule, and side effects requiring medical attention (pain medications may be prescribed for continued pain and muscle spasm; laxatives may be prescribed for prevention of constipation)
___ infection prevention
___ signs and symptoms of postoperative infection
___ signs and symptoms of CSF drainage
___ when and how to report signs and symptoms of complications
___ recommended alterations in life-style to prevent recurrence of back problems
___ comfort measures
___ correct body mechanics
___ use of pain-relief measures, including prescribed medications
___ postsurgical activity restrictions
___ date, time, and location of follow-up appointments
___ how to contact the doctor.

DOCUMENTATION CHECKLIST
Using outcome criteria as a guide, document:
___ clinical status on admission
___ significant changes in status, especially regarding motor or sensation deficits, headaches, and weakness
___ results of myelography, spine X-ray, CT scan, electromyelography, MRI, and hemoglobin and hematocrit testing
___ episodes of muscle spasms, severe pain at surgical incision site or in extremities
___ pain-relief measures
___ nutritional intake
___ elimination habits
___ preoperative teaching
___ patient/family teaching
___ discharge planning.

ASSOCIATED CARE PLANS
Ineffective Individual Coping
Knowledge Deficit
Low Back Problems
Pain
Surgical Intervention

REFERENCES
Brodt, Dagman. *Medical-Surgical Nursing and the Nursing Process: A Study and Review Book.* Boston: Little, Brown & Co., 1986.

Carpenito, L. *Nursing Diagnosis: Application to Clinical Practice.* Philadelphia: J.B. Lippincott Co., 1983.

Devoti, A.L. "Lumbar Laminectomy: Diagnosis to Discharge," *Journal of Neurosurgical Nursing* 15(3):140-43, June 1983.

Farrell, Jane. *Illustrated Guide to Orthopedic Nursing*, 3rd ed. Philadelphia: J.B. Lippincott Co., 1986.

Hickey, J.V. *The Clinical Practice of Neurological and Neurosurgical Nursing.* Philadelphia: J.B. Lippincott Co., 1986.

Kneisl, Carol R., and Ames, Sue A. *Adult Health Nursing: A Biopsychosocial Approach.* Menlo Park, Calif: Addison-Wesley Publishing Co., 1986.

Swearingen, Pamela L. *Manual of Nursing Therapeutics: Applying Nursing Diagnoses to Medical Disorders.* Menlo Park, Calif.: Addison-Wesley Publishing Co., 1986.

Ulrich, Susan, et al. *Nursing Care Planning Guides: A Nursing Diagnosis Approach.* Philadelphia: W.B. Saunders Co., 1986.

Myasthenia Gravis

DRG information
DRG 12 [Medical DRG] Degenerative Nervous System
 Disorders.
 Mean LOS = 6.9 days

Introduction
DEFINITION AND TIME FOCUS
Myasthenia gravis (MG) is a chronic debilitating disease resulting from defective transmission of nerve impulses at the neuromuscular junction. Characterized by
remissions and exacerbations of progressive muscle
weakness, MG is estimated to occur in 1 out of 10,000
to 50,000 persons and affects more women than men.
Peak incidence occurs during the 20s and 30s. When
full-blown, MG causes complete dependence.

 MG usually is treated pharmacologically. If symptoms persist despite medication, plasmapheresis may be
used to remove autoantibodies. Thymectomy may be
performed in patients with thymomas or thymic hyperplasia because these abnormal cells may trigger an autoimmune reaction; thymus gland removal decreases
the response to new antigens. This clinical plan focuses on the patient admitted for initial diagnosis and
pharmacologic treatment of MG.

ETIOLOGY/PRECIPITATING FACTORS
• an autoimmune syndrome
• antibodies to acetylcholine receptors, reducing number
of functional receptors on muscle cells
• smoking
• alcohol consumption
• cold weather
• prolonged exposure to sun
• stress
• menstruation
• pregnancy
• influenza

Focused assessment guidelines
NURSING HISTORY (Functional health pattern findings)

Health perception–health management pattern
• may report vague symptoms in the absence of objective findings
• may report or exhibit *weak muscles, especially those involved in chewing, swallowing, and speaking*
• may report or exhibit weakness of facial and extra-
ocular muscles (may also complain of diplopia)
• may report breathlessness (related to respiratory muscle weakness)
• may report *fatigue, with partial improvement of muscle
strength with rest*

• may report or exhibit weakness that is restricted to
specific muscle groups or generalized and symmetrical
or asymmetrical
• may report increased weakness with repetitive use of
the muscle group

Nutritional-metabolic pattern
• may report difficulty in swallowing that worsens
toward the end of meals
• may report weight loss related to decreased intake

Elimination pattern
• may report constipation

Activity-exercise pattern
• may report increasing fatigue with delayed muscle-
strength recovery
• may report sedentary life-style since onset of symptoms

Self-perception–self-concept pattern
• may present self as helpless and unable to complete
any physical tasks
• may present self as tired or depressed

Role-relationship pattern
• may report that emotional stress exacerbates symptoms

Sexuality-reproductive pattern
• may describe impotence

Coping-stress tolerance pattern
• may report coping with symptoms by resting
• may display manifestations of ineffective coping
(for example, frustration, denial, and anger)
• may report that stress worsens symptoms

Value-belief pattern
• may have delayed seeking attention because of the
vagueness and transience of symptoms
• may have another autoimmune disease, such as lupus
erythematosus, rheumatoid arthritis, or thyrotoxicosis,
and may believe that MG symptoms are manifestations
of the other disease

PHYSICAL FINDINGS
General appearance
• expressionless
• fatigued

Pulmonary
• dyspnea
• limited chest excursion
• possibly decreased tidal volume, vital capacity, and inspiratory force

Gastrointestinal
• hypoactive bowel sounds (less common)
• constipation (less common)

Neurologic
• *ptosis* (worsened with upward gaze), squinting, and nystagmus
• attempts to smile look snarllike
• high-pitched, nasal voice
• progressive weakening of voice during conversation
• poorly articulated speech
• normal sensory findings

Musculoskeletal
• difficulty sitting upright, holding head up, and reaching above head
• facial drooping
• mouth hanging open
• dysphasia
• dysphagia

DIAGNOSTIC STUDIES
• arterial blood gas (ABG) levels—may reveal hypoxemia and/or hypercarbia related to ineffective ventilation
• white blood cell count—may reveal leukocytosis related to pulmonary infection
• triiodothyronine and thyroxine—normal levels rule out possible thyroid etiology of muscle weakness; abnormally high or low levels do not exclude MG; a small percentage of MG patients also have thyroid abnormalities
• magnesium—may be low because of protein-calorie malnutrition
• *edrophonium test*—when 2 to 10 mg of edrophonium chloride (Tensilon) is administered I.V., *marked improvement in muscle strength within 60 seconds is diagnostic of MG*
• electromyelogram—shows rapid decreases in evoked muscle action potentials
• Computed tomography scan or chest X-ray—may reveal thymoma or thymic hyperplasia

POTENTIAL COMPLICATIONS
• airway obstruction
• respiratory arrest
• aspiration
• myasthenic crisis
• cholinergic crisis
• corneal abrasion or ulceration

Collaborative problem: *Muscle weakness related to reduced number of acetylcholine receptors*

NURSING PRIORITY: Promote optimal muscle strength.

Interventions

1. *Administer anticholinesterase medication* orally three or four times per day, 30 to 60 minutes before meals, as ordered. Give with milk. Observe for such effects as:
• therapeutic—increased muscle strength
• underdosage—continuation or worsening of myasthenic symptoms (such as weakness, ptosis, dyspnea, nd dysphagia)
• overdosage—cholinergic symptoms (same as myasthenic plus increased salivation; vomiting; diarrhea; fasciculation; and increased pulmonary secretions).

2. *Keep an emergency airway nearby as well as suctioning and ventilation equipment.* Monitor ABG measurements, as ordered.

Rationales

1. Anticholinesterases slow the breakdown of acetylcholine at the neuromuscular junction, promoting better impulse transmission to muscles and facilitating chewing and swallowing during meals. Milk prevents gastric irritation. The margin between therapeutic effects, underdosage, and overdosage is variable. Anticholinesterase need may fluctuate, depending on stresses (such as emotions or infection) and the effects of other therapies.

Underdosage may precipitate myasthenic crisis, an abrupt exacerbation of motor weakness caused by inadequate impulse transmission at the neuromuscular junction. Overdosage may precipitate cholinergic crisis, an abrupt exacerbation of motor weakness caused by prolonged action of acetylcholine at the neuromuscular junction.

Underdosage and overdosage are difficult to differentiate because most of the signs and symptoms are identical. The presence of parasympathetic effects helps to identify the overdosage state but is not absolutely diagnostic. The edrophonium (Tensilon) test may be used to definitively differentiate underdosage from overdosage.

2. Anticholinesterase overdosage or underdosage leads to respiratory muscle weakness that might require artificial ventilation. ABG measurements provide objective evidence of the adequacy of ventilation.

Interventions *continued*

3. *Keep atropine sulfate nearby.*

4. Periodically assess muscle strength by having the patient maintain a steady upward gaze and by assessing the volume of fluid the patient can drink through a straw.

5. Keep a daily log of periods of fatigue and times of increased and decreased muscle strength.

6. Contact the doctor if the patient says that more or less medication is needed.

7. Administer such medications as succinylcholine and pancuronium, with caution, as ordered.

8. Observe for muscle weakness after the administration of aminoglycoside antibiotics or antiarrhythmic medications, especially quinidine and procainamide.

9. Additional individualized interventions: _____
_____
_____

Rationales *continued*

3. Atropine sulfate is the antidote for anticholinesterase overdosage (cholinergic crisis).

4. MG commonly affects eye muscles the most. After 1 minute of upward gazing, progressive drooping of eyelids may occur. Drinking through a straw requires repetitive use of the facial and swallowing muscles.

5. This information helps the doctor adjust the medication dosage and schedule it for optimal patient benefit.

6. MG patients on long-term medication therapy often can detect over- or underdosage before clinical signs appear.

7. MG patients are more sensitive to the effects of curariform drugs.

8. MG patients are sensitive to the neuromuscular blocking effects of the aminoglycosides and Class Ia antiarrhythmics.

9. Rationale: _____
_____
_____

Outcome criteria

Within 12 hours of admission, the patient will show:
• muscle strength adequate to support ventilation, manifested by pH > 7.35 and $PaCO_2$ < 45 mm Hg.

Within 2 days of admission, the patient will show:
• improved muscle strength and the ability to turn self in bed and assist with transfer to chair.

Collaborative problem: *Potential aspiration related to impaired swallowing*

NURSING PRIORITY: Prevent aspiration.

Interventions

1. *Plan mealtimes to coincide with peak anticholinesterase effects.*

2. Ask the patient for self-evaluation of swallowing ability, and order foods of appropriate consistency: liquid, pureed, soft, or regular. Give the patient nothing by mouth if swallowing is severely impaired.

3. Provide rest periods during meals.

4. Have suctioning equipment at the patient's bedside. Stay with the patient during meals.

5. Teach the patient and family what steps to take if choking or aspiration occurs, such as back blows, abdominal thrusts, and nasotracheal suction.

Rationales

1. Oral anticholinesterase medications achieve full effect within 60 minutes of administration. The duration of action ranges from 2 to 8 hours. The potential for aspiration increases when anticholinesterase levels are low.

2. Subjective evaluation of swallowing is generally accurate. This also allows the patient to participate in decision making, thus keeping a sense of control.

3. Chewing and swallowing make repetitive use of the same muscle groups.

4. Death commonly results from respiratory complications secondary to aspiration.

5. Back blows and abdominal thrusts loosen food obstructing the airway. Suctioning stimulates coughing and removes sputum and debris.

(continued)

Interventions *continued*

6. Additional individualized interventions: _____
_____
_____

Rationales *continued*

6. Rationale: _____
_____

Outcome criteria

Throughout the period of hospitalization, the patient:
• will not aspirate.

By the time of the patient's discharge, the family:
• will demonstrate airway clearance procedures.

Nursing diagnosis: *Activity intolerance related to muscle fatigue*

NURSING PRIORITY: Minimize fatigue and promote a tolerable level of activity.

Interventions

1. *Identify sources of excess energy consumption,* such as frequent telephone conversations, reading, watching television, or chewing hard or tough food.

2. *Space bathing, grooming, and other activities throughout the day to avoid fatigue.*

3. Rearrange the environment to keep frequently used items close by.

4. Plan a rest period before each meal. Keep meals small.

5. Additional individualized interventions: _____
_____
_____

Rationales

1. Minimizing unnecessary actions helps conserve strength.

2. Muscles weaken rapidly when used repetitively. Several short rest periods may be more effective in restoring muscle strength than one longer rest period.

3. Keeping frequently used items within easy reach minimizes unnecessary muscle use.

4. The muscles used in chewing and swallowing weaken quickly.

5. Rationale: _____
_____

Outcome criteria

Within 2 days of admission, the patient will:
• show little or no fatigue.

Within 5 days of admission, the patient will:
• be able to perform activities of daily living (ADLs) without assistance.

Nursing diagnosis: *Ineffective airway clearance related to decreased inspiratory force and increased secretion production*

NURSING PRIORITY: Maintain a patent airway.

Interventions

1. Demonstrate the cascade cough by having the patient take a deep breath, cough three or four times after the same inhalation, and repeat several times until the cough is productive.

2. Encourage the patient not to suppress coughs.

Rationales

1. A deep breath followed by a single long, harsh cough is ineffective in airway clearance because it frequently causes bronchospasm. The cascade cough mimics the normal cough. It is effective because it moves sputum farther up the bronchial tree with each successive cough.

2. Because of pain or unpleasant sensations, the patient may try to stop the cough response to airway irritation.

Interventions *continued*

3. Perform chest physiotherapy (CPT) and suction every 2 to 4 hours, as needed. Evaluate lung sounds to judge efficacy.

4. Additional individualized interventions: _____
_____
_____

Outcome criteria
Within 12 hours of admission, the patient will:
• have arterial PO_2 > 50 mm Hg.
Within 5 days of admission, the patient will:
• show clearing or absence of rhonchi

Rationales *continued*

3. CPT mechanically loosens secretions; suctioning helps remove them. Effective CPT clears secretions.

4. Rationale: _____
_____
_____

• expectorate any sputum produced
• have a temperature under 101.3° F. (38.5° C.).

Nursing diagnosis: *Ineffective breathing pattern related to muscle fatigue*

NURSING PRIORITY: Promote adequate ventilation.

Interventions

1. *Monitor and document the respiratory rate and depth every 2 hours.* Observe for changes.

2. *Measure vital capacity, tidal volume, and inspiratory force before and 1 hour after administration of anticholinesterase medications.* Alert the doctor if the patient's vital capacity falls below 10 ml/kg, if tidal volume falls below 5 ml/kg, or if inspiratory force falls below −20 cmH_2O or a pattern of decreasing values occurs.

3. Additional individualized interventions: _____
_____
_____

Rationales

1. Changes in rate and depth are clues to impending respiratory muscle failure.

2. A therapeutic dose of anticholinesterase medication results in increased vital capacity, tidal volume, and inspiratory force. Both underdosage and overdosage result in muscle weakness, which is reflected as decreased vital capacity, tidal volume, and inspiratory force. Values that do not improve with I.V. administration of an anticholinesterase indicate the need for intubation and mechanical ventilation.

3. Rationale: _____
_____
_____

Outcome criteria
Within 12 hours of admission, the patient will have:
• no dyspnea
• arterial PCO_2 < 50 mm Hg
• arterial PO_2 > 50 mm Hg
• a respiratory rate < 30/minute.

Within 24 hours of admission, the patient will have:
• a regular breathing pattern
• a vital capacity > 15 ml/kg
• a tidal volume > 5 ml/kg
• an inspiratory force > −20 cmH_2O.

Nursing diagnosis: *Impaired verbal communication related to fatigue of facial and respiratory muscles*

NURSING PRIORITY: Establish effective communication.

Interventions

1. Avoid frequent or long conversations with the patient.

2. Provide alternate methods of communication, such as paper and pencil or a word board.

Rationales

1. Facial and respiratory muscles are easily fatigued.

2. Alternate methods allow communication without using facial and respiratory muscles.

(continued)

Interventions *continued*

3. Additional individualized interventions: _____

_____

_____

Rationales *continued*

3. Rationale: _____

_____

_____

Outcome criterion
Within 24 hours of admission, the patient will:
• communicate needs.

Nursing diagnosis: *Nutritional deficit related to decreased oral intake*

NURSING PRIORITY: Maintain adequate oral nutrition.

Interventions

1. Perform a nutritional assessment on admission including:
• height and weight
• midarm circumference measurement
• triceps skin-fold measurement
• arm muscle circumference calculation
• creatinine height index.

2. Provide a diet with the proper balance of protein, fat, carbohydrate, and calories.

3. Serve the main meal in the morning.

4. Provide liquids in a cup.

5. Have the patient sit erect during meals.

6. Record all food and nutritional supplements consumed. Evaluate protein, calorie, vitamin, and mineral intake.

7. Consult with a dietitian about nutritional supplements, tube feedings, and total parenteral nutrition, if indicated.

8. Additional individualized interventions: _____

_____

_____

Rationales

1. These parameters indicate nutritional status, which affects muscle performance.

2. A balanced diet meets nutritional needs while keeping the respiratory quotient at a normal level (0.8). (The respiratory quotient [RQ]—the ratio of carbon dioxide [CO_2] produced to oxygen consumed during metabolism—indicates the patient's ability to increase ventilation to remove excess CO_2 produced by a large carbohydrate intake. If RQ is abnormal, the work load caused by this increased CO_2 production may precipitate respiratory failure.)

3. The muscles used for chewing are stronger in the morning.

4. It is difficult to drink with a straw if facial muscles are weak.

5. Sitting erect facilitates the swallowing reflex.

6. This record of consumption provides the basis for dietary assessment; its evaluation forms the basis for further planning.

7. The dietitian's expertise helps meet the MG patient's special nutritional needs.

8. Rationale: _____

_____

_____

Outcome criteria
Within 2 days of admission, the patient will:
• have arterial PCO_2 levels within normal limits.

Within 5 days of admission, the patient will:
• have no nontherapeutic weight loss > 10% of baseline body weight.

Nursing diagnosis: *Knowledge deficit related to required life-style adjustments and new medications*

NURSING PRIORITY: Provide the knowledge needed for self-care.

Interventions

1. *Teach the patient and family about the disease process and its implications.* Find out what the doctor has stated, and reinforce that explanation. Clarify misconceptions. Stress the fluctuating nature of MG and the value of informed self-care.

2. *Instruct about factors that may precipitate crisis:* stress, infection, smoking, alcohol, exposure to cold or heat, pregnancy, and medication overdosage or underdosage.

3. *Teach the patient and family signs and symptoms of crises* that may require notifying the doctor or nurse, including: nausea, vomiting, diarrhea, abnormal sweating, increased salivation, irregular or slow heartbeat, muscle weakness, or severe abdominal pain.

4. *Teach the patient about medications,* particularly:
• the importance of following the schedule exactly if the patient is to be discharged on a fixed anticholinesterase schedule
• the parameters within which the patient may adjust the dosage if following an on-demand anticholinesterase schedule
• signs of overdosage and underdosage
• the significance of alterations in GI function (such as nausea, cramping, diarrhea, or constipation)
• the need to check with the doctor before taking any additional medications, including over-the-counter medications.

5. Demonstrate how to keep a medication response log.

6. Provide information about how to obtain a Medic Alert bracelet or pendant.

7. Teach ways to cope with decreased activity tolerance (obtain specifics from the Myasthenia Gravis Foundation or consult Rudy [1984]), including the following:
• conserving energy (for example, by using clothing that is easy to put on on)
• spacing activities
• instituting safety precautions (such as hand rails in the tub or by the commode).

Rationales

1. Because of its chronicity, MG requires a well-informed, motivated patient and family for best management. The doctor's initial explanation may have been "blocked" or misinterpreted because of anxiety. Congruent explanations from the doctor and nurse increase confidence in caregivers.

2. The patient and family must be aware of risk factors in order to avoid them. Involving the patient in self-management may help restore a sense of control and provide reassurance that MG does not affect intellectual capacity.

3. The signs and symptoms of myasthenic and cholinergic crises are similar. Both underdosage and overdosage of anticholinesterases can cause life-threatening respiratory insufficiency.

4. A knowledgeable, confident patient and family are crucial to successful management of MG. GI dysfunction may result from long-term anticholinesterase therapy or may represent anticholinesterase toxicity. If a doctor rules out the latter, the patient may be helped by small meals, altered fluid intake, antiemetics, or other interventions.
   Many medications, such as narcotics, sedatives, quinidine, and aminoglycoside antibiotics, interfere with neuromuscular transmission.

5. The medication response log helps the doctor adjust medication dosages if needed.

6. In an emergency, it is essential that those providing care know the patient's name, diagnosis, current medication dosages, and the doctor's name and number.

7. Learning methods to cope with this chronic disease may reduce frustration, decrease exacerbations, and restore self-esteem.

(continued)

Interventions *continued*

8. Provide the following address:
The Myasthenia Gravis Foundation
15 East 26th Street
New York, NY 10010.

9. Additional individualized interventions: _____

_____

_____

Outcome criteria
Within 5 days of admission, the patient will:
• list signs and symptoms that should be reported to the doctor or nurse promptly
• know how to order a Medic Alert bracelet or pendant
• begin maintaining a medication response log.

Rationales *continued*

8. The Myasthenia Gravis Foundation provides direct services to patients and families.

9. Rationale: _____

_____

_____

By the time of discharge, the patient will:
• list four factors that may precipitate a crisis
• verbalize intent to follow the medication schedule exactly as prescribed
• verbalize ways to cope with decreased activity tolerance.

Discharge planning
NURSING DISCHARGE CRITERIA
Upon discharge, documentation shows evidence of:
• ABG levels within normal limits
• absence of fever
• absence of airway-compromising dysphagia for at least 48 hours
• ability to tolerate adequate nutritional intake
• absence of cardiovascular and pulmonary complications
• ability to tolerate at least a minimum activity level
• ability to perform ADLs independently or with minimal assistance
• ability to understand and maintain medication response log
• adequate home support
• referral to home care or nursing home if indicated by progression of disease, lack of availability of home support, and potential for needing emergency care.

Additional discharge planning information: Because of the age-group and sex that MG usually strikes and the chronicity of the illness, it is essential that the patient's home situation be carefully assessed. In many cases there are considerable problems associated with child care, finances, and ability to cope with the alteration in living pattern. The mid- and end-stage disease patients often need nursing home placement or around-the-clock home care assistance if they can afford it. A referral to social service should be expected with every MG patient.

PATIENT/FAMILY DISCHARGE TEACHING CHECKLIST
Document evidence that patient/family demonstrates understanding of:
__ nature of disease and implications
__ signs and symptoms of myasthenic and cholinergic crises
__ activity recommendations/limitations
__ airway clearance procedures
__ for all discharge medications: purpose, dosage, administration schedule, and side effects requiring medical attention (usual discharge medications include an anticholinesterase)
__ community resource and support groups
__ how and where to obtain an emergency identification (Medic Alert) card or bracelet
__ when and how to access the emergency medical system
__ date, time, and location of follow-up appointments
__ how to contact doctor.

DOCUMENTATION CHECKLIST
Using outcome criteria as a guide, document:
__ clinical status on admission
__ significant changes in status
__ responses to medications
__ periods of fatigue or increased weakness
__ swallowing ability
__ respiratory parameters before and after medication administration
__ activity tolerance
__ patient/family teaching
__ discharge planning.

ASSOCIATED CARE PLANS
Grief/Grieving
Ineffective Family Coping
Ineffective Individual Coping
Knowledge Deficit
Total Parenteral Nutrition

REFERENCES

Blazey, M.E., et al. "Nutritional Assessment of Protein Status," *Dimensions of Critical Care Nursing* 5(6):328-32, November/December 1986.

Hickey, Joanne V. *The Clinical Practice of Neurological and Neurosurgical Nursing,* 2nd ed. Philadelphia: J.B. Lippincott Co., 1985.

Kinney, A.B., and Gokey, M.J. "Myasthenia Gravis," in *Nursing: Body, Mind, Spirit,* 2nd ed. Edited by Kenner, C.V., et al. Boston: Little, Brown & Co., 1985.

Mitchell, Pamela, et al. *Neurological Assessment and Nursing Practice.* New York: Appleton & Lange, 1983.

Noroian, E.L. "Myasthenia Gravis: A Nursing Perspective," *Journal of Neuroscience Nursing* 18(2):74-80, April 1986.

Piper, B.F. "Fatigue," in *Pathophysiological Phenomena in Nursing: Human Response to Illness.* Edited by Carrieri, Virginia K., et al. Philadelphia: W.B. Saunders Co., 1986.

Rowland, L.P. "Diseases of Chemical Transmission at the Nerve-Muscle Synapse: Myasthenia Gravis and Related Syndromes," in *Principles of Neural Science,* 2nd ed. Edited by Kandel, E.R., and Schwartz, J.H. New York: Elsevier, 1985.

Rudy, Ellen B. *Advanced Neurological and Neurosurgical Nursing.* St. Louis: C.V. Mosby Co., 1984.

Traver, G.A. "Ineffective Airway Clearance: Physiology and Clinical Application," *Dimensions of Critical Care Nursing* 4(4):198-208, July/August 1985.

Multiple Sclerosis

DRG information

DRG 13 [Medical DRG] Multiple Sclerosis and
Cerebellar Ataxia.
Mean LOS = 7.2 days

Additional DRG information: Patients with multiple sclerosis (MS) are most often admitted to an acute care setting for *complications,* such as pneumonia or bowel or bladder dysfunction. However, in the past 5 years, some neurologists have been admitting MS patients for trials of various I.V. medications used to counteract MS symptoms. Only in these rare circumstances would MS be the principal diagnosis. More commonly, an MS patient would be diagnosed with another illness, and the DRG would be one related to the principal diagnosis.

Introduction

DEFINITION AND TIME FOCUS

MS is a relatively common inflammatory, degenerative, chronic disease of the central nervous system (CNS). Approximately 500,000 cases occur in the United States each year. The disease is characterized by recurrent inflammatory reactions and the formation of sclerotic plaques throughout the CNS, interfering with normal impulse conduction and eventually causing irreversible neurologic deficits. Exacerbations and remissions are common, with some symptoms appearing only briefly or intermittently. The prognosis is variable: approximately one third of patients experience minimal disability and can continue most normal activities; the remaining two thirds have moderate to severe limitations and are susceptible to complications associated with relative or absolute immobility. MS affects women about five times as frequently as men and most often is diagnosed when the patient is aged 20 to 40. This clinical plan focuses on the MS patient admitted for diagnosis or management during an acute episode of the disease.

ETIOLOGY/PRECIPITATING FACTORS

Theories under study include:
• nutritional deficiencies
• excessive dietary animal fat
• heavy metal poisoning
• vascular disturbances
• acute viral infection
• viruses that invade the host early in life but remain dormant in the body for years before symptoms develop (results of slow-virus research studies bear some resemblance to the effects of MS)
• allergic or CNS hypersensitivity response to a common virus (90% of MS patients have high concentrations of measles antibodies in cerebrospinal fluid [CSF])
• immunologic disorder, particularly of cell-mediated immunity
• autoimmune response (immune cells are found in the demyelinated plaques)
• genetic and environmental predisposition
• stress, trauma, pregnancy, or fever (may precipitate incidence or exacerbation).

Focused assessment guidelines

NURSING HISTORY (Functional health pattern findings)

Health perception–health management pattern
• onset generally between ages 20 and 40
• typically reports a history of *symptom-recovery cycles:* mild, transient symptoms occurring in one body part, then subsiding, with patient continuing to see self as healthy until appearance of symptoms in another part of body
• may report that symptom-recovery cycles have been increasing in frequency and severity
• may report a history of *remission-exacerbation cycles* of symptoms

Nutritional-metabolic pattern
• typically describes *difficulty chewing food*
• may report exhaustion from effort of eating
• may report choking (dysphagia) episodes (from poor muscle control)

Elimination pattern
• *may report constipation, impaction, or incontinence* (related to weakness or spasticity of anal sphincter)
• *may report urgency, frequency, or retention* (from loss of bladder sphincter control)

Activity-exercise pattern
• *may report spasticity and weakness of limbs*
• *may report weakness and fatigue with activity*

Sleep-rest pattern
• initially, reports that rest reduces symptoms
• later, may report that spasticity interrupts sleep

Cognitive-perceptual pattern
• describes *diplopia and (commonly) eye pain*
• may exhibit mentation disorders, such as impaired judgment and failure to comprehend or conceptualize

Self-perception–self-concept pattern
• may discuss feelings of diminished self-worth as job performance becomes impaired (psychosocial disequilibrium)
• family may report patient emotional lability

Role-relationship pattern
• may relate increased dependence on others as disease progresses

Sexuality-reproductive pattern
• if male, may report occasional impotence
• if female, may report alterations in vaginal sensation

Coping-stress tolerance pattern
• may report difficulty adjusting to disease process if diagnosed in early to middle adult life (prime productive years)
• may report usual coping mechanisms effective, if in remission phase early in disease process, or ineffective, if exacerbation cycles become more frequent and symptoms more disabling

Value-belief pattern
• may have ignored mild, transient symptoms (denial), only to seek medical attention later when recurring symptoms became more severe

PHYSICAL FINDINGS
Gastrointestinal
• *impaction or incontinence*

Neurologic
• classic triad: *nystagmus, intention tremors, and scanning (slow, monotonous, slurred) speech* (Charcot's triad)
• loss of coordination
• ataxia
• paralysis
• cranial nerve impairment
  □ evidence of *optic neuritis with visual field deficits*
  □ presence of blind spot
  □ nystagmus (as noted above)
  □ dysarthria
  □ scanning speech (as noted above)
  □ dysphagia
  □ *loss of facial muscle control*
• Lhermittes's sign—sudden "shock wave" down the body on forward neck flexion
• *hyperreflexic deep tendon reflexes*

• sensory loss, including paresthesia
• decreased vibratory sensation
• decreased or absent proprioception

Musculoskeletal
• spasticity
• *reduced mobility*
• contractures (related to immobility)

Genitourinary
• *incontinence*

Integumentary
• reddened pressure points, skin breakdown (effects of immobility)

DIAGNOSTIC STUDIES
• *electrophoresis—elevated oligoclonal banding of immunoglobulin G in 90% of patients* (contributes evidence for differential diagnosis of MS)
• hematology—gamma globulin levels abnormally high, reflecting increased immune system activity
• *evoked response potentials—delayed response after adequate stimulus of visual, auditory, or somatosensory mechanism* suggests MS
• *computed tomography (CT) scan—may indicate lesion of CNS white matter, atrophy, or ventricular enlargement*
• lumbar puncture—increased protein and white blood cells in CSF
• core hyperthermia—use as a diagnostic procedure is controversial because results may resemble symptoms of other CNS diseases; increasing body core temperature to 102° F. (38.9° C.) causes marginal conduction to become incomplete or blocked; besides being diagnostically inconclusive, the test presents some risk to the patient

POTENTIAL COMPLICATIONS
(associated with immobility)
• phlebitis
• urinary tract infection
• respiratory tract infection
• thromboembolic phenomena

Nursing diagnosis: *Impaired physical mobility related to disease process (demyelinization)*

NURSING PRIORITIES: (a) Preserve maximum physical functioning and (b) protect from effects of immobility.

Interventions	Rationales
1. *Provide rest; prevent fatigue.*	1. Rest seems to alleviate symptoms; fatigue may worsen symptoms.

(continued)

Interventions *continued*

2. *Begin a physical therapy program, as ordered:*
• active and passive range-of-motion exercises
• limb splints
• gait training
• leg weights and heavy shoes for balance during weight bearing
• swimming.

3. *Medicate, as ordered, to control pain and muscle spasm.* Observe precautions and watch for side effects, including:
• diazepam (Valium)—observe for increased fatigue, sedation, confusion, or depression
• dantrolene sodium (Dantrium)—monitor liver function studies (serum glutamic-oxaloacetic transaminase and serum glutamic-pyruvic transaminase), as ordered, and observe for jaundice or other signs of liver damage as well as for drowsiness or increased weakness
• baclofen (Lioresal)—observe for increased fatigue, drowsiness, or dizziness.

4. *Assess lung sounds* at least every 8 hours. Report crackles, rhonchi, decreased breath sounds, or other abnormal findings promptly. Encourage use of the incentive spirometer, as ordered, or other pulmonary hygiene measures.

5. Teach the patient the need for specific mobility aids, such as a cane, a walker, crutches, or a wheelchair.

6. *Instruct the patient in safety measures* to prevent injury related to sensory loss:
• use of a thermometer to test water temperature
• use of gloves in inclement weather
• use of an eye patch to alleviate eye disturbances
• use of safe kitchen utensils to prevent burns.

7. *Frequently assess skin and bony prominences for pressure signs.* Reposition the patient to alleviate pressure effects. Teach the patient and family how to assess skin and minimize pressure.

8. *Minimize the cardiovascular effects of immobility,* using the following measures:
• Use antiembolism stockings.
• Teach leg exercises to increase venous return.
• Check indices of peripheral circulation—pulses, color, temperature, sensation, mobility, and capillary refill time.
• Note dependent edema.

Rationales *continued*

2. Exercising prevents joint contractures and improves muscle tone. Circulation improves with musculoskeletal activities. A sense of achievement can be attained as exercise endurance increases.

3. Medications (antidepressants, analgesics, and antispasmotics) relax the patient by relieving pain and spasm, promoting comfort, and permitting physical activity. Side effects of these medications may make their benefits of questionable value in some MS patients. Reduced muscle tone may contribute to increased weakness and risk of injury.

4. Immobility contributes to stasis of lung secretions, predisposing MS patients to development of infections and other complications related to inadequate chest excursion.

5. Teaching the patient the importance of aids helps facilitate adjustment to using them. Although adjustment to them may be difficult, aids can prevent injury and offer the patient a sense of security while mobile.

6. Impaired sensory perception may cause injury. Especially significant is the effect of temperature changes: increased core temperature has the potential of accentuating the MS symptoms by blocking impulse conduction.

7. Frequent assessment and treatment of pressure areas is necessary because immobility predisposes the patient to circulatory impairment and resultant skin breakdown. Frequent position changes redistribute pressure. Teaching the patient and family may avert postdischarge problems.

8. Immobility influences all systems. Increasing venous return may reduce venous stasis and the risk of thromboembolism. Identifying arterial insufficiency helps ensure peripheral oxygenation. Edema suggests decreased peripheral circulation and the need for prompt limb elevation.

Interventions *continued*

9. Medicate, as ordered, with the following medications, observing for untoward effects and providing appropriate patient teaching:

• adrenocorticotropic hormone or corticosteroids—observe for excessive weight gain and signs of bleeding, infection, or gastric distress. Caution the patient not to stop taking the medication abruptly without consulting the doctor.

• immunosuppressant drugs: Caution the patient about the increased risk of infection, and review infection signs and symptoms and precautionary measures with the patient.

10. Use stress reduction techniques, such as deep breathing, progressive relaxation, or visualization, when appropriate.

11. Additional individualized interventions: _____

_____

_____

Rationales *continued*

9. Numerous medical therapies are under investigation. Medication therapy varies widely, depending on patient status and doctor preference.

• These drugs may reduce the length of exacerbations. Sudden withdrawal from corticosteroids may precipitate adrenal insufficiency.

• Immunosuppressants are still of questionable value for long-term MS therapy but may offer longer-lasting effects than corticosteroids.

10. Stress may precipitate an acute episode.

11. Rationale: _____

_____

_____

Outcome criteria

Within 3 days of admission, the patient will:
• recognize own need for rest
• determine individual need for medication
• show no evidence of skin breakdown or other effects of immobility.

Within 5 days of admission, the patient will:
• recognize the need for mobility assistance
• list three safety measures
• function at or above admission level.

Nursing diagnosis: *Altered bowel and bladder function* related to disease process (demyelinization)*

NURSING PRIORITY: Maintain bowel and bladder function.

Interventions

1. *Assess and record the patient's pattern of bowel and bladder function. Identify any dysfunctional pattern.*

2. *Evaluate dietary habits.* Determine the need for high-fiber, high-bulk foods.

3. *Increase and record fluid intake* as appropriate.

4. *Initiate a bowel or bladder program*, as appropriate—for example, manual extraction, stimulation, Credé's maneuver, or an indwelling (Foley) catheter. Consult protocols for rehabilitation and bowel or bladder retraining.

Rationales

1. MS may cause elimination problems from decreased peristalsis. Evaluation of the patient's status allows for decision making about an elimination program; for example, is the elimination problem constipation or retention?

2. A regulated diet high in fiber and bulk promotes normal peristalsis to move bowel contents through the alimentary canal.

3. Increased fluid intake facilitates absorption and promotes peristalsis.

4. Mechanical or manual assistance may be necessary to overcome the effects of demyelinization on elimination. Protocols vary among institutions.

(continued)

*non-NANDA diagnosis

Interventions *continued*

5. Medicate, as ordered, by providing laxatives, stool softeners, and propantheline bromide (Pro-Banthine).

6. Prevent exposure to infection. If infection is present, treat it vigorously.

7. *Teach the patient a bowel and bladder program* for elimination management at home, suggesting the following guidelines:
• Establish regular voiding times.
• Utilize Credé's maneuver.
• Restrict fluids at night or before trips.
• Observe for signs of infection.
• Utilize suppositories, as ordered.
• Maintain adequate fluid and fiber intake.
• Monitor times and consistency of bowel movements.

8. Additional individualized intervention: _____
_____
_____

Outcome criteria
Within 5 days of admission, the patient will:
• comply with dietary recommendations

Rationales *continued*

5. Medication may be required to adjust bowel absorption of metabolites and to reduce bowel spasticity problems.

6. The patient with MS is at increased risk for recurring infection, especially if urinary retention is evident. (Urinary stasis is a precursor to urinary tract infection.)

7. In many cases, the patient can manage an effective elimination regimen at home; when possible, this reestablishes a sense of independence and control.

8. Rationale: _____
_____
_____

• have satisfactory bowel and bladder elimination restored
• list measures to maintain effective elimination.

Nursing diagnosis: *Potential sexual dysfunction related to fatigue, decreased sensation, muscle spasm, and/or urinary incontinence*

NURSING PRIORITIES: (a) Promote healthy sexual identity and (b) teach ways to minimize the effects of disease on sexual functioning.

Interventions

1. *Assess the effects of MS on the patient's sexual function.* During the admission interview, ask the patient how the disease has affected his or her sexual performance.

2. *Encourage the patient and spouse or partner to share sexual concerns.* Offer to be available as a resource, or refer the couple to another health professional.

3. *Offer specific suggestions* for identified problems, such as teaching the patient to:
• Initiate sexual activity when energy levels are highest.
• Try different positions (for example, side-lying) if muscle spasm makes leg abduction difficult or if weakness limits activity.

Rationales

1. MS is extremely variable in its course and effects. The patient may be hesitant to broach the subject of sexuality. Gentle, matter-of-fact questioning during routine assessment provides the patient an opportunity to voice concerns.

2. Even couples who have no difficulty communicating in most areas may find it hard to verbalize feelings related to sexuality. Health professionals who are comfortable discussing sexual issues may be able to facilitate dialogue in a nonthreatening way.

3. Patients need concrete information on specific problems.
• Fatigue contributes to decreased libido.

• Muscle spasms commonly affect hip abductor and adductor muscles. Some sexual positions require less energy expenditure.

Interventions *continued*

• Empty the bladder before sexual activity. Pad the bedding, as necessary, to protect against wetness.

• Try oral or manual stimulation if intercourse is difficult or unsatisfying.

4. Encourage expressions of affection between patient and partner. If ongoing dysfunction has created anxiety about sexual encounters, suggest affectionate "play" sessions without intercourse as the goal.

5. Emphasize the importance of discussing birth control and family planning with a doctor.

6. Additional individualized interventions: _____
_____
_____

Rationales *continued*

• Urinary incontinence is more common during intercourse or masturbation.

• The MS patient may find intercourse less satisfying than before because decreased sensation makes orgasm more difficult to achieve.

4. Sexuality involves more than the act of coitus. Emphasis on playful, affectionate exchanges between partners helps reduce anxiety, promotes trust and improves the patient's body image and self-esteem.

5. Use of an intrauterine device may be contraindicated in a female patient with MS because decreased sensation may cause complications to go undetected. Birth control pills may exacerbate MS symptoms. The familial tendency to develop MS and lack of prenatal screening for the disease may be significant factors for the patient considering having a child because women of childbearing age are the primary victims of the disease.

6. Rationale: _____
_____
_____

Outcome criteria

During the admission interview, the patient will:
• identify sexual concerns.

Throughout the period of hospitalization, the patient will:
• initiate affection, especially with partner.

By the time of discharge, the patient will:
• list three measures to minimize sexual dysfunction.

Nursing diagnosis: *Disturbed self-concept: body image, self-esteem, role performance, related to progressive, debilitating effects of disease*

NURSING PRIORITY: Promote a healthy self-image and a realistic acceptance of limitations.

Interventions

1. *Encourage the patient to participate in all decisions* related to care planning. Discourage overdependent behavior patterns. Help the patient set goals and work toward them.

2. *Facilitate the expression of feelings* related to losses. Avoid overly cheerful responses while maintaining a positive outlook. See the "Grief/Grieving" and "Ineffective Individual Coping" care plans, pages 41 and 51.

Rationales

1. Active participation fosters a sense of control and increases self-esteem. Patients with MS experience loss of control in many areas; encouraging responsibility for self-care helps them maintain dignity and independence. Goal setting aids in maintaining hope.

2. The patient suffering from a chronic debilitating disease may see each hospitalization as a further step in disease progression and loss of control. Healthy grieving is a realistic response to multiple losses and a normal part of the process of acceptance. Overly cheerful responses indicate a lack of understanding of the profound changes MS entails for the patient. Empathy and realistic optimism, in contrast, show respect for the patient. The general care plans noted suggest other interventions that may be helpful for patients with MS.

(continued)

Interventions *continued*

3. Work with the family to promote maximal patient participation in familiar family roles and rituals or to identify new family roles of value for the patient, such as humorist, correspondent, or arbitrator.

4. During care activities, encourage the patient to touch affected body parts, perform self-lifting activities as much as possible, and participate in grooming and wardrobe selection.

5. *Provide recognition for goals achieved.* Acknowledge evidence of inner strengths and growth as well as external achievements; for example, notice difficult emotional issues the patient has dealt with positively as well as activity goals achieved.

6. Additional individualized interventions: _____

_____

_____

Rationales *continued*

3. Disease progression and an increasing sense of helplessness are compounded by the inability to fulfill familiar family roles. Encouraging family recognition and support of these roles minimizes role-loss distress. Physical disability may nevertheless allow assumption of new roles within the family, thus helping the patient maintain a sense of self-worth.

4. Acceptance of altered body image and function is essential to a healthy self-concept. Touching one's body and becoming familiar with its limitations is the first step toward acceptance. Grooming promotes a positive self-concept.

5. Chronic progressive disease may narrow a patient's world view severely. Recognition of struggles and achievements decreases the sense of isolation and aloneness. Patients can teach nurses much that may help them care for other patients. Acknowledgment of this gift may help provide a sense of meaning in difficult times and extend the patient's outlook toward others.

6. Rationale: _____

_____

_____

Outcome criteria

Throughout the period of hospitalization, the patient will:
• participate actively in care planning
• verbalize feelings related to losses

• participate in family activities to the extent possible
• show interest in appearance and grooming
• initiate independent activities
• show an interest in others.

Nursing diagnosis: *Altered family processes related to progressive, debilitating effects of disease on family members and resultant alteration in role-related behavior patterns*

NURSING PRIORITY: Maintain family integrity while facilitating a healthy adjustment to necessary role changes.

Interventions

1. *Assess the family system* by observing family members' interaction with the patient, encouraging family participation in care activities, and talking with family members individually or as a group about changes brought about by the disease. See the "Ineffective Family Coping" care plan, page 47.

2. Encourage family members to "trade off" in the care provision role, as necessary.

Rationales

1. Chronic diseases can have a devastating effect on families as well as on affected individuals. As the primary support system for most patients, families must be supported and considered in care planning. Open discussion among family members facilitates mutual supportiveness and understanding. The care plan noted provides interventions especially helpful for families in (or at risk for) crisis.

2. As the disease progresses, the patient becomes more dependent on others for care. Sharing care responsibilities helps prevent burnout, provides variety in care routines, and facilitates mutual understanding.

Interventions *continued*

3. Help the family understand and accept mental changes, if present.

4. Promote healthy habits for family members: urge adequate rest, dietary intake, exercise, and relaxation.

5. Help the family plan changes in the home environment to facilitate care for the patient: structural changes (ramps, rails); rearrangement of furnishings and supplies to allow easy patient access; transportation/care arrangements through a social services referral; and the availability of special supplies for incontinence.

6. Additional individualized interventions: _____
_____
_____

Outcome criteria
By the time of discharge, family members will:
• appear healthy and well rested

Rationales *continued*

3. From 40% to 60% of MS patients exhibit alterations in mental function, ranging from inattention and euphoria (early in the disease) to irritability, depression, disorientation, and loss of memory (later in the disease). Understanding that these symptoms are part of the disease process and not intentional helps minimize distress for both patient and family.

4. Adequate sleep, food, exercise, and relaxation are essential if family members are to remain strong, supportive, and capable of caring for the patient and each other. Guilt feelings may preclude meeting their own needs unless health care providers offer encouragement.

5. Gradual progression of the disease may overwhelm the family with new demands unless careful planning is initiated. Social services may be able to offer numerous resources for patient and family support at home through volunteer, charitable, church, or public institutions.

6. Rationale: _____
_____
_____

• participate actively in the patient's care
• participate in home care planning.

Discharge planning
NURSING DISCHARGE CRITERIA
Upon discharge, documentation shows evidence of:
• stable vital signs
• absence of fever
• absence of pulmonary or cardiovascular complications
• ability to manage bowel and bladder functioning independently or with minimal assistance
• absence of signs and symptoms of urinary tract infection
• ability to transfer and ambulate at prehospitalization levels or with minimal assistance, using appropriate assistive devices, as ordered
• ability to tolerate adequate nutritional intake
• control of muscle spasms and pain with oral medications
• adequate home support system or referral to home care or a nursing home if indicated by inadequate home support system or inability to perform self-care.

PATIENT/FAMILY DISCHARGE TEACHING CHECKLIST
Document evidence that patient/family demonstrates understanding of:
__ course and nature of MS
__ physical therapy program
__ all discharge medications' purpose, dosage, admin-

istration schedule, and side effects requiring medical attention (usual discharge medications include corticosteroids, antispasmodics, and stool softeners)
__ mobility assistance equipment
__ safety instructions for protection from injury related to sensory deficits
__ information regarding problems associated with immobility
__ stress reduction techniques
__ community resources
__ recommended therapeutic diet
__ bowel and bladder program
__ avoidance of exposure to infection.

DOCUMENTATION CHECKLIST
Using outcome criteria as a guide, document:
__ clinical status on admission
__ significant changes in clinical status
__ pertinent laboratory data and diagnostic findings
__ physical therapy program/activity tolerance
__ administration of medications
__ nutritional intake
__ fluid intake and output
__ bowel and bladder function
__ patient/family teaching
__ discharge planning.

ASSOCIATED CARE PLANS
Grief/Grieving
Ineffective Family Coping
Ineffective Individual Coping

REFERENCES
Alfaro, Rosalinda. *Application of Nursing Process: A Step-by-Step Guide to Care Planning.* Philadelphia: J.B. Lippincott Co., 1986.

Bullock, Barbara L., et al. *Pathophysiology: Adaptations and Alterations in Function.* Boston: Little, Brown & Co., 1984.

DeYoung, Sandra. *The Neurologic Patient.* Englewood Cliffs, N.J.: Prentice-Hall, 1983.

Iyer, Patricia W., et al. *Nursing Process and Nursing Diagnosis.* Philadelphia: W.B. Saunders Co., 1986.

The Nervous System. The Human Body Series. New York: Torstar Books, Inc., 1985.

Patrick, Maxine L., et al. *Medical-Surgical Nursing: Pathophysiological Concepts.* Philadelphia: J.B. Lippincott Co., 1986.

Raffensperger, Ellen. *Clinical Nursing Handbook.* Philadelphia: J.B. Lippincott Co., 1986.

Riley, Mary A., and Beltran, Mary J. *Clinical Nursing Interventions With Critical Elements.* New York: John Wiley & Sons, 1986.

Rudy, Ellen B. *Advanced Neurologic and Neurosurgical Nursing.* St. Louis: C.V. Mosby Co., 1984.

Samonds, R.J., and Cammermeyer, M. "The Patient with Multiple Sclerosis," *Nursing85* 15(9):60-64, September 1985.

Retinal Detachment

DRG information

DRG 36 [Surgical DRG] Retinal Procedures.
  Mean LOS = 3.1 days
DRG 46 [Medical DRG] Other Disorders of the Eye.
  Age greater than 17 with Complication or
  Comorbidity (CC).
  Mean LOS = 3.8 days
DRG 47 [Medical DRG] Other Disorders of the Eye.
  Age greater than 17 without CC.
  Mean LOS = 2.5 days
DRG 48 [Medical DRG] Other Disorders of the Eye.
  Age 0 to 17.
  Mean LOS = 2.9 days

Additional DRG information: If retinal detachment cannot or should not be repaired surgically, DRG 46, 47, or 48 would be used. If surgery is attempted, DRG 36 would be used. Although the mean LOS for each DRG is between 2.5 and 3.8 days, it would not be unusual for a patient with a retinal detachment to be discharged the day of or the day after the surgical procedure. Therefore, the patient's home support system should be carefully analyzed and a referral to home care should *always* be considered.

Introduction

DEFINITION AND TIME FOCUS

Retinal detachment (RD) is the separation of the neural retinal layer (rods and cones) from the pigment epithelium layer of the retina. RD most commonly results from the entry of vitreous humor (a liquid) through a hole or tear into the potential space between the layers. Blindness can occur unless the separation is treated surgically. This clinical plan focuses on the patient admitted for surgical treatment of RD.

ETIOLOGY/PRECIPITATING FACTORS

• myopic eye, causing thinness of the retina and vitreous degeneration
• aphakic eye (absent lens), causing distortion of the eye
• degenerative systemic or eye disease (hypertension, diabetic retinopathy, or tumors) that causes separation or traction on the retina from holes, hemorrhage, or anatomic distortion
• trauma to the head or eye that causes tearing (ripping) of the retina
• strenuous physical exertion that causes separation from increased pressure within the eye

Focused assessment guidelines

NURSING HISTORY (Functional health pattern findings)

Health perception–health management pattern

• may report *vision loss: unilateral and blurred, like a veil or like a blind being drawn over the eye*
• may report *flashing lights*, usually lasting seconds
• may report *floating spots* (floaters)—typically, red blood cells (RBCs)
• may be under treatment for diabetes mellitus, hypertension, or an eye condition
• may have a black eye or a history of head trauma
• if over age 40, may be at higher risk

Activity-exercise pattern

• may report an incident of heavy straining coinciding with onset of vision changes

Cognitive-perceptual pattern

• may not recall or relate present condition to previous ocurrence of blow to head or eye
• *usually does not report pain*

Self-perception–self-concept pattern

• may express fears about the effects of loss of vision on mobility and work

Role-relationship pattern

• may express concern about ability to take care of family

Value-belief pattern

• may express disbelief over suddenness of vision loss

PHYSICAL FINDINGS

Cardiovascular

• hypertension

Neurologic

• *usually a sudden decrease in central and peripheral vision*

Integumentary

• if RD was caused by trauma, may have bruising around eyes

Musculoskeletal

• hesitancy, awkwardness during ambulation

DIAGNOSTIC STUDIES
• laboratory data—usually reflect no significant abnormalities
• *direct and indirect opthalmoscopic measurements—show a bulging and hanging retina, curved reddish tear(s), and floating RBCs*
• *visual field and acuity examinations—will show unilateral vision loss* opposite the area of detachment
• biomicroscopy—may indicate proliferation of cells along retinal and vitreous surfaces (proliferative vitreoretinopathy)
• ultrasonography—will identify areas of detachment

POTENTIAL COMPLICATIONS
• permanent loss of vision
• extension of RD
• RD in other eye
• retinal hemorrhage
• infection (scleral, choroidal, or retinal)
• intolerance to scleral circling or buckling devices (bands or implants that serve to indent the eye inward)
• referred pain to face and head on affected side
• exposure of sutures or implanted devices
• endophthalmitis (inflammation of the inner eye)
• vitreal fibroblastic growth
• sympathetic ophthalmia in the other eye

Collaborative problem: *Potential further loss of vision related to extension of detachment while awaiting surgical intervention*

NURSING PRIORITY: Prevent or minimize further vision loss during the preoperative period.

Interventions

1. *Evaluate and document visual acuity and visual fields on admission, every 2 hours, and as needed.*

2. *Restrict movement.* Place the patient on continuous bed rest. Position the head with the affected area lowermost.

3. Pad one or both eyes, as ordered, either continuously or intermittently.

4. Additional individualized interventions: _____
_____
_____

Rationales

1. Changes in visual acuity and visual fields may indicate worsening detachment. Sudden loss of central vision, such as inability to read, may indicate detachment in the macular area. Increased blurring or number of floaters may indicate hemorrhage.

2. Rest decreases the risk of further detachment. A dependent position helps reattachment by gravity.

3. Eye pads rest the eyes and prevent rapid eye movements, which may increase fluid accumulation between the retinal layers.

4. Rationale: _____
_____
_____

Outcome criteria
Throughout the preoperative period, the patient will:
• show no further vision loss
• maintain activity and position limitations.

Collaborative problem: *Potential loss of vision related to postoperative extension of tear or detachment and nonapproximation of retinal layers; retinal hemorrhage; or eye infection*

NURSING PRIORITY: Prevent complications that could cause further vision loss postoperatively.

Interventions

1. *Verify specific postoperative positioning restrictions with the doctor.* Inform the patient about the restrictions. Place the patient on bed rest or limited activity for 1 to 2 days. Position the head with detached area lower-

Rationales

1. Rest decreases the risk of redetachment while the area is healing. Maintaining the affected area in a dependent position aids approximation of the layers and development of adhesion scars. The air bubble provides

Interventions *continued*

most, unless an air bubble has been injected. Position a patient who has an air bubble (injected into the eye cavity) so that the air bubble will rise against the detachment and remain there (usually this requires a facedown position with the head turned to the side just enough for the patient to breathe); maintain the facedown position for several days while the patient is in bed, eating, using the commode, or ambulating.

2. Teach the patient to avoid quickly executed head movements such as jerking (hair combing, face washing, teeth brushing, head turning, shampooing, coughing); rapid eye movements, such as those involved in reading or doing crafts; vomiting; and Valsalva's maneuver.

3. After eye pads are changed (within 1 to 2 days), instruct the patient to report any vision changes or other physical symptoms immediately.

4. Give antiemetics, as needed, for nausea.

5. Give antibiotics, as ordered, to prevent infection.

6. Monitor continuously for such complications as retinal hemorrhage, evidenced by vision changes and the appearance of floaters.

7. Incorporate relevant teaching into all interventions.

8. Additional individualized interventions: _____
_____
_____

Rationales *continued*

traction against the area and promotes adherence of the layers. The air bubble will be absorbed into the surrounding tissue in 5 to 10 days.

2. Jerking head movements, rapid eye movements, vomiting, Valsalva's maneuver, and other quickly executed activities will increase intraocular pressure—and the risk of redetachment.

3. Changes in visual fields or vision acuity may indicate redetachment.

4. Vomiting increases intraocular pressure and can cause redetachment.

5. Infection increases the risk of vision loss.

6. Complications such as hemorrhage can increase the risk of nonapproximation of retinal layers.

7. A knowledgeable patient is more likely to comply with recommendations and to recognize complications.

8. Rationale: _____
_____
_____

Outcome criteria

Within the immediate postoperative period, the patient will:
• show no further vision loss
• have no nausea or vomiting
• maintain position and activity limitations

• remain free of complications, such as hemorrhage or infection.
Within 3 days of surgery, the patient will:
• describe signs and symptoms of retinal redetachment.

Nursing diagnosis: *Eye pain related to a postoperative inflammatory process*

NURSING PRIORITY: Relieve eye pain.

Interventions

1. *Assess the patient for pain* immediately after surgery and every 2 hours thereafter.

2. Medicate as needed with analgesics, as ordered. Document pain episodes and medication.

3. Apply moist compresses, as ordered.

Rationales

1. Mild pain is expected after surgical manipulation of the eye; however, an increase or a sudden change in pain may indicate complications, such as retinal hemorrhage.

2. Pain increases intraocular pressure and the risk of redetachment.

3. Moist compresses reduce swelling and relieve pain.

(continued)

Interventions *continued*

4. Keep the room dark and quiet immediately after surgery and as needed.

5. Avoid direct pressure to the eyeball.

6. Additional individualized interventions: _____
_____
_____

Rationales *continued*

4. Reduced light and noise may diminish the effects of photophobia caused by mydriatics and swelling.

5. External pressure may increase intraocular pressure, pain, and risk of redetachment.

6. Rationale: _____
_____
_____

Outcome criteria
Within 1 day postoperatively, the patient will:
• verbalize the absence or relief of pain

• have no swelling
• show a relaxed posture and facial expression.

Nursing diagnosis: *Impaired physical mobility related to position and activity limitations*

NURSING PRIORITY: Prevent complications related to immobility.

Interventions

1. See the "Surgical Intervention" care plan, page 71.

2. Encourage isometric exercises, deep breathing, and range-of-motion (without head movement) exercises every hour while the patient is awake. Caution the patient to avoid coughing and Valsalva's maneuver during exercise.

3. Consult the doctor regarding activity progression. Maintain the head in the desired dependent position while the patient is ambulating, as ordered.

4. Instruct the patient about postdischarge activity restrictions, typically:
• moderate, unhurried activities for the first few weeks, avoiding jerking the head or straining (as caused by reading, shampooing, bending the head below the waist, or driving)
• depending on ocular status, light activities by 3 weeks (such as light secretarial work)
• by 6 weeks, heavy work, sex, and exercise.

5. Additional individualized interventions: _____
_____
_____

Rationales

1. The "Surgical Intervention" care plan contains general interventions related to postoperative immobility.

2. These activities will prevent venous stasis, skin breakdown, and atelectasis. Note: Coughing is contraindicated because, like Valsalva's maneuver, it increases intraocular pressure.

3. Most patients are ambulatory by the 2nd postoperative day, but activity prescriptions vary. Maintaining a dependent head position will aid in scar formation and adherence of retinal layers.

4. Abrupt or vigorous changes in position associated with activity increase the risk of redetachment. Lowering the head below the waist or leaning over a bowl to shampoo hair increases intraocular pressure and jeopardizes reattachment. Gradual activity progression allows activity increase to parallel healing.

5. Rationale: _____
_____
_____

Outcome criteria
Within 3 days postoperatively, the patient will:
• have no skin breakdown
• exhibit clear lungs
• show no further vision loss.

Nursing diagnosis: *Potential injury related to vision loss and/or eye pads*

NURSING PRIORITY: Prevent injuries.

Interventions

1. Preoperatively, postoperatively, and as needed, provide orientation to the room, including the bathroom, call light, telephone, bed controls, side rails, and position of furniture.

2. Explain procedures continuously as they are done.

3. Document vision limitations on the cardex.

4. Additional individualized interventions: _____
_____
_____

Rationales

1. Knowledge of the location of furniture and equipment needed for activities of daily living (ADLs) will help prevent patient falls and injuries.

2. Continuous explanations relieve the patient's anxiety about not being able to see; they also help the patient anticipate the nurse's touch during procedures.

3. A cardex record will be available to other personnel to aid in providing continuity of care.

4. Rationale: _____
_____
_____

Outcome criteria

By the time of surgery, the patient will:
• be oriented to the environment.

Within 2 hours postoperatively, the patient will:
• be reoriented to the environment.

During hospitalization, the patient will:
• be free of injury
• be able to perform ADLs in the hospital room with minimal assistance.

Nursing diagnosis: *Anxiety related to fear of blindness*

NURSING PRIORITIES: (a) Reduce anxiety to a tolerable level, and (b) provide realistic reassurance about vision status.

Interventions

1. During the provision of care, elicit and accept the patient's expressions of fear and anxiety. Help the patient identify and prioritize problems. Also, see the "Ineffective Individual Coping" care plan, page 51.

2. Offer realistic reassurance as indicated by the patient's condition.

3. If the eye or eyes are patched, check the patient frequently, anticipate needs, speak when approaching the bedside, and use touch to offer reassurance.

4. Additional individualized interventions: _____
_____
_____

Rationales

1. The threat of blindness implies alteration in almost all aspects of the patient's life. Identifying the most significant components of the threat helps the patient regain control and initiate contingency planning. The "Ineffective Individual Coping" care plan contains general measures for relieving anxiety.

2. A large majority of retinal reattachments are sucessful in restoring vision.

3. Inability to see increases the sense of helplessness and isolation, further contributing to anxiety. Speaking on approach alerts the patient to the nurse's presence. Reassurance is often conveyed by nonverbal behavior; because the patient cannot perceive the usual visual cues, touch may be especially meaningful.

4. Rationale: _____
_____
_____

Outcome criteria

Within 3 days postoperatively, the patient will:
• have a relaxed facial expression

• identify specific fears related to fear of blindness
• verbalize a realistic perception of the prognosis.

Nursing diagnosis: *Diversional activity deficit (boredom, isolation) related to postoperative activity limitation*

NURSING PRIORITY: Promote allowable activities.

Interventions

1. Provide diversional activities that do not cause rapid eye movement or head jerking, such as radio, television, conversation, books, and visitors, considering activity restrictions.

2. Additional individualized interventions: _____
_____
_____

Rationales

1. Such activities will help heal the retinal layers while relieving boredom and reducing isolation.

2. Rationale: _____
_____
_____

Outcome criteria
Throughout the period of hospitalization, the patient will:
• accept activity restriction

• have no further vision loss or other complications
• spend time daily visiting with friends and family.

Discharge planning
NURSING DISCHARGE CRITERIA
Upon discharge, documentation shows evidence of:
• absence of infection
• absence of pain
• ability to manage ADLs with minimal limitations
• ability to ambulate (same as before hospitalization) with minimal assistance
• stable vital signs
• absence of pulmonary or cardiovascular complications
• expected amount of restored vision or ability to accept vision deficit
• ability to follow activity restrictions
• adequate home support system
• referral to home care if support system is inadequate or if further teaching and observation of progress are warranted
• knowledge of how to contact community resources that offer support to visually impaired persons (if vision is permanently impaired).

PATIENT/FAMILY DISCHARGE TEACHING CHECKLIST
Document evidence that patient/family demonstrates understanding of:
__ extent of vision loss (if any) and expected time period needed for further return of vision
__ all discharge medications' purpose, which eye to medicate, dosage, administration schedule, and side effects requiring medical attention; usual discharge medications include mydriatics

__ activity limitations
__ signs and symptoms indicating redetachment, such as changes in vision or seeing floaters or flashes of light
__ date, time, and location of follow-up appointments
__ (if appropriate) community resources for the visually impaired.

DOCUMENTATION CHECKLIST
Using outcome criteria as a guide, document:
__ clinical status on admission
__ significant changes in status
__ pertinent laboratory and diagnostic test findings
__ vision changes
__ pain-relief measures
__ activity and position restrictions
__ nutritional intake
__ other therapies
__ patient/family teaching
__ discharge planning.

ASSOCIATED CARE PLANS
Grief/Grieving
Ineffective Individual Coping
Knowledge Deficit
Pain
Surgical Intervention

REFERENCES

Boyd-Monk, Heather. "Retinal Detachment and Vitrectomy: Nursing Care," *The Nursing Clinics of North America* 16:433-51, September 1981.

Brunner, Lillian, and Suddarth, Doris, eds. *Lippincott Manual of Nursing Practice,* 4th ed. Philadelphia: J.B. Lippincott Co., 1986.

Carnevali, Doris L., and Patrick, Maxine. *Nursing Management for the Elderly.* Philadelphia: J.B. Lippincott Co., 1979.

Cavalier, Jacqueline P. "When Moments Count...The Two Eye Emergencies that Demand Instant Intervention," *RN* 44:41-43, November 1981.

Glover, Sarah F. "Update on Scleral Buckling: A Fight for Sight," *Today's OR Nurse* 8(1): 8-12, January 1986.

Lewis, S., and Collier, I. *Medical-Surgical Nursing: Assessment and Management of Clinical Problems.* New York: McGraw-Hill Book Co., 1983.

Long, B.C., and Phipps, W.J. *Essentials of Medical-Surgical Nursing: A Nursing Process Approach.* St. Louis: C.V. Mosby Co., 1985.

Parker, Paula J. "Scleral Rupture," *Journal of Ophthalmic Nursing & Technology* 5(2):44-46, March/April 1986.

"The Retinal Effects of a Shiner," *Emergency Medicine* 13:57-61, December 1981.

Sheehy, Susan B. *Emergency Nursing: Principles and Practice.* St. Louis: C.V. Mosby Co., 1985.

Swearingen, Pamela L. *Manual of Nursing Therapeutics: Applying Nursing Diagnoses to Medical Disorders.* Menlo Park, Calif.: Addison-Wesley Publishing Co., 1986.

Tumulty, Gail, and Resler, Marion M. "Eye Trauma," *American Journal of Nursing* 84(6):740-44, June 1984.

Welch, Judith, and Tyler, Judith. "Emergency! Dealing with Eye Injuries," *RN* 47(3):53-54, March 1984.

Whitton, Sally. "Managing Detachment with Retinal Tacks," *Journal of Ophthalmic Nursing & Technology* 5(3):91-93, May/June 1986.

Glaucoma

DRG information

DRG 38 [Surgical DRG] Primary Iris Procedure.
  Mean LOS = 2.2 days
DRG 45 [Medical DRG] Neurological Eye Disorders
  [low tension glaucoma].
  Mean LOS = 3.3 days
DRG 46 [Medical DRG] Other Disorders of the Eye.
  Age greater than 17 with Complication or
  Comorbidity (CC) [associated with disorders of
  the lens or borderline glaucoma].
  Mean LOS = 3.8 days

Additional DRG information: Patients with DRGs 38,
45, and 46 are rarely admitted to acute-care facilities
today. DRG 38 patients are most often admitted to
same-day surgery units or have their procedures done
on an outpatient basis. This may be of concern because
it reduces the amount of time available for teaching and
evaluation of the patients' ability to follow discharge instructions. Documentation must contain evidence of adequate home support to assist the patient postdischarge.
A referral to home care should always be considered.
DRGs 45 and 46 are treated in the acute-care setting
if CC necessitates admission.

Introduction
DEFINITION AND TIME FOCUS
Glaucoma is the progressive loss of visual fields resulting from increased intraocular pressure, which dam-
ages the optic nerve. The increased intraocular
pressure results from an imbalance between the formation and absorption of aqueous humor. Simple chronic
glaucoma is characterized by a gradual loss of peripheral vision, eventually leading to total vision loss,
whereas the less common acute angle-closure glaucoma
is usually characterized by a severe vision loss within
a few hours of onset. This clinical plan focuses on patients admitted for definitive diagnosis and management of both types of glaucoma. Simple chronic glaucoma is sometimes referred to as open-angle or primary
open-angle glaucoma. Other terms for acute angle-closure glaucoma include acute (congestive) glaucoma,
narrow-angle glaucoma, and angle-closure or primary
angle-closure glaucoma.

ETIOLOGY/PRECIPITATING FACTORS
• simple chronic glaucoma—severe myopia; degenerative
changes in the eye; swollen cataracts; ocular trauma,
infection, tumor, inflammation, or hemorrhage; other
factors that can narrow the trabecular meshwork openings, thus increasing resistance to aqueous humor
drainage and raising intraocular pressure; and genetic
predisposition

• acute angle-closure glaucoma—darkness; excitement,
mydriatic medications, and other factors that can dilate
the pupils, pushing the iris against the trabecular
meshwork, thus blocking the drainage of aqueous humor through the anterior-chamber angle and increasing
intraocular pressure

Focused assessment guidelines
NURSING HISTORY (Functional health pattern findings)

Health perception–health management pattern
• simple chronic glaucoma—slow onset, initially without
symptoms, but then developing early symptoms, such
as *gradual loss of peripheral vision (tunnel vision), slightly
blurred vision*, persistent dull eye pain or tired feeling in
the eye, or failure to detect color changes (particularly
blue-green); later symptoms include blurred vision, haloes around lights, morning headaches that disappear
shortly after arising, or pain behind eyeball
• acute angle-closure glaucoma—may report *sudden onset of severe eye pain* radiating to head, sudden blurred
vision progressing to severe loss of vision within a few
hours, decreased light perception, or colored haloes
around lights
• may have a history of frequent changes of eyeglasses
after age 40 or of severe myopia
• if over age 40, female, black, diabetic, or with a family history, at increased risk

Nutritional-metabolic pattern
• acute angle-closure glaucoma—may report *nausea,
vomiting, or abdominal pain*

Activity-exercise pattern
• may report fatigue in performing activities of daily
living (ADLs)
• may report decreased time spent in leisure activities
• may report self-care deficit, such as inadequate
grooming
• may report alterations in mobility, such as bumping
into people or objects and hesitancy in walking in unfamiliar environments

Sleep-rest pattern
• may report difficulty adjusting to darkness
• may report eye pain at night or in the early morning

Self-perception–self-concept pattern
• may present self as most concerned about ability to be
independent

Role-relationship pattern
• may report a history of decreased ability to cope with
ADLs

• may report a decreased ability to maintain social, job, and family roles
• may report increased isolation from other people

Value-belief pattern
• may have delayed seeking medical attention because of gradual development of symptoms
• when stable, may find it difficult to comprehend or believe that lifelong treatment will be required (denial)

PHYSICAL FINDINGS
Gastrointestinal
With acute angle-closure glaucoma:
• nausea
• vomiting
• abdominal pain

Neurologic
• *increased intraocular pressure*
• cupping of optic disk
• visual field losses with scotomas (blind spots)
• optic disk degeneration
• whiteness of optic nerve disk
• white or gray appearance of cornea
• shallow anterior chamber
• in addition (with acute angle-closure glaucoma), fixed and dilated pupil, corneal edema, hazy appearance to cornea, headache, and reddened eye

Musculoskeletal
• pained or anxious facial expression
• fatigue
• hesitancy in walking

DIAGNOSTIC STUDIES
• ophthalmoscopy—shows a white optic disk with cupping and displaced and depressed large retinal vessels
• tonometry—shows corneal indentation consistent with elevated intraocular pressure; values above 22 mm Hg indicate glaucoma, although individual norms vary
• gonioscopy—shows characteristic changes over time, small defects progressing to larger visual field defects (may have 20/20 central vision); optic disk becomes wider, deeper, and paler; impending angle closure may appear before rise in intraocular pressure
• tonography—shows the characteristic changes: a flat graphic tracing with increased intraocular pressure
• visual field determination—shows characteristic loss of visual field; also shows location, size, and density of scotomas

POTENTIAL COMPLICATIONS
• total blindness
• trauma or self-injury
• nutritional deficits
• failure to thrive
• social isolation

Collaborative problem: *Potential increased intraocular pressure related to noncompliance with the medication regimen, use of medication causing increased intraocular pressure, or the effect of environmental variables*

NURSING PRIORITY: Prevent or minimize increases in intraocular pressure.

Interventions

1. *Assess for the presence of, or any increase in, eye pain, pain around orbit, blurred vision, reddened eye, abdominal pain, nausea, vomiting, and neurologic changes,* on admission and as needed.

2. *Evaluate the visual fields* on admission and as needed.

3. *Assess for use of medications before hospitalization* by obtaining a comprehensive list of all current and past medications taken by the patient. Validate with the doctor the continued use of medications during hospitalization.

Rationales

1. A change from baseline assessment data may indicate increasing intraocular pressure, affecting optic nerve function. With acute angle-closure glaucoma, this may indicate an emergency situation.

2. Progressive visual field losses indicate increasing intraocular pressure. Detection of subtle changes may require the use of special equipment.

3. Use of certain medications can precipitate an acute episode; many preparations can produce increased intraocular pressure, including:
• steroids (all types)
• oral and nasal inhalants
• amphetamines
• nasal decongestants (oral or spray)
• nonprescription diet capsules or tablets
• anticholinergics
• antihistamines
• antidiarrheal agents
• some antidepressant drugs
• nonsteroidal anti-inflammatory drugs.

(continued)

Interventions *continued*

4. *Administer and document ocular medications,* as ordered.

5. Evaluate medications' effectiveness and observe for the presence of major side effects, including:
• cholinergics—headache, excessive salivation, diaphoresis, nausea, and vomiting
• adrenergics—headache, tachycardia, and tremors
• carbonic anhydrase inhibitors—paresthesias, anorexia, nausea, fatigue, and impotence
• beta-adrenergic blockers—bradycardia, hypotension, fatigue, and depression
• hyperosmotics—dehydration.

6. Assess for signs and symptoms of decreased tolerance to ocular medications related to prolonged medical therapy: increased blurring of vision; increased headache; nausea; fixed and dilated pupil; increased blood pressure; allergic reaction; and asthmatic attack.

7. Minimize stressful events.

8. Use noninvasive techniques to reduce intraocular pressure.

9. Prepare the patient for diagnostic testing.

10. Additional individualized interventions: _____
_____
_____

Outcome criteria
By the time of discharge, the patient will:
• show no signs or symptoms of increased intraocular pressure
• show no further decrease in vision

Rationales *continued*

4. Consistent and timely use of medications will decrease intraocular pressure. Common medications used singly or in combination include:
• cholinergics (parasympathomimetics), such as pilocarpine hydrochloride and carbachol, to facilitate aqueous outflow
• adrenergics (sympathomimetics), such as epinephrine, to decrease aqueous humor production and increase aqueous outflow
• carbonic anhydrase inhibitors, such as acetazolamide (Diamox) (an oral agent), and beta-adrenergic blockers, such as timolol maleate, to reduce secretion of aqueous humor
• hyperosmotics, such as mannitol, used preoperatively to reduce intraocular pressure by reducing the volume of intraocular fluid.

5. If symptoms persist or increase, intraocular pressure is probably increasing, and the doctor needs to be notified. Undesirable side effects may compromise other body systems.

6. An increase in signs and symptoms may indicate that the prescribed medication is no longer effective and intraocular pressure is rising. The doctor needs to be notified immediately.

7. Stress—worry, fear, excitement, or anger—increases intraocular pressure. Anticipating and preventing stress reactions helps maintain intraocular pressure at a safe level.

8. Meditation, rest, a quiet environment, and a decrease in stimuli help decrease stress and, thus, intraocular pressure.

9. Some diagnostic tests, such as tonometry, involve application of direct pressure to the eyeball. These may be done repeatedly, at different times of the day, to assess intraocular pressure. Thorough explanations of tests may decrease the patient's anxiety and ensure compliance during the procedures.

10. Rationale: _____
_____
_____

• list three signs of increased intraocular pressure
• list three techniques to minimize an intraocular pressure increase.

Nursing diagnosis: *Eye pain related to progressive pressure on the optic nerve*

NURSING PRIORITY: Minimize or relieve eye pain.

Interventions

1. On admission, *assess the patient for eye pain* presence and degree.

2. Monitor the patient every 2 hours while awake for the occurrence of, or an increase in, eye pain.

3. On admission, *teach the patient to report any eye pain or change in symptoms.*

4. Assess for associated signs and symptoms, such as blurred vision, nausea, vomiting, abdominal pain, or neurologic changes.

5. *Administer eye medications,* as ordered. Document administration.

6. *Administer analgesics* judiciously, as ordered, and document. Assess pain relief 30 minutes after administering medication.

7. Use noninvasive pain-relief measures as well as medications. See the "Pain" care plan, page 64, for details.

8. Help the patient identify and modify causes of stress.

9. Explain unfamiliar procedures and new events.

10. Additional individualized interventions: _____
_____
_____

Rationales

1. Eye pain in the glaucoma patient indicates increased intraocular pressure.

2. Increased eye pain, or the occurrence of eye pain not present previously, may indicate increasing intraocular pressure.

3. Early intervention is essential in preventing further damage to the optic disk.

4. The patient may not report pain, but observation of associated signs or symptoms may facilitate early intervention. Without early intervention, eye pain will eventually occur. Listed signs and symptoms may indicate increasing intraocular pressure or an episode of acute angle-closure glaucoma. Even if the patient does not report an increase in symptoms, observations should also be made regarding hesitancy in walking, bumping into people or walls, or exhibiting new bruises from hitting objects.

5. Eye medications are administered to permit better drainage of aqueous humor and to decrease the amount of humor produced. Consistent, accurate medication administration will reduce intraocular pressure and may prevent eye pain.

6. Continued pain can cause increased anxiety and stress, leading to increased intraocular pressure.

7. Alternate measures such as cold eye compresses may decrease painful eye spasms. Relaxation techniques and meditation, as well as a quiet room with decreased stimuli, may reduce the perception of pain stimuli.

8. Stress may increase intraocular pressure. Knowledge and modification of individual stressors, such as worry, fear, anxiety, and anger, may decrease intraocular pressure and pain.

9. Patients who are well prepared for new procedures and events experience less stress.

10. Rationale: _____
_____
_____

Outcome criteria

Within 30 minutes of the occurrence of intraocular pain, the patient will:
• verbalize the absence or relief of pain.

By the time of discharge, the patient will:
• practice selected noninvasive pain-relief measures
• identify stressors that may increase pain.

Nursing diagnosis: *Potential for injury related to decreased visual fields, medically induced blurred vision, use of eye patches, and hesitancy in walking*

NURSING PRIORITY: Prevent patient injury.

Interventions

1. *Assess the patient's vision.* Document blurred vision, the amount of peripheral vision, blindness, or patched eyes.

2. *Assess for and document signs of decreasing vision* (each shift).

3. *Orient the patient to the environment.*

4. Rearrange the environment, with the patient's assistance, so that the patient has a maximum field of vision.

5. Illuminate the room adequately, and provide a night light.

6. Place the bed in a low position with the wheels locked.

7. Teach the patient the side effects of medications.

8. Encourage asking for assistance, as needed. Instruct the patient to avoid activities that may increase intra-ocular pressure, such as coughing, vomiting, bending at the waist, squeezing the eyes, and Valsalva's maneuver when straining at stool.

9. Additional individualized interventions: _____ _____ _____

Rationales

1. Unable to see all or part of the environment as a re-sult of tunnel vision or blurred vision, the patient may knock objects over, bump into them, or fall over them. Awareness of the patient's limitations helps determine the level of teaching needed about environmental haz-ards and the necessity for rearranging the environment.

2. As the patient's visual acuity decreases, the poten-tial for injury increases.

3. A thorough knowledge of surroundings, including the call system and available nurse assistance, decreases the possibility of falls or injury.

4. Placing objects within reach and sight of the patient will decrease the potential for self-injury and feelings of dependence on the health team. Thereafter, the envi-ronment should never be rearranged without first noti-fying the patient. Move unneeded objects out of the room so that the patient will not fall over them or bump into them.

5. When a patient has blurred or decreased vision, it is even more difficult to see in a dimly lit room. Appropri-ate lighting will facilitate safety and decrease the pa-tient's risk of self-injury.

6. The patient has less potential for injury if the bed is at an appropriate level at all times.

7. Knowledge that vision may be further impaired after medication administration will alert the patient to the need for increased safety measures.

8. Calling for assistance may prevent the patient from falls and injuries, and instruction may keep the patient from engaging in activities that will increase intraocu-lar pressure.

9. Rationale: _____ _____ _____

Outcome criteria
By the time of discharge, the patient will:
• have experienced no falls or injuries

• list safety measures necessary to prevent injury
• adjust to limitations on movement and activity.

Nursing diagnosis: *Fear related to previous vision losses, possible surgery, and possible total blindness*

NURSING PRIORITY: Comfort and support the patient.

Interventions

1. Encourage expression of feelings.

2. Provide a quiet environment.

3. Explain the need for frequent administration of ocular medications, for tonometry readings, and for frequent physical assessments.

4. Support preferred coping styles.

5. Explore the patient's strengths, and introduce resources to cope with the fear of blindness.

6. Observe for excessive stress levels resulting from fear.

7. Observe for evidence of a positive response to therapy.

8. Additional individualized interventions: _____
_____
_____

Rationales

1. Expressing fear, perhaps along with associated feelings of anger and helplessness, may assist the patient in coping. For the nurse, listening attentively, providing consistency in caregivers, reassuring the patient that the nurse will be available, and communicating sensitivity to the patient's problem will encourage ventilation of feelings. Reinforcing that the patient's response is appropriate will assist in developing the trust necessary for sharing of feelings.

2. With the sudden onset of symptoms and the presence of pain, as in acute angle-closure glaucoma, the patient may be very frightened. A quiet and distraction-free environment may reduce the patient's stress while facilitating the effect of prescribed medications. As intraocular pressure and symptoms subside, fear may decrease.

3. Explaining each step of the therapy may reduce the patient's fear of the unknown and help him adjust to the new routines.

4. Ascertaining how the patient normally copes with fear and encouraging the use of those coping strategies, while offering comfort and support, may help reduce the fear. Offering feedback about the patient's expressed feelings and supporting realistic perceptions may help him cope more realistically with the fear of blindness.

5. Focusing on the patient's strengths and capabilities may help the patient recognize the ability to cope with the fear and the future regardless of outcome. So may introducing the patient to a person coping successfully with glaucoma.

6. The patient may become stressed to the point of incapacitation. Early intervention is needed to prevent this reaction, because the procedures and possible surgery require the participation of a calm, relaxed patient.

7. Reduced fear and increased comfort indicate the patient is responding in a positive manner and is coping effectively with fear.

8. Rationale: _____
_____
_____

Outcome criteria

Within 2 days of admission, the patient will:
• verbalize fears

• exhibit calm, relaxed facial expression, body movements, and behavior.

Nursing diagnosis: *Knowledge deficit related to the disease and the impending surgery*

NURSING PRIORITY: Increase the patient's knowledge about the surgical experience.

Interventions

1. Provide preoperative teaching for the patient who will have eye surgery. (See the "Surgical Intervention" care plan, page 71, for details.) Assess the patient's level of knowledge regarding the disease, and incorporate relevant pathophysiology into the teaching, as needed, to correct any misconceptions.

2. Explain laser iridotomy or laser trabeculoplasty if either technique will be used.

3. Explain surgical iridectomy or trabeculectomy if one of these techniques will be used.

4. Provide instruction about postoperative routine, precautions, and signs of complications.

5. Maintain patient comfort.

6. Prevent infection by washing hands before and after administering eye drops or changing a patch, keeping the tip of the eyedropper sterile, and checking the eye patch regularly for drainage. Change the patch as ordered. Provide associated teaching.

7. Additional individualized interventions: _____
_____
_____

Rationales

1. The patient having eye surgery will be awake and must be calm and relaxed to cooperate during the procedure. Information about the specific procedure and correction of misconceptions allays anxieties and helps ensure better cooperation. Nonpharmacologic treatments for glaucoma include classic surgical (cutting) techniques, such as iridectomy and trabeculectomy, and laser techniques (iridotomy and trabeculoplasty). Surgery is usually necessary with acute angle-closure glaucoma.

2. This noninvasive alternative to surgery may be less frightening to the patient because it involves less risk, is more cost-effective, and can be done on an outpatient basis. Posttreatment discomfort is usually limited to headaches and blurred vision for the first 24 hours. Glaucoma medications are continued at least until the first check-up.

3. Iridectomy is used for acute angle-closure glaucoma; trabeculectomy or iridectomy is used for simple chronic glaucoma.

4. The patient's understanding of the postoperative routine will help avoid complications, such as intraocular hemorrhage, increased intraocular pressure, and injury. Intraocular hemorrhage may be related to improper positioning and/or increased intraocular pressure. Intraocular pressure can be increased by sneezing, coughing, bending, vomiting, straining with bowel movement, or lifting heavy objects. The potential for injury is increased because of wearing of the eye patch, possible poor vision in the unoperated eye, and frustration from dependence on others and restricted activities.

5. Postoperatively, the eye will be sensitive to light after removal of the eye patch. Medicating as needed and encouraging the patient to dim room lights and to wear dark glasses assists in maintaining comfort.

6. Eye infection may cause vision loss and negate the effects of surgery.

7. Rationale: _____
_____
_____

Outcome criteria

By the day of surgery, the patient will:
• verbalize understanding of preoperative instructions
• verbalize understanding of surgery and postoperative routines

• identify signs of postoperative complications and list ways to prevent them.

By the time of discharge, the patient will have:
• demonstrated the proper technique for administration of eye drops.

Discharge planning

NURSING DISCHARGE CRITERIA

Upon discharge, documentation shows evidence of:
• stable intraocular pressure within acceptable limits, controlled by ocular medications or surgery
• healthy coping behaviors regarding vision loss and possibility of total blindness
• an understanding of glaucoma, glaucoma management, and signs and symptoms of increasing intraocular pressure
• an understanding of the pharmacologic regimen and the reasons for a lifelong commitment to it.

PATIENT/FAMILY DISCHARGE TEACHING CHECKLIST

Document evidence that patient/family demonstrates understanding of:

___ all discharge medications' purpose, dosage, which eye to receive medication, administration schedule and technique, and side effects requiring medical attention; usual discharge medications include adrenergics, cholinergics, carbonic anhydrase inhibitors, and beta-adrenergic blockers

___ infection prevention

___ need to avoid nonprescription medications

___ need to avoid use of mydriatic or cycloplegic medications that dilate the pupils

___ signs and symptoms indicating increasing intraocular pressure, such as aching around the eye or any changes in vision

___ date, time, and location of follow-up appointments and importance of lifelong medical supervision

___ when and how to report any reappearance of symptoms or stressful events to the ophthalmologist

___ safety precautions in taking eye medications, such as carrying medications when away from home, having a reserve bottle of eye drops at home, and knowing which local pharmacies are open late in case of emergency

___ factors that increase potential for injury

___ need to assess safety of home environment

___ safety measures to use or the need for assistance when performing tasks or activities that require clear vision

___ circumstances that may increase intraocular pressure, such as emotional upsets, fatigue, constricting clothing, heavy exertion, upper respiratory infections, and sexual activity

___ recommended activities and precautions, such as exercise in moderation, moderate use of eyes for reading and watching television, maintenance of regular bowel habits, and no driving for 2 hours after administration of ocular drugs

___ transportation alternatives

___ ways to mobilize support systems

___ ways to adjust to social situations in view of loss of vision and need to follow medication routine

___ need for potassium supplement or high-potassium foods if acetazolamide (Diamox) is prescribed

___ (if readmitted to the hospital) need to alert health team about glaucoma diagnosis and continued need for prescribed eye drops

___ importance of wearing a medical identification tag indicating patient has glaucoma.

DOCUMENTATION CHECKLIST

Using outcome criteria as a guide, document:

___ clinical status on admission

___ significant changes in status, especially regarding vision, headaches, and eye pain

___ results of ophthalmoscopy, tonometry, gonioscopy, tonography, and visual field determination

___ episodes of eye pain or headache

___ episodes of nausea, vomiting, or abdominal pain

___ pain-relief measures

___ serial tonometry results

___ surgery or ocular medication management

___ nutrition intake

___ patient/family teaching

___ discharge planning.

ASSOCIATED CARE PLANS

Grief/Grieving
Ineffective Individual Coping
Knowledge Deficit
Pain
Surgical Intervention

REFERENCES

Brunner, Lillian, and Suddarth, Doris, eds. *Lippincott Manual of Nursing Practice*, 4th ed. Philadelphia: J.B. Lippincott Co., 1986.

Campbell, Claire. *Nursing Diagnosis and Intervention in Nursing Practice*, 2nd ed. New York: John Wiley & Sons, 1984.

Carnevali, D.L., and Patrick, Maxine. *Nursing Management for the Elderly*, 2nd ed. Philadelphia: J.B. Lippincott Co., 1986.

Carpenito, L. *Nursing Diagnosis: Application to Clinical Practice*. Philadelphia: J.B. Lippincott Co., 1983.

Goldstein, J. "Ocular Side Effects of Systemic Drugs: A Physical Assessment Guide for the Ophthalmic Medical Assistant," *Journal of Ophthalmic Nursing and Technology* 5(3):103-06, May/June 1986.

Kapperud, M.J. *The Aging Eye: A Guide for Nurses*. Minneapolis: The Minnesota Society for the Prevention of Blindness and Preservation of Hearing, 1983.

Kilroy, J.L. "Care and Teaching of Patients with Glaucoma," in *The Nursing Clinics of North America: Ophthalmic Nursing*. Edited by Boyd-Monk, H. Philadelphia: W.B. Saunders Co., 1981.

Lewis, S.M., and Collier, I. *Medical Surgical Nursing: Assessment and Management of Clinical Problems*. New York: McGraw-Hill Book Co., 1983.

Long, B.C., and Phipps, W.J. *Essentials of Medical-Surgical Nursing: A Nursing Process Approach*. St. Louis: C.V. Mosby Co., 1985.

Resler, M.M., and Tumulty, Gail. "Glaucoma Update," *Americal Journal of Nursing* 83(5):752-56, May 1983.

Radical Neck Dissection

DRG information

DRG 76 [Surgical DRG] Other Respiratory System
O.R. Procedures. With Complication or
Comorbidity (CC).
Mean LOS = 8.8 days

DRG 77 [Surgical DRG] Other Respiratory System
O.R. Procedures. Without CC.
Mean LOS = 4.3 days
Principal diagnoses include:
• excision of regional lymph nodes
• excision and/or operation/repair of larynx
• tracheostomy.

DRG 400 [Surgical DRG] Lymphoma or Leukemia with
Major O.R. Procedure.
Mean LOS = 11.2 days
Principal diagnoses include:
• malignant neoplasm of lymph nodes
• lymphosarcoma.

Additional DRG information: Radical neck dissection
(RND) has a number of alternative DRGs, depending on
the cause of the RND. The DRG assigned will depend
on the cause for the surgery (that is, where the cancer
is located), not on the extent of the surgery (that is,
tracheostomy or laryngectomy) or how radical a dissection is performed.

Introduction

DEFINITION AND TIME FOCUS

RND is a surgical procedure performed for cancers of
the head and neck. Normally, RND involves the surgical removal of:
• lymph nodes in the neck
• lymphatic vessels
• the sternocleidomastoid muscle
• the internal jugular vein
• the spinal accessory nerve (innervates the
trapezius muscle)
• the submandibular salivary gland
• the tail of the parotid gland.

When RND is combined with removal of a tumor located in the mouth, pharynx, or larynx (a common occurrence), a tracheostomy is usually created. If a total
laryngectomy is performed, the tracheostomy will be
permanent, and the common opening between the trachea and the pharynx will be surgically closed. A patient who does not require total laryngectomy may
have a temporary tracheostomy until surgical or radia-
tion-related edema subsides. Such a patient is commonly returned postoperatively to the intensive care
unit (ICU) initially. This clinical plan focuses on the immediate preoperative period and the post-ICU phase of
postoperative care for the patient undergoing RND.

ETIOLOGY/PRECIPITATING FACTORS

RND is performed for the removal of:
• primary malignant tumors of the mouth, pharynx,
or larynx
• skin lesions (melanomas).
    Risk factors associated with the development of
these cancers include:
• heavy use of alcohol and cigarettes (oral and laryngeal cancer)
• pipe or cigar smoking (oral cancer)
• tobacco chewing (oral cancer)
• exposure to nickel or wood dust or woodworking
chemicals (nasopharyngeal cancer)
• fair complexion and long-term or frequent sun exposure (melanoma).

Focused assessment guidelines

NURSING HISTORY (Functional health pattern findings)

Health perception–health management pattern
• *history of heavy cigarette smoking, alcohol abuse, or both*
• may have had radiation or chemotherapy (for head and
neck cancer)
• may have history of previous head or neck cancer

Nutritional-metabolic pattern
• may report *weight loss*
• may report dysphagia, sore throat, or difficulty chewing
• may report no appetite
• may have a history of skin lesions (basal cell)

Sleep-rest pattern
• may report *fatigue*

Cognitive-perceptual pattern
• may report *change in taste sensation*
• may report neck pain (rare)

Self-perception–self-concept pattern
• views self as *strong, active, easy-going individual* or
may be *very passive**
• may report voice change

Role-relationship pattern
• may describe self as *depending on no one else**
• may be head of household
• may have a history of sporadic employment related
to alcoholism*

Coping–stress tolerance pattern
• may have delayed seeking treatment (denial)
• may show *tendency to avoid issues requiring a decision**
• may have *only spouse or friend as major support system*

*based on author's clinical experience

Value-belief pattern
• views disease as life-threatening
• wants to have surgery in order to return to usual activities
• if melanoma patient, may have difficulty accepting seriousness of disease and need for radical surgery

PHYSICAL FINDINGS
Pulmonary
• productive cough or wheezing
• hoarseness
• difficulty breathing

Gastrointestinal
• *nonhealing ulcer in oral cavity*
• may be edentulous or have poor oral hygiene

Neurologic
• otalgia (ear pain)

Integumentary
• *melanoma*

Musculoskeletal
• *lump on neck*

DIAGNOSTIC STUDIES
• blood studies, including complete blood count and electrolyte determinations—used for preoperative baseline studies; findings usually within normal limits; de-creased albumin levels indicate altered nutrition; elevated or depressed white blood cell (WBC) count may indicate immune system's response to disease process or stage of recovery from radiation therapy or chemotherapy
• liver function test—used to rule out liver disease preoperatively
• chest X-ray—may show metastasis or pulmonary disease
• *head and neck X-rays or computed tomography (CT scan)—done to identify location and extent of tumor and metastasis to sinuses, neck, or brain*
• *panendoscopy and biopsy—define tumor type and extension of tumor*
• barium swallow—if dysphagia is present, defines involvement of pharynx, epiglottis, or esophagus
• lymphoscintigraphy (for melanoma patient)—identifies involved lymph nodes and drainage pathways
• laryngogram—if hoarseness is present, defines area of involvement in larynx and extent of airway obstruction
• abdominal CT scan—may demonstrate metastasis to abdominal organs
• upper or lower GI series—may demonstrate metastasis to esophagus or digestive system

POTENTIAL COMPLICATIONS
• airway obstruction
• carotid artery rupture
• cutaneous or tracheoesophageal fistula formation

Nursing diagnosis: *Preoperative knowledge deficit related to unfamiliar diagnosis and surgical procedure*

NURSING PRIORITY: Supplement the patient's and family's knowledge of impending surgery.

Interventions

1. See the "Knowledge Deficit" and "Surgical Intervention" care plans, pages 56 and 71.

2. On patient admission, *assess knowledge base.* Encourage questions. Help the patient and family to identify concerns and methods to cope with them. As appropriate, *explain and illustrate the signs and symptoms of head and neck cancer, the planned treatment, and the expected postoperative outcomes.* The usual postoperative expectations include a bulky neck dressing, ICU care until the patient is stabilized, a nasogastric (NG) tube, intubation or tracheostomy, skin catheters, and skin graft and donor sites. Document the patient's and family's level of understanding and their response.

Rationales

1. These care plans contain general interventions for surgical patients and those with knowledge deficits.

2. Knowledge of expected events decreases anxiety and gives a sense of control. Providing information helps the patient and family focus questions on areas not understood. Individuals differ in the amount of detail desired: some may request pictures or samples of tubes. Airway management postoperatively varies, but most patients have a temporary tracheostomy until edema subsides. The temporary tracheostomy is usually closed within approximately 2 weeks postoperatively, depending on the patient's status. If the patient will be undergoing radiation therapy, the tracheostomy may be maintained for a longer period. The patient undergoing total laryngectomy will have a permanent tracheostomy.

(continued)

Interventions *continued*

3. Additional individualized interventions: _____
_____
_____

Rationales *continued*

3. Rationale: _____
_____
_____

Outcome criteria

Before surgery, the patient will:
• state the reason for surgery and outcome expectations
• exhibit a decreased anxiety level.

Before surgery, the family will:
• explain or list their greatest concern and at least one way they will deal with it.

Nursing diagnosis: *Ineffective coping: avoidance related to inaccurate perception of health status*

NURSING PRIORITY: Promote accurate perception of health status and of available resources for health promotion.

Interventions

1. On admission, *determine the time lapse between when initial symptoms appeared and when treatment was sought.* Explain the common signs and symptoms. Allow expression of guilt, resentment, and regret if treatment was delayed because of patient denial or avoidance. Emphasize that treatment *is* occurring now.

2. *Evaluate for potential alcohol dependence.* As part of the admission interview, question the patient specifically, directly, and matter-of-factly about alcohol consumption, noting the time of the last drink. Observe for periorbital edema and ecchymoses or abrasions in various stages of healing. Be alert to any excessive use of such toiletries as mouthwash.

3. *Assess for signs and symptoms of alcohol withdrawal syndrome,* as follows:
• mild (4 to 16 hours after the last drink)—tremors, agitation, tachycardia, vomiting, hypertension, diarrhea
• moderate (1 to 3 days later)—profuse diaphoresis, seizures, hallucinations, incontinence
• severe (variable onset, usually about 72 hours after the last drink)—delirium tremens, hyperthermia, violent behavior, extreme blood pressure changes, disorientation.
   Notify the doctor if withdrawal is suspected, and institute sedative therapy, as ordered, along with any other medical measures.

4. Postoperatively, *teach risk factors* of head and neck cancer, and document the patient's level of understanding.

Rationales

1. Time lapse may indicate denial as the primary coping method. Initial symptoms are often mild and may be easily ignored. Verbalization decreases unnecessary guilt if treatment was delayed.

2. Alcohol dependence is a typical finding in this patient group and must be identified for early assessment and treatment of withdrawal symptoms. Specific questioning may unmask hidden alcoholism; although these patients tend to underestimate their consumption, they usually can and will accurately identify the time of their last drink. Periorbital edema suggests fluid retention, possibly related to excessive alcohol consumption. Lesions in various stages may be a sign of frequent falls because of intoxication. Patients may attempt to fend off withdrawal symptoms by using alcohol-laden toiletries while hospitalized.

3. Severe alcohol withdrawal syndrome is a potentially life-threatening occurrence that may be prevented with early intervention. Sedation (usually with benzodiazepines) may prevent the syndrome's progression. Untreated, severe alcohol withdrawal (delirium tremens) may result in myocardial infarction, cerebrovascular accident, or other serious complications.

4. A review of risk factors provides a baseline for discussion and planning to eliminate known risks.

Interventions continued

5. Before discharge, *offer resources available for smoking cessation and alcohol rehabilitation,* and document the plan for follow-up.

6. Additional individualized interventions: _____
_____
_____

Outcome criterion
By the time of discharge, the patient will:
• state one action to decrease the risk of recurrence of head and neck cancer.

Rationales continued

5. Major life-style changes require support and follow-up. Smoking and alcohol intake are major risk factors for the recurrence of head and neck cancer.

6. Rationale: _____
_____
_____

Nursing diagnosis: *Disturbed role performance related to muscle weakness or job disruption*

NURSING PRIORITY: Advise the patient of available resources for job adjustment.

Interventions

1. Preoperatively, *assess the physical requirements of the patient's job,* especially noting any heavy lifting or use of shoulder muscles. Have the patient and family discuss work options with the patient's employer. Involve a social worker or vocational rehabilitation specialist.

2. Before discharge, document a plan for alternative employment or disability follow-up.

3. Additional individualized interventions: _____
_____
_____

Outcome criteria
Before surgery, the patient will:
• express minimal anxiety about work and finances.

Rationales

1. The patient may be unaware of surgery's effect on his or her job performance. Planning preoperatively minimizes postoperative distress about changed abilities or activity restrictions. A social worker or vocational rehabilitation specialist may offer new options.

2. Finances and job security may be major obstacles to compliance with the total treatment plan if not addressed before discharge.

3. Rationale: _____
_____
_____

By the time of discharge, the patient will:
• state a plan for vocational rehabilitation.

Nursing diagnosis: *Pain related to edema, intubation, and surgical wound*

NURSING PRIORITY: Relieve postoperative pain.

Interventions

1. See the "Pain" general care plan, page 64.

2. *For headache, medicate as ordered* and document promptly. *Elevate the head of the bed at all times.*

3. For a sore throat, administer mouth care before meals, and offer fluids every 1 to 2 hours.

Rationales

1. This care plan contains general interventions for pain management.

2. Postoperative headache may be caused by edema related to loss of lymphatics and the jugular vein. The semi-upright position facilitates fluid drainage and decreases pressure.

3. Fluids bathe the oral mucosa and stimulate salivary flow.

(continued)

Interventions continued

4. *For shoulder pain, support the arm and shoulder at all times;* teach the patient support methods; and medicate promptly, as ordered, at the onset of pain and before ambulation or activities of daily living (ADLs). Document all measures taken.

5. Additional individualized interventions: _____
_____
_____

Rationales continued

4. Adequate support decreases tension on the surgical site and maintains body alignment. Analgesics decrease pain, facilitating resumption of therapeutic activity.

5. Rationale: _____
_____
_____

Outcome criteria
Throughout the postoperative period, the patient will:
• verbalize absence or relief of pain
• exhibit relaxed posture and facial expression.

Nursing diagnosis: *Potential ineffective airway clearance related to edema and excessively thick secretions postoperatively*

NURSING PRIORITIES: (a) Prevent airway obstruction, and (b) facilitate secretion removal.

Interventions

1. In the immediate postoperative period, *assess and document upper airway patency, the presence and consistency of secretions, and the patient's ability to effect airway clearance.*

2. *If a tracheostomy is present, provide humidification* and oxygen, as ordered. *Suction the patient* according to secretion amounts and consistency, possibly as often as every hour in the first 24 hours postoperatively.

3. *Assess the wound site for increasing edema,* reevaluating upper airway patency and documenting changes at least hourly for the first 24 hours postoperatively. Note and report any choking sensation, sense of apprehension, change in respiratory rate or depth, and increased upper airway sounds or tracheal shift.

4. If the patient has a permanent tracheostomy, teach the patient and at least one family member the skills necessary for home care. Include the following points:
• adequate humidification
• suctioning
• tube cleaning
• emergency reinsertion of the tube if it dislodges
• stoma covering
• need to cover the stoma when showering
• need to carry medical alert identification.

5. Additional individualized interventions: _____
_____
_____

Rationales

1. The effects of surgery and intubation alter airway patency and secretion consistency. Patients vary in their ability to cough out secretions.

2. A tracheostomy bypasses the normal humidification function of the nose, so the patient requires supplemental humidity to liquefy secretions. The need for suctioning varies, depending on the duration of intubation, preoperative lung status, and the individual response to the tracheostomy.

3. Early signs of upper airway obstruction are subtle and progressive and may be related to pressure on the trachea from increasing edema at the wound site. If edema causes airway compromise, immediate medical intervention is required.

4. Skill at home care reduces the patient's and family's anxiety and increases the sense of competence to cope with the life-style changes created by the surgery. Suctioning and cleaning are necessary to maintain airway patency. An emergency plan for tube dislodgement may help avert panic if this complication occurs. A stoma covering prevents aspiration of dust or insects, and covering the stoma during showering and avoiding water sports prevents aspiration of water. Medical alert identification will save precious time in establishing an appropriate airway if the patient suffers a cardiac arrest or airway compromise.

5. Rationale: _____
_____
_____

Outcome criteria

Within 48 hours postoperatively, the patient will:
• effectively clear the airway with minimal assistance.

Throughout the postoperative period, the patient will:
• maintain airway patency.

By the time of discharge, the patient and family will:
• demonstrate the correct technique for suctioning and for cleaning the tube

• verbalize a plan for emergency airway maintenance.

By the time of discharge, the patient will:
• identify ways to avoid aspiration
• verbalize the intent to obtain medical alert identification.

Nursing diagnosis: *Impaired swallowing related to decreased strength of muscles involved in mastication, edema, tracheostomy tube, or esophageal sutures**

NURSING PRIORITIES: (a) Prevent aspiration and (b) promote adequate intake.

Interventions

1. *Teach the patient to use oral suction equipment, and keep it at the bedside continuously.*

2. *Be present during meals,* and teach the following: the "supraglottic swallow" (if the patient has a tracheostomy); use of soft foods and frequent, small feedings (if the patient underwent total laryngectomy); and placement of food in the area of the mouth unaffected by surgery. *Encourage persistence in swallowing,* and document progress.

3. Additional individualized interventions: _____

Rationales

1. An increase in the amount of secretions is common after this surgery and difficult to handle if swallowing is impaired. Saliva flows continually; patient control of suction decreases anxiety and minimizes the risk of choking.

2. The "supraglottic swallow" protects the airway and decreases the potential for aspiration. The sequence is usually: cough, take a breath, take food, swallow, cough, swallow, and breathe. Soft foods and frequent feedings gradually stretch the esophageal suture site and encourage muscle relaxation. Swallowing success is increased when food is controlled in the mouth; inspection of the mouth after swallowing indicates areas of weakness and helps determine the optimal site for food placement. Initial attempts may be unsuccessful and discouraging unless support is given. New techniques require practice to be effective.

3. Rationale: _____

Outcome criteria

Throughout the postoperative period, the patient will:
• exhibit no aspiration
• use suction equipment effectively.

By the time of discharge, the patient will:
• control oral secretions without using suction
• use a modified eating technique effectively.

Nursing diagnosis: *Potential for injury related to uncompensated sensory deficit (decreased sense of temperature, sense of touch, and hearing on side of surgery)*

NURSING PRIORITIES: (a) Prevent injury and (b) maintain sensory function.

Interventions

1. See the "Skin Grafts" care plan, page 322.

Rationales

1. This care plan contains interventions for skin graft care.

(continued)

---

*This diagnosis applies to patients who have had combined surgery, including RND.

Interventions *continued*

2. *Maintain continuous suction on drainage catheters:* the recommended level is 100 to 120 mm Hg. When the patient ambulates, use a portable drain collector. Interrupt suction to assess the system's patency every 1 to 2 hours for the first 48 hours, then every 4 hours until drains are removed.

3. *Observe and document wound drainage* every 8 hours. Report abnormalities, especially any sudden increase in the amount of drainage. Instruct the patient and family on the importance of careful observation.

4. *If infection or a fistula occurs, determine the need for placing the patient on carotid artery rupture precautions.* These vary among institutions but always include avoidance of cough, sudden head movements, and Valsalva's maneuver.
   Ensure that supplies are placed at the bedside as follows:
• towels, packing, and dressings
• hemostats and clamps
• gowns and gloves
• suture materials
• a light source
• a laryngoscope and cuffed endotracheal and tracheostomy tubes
• suction equipment.

5. *If carotid rupture occurs, stay with the patient, call for help, apply direct pressure if the hemorrhage site is visible, and maintain airway patency* by orotracheal suctioning if hemoptysis is present.

6. *Inspect and document changes in the wound site,* especially noting redness, pallor, and increasing edema. Report abnormalities.

7. Cleanse the suture line, as ordered, and document changes. The usual care involves using hydrogen peroxide with sterile swabs for crust removal three or four times daily, followed by a thin application of bactericidal ointment to the suture line.

8. Support the patient's shoulder and arm at all times. Begin range-of-motion exercises, as ordered.

Rationales *continued*

2. Negative pressure is required to facilitate clot and fluid removal from the surgical wound. Inadequate suction may cause drain blockage and result in excessive edema, airway obstruction, or both.

3. A dramatic increase in bloody drainage may indicate impending carotid artery rupture. This is most likely to occur in the immediate postoperative period or later if infection or fistula formation occurs near the carotid artery. An increase in clear fluid or a change to milky drainage may indicate infection or fistula formation. Usually, drainage is less than 100 ml every 8 hours for the first 2 days, then less than 20 ml every 8 hours on succeeding days.

4. Exposure of the carotid artery may occur if surrounding tissues are damaged by infection or if fistula formation delays the healing process. Artery rupture is a life-threatening complication requiring immediate medical intervention. Prior assembly of needed supplies facilitates prompt intervention if rupture occurs.

5. Most patients remain awake during carotid artery rupture. External pressure on a visible site controls the hemorrhage temporarily until medical personnel arrive. A common pathway for an internal hemorrhage is the trachea.

6. Redness or pallor may indicate tension on the area, requiring arm, shoulder, or neck repositioning or adjustment of tracheostomy ties or the oxygen collar. Increasing edema may indicate inadequate or blocked drainage tubes.

7. Cleansing facilitates the healing process and decreases the potential for infection. Controversy continues regarding the relative effectiveness of available bactericidal preparations.

8. Proper body alignment promotes healing and decreases tension on the surgical site. Innervation to the muscle is lost, but the muscle mass remains and requires exercise to prevent atrophy.

Interventions *continued*

9. Teach the patient to exercise care concerning the surgical site when performing ADLs. Also teach the male patient to visualize the neck when shaving rather than depending on touch. Emphasize the importance of testing food temperatures before eating. Discourage the use of heat for relief of shoulder pain.

10. Additional individualized interventions: _____

_____

_____

Rationales *continued*

9. Numbness increases the risk of accidental injury while shaving and eating. Heat should not be used to treat shoulder pain, because temperature awareness is impaired after surgery.

10. Rationale: _____

_____

_____

Outcome criteria

Within 5 days postoperatively, the patient will:
• exhibit less than 20 ml of drainage every 8 hours
• exhibit wound site with decreased redness, no pallor, no increased edema, and minimal areas of crusting.

Throughout the postoperative period, the patient will:
• keep shoulder and arm effectively supported

• receive immediate intervention if the carotid artery ruptures.

By the time of discharge, the patient will:
• protect the wound site effectively during ADLs
• identify areas of numbness and state protective measures for each area.

Nursing diagnosis: *Nutritional deficit related to anorexia and impaired swallowing*

NURSING PRIORITY: Optimize nutritional intake.

Interventions

1. On patient admission, document height, weight, weight loss, intake pattern, and food consistency tolerances.

2. *Consult a dietitian* for a thorough nutritional assessment to calculate needed calorie and protein requirements.

3. *Monitor and document intake* at each mealtime. Supplement the diet as needed. Administer enteral feedings, as ordered, and document the patient's response.

4. Weigh the patient twice weekly, and document.

5. Administer mouth care or an analgesic, as ordered, before mealtimes.

6. Additional individualized interventions: _____

_____

_____

Rationales

1. Weight and weight loss help establish the patient's current nutritional status. Intake patterns and food consistency tolerances provide a focus for dietary planning.

2. Nutritional requirements are increased in disease and during treatment. The dietitian's expertise helps meet individual patient needs.

3. To achieve the required high calorie and protein intake, additional feedings are often necessary. Individual patients respond differently to enteral feedings, and frequent adjustment is required.

4. Weight changes indicate progress or the need for adjustment to meet body requirements.

5. Good oral hygiene enhances food appeal when appetite is poor. Analgesics may be indicated if pain keeps the patient from eating.

6. Rationale: _____

_____

_____

Outcome criteria

Throughout the postoperative period, the patient will:
• experience no further weight loss

• have nutritional intake meeting calculated calorie and protein requirements.

Nursing diagnosis: *Alteration in oral mucous membrane related to intake restrictions and NG tube*

NURSING PRIORITIES: (a) Minimize mucous membrane damage and (b) promote healing.

Interventions

1. While the patient is restricted from taking food or fluids, provide mouth care every 2 hours, as ordered.

2. After oral intake is resumed, provide mouth care after meals and at bedtime.

3. If oral suture lines are present, perform mouth care using a power spray, according to protocol and as ordered. Document the appearance of the oral cavity, and note changes.

4. Additional individualized interventions: _____
_____
_____

Rationales

1. Mouth care stimulates salivary flow and decreases pooling of saliva, which fosters bacterial growth. Usually, care involves half-strength hydrogen peroxide and normal saline solution.

2. Food trapped in the altered oral cavity serves as a medium for bacterial growth and must be removed to prevent infection.

3. Crusting requires power-spray pressure for adequate removal.

4. Rationale: _____
_____
_____

Outcome criteria

Throughout the postoperative period, the patient will:
• exhibit pink and moist mucous membranes
• exhibit no signs and symptoms of infection.

Nursing diagnosis: *Impaired verbal communication related to oral surgery, tracheostomy, and edema**

NURSING PRIORITIES: (a) Maximize communication and (b) minimize patient frustration.

Interventions

1. Before surgery, *help the patient determine postoperative methods of communication.* Document the methods chosen; options include:
• pencil and paper on a clipboard
• a "magic slate"
• a communication board or set of cards with pictures of commonly needed items
• an electrolarynx device (for later postoperative stages).

2. Postoperatively, *tag the call system* "patient cannot talk." Explain to the patient and family that the call system can still be used.

Rationales

1. Use of alternative communication methods that the patient chooses decreases anxiety and facilitates communication. Some patients may prefer pencil and paper because the "magic slate" may be associated with childlike feelings of helplessness. A communication board or picture cards may be partially prepared by the patient preoperatively, increasing his or her sense of self-control. Electrolaryngeal devices for laryngectomees are usually not used until 5 to 7 days postoperatively, so another method will be needed initially.

2. This alerts the secretary or nurse to the high priority of a call. The patient is assured that his needs will be met.

Interventions *continued*

3. Postoperatively, assess and document if the patient has decreased hearing on the surgical side. If so, speak to the patient on the unaffected side. Do not shout. Use active listening skills at the bedside.

4. Before replying, allow the patient using a communication device to finish writing out his or her thoughts.

5. Obtain a speech therapy consult, as ordered.

6. Teach the patient with a tracheostomy to cover the opening when speaking, according to protocol or as ordered.

7. Additional individualized interventions: _____
_____
_____

Rationales *continued*

3. Edema may temporarily block the ear canal. Inability to speak does not necessarily indicate deafness; shouting may intimidate or annoy the patient. Standing near the patient when speaking or listening facilitates communication.

4. This prevents incorrect second-guessing and allows the patient to express feelings adequately.

5. Speech therapy exercises improve speech clarity.

6. This prevents air leakage around the trachea, which decreases speech clarity and volume.

7. Rationale: _____
_____
_____

Outcome criteria

Throughout the period of hospitalization, the patient will:
• maintain communication
• experience minimal frustration with communication.

Nursing diagnosis: *Self-care deficit: bathing/hygiene, dressing/grooming related to muscle weakness, pain and uncompensated neuromuscular impairment*

NURSING PRIORITIES: (a) Maximize the patient's self-care ability, and (b) encourage the use of affected muscles.

Interventions

1. Postoperatively, *demonstrate methods to compensate for loss of function,* including use of the unaffected arm and shoulder to bathe, comb hair, and dress by putting clothing on the affected side first.

2. *Medicate with an analgesic,* as ordered, before the start of activities.

3. Teach strengthening exercises, as ordered, and document progress. Facilitate referral to a physical therapist for an ongoing activity plan.

4. Additional individualized interventions: _____
_____
_____

Rationales

1. Initial weakness may discourage the patient from using the unaffected arm and shoulder to the fullest advantage.

2. This encourages arm exercise without pain.

3. Exercises can partially train the muscle to tense, offsetting some of the shoulder drop that occurs with lost innervation. The physical therapist's expertise helps in planning rehabilitation.

4. Rationale: _____
_____
_____

Outcome criterion

Within 5 days postoperatively, the patient will:
• be able to bathe and dress with minimal help.

Nursing diagnosis: *Family coping: potential for growth related to successful management of situational crisis (prolonged treatment for head and neck cancer)*

NURSING PRIORITY: Support the family.

Interventions

1. *Assess and document the family's reactions to and feelings* about the patient's illness, care, and future needs. Allow the family time and space away from the patient to verbalize their feelings and concerns.

2. Discuss with the patient and family the dietary, activity, and life-style modifications needed as a result of surgery or any future treatment plans, such as radiation therapy or chemotherapy. Document the course of action agreed upon by the patient and family.

3. Postoperatively, teach the patient and family skills needed after discharge, such as preparation of a high-calorie, high-protein diet; enteral feeding; dressing changing (if a fistula develops); special mouth care, as ordered; and tracheostomy care and suctioning. Discuss signs and symptoms of possible complications and a plan of action should complications occur. If a tracheostomy is present, provide referral for home care follow-up.

4. Arrange for a visit by a person with similar experience, if the patient desires. Document the patient's and family's response to the visit.

5. Initiate and document referral to appropriate community resource groups, such as home health care, a cancer support group, a smoking cessation group, or an alcoholism support group.

6. Additional individualized interventions: _____
_____
_____

Rationales

1. Verbalization facilitates the family's ability to identify strengths and plan for posthospital patient care.

2. Planning for changes decreases anxiety surrounding discharge home. Often, the initial symptoms of head and neck cancer require changes in diet. Family members may have already made these changes and identified others; in this case, the family may simply need reassurance that their plans are appropriate.

3. Instruction, demonstration, and practice of home-care skills enable the patient and family to effectively meet needs after discharge. Familiarity with procedures increases self-care abilities and the confidence of both the patient and family. Explanation of potential problems and possible solutions relieves anxiety and encourages early assessment and prompt treatment of complications.

4. Common problems and helpful solutions can be identified by a peer, benefiting both the patient and family.

5. Support groups strengthen and expand the patient's and family's coping resources.

6. Rationale: _____
_____
_____

Outcome criteria

By the time of discharge, family members will:
• state the plan for support after discharge
• demonstrate skills needed for home care—dietary management, wound care, and mouth care

• verbalize plans for required life-style modifications related to current or future treatments
• identify the most common complication and state the plan of action should this complication occur.

Nursing diagnosis: *Potential disturbed self-concept: body image related to change in physical appearance and to functional limitations*

NURSING PRIORITY: Encourage acceptance of change and limitations.

Interventions

1. See the "Grief/Grieving" and "Ineffective Family Coping" care plans, pages 41 and 47.

Rationales

1. These care plans contain interventions helpful in coping with potential body-image disturbance.

Interventions *continued*

2. After surgery, *demonstrate acceptance of the patient's appearance by looking directly at him or her* when speaking and giving care.

3. *Discuss and document family reactions to appearance changes* and acceptance needed by patient.

4. *By the second postoperative day, ambulate the patient outside the room.*

5. *Prepare the patient for the wound site's appearance, and discuss the healing process.*

6. *Prepare the patient for possible social rejection after discharge.* Discuss and document feelings and responses.

7. Encourage prescribed exercises to strengthen the shoulder muscle.

8. Additional individualized interventions: _____
_____
_____

Outcome criteria
Within 2 days postoperatively, family members will:
• accept the patient's appearance and give positive support.

Rationales *continued*

2. Patients sense nonverbal communication. An initial positive response to the patient's changed appearance strengthens self-esteem.

3. Awareness of patient needs helps the family give adequate support.

4. Early ambulation outside the room environment encourages adjustment to changes.

5. Initial appearance is distorted until healing is complete. Preparing the patient in advance minimizes distress over the wound site's appearance.

6. Acquaintances may have limited experience with facial surgery, and the patient should be prepared for their responses. Previous discussion of possible reactions may help minimize the painfulness of such encounters.

7. The muscle can be strengthened to offset shoulder drop.

8. Rationale: _____
_____
_____

By the time of discharge, the patient will:
• show beginning acceptance of body changes and limitations
• verbalize a method for dealing with rejection.

Discharge planning
NURSING DISCHARGE CRITERIA
Upon discharge, documentation shows evidence of:
• stable vital signs
• absence of fever
• absence of life-threatening dysphagia
• absence of pulmonary and cardiovascular complications
• hemoglobin and WBC levels within normal parameters
• a healing wound with drainage amount within expected parameters and no evidence of bloody or purulent drainage
• completion of a diagnostic workup for evidence of cancer
• ability to tolerate adequate oral nutrition
• ability to perform wound care, dressing changes, and exercise program independently or with minimal assistance
• ability to perform ADLs and ambulate at prehospitalization level
• ability to control pain using oral medications
• adequate home support system or referral to home care if indicated by patient's inability to perform ADLs, ambulate, and care for wound as directed.

Additional information to be documented if the patient has undergone a laryngectomy or a tracheostomy:
• ability to communicate adequately
• ability to perform tracheostomy care independently or with minimal assistance
• ability to perform emergency tracheostomy care if the entire tracheostomy apparatus becomes dislodged
• automatic referral to home care or nursing home care if indicated by inadequate home support system and patient's inability to independently perform tracheostomy care.

PATIENT/FAMILY DISCHARGE TEACHING CHECKLIST
Document evidence that patient/family demonstrate understanding of:
__ extent of disease and surgery, and implications
__ caloric requirements and dietary modifications
__ wound care
__ mouth care
__ schedule for resuming activities and returning to work
__ common changes in feelings post-RND

___ signs and symptoms of disease recurrence
___ all discharge medications' purpose, dose, administration schedule, and side effects requiring medical attention (usual discharge medications include an analgesic and an antibiotic)
___ date, time, and location of follow-up appointments
___ how to contact doctor
___ need for smoking-cessation program or alcoholism rehabilitation, as needed
___ community resources for speech rehabilitation, physical therapy, and support
___ when and how to activate emergency medical system.

DOCUMENTATION CHECKLIST

Using outcome criteria as a guide, document:
___ clinical status on admission
___ significant changes in status
___ pertinent laboratory and diagnostic test findings
___ pain-relief measures
___ wound site appearance and drainage
___ other therapies: mouth care and wound care
___ nutritional intake
___ patient/family teaching
___ discharge planning.

ASSOCIATED CARE PLANS

Death and Dying
Grief/Grieving
Ineffective Family Coping
Ineffective Individual Coping
Pain
Skin Grafts
Surgical Intervention

REFERENCES

Carpenito, L.J. *Nursing Diagnosis: Application to Clinical Practice.* Philadelphia: J.B. Lippincott Co., 1983.

Duke University Hospital Nursing Services. *Guidelines for Nursing Care: Process and Outcome.* Philadelphia: J.B. Lippincott Co., 1983.

Griffin, C.W., and Lockhart, J.S. "Learning to Swallow Again." *American Journal of Nursing* 87(3):314-17, March 1987.

Sigler, B.A. "Nursing Care for Head and Neck Tumor Patients," in *Comprehensive Management of Head and Neck Tumors.* Edited by Thawley, S.E., et al. Philadelphia: W.B. Saunders Co., 1987.

Strasen, L. "Acute Alcohol Withdrawal Syndrome in the Critical Care Unit," *Critical Care Nurse* 2(6):24-31, November/December 1983.

Thompson, J.M., et al, eds. *Clinical Nursing.* St. Louis: C.V. Mosby Co., 1986.

Asthma

DRG information

DRG 96 [Medical DRG] Bronchitis and Asthma.
>Age greater than 17. With Complication or Comorbidity (CC).
>Mean LOS = 6.0 days
>Principal diagnoses include:
>• bronchitis [acute and chronic]
>• asthma.

DRG 97 [Medical DRG] Bronchitis and Asthma.
>Age greater than 17 to 69. Without CC.
>Mean LOS = 4.9 days

DRG 98 [Medical DRG] Bronchitis and Asthma.
>Age 0 to 17.
>Mean LOS = 3.0 days

Additional DRG information: These DRGs, as well as many others having to do with respiratory disease, are very difficult to code accurately because of numerous coding nuances. The coders depend entirely on the medical record to determine the correct DRG. All DRGs listed above have very low relative weights, making them very low in reimbursement. However, a patient presenting with these disorders and arterial blood gas (ABG) levels within certain abnormal parameters may be legitimately coded respiratory failure, which has a much higher weight and reimbursement. Also, if asthma is caused by a bacterium or another organism, the DRG would fall under a high-paying DRG. Nurses also should be aware that it is important to document any condition that would count as a comorbidity, because comorbidity places the patient in a higher-paying DRG.

Introduction

DEFINITION AND TIME FOCUS

Asthma is characterized by increased responsiveness and hyperreactivity of the tracheal and bronchial smooth muscle to various stimuli, resulting in widespread narrowing of the airways (bronchoconstriction), increased mucus production, mucosal inflammation and edema, and airflow obstruction. These changes are reversible, either spontaneously or as a result of therapy. Between asthma attacks, the individual may remain symptom-free. Attacks vary in severity, from mild obstruction to profound respiratory failure. Status asthmaticus is a nonspecific term used when severe obstruction is unrelieved by usual medical treatment.

Two types of asthma exist:
• extrinsic asthma—childhood onset, often disappearing in the adult; positive family history; usually seasonal; multiple well-defined allergies; positive response to allergy skin testing (indicative of an antigen-antibody response)

• intrinsic asthma—seen in adults after age 30; may be more severe in nature and continuous; associated with a history of recurrent respiratory tract infections; multiple nonspecific conditions can provoke an attack; negative response to allergy skin testing.

The adult patient admitted to the acute care setting usually has intrinsic asthma and is in acute respiratory distress. This care plan focuses on the patient admitted after self-management and/or after doctor outpatient intervention has failed to terminate an asthma attack.

ETIOLOGY/PRECIPITATING FACTORS

• acute episode may be precipitated by any of numerous etiologic agents:
>☐ infection (viral or bacterial)
>☐ environmental exposure to a nonspecific allergen (such as second-hand smoke, dust, or cleaning compounds)
>☐ chronic sinusitis
>☐ weather changes (such as, heat, cold, fog, or wind)
>☐ exercise
>☐ regurgitation
>☐ psychogenic factors
>☐ ingestion of aspirin (aspirin-sensitive individuals may also be sensitive to indomethacin; mefenamic acid; or tartrazine [yellow dye], an ingredient found in many medications)

• airway response to the precipitating agent may be immediate or delayed

Focused assessment guidelines

NURSING HISTORY (Functional health pattern findings)

Health perception–health management pattern

• may report *increasing shortness of breath*, stated as "can't catch breath," "can't inhale," or "hyperventilating"
• may report chest tightness
• describes a *panicky, suffocating feeling* (typically resists oxygen mask)
• may report *increased coughing*, often dry and nonproductive, that leaves patient short of breath
• may report change in sputum production, usually less sputum mobilization (patient still produces sputum but is unable to raise it)
• attack may have been in progress for some time before admission to the acute-care setting; patient may report *increasing fatigue* and inability to handle the attack with prescribed and nonprescribed measures
• may no longer be complying with prescribed treatments

• reports using inhalers (either prescription or nonprescription type), continuously, without benefit
• may identify certain events or environmental factors as major contributors to the attack's development

Sleep-rest pattern
• may state that cough disturbs sleep

Nutritional-metabolic pattern
• may report *dehydration* (from shortness of breath, use of oral breathing, or reluctance to drink water)
• typically has not eaten since onset of the attack because of preoccupation and shortness of breath; may complain of nausea, which may be related to medication use or abuse
• if a chronic corticosteroid user, may report weight gain

Activity-exercise pattern
• may report ongoing exercise limitations because participation in exercise can precipitate wheezing and shortness of breath
• if exercise is limited, may report difficulty maintaining desired level of physical conditioning

Cognitive-perceptual pattern
• may be able to describe complex strategies for self-management during an acute attack, but may report inability to put them in effect during an actual attack, when panic may overwhelm problem-solving skills and hypoxemia may impair thinking

Role-relationship pattern
• if an attack is experienced in public, may shy away from public events and activities because of embarrassment from severe dyspnea and cough; may also report that laughing can precipitate an attack
• may report that spouse or partner as well as family and social groups precipitate attacks by use of environmental irritants such as smoking

Self-perception–self-concept pattern
• if on maintenance corticosteroid therapy, may report changes in body image related to cushingoid effects of medications; may become very discouraged with appearance and inability to prevent or alter physiologic changes

Coping–stress tolerance pattern
• may describe fluctuations in emotions, such as:
  □ denial of problem (may ignore potential irritants by refusing to give away a pet, to stop smoking, or to remove offending furniture; may maintain ignorance of medication routines and self-management strategies)
  □ anger (may blame others for precipitating attack; may describe asthma as a "kid's disease"; may not feel past health habits justify extent of disease)

PHYSICAL FINDINGS
Physical parameters, which vary with the severity of an attack, are good indicators of treatment outcomes.

General appearance
• *anxious; maintains upright position*
• fever if infection is present

Neurologic
• *initially hyperalert, awake, and oriented; may become progressively less alert, although awake and oriented, as fatigue progresses*
• restlessness (from hypoxemia)
• lethargy (from increased carbon dioxide [CO_2] levels)

Integumentary
• *color initially good;* may be flushed; cyanosis a late, unreliable sign
• *diaphoresis*
• *mucous membranes dry* from rapid oral breathing and dehydration

Cardiovascular
• *sinus tachycardia* (related to bronchodilating medications and stress response)
• *mild to moderate hypertension* (related to medications and anxiety)
• paradoxical pulse becoming more pronounced (greater than 15 mm Hg) as air trapping increases
• potential dysrhythmias

Respiratory
• *use of accessory neck muscles during breathing,* becoming more pronounced as severity of obstruction worsens
• *respiratory rate less than 30 breaths/minute, increasing as attack worsens but possibly lessening with fatigue*
• *prolonged exhalations*
• *wheezing* noted; may be audible from a distance (timing varies with stage of severity: initially, expiratory then inspiratory-expiratory, finally no wheezing—"silent" chest is indicative of critical airflow limitation)
• *cough,* possibly *decreased sputum production* (increased production a positive sign: color can be yellow, sputum thick or crusted)
• speech pattern changes to monosyllabic as airflow limitation worsens

DIAGNOSTIC STUDIES
• *ABG measurements*—may be obtained only in severe or prolonged attack; *hypoxemia always present; CO_2 level used to stage attack's progress:*
  □ stage 1: decreased PO_2 and PCO_2 levels (hyperventilation)
  □ stage 2: decreased PO_2 level, normal PCO_2 level (increased fatigue)
  □ stage 3: decreased PO_2 level (<50 mm Hg), increased PCO_2 level (critical hypoventilation and fatigue)

• sputum specimens—Gram stain used to detect presence of treatable organisms; eosinophil smear done if allergens are suspected as primary etiology; culture and sensitivity testing difficult to obtain because mucus is initially thick, tenacious, and difficult to mobilize; casts and plugs are present when sputum is mobilized

• complete blood count and differential—white blood cell (WBC) count increased with infection; eosinophil count increased with allergy

• *serum electrolyte levels—potassium level invariably decreased*

• theophylline level—may be necessary in acute phase if patient may have treated self extensively with non-prescription and prescription remedies; normal level 10 to 20 mcg/ml; an elevated level may indicate medication misuse; a decreased level may indicate noncompliance

• *chest X-ray—shows hyperinflation;* air trapping decreases as airflow obstruction improves; between attacks, hyperinflation resolves; infiltrates are present if infection is major etiology

• pulmonary function testing (PFT)—not usually performed during an acute attack; measures of airflow rate, peak expiratory flow rate (PEFR), and forced expiratory flow rate in 1 second (FEV_1) are less than 25% of predicted value in severe obstruction; full PFT demonstrates dramatic response to bronchodilators; methacholine or histamine challenge provokes increased airway resistance

• allergen skin test—negative; positive skin test does not necessarily indicate that a respiratory response will be produced if exposure occurs

POTENTIAL COMPLICATIONS
• cardiopulmonary arrest
• cardiac dysrhythmias
• rib fractures (from violent coughing)
• pneumothorax
• atelectasis
• pneumonia
• drug overdose related to noncompliance or knowledge deficit about medication use during an acute attack

Collaborative problem: *Potential status asthmaticus or pulmonary arrest related to airway obstruction, hypoxemia, and progressive fatigue*

NURSING PRIORITIES: (a) Maintain effective airway clearance, and (b) promote an efficient breathing pattern.

Interventions

1. *Administer oxygen via nasal cannula, 2 to 3 liters/minute or more, as ordered.*

2. *Administer fluid therapy* orally or intravenously, as ordered. The usual fluid goal, 2 to 3 liters every 24 hours, may vary with the patient's age and general status.

3. *Monitor patient status continuously until it stabilizes.* Parameters to monitor include level of consciousness, skin color and moisture, speech pattern, use of accessory muscles for breathing, breath sounds, sputum production, respiratory rate, pulse blood pressure, and paradoxical pulse. Obtain ABG measurements, as ordered, and expiratory flow rates. Thoroughly document findings. Report changes that indicate deteriorating status.

4. *Be especially alert for signs of a potentially fatal attack,* and promptly report any to the doctor. Such signs include:
• previous severe asthma attacks
• FEV_1 < 500 cc or PEFR < 100 liters/minute
• little or no response to bronchodilator therapy in 1 hour, as evidenced in flow rate measurements
• altered level of consciousness

Rationales

1. Hypoxemia is always present in an acute asthma attack because of ventilation-perfusion imbalance. Supplemental oxygen decreases the work of breathing and reduces potential cardiac dysfunction.

2. The patient is usually dehydrated on admission. Hydration promotes expectoration of thickened sputum and minimizes development of impacted mucus.

3. Parameters vary with the attack's severity, the patient's response to treatment, and patient fatigue. Because of physiologic instability, parameters may change rapidly.

4. One or more of the items cited may forewarn of a fatal attack. Prompt, aggressive therapy is necessary to forestall pulmonary arrest.

(continued)

Interventions *continued*

- cyanosis
- PO$_2$ < 50 mm Hg
- PCO$_2$ > 45 mm Hg
- pulsus paradoxus
- EKG abnormality
- pneumothorax.

5. *Administer pharmacologic agents,* as ordered. The medication regimen varies but typically includes:

- bronchodilators, such as beta-adrenergics and theophylline. Beta-adrenergic agents (epinephrine, terbutaline, isoproterenol, and metaproterenol) are given subcutaneously, inhaled from a pressurized canister or nebulizer, or taken orally; observe for such side effects as nervousness or hypertension. Theophylline (xanthine) preparations, such as aminophylline, are initially given I.V. and then orally; observe for and report any dysrhythmias, tachycardia, hypotension, vomiting, or other side effects.
- corticosteroids. These are initially given I.V., then orally, with tapering as soon as possible. Aerosolized corticosteroids, with or without oral agents, may be used in some patients.

6. *Initiate measures to alleviate panic, ensure safety, and promote relaxation.* Place the patient in an upright position with adequate support; promote exhalation of trapped air by instructing the patient to prolong the exhalation phase of breathing and to exhale without force; maintain a calm, reassuring attitude; reduce environmental stimulation, if possible.

7. *Monitor therapeutic medication levels, and assess for associated electrolyte and glucose imbalances* daily, as ordered. Report abnormal findings.

8. *Initiate measures to mobilize sputum,* such as postural drainage and percussion, suctioning if necessary, and controlled cough. Caution: Each of these measures can intensify hypoxemia. Use supplemental oxygen, temporarily increasing the liter flow if any evidence of respiratory distress is observed.

9. *Monitor fluid balance,* noting intake and output, weight, skin turgor, condition of mucous membranes, characteristics of sputum, presence or absence of edema, and urine specific gravity and hematocrit levels. Document and report abnormalities.

Rationales *continued*

5. Although some patients can control symptoms using relaxation techniques, pharmacologic intervention is usually necessary and is more effective before the attack becomes severe or prolonged.
- Adenosine 3':5'-cyclic phosphate (c-AMP) is a chemical mediator that controls bronchodilation. Beta-adrenergics and xanthines stimulate production, or prevent destruction, of c-AMP and thus produce bronchodilation. Effectiveness varies with blood level.

- Corticosteroids (I.V. or oral) are believed to reduce inflammation, thereby reducing edema in bronchial mucosa. Aerosolized corticosteroids may provide beneficial effects while minimizing side effects, since they are delivered directly to the affected tissues.

6. Acutely asthmatic patients experience extreme anxiety and panic. They may attempt to alleviate discomfort with counterproductive posturing and breathing patterns and with restless activity. Characteristically, the harder the patient attempts to breathe, the less productive the effort, with increased air trapping. Prolonged exhalation facilitates a relaxed expiratory effort and reduces air trapping.

7. Establishment of a therapeutic medication regimen requires ongoing monitoring of drug levels and electrolyte status as the patient is rehydrated and stabilized. Theophylline clearance may be impaired, or electrolyte or glucose levels may be altered, or both—especially in patients with cardiac disease, hypertension, or liver disease, or in those using other medications.

8. Once hydration is initiated, the patient must mobilize the thick, crusty mucus rapidly to prevent bronchial plugging. Because of fatigue, the patient may need assistance in this process.

9. During an asthma attack, profuse diaphoresis and tachypnea cause fluid loss. Because the patient is usually too dyspneic and panicky to take oral fluids, significant dehydration may rapidly ensue. I.V. fluid replacement must be individualized and monitored carefully; otherwise, aggressive hydration may lead to fluid overload in patients with compromised cardiovascular status.

Interventions *continued*

10. Do not administer narcotics or sedatives.

11. *Observe for indicators of the need for intubation*, such as fatigue, further reduction in thoracic expansion, decreasing level of consciousness, PCO$_2$ level increased >10 mm Hg above the resting level, severe hypoxemia, and decreasing breath sounds. Alert the doctor immediately if these indicators are noted.

12. Additional individualized interventions: _____

_____

Rationales *continued*

10. The patient may be anxious but this is related to hypoxemia. Sedation depresses the respiratory drive and promotes hypoventilation.

11. When the work of breathing becomes overwhelming, exhaustion results. If intubation and mechanical ventilation are not initiated promptly, pulmonary arrest can ensue.

12. Rationale: _____

_____

Outcome criteria
Within 1 hour of beginning therapy, the patient will:
• show an improved flow rate (FEV$_1$ and PEFR)
• mobilize sputum
• exhibit reduced anxiety with maintenance of a normal level of consciousness
• have reduced hypoxemia, with maintenance of PCO$_2$ level at or below normal.

Once stabilized, the patient will:
• have improved breath sounds
• decrease use of accessory muscles for breathing
• exhibit stable vital signs within normal limits for this patient
• have improved ABG measurements.

Nursing diagnosis: *Potential social isolation related to activity-induced shortness of breath; irritants; and change in body image*

NURSING PRIORITY: Improve the patient's ability to prevent or cope with breathing difficulties.

Interventions

1. After resolution of the acute episode, discuss and demonstrate (through roleplaying) assertive strategies to be used when the patient must confront an environmental irritant (such as second-hand smoke). Have the patient return the demonstration.

2. Demonstrate strategies to be used during a coughing episode (for example, controlled cough technique or "huff" coughing) and for acute shortness of breath occurring during an activity (for example, upright and forward posturing, with shoulder relaxation and prolonged exhalation). Coach the patient in using these strategies.

3. Discuss with the patient medication side effects, such as anxiety and tremor from bronchodilators or moon face, loss of muscle tissue, and a tendency to bruise from corticosteroids. Encourage ventilation of frustrations about their impact on socialization.

4. Help the patient identify personal factors that may precipitate attacks or contribute to them. Observing dietary intake, medications, emotional state, and environmental factors before an attack may provide clues about an individual's triggering mechanisms.

Rationales

1. The patient will be more likely to implement an assertive, nonaggressive strategy for dealing with potentially hazardous situations if several alternative responses are provided. Patients often do not realize that they have a right to request environmental changes or do not know how to make such requests.

2. Breathing strategies reduce forceful exhalation, which occurs during cough or acute shortness of breath and results in increased airway obstruction.

3. Although nothing can be done to eliminate these side effects, compliance with the prescribed regimen may be improved if the patient vents his feelings about the side effects to an understanding professional.

4. Once specific trigger factors have been pinpointed, the patient can take steps to minimize or reduce exposure to them.

(continued)

Interventions *continued*

5. Emphasize the importance of adequate daily fluid intake.

6. Additional individualized interventions: _____
_____
_____

Outcome criteria
By the time of discharge, the patient will:
• demonstrate appropriate breathing techniques during activity-induced shortness of breath or coughing episodes
• describe assertive strategies for dealing with environmental irritants

Rationales *continued*

5. Dry mucous membranes may precipitate an attack. Dehydration worsens airway obstruction related to tenacious sputum.

6. Rationale: _____
_____
_____

• realistically describe body image changes related to medication side effects, while continuing to comply with the medication regimen
• identify factors that may trigger attacks.

Discharge planning
NURSING DISCHARGE CRITERIA
Upon discharge, documentation shows evidence of:
• WBC count within normal parameters
• oxygen and I.V. therapy discontinued for at least 24 to 48 hours
• stable vital signs
• ABG measurements within expected parameters
• absence of cardiovascular and pulmonary complications (such as dysrhythmias or atelectasis)
• tolerance of and response to oral medication regimen
• absence of dehydration signs and symptoms
• ability to tolerate adequate nutritional intake
• absence of acute shortness of breath on exertion
• ability to ambulate and perform activities of daily living at prehospitalization level
• adequate home support or referral to home care if indicated by inadequate home support system or patient's inability to perform self-care.

PATIENT/FAMILY DISCHARGE TEACHING CHECKLIST
Document evidence that patient and family demonstrate understanding of:
___ factors that trigger an asthma attack (specific to the individual patient, if possible)
___ home and work environment assessment and modifications to counter potential irritants
___ preventive measures for use when irritant exposure is unavoidable
___ clinical manifestations of an impending attack
___ relaxation and breathing exercises to improve control during an attack
___ all discharge medications' purpose, dose, administration schedule, and side effects requiring medical

attention (usual discharge medications include bronchodilators and corticosteroids)
___ purpose and use of over-the-counter medications (bronchodilating medications, expectorants, cough suppressants, cold remedies or sleep remedies) as well as precautions to take when using them
___ bronchial hygiene measures: indications, schedule, and use
___ use and cleaning of respiratory therapy equipment
___ self-management plan, including decision-making strategies for beginning or mild attacks and an emergency plan for severe or progressing attacks
___ hydration requirements
___ controlled cough technique
___ exercise recommendations and limitations, if any
___ measures to control shortness of breath when performing activities
___ need for flu and pneumococcus vaccine
___ date, time, and location of follow-up appointment
___ how to contact doctor.

DOCUMENTATION CHECKLIST
Using outcome criteria as a guide, document:
___ clinical status on admission
___ significant changes in status
___ pertinent laboratory and diagnostic test findings
___ institution of therapeutic modalities, including patient reponse
___ respiratory status (each shift)
___ oxygen therapy
___ medications
___ hydration status, fluid intake and output
___ patient and family teaching
___ discharge planning.

ASSOCIATED CARE PLANS
Fluid and Electrolyte Imbalances
Ineffective Individual Coping
Knowledge Deficit

REFERENCES
Elpern, E. "Asthma Update: Pathophysiology and Treatment," *Heart & Lung* 9(4):665, July/August 1980.

Fuchs, P.L. "Asthma: Physiology, Signs and Symptoms," *Nursing83* 12(12):36, December 1983.

Janson-Bjerklie, S. "The Role of Emotions and Suggestion in Triggering Asthma," *Respiratory Therapy* 13(3):17, 25, 28, May/June 1983.

Mancini, M.R., et al. "Fighting the Frustrations of Status Asthmaticus," *Nursing82* 12(3):58-63, March 1982.

Rifas, E. "Teaching Patients to Manage Acute Asthma: The Future Is Now," *Nursing83* 13(4):77, April 1983.

Summer, W.R. "Status Asthmaticus," *Chest* 87(1):87 (Supp.), January 1985.

Chronic Obstructive Pulmonary Disease

DRG information

DRG 88 [Medical DRG] Chronic Obstructive
Pulmonary Disease.
Mean LOS = 6.3 days
Principal diagnoses include:
• bronchiectasis [congenital]
• bronchitis [obstructive chronic]
• emphysema
• chronic respiratory conditions due to
fumes or vapors.
This DRG is frequently seen in acute care.
Also, patients are frequently readmitted within
15 days of previous hospitalization.

DRG 89 [Medical DRG] Simple Pneumonia and Pleurisy.
Age greater than 17. With Complication or
Comorbidity (CC).
Mean LOS = 7.2 days
Principal diagnoses include:
• bronchopneumonia
• influenza with pneumonia
• bacterial pneumonia
• pneumonia with organism unspecified.

DRG 96 [Medical DRG] Bronchitis and Asthma.
Age greater than 17. With CC.
Mean LOS = 6.0 days

DRG 97 [Medical DRG] Bronchitis and Asthma.
Age greater than 17. Without CC.
Mean LOS = 4.9 days

Introduction

DEFINITION AND TIME FOCUS

Chronic obstructive pulmonary disease (COPD) is a diagnostic category applied to patients whose primary respiratory difficulty involves exhalation of air. This care plan focuses on two diseases, emphysema and chronic bronchitis. (Asthma, another disorder sometimes included in COPD, is covered in a separate care plan.)
• Emphysema is defined as permanent, nonreversible destruction of alveoli, resulting in dyspnea inappropriate for age and level of exertion.
• Chronic bronchitis (inflammation of the bronchi) is characterized by a chronic productive cough resulting from hyperplasia of mucus-producing cells and increased mucus production.
    Few patients have a "pure" disease process; most experience a combination of symptoms.
    Commonalities in the stable state include:
• difficulty exhaling because of airway collapse, especially noted with effort (the harder the patient tries to exhale, the less he can)
• air trapping with hyperinflation
• dyspnea
• history of smoking
• hypersensitivity of the airways to a variety of stimuli
• difficulty handling secretions.

Commonalities during an exacerbation include ventilation-perfusion imbalance resulting in:
• increased work of breathing
• increased myocardial work
• hypoxemia
• carbon dioxide retention.
    This care plan focuses on the COPD patient who is admitted to the acute-care setting with exacerbation of the disease and failure of prescribed therapies to control the symptoms.

ETIOLOGY/PRECIPITATING FACTORS

• exacerbation precipitated most commonly by an infectious process, viral or bacterial; other common precipitants include exposure to environmental pollutants (second-hand smoke, dust, or cleaning compounds), exercise, and weather changes (heat, cold, fog, or wind)

Focused assessment guidelines

NURSING HISTORY (Functional health pattern findings)

Health perception–health management pattern

• complains of *greater than normal shortness of breath*, with inability to control symptoms with prescribed or nonprescribed therapies
• may report increased fatigue and feel unable to cope with this crisis
• may report increasing anxiety and panic
• may report increasing difficulty mobilizing and eliminating sputum

Nutritional-metabolic pattern

• may report *anorexia*
• may report inability to eat and digest without shortness of breath
• may report nausea, possibly associated with medications
• may report bloating, especially after eating foods noted for causing flatulence
• may report difficulty complying with therapeutic recommendation to drink at least 2 qt water per day
• may report symptoms of fluid and electrolyte disturbance, such as weakness, lethargy, confusion, weight changes, and muscle cramping

Activity-exercise pattern

• complains of *shortness of breath with even minimal exertion or when performing activities of daily living*
• may be aware of ability to control shortness of breath and panic with breathing maneuvers but may report forgetting this ability in crisis

Sleep-rest pattern

• reports *sleep pattern disturbance*
• may report having slept in an upright posture (usually in a reclining chair) during the previous night's exacerbation

• may report bouts of shortness of breath during the night, relieved by bronchial hygiene and expectoration of secretions
• may report trouble getting to sleep and nervousness
• may report chronic fatigue and sleepiness during the day
• may report nocturia (may be related to medications)
• may report morning headache

Cognitive-perceptual pattern
• may report *fluctuating compliance with therapeutic regimen* (may perceive regimen as complex and difficult to fully understand and follow)

Role-relationship pattern
• may report *multiple role changes, resulting in depression, isolation, and increased dependence*
• may report *difficulty verbalizing feelings* because emotions intensify shortness of breath

Sexuality-reproductive pattern
• may report complex interpersonal role changes with spouse or partner (if one is present), with decreased desire for and frequency of sexual activity because of shortness of breath actual or feared

Coping–stress tolerance pattern
• may have difficulty expressing either positive or negative emotions because of shortness of breath
• may report acting erratically, alternately passive, angry, abusive, or manipulative, with wide mood fluctuations

Value-belief pattern
• may report ambivalence about staff using resuscitative measures that patient realizes (possibly from past experience) may become necessary during this hospitalization but may not ultimately improve the quality of life

PHYSICAL FINDINGS
General appearance
• *apprehensive and anxious;* maintains upright, tense posture
• panics easily if activity is requested
• emphysema—cachectic; chronic bronchitis—plethoric

Cardiovascular
• typically, *rapid pulse* because of medications; expected upper limit for medication-induced tachycardia <120 beats/minute
• atrial fibrillation (common dysrhythmia of COPD)
• signs of cor pulmonale and right heart failure (edema, jugular venous distention, or crackles)

Pulmonary
• *accentuated accessory neck muscles*
• *barrel chest* from hyperinflation
• *decreased breath sounds bilaterally*
• *prolonged expiratory phase*
• cough with sputum production; hallmark of emphysema: sputum appearance (tapiocalike plugs); hallmark

of chronic bronchitis: copious amounts of sputum
• rhonchi if secretions are copious; crackles if heart failure or pneumonia is present (crackles are not a common or expected finding in COPD)
• chronic sinus drainage with accompanying sinus pain (may be source of recurring infections)

Neurologic
• anxious
• if hypoxemic, restless
• if PCO_2 levels are increased, lethargic and sleepy

Integumentary
• skin becomes discolored (mottled and cyanotic) easily during coughing spells, strenuous activity, or episodes of acute shortness of breath

DIAGNOSTIC STUDIES
• *arterial blood gas (ABG) measurements—derangements vary with disease type*
  ◻ *hypoxemia*—most common; becomes more pronounced with exercise; when stable, PO_2 level should be between 55 and 65 mm Hg, because a COPD patient may have a reduced respiratory drive when PO_2 level is greater than 65 mm Hg; in acute exacerbation, PO_2 level commonly falls below 55 mm Hg
  ◻ *increased carbon dioxide (CO_2) level*—in stable COPD patient, PCO_2 level should be maintained at 50 mm Hg or less; during exacerbation, PCO_2 level above 50 mm Hg is very common
  ◻ acid-base imbalance—in stable state, respiratory acidosis is compensated; during exacerbation, both respiratory and metabolic acidosis may be present
• sputum specimens—if infection is suspected, Gram stain and culture and sensitivity tests are done to determine appropriate antibiotic
• theophylline level—normal: 10 to 20 mcg/ml; may be elevated if patient has readjusted theophylline dose or taken over-the-counter medications
• alpha$_1$-antitrypsin assay—uncommon; performed to determine alpha$_1$-antitrypsin deficiency in young patients suspected of emphysema
• other tests—white blood cell count, hematocrit values, and serum electrolyte levels, according to suspected etiology
• *chest X-ray—shows hyperinflation* with flattening of the diaphragm caused by air trapping in the chest, that may worsen during exacerbation; may also show infiltrates, depending on cause of exacerbation
• pulmonary function testing—usually not performed in acute exacerbation state; common findings in stable state include:
  ◻ reduced expiratory flow rates, especially with effort; more pronounced airway obstruction as patient tries harder to exhale
  ◻ some response to bronchodilators in patients with chronic bronchitis; no response in patients with emphysema
  ◻ decreased diffusion capacity in patients with emphysema predominating

POTENTIAL COMPLICATIONS
- acute respiratory failure
- cardiac dysrhythmias
- depressed brain function; permanent brain injury
- other organ injury (for example, kidney)
- pneumonia
- pneumothorax
- cor pulmonale

Collaborative problem: Respiratory failure (PO_2 level less than 50 mm Hg, with or without PCO_2 level greater than 50 mm Hg) related to ventilation-perfusion imbalance

NURSING PRIORITIES: (a) Maintain adequate airway clearance, (b) reverse hypoxemia and CO_2 retention, (c) maintain optimum environment for adequate function of patient's limited respiratory reserves, and (d) resolve precipitating events.

Interventions

1. *Obtain and report* ABG measurements as needed to determine a baseline for the patient; to monitor the appropriateness of therapy; and to determine the effect of an acute episode (indicated if the patient becomes somnolent or increasingly restless or has a sudden personality change).

2. *Administer oxygen* as ordered, generally 2 to 3 liters per minute. Maintain oxygen delivery during activity.

3. *Administer pharmacologic agents,* as ordered, which may include:
- bronchodilators

- antibiotics
- corticosteroids

- expectorants.

Monitor therapeutic levels as indicated.

4. *Perform bronchial hygiene measures,* as ordered. *Assess lung sounds* before and after all treatments and at least every 4 hours when the patient is awake. Report and document the effectiveness of any or all of the following treatments: aerosols, intermittent positive-pressure breathing, postural drainage and percussion, and suctioning (if the coughing mechanism is inadequate).

5. *Maintain fluid intake* at 2 to 3 qt water per day.

Rationales

1. ABG evaluations are the only reliable way of assessing the patient's oxygenation and CO_2 status. No formula exists for determining the precise percentage of oxygen a patient needs because the appropriateness of the oxygen dosage can be evaluated only by serial ABG determinations.

2. COPD patients may have an altered regulation-of-respiration mechanism. Instead of responding to an elevated CO_2 level (normal response), the COPD patient may respond only to a need for oxygen. Low percentages of oxygen are less likely to decrease the respiratory drive. Oxygen demand increases with activity.

3. Pharmacologic agents are ordered on the basis of etiology.
- Adenosine 3':5'-cyclic phosphate (c-AMP) is a chemical mediator that controls bronchodilation. Bronchodilators (sympathomimetics and xanthines) stimulate production or prevent destruction of c-AMP, thereby producing bronchodilation. Effectiveness varies with blood level.
- Antibiotics are ordered for the specific organism.
- Corticosteroids (I.V. or oral) are believed to reduce inflammation.
- Expectorants may be used as an adjunct to water and fluid therapy.

4. Ventilation-perfusion abnormalities are the major reason for respiratory failure in the COPD patient. Bronchial hygiene measures open obstructed airways for more effective ventilation and help the already compromised system perform cleansing while conserving oxygen reserves.

5. Sputum viscosity is related to the patient's hydration status. Water is the most physiologically compatible expectorant.

Interventions *continued*

6. *Monitor, document, and report signs of infection or further deterioration in respiratory status,* such as an increase or decrease of sputum, changes in the sputum's color or consistency, fever, increased shortness of breath, and changes in breath sounds.

7. If possible, *reduce or eliminate environmental irritants:* encourage smoking cessation, and do not use (or allow roommates or visitors to use) hair, deodorant, or room-freshening sprays or strong fragrances near the patient.

8. Additional individualized interventions:_____

_____

_____

Rationales *continued*

6. Routine monitoring and accurate documentation on a shift-by-shift basis will allow early detection of subtle changes in the patient's condition that might signal illness progression.

7. Numerous environmental substances and sprays can cause airway irritation in the COPD patient (especially when the airways are already vulnerable) and exacerbate the condition.

8. Rationale:_____

_____

_____

Outcome criteria
Within 48 hours of admission, the patient will:
• exhibit PO_2 level greater than 50 mm Hg, with or without supplemental oxygen
• exhibit a PCO_2 level within the patient's normal range, typically less than 50 mm Hg
• exhibit fewer and shorter periods of acute shortness of breath.

By the time of discharge, the patient will:
• exhibit reduced evidence of infection or environmental irritation
• easily expectorate clear or white, thin sputum
• have lungs clear to auscultation, without rhonchi or crackles.

Nursing diagnosis: *Ineffective breathing pattern related to emotional stimulation, fatigue, or blunting of respiratory drive*

NURSING PRIORITY: Maintain an effective breathing pattern.

Interventions

1. *Reduce the work of breathing and lessen depletion of oxygen reserves* through teaching and by promoting relaxation as follows:
• Position the patient for comfort (upright may be best, with a pillow under the elbows and the patient leaning on the overbed table).
• Remind the patient to relax the shoulders and neck muscles.
• Instruct the patient to prolong the exhalation phase of breathing.
• Sit with the patient and encourage breathing in a rhythmic pattern.
• Use a calm, unhurried manner.

2. *Teach and help the patient perform breathing exercises and coordinate breathing with activity.*

3. *Pace all activities* according to periods of maximum bronchodilation and peak energy. Encourage energy conservation.

4. Instruct the patient in breathing techniques to use when expressing feelings that create shortness of breath (controlled cough technique or bronchial hygiene measures for public use).

Rationales

1. Inhalation normally requires muscle work and energy expenditure. Exhalation is ordinarily passive, not requiring extra energy and oxygen, but because the COPD patient in distress uses oxygen for both inhalation and exhalation, a large amount of oxygen from each inhalation is used to take and expel the next breath. Also, because of the anxiety caused by shortness of breath, the COPD patient tends to tighten muscle groups, thus using even more oxygen. Relaxation and easy, prolonged exhalation allow the COPD patient to maximize lung expansion while minimizing energy and oxygen expenditures. Although the COPD patient may know the value of breathing techniques, he or she may forget them in a crisis and need the active assistance of the nurse to regain control.

2. Breath-holding during exertion dramatically increases the COPD patient's shortness of breath.

3. Pacing allows activity while conserving energy reserves.

4. Any expression of emotion, such as happiness, anger, or sadness, affects respiratory patterns and may increase shortness of breath in the COPD patient.

(continued)

Interventions *continued*

5. Avoid the use of sedatives or narcotics.

6. Additional individualized interventions: _____
_____
_____

Rationales *continued*

5. These agents will further depress the respiratory centers and may provoke respiratory arrest.

6. Rationale: _____
_____
_____

Outcome criteria

Immediately upon admission, after coaching by nurse, the patient will:
• resume continuous use of breathing techniques.

Within 24 hours, the patient will:
• pace activities to coincide with periods of maximum bronchodilation and peak energy.

Nursing diagnosis: *Nutritional deficit related to shortness of breath during and after meals and to the side effects of medications*

NURSING PRIORITIES: (a) Maintain adequate caloric and nutritional intake, (b) reduce deterrents to eating, and (c) optimize environmental conditions to increase appetite.

Interventions

1. *Use supplemental oxygen during mealtimes,* as ordered.

2. *Arrange to perform bronchial hygiene measures before meals.* Follow oral hygiene measures with mouth care. Remove secretions from the eating area in the room.

3. *Provide frequent, small meals.*

4. *Monitor the patient's weight and nutritional intake daily.*

5. *Obtain a dietary consultation as soon as the patient can take foods or fluids,* with special attention to needs for:
• high-protein, low-carbohydrate, high-fat supplements

• elimination of gas-producing foods from diet

• consideration of the patient's food preferences and conformation to any dietary restrictions, such as limiting salt.

Rationales

1. The act of eating requires oxygen. Supplemental oxygen during meals will bolster oxygen reserves.

2. Performing hygiene measures before meals will ensure maximum bronchodilation and reduce activity-related ventilation-perfusion imbalance that may cause hypoxemia. The presence of sputum may decrease appetite.

3. Small meals require less oxygen for the eating and digestive processes.

4. During periods of exacerbation, metabolic demands may increase, creating an increased demand for calories to maintain weight. Daily assessment detects the need for dietary supplements to prevent further depletion.

5. Early dietary consultation can prevent future complications from further debilitation.

• COPD patients have an increased respiratory rate and increased work of breathing, resulting in greater metabolic demands. A diet with a low calorie-to-nitrogen ratio will meet metabolic demands without increasing CO_2 production (as occurs with a high-calorie diet).
• Abdominal distention can cause diaphragmatic compression, increasing the sensation of shortness of breath.
• The dietitian's expertise can be invaluable in devising a nutritional plan the patient will follow.

Interventions *continued*

6. Additional individualized interventions: _____
_____
_____

Outcome criteria
Within 48 hours of admission, the patient will:
• take meals without episodes of acute shortness of breath.

Rationales *continued*

6. Rationale: _____
_____
_____

By the time of discharge, the patient will:
• have stabilized weight.

Nursing diagnosis: *Impaired mobility related to shortness of breath, avoidance of physical activity with resultant muscle weakness, deconditioning, depression, and (possibly) exercise-related hypoxemia*

NURSING PRIORITY: Promote a gradual return to an optimal level of activity, with absent or controlled episodes of acute shortness of breath. (Note: Progress on this priority will depend on resolving the exacerbation and its precipitating factors.)

Interventions

1. *Instruct the patient in breathing techniques to use when performing activities of daily living (ADLs):* slow and relaxed exhalation, avoidance of breath-holding, and relaxation of accessory muscles. (For more information, and pictures of these techniques for use during instruction, contact the local American Lung Association chapter.)

2. *Administer oxygen during activity,* as ordered.

3. *Before recommending an activity level, assess for stable ABG measurements and level of fitness* (the pulmonary function or respiratory therapy department can assist in determining appropriate exercise assessment).
    Also assess for other factors contributing to inactivity, such as family relationships, concomitant diseases (for example, arthritis), or environmental conditions.

4. *Before beginning a walking schedule, teach the patient how to control shortness of breath when walking.* This includes telling the patient to "stop, lean back, position hips against a sturdy object (wall), and stand with feet apart" when shortness of breath occurs.

5. *Develop and implement a daily walking schedule,* increasing time and distance as tolerated.

6. *Before, during, and after walking, monitor the patient's response to the exercise.* Document these parameters along with the time and distance walked: blood pressure (before and after), pulse rate and rhythm, color, respiratory rate, and degree of shortness of breath.

Rationales

1. Breathing techniques taught to COPD patients can facilitate full exhalation, thereby promoting removal of stale air, increasing ventilatory efficiency, and permitting a wider range of physical activity.

2. Increased activity requires supplemental oxygen.

3. If undertaken prematurely, increased activity may worsen the exacerbation. The patient is unlikely to adhere to an activity prescription that is inappropriate in terms of ABG measurements or level of fitness or that ignores other deterrents to activity.

4. Gaining control over shortness of breath episodes improves the patient's confidence in walking independently.

5. Implementation of a walking schedule should be started in the hospital, if possible, so that the patient can be observed and coached in appropriate breathing techniques.

6. If a patient is experiencing desaturation or acidosis during the walk, these events will be reflected in vital sign changes. More sophisticated exercise testing may be needed to determine the extent of disability and the appropriate therapy.

(continued)

Interventions *continued*

7. Additional individualized interventions: _____

_____

_____

Rationales *continued*

7. Rationale: _____

_____

_____

Outcome criteria

Throughout the period of hospitalization, the patient will:
• increase the ability to ambulate over longer time and distance without shortness of breath, pulse changes (rate or rhythm), blood pressure drop, or a color change.

By the time of discharge, the patient will:
• demonstrate the method for controlling activity-related shortness of breath.

Nursing diagnosis: *Sleep pattern disturbance related to bronchodilator medications (stimulant effect), bouts of nocturnal shortness of breath, depression, and anxiety*

NURSING PRIORITY: Minimize sleep disruption.

Interventions

1. Identify the patient's normal sleep pattern as well as the abnormal pattern being experienced.

2. Consult with the doctor about adjusting medications to optimize bronchodilation yet minimize stimulant effects.

3. Instruct the patient in performing the bronchial hygiene regimen before retiring and as needed for bouts of nocturnal dyspnea.

4. Administer oxygen therapy during the night, as ordered.

5. During hospitalization, monitor the patient's bouts of sleeplessness, including degree of shortness of breath, pulse rate and rhythm, respiratory rate, and breath sounds. Observe which treatments seem to provide the most benefit.

6. Instruct the patient in relaxation techniques to be used at bedtime. (Sleeping medications should not be used by COPD patients unless specifically ordered by the pulmonary physician.)

7. Additional individualized interventions: _____

_____

_____

Rationales

1. The patient may have misconceptions about normal and abnormal sleeping patterns. Discussion may clarify factors contributing to sleep disturbance.

2. Bronchodilators vary in their stimulant properties. Stimulants may cause myocardial irritability, nervousness, and anxiety and may increase oxygen demand.

3. Bouts of nocturnal shortness of breath are often unavoidable; the best alternative is to teach the patient how to deal with such an episode effectively.

4. PaO_2 levels decrease in all people at night. Although most people can tolerate the decrease, the already-hypoxemic COPD patient cannot tolerate any further decrease, because hypoxemia-induced pulmonary vasoconstriction can precipitate or exacerbate cor pulmonale.

5. Observation of a sleeplessness episode and its resolution may provide clues for further prevention. Discussing your observations can help the patient learn to deal with future episodes.

6. Relaxation techniques can promote sleep and minimize oxygen demands. Sleeping medications may depress respirations in the already compromised patient.

7. Rationale: _____

_____

_____

Outcome criteria

By the time of discharge, the patient will:
• report less frequent episodes of nocturnal shortness of breath
• sleep throughout the night, without early-morning headache or excessive drowsiness during the day

• fall asleep easily at night
• report an improved sleep pattern and/or more easily controlled episodes of nocturnal shortness of breath, or both.

Nursing diagnosis: *Potential for injury related to failure to recognize signs and symptoms indicating impending exacerbation*

NURSING PRIORITY: Teach the patient to recognize an impending exacerbation and to seek appropriate treatment.

Interventions

1. *Teach the signs and symptoms of an impending exacerbation,* including:
• increased or decreased sputum amount
• change in the color or character of sputum over a 24-hour period
• fever (based on baseline normal temperature)
• restlessness or inability to sleep lasting more than one night
• increased fatigue or sleepiness.

2. *Emphasize the need to notify the doctor promptly* if these symptoms occur, rather than altering the medication regimen on one's own.

3. *Caution the patient to avoid overmedication with prescription drugs or over-the-counter remedies.*

4. Additional individualized interventions: _____
_____
_____

Rationales

1. Early detection and intervention increase the likelihood of successful reversal or control of the episode.

2. Appropriate intervention requires medical judgment.

3. Overuse of some medications, such as bronchodilators, may actually worsen the exacerbation by increasing oxygen demands. Over-the-counter remedies may contain substances, such as ephedrine, that potentiate or counteract the therapeutic effects of prescribed medication.

4. Rationale: _____
_____
_____

Outcome criteria

By the time of discharge, the patient will:
• list four indicators of an impending exacerbation

• correctly identify the rationale for notifying the doctor before adjusting the medication regimen.

Nursing diagnosis: *Altered sexuality patterns related to shortness of breath, change in body image, deconditioning, change in relationship with spouse or partner, and side effects of medications*

NURSING PRIORITY: Help the patient and spouse (or partner) to discuss feelings and determine realistic expectations.

Interventions

1. Establish rapport with the patient and spouse (or partner). Discuss with them their feelings concerning changes in sexual functioning.

Rationales

1. A sense of rapport makes discussion of this often-sensitive topic more comfortable. Discussion will help clarify the issues involved and the expectations held by the patient and spouse (or partner).

(continued)

Interventions *continued*

2. Help the patient learn or arrange therapeutic modalities (including medication schedule, oxygen level, bronchial hygiene, energy conservation) to optimize the ability to function sexually, as desired.

3. Additional individualized interventions: _____

_____

_____

Rationales *continued*

2. As with other activity areas, the patient must learn to optimize therapies to accomplish desired goals.

3. Rationale: _____

_____

_____

Outcome criterion
By the time of discharge, the patient will:
• describe ways to use therapies for maximum benefit in order to engage in sexual activity.

Discharge planning
NURSING DISCHARGE CRITERIA
Upon discharge, documentation shows evidence of:
• absence of fever and other signs of infection
• ABG levels within acceptable parameters
• absence of cardiovascular or pulmonary complications
• minimal shortness of breath
• lung sounds clear or as usual for patient when not in exacerbation state
• ability to tolerate ambulation with minimal limitations, same as before exacerbation and hospitalization
• ability to perform ADLs independently (or with minimal assistance) at preexacerbation level
• ability to tolerate diet with minimal shortness of breath
• stabilized weight (within 5 lb of normal weight)
• adequate home support system or referral to home care if indicated by inadequate home support, inability to perform ADL at preexacerbation level, or need for continued assistance with bronchial hygiene measures.
   Note: It is important for nurses to be aware that patients with COPD will not be "normal" when discharged. Therefore, discharge evaluation should relate to the patient's condition before the exacerbation. The most important thing to document is the absence of acute infection, but nurses also need to be alert to ABG levels on discharge. ABG levels must be within acceptable parameters, because abnormal levels on discharge commonly precipitate readmission within a short time.

PATIENT/FAMILY DISCHARGE TEACHING CHECKLIST
Document evidence that patient/family demonstrates understanding of:
__ practical energy conservation and breathing techniques
__ signs and symptoms of infection or exacerbation
__ for all discharge medications: purpose, dose, administration schedule, and side effects requiring medical attention (usual discharge medications include bronchodilators, corticosteroids, antibiotics, and expectorants)

__ bronchial hygiene measures
__ use, care, and cleaning of needed respiratory equipment
__ need for drinking 2 to 3 qt water per day
__ dietary restrictions
__ daily weight monitoring
__ avoidance of exposure to infections and need for flu vaccination
__ avoiding lung irritants, such as cold air, second-hand smoke, sprays, and dust
__ exercise prescription
__ referral to community agencies, as appropriate (such as Meals on Wheels, American Lung Association, Better Breathers Club, respiratory equipment company and name of representative, Lifeline telephone service, home care agency, and smoking cessation group)
__ date, time, and location of next appointment
__ how to contact doctor.

DOCUMENTATION CHECKLIST
Using outcome criteria as a guide, document:
__ clinical status on admission
__ significant changes in status
__ pertinent laboratory and diagnostic tests, such as ABG levels
__ episodes of shortness of breath, including physical assessment parameters during each episode, treatment modality administered, and treatment outcome
__ respiratory status per shift, including breath sounds; character of cough; and character, color, and amount of sputum
__ administration and outcome of therapeutic modalities given
__ nutritional intake
__ fluid intake
__ exercise ability and activity
__ patient/family teaching
__ discharge planning.

ASSOCIATED CARE PLANS
Death and Dying
Fluid and Electrolyte Imbalances
Grief/Grieving
Ineffective Individual Coping
Knowledge Deficit
Pneumonia

REFERENCES
Gift, A.G., et al. "Psychologic and Physiologic Factors Related to Dyspnea in Subjects with Chronic Obstruction Pulmonary Disease," *Heart & Lung* 15(6):595-601, November 1986.
Moser, K., and Spragg, R.G. *Respiratory Emergencies.* C.V. Mosby Co., 1982.
Shapiro, B.A., et al. *Clinical Application of Respiratory Care*, 3rd ed. Chicago: Year Book Medical Pubs., 1985.
Woldum, K.M., et al. *Patient Education: Tools for Practice*. Rockville, Md.: Aspen Publishing, 1985.

Lung Cancer

DRG information

DRG 76   [Surgical DRG] Other Respiratory System O.R. Procedure. With Complication or Comorbidity.
Mean LOS = 8.8 days

DRG 82   [Medical DRG] Respiratory Neoplasms.
Mean LOS = 6.4 days

DRG 410 [Medical DRG] Chemotherapy.
Principal diagnosis: maintenance chemotherapy.
Mean LOS = 2.4 days

DRG 412 [Medical DRG] History of Malignancy with Endoscopy.
Main LOS = 2.0 days

Introduction

DEFINITION AND TIME FOCUS

Lung cancer is a condition of aberrant cellular growth causing morphologic tissue changes within the lung. It causes 22% of all cancer in men and 35% of all cancer-related deaths in men. It is responsible for 9% of all cancer in women and 17% of all cancer-related deaths in women.

Tumors may be primary (original) or secondary (from distant metastasis). The most common types of primary lung cancer are squamous cell carcinoma (40% to 50% of cases), adenocarcinoma (25% of cases), small cell anaplastic carcinoma (20% to 25% of cases), and large-cell anaplastic carcinoma (< 15%).

Surgical resection, lobectomy, or pneumonectomy may be performed alone or in combination with radiation therapy, chemotherapy, or both to treat lung cancer. However, the 5-year survival rate for persons with this disease is below 10% regardless of the treatment used. This clinical plan focuses on the patient who has been admitted to an acute-care center with primary lung cancer and who is receiving chemotherapy as an initial treatment.

ETIOLOGY/PRECIPITATING FACTORS

• cigarette smoking
• exposure to carcinogens, such as asbestos, pollution, pitchblende, metals, or chemicals
• genetic predisposition

Focused assessment guidelines

NURSING HISTORY (Functional health pattern findings)

Health perception–health management pattern
• likely to report *history of heavy smoking*
• may report *dyspnea associated with activity or anxiety;* degree of dyspnea may be disproportionate to overall clinical picture

• may complain of *chest pain aggravated by deep breathing* (if pleura involved), *cough* (may be nocturnal), *rust-streaked or purulent sputum, or hemoptysis*
• if more than age 45 and male, at increased risk
• may complain of shoulder or arm pain if brachial plexus involved
• hoarseness common with laryngeal involvement
• may report easy bleeding from minor trauma, and slowed clot formation (cancer inhibits Factor VIII [anti-hemophilic factor] activity)
• probably did not feel a need to seek medical assistance until cough, dyspnea, weakness, and weight loss caused patient to sense that "something was wrong"

Nutrition-metabolic pattern
• may report *significant weight loss, anorexia,* early satiety, changes in taste sensation, or reduced sensitivity to sweets

Elimination pattern
• may report constipation accompanied by abdominal discomfort or diarrhea

Activity-exercise pattern
• may report *general fatigue and weakness*

Sleep-rest pattern
• may report sleep disturbed by cough

Self-perception–self-concept pattern
• loss of ability to carry out routine activities may precipitate questioning of self-worth and a feeling of powerlessness
• may express fear related to diagnosis, physical disabilities, and possible death

Role-relationship pattern
• may describe inability to assume family tasks, occupational role, and so forth
• may report feelings of loss related to changing roles and possible death
• may report loss of a significant relationship before diagnosis

Sexuality-reproductive pattern
• may report inability to be sexually active without experiencing dyspnea

Coping–stress tolerance pattern
• usually reports feeling depressed or despondent

Value-belief pattern
• may express feeling of personal control over circumstances (commonly experienced by individuals with above-average chances of successful remission)

• may equate cancer with death (commonly experienced by individuals with below-average chances of successful remission)

PHYSICAL FINDINGS
Cardiovascular
• rapid pulse rate if anemia is present
• dysrhythmias if cardiac involvement is present
• edema of face or neck or distended neck veins if superior vena cava syndrome is present

Pulmonary
• *cough* (may be nocturnal)
• *rust-streaked or purulent sputum*
• *crackles, wheezes, and friction rub* in affected lung
• hoarseness if vocal cord involvement is present
• clubbing of fingers

Neurologic
• headache, mental confusion, and unsteady gait if central nervous system involvement is present
• diminished deep tendon reflexes
• decreased mental alertness if anemia and hypoxemia are present

Musculoskeletal
• pathologic fractures with metastasis

DIAGNOSTIC STUDIES
• *carcinoembryonic antigen titer—high levels* may be useful to monitor treatment responses; 50% of patients may have false-negative titers
• *arterial blood gas (ABG) measurements—may reveal hypoxemia*
• *hemoglobin values—may be low from anemia*
• *hematocrit values—may be low from anemia*
• *platelet count—may be low from bone marrow suppression*
• *white blood cell (WBC) count—may be low from bone marrow suppression*
• sputum collection for cytology—may be useful to determine cell type (according to continuum of classes from normal to malignant)
• *serum albumin level—hypoalbuminemia may indicate malnutrition*

• serum creatinine level—indicates alterations in renal function related to chemotherapy
• 24-hour urine creatinine test—nutritional index, indicates changes in lean body weight when compared with individual's height; also indicates alterations in renal function related to chemotherapy
• *chest X-ray—may reveal tumor position;* usually does not show early tumor involvement
• *computed tomography scan—outlines size, shape, and position of tumor*
• bronchoscopy—useful in diagnosing centrally located lesions
• mediastinoscopy—needle biopsy of nodes useful in diagnosis and tumor staging
• radioisotopic scans—performed to assess for metastasis
• scalene node biopsy—performed to determine lymphatic involvement

POTENTIAL COMPLICATIONS
From lung cancer:
• pleural effusion
• pneumonitis
• cardiac failure or dysrhythmias
• brachial plexus involvement
• Cushing's syndrome
• hypercalcemia
• syndrome of inappropriate antidiuretic hormone
• peripheral neuritis
• central nervous system (CNS) degeneration
• dermatomyositis
• superior vena cava syndrome
• paralysis of diaphragm
• pathologic fractures
• disseminated intravascular coagulation
From chemotherapy:
• bone marrow suppression
• immunosuppression
• renal tubular necrosis
• liver toxicity
• cardiotoxicity
• pulmonary toxicity
• neurotoxicity
• sterility

Collaborative problem: *Hypoxemia related to aberrant cellular growth of lung tissue, bronchial obstruction, increased mucus production, and/or pleurisy*

NURSING PRIORITY: Optimize oxygen availability to cells.

Interventions

1. *Initiate ABG measurements* on admission, and *monitor for changes in PO_2* daily or as clinical condition changes, as ordered.

Rationales

1. The partial pressure of oxygen (PO_2) indicates the amount of pressure being exerted against an artery by oxygen. A decreased PO_2 reflects increased hypoxemia.

(continued)

Interventions *continued*

2. *Administer humidified oxygen* continuously, via mask, as ordered and according to nursing judgment.

3. *Elevate the head of the bed during dyspneic episodes.*

4. *Evaluate and document breath sounds, respiratory rate, and chest movements* every 8 hours or more frequently, based on the patient's condition. Observe for dyspnea: complaints of difficulty breathing, shortness of breath, flaring nostrils, and intercostal retractions on inspiration or bulging on expiration.

5. *During dyspneic episodes, stay with the patient, explain all procedures, and support the patient and family.* Control the impulse to increase the oxygen rate or concentration over the prescribed level; counsel the patient and family accordingly.

6. *Encourage the patient to stop or decrease smoking.*

7. *Teach pursed-lip breathing and relaxation techniques.*

8. Additional individualized interventions: _____
_____
_____

Rationales *continued*

2. Oxygen administered at higher-than-room-air concentrations increases the oxyhemoglobin saturation of available red blood cells. An increase in hemoglobin saturation increases the amount of oxygen available for cellular metabolism if circulation is not impaired. Patients with lung cancer frequently need high concentrations of oxygen that can be provided only by mask or mechanical ventilation. An oxygen humidifier decreases the drying effect on the respiratory mucosa caused by oxygen administration.

3. Elevating the head of the bed aids respiratory movement by allowing gravity to displace abdominal organs downward, thus decreasing pressure on the diaphragm.

4. Dyspnea is a subjective finding that indicates hypoxemia. Abnormal findings common in patients with lung tumors include crackles, bronchial breath sounds, pleural friction rubs, and decreased breath sounds.

5. Feelings of dyspnea are often associated with anxiety and fear of impending death. Anxiety may be decreased if the patient feels in control and has confidence in caregivers. Increasing oxygen levels may remove the hypoxic stimulus to respiration in patients with chronic obstructive pulmonary disease; cause carbon dioxide narcosis if a face mask is used; or precipitate oxygen toxicity.

6. Smoking increases mucus production, irritates respiratory mucosa, and decreases oxyhemoglobin saturation.

7. Pursed-lip breathing increases end-expiratory pressure and helps prevent alveolar collapse. Controlled breathing and relaxation decrease the anxiety associated with dyspnea.

8. Rationale: _____
_____
_____

Outcome criteria
Within 1 week of admission, the patient will:
• exhibit less dyspnea while at rest
• use pursed-lip breathing and relaxation procedures
• decrease smoking by one-half or more compared to preadmission rate.

Collaborative problem: *Potential hemorrhage related to depression of platelet production by chemotherapy*

NURSING PRIORITY: Prevent or minimize hemorrhage.

Interventions

1. *Caution the patient to report any bleeding immediately,* including petechiae, ecchymoses, and oozing wounds.

2. *Initiate and monitor serum platelet counts* before, during, and after chemotherapy, as ordered.

3. Caution the patient to use a soft toothbrush or a Water Pic for oral hygiene and to avoid spicy foods.

4. Teach the patient to monitor urine and stools for bleeding signs and to report any that occur immediately.

5. Instruct the patient to use an electric razor for shaving or to grow a beard (unless alopecia is present).

6. Administer medications to suppress menses, as ordered.

7. Teach the patient to report any headaches, dizziness, or feelings of light-headedness immediately.

8. Avoid I.M. injections. If they are unavoidable, apply pressure for at least 5 minutes after the injection.

9. Avoid administering aspirin and aspirin-containing medications.

10. Apply ice packs to bleeding areas.

11. Administer stool softeners, as ordered.

12. Additional individualized interventions: _____
_____
_____

Rationales

1. Hemorrhage may occur rapidly. The patient may be able to assume some responsibility for observing for signs of bleeding. Petechiae, ecchymoses, and oozing wounds are signs of clotting problems.

2. Chemotherapeutic agents suppress bone marrow and affect platelet production. A patient with a platelet count lower than $20,000/mm^3$ is at high risk for hemorrhage.

3. Oral mucosa may bleed if irritated from flossing or use of a hard toothbrush or a toothpick. Spicy foods also may irritate oral mucosa.

4. Tea-colored (cola-colored) urine or black, tarry, or blood-streaked stools indicate bleeding.

5. Use of nonelectric razors increases the risk of lacerating skin while shaving.

6. Prolonged menstrual bleeding may cause severe blood loss.

7. CNS bleeding may cause headaches, dizziness, or light-headedness. Dizziness and light-headedness also may indicate hypovolemia.

8. Decreased platelet counts prolong clotting time. Direct pressure for 5 minutes should stop active bleeding in most patients.

9. Aspirin decreases platelet aggregation and increases clotting time.

10. Ice causes peripheral vasoconstriction, decreasing the amount of blood flow to the area and decreasing the risk of significant hemorrhage.

11. Stool softeners promote formation of soft stools, which decrease the risk of tearing the rectal mucosa. Soft stools also help minimize straining on defecation, which increases intracranial pressure and may lead to intracranial bleeding.

12. Rationale: _____
_____
_____

Outcome criteria

Within 1 week of admission, the patient will:
• exhibit vital signs within normal limits

• have no evident bleeding
• employ safety measures to prevent bleeding.

Nursing diagnosis: *Pain associated with involvement of peripheral lung structures; metastasis; and/or chemotherapy*

NURSING PRIORITY: Relieve pain and promote comfort.

Interventions

1. *Instruct the patient to report pain or feelings of discomfort immediately.*

2. *Monitor the patient continually for signs of pain or discomfort,* such as facial grimaces, splinting of the chest (painful area), diaphoresis, or restlessness.

3. *Involve the patient in pain-control strategies* by using imagery and relaxation techniques. See the "Pain" care plan, page 64, for details.

4. *Administer pain medication,* as needed, according to a set schedule or according to medical protocol and nursing judgment. Teach the patient or a family member the procedure to use for administering pain medication after discharge.

5. Additional individualized interventions: _____
_____
_____

Rationales

1. Interventions administered early in the pain experience provide more effective relief than measures employed after the pain has peaked.

2. The patient may not report any feelings of pain or discomfort. Careful observation may detect nonverbal indications that the patient is in pain.

3. Use of cognitive measures may decrease pain perception. The "Pain" care plan contains general interventions for pain.

4. Pain medication ordered for a terminally ill patient may be given more frequently and in larger doses than routinely recommended (the patient receiving the medication over a prolonged period of time may develop an increased tolerance). A set schedule may improve ongoing pain control, because analgesics are more effective if given before pain becomes severe. Self- (or family) administration of medication enables the patient to control pain at home.

5. Rationale: _____
_____
_____

Outcome criteria

Within 1 hour of admission, the patient will:
• verbalize pain relief
• show a relaxed facial expression
• assume a relaxed posture.

Within 1 week of admission, the patient will:
• request pain-relief medication before pain peaks

• state a feeling of increased sense of control over pain.

Within 1 week of admission, the patient or a family member will:
• demonstrate the correct procedure for pain medication administration.

Nursing diagnosis: *Potential infection related to immunosuppression from chemotherapy and malnutrition*

NURSING PRIORITY: Prevent infection.

Interventions

1. *Observe strict medical and surgical asepsis* with wound care, puncture sites, or any invasive procedures.

2. *Monitor and record temperature* every 8 hours. Report even slight temperature elevations.

Rationales

1. The immunosuppressed patient easily contracts infections because of diminished host defenses. Maintenance of strict medical and surgical asepsis decreases the risk of exposing the patient to pathogenic organisms.

2. Elevated temperature is a sign of infection. The immunosuppressed patient may show slight or no temperature elevation even when extensive infection is present.

Interventions *continued*

3. *Instruct the patient to avoid crowds and persons with infections.* Do not place the patient in reverse isolation unless a laminar airflow room (or other method) is available.

4. *Monitor WBC counts before, during, and after chemotherapy,* as ordered.

5. Initiate routine cultures of stool, urine, sputum, nasopharynx, oropharynx, and skin, as ordered.

6. Additional individualized interventions: _____

_____

_____

Rationales *continued*

3. The risk of infection is increased when a patient is exposed to individuals with contagious diseases. Reverse isolation is usually not effective unless laminar airflow is used, because airborne organisms can still enter the patient's room.

4. Chemotherapy causes bone marrow depression, which may decrease the WBC count. WBC (granulocyte) counts below 1,000/mm^3 increase the patient's risk of infection.

5. Cultures provide information about bacterial colony growth that may produce infection. Early information about possible causes of infection guides the doctor in prescribing appropriate antibiotic therapy.

6. Rationale: _____

_____

_____

Outcome criteria

Within 1 hour of admission, the patient will:
• isolate self from infected family members or friends.

Within 1 week of admission, the patient will:
• present no signs of infection

• have normal temperature
• present no growth from cultures.

Nursing diagnosis: *Potential sensory-perceptual alteration related to peripheral neuropathies caused by chemotherapy*

NURSING PRIORITY: Minimize sensory-perceptual deficits caused by chemotherapy.

Interventions

1. *Assess, document, and report deficits in neurologic functioning,* including reports of paresthesias, abnormal deep tendon reflexes, or signs of foot drop.

2. *Discontinue or decrease the chemotherapy dosage, depending on the severity of neuropathies,* as ordered.

3. Explain that changes in sensation are related to chemotherapy, and allow the patient to express fears related to this situation.

4. *Protect the area of decreased sensory perception from injury:* use a bath thermometer; assess the skin every 8 hours for signs of trauma; apply dressings to injured areas; use a night light; and avoid clutter in areas of activity to prevent abrasions, contusions, or falls.

5. Additional individualized interventions: _____

_____

_____

Rationales

1. Chemotherapeutic agents such as vincristine (Oncovin) may cause peripheral neuropathies.

2. Discontinuation or dosage reduction of vinca alkaloids may reverse adverse neurologic effects. Discontinuation of medication will prevent further development of neuropathies related to medication administration.

3. Fear may be reduced when the reality of a situation is confronted.

4. Decreased perception at sensory nerve endings may reduce ability to judge temperature and pressure and may also reduce pain sensation. Knowledge of methods to prevent injury reduces the potential for injury.

5. Rationale: _____

_____

_____

Outcome criteria
Within 1 week of admission, the patient will:
• have no complaints of paresthesias

• exhibit no evidence of foot drop
• have normal deep tendon reflexes.

Nursing diagnosis: *Nutritional deficit related to cachexia associated with tumor growth, anorexia, changes in taste sensation, or stomatitis*

NURSING PRIORITIES: (a) Minimize weight loss and (b) promote return to optimum body weight.

Interventions

1. *Within 24 hours of admission, estimate required protein needs* based on ideal body weight and serum total protein level.

2. *With the dietitian, develop diet plans* based on calculated dietary needs and the patient's food preferences.

3. *Increase dietary protein levels* by adding powdered milk to gravies, puddings, and milk products.

4. *Provide small, frequent feedings.*

5. *Document weight* weekly.

6. *Provide antiemetics,* as ordered, before administration of chemotherapeutic agents. To reduce nausea, provide diversional activities during chemotherapy and encourage the patient to lick salt or a lemon slice or sip sweetened ice water.

7. Assess oral mucosa for stomatitis daily and document.

8. Provide a mild mouthwash with viscous lidocaine before meals.

9. Rinse the patient's mouth with water or diluted hydrogen peroxide after meals.

Rationales

1. Caloric needs are altered by cancer-related cachexia. Serum total protein level reflects the status of visceral protein stores. Protein needs for a patient with cancer are calculated as 1g/kg of ideal body weight (1 gram of protein = 30 kcal).

2. Patient participation allows some feeling of control. Nutrition intake should increase if the patient's likes and dislikes are considered in planning meals.

3. Powdered milk increases protein content without increasing bulk.

4. Small, frequent feedings increase total intake for the patient who experiences early satiety, common in patients with cancer.

5. An accurate data base allows accurate assessment of changing nutritional needs. Patients with cancer commonly experience significant weight loss.

6. The effects of chemotherapy on CNS and gastric mucosa may induce vomiting. Prochlorperazine (Compazine), droperidol (Inapsine), and haloperidol (Haldol) are effective antiemetics. Marijuana and tetrahydrocannabinol are being studied for control of nausea and vomiting. Nausea associated with chemotherapy may be psychogenic (it sometimes occurs before chemotherapy is administered); diversional activities may distract the patient's attention and reduce nausea. The taste of lemon, salt, or sugar relieves feelings of nausea in some persons.

7. Chemotherapeutic agents, such as methotrexate and fluorouracil, may cause stomatitis. Chemotherapeutic agents affect cells that undergo rapid replication, such as those in the GI system. Stomatitis interferes with the ability to eat.

8. The local anesthetic action of lidocaine decreases oral discomfort experienced during meals.

9. Rinsing and cleansing with water or hydrogen peroxide reduces the bacterial count in the mouth and decreases the risk of infection.

Interventions *continued*

10. Lubricate the patient's lips with petrolatum.

11. Assess oral mucosa daily for signs of lesions from superimposed infections, such as *Candida*.

12. Instruct the patient to rinse the mouth with yogurt or buttermilk, then swallow it three times a day.

13. Administer oral nystatin, as ordered.

14. Additional individualized interventions: _____

_____

Rationales *continued*

10. Lubrication with petrolatum reduces lip drying and cracking.

11. *Candida* is an opportunistic organism that may cause infection in an immunosuppressed individual.

12. Yogurt and buttermilk restore to the GI tract the natural flora destroyed by chemotherapeutic agents. Growth of opportunistic organisms is decreased if normal flora are maintained.

13. Oral nystatin is effective against candidal infections.

14. Rationale: _____

_____

Outcome criteria

Within 1 week of admission, the patient will:
• gain approximately 2 lb
• plan meals appropriately, with or without family assistance

• have no nausea or vomiting
• exhibit pink oral mucosa, with no lesions.

Nursing diagnosis: *Constipation or diarrhea related to chemotherapy*

NURSING PRIORITY: Promote normal bowel elimination.

Interventions

1. *Assess and document bowel elimination patterns* on admission. Determine usual bowel elimination patterns before chemotherapy.

2. *Administer antidiarrheal medication,* such as diphenoxylate hydrochloride with atropine sulfate (Lomotil), as ordered.

3. *Assess for signs of paralytic ileus* (such as diminished or absent bowel sounds and abdominal discomfort) every 8 hours. If present, report them to the doctor immediately.

4. Prevent constipation by increasing dietary fiber, providing warm fluids, and promoting the optimum amount of exercise.

5. Administer stool softeners, as ordered.

6. Additional individualized interventions: _____

_____

Rationales

1. Chemotherapeutic agents may cause constipation or diarrhea. Information about previous bowel elimination patterns determines the norm for bowel elimination during hospitalization.

2. Lomotil is effective as an antidiarrheal because of its anticholinergic activity, which slows gastric motility.

3. Paralytic ileus is a medical emergency that may be precipitated by chemotherapeutic agents such as vincristine.

4. Bran, raw vegetables, fruits, and whole grain breads provide dietary fiber and promote bowel elimination. Liquids increase peristalsis. Exercise causes abdominal muscle contraction and promotes bowel elimination.

5. Stool softeners promote bowel elimination by increasing the water content of stools and easing their passage.

6. Rationale: _____

_____

Outcome criteria
Within 1 week of admission, the patient will:
• maintain regular bowel elimination
• have soft stools.

Nursing diagnosis: *Potential altered urinary elimination patterns related to possible development of renal toxicity or hemorrhagic cystitis from chemotherapy*

NURSING PRIORITY: Maintain normal urinary elimination patterns.

Interventions

1. *Assess and document urinary elimination patterns* on admission.

2. *Force fluids and administer allopurinol* before administration of chemotherapeutic agents, as ordered.

3. *Alkalinize the patient's urine* before and during chemotherapy to prevent formation of uric acid calculi.

4. *Monitor serum creatinine and 24-hour urine creatinine* laboratory studies, as ordered, before chemotherapy.

5. Additional individualized interventions: _____
_____
_____

Rationales

1. Accurate assessment provides direction for developing an appropriate care plan.

2. Cyclophosphamide may cause hemorrhagic cystitis. Methotrexate may cause renal toxicity. Increasing fluid intake increases the glomerular filtration rate and reduces the risk of potentially toxic renal effects caused by chemotherapy. Allopurinol decreases formation of uric acid calculi from chemotherapy by inhibiting uric acid synthesis.

3. Uric acid excretion is increased in acidic urine, and chemotherapy may cause formation of uric acid calculi. Fruits (for example, oranges, tomatoes, and grapefruit), vegetables, and milk increase urine alkalinity and decrease the risk that uric acid calculi will form.

4. Serum creatinine and 24-hour urine creatinine studies provide information about renal function. Creatinine should be cleared by kidneys that are functioning normally.

5. Rationale: _____
_____
_____

Outcome criteria
Within 1 week of admission, the patient will:
• have urine output within normal limits

• have amber-colored urine
• have no pain with urination.

Nursing diagnosis: *Activity intolerance related to weakness from cachexia, alteration in protein metabolism, muscle wasting, or hypoxia*

NURSING PRIORITY: Optimize activity level without inducing dyspnea.

Interventions

1. Immediately on admission, *determine what activities the patient can tolerate without dyspnea.*

2. Instruct the patient to organize activities so that tasks are spaced in manageable units.

Rationales

1. Dyspnea occurs as energy requirements exceed oxygen availability. Information about dyspnea-free activities guides activity recommendations.

2. Activities performed without fatigue promote feelings of comfort and decrease dyspnea.

Interventions *continued*

3. Teach the use of proper body mechanics to decrease the amount of energy expenditure associated with performing activities of daily living (ADLs): explain the need to slide objects rather than carry them, keep the work field close to the body, sit to work when possible, allow gravity to help, and avoid unnecessary bending or reaching.

4. Additional individualized interventions: _____
_____
_____

Rationales *continued*

3. The use of proper body mechanics reduces energy requirements for tasks.

4. Rationale: _____
_____
_____

Outcome criteria
Within 1 week of admission, the patient will:
• manage activities with less dyspnea
• perform ADLs with minimal assistance.

Nursing diagnosis: *Sleep pattern disturbance related to being awakened by nocturnal cough*

NURSING PRIORITY: Optimize sleep patterns.

Interventions

1. *Assess and document sleep patterns* on admission. Discuss sleep patterns that were present before diagnosis.

2. *Provide quick, efficient assistance with respiratory hygiene* during coughing that disrupts sleep.

3. *Instruct the patient to sleep with the head elevated.*

4. *Exercise caution in administering sedatives and hypnotics.*

5. Additional individualized interventions: _____
_____
_____

Rationales

1. Sleep pattern goals should be based on the patient's perception of his or her normal sleep patterns. Sleep disruption, often present after diagnosis because of psychological distress, robs the patient of energy needed to cope with the illness.

2. Sleep disturbance is minimized if care is provided quickly and efficiently.

3. Head elevation while sleeping will ease the work of breathing by decreasing pressure on the diaphragm.

4. Sedatives and hypnotics may blunt respiratory drive and worsen hypoxia.

5. Rationale: _____
_____
_____

Outcome criterion
Within 3 days of admission, the patient will:
• report 8 to 10 hours of sleep/24 hours, including 4 hours of uninterrupted sleep.

Nursing diagnosis: *Disturbed self-concept: body image and self-esteem, related to weight loss, cough, sputum production, loss of hair, and changes in role*

NURSING PRIORITY: Promote a positive self-concept.

Interventions

1. *Approach the patient with an accepting attitude.*

Rationales

1. An individual needs to experience acceptance from others if he is to develop a positive self-concept.

(continued)

Interventions *continued*

2. *Assess and document attitudes and responses* that provide data related to the patient's self-concept and role changes.

3. *Encourage the patient and family to ventilate feelings.*

4. Discuss methods to accentuate the patient's positive features and minimize evidence of weight loss through changes in hairstyle and clothing.

5. Encourage the use of a portable disposal unit for discarding tissues and sputum.

6. Encourage frequent contact, personal or by telephone, with significant others.

7. Discuss probable hair loss before chemotherapy is started. With the patient's permission, cut hair before hair loss occurs. Natural hair may be used to fashion a wig, or the patient can be fitted for a wig before hair loss. The patient may want to wear a cap instead of a wig.

8. Remind the patient that hair loss is not permanent and that hair regrows after the last dose of chemotherapeutic agent.

9. Explain to the patient about scalp tourniquets and scalp hypothermia treatments that may be used to diminish hair loss. Inform the patient that these procedures are time-consuming and may be unsuccessful.

10. Additional individualized interventions: _____
_____
_____

Rationales *continued*

2. Accurate assessment of the patient's self-concept facilitates development of appropriate care plans.

3. Expression of feelings promotes honest, open relationships.

4. Clothing that fits well without accentuating weight loss improves general feelings of well-being. A well-groomed appearance improves self-concept.

5. Knowing how to dispose of unsightly tissues and sputum improves the patient's feelings of control and increases self-esteem.

6. Contact with others minimizes feelings of isolation and improves self-concept.

7. Knowledge about forthcoming hair loss will decrease the anxiety associated with it. Hair loss is more manageable when hair is short. Use of a wig or cap helps minimize the impact of hair loss on body image and self-esteem.

8. Hair regrowth usually begins within a few days to a few weeks after the last dose of chemotherapeutic agent. Note: New hair may be different in color and texture. Hair loss may affect all areas of the body, not just head hair.

9. Scalp tourniquets and scalp hypothermia treatments diminish the contact of chemotherapeutic agents with hair follicles and may decrease hair loss. Patients should be allowed to make informed choices.

10. Rationale: _____
_____
_____

Outcome criteria
Within 1 week of admission, the patient will:
• wear well-fitting clothes
• express the desire to purchase a wig or wear a cap

• initiate interaction with friends, family, and health care providers.

Nursing diagnosis: *Altered sexuality patterns related to dyspnea and possible sterility*

NURSING PRIORITIES: (a) Promote acceptance of optimal expressions of sexuality, and (b) promote long-range plans for childbearing, if desired.

Interventions

1. During initial assessment, *discuss any changes in patterns of sexual expression* that have resulted from the diagnosis and treatments.

Rationales

1. Open discussion helps the patient to develop realistic goals and expectations related to sexual expression.

Interventions continued

2. *Help the patient and spouse (or partner) to discuss their desires for sexual expression and intimacy.* Help them differentiate the two needs and stress the importance of love and affection in maintaining a sense of closeness with each other.

3. *Discuss options for sexual expression within the patient's physical limitations.* For example, if intercourse is fatiguing or impossible for physical reasons, and if the couple is receptive, suggest alternate forms of sexual and sensual expression that appeal to all senses, such as massage with scented oils, listening to music, sharing foods with various tastes and textures, and reading romantic literature.

4. *Encourage the use of supplemental oxygen during intercourse.*

5. *Provide privacy* for the patient and spouse (or partner) to maintain intimacy through such activities as private discussions and affectionate cuddling, if desired.

6. Explain that reduced sexual responsiveness may be associated with fatigue or chemotherapy.

7. Explain that chemotherapy may cause sterility. If appropriate, discuss sperm banking before chemotherapy. Inform the patient that childbearing plans should be postponed for at least 18 months after the last dose of chemotherapeutic agent.

8. Additional individualized interventions: _____
_____
_____

Rationales continued

2. Honest, caring communication between partners about their sexual needs facilitates adjustment to cancer's impact on sexuality. Differentiating the desire for sexual activity from the desire for emotional closeness may allow the couple to focus on the strengths in their relationship rather than on a loss of a specific sexual activity.

3. Sexual expression is closely tied to self-esteem, and patients and their spouses (or partners) may find that their self-esteem suffers when they can no longer participate in intercourse. Knowledge of alternate methods of sexual and sensual gratification can restore sexual intimacy and increase self-esteem when intercourse is no longer an option.

4. Increased oxygen demands are associated with exercise.

5. Intimacy is encouraged when individuals share uninterrupted time together.

6. Knowing the reasons for reduced sexual responsiveness decreases anxiety about sexuality.

7. Chemotherapy may affect gonadal function and diminish sperm and ovum production. Sperm may be saved in sperm banks for future fertilization. Changes in sperm and ovum resulting from chemotherapy should be reversed by 18 months after the end of chemotherapy. Although the prognosis for these patients may be poor, discussion of future plans may help maintain hope.

8. Rationale: _____
_____
_____

Outcome criteria
Within 1 week of admission, the patient and a spouse (or partner) will:
• discuss the desire for sexual expression and intimacy
• request time for privacy.

Discharge planning
NURSING DISCHARGE CRITERIA
Upon discharge, documentation shows evidence of:
• absence of fever and pulmonary or cardiovascular complications
• stable vital signs
• absence of infection
• nausea or vomiting and diarrhea controlled by oral medications

• absence of signs and symptoms indicating dehydration
• absence of signs and symptoms indicating renal dysfunction
• ability to tolerate adequate nutritional and fluid intake
• ability to control pain using oral and subcutaneous medication
• absence of bowel complications
• coughing controlled by medication

• minimal use of oxygen to assist breathing; ability to demonstrate or verbalize proper oxygen administration technique, including how to acquire oxygen for home use
• ability to tolerate ADLs and ambulation with minimal difficulty
• adequate home support system or, if appropriate, referral to hospice, home care, or both
• knowledge of community support programs.

PATIENT/FAMILY DISCHARGE TEACHING CHECKLIST
Document evidence that patient and family demonstrate understanding of:
___ diagnosis
___ effects of chemotherapy
___ prevention, detection, and management of bleeding
___ use of supplemental oxygen
___ smoking cessation
___ breathing exercises
___ all discharge medications' purpose, dose, administration schedule, and side effects requiring medical attention; usual discharge medications include analgesics, antiemetics, and stool softeners or antidiarrheals, as appropriate
___ pain-relief measures
___ signs of infection and methods to prevent infection
___ signs of neurologic changes
___ dietary modifications
___ measures to control nausea and vomiting
___ measures to promote normal renal function
___ measures to decrease dyspnea
___ measures to minimize effects of changing body image
___ plans for sexual expression
___ date, time, and location of follow-up appointments
___ how to contact doctor
___ when and how to seek emergency medical care
___ community resources.

DOCUMENTATION CHECKLIST
Using outcome criteria as a guide, document:
___ clinical status on admission
___ significant changes in status
___ pertinent laboratory and diagnostic test findings
___ response to chemotherapy
___ episodes of dyspnea
___ oxygen therapy
___ bleeding episodes
___ nutritional status
___ bowel elimination
___ urine elimination
___ activity tolerance
___ sleep patterns
___ patient and family teaching
___ discharge planning.

ASSOCIATED CARE PLANS
Death and Dying
Grief/Grieving
Ineffective Family Coping
Ineffective Individual Coping
Knowledge Deficit
Pain

REFERENCES
Bakemeier, R.F. "Basic Concepts of Cancer Chemotherapy and Principles of Medical Oncology," in *Clinical Oncology: A Multidisciplinary Approach,* 6th ed. Edited by Rubin, P.R. Rochester, N.Y.: University of Rochester School of Medicine and Dentistry, 1983.

Campbell, C. *Nursing Diagnosis and Intervention in Nursing Practice,* 2nd ed. New York: John Wiley & Sons, 1984.

Gordon, M. *Nursing Diagnosis: Process and Application.* New York: McGraw-Hill Book Co., 1982.

Harbert, J., et al. *Comprehensive Psychiatric Nursing,* 2nd ed. New York: McGraw-Hill Book Co., 1978.

Henshaw, E.C., and Schloerb, P.R. "Nutrition and the Cancer Patient," in *Clinical Oncology: A Multidisciplinary Approach,* 6th ed. Edited by Rubin, P.R. Rochester, N.Y.: University of Rochester School of Medicine and Dentistry, 1983.

Houtte, P.V., et al. "Lung Cancer," in *Clinical Oncology: A Multidisciplinary Approach,* 6th ed. Edited by Rubin, P.R. Rochester, N.Y.: University of Rochester School of Medicine and Dentistry, 1983.

Lewis, C.M. *Nutrition and Nutrition Therapy in Nursing.* East Norwalk, Conn.: Appleton-Century-Crofts, 1986.

Long, B.C., and Phipps, W.J., eds. *Essentials of Medical Surgical Nursing: A Nursing Process Approach.* St. Louis: C.V. Mosby Co., 1985.

Maxwell, M.B. "Dyspnea in Advanced Cancer," *American Journal of Nursing* 85(6):672-77, June 1985.

Vredevoe, D.L., et al. *Concepts of Oncology Nursing.* Englewood Cliffs, N.J.: Prentice Hall, 1981.

Pneumonia

DRG information

DRG 89 [Medical DRG] Simple Pneumonia.
Age greater than 17. With Complication
or Comorbidity (CC).
Mean LOS = 7.2 days
Principal diagnoses include:
• bronchopneumonia, organism unspecified
• influenza with pneumonia
• pleurisy without effusion
• bacterial pneumonia
• Haemophilus pneumonia
• streptococcal pneumonia
• pneumococcal pneumonia
• viral pneumonia.
DRG 90 [Medical DRG] Simple Pneumonia.
Age greater than 17. Without CC.
Mean LOS = 5.9 days
DRG 91 [Medical DRG] Simple Pneumonia.
Age 0 to 17.
Mean LOS = 4.9 days

Introduction

DEFINITION AND TIME FOCUS
Respiratory infections account for a significant number of hospitalizations each year, particularly among the very old and the very young—the two groups most susceptible to serious respiratory illness. Respiratory infections include bacterial pneumonias (most commonly caused by pneumococci), viral pneumonias (most commonly caused by influenza and other viral diseases), tuberculosis, lung abscesses, fungal infections, bronchitis from various etiologies, and pulmonary empyema developed as a result of another disorder. Since the advent of antibiotic therapy, patients are hospitalized for treatment less commonly today than in the past. Four factors are significant in determining the need for inpatient care: the patient's age, the presence of underlying disease, the nature and severity of the patient's signs and symptoms, and the presence of immunosuppression.

This care plan focuses on the patient with pneumonia who is admitted to the medical-surgical setting for diagnosis and treatment. Similar nursing interventions are applicable to most patients with respiratory infections of other types.

ETIOLOGY/PRECIPITATING FACTORS
• for community-acquired disease:
   □ in otherwise healthy people, a particularly virulent organism or a high level of exposure
   □ in the elderly population, chronic obstructive pulmonary disease, alcoholism, influenza, pulmonary neoplasms, congestive heart failure, altered consciousness, or swallowing disorders
   □ usual organisms include viruses, pneumococci, or *Mycoplasma pneumoniae*

• for nosocomial disease:
   □ compromised pulmonary defense mechanism resulting from immunosuppression, ongoing poor nutritional status, structural defects in the mucosal lining of the respiratory tract, or a depressed cough reflex; also, use of an endotracheal or tracheostomy tube
   □ usual organisms include staphylococci, *Klebsiella pneumoniae*, and *Pseudomonas aeruginosa*

Focused assessment guidelines
The manifestations of respiratory infections vary considerably, depending on the degree of inflammation present, the stage of the disease process, and the type of pathogenic organism involved.

NURSING HISTORY (Functional health pattern findings)

Health perception–health management pattern
• complains of *fatigue, malaise, and respiratory symptoms,* such as cough, pleurisy (chest pain with inspiration), and sputum production
• if disease is community-acquired, may report a recent bout of upper respiratory infection or sinus disease; self-treatment common—may have used outdated antibiotics (prescribed for a previous illness), over-the-counter medications, or both
• may report smoking history, alcohol abuse, or multiple stressors contributing to overall fatigue
• if disease is of nosocomial origin, may not have been admitted for a primary respiratory disorder but may have multiple risk factors, such as activity restriction, depressed inspiratory effort, depressed cough reflex, and use of respiratory equipment or an artificial airway

Nutritional-metabolic pattern
• reports *anorexia* during illness; may report poor nutrition before onset of respiratory illness

Activity-exercise pattern
• may report *limited activity because of fatigue and shortness of breath*

Sleep-rest pattern
• may report fatigue with *inability to "catch up" on needed rest*
• *if cough is present, it may disturb sleep*

Cognitive-perceptual pattern
• in community-acquired disease, may wonder why the illness occurred when patient was in good physical condition; does not relate subtle increased amounts of stress in life to present illness (stresses may include excessive exercise); may have delayed seeking medical attention because the illness seemed like "just a little cold"

• in nosocomial disease, patient and family may not understand connection between the primary reason for hospitalization and the present illness

PHYSICAL FINDINGS
General appearance
• *fever—low-grade or with shaking chills,* depending on pathogenic organism (check patient's "normal" temperature, because "low-grade" fever may actually represent a significant elevation in some persons, such as the elderly)

Pulmonary
• *crackles*
• *decreased breath sounds* over area of infection
• *increased respiratory rate*
• *shallow, labored breathing* (often no shortness of breath reported)
• possible abnormal bronchial breath sounds heard on auscultation over area of consolidation
• fremitus—normal or increased
• possible cough
• possible sputum production and rhinorrhea—character, color, and odor of secretions depend on pathogenic organism (generally, viral organisms produce clear secretions, whereas bacterial organisms produce discolored and purulent secretions)

Gastrointestinal
• possible vomiting

Integumentary
• warm, moist skin
• possible cyanosis, pallor, or flushing

Lymphoreticular system
• possible cervical lymphadenopathy or tenderness in salivary glands

Musculoskeletal
• weakness

DIAGNOSTIC STUDIES
• arterial blood gas (ABG) measurements—may show

hypoxemia; possible *hypocapnea* related to increased minute volume in response to hypoxemia
• sputum specimen (Gram stain, culture and sensitivity testing, or both)—performed to identify causative organisms; may be difficult to differentiate between colonization by an organism that is not the primary cause of infection and the pathogenic organism; even isolation of a specific pathogen is not necessarily proof of the parenchymal disease's etiology
• transtracheal aspiration—may be performed in an attempt to obtain a "pure" sputum specimen for examination, one uncontaminated by saliva or mouth flora; an increased number of polymorphonuclear cells with few squamous cells is considered indicative of a valid specimen
• blood culture—may show matching of organism in sputum and blood, increasing likelihood that organism is causative pathogen
• bronchoscopy—may be performed to obtain a sputum specimen; to identify the problem; or therapeutically, to clear the airways
• *chest X-ray*—shows *pulmonary infiltrates* in affected areas from inflammatory process (occasionally clear); may show pleural effusion
• thoracentesis—done to identify organism if significant pleural fluid is present on chest X-ray and sputum specimen is unobtainable
• pulmonary function tests—forced vital capacity decreased
• white blood cell (WBC) count—may be elevated but does not contribute specifically to diagnosis

POTENTIAL COMPLICATIONS
• severe hypoxemia
• adult respiratory distress syndrome (ARDS)
• empyema
• sepsis
• lung abscess
• pulmonary embolism
• pneumothorax
• pericarditis
• meningitis

Collaborative problem: *Potential hypoxemia related to inflammatory response to pathogen and inadequate airway and alveolar clearance*

NURSING PRIORITY: Optimize oxygenation and airway and alveolar clearance.

Interventions

1. *Administer oxygen therapy,* as ordered. Document therapy on initiation and per shift.

Rationales

1. Until airway and alveolar clearance is achieved, supplemental oxygen is necessary to reduce the system's need to maintain high minute volumes. Although high minute volumes help compensate for hypoxemia, they may contribute to respiratory fatigue and, ultimately, respiratory failure. The usual administration method is 1 to 6 liters/minute by nasal cannula.

Interventions *continued*

2. *Maintain oxygen therapy during activity,* such as ambulation to the bathroom. Note activity tolerance, observing for increased fatigue, tachypnea, cyanosis, tachycardia, and other signs of impaired oxygenation.

3. *Administer and document antibiotic therapy,* as ordered. Monitor the results of indicated blood level studies. Monitor and document the antibiotic's side effects. (Also see the "Osteomyelitis" care plan, page 309.)

4. *Evaluate patient progress and document parameters* once per shift and as needed: sputum character and color; presence or absence of cough; temperature; pulse; respiratory rate; skin color; level of consciousness; breath sounds; and activity tolerance.

5. Collect sputum specimens in the recommended manner. Maintain a sterile collection cup. Upon expectoration of lower respiratory tract secretions, send the specimen to the laboratory immediately to prevent overgrowth of normal oral flora that are always present in a sputum specimen. If necessary, ask the respiratory therapy department to perform a sputum induction to collect a good specimen.

6. *Perform noninvasive measures to promote airway clearance:*
• The patient who is able to cooperate should deep-breathe and cough each hour and use an incentive spirometer, as ordered.
• If the patient is unable to cooperate, perform artificial sighing and coughing each hour, using an Ambu bag.
• Perform postural drainage and percussion with vibration every 4 hours or as ordered.

7. *Perform nasotracheal suctioning* if the patient cannot cough effectively. Suction as needed, as indicated by rhonchi heard over the major airways.

8. Use increased levels of supplemental oxygen before and during airway clearance procedures.

9. *Encourage the patient to increase fluid intake* to at least 2,000 ml/day.

Rationales *continued*

2. Increased activity levels increase oxygen demands and further tax the already compromised system.

3. The antibiotic of choice is determined by the type of pathogen identified. Optimum antibiotic blood levels, necessary to achieve desired results, vary among individuals. (The "Osteomyelitis" care plan contains a detailed discussion of selected antibiotics' side effects.) Some side effects require alterations in medication levels or type of therapy to prevent immediate or long-term complications.

4. Changes in level of consciousness, such as increased restlessness or lethargy, can indicate deterioration and impending respiratory failure. Other parameters should improve if antibiotic and airway clearance therapy is effective.

5. Appropriate antibiotic therapy depends on accurate pathogen identification.

6. Purulent infectious secretions are produced in the airways and alveoli. Noninvasive clearance measures facilitate movement of secretions upward toward the major airways, where they can be expectorated or suctioned.

7. Nasotracheal suctioning is effective only if secretions are within reach of the suction catheter, typically above the carina (which is at the level of Louis' angle). Because nasotracheal suctioning can damage the tracheal mucosa, it should not be done unless secretions are within reach.

8. All of the measures used to assist airway clearance may intensify hypoxemia while they are being performed, especially if the patient has concomitant cardiovascular disease. Supplemental oxygen can be maintained via nasal prongs during nasotracheal suctioning.

9. Sputum's viscosity is related to the patient's overall hydration status. Fever contributes to dehydration. Adequate fluid intake promotes thinner secretions that can be expectorated more easily, decreasing the chance of hypoxemia related to sputum "plugs" in airway.

(continued)

Interventions *continued*

10. *Encourage small, frequent, high-protein, high-calorie meals.* (If the patient cannot eat, begin total parenteral nutrition, as ordered.)

11. *Monitor ABG levels,* as ordered and as needed, if dyspnea increases or respiratory effort is inadequate. Report abnormalities immediately, and prepare the patient for possible ventilatory support.

12. Additional individualized interventions: _____
_____
_____

Rationales *continued*

10. Protein and calorie malnutrition may contribute to impaired humoral and cell-mediated host defenses. Malnutrition also weakens the patient, contributing to a less vigorous respiratory effort.

11. Indications of severe hypoxemia and developing ARDS include a dropping PO_2 level despite a stable or increasing level of supplemental oxygen.

12. Rationale: _____
_____
_____

Outcome criteria
Within 2 days of admission, the patient will:
• easily expectorate sputum with less purulent appearance
• exhibit decreased crackles
• demonstrate pulmonary hygiene measures hourly while awake

• exhibit increased vigor and ability to perform self-care measures
• have no fever
• take oral fluids to recommended level
• have adequate dietary intake.

Nursing diagnosis: *Pain related to fever and pleuritic irritation*

NURSING PRIORITY: Minimize discomfort while promoting adequate oxygenation.

Interventions

1. See the "Pain" general care plan, page 64.

2. Administer antipyretics, analgesics, or both, as ordered and as needed. Use caution in administering sedatives or narcotics, if ordered. Document response.

3. Teach the patient to splint the chest wall with hands or pillows, as needed, while coughing, deep-breathing, or performing other pulmonary hygiene measures.

4. Provide a heating pad or hot packs to areas of chest wall discomfort, as ordered.

5. Additional individualized interventions: _____
_____
_____

Rationales

1. This care plan contains interventions for the care of patients in pain.

2. Pleuritic pain and discomfort from fever may be so severe that the patient inhibits thoracic expansion to minimize pain, thus contributing to atelectasis, hypoventilation, inadequate airway clearance, and hypoxemia. Sedatives or narcotics may cause respiratory depression.

3. Splinting may help reduce unnecessary associated chest wall movement, which contributes to pain. Providing support for painful areas helps promote fuller chest expansion despite discomfort.

4. Heat reduces inflammation and promotes muscle relaxation.

5. Rationale: _____
_____
_____

Outcome criteria
Within 24 hours of admission, the patient will:
• demonstrate splinting technique while performing pulmonary hygiene measures (if stable)

• state that pain relief was obtained with medication
• demonstrate adequate chest expansion during inspiratory effort.

Nursing diagnosis: *Knowledge deficit related to home care and preventive measures*

NURSING PRIORITY: Teach home care and preventive measures.

Interventions

1. Emphasize the importance of an ongoing pulmonary hygiene regimen. Teach the patient and family techniques for home use, based on the patient's condition and capabilities at discharge.

2. Teach the importance of rest during convalescence at home.

3. Review prophylactic measures, including the following:
• avoidance of exposure to respiratory irritants (smoke, dust, and chemical sprays)
• avoidance of crowds and persons with known infections, whenever possible
• awareness of mode of transmission (usually airborne)—increased concentrations of pathogens in saliva and sputum
• need for influenza vaccination, once the patient is stable, if recommended by the doctor.

4. Teach the patient and family the importance of promptly reporting symptoms that may indicate recurrence: headache, fever, dyspnea, chest pain, or other symptoms of "colds" or the "flu."

5. Additional individualized interventions: _____
_____
_____

Rationales

1. Deep-breathing exercises should be continued at home for at least 4 to 6 weeks to help reduce atelectasis and promote healing. Further pulmonary hygiene measures on an ongoing basis may be indicated for patients with coexisting conditions, such as emphysema, that are associated with a higher incidence of recurrence.

2. Respiratory infections place significant stresses on the body. Overexertion may further tax compromised defenses. Rest promotes healing.

3. Persons recovering from respiratory infections tend to be susceptible to other infections and are also at increased risk for recurrence after healing takes place. Preventive measures may help the patient avoid further illness.

4. Early and appropriate treatment of respiratory infections results in shorter periods of illness. In the elderly and other high-risk groups, delay in reporting symptoms is associated with higher mortality.

5. Rationale: _____
_____
_____

Outcome criteria
By the time of discharge, the patient will:
• demonstrate effective pulmonary hygiene measures for home use
• list three preventive measures
• list three symptoms indicating possible recurrence.

Discharge planning
NURSING DISCHARGE CRITERIA
Upon discharge, documentation shows evidence of:
• absence of pulmonary or cardiovascular complications (dullness on auscultation may still be present)
• ABG levels and WBC count within normal parameters
• absence of fever for at least 24 hours
• clearing pleural effusion on chest X-ray
• decreasing sputum production
• no need for supplemental oxygen for at least 48 hours
• absence of I.V. antibiotics for 24 to 48 hours
• ability to tolerate adequate dietary and fluid intake
• ability to control pain using oral medications
• ability to ambulate and perform activities of daily living same as before hospitalization

• adequate home support system or referral to home care or a nursing home if indicated by an inadequate home support system or patient's inability to care for self.

PATIENT/FAMILY DISCHARGE TEACHING CHECKLIST
Document evidence that patient/family demonstrates understanding of:
___ all discharge medications' purpose, dose, administration schedule, and side effects requiring medical intervention (usual discharge medications include antibiotics; patient may be discharged with a bronchodilator if infectious agent has been very irritating to mucous membranes)

__ recommended dietary plan and need for ongoing
fluid intake
__ realistic plan for rest and activity
__ care and use of oxygen equipment, if required for
home use
__ pulmonary hygiene measures
__ preventive measures to avoid recurrence
__ symptoms to report to health care provider
__ date, time, and location of follow-up appointments
__ how to contact doctor.

DOCUMENTATION CHECKLIST
Using outcome criteria as a guide, document:
__ clinical status on admission
__ significant changes in status
__ pertinent diagnostic findings
__ ABG test results
__ pain-relief measures
__ nutrition and fluid intake
__ oxygen therapy
__ airway clearance measures and results
__ patient and family teaching
__ discharge planning.

ASSOCIATED CARE PLANS
Chronic Obstructive Pulmonary Disease
Fluid and Electrolyte Imbalances
Geriatric Considerations
Ineffective Individual Coping
Knowledge Deficit
Pain

REFERENCES
Belshe, R."Viral Respiratory Disease in the Intensive
Care Unit," *Heart & Lung* 15(3):226, May 1986.
Frame, P.T. "Acute Infectious Pneumonia in the Adult,"
Respiratory Care 28(1):100, January 1983.
Gleckman, R.A. "Community-Acquired Pneumonia in
the Geriatric Patient," *Hospital Practice* 20(3):57,
March 1985.
Luckmann, J., and Sorensen, K.R. *Medical-Surgical
Nursing: A Psychophysiologic Approach*, 2nd ed. Phila-
delphia: W.B. Saunders Co., 1980.
Stratton, C.W. "Bacterial Pneumonias—An Overview
with Emphasis on Pathogenesis, Diagnosis, and
Treatment," *Heart & Lung* 15(3):226, May 1986.
Tafuro, P., et al. "Approach to Hospital-Acquired Pneu-
monias," *Heart & Lung* 13(5):482, September 1984.

Acute Myocardial Infarction

DRG information
DRG 121 [Medical DRG] Circulatory Disorders. With
    AMI and Cardiovascular Complication.
    Discharged Alive.
    Mean LOS = 9.4 days
DRG 122 [Medical DRG] Circulatory Disorders. With
    AMI. Without Cardiovascular Complication.
    Discharged Alive.
    Mean LOS = 7.3 days

Introduction
DEFINITION AND TIME FOCUS
Acute myocardial infarction (AMI) is necrosis (death)
of the myocardium resulting from an interrupted or diminished supply of oxygenated blood from the coronary
arteries. This clinical plan focuses on the patient with
a diagnosis of AMI who has been transferred from the
coronary care unit (CCU) to an intermediate care unit.

ETIOLOGY/PRECIPITATING FACTORS
The underlying disease process is usually atherosclerosis resulting in coronary occlusion or thrombosis, although severe coronary spasm may also be a cause.
    Precipitators include:
• factors that increase myocardial oxygen demand, including physical exertion, emotional stress, heavy
meals, tachycardia, hyperthyroidism, hypertension, valvular insufficiency, and pregnancy
• factors that decrease myocardial oxygen supply, including vasoconstriction, smoking, air pollution, anemia,
bradycardia, hypotension, and sleep.

Focused assessment guidelines
NURSING HISTORY (Functional health pattern findings)

Health perception–health management pattern
• may have *history of chest pain or previous infarction*
• may be *under treatment for hypertension, diabetes mellitus, congestive heart failure (CHF), dysrhythmias,* hyperthyroidism, or anemia
• may have *cardiac risk factors,* such as smoking, obesity, hyperlipidemia, high-stress occupation, sedentary
life-style, or positive family history
• if male, over 40, and white, is at increased risk
• if female and postmenopausal, is at increased risk
• may be noncompliant with treatment program (diet,
exercise, and medication)

Nutritional-metabolic pattern
• usually describes *diet high in calories, fat, and salt*

Elimination pattern
• may report constipation

Activity-exercise pattern
• may report lack of energy for personal care and
activities
• commonly describes *sedentary life-style,* lack of regular
exercise, and lack of leisure activities

Sleep-rest pattern
• may report difficulty sleeping because of unfamiliar
surroundings, noise, or anxiety
• may report need for frequent rest periods

Cognitive-perceptual pattern
• may report recurring chest pain

Self-perception–self-concept pattern
• may express realization of vulnerability and mortality

Role-relationship pattern
• may express concern over inability to continue in
usual family roles
• may express concern for family's ability to manage
• may express concern about ability to return to work
• may express financial concerns

Sexuality-reproductive pattern
• may express concern about decreased libido and resumption of sexual activities

Coping–stress tolerance pattern
• usually *Type A personality* (aggressive, ambitious,
competitive, work-oriented, time-driven, impatient,
and hostile)
• usually anxious, expressing fear of sudden death, loss
of employment, and loss of independence
• may be depressed over losses
• may deny seriousness of illness

Value-belief pattern
• may express need for spiritual counseling

PHYSICAL FINDINGS
Cardiovascular
• normal sinus rhythm or controlled dysrhythmias
• S₃ or S₄ (less common)
• hypotension (related to medications)

Pulmonary
• shortness of breath
• crackles (less common)
• tachypnea secondary to pain or anxiety

Musculoskeletal
• weakness
• fatigability

DIAGNOSTIC STUDIES

• *cardiac enzymes—after an infarct, creatine phosphokinase levels should return to normal within 3 to 4 days, lactic dehydrogenase levels within 7 to 10 days; sustained or regained elevations indicate continued or further cell death (expanding or recurrent infarction)*
• electrolyte levels—should be within normal limits; however, hypokalemia is not uncommon because of diuretic therapy
• cholesterol and triglyceride levels—may be elevated
• blood urea nitrogen and creatinine levels—should be within normal ranges; however, may be elevated if blood supply to kidneys is diminished
• serum drug levels—should be within therapeutic range
• white blood cell count—should be returning to normal 5 to 7 days after infarct
• erythrocyte sedimentation rate—may remain elevated for several weeks
• chest X-ray—may show cardiomegaly; if CHF is present, may show lung congestion, pleural effusion, and pulmonary edema
• telemetry—may show dysrhythmias
• *12-lead EKG—abnormal ST segment elevation, signifying ischemia, and depressed or inverted T wave, indicating injury, may be present for days to weeks or longer; abnormal Q waves, signifying necrosis, may remain indefinitely*

• echocardiography—may show valvular dysfunction, mural thrombi, dilated chambers, abnormal wall motion, and decreased cardiac output
• exercise stress test—submaximal tests, used to measure exercise capacity and to help set guidelines for an activity and exercise program, may show intolerance, as evidenced by dysrhythmias, chest pain, shortness of breath, claudication, ST segment changes, and blood pressure changes
• thallium scan—used to detect location and extent of infarction and scarring; when performed during exercise, can reveal ischemic areas that are adequately perfused at rest

POTENTIAL COMPLICATIONS

• pulmonary edema
• thromboembolism
• ventricular aneurysm
• extension of the infarction
• recurrent myocardial infarction
• dysrhythmias
• angina
• CHF
• valvular dysfunction
• Dressler's (postmyocardial infarction) syndrome
• shoulder-hand syndrome

Nursing diagnosis: *Activity intolerance related to myocardial ischemia, decreased contractility, and/or dysrhythmias*

NURSING PRIORITIES: (a) Minimize the risk of further infarction, and (b) implement safe measures to increase activity or exercise tolerance.

Interventions

1. Using telemetry, *continuously monitor heart rate rhythm, and conduction,* as ordered. Document every 4 hours.

2. *Promote physical comfort and rest.*

3. *Prohibit smoking and intake of stimulants,* such as coffee, tea, and other extremely hot fluids.

Rationales

1. A myocardial infarction may produce dysrhythmias by promoting reentry and increased automaticity. Early detection allows for prompt treatment and prevention of life-threatening dysrhythmias. Activity or exercise may precipitate new dysrhythmias, or a change in preexisting dysrhythmias, which can result in decreased cardiac output.

2. Rest reduces myocardial oxygen needs and allows the heart to heal. Physical comfort reduces anxiety as well as oxygen demand. Controlling the extent of myocardial ischemia limits the infarction's size.

3. Stimulants increase the heart rate, thus increasing oxygen demands. Smoking decreases oxygen availability because hemoglobin molecules have a greater affinity for carbon monoxide (present in smoke) than they do for oxygen.

Interventions *continued*

4. *Encourage performance of activities of daily living (ADLs) and diversional activities,* as permitted and tolerated. Allow as much decision making by the patient as possible.

5. *Implement the prescribed activity or exercise program* according to unit protocol, starting with low-energy-requirement activities, such as range-of-motion (ROM) exercises, and progressing to full self-care.

6. *Assess and document intolerance to activity or exercise,* as evidenced by:
• a pulse rate greater than 110 or increased more than 20 beats/minute over baseline
• a pulse rate that does not return to baseline within 5 minutes
• new dysrhythmias or a change in preexisting dysrhythmias
• a blood pressure decrease during activity
• chest pain, diaphoresis, or dyspnea
• dizziness, increased weakness or fatigue, or syncope
• ST segment elevation (if monitored).
Monitor vital signs before and after activity or exercise and every 5 to 15 minutes during each session, depending on the patient's tolerance.

7. *Stress the importance of avoiding Valsalva's maneuver and isometric exercises.*

8. *Provide supplemental oxygen,* as ordered, using nursing judgment.

9. *Administer vasodilators,* as ordered, and monitor the patient's response. Also monitor for side effects, particularly hypotension.

10. *Teach the patient to monitor pulse rate* before and after activity or exercise.

11. *Stress the importance of compliance with the activity or exercise program and with rest requirements.*

Rationales *continued*

4. Participation in ADLs and diversional activities increases the patient's sense of well-being and decreases anxiety. Making decisions about care activities and the timing of care, when possible, increases the patient's sense of control.

5. Progressive activity increases the heart's strength and collateral circulation. Alternating activity or exercise with rest periods prevents fatigue. Performing initial activities requiring lower increases in heart rate and blood pressure avoids oxygen demand disproportionate to the available oxygen supply. Early ROM exercises decrease the risk of thromboembolism and other deleterious effects of bed rest.

6. Exercise places an increased demand on the heart that it may not be able to meet. Myocardial infarction decreases contractility. Cardiac output may be reduced, resulting in decreased blood pressure and decreased tissue perfusion. The heart rate may increase as a compensatory mechanism to maintain cardiac output. The absence or presence of symptoms can guide the progression or cessation of the activity or exercise program.

7. Valsalva's maneuver may lead to bradycardia and a corresponding decrease in cardiac output and tissue perfusion. Isometric exercises cause a greater increase in blood pressure and heart rate than isotonic exercises do, because sustained muscle tension impedes blood flow. The resultant increase in afterload increases myocardial work and myocardial oxygen demand.

8. The healing myocardium requires a constant supply of oxygen. Supplemental oxygen increases arterial oxygen tension and may increase activity tolerance.

9. Vasodilators dilate coronary arteries and peripheral blood vessels, thus increasing myocardial oxygen supply while decreasing demand.

10. Pulse rate best reflects the cardiac work required during activity or exercise.

11. Compliance is necessary to improve healing of the myocardium and to prevent a sudden increase in oxygen demand. Fatigue is to be avoided because fatigued muscles require increased oxygen.

(continued)

Interventions *continued*

12. Encourage family and friends to support the patient's activity or exercise improvements.

13. Additional individualized interventions: _____

_____

_____

Outcome criteria
By the time of discharge, the patient will:
• present vital signs within normal limits
• show independence in self-care activities

Rationales *continued*

12. Support from family and friends, as well as health care professionals, can motivate the patient to increase activity or exercise in accordance with the therapeutic plan and individual tolerance.

13. Rationale: _____

_____

_____

• show independence in ambulation
• comply with the recommended activity or exercise program.

Nursing diagnosis: *Potential ineffective coping related to anxiety, denial, or depression*

NURSING PRIORITY: Encourage healthy coping.

Interventions

1. *Encourage verbalization of feelings.*

2. *Anticipate feelings* of denial, shock, anger, anxiety, and depression.

3. *Explain the grieving process* to the patient and family.

4. Evaluate the meaning of the person's altered body image and role responsibilities.

5. *Assess daily for indicators of anxiety,* such as apprehensive expression, tense posture, continuous talking, difficulty remembering explanations, sweating palms, tachycardia, shaking voice, tremulousness, disturbed sleep, and indecision.
• Introduce yourself and other caregivers to the patient and family.

• Assign a primary care nurse, and limit the number of other nurses caring for the patient.
• Care for the patient calmly and confidently.

• Explain the purpose and routine nature of frequent assessments.

• Repeat explanations as necessary.

Rationales

1. The patient may think his reactions are bizarre or otherwise inappropriate and may need "permission" to verbalize them.

2. These are normal responses to loss. They may become exaggerated in the face of overwhelming, life-threatening experiences and intense psychological threats.

3. The patient and family may be bewildered and alarmed about their emotional responses.

4. Patients may respond in various ways because of the unique meaning of losses to each. These ways are described further in the sections that follow.

5. Systematic assessment and comparison with previous findings increases the likelihood that coping problems will be detected early. Anxiety may result from fear of the unknown, unfamiliar surroundings, unfinished business, or other causes.
• Introductions reduce the depersonalization of the hospital environment and lay the foundation for establishing rapport and trust.
• Continuity of caregivers promotes trust.

• Calm, confident behavior provides nonverbal reassurance that the caregiver is competent.
• Explaining that frequent assessments are routine reassures the patient that his condition is not necessarily deteriorating.
• Anxiety interferes with memory; repetition enhances learning.

Interventions *continued*

• Orient the patient to the unit environment.

• Administer minor tranquilizers, as ordered, using nursing judgment. Document.

• Help the patient to explore alternatives for resolving unfinished business.

6. *Assess daily for indicators of denial,* such as refusal to discuss the infarct, minimal acceptance of its significance, apparent lack of concern about status, verbal acknowledgment that the infarct has occurred but disregard of diet and activity restrictions, and ongoing attempts to continue conducting business.
• *Evaluate the impact of denial on the patient's health.*

• If the patient verbalizes denial, listen nonjudgmentally.

• If the denial is being expressed through acting-out behavior, document, express concern, and promote greater control over the environment. Involve the patient in solving the problem, compromising and modifying restrictive aspects of the care plan, and allow choices where appropriate.

• Be alert for topics the patient consistently fails to raise or refuses to discuss when prompted.

• Encourage the patient to focus on remaining abilities.

• Encourage the resumption of full self-care, as physical abilities allow.

• Consult psychiatric resources for further assistance, if needed.

7. *Assess daily for indicators of depression,* such as verbalized concern about "damaged heart"; focus on past physical accomplishments; expression of negative feelings about the body; verbalized feelings of sadness, helplessness, or hopelessness; lack of appetite; insomnia or excessive sleeping; psychosomatic complaints (such as headache, neckache, backache, or stomachache); apathy; frequent crying episodes (or desire to cry); and poor personal hygiene.

Rationales *continued*

• Orientation to the unit environment increases the predictability of experiences, reducing the patient's need for vigilance (wary watchfulness) and helping the patient learn the "patient role."

• Minor tranquilizers may help calm the patient during periods of physiologic instability but can interfere with psychological adjustment by creating an air of unreality and by disturbing rapid-eye-movement (REM) sleep. Usually, diazepam (Valium) is given.

• The patient may be "locked into" the need to keep appointments, conduct business, and so forth, and may need assistance in determining realistic ways to handle such situations. The patient may also need such reassurance as "It's OK to let go" and "People will understand that your health needs come first now."

6. Early detection allows interventions promoting prompt resolution of depression. Denial may be associated with the patient's current grieving process or previous coping pattern.

• Some denial is normal and may be a healthy initial response to an overwhelming situation. Denial that promotes self-destructive behavior, however, requires intervention.

• Confronting denial and forcing the patient to "face facts" before he or she is ready to cope with them may precipitate distraught behavior.

• These interventions promote a greater sense of control for the patient and thus are more likely to be successful in promoting behavioral changes than are confrontation and threats.

• The patient may avoid topics that are especially anxiety-producing.

• The patient may become preoccupied with or panicky about perceived losses and may need encouragement to focus on strengths.

• Enforced dependence contributes to low self-esteem.

• A psychiatric clinical specialist, psychiatrist, or social worker can provide additional insight and guidelines for further intervention.

7. Accurate interpretation of cues increases the likelihood of selecting appropriate nursing interventions. Depression is most likely to result from body-image change and altered role performance.

(continued)

Interventions *continued*

• Assess for and document specific psychological, spiritual, and pathophysiologic causes of depression as well as the depressive effects of medications.

• Assess and document the patient's sleep pattern. Promote restful sleep by grouping procedures, minimizing external stimuli, and providing relaxation measures at bedtime.

• Encourage verbalization of feelings and crying.

• Assist with realistic problem solving.

• When pessimism is expressed, point out hopeful aspects of the situation.

• Encourage physical activity, as appropriate, and document responses.

• Help the patient identify and implement enjoyable diversions.

• Share updated information on the patient's status, as appropriate. Emphasize even small signs of progress.

8. Additional individualized interventions: _____

_____

_____

Rationales *continued*

• Treatment of depression is likely to be most effective when it focuses on specific causative factors and patient concerns.

• Depression may contribute to sleep disturbances (especially feeling less than fully rested on awakening). Depression also can result from deprivation of REM sleep.

• Sharing feelings can help the patient identify causes of depression. Because crying is discouraged in American society, the patient may need permission and active encouragement to release pent-up tears.

• The patient who has mental "tunnel vision" may need help identifying options and evaluating their advantages and disadvantages.

• Depression may be self-perpetuating. Focusing on hopeful, positive factors may encourage the patient to break the cycle of depressive rumination.

• Depression is immobilizing, and lack of activity reinforces depression. Mood elevation often follows resumption of physical activity.

• Boredom may encourage an unhealthy preoccupation with illness. Pleasurable diversions include reading, doing crossword puzzles, listening to music, participating in arts and crafts (which involve the patient directly), and watching television (a more passive activity).

• A depressed person tends to focus only on negative thoughts. Emphasizing even small status gains may help the patient recognize signs of recovery.

8. Rationale: _____

_____

_____

Outcome criteria
Within 3 days of admission to the intermediate care unit, the patient will:
• appear less anxious by exhibiting a calm expression, relaxed posture, dry palms, steady voice and hands, no tremors, and a normal heart rate. Patient will also sleep easily, have no morning insomnia, be comfortable with silences, and be able to recall explanations and make reasonable decisions.
• confront denial, if present, and express concern about the heart attack by discussing problems, gradually showing other signs of grief (such as crying, anxiety, or anger), taking responsibility for cooperating with the health plan, and allowing others to take over business affairs
• exhibit less depression, if present, and participate in self-care, show a return of appetite, sleep restfully, openly discuss problems, talk about feelings without uncontrollable crying, express interest in learning about life-style modifications, make appropriate decisions, and express an intention to use available resources.

Nursing diagnosis: *Altered sexuality pattern related to physical limitations secondary to tissue ischemia and medications*

NURSING PRIORITY: Provide information to the patient and spouse (or partner) regarding resumption of sexual activity.

Interventions

1. *Obtain a sexual history,* including incidence of chest pain during or after foreplay and intercourse.

Rationales

1. The history provides baseline information and identifies previous sexual problems.

Interventions *continued*

2. Encourage the patient and spouse (or partner) to verbalize fears and anxieties. Provide time for joint and individual discussion.

3. Be aware of personal feelings about sexuality and if you are too uncomfortable to counsel the couple effectively, make an appropriate referral.

4. Provide printed material about AMI and resumption of sexual activities.

5. Inform the patient that some medications can cause impotence or decrease libido. Encourage discussion with the doctor if such problems occur.

6. Discuss ways to decrease the effects of sexual activity on the cardiovascular system—for example, medications and positioning.

7. Emphasize that sexual activity should be avoided after large meals or excessive alcohol intake, in extreme temperatures, and under conditions of fatigue or increased stress.

8. As ordered, *evaluate activity tolerance* by means of low-level treadmill exercise testing or two-flight stair climbing, followed by a resting EKG.

9. Teach symptoms that should be reported to the doctor if they occur during foreplay or intercourse, particularly increased heart rate and respirations persisting 10 minutes after activity, extreme fatigue the day after sexual activity, and chest pain during intercourse.

10. Additional individualized interventions: _____
_____
_____

Rationales *continued*

2. Verbalizing fears and anxieties may help identify important issues and allow an opportunity to correct misconceptions.

3. Unawareness of personal feelings may inhibit sensitivity to sexual concerns. The couple may sense the caregiver's discomfort and become inhibited about expressing their concerns.

4. Accurate information may allay fears and anxieties and dispel misconceptions. Providing printed material will avoid misinterpretation and may increase the likelihood of resumption of sexual activity.

5. Patient awareness of possible pharmacologic causes of sexual dysfunction helps decrease anxiety. Some commonly used medications that can have these side effects are antihypertensives (such as methyldopa, reserpine, guanethidine, and clonidine); diuretics (such as spironolactone and hydrochlorothiazide); and beta blockers (such as propranolol and nadolol).

6. Nitroglycerin or another vasodilator may be prescribed for use before intercourse, to reduce the heart's workload. Some positions require less myocardial work than others.

7. Digestion of a large meal requires increased splanchnic blood flow and, therefore, increases cardiac workload. In low doses, alcohol increases heart rate and cardiac output; in higher doses, alcohol causes myocardial depression and corresponding decreases in heart rate and cardiac output. Stress causes catecholamine release, thus increasing cardiac workload and oxygen demand.

8. These tests provide specific information that can be used in counseling and as a guide for resuming sexual activity. The myocardial oxygen requirement for two-flight stair climbing is similar to that required for sexual activity. Walking on a treadmill at 3 to 4 miles/hour without EKG changes or excessive increases in blood pressure and heart rate indicates that the patient is more than able to meet the cardiac work requirements of sexual activity.

9. These symptoms indicate that the activity is too strenuous and that the increased myocardial oxygen demand is not being met.

10. Rationale: _____
_____
_____

Outcome criteria

Within 1 week of admission to unit, the patient will:
• verbalize understanding of sexual activity's effects on cardiovascular function

• list three recommendations for minimizing myocardial stress during sexual activity.

Nursing diagnosis: *Knowledge deficit related to newly diagnosed complex disease process and to therapy*

NURSING PRIORITY: Assist in identifying cardiac risk factors and ways to modify life-style.

Interventions

1. For the patient to understand the disease process:

• *Describe the basic anatomy and physiology of the heart, the atherosclerotic process, and the pathophysiology of chest pain and AMI.*
• *Discuss angina's symptoms and what to do if angina occurs.* Instruct the patient to call the doctor if chest pain is unrelieved by nitroglycerin (see *Medication Therapy for Coronary Artery Disease* for guidelines).
• *Instruct the patient about medication therapy* (see *Medication Therapy for Coronary Artery Disease*).

2. For the patient to implement necessary dietary modifications:
• Explain the rationale for a diet low in calories (if the patient is obese), saturated fats, and salt.

• Take a dietary history, and help the patient identify eating patterns.
• *Have the dietitian help the patient plan a reduced-calorie, -fat and -salt diet* that fits his or her life-style, culture, and socioeconomic status.
• *Discuss the role of exercise* in reducing weight, blood pressure, and serum lipid levels.
• Stress the need for the entire family to follow the modified diet.

• Give information about antilipid medications (if prescribed), including action, dosage, scheduling, and side effects.
• Provide a list of weight-reduction programs, if appropriate.
• *Give printed diet information for home use.*

3. For the patient to understand the importance of hypertension management:

Rationales

1. The patient who understands the disease process is more likely to implement therapeutic recommendations successfully.
• Comprehension of AMI's pathophysiology provides a basis for understanding therapeutic approaches.

• The prepared patient is more likely to react appropriately when angina recurs.

• Accurate information dispels misconceptions, reduces anxiety, and increases patient compliance.

2. Obesity, hypertension, and hyperlipidemia greatly increase the risk of coronary heart disease (CHD).
• Reducing weight and salt intake helps decrease blood pressure. Reducing saturated fat intake decreases blood lipid levels and increases the level of high-density lipoproteins (HDLs), which protect against atherosclerosis. Explanations improve patient compliance.
• The dietary history provides baseline information and identifies patterns that need change.
• The patient is more apt to adhere to a prescribed diet if it is acceptable and affordable.

• Exercise decreases blood pressure, weight, triglyceride levels, and anxiety. It also increases HDL levels.
• There is a familiar tendency for the development of obesity, hypertension, and hyperlipidemia. Compliance is more likely if the patient can continue sharing family meals.
• Antilipid medications are used to inhibit lipid synthesis. Information about medications will help the patient assume responsibility for self-care.
• Programs can provide motivation and increase compliance.
• Giving the patient printed material will avoid misinterpretation and increase compliance.

3. Hypertension is a significant predictor of CHD: the risk of heart disease increases in direct proportion to increases in systolic and diastolic blood pressure.

(continued on page 200)

MEDICATION THERAPY FOR CORONARY ARTERY DISEASE

Drug	Action	Administration	Patient instructions	Possible side effects
Vasodilator (e.g., nitroglycerin or long-acting nitrates)	Primarily dilates peripheral blood vessels, reducing myocardial workload	Can be given by mouth before meals. Sublingual: 1 tablet every 5 minutes for a maximum of three tablets; if no relief, call doctor.	Take prophylactically before activities, if ordered, or at onset of chest pain. Take sitting or lying down to prevent postural hypotension. If no relief after three tablets, do not drive self to hospital: call an ambulance. Keep record of number of tablets taken. Check expiration date. Carry nitroglycerin at all times. Wear Medic-Alert bracelet. Avoid alcohol, which has added vasodilating effect. Replace tablets at 4 months. If ointment or patch is prescribed, instruct in correct application, skin care, site rotation, and frequency of change.	Transient headache, flushing, faintness, dizziness, or hypotension
Beta blocker (e.g., propranolol)	Blocks catecholamines' effect to decrease blood pressure, heart rate, and contractility; also decreases automaticity to slow sinus rate and suppress ectopic beats	By mouth, before meals	Monitor pulse rate and blood pressure; report pulse rate under 60 beats/minute, irregular, or changed. Do not stop abruptly—may precipitate chest pain or myocardial infarction.	Bradycardia, hypotension, dizziness, nausea, vomiting, diarrhea, or bronchoconstriction
Calcium channel blocker (e.g., verapamil)	Blocks transport of calcium across cell membrane, resulting in vasodilation and decreased contractility; verapamil also increases refractory period of atrioventricular node and decreases sinoatrial node rate	By mouth, 1 hour before meals or 2 hours after meals	Monitor pulse rate and blood pressure; report pulse rate under 50 beats/minute.	Postural hypotension, bradycardia, headache, dizziness, syncope, nausea, edema, or constipation
Inotropic agent (e.g., digoxin)	Slows conduction; increases contractility and automaticity	By mouth (after I.M. or I.V. loading dose)	Check pulse rate before taking. Report pulse rate under 60 beats/minute, irregular, or changed; stop medication and call doctor, if anorexic longer than 1 day.	Anorexia, nausea, vomiting, diarrhea, bradycardia, dysrhythmias, fatigue, weakness, dizziness, headache, blurred vision, hypokalemia, renal disease, hypothroidism, and other disease processes that may increase serum digoxin levels

Interventions *continued*

• *Explain the risks of high blood pressure.*

• *Discuss medication therapy,* including action, dosage, scheduling, and side effects, such as electrolyte imbalances, sexual dysfunction, orthostatic hypotension, lethargy, headache, flushing, nausea, vomiting, and palpitations.

• *Describe ways to reduce salt intake,* based on the diet history.

• *Emphasize the need for follow-up visits.*

• *Provide printed information* about antihypertensive medications.

• *Stress the importance of contacting the doctor if any of these symptoms occur:* chest pain, dizziness, headache, blurred vision, edema, nausea, vomiting, nose bleeds, or shortness of breath.

4. For the patient to understand the importance of smoking cessation:

• *Explain the rationale for quitting.*

• Discuss the benefits of not smoking.

• *Help the patient identify needs currently met by smoking, then explore substitute options.*

• Discuss with the patient's spouse, partner, or significant others the need to assist and support the patient's efforts to stop smoking.

• Provide a list of community stop smoking programs.

Rationales *continued*

• *Hypertension increases afterload and makes the heart increase its rate and force of contraction over a period of time. Left ventricular hypertrophy occurs, resulting in an increase in cardiac workload and oxygen demand. Also, a structural change in the coronary arteries accelerates atherosclerosis.*

• Noncompliance is often a problem with antihypertensive medication therapy. Lack of symptoms attributable to hypertension makes it difficult to convince patients they have a serious health problem requiring lifelong treatment and follow-up care; the appearance of side effects may further increase noncompliance. The patient should know that the doctor can change medications or dosage if side effects do occur.

• Reduced salt intake decreases fluid volume and myocardial workload. Although the relationship between salt intake and hypertension is not well understood, a reduced intake in susceptible people is known to decrease blood pressure. Excessive salt intake causes fluid retention, which increases blood volume and peripheral vascular resistance and can lead to elevated blood pressure. Reducing salt intake also enhances the effectiveness of most antihypertensives.

• Follow-up visits provide opportunities to monitor blood pressure, response to medication and other forms of treatment, and early development of complications.

• Giving the patient printed material will avoid misinterpretation and increase compliance.

• These symptoms, indicating increased hypertension, or cardiac failure, or both, require therapeutic intervention.

4. Smoking increases the risk of premature heart disease by three to six times; cessation of smoking markedly decreases that risk.

• Smoking causes vasoconstriction, alters coagulation, and increases carbon monoxide levels and platelet aggregation. Also, nicotine (a stimulant) increases heart rate and the occurrence of dysrhythmias.

• This makes smoking cessation during hospitalization a growth-promoting experience. The many benefits include an improved sense of smell, an improved ability to taste, improved lung function, monetary savings, increased longevity, and gratitude from nonsmokers.

• Smoking satisfies complex needs. For a stop smoking program to be successful, it must address those needs, ideally meeting them with less harmful substitutes.

• Support from other people provides motivation and encouragement to stop smoking.

• These programs offer support, motivation, and methods to help the patient.

Interventions *continued*

5. For the patient to understand the importance of stress reduction:
• *Discuss stress and its effect on the cardiovascular system.*

• *Help the patient to identify stressors* and to learn health-promoting behaviors.

• *Identify the characteristics of Type A behavior exhibited by the patient,* and review their relationship to AMI.
• *Teach stress reduction techniques,* such as progressive relaxation, guided imagery, and aerobic exercise within recommended guidelines. Provide referral to an outpatient stress reduction program, as needed, and to a cardiac rehabilitation program, where available.

6. Additional individualized interventions: _____
_____
_____

Rationales *continued*

5. Stress is an important risk factor for AMI recurrence.
• Tension and psychological stress cause sympathetic stimulation, raising blood pressure and increasing the pulse rate and cardiac workload.
• Behavior modification is necessary for stress reduction and promotion of optimal health. The program should include specific and regular times for recreation and relaxation.
• Correlations exist between Type A behavior patterns and the prevalence of CHD.
• Decreasing stress reduces myocardial oxygen demands and increases the patient's feeling of well-being.

6. Rationale: _____
_____
_____

Outcome criteria

By the time of discharge, the patient will:
• verbalize knowledge of preventive health measures
• verbalize a willingness to adhere to prescribed therapy
• list personal risk factors
• explain the rationale for dietary modifications

• identify specific ways to reduce salt and fat intake
• have begun a smoking cessation program, if appropriate
• identify two personal stressors and ways to cope with them
• verbalize understanding of the medication regimen.

Discharge planning
NURSING DISCHARGE CRITERIA
Upon discharge, documentation shows evidence of:
• absence of chest pain
• tolerance of activity without signs of orthostatic hypotension, dyspnea, pain, or shortness of breath
• angina controlled by medication
• absence of oxygen therapy for at least 48 hours before discharge
• EKG within expected parameters
• dysrhythmias (if present) controlled by oral medication
• I.V. lines discontinued for at least 48 hours before discharge
• ability to tolerate ambulation and perform activities of daily living
• vital signs within expected parameters for at least 48 hours before discharge
• absence of fever and of pulmonary or cardiovascular complications
• blood chemistries and laboratory values within expected parameters
• ability to tolerate diet and any diet restrictions
• normal elimination pattern
• referral to outpatient cardiac rehabilitation program (if applicable).

PATIENT/FAMILY DISCHARGE TEACHING CHECKLIST
Document evidence that patient and family demonstrate understanding of:
___ AMI disease process and implications
___ accuracy in measuring radial pulse rate
___ all discharge medications' purpose, dosage, administration schedule, and side effects requiring medical attention (usual discharge medications include nitrates, beta blockers, antidysrhythmics, calcium antagonists, antihypertensives, and inotropes).
___ need for risk modification
___ prescribed diet
___ prescribed activity or exercise program
___ need for regularly scheduled rest periods
___ signs and symptoms to report to health care provider
___ need for follow-up care
___ when to resume sexual activity
___ availability of community resources
___ how to contact doctor.

DOCUMENTATION CHECKLIST
Using outcome criteria as a guide, document:
___ status on admission to intermediate care unit
___ significant changes in status

___ pertinent laboratory and diagnostic test findings
___ telemetry monitoring
___ chest pain episodes
___ interventions for pain relief
___ dietary intake and output
___ medical management therapies, including
    medications
___ emotional status
___ activity tolerance
___ patient and family teaching
___ discharge planning.

ASSOCIATED CARE PLANS
Death and Dying
Fluid and Electrolyte Imbalances
Geriatric Considerations
Grief/Grieving
Ineffective Family Coping
Ineffective Individual Coping
Knowledge Deficit
Pain

REFERENCES
Andreoli, Kathleen, et al. *Comprehensive Cardiac Care: A Text for Nurses, Physicians, and Other Health Practitioners*, 5th ed. St. Louis: C.V. Mosby Co., 1983.

Carpenito, L. *Nursing Diagnosis: Application to Clinical Practice*. Philadelphia: J.B. Lippincott Co., 1983.

Gordon, Margory. *Nursing Diagnosis: Process and Application*. New York: McGraw-Hill Book Co., 1982.

Sadler, Diane. *Nursing for Cardiovascular Health*. East Norwalk, Conn.: Appleton-Century-Crofts, 1984.

Thompson, June, et al. *Clinical Nursing*. St. Louis: C.V. Mosby Co., 1986.

Ulrich, Susan, et al. *Nursing Care Planning Guides: A Nursing Diagnosis Approach*. Philadelphia: W.B. Saunders Co., 1986.

Underhill, Sandra, et al. *Cardiac Nursing*. Philadelphia: J.B. Lippincott Co., 1982.

Angina Pectoris

DRG information
DRG 140 [Medical DRG] Angina Pectoris.
 Mean LOS = 4.1 days

Introduction
DEFINITION AND TIME FOCUS
Angina pectoris—transient insufficient coronary blood flow caused by obstruction or constriction of the coronary arteries—is characterized by brief episodes of retrosternal chest pain, commonly felt beneath the middle and upper thirds of the sternum. In angina, cells within the heart muscle do not die, as they do in myocardial infarction (MI), because the hypoxia is transient. Angina often is categorized into classic angina and Prinzmetal's angina. These categories differ according to etiology, precipitating factors, descriptions of pain, and EKG findings, as described in the sections that follow. This clinical plan focuses on the patient admitted to a medical-surgical unit for diagnosis and medical management during an initial acute attack.

ETIOLOGY/PRECIPITATING FACTORS
Classic angina:
• any condition that decreases oxygen delivery by the coronary arteries, increases the cardiac workload, or increases myocardial need for oxygen—for example, atherosclerosis, severe aortic stenosis, mitral stenosis or regurgitation, hypotension, hyperthyroidism, marked anemia, and ventricular dysrhythmias
• classic coronary artery disease risk factors—for example, physical or emotional stress, physical inactivity, obesity, smoking, increased serum cholesterol level (above 200 mg/dl), and diabetes mellitus
• genetic factors—for example, hypertension and Type II familial hyperlipoproteinemia
 Prinzmetal's angina:
• coronary artery spasm

Focused assessment guidelines
NURSING HISTORY (Functional health pattern findings)

Health perception–health management pattern
• *reports sudden onset of substernal chest pain, pressure, or both; not sharply localized*—may radiate to arms, shoulders, neck, jaw, upper abdomen; untreated, lasts usually 2 to 5 minutes, not more than 30 minutes
• typically describes pain as "pressure," "tightness," "aching," or "squeezing," with rest or nitroglycerin providing relief
• with classic angina, typically reports recent emotional stress, heavy exercise, a large meal, or exposure to cold

• with Prinzmetal's angina, typically reports cyclical pain in absence of precipitating factors
• may be under treatment for hypertension, hyperlipidemia, or diabetes mellitus
• may have left ventricular hypertrophy
• may be obese or smoke cigarettes
• may have history of chronic stress, Type A behavior, sedentary life-style
• white men over age 40, white women over age 50, and black men and women under age 45 with hypertension are at increased risk

Nutritional-metabolic pattern
• *may report nausea or indigestion*
• may report feeling of fullness
• when stable, likely to report diet high in calories, cholesterol, saturated fat, and caffeine
• may report pain episode after large, heavy meal

Activity-exercise pattern
• typically describes *shortness of breath* during chest pain episode
• when stable, commonly reports sedentary life-style with only sporadic exercise
• may report transient chest pain episodes during increased activity, alleviated by rest

Sleep-rest pattern
• when stable, may report sleep disturbance such as chest pain during dreaming or when lying flat

Cognitive-perceptual pattern
• *may report feeling of impending doom* during chest pain

Self-perception–self-concept pattern
• may appear to have difficulty believing something is physically wrong during pain-free intervals

Role-relationship pattern
• *may report family history of coronary artery disease*
• may report perception that others are dependent on him or her
• may be involved in multiple high stress roles, such as business executive, president of community group, parent of teenager
• commonly concerned that hospitalization will prevent resumption of occupation and life-style routine

Sexuality-reproductive pattern
• may have history of oral contraceptive use
• may report previous chest pain episodes during sexual activity
• may verbalize concern over resuming normal sexual relations

Coping–stress tolerance pattern
• *typically shows Type A personality traits*—for example, overreaction to stress, exaggerated sense of urgency, excessive aggressiveness, and competitiveness
• may be in high-stress occupation
• *typically has delayed securing medical attention* because chest pain subsided with rest (denial)

Value-belief pattern
• may display compulsive striving for achievement

PHYSICAL FINDINGS
Cardiovascular
• *increased heart rate*
• elevated blood pressure at onset of pain
• dysrhythmias
• S_3 and S_4 gallop
• transient jugular venous pressure elevations

Pulmonary
• *shortness of breath* during chest pain episode
• abnormal breath sounds, particularly crackles

Neurologic
• anxiety
• restlessness

Integumentary
• cool, clammy skin
• diaphoresis

Musculoskeletal
• *pained facial expression*
• clenched fists
• tense, rigid posture

DIAGNOSTIC STUDIES
• *cardiac enzyme and isoenzyme levels*—no elevations, or minor elevations without pattern characteristic of AMI

• complete blood count—may show decreased hemoglobin, hematocrit, and red blood cell levels, suggesting anemia-induced angina
• serum cholesterol, lipid profile—may be elevated, indicating increased risk for coronary artery disease
• serum electrolyte levels—used to determine imbalances, particularly in potassium levels, that can cause cardiac rhythm disturbances
• serum drug levels—may indicate toxic or subtherapeutic levels of cardiotonics or antidysrhythmics
• *12-lead EKG—resting EKG usually normal in angina; ischemic changes during chest pain:* classic angina, inversion of T waves and ST depression; Prinzmetal's angina, ST elevation
• treadmill or exercise test—may reveal chest pain and EKG signs of ischemia on exertion, especially ST- and T-wave changes; ventricular dysrhythmias; and downsloping ST segment or horizontal ST segment depression
• myocardial perfusion studies—may show ischemic areas of the myocardium, imaged with thallium 201, as cold spots
• echocardiogram—may illustrate abnormal structural problems, such as valvular disease or stenoses
• cardiac catheterization and angiography—used to visualize blockage and to demonstrate patency of coronary arteries and ability of coronary vessels to provide adequate perfusion to myocardium

POTENTIAL COMPLICATIONS
• sudden death
• myocardial infarction (MI)
• intractable, unstable, or crescendo angina
• dysrhythmias, especially ventricular
• decreased ventricular function

Nursing diagnosis: *Chest pain related to myocardial ischemia*

NURSING PRIORITY: Identify and relieve chest pain.

Interventions

1. *Assess and document chest pain episodes* according to the following criteria: location, duration, quality (on a scale of 1 to 10), precipitating factors, aggravating factors, alleviating factors, and associated signs and symptoms.

2. *Assess the patient for nonverbal signs of chest pain:* restlessness; clenched fists; rubbing of the chest, arms, or neck; chest clutching; and facial flushing or grimacing.

Rationales

1. Many conditions can produce chest pain. The nurse must carefully assess the type of chest pain in order to differentiate angina from pain related to other causes, such as pleuritic, gastric, or musculoskeletal disorders.

2. Patients differ in the ways they express pain and in the meaning pain has for them. Denial of cardiac symptoms is common initially. An increase or change in the degree or intensity of pain may indicate increasing myocardial ischemia.

Interventions continued

3. *Obtain a 12-lead EKG immediately during acute chest pain.*

4. *Medicate promptly at the onset of pain with sublingual nitroglycerin, as ordered.* (The typical protocol is 0.15 to 0.6 mg per tablet every 5 minutes to a maximum of three tablets.) Assess pain relief after 15 to 20 minutes. Evaluate and document blood pressure, pulse rate, respirations, and pain before and after pain medication. If the pain is unrelieved after 15 to 20 minutes (or after three tablets), notify the doctor immediately.

5. *Implement measures to improve myocardial oxygenation:* institute oxygen therapy, place the patient on bed rest in semi- to high Fowler's position, and minimize environmental noise and distractions.

6. Stay with the patient during chest pain episodes.

7. *Monitor and document the therapeutic effects of beta blockers* (such as propranolol, metoprolol, and nadolol) *and calcium channel blockers* (such as verapamil and nifedipine). Monitor for bradycardia, hypotension, dysrhythmias, signs and symptoms of congestive heart failure, constipation, and exacerbation of ischemic symptoms from medication therapies.

8. *Establish and maintain I.V. access.*

9. Additional individualized interventions: _____
_____
_____

Outcome criteria
Within 30 minutes of chest pain onset, the patient will:
• verbalize absence or relief of pain
• display relaxed facial expression and body posture
• display normal depth and rate of respirations
• show no restlessness, grimacing, or other signs and symptoms of pain.

Rationales continued

3. Resting EKGs are usually normal in the patient with myocardial ischemia. Ischemic changes may be noted on the EKG only during periods of actual chest pain.

4. Nitrates decrease myocardial oxygen demands by causing vasodilation, which reduces preload and afterload and thus decreases cardiac workload and oxygen consumption. Pain unrelieved by nitroglycerin suggests extended ischemia or myocardial necrosis development.

5. These measures reduce the heart's oxygen demand and help alleviate the chest pain and ensuing anxiety. Chest and head elevation makes lung ventilation easier by permitting the lungs and respiratory muscles to function without being cramped. Sitting with the shoulders slightly pulled back allows unrestricted movement of the diaphragm. Decreasing anxiety reduces circulating catecholamine levels, thus decreasing blood pressure and myocardial oxygen consumption.

6. The presence of a competent caregiver may decrease anxiety and promote patient comfort. It also allows for immediate intervention if problems occur.

7. Beta blockers block the myocardial response to sympathetic stimulation, thus decreasing oxygen demand and preventing or relieving anginal pain. Beta blockers also decrease heart rate, blood pressure, and myocardial contractility. Calcium channel blockers dilate the coronary arteries, thus decreasing coronary artery spasm and improving myocardial perfusion.

8. I.V. access is necessary for possible emergency medication administration or until the differential diagnosis is completed. The usual order is for a Heparin Lock or dextrose 5% in water to keep the vein open.

9. Rationale: _____
_____
_____

Within 1 hour of chest pain onset, the patient will:
• display vital signs within normal limits
• increase participation in appropriate activities
• show no life-threatening dysrhythmias.

Collaborative problem: *Potential dysrhythmias or myocardial infarction related to myocardial hypoxia and ischemia*

NURSING PRIORITIES: (a) Optimize cardiac oxygenation and perfusion, and (b) decrease myocardial oxygen demands.

Interventions

1. *Monitor, report, and document signs and symptoms of dysrhythmias*—such as irregular apical pulse, pulse deficit, pulse rate below 60 or above 100 beats/minute, syncope, dizziness, palpitations, chest "fluttering," or abnormal configurations on rhythm strips or 12-lead EKGs.

2. *Administer antidysrhythmic medications*, as ordered, noting and documenting their effectiveness and side effects.

3. *Decrease myocardial oxygen demands* by restricting activity (based on the dysrhythmia's severity), maintaining oxygen therapy, and providing a calm, supportive environment.

4. *Monitor, report, and document signs and symptoms of inadequate tissue perfusion*—such as decreasing blood pressure; cool, clammy skin; cyanosis; diminished peripheral pulses; decreased urine output; increased restlessness and agitation; or respiratory distress.

5. *Monitor and report signs and symptoms of developing MI*—such as chest pain lasting longer than 30 minutes and unrelieved by administration of short-acting nitrate; elevation of creatine phosphokinase (CPK) isoenzymes; ST segment elevation; pathological Q wave on a 12-lead EKG.

6. Additional individualized interventions: _____
_____
_____

Rationales

1. Ventricular irritability secondary to myocardial ischemia can lead to life-threatening ventricular dysrhythmias. Prompt dysrhythmia identification is essential for stabilizing the patient's cardiovascular condition.

2. Common antiarrhythmic medications include lidocaine, procainamide, quinidine, bretylium, and atropine. Lidocaine is the medication of choice for dangerous premature ventricular contractions (more than 6/minute, sequential, multifocal, or early diastolic), which are common with myocardial hypoxia and ischemia.

3. Activities that increase myocardial oxygen demands may potentiate dysrhythmia development by promoting increased automaticity and impeding electrical conduction through the myocardium.

4. Dysrhythmias may lead to decreased cardiac output, resulting in inadequate tissue perfusion. Prompt recognition is essential to minimize damage and complications.

5. When myocardial ischemia is severe or prolonged, irreversible injury (tissue necrosis) occurs. Chest pain that does not respond to nitroglycerin within 30 minutes strongly suggests MI.

6. Rationale: _____
_____
_____

Outcome criteria

Within 30 minutes of chest pain onset, the patient will:
• verbalize relief of chest pain
• have stable vital signs.

Within 24 hours of admission, the patient will:
• display an apical or radial pulse rate of 60 to 100 beats/minute
• show normal sinus rhythm on EKG or pharmacologically controlled dysrhythmias
• have no syncope, palpitations, or skipped beats
• have no pulse deficit.

Within 3 days of admission, the patient will:
• have no elevation of cardiac enzymes
• have a resting EKG negative for ST elevation and Q waves
• have normal blood pressure, pulse, and respirations
• display clear lungs
• maintain normal urine output.

Nursing diagnosis: *Activity intolerance related to development of chest pain on exertion*

NURSING PRIORITY: Promote gradual activity restoration, balancing myocardial oxygen supply and demand.

Interventions

1. *Instruct the patient to cease immediately any activity that precipitates chest pain.* If chest pain occurs, maintain the patient in Fowler's position, and administer oxygen therapy, as ordered.

2. *Instruct the patient to avoid activities that create a Valsalva's maneuver,* such as straining to have a bowel movement or heavy lifting and straining.

3. *Document activity tolerance, and instruct the patient to increase activity gradually;* monitor pulse rate before and after activity; use development of chest pain, fatigue, or marked tachycardia as an indication for stopping; and pace activities to avoid sudden energy bursts.

4. *Promote physical rest and emotional comfort.*

5. Additional individualized interventions: _____
_____
_____

Rationales

1. Pain is often relieved by stopping the physical activity that preceded its onset. Changing from a supine to a sitting position decreases central blood volume because blood pools in the extremities, reducing the heart's oxygen demand. Fowler's position allows maximum lung expansion; oxygen therapy decreases the heart's workload.

2. Valsalva's maneuver induces parasympathetic stimulation, which can cause bradycardia and decrease cardiac output, leading to increased ischemia.

3. Physical activity increases myocardial oxygen demand and can precipitate chest pain. An individual activity prescription is determined for each patient to maintain cardiovascular stability and prevent fatigue.

4. Fear and anxiety increase sympathetic nervous system responses, thus increasing myocardial oxygen demand. Relaxation increases the patient's ability to cooperate and to participate in therapeutic activities.

5. Rationale: _____
_____
_____

Outcome criteria

Within 24 hours of admission, the patient will:
• rest comfortably
• tolerate bed rest without chest pain.

Within 72 hours of admission, the patient will:
• ambulate to the bathroom and chair without chest pain
• have normal bowel elimination without straining.

Nursing diagnosis: *Altered health maintenance related to presence of cardiovascular risk factors*

NURSING PRIORITY: Minimize the development of complications from modifiable risk factors.

Interventions

1. *Teach the patient about factors that may precipitate anginal attacks after discharge*—such as strenuous exercise, changes in sexual habits or partners, exposure to extreme cold, strong emotions, stress, or smoking. Teach ways to decrease the possibility of chest pain—such as using sublingual nitroglycerin prophylactically; monitoring pulse rate before and after activity; and stopping activity if chest pain, dyspnea, or palpitations ensue. Use the patient's own experience as a basis for teaching. Document the patient's response to teaching.

Rationales

1. Teaching the patient ways to avoid precipitating anginal attacks will decrease anxiety and may increase participation in self-care. Controlling risk factors may minimize the disease's progress and lessen its impact on the patient's life-style. Relating teaching to the patient's own experience capitalizes on the teaching principle that adults learn better when material is relevant to their needs and integrated with prior experience.

(continued)

Interventions *continued*

2. Instruct the patient on nutritional modifications to maintain a diet low in saturated fat and cholesterol and to achieve ideal body weight. Document current height and weight.

3. Provide six light meals per day rather than three heavy ones.

4. Encourage elimination from the diet of foods and beverages high in caffeine.

5. Discourage cigarette smoking.

6. Instruct the patient in stress-reduction techniques.

7. Start the patient on a cardiovascular fitness regimen when approved by the doctor.

8. Additional individualized interventions: _____
_____
_____

Rationales *continued*

2. Exacerbation of coronary artery disease may be related to increased dietary intake of cholesterol, which contributes to increased plaque formation and narrowing of coronary arteries. Obesity elevates blood pressure and places a greater workload on the heart.

3. Although subject to debate, large meals are believed by some to require an increased blood supply to the GI tract for digestion, thereby increasing myocardial work. An anginal attack may be precipitated by a large, heavy meal. Small meals are also more comfortable for the patient.

4. Coffee, tea, chocolate, and colas contain varying amounts of caffeine, which is a myocardial stimulant that increases myocardial oxygen consumption.

5. Nicotine causes vasoconstriction, is a cardiac stimulant, and reduces oxygen availability.

6. Unresolved anxiety and a stressful life-style increase myocardial oxygen demands, so they are risk factors in the development and exacerbation of cardiovascular disease. Decreasing stress levels may decrease circulating catecholamine levels, thus decreasing blood pressure and overall myocardial oxygen consumption.

7. Supervised exercise rehabilitation enhances cardiovascular fitness while minimizing the chance of another cardiac event.

8. Rationale: _____
_____
_____

Outcome criteria
Within 3 days of admission, the patient will:
• verbalize knowledge of diet, life-style, and health habit modifications

• indicate specific plans made for appropriate life-style modifications
• eliminate smoking.

Discharge planning
NURSING DISCHARGE CRITERIA
Upon discharge, documentation shows evidence of:
• absence of chest pain, or angina controlled by oral or sublingual medications
• stable vital signs for at least 48 hours before discharge
• absence of fever and pulmonary or cardiovascular complications
• ability to perform activities of daily living and ambulate without chest pain

• blood chemistry studies within expected parameters
• normal sinus rhythm or pharmacologically controlled dysrhythmias
• ability to tolerate activity at prescribed levels
• ability to tolerate diet and dietary restrictions
• normal voiding and bowel movements
• ability to verbalize activities that may precipitate angina
• referral to outpatient cardiac programs (if applicable).

PATIENT/FAMILY DISCHARGE TEACHING CHECKLIST

Document evidence that patient and family demonstrate understanding of:
___ the clinical condition's pathophysiology and implications
___ recommended modifications of risk factors: smoking, stress, obesity, lack of exercise, diet high in fat and cholesterol
___ prescribed dietary modifications
___ resumption of daily activities
___ all discharge medications' purpose, dose, administration schedule, side effects, toxic effects (usual discharge medications include nitrates, beta blockers, calcium channel blockers, or antilipid drugs)
___ common emotional adjustments
___ community resources for life-style and risk factor modification, such as stress- and weight-reduction groups, cardiac exercise programs, and smoking cessation programs
___ signs and symptoms indicating need for medical attention, such as chest pain unrelieved by three nitroglycerin tablets within 20 minutes, onset of new pattern of anginal attacks, palpitations or skipped beats, syncope, dyspnea, or diaphoresis
___ date, time, and location of follow-up appointments
___ how to contact doctor.

DOCUMENTATION CHECKLIST

Using outcome criteria as a guide, document:
___ clinical status on admission
___ significant changes in status
___ chest pain episodes—precipitating, aggravating, and alleviating factors
___ pertinent laboratory and diagnostic test results
___ pain-relief measures
___ oxygen therapy
___ I.V. therapy
___ use of protocols
___ nutritional intake
___ response to medications
___ emotional response to illness; coping skills
___ activity tolerance
___ patient and family teaching
___ discharge planning.

ASSOCIATED CARE PLANS

Acute Myocardial Infarction
Ineffective Individual Coping
Knowledge Deficit
Pain

REFERENCES

Cardiac Problems. Nurse Review Series. Springhouse, Pa.: Springhouse Corp., 1986.
Cardiovascular Care Handbook. Springhouse, Pa.: Springhouse Corp., 1986.
Carpenito, L. *Handbook of Nursing Diagnosis.* Philadelphia: J.B. Lippincott Co., 1985.
Gordon, M. *Manual of Nursing Diagnosis 1984-1985.* New York: McGraw-Hill Book Co., 1985.
Huang, S.L., et al. *Coronary Care Nursing.* Philadelphia: W.B. Saunders Co., 1983.
Mahoney, E., and Flynn, J. *Handbook of Medical-Surgical Nursing.* New York: John Wiley & Sons, 1983.
Raffensperger, E., et al. *Quick Reference to Medical-Surgical Nursing.* Philadelphia: J.B. Lippincott Co., 1983.
Sadler, D. *Nursing for Cardiovascular Health.* East Norwalk, Conn.: Appleton-Century-Crofts, 1984.
Ulrich, S., et al. *Nursing Care Planning Guides: A Nursing Diagnosis Approach.* Philadelphia: W.B. Saunders Co., 1986.
Underhill, S., et al. *Cardiac Nursing.* Philadelphia: J.B. Lippincott Co, 1982.

Congestive Heart Failure

DRG information

DRG 127 [Medical DRG] Heart Failure and Shock.
　　　Mean LOS = 6.2 days

Additional DRG information: DRG 127 is the most prevalent DRG across the United States: 4.9% of all PPS discharges fall into this category; however, it is important to note that heart failure is a diagnosis that commonly accompanies other diagnoses, especially other cardiac diagnoses. In these cases, DRG 127 would most likely not be the principal DRG.

Introduction

DEFINITION AND TIME FOCUS

Heart failure is the inability of the heart to provide cardiac output sufficient to meet metabolic demands of the body. Congestive heart failure (CHF) is circulatory congestion from heart failure. This clinical plan focuses on the care of the patient admitted to a medical-surgical unit for:
• treatment of an episode of CHF from an exacerbation of a chronic condition
• postcoronary care unit care for CHF resulting from an acute event (such as acute myocardial infarction [AMI]).

ETIOLOGY/PRECIPITATING FACTORS

• conditions that alter effective contraction of the heart muscle, such as cardiomyopathies, ischemic cardiac disease, ventricular aneurysms, or constrictive pericarditis
• conditions that increase fluid volume and lead to circulatory overload (increased preload), such as too-rapid infusion of I.V. fluids, increased sodium intake, or inadequate diuretic therapy
• conditions that alter cardiac rhythm, such as severe bradycardia in the presence of decreased contractility, or tachycardia severe enough to decrease cardiac filling time and diminish cardiac output
• conditions that increase resistance to movement of blood from the heart (increased afterload), such as arteriosclerotic heart disease, hypertensive heart disease, or pulmonary hypertension
• conditions that interfere with orderly movement of blood through the heart, such as valvular diseases causing insufficiency or stenosis
• conditions that increase tissue demands for oxygen beyond the heart's capabilities, such as hyperthyroidism, fever, pregnancy, or anemia

Focused assessment guidelines

NURSING HISTORY (Functional health pattern findings)

Health perception–health management pattern

• occasionally, episode may have occurred in response to an acute event such as an AMI, and patient may have no experience with signs and symptoms
• more commonly, may be under long-standing treatment for heart failure or an underlying precipitating disease such as hypertensive heart disease
• occasionally, may give indications of noncompliance with dietary restrictions, medications, or activity restrictions
• commonly complains of *peripheral edema*

Nutritional-metabolic pattern

• *anorexia* common; occasionally, reports nausea or vomiting from congestion of peripheral circulation or from medication side effects
• occasionally, weight loss and cachexia may be present from decreased caloric intake and poor nutrient absorption

Elimination pattern

• may report *altered urinary patterns* (from diuretic treatment or decreased blood flow to kidneys)
• occasionally, may report constipation (from edema of the GI tract)

Activity-exercise pattern

• commonly reports *inability to participate in active exercise or leisure activities*
• occasionally reports difficulty participating in everyday activities from fatigue or shortness of breath

Sleep-rest pattern

• commonly reports *disturbed sleep patterns* from dyspnea and nocturia
• commonly reports sleeping on 2 or 3 pillows (from *orthopnea*)
• occasionally reports *paroxysmal nocturnal dyspnea*

Cognitive-perceptual pattern

• occasionally demonstrates lack of understanding of problem and treatment protocols (if heart failure is caused by an acute event)
• occasionally reports headaches, confusion, or memory impairment

Self-perception–self-concept pattern

• occasionally describes disturbances in body image related to edema and decreased activity level

Role-relationship pattern

• commonly describes *difficulty fulfilling role responsibilities* because of fatigue, weakness, or decreased activity tolerance

Sexuality-reproductive pattern

• may report decreased libido and impotence or orgasmic dysfunction related to fatigue or medications

Coping–stress tolerance pattern
• may report anxiety related to shortness of breath
• occasionally complains of anxiety related to chronic illness
• occasionally grieves for loss of former level of health and loss of former roles and function
• occasionally anticipates premature death

PHYSICAL FINDINGS
Cardiovascular
• *tachycardia*
• *S$_3$ heart sound*
• *S$_4$ heart sound with summation gallop* (with tachycardia)
• atrial and ventricular dysrhythmias
• *jugular vein distention*
• systolic murmur (in advanced CHF)
• decreased peripheral pulses

Pulmonary
• *dyspnea*
• *crackles*
• nonproductive cough
• progressive bilateral diminishing of breath sounds, beginning at bases

Neurologic
• increased irritability
• impaired memory
• confusion (rare)

Gastrointestinal
• *abdominal distention*
• vomiting
• tenderness over liver

Renal
• *decreased urine output*

Integumentary
• *edema* in dependent areas, such as feet and sacrum
• cyanosis
• clubbing of fingers (in long-standing chronic failure)

Musculoskeletal
• *weakness and easy fatiguability*
• muscle wasting (rare)

DIAGNOSTIC STUDIES
• *serum electrolyte levels—electrolyte imbalances may occur* from fluid shifts, diuretic therapy, or response of organ systems to decreased oxygen supply and increased congestion
  □ hyponatremia: volume overload in CHF causes dilutional hyponatremia; sodium restriction and diuretics may also lead to low serum sodium as well
  □ hypokalemia: most of the common diuretics cause potassium loss
  □ hyperkalemia: can occur with oliguria or anuria
• *arterial blood gas (ABG) measurements*
  □ *lowered* PO$_2$ related to pulmonary congestion
  □ *elevated* PCO$_2$ (respiratory acidosis) may be from pulmonary edema or hypoventilation
• prothrombin time (PT), partial thromboplastin time (PTT)—obtained for baseline before beginning anticoagulant therapy or to evaluate clotting status if patient already on anticoagulants
• *blood urea nitrogen (BUN) and creatinine levels—*elevated from decreased renal function
• *bilirubin, aspartate aminotransferase (AST, formerly serum glutamic-oxaloacetic acid or SGOT), lactic dehydrogenase (LDH) levels—elevated from decreased liver function*
• urinalysis—reveals proteinuria and elevated specific gravity
• *chest X-ray—cardiac silhouette commonly enlarged in CHF;* can demonstrate redistribution of pulmonary blood flow by revealing distention of the pulmonary veins; commonly shows interstitial and alveolar edema
• electrocardiogram (EKG)—nonspecific diagnostically, but useful in identifying rhythm disturbances, conduction defects, axis deviations, and hypertrophy
• echocardiography—can identify valvular abnormalities, chamber enlargement, abnormal wall motion, hypertrophy, pericardial effusions, and mural thrombi

POTENTIAL COMPLICATIONS
• cardiogenic shock
• pulmonary edema
• myocardial infarction
• dysrhythmias
• thrombolytic complications
• renal failure
• liver failure

Collaborative problem: *Decreased cardiac output related to decreased contractility, altered heart rhythm, fluid volume overload, or increased afterload*

NURSING PRIORITY: Maintain optimum cardiac output.

Interventions

1. *Monitor and document heart rate and rhythm, heart sounds, blood pressure, pulse pressure, and the presence or absence of peripheral pulses.* Compare to the baseline assessment. Report abnormalities to the doctor, particularly tachycardia, a new S$_3$ heart sound or systolic

Rationales

1. One of the earliest signs of worsening failure is increased heart rate. The presence of a new S$_3$ heart sound or a systolic murmur may reflect increased fluid volume, leading to increased cardiac congestion and failure. Decreased blood pressure can reflect decreased

(continued)

Interventions *continued*

murmur, hypotension, decreased pulse pressure or pulse loss, or increased irregularity of cardiac rhythm.

2. *Administer cardiac medications,* as ordered, and document the patient's response. Observe for therapeutic and side effects:

• inotropic agents (digitalis derivatives)—monitor for anorexia, pulse rate below 60 beats/minute or above 100 beats/minute, irregular heart rate, nausea, vomiting, and visual disturbances. Withhold the dose and contact the doctor if any of these signs occur.

• diuretics such as hydrochlorothiazide (Diuril) and furosemide (Lasix)—monitor for hypovolemia and hypokalemia. (See the "Fluid and Electrolyte Imbalances" care plan, page 21, for details.)

• nitrates such as isosorbide dinitrate (Isordil)—monitor for signs of hypovolemia.

• afterload reducers (vasodilators) such as hydralazine (Apresoline)—monitor for hypotension.

3. *Observe for signs and symptoms of hypoxemia,* such as confusion, restlessness, dyspnea, dysrhythmias, tachycardia, and cyanosis. *Ensure adequate oxygenation* with proper positioning and administration of supplemental oxygen, as ordered.

4. *Ensure adequate rest* by monitoring the noise level, limiting visitors, coordinating diagnostic tests (such as by ordering multiple blood tests on one blood sample rather than by obtaining separate samples, when possible), and spacing therapeutic interventions.

5. *Monitor fluid status:*

Rationales *continued*

cardiac output due to decreased myocardial contractility or overdiuresis. Diminished pulse pressure or peripheral pulse loss can indicate a decrease in cardiac output. Increased irregularity of heart rhythm can reflect an increased number of premature atrial or ventricular contractions—signs of increasing failure or medication toxicity.

2. Pharmacotherapeutic agents may relieve CHF by altering preload, contractility, or afterload—major determinants of cardiac output. However, many of these agents have narrow therapeutic ranges or side effects that can worsen the underlying disease process.

• Inotropic agents increase contractility but also can increase myocardial oxygen consumption and cardiac work, thereby contributing to increasing CHF. Digitalis, one of the most common medications used, has a narrow therapeutic range. Early toxic side effects include anorexia; later, severe bradydysrhythmias, tachydysrhythmias, and irregular cardiac rhythms can compromise cardiac output. These and the noncardiac signs of digitalis toxicity are more common in patients with decreased renal function.

• Diuretics decrease preload but can cause true hypovolemia, from excessive fluid loss, or hypokalemia, from potassium loss.

• Nitrates cause venodilation, reducing preload but also placing the patient at risk for relative hypovolemia from redistribution of blood volume to the periphery.

• Afterload reducers lower resistance to ventricular ejection but may lower blood pressure to such an extent that organ perfusion suffers.

3. The semi-Fowler's position prevents abdominal organs from pressing on the diaphragm and permits more complete movement. In a severely dyspneic patient, an upright position permits use of accessory muscles for breathing. An upright position also causes redistribution of blood flow to dependent areas, decreasing the amount of blood returning to the heart and reducing preload in a patient with volume overload. A patient who has difficulty maintaining an arterial oxygen level (PaO$_2$) above 60 mm Hg may benefit from supplemental oxygen.

4. Rest reduces myocardial oxygen consumption.

5. Fluid volume may be increased due to inability of the heart to maintain adequate flow and pressure through the kidneys. Increasing lung and peripheral congestion is a sign of increasing failure.

Interventions *continued*

• Obtain accurate daily weights.

• Maintain an accurate intake and output record.

• Assess the lung sounds for crackles, decreased sounds, and a change from vesicular to bronchial breath sounds.

• Assess dependent areas for edema. Assess for increasing dyspnea.

• Assess for signs of dehydration.

6. Assess the patient's mental status for increasing confusion.

7. Decrease fear and anxiety by providing information and by eliciting the patient's concerns and responding to them. See the "Ineffective Individual Coping" care plan, page 51, for details.

8. Additional individualized interventions: _____

_____

Rationales *continued*

• A rapid gain of 1 to 2 lb/day indicates fluid retention and the need for increased diuretics.

• Accurate intake and output records can alert care providers to early fluid excess.

• Crackles, decreased sounds, and bronchial breath sounds indicate fluid in the lungs and signal increasing left-sided failure.

• Dependent edema and dyspnea are signs of increasing right-sided failure.

• Fluid volume may be decreased due to overdiuresis.

6. When cardiac output is decreased, cerebral perfusion suffers, producing confusion.

7. Fear and anxiety activate the sympathetic nervous system and increase heart rate, myocardial contractility, and vasoconstriction. All these factors increase myocardial oxygen consumption. The "Ineffective Individual Coping" care plan contains general interventions to reduce anxiety.

8. Rationale: _____

_____

Outcome criteria

By the time of discharge, the patient will:
• exhibit heart rate under 100 beats/minute
• have warm, dry skin
• exhibit optimal systolic blood pressure, as manifested by capillary refill time of less than 3 seconds, and minimal or absent peripheral edema
• have no S₃ heart sound

• have stable cardiac rhythm with any life-threatening dysrhythmias under control
• have lungs clear to auscultation
• perform activities of daily living (ADLs) without incapacitating dyspnea
• have mental status within normal limits for this patient.

Nursing diagnosis: *Fluid and electrolyte imbalance* related to CHF, decreased renal perfusion, and diuretic therapy*

NURSING PRIORITY: Optimize and monitor volume status and electrolyte balance.

Interventions

1. See the "Fluid and Electrolyte Imbalances" care plan, page 21.

2. *Monitor creatinine and BUN levels* and report increasing values.

3. *Monitor sodium and potassium levels.* Report abnormal values and signs of imbalances.

Rationales

1. The "Fluid and Electrolyte Imbalances" care plan contains generalized interventions for these disorders.

2. Decreased renal perfusion from worsening failure is reflected in creatinine and BUN levels. The BUN level rises disproportionately, and the BUN:creatinine level ratio can change from the norm of 10:1 to as high as 40:1.

3. Hyponatremia can cause decreased blood pressure, confusion, headache, and convulsions. Hypokalemia can lead to weakness, fatigue, ileus, and ventricular fibrillation. Hyperkalemia can lead to bradycardia and ventricular asystole.

(continued)

*Non-NANDA diagnosis

Interventions *continued*

4. Additional individualized interventions: _____

_____

_____

Rationales *continued*

4. Rationale: _____

_____

_____

Outcome criterion

By the time of discharge, the patient will:
• exhibit sodium, potassium, creatinine, and BUN levels within expected parameters.

Nursing diagnosis: *Activity intolerance related to bed rest and decreased cardiac output*

NURSING PRIORITIES: (a) Prevent complications of bed rest, and (b) increase activity level without detrimentally increasing cardiac workload.

Interventions

1. *Determine cardiac stability* by evaluating blood pressure, heart rhythm and rate, and indicators of oxygenation such as level of consciousness and skin color.

2. *When the patient is stable, institute a graduated activity program* according to unit protocol. Begin with regular position changes and range-of-motion (ROM) exercises during bed rest. Then, as tolerated, progress to active ROM exercises and out-of-bed activities such as chair sitting and ambulating.

3. *Evaluate patient tolerance as new activities are introduced.* Monitor blood pressure and pulse; respiratory rate, pattern, and depth; level of consciousness and coordination; and verbalizations about energy and strength.
    Discontinue any activity, and resume it later at a slower pace if any of the following signs occur:
• pulse rate >30 beats/minute above resting level (or >15 beats/minute if on beta blockers)
• systolic blood pressure 15 mm Hg or more below resting level
• diastolic blood pressure 10 mm Hg or more above resting level
• new or increased pulse irregularity
• dyspnea, slowed respiratory rate, or shallow respirations
• decreased level of consciousness, or loss of coordination
• chest or leg pain
• fatigue disproportionate to the activity
• profound weakness.

Rationales

1. Activity causes increased myocardial contractility, heart rate, blood pressure, and myocardial oxygen consumption. If activity is begun with a condition that compromises cardiac output (for example, tachycardia or severe dysrhythmias), cardiac output will be reduced further.

2. Bed rest has many detrimental effects, including cardiac deconditioning, increased risk of atelectasis and pneumonia, and skin breakdown. It also promotes venous stasis, which increases the risk of thromboembolism already faced by CHF patients due to depressed myocardial contractility and atrial fibrillation—a dysrhythmia common in CHF due to atrial distention. Position changes and exercises that involve muscle contraction and change in muscle length (such as active or passive limb flexion) improve peripheral circulation and lessen the risk of thromboembolism and other adverse effects from immobility.

3. A too-rapid rate of activity progression can exacerbate failure, myocardial ischemia, or peripheral vascular insufficiency. It also may cause hypotension, syncope, cardiovascular collapse, or other catastrophies. At the very least, a too-rapid progression may cause a psychological setback if the patient feels expected to meet unrealistic standards.

Interventions *continued*

4. Alternate activity with rest periods.

5. *Administer anticoagulants,* as ordered. Monitor appropriate coagulation studies and report results that exceed set limits.

6. *Avoid conditions associated with Valsalva's maneuver* (forced expiration against a closed glottis), including:
• moving in bed while breath-holding—teach the patient to exhale when changing position
• straining at stool—increase dietary fiber, provide prune juice, and administer a stool softener if necessary and as ordered.

7. Additional individualized interventions: _____

_____

_____

Rationales *continued*

4. Bed rest and inactivity cause cardiac and muscle deconditioning. Initially, even short periods of activity can induce symptoms of cardiac compromise.

5. Heparin inactivates thrombin, preventing formation of fibrin clots. The therapeutic PTT should be 2 to 2½ times normal. Warfarin sodium (Coumadin) interferes with vitamin K production, decreasing synthesis of several clotting factors. The therapeutic PT should be 1½ to 2½ times the normal value.

6. Valsalva's maneuver increases intrathoracic pressure and decreases blood return to the heart. When the breath is released, there is a reflex increase in venous return. Valsalva's maneuver has been associated with syncope and premature ventricular contractions.

7. Rationale: _____

_____

_____

Outcome criteria

By the time of discharge, the patient will:
• exhibit no evidence of thrombophlebitis or pulmonary embolism
• maintain a normal bowel pattern
• perform self-care activities—feeding, bathing, and

dressing independently—with no significant change in heart rate or blood pressure
• walk in hall with no significant change in heart rate and blood pressure and no complaints such as chest pain or profound fatigue.

Nursing diagnosis: *Nutritional deficit related to decreased appetite and possible dislike of a low-sodium diet*

NURSING PRIORITY: Ensure appropriate intake of nutrients for healing and for increasing activity.

Interventions

1. *Keep a daily record of caloric intake* to ensure an adequate amount of calories. Consult with the dietitian to identify caloric needs.

2. *Assess the patient's dietary preferences,* and plan meals to meet treatment requirements and patient needs.

3. Additional individualized interventions: _____

_____

_____

Rationales

1. Caloric needs vary with each patient's stage of illness, activity level, and weight in relation to ideal body weight.

2. A low-sodium diet reduces cardiac preload by lessening water retention. Unfortunately, low-sodium diets are often unpalatable to patients accustomed to seasoned foods. A patient may be more willing to comply with changes if dietary preferences are considered whenever possible.

3. Rationale: _____

_____

_____

Outcome criterion

By the time of discharge, the patient will:
• meet daily caloric intake requirements as determined

by actual caloric intake compared with recommended caloric intake.

Nursing diagnosis: *Knowledge deficit related to complex disease process and treatment*

NURSING PRIORITY: Prepare patient to implement necessary life-style modifications.

Interventions

1. *Once the patient is stable, institute a structured teaching plan.* See the "Knowledge Deficit" care plan, page 56, for details of the teaching process.

2. *Briefly explain the pathophysiology of heart failure.* Relate the explanation to the patient's signs and symptoms.

3. *Explain the rationale for dietary restrictions* such as a low-sodium diet, avoidance of salty foods, and not adding salt to foods. Provide a list of high-sodium foods to avoid and suggest alternative seasonings, such as lemon juice and herbs. Recommend low-sodium cookbooks. Engage the patient's spouse or partner in the teaching plan. Capitalize on the dietitian's expertise in teaching dietary adjustments.

4. *Explain the rationale for activity restrictions.* Provide specific information about recommended activities. Teach the patient to monitor his or her own activity tolerance, such as pulse taking before and after activity, and self-monitoring for signs and symptoms. (See the "Activity intolerance" nursing diagnosis in this care plan for details.)

5. *Teach about medications* to be taken after discharge— typically inotropes, diuretics, vasodilators, or anticoagulants. Provide information sheets, and review the medications' purpose, dosage, schedule, side effects, and toxic effects. Stress the importance of taking doses on time. Suggest a pillbox labeled with days and times for doses.

6. *Emphasize the importance of self-monitoring* for signs and symptoms of increasing failure, such as ankle or leg swelling, breathlessness, tachycardia, and new or increased pulse irregularity.

7. *Discuss with the patient and family an emergency care plan,* if needed, including:
• a Medic Alert bracelet
• circumstances under which to call the Emergency Medical System (EMS), such as severe chest pain, marked difficulty breathing, and cessation of breathing
• EMS access
• cardiopulmonary resuscitation (CPR) classes for the family.

Rationales

1. Teaching is more efficient and effective when planned than when haphazard. The "Knowledge Deficit" care plan contains specifics on assessing readiness to learn and on teaching methodologies.

2. An adult learns best when the value of the information is explicitly identified in relation to his or her own situation. Relevant information is helpful, but excessive detail can overwhelm and confuse the person.

3. Successful management of CHF is multifaceted and requires lifelong life-style modifications; one of the most difficult is making dietary adjustments. Understanding the rationale behind dietary restrictions may help establish and maintain the motivation necessary for persevering in life-style adjustments.

4. Vague admonitions to "take it easy" leave the patient confused and uncertain about safe activities and may impair adjustment to an altered life-style, thus creating a "cardiac cripple." Providing specific information (which varies with patient condition and unit protocol) lessens uncertainty and facilitates adjustment to recommended activity levels.

5. Successful CHF management often requires multiple medications. Understanding their purpose may increase the patient's motivation to take them, and comprehending dosage may increase dosage accuracy. A pillbox decreases likelihood of confusion or forgotten doses.

6. Early detection of increasing failure is crucial to identify disease progression or the need to adjust the therapeutic regimen. The patient can best identify subtle physiologic changes.

7. The patient with heart failure is at increased risk for other cardiovascular complications such as myocardial infarction or cardiac arrest. Preplanning for a possible emergency situation increases the likelihood of prompt, appropriate action if one occurs.

Interventions *continued*

8. Review the plan for follow-up care—the doctor and clinic and the date, time, and location of the next appointment.

9. Additional individualized interventions: _____

_____

_____

Rationales *continued*

8. The ongoing disease process requires consistent follow-up care for optimal management.

9. Rationale: _____

_____

_____

Outcome criteria
By the time of discharge, the patient will:
• state intent to follow dietary recommendations
• correctly take own pulse
• list five signs or symptoms of activity intolerance

• correctly identify details of discharge medications
• verbalize understanding of when to access EMS
• have a record of the details about follow-up appointments.

Nursing diagnosis: *Potential noncompliance related to complicated treatment regimen, possible health beliefs, or possible negative relationship with caregivers**

NURSING PRIORITY: Maximize compliance.

Interventions

1. *Observe for possible indicators of noncompliance,* such as exacerbation of signs and symptoms, development of complications, failure to keep health appointments, reports of behavior contrary to health recommendations, failure to seek health care attention when indicated, despairing remarks about health status, or belligerent exchanges with caregivers.

2. *Evaluate the extent and result of noncompliance.*

3. *Differentiate true noncompliance from nonadherence to the therapeutic regimen from other causes* such as knowledge deficit, unsupportive family, memory deficits, medication or treatment side effects unacceptable to the patient, transportation difficulties, denial, poor self-esteem, or self-destructive behavior.
   Consult the "Ineffective Individual Coping" care plan, page 51; the "Knowledge Deficit"care plan, page 56; and the "Potential ineffective coping" nursing diagnosis, page 194, for further suggestions. Take appropriate steps (such as teaching or referring for social services) as indicated.

Rationales

1. Noncompliance can have serious health repercussions. Early identification of a possible problem increases the likelihood of a successful resolution.

2. If noncompliance is limited to areas of minor consequence in the overall care plan, no further action may be necessary.

3. Numerous problems may masquerade as noncompliance. Accurate differentiation of problems increases the likelihood of appropriate interventions and resolution. The care plans listed provide additional details.

(continued)

*Note: Noncompliance currently is defined by NANDA as the informed decision not to follow a prescribed treatment regimen. As such, it is more limited than just deviation from therapeutic recommendations. The diagnosis is controversial; many nurses believe it is value-laden and thus inappropriate. Our intent is not to label a patient negatively but instead to use the term in a neutral way to describe the situation in which a person makes an informed decision not to follow caregivers' recommendations. Because we respect the patient's right to self-determination, we recognize that patients have a right to refuse therapy. Our goal is to help the nurse identify and eliminate causative factors that may be confused with noncompliance so that the diagnosis is not applied prematurely, the patient's rights are protected, and the potential for future compliance remains a viable option.

Interventions *continued*

4. Initiate discussion of the situation with the patient, family, and other caregivers, involving a psychiatric clinician or other health care team members as needed.

5. *Explicitly express concern for the patient as a person.*

6. *Emphasize the seriousness of CHF and the importance of self-care.* Use the patient's own situation to explain how noncompliance affects health, and emphasize the positive effects of adherence.

7. Discuss the following with the patient:
• life priorities
• personal perception of prognosis
• feelings about the length of the illness
• the general complexity of treatment
• degree of confidence in caregivers
• health care beliefs.

8. Consider the patient's cultural and spiritual background.

9. Ask the patient about his or her level of satisfaction with caregivers. Also, examine caregivers' attitudes: if nontherapeutic, consider either helping caregivers to establish more positive attitudes or substituting other caregivers.

10. *Validate conclusions about reasons for behavior with the patient and significant others.*

11. Collaborate with other caregivers to reevaluate the goals and implementation methods of the care plan. Consider possible modifications or revisions.

12. Search for alternate solutions. Ask what the patient wants or is willing to do to bring about agreement to the plan.

13. Use creative negotiation strategies to set goals with the patient. Consider changing the scope of the agreement, shortening its length, or making trade-offs.

Rationales *continued*

4. All members of the care team may contribute insights and observations helpful in reevaluation of the care plan.

5. Expression of human caring and warmth may help break the cycle of negativity, if present, and free up emotional energy for improved self-care. Nurturing behavior also may help establish rapport and trust.

6. Disbelief in the seriousness of the illness has been linked with noncompliance. Examples that incorporate personal experiences are most relevant and effective in making points "come alive" in a meaningful way.

7. Apparent deliberate noncompliance may actually reflect preoccupation with more pressing needs, such as food and shelter. The patient's perception of expected outcomes may be incongruent with caregivers', reflecting an overly pessimistic view. Prolonged illness, complex treatment, lack of confidence in caregivers, and health care beliefs different from caregivers' beliefs increase the likelihood of noncompliance.

8. Recommending treatment that clashes with cultural or spiritual beliefs is usually unacceptable.

9. The patient's level of dissatisfaction with caregivers influences noncompliance. Caregivers' negative (such as cynical or punitive) attitudes resulting from frustration may be amenable to change through ventilation and peer support. Negative attitudes resulting from "burnout" or personality clashes, however, may not be immediately modifiable and may be best dealt with by removing the caregivers from the situation.

10. Labeling a patient noncompliant may stigmatize the patient and affect future caregivers' behavior. Obtaining feedback about the accuracy of identified reasons for behavior helps avoid erroneous assumptions and inappropriate interventions.

11. Insisting on a plan to which the patient objects may cause the situation to degenerate into a power struggle between patient and caregivers. Flexibility and adaptability are more likely to achieve the desired ends.

12. Focusing on what the patient wants or is willing to do interrupts negativism and recasts the situation in a positive light. Such refocusing may free up energy for creative problem solving and increase the patient's sense of control.

13. If full agreement is not possible, partial or temporary agreement may be. The patient may be willing to trade off compliance in one area (for example, medications) for greater freedom in another (for example, food intake).

Interventions *continued*

14. *If the patient makes an informed choice not to follow the recommendations, and if negotiation is not possible:*
• *Avoid punitive responses, and accept the decision.*

• Keep open the option for future treatment if the patient undergoes a change of mind.
• Respect the patient's readiness to die, if present.

15. Additional individualized interventions: _____
_____
_____

Rationales *continued*

14. Patients have the right of self-determination.

• Exhibiting rejecting or other punitive behavior when the patient exercises the right of self-determination shows disrespect for the patient and may provoke termination of any further contact with health care resources.
• As the patient's condition changes with time, resistance to recommendations may soften.
• Every human being deserves the right to die with dignity. The decision to refuse care may be a rational choice to live out the remaining period of life in a manner particularly meaningful to the patient.

15. Rationale: _____
_____
_____

Outcome criteria
Within 2 days of admission, the patient will:
• identify areas of potential noncompliance
• identify reasons for noncompliance

• verbalize willingness and ability to follow modified therapeutic plan, when possible.

Discharge planning
NURSING DISCHARGE CRITERIA
Upon discharge, documentation shows evidence of:
• stable vital signs
• absence of fever and pulmonary or cardiovascular complications
• ability to tolerate adequate nutritional intake
• stable cardiac rhythm with dysrhythmias controlled
• shortness of breath no worse than before exacerbation of CHF
• peripheral edema within acceptable limits or no worse than patient normally exhibits
• ABG measurements within acceptable parameters
• clear lung fields as shown by chest X-ray within 48 hours of discharge
• absence of supplemental oxygen for at least 48 hours before discharge
• absence of signs and symptoms indicating dehydration
• mental status within normal limits for patient
• laboratory values within expected parameters
• absence of urinary or bowel dysfunction
• ability to perform ADLs and ambulate same as before hospitalization
• adequate home support system, or referral to home care if indicated by inadequate home support system or patient's inability to perform ADLs
• referral to community support group for heart failure patients.

PATIENT/FAMILY DISCHARGE TEACHING CHECKLIST
Document evidence that patient and family demonstrate understanding of:
__ disease process and implications
__ signs and symptoms of increasing failure
__ all discharge medications' purpose, dosage, administration schedule, and side effects requiring medical attention (usual discharge medications include inotropes, diuretics, vasodilators, or anticoagulants)
__ dietary restrictions
__ activity restrictions
__ plan for follow-up care
__ plan for emergency care
__ how to contact doctor.

DOCUMENTATION CHECKLIST
Using outcome criteria as a guide, document:
__ clinical status on admission
__ significant changes in clinical status
__ pertinent laboratory and diagnostic findings
__ intake and output
__ nutritional intake
__ response to activity progression
__ response to illness and hospitalization
__ response of family to illness
__ patient and family teaching
__ discharge planning.

ASSOCIATED CARE PLANS
Acute Myocardial Infarction
Chronic Renal Failure
Death and Dying
Fluid and Electrolyte Imbalances
Grief/Grieving
Ineffective Individual Coping
Knowledge Deficit

REFERENCES
Guzzetta, C., and Dossey, B. *Cardiovascular Nursing: Bodymind Tapestry*. St. Louis: C.V. Mosby Co., 1984.
Holloway, N. *Nursing the Critically Ill Adult*. Menlo Park, Calif.: Addison-Wesley Publishing Co., 1979.
Kim, M.J., and Morita, D.A. *Classification of Nursing Diagnosis: Proceedings of the Third and Fourth National Conferences*. McGraw-Hill Book Co., 1982.
Lavin, M.A. "Bed Exercises for Acute Cardiac Patients," *American Journal of Nursing* 73(7):1226-27, July 1973.
Michaelson, C.R. *Congestive Heart Failure*. St. Louis: C.V. Mosby Co., 1983.
Sackett, D.L., and Haynes, R.B. *Compliance with Therapeutic Regimens*. Baltimore: Johns Hopkins University Press, 1976.
Whittaker, A.A. "Acute Renal Dysfunction: Assessment of Patients at Risk," *Focus on Critical Care* 12(3):12-17, June 1985.

Permanent Pacemaker Insertion

DRG information

DRG 115 [Surgical DRG] Permanent Cardiac Pacemaker Implant. With AMI, Heart Failure, or Shock.
Mean LOS = 12.8 days

DRG 116 [Surgical DRG] Permanent Cardiac Pacemaker Implant. Without AMI, Heart Failure, or Shock.
Mean LOS = 6.6 days

Introduction
DEFINITION AND TIME FOCUS
The insertion of a permanent pacemaker is a procedure that may be required when the patient is symptomatic from decreased cardiac output secondary to irreversible or uncontrolled dysrhythmias. Irreversible bradycardia results from atrioventricular (AV) heart block (typically Mobitz Type II second-degree or third-degree), sinus bradycardia, sinus arrest, or sinoatrial (SA) block. Tachydysrhythmias unresponsive to treatments also may benefit from a permanent pacemaker, as may sick sinus (tachycardia-bradycardia) syndrome.

This clinical plan focuses on managing the patient who has had a permanent pacemaker inserted by a transvenous approach. The lead is inserted through a vein—commonly the cephalic, jugular, or subclavian—and positioned with fluoroscopy in the right ventricle. Lead attachment to the endocardium is either passive, with fibrosis occurring at the contact point, or active, with the lead screwed into the muscle. A subcutaneous pocket is made in the upper chest or abdominal region, and the pulse generator box is placed into it. The distal end of the lead is connected under the skin to the generator box. The procedure is commonly done under local anesthesia.

ETIOLOGY/PRECIPITATING FACTORS
• idiopathic sclerotic degeneration of the SA node
• coronary artery disease, especially with significant disease or infarction involving the artery to the SA node (right coronary artery in 55% of the population, circumflex in 45%) or the AV node (right coronary artery in 90%, circumflex in 10%)
• rheumatic heart disease
• cardiomyopathy
• congenital heart disease—for example, ventricular septal defect or transposition of the great vessels
• cardiac surgical trauma or edema affecting the conduction system
• myocarditis

Focused assessment guidelines
NURSING HISTORY (Functional health pattern findings
Note: Findings vary, depending on the underlying pathophysiologic condition requiring insertion of an artificial pacemaker.

Health perception–health management pattern
• may report *syncope, dizziness, and light-headedness* (Adams-Stokes disease)
• may be under treatment for *dysrhythmias*
• may also be under treatment for angina, atherosclerosis, hypertension, or congestive heart failure
• may report a history of myocardial infarction (MI), congenital heart disease, or cardiac surgery
• typically an elderly male

Nutritional-metabolic pattern
• may report swelling of extremities and weight gain

Activity-exercise pattern
• may report shortness of breath, fatigue, and activity intolerance

Cognitive-perceptual pattern
• may report chest pain
• may report palpitations

Self-perception–self-concept pattern
• may express concern over anticipated changes in body image and functioning
• may express concern over follow-up care and restrictions

PHYSICAL FINDINGS
(before pacemaker insertion)

Cardiovascular
• *dysrhythmias*—bradycardia, irregular rhythms, or (uncommonly) tachycardia
• *hypotension*
• venous engorgement or jugular vein distention
• S_3 or S_4 heart sounds
• decreased peripheral pulses
• slow capillary refill

Pulmonary
• crackles
• shortness of breath
• paroxysmal nocturnal dyspnea

Neurologic
• *dizziness*
• *syncope*
• convulsions

Integumentary
• cool, clammy skin
• edema

Renal
• weight gain (from fluid retention)

Gastrointestinal
• liver enlargement
• positive hepatojugular reflux

DIAGNOSTIC STUDIES
• electrolyte panel—used to rule out disturbances affecting cardiac conduction and contractility (hypokalemia or hyperkalemia, and hypocalcemia or hypercalcemia)
• serum drug levels—may reveal subtherapeutic or toxic medication levels that may affect heart rate and rhythm (medications that may affect heart rate or rhythm include digoxin, quinidine, beta blockers, calcium channel blockers, narcotics, and some psychotropics and antihypertensives)
• blood urea nitrogen and creatinine levels—may reflect low renal perfusion from low cardiac output

• triiodothyronine (T_3) and thyroxine (T_4) levels—may be low, indicating that hypothyroidism may be depressing cardiac impulse formation or conduction
• 12-lead EKG—may reveal electrical activity not obvious in a single-lead rhythm strip and may help identify the dysrhythmia
• Holter monitor—may be used to confirm sick sinus syndrome or other transient dysrhythmias
• chest X-ray—may show cardiac enlargement
• electrophysiology studies—may allow induction and identification of symptom-causing dysrhythmias

POTENTIAL COMPLICATIONS
• dysrhythmias
• infection
• thrombosis or embolism
• tamponade or perforation of myocardium
• hematoma or hemorrhage
• lead fracture
• pneumothorax
• hiccups (diaphragmatic pacing)
• tricuspid insufficiency
• painful subcutaneous pocket or pocket erosion

Collaborative problem: *Potential dysrhythmias related to pacemaker malfunction or catheter displacement*

NURSING PRIORITY: Maintain optimal cardiac rhythm.

Interventions

1. *Initiate constant EKG monitoring* for 48 to 72 hours after pacemaker insertion or as ordered. Keep alarms on at all times. Set the low limit at 3 beats less per minute than the pacer setting. Set the high limit 10 beats/minute above the anticipated maximum cardiac rate. Place monitoring electrodes 2″ (5 cm) away from the generator box. Change the monitoring electrode sites if the pacer appears to be malfunctioning.

2. *Document in the care plan the type and rate of the pacer and the intrinsic rate and rhythm.*

3. *Record and document rhythm strips* every shift. Mount them in the chart. Analyze the strips: Appropriately paced beats will show a pacer spike artifact followed by a depolarization wave that differs from the intrinsic waveform. Notify the doctor promptly if problems occur with impulse initiation or conduction:

• failure to sense—pacer spikes occurring despite an intrinsic rate higher than the pacer setting

Rationales

1. Continuous monitoring facilitates early problem detection. If the pacemaker is functioning properly, the cardiac rate should not go below the pacer setting. The potential for tachydysrhythmias cannot be ignored. Monitoring electrodes placed near the generator box or in lead locations where the EKG amplitude is small may result in failure to record intrinsic beats.

2. This information is necessary for correct EKG interpretation.

3. Systematic documentation provides an objective, organized means of analyzing pacer activity. Waveforms of paced and intrinsic beats differ because of independent conduction paths.

• The sensitivity setting may be such that the pacemaker does not consistently detect intrinsic low-amplitude cardiac electrical activity. Failure to sense also may result from fibrosis at the lead tip, lead fracture, or a dislodged lead. Failure to sense may result in inappropriate, unnecessary pacing and may cause "R on T phenomenon," in which a QRS complex falls on the preceding T wave, triggering ventricular tachycardia or ventricular fibrillation.

Interventions continued

• failure to capture—pacing spikes not followed by cardiac depolarization

• failure to pace—absence of pacing spikes when the intrinsic rate is below the pacer setting.

4. *Obtain 12-lead simultaneous EKG recordings* daily for 3 days and as needed.

5. *Administer cardiac medications,* as ordered, and document their effectiveness and side effects.

6. *Monitor blood pressure, apical pulse, and respirations* every 4 hours or as ordered.

7. *Maintain and document I.V. line patency,* as ordered.

8. *Maintain bed rest with turning limitations and with the head of the bed elevated 30 to 45 degrees* for 48 to 72 hours or as ordered.

9. If restricted use of the affected arm is ordered, perform limited passive range-of-motion (ROM) exercises with the arm every hour during the first 24 hours postoperatively.

10. Assess daily chest X-ray for 3 days.

11. Additional individualized interventions: _____

_____

_____

Outcome criteria
Immediately postoperatively and throughout the period of hospitalization, the patient will:
• display a cardiac rate no less than pacemaker setting
• display EKG evidence of appropriate pacer sensing, firing, and capturing
• have stable vital signs that are within normal limits.

Rationales continued

• Failure to capture may result when the voltage of the pacemaker stimulus is insufficient to trigger depolarization. It may result from fibrosis at the lead-myocardial junction, the effect of cardiac drugs, electrolyte imbalance, or a dislodged or malpositioned lead.

• Failure to pace may result from a fractured lead wire, malfunction at the lead generator connection, power source depletion, or oversensing—the sensing of noncardiac electrical activity, such as muscle activity near the generator box, power lines, other sources of electrical noise, or cross talk in dual chamber pacemakers.

4. A 12-lead recording is more definitive in showing pacer function and cardiac electrical activity than a single-lead rhythm strip. Simultaneous tracings help to confirm pacing spikes and intrinsic beats that may vary in amplitude in different leads and therefore may not be obvious in one particular lead.

5. Cardiac medications may be indicated for treatment of underlying cardiac problems, such as coronary artery or valvular disease.

6. Deviation from baseline vital signs may indicate pacer failure or other complications.

7. The I.V. line may be needed to administer emergency medications.

8. With passive lead placement, activity and positioning limitations are needed temporarily to maintain lead placement until fibrosis develops around the electrode tip and anchors it in place. Limitation may be less restrictive if lead has been actively attached.

9. Movement restrictions may be ordered to reduce the chance of lead displacement. Passive ROM exercises may prevent frozen shoulder.

10. Chest X-rays may be used to confirm lead placement.

11. Rationale: _____

_____

_____

Within 3 days postoperatively, the patient will:
• have decreased or eliminated signs and symptoms of low cardiac output (if present preoperatively)
• visit the pacemaker clinic for a definitive check of pacemaker functioning.

Nursing diagnosis: *Potential for infection related to surgical disruption of skin barrier*

NURSING PRIORITIES: (a) Promote incisional healing by primary intention, and (b) prevent or promptly detect infection.

Interventions

1. *Check the primary dressing for drainage.* Circle any drainage, and write the date and time when first discovered.

2. *Reinforce the primary dressing* as needed for 24 hours. Do not change the primary dressing without an order from the doctor.

3. *Check the incision, after removing the primary dressing,* for excessive redness, swelling, warmth, and drainage.

4. *Perform wound care,* as ordered.

5. Administer antibiotics, as ordered.

6. *Monitor body temperature* every 4 hours. Notify the doctor if the oral temperature exceeds 100° F. (37.8° C.).

7. Monitor the white blood cell (WBC) count, as ordered.

8. Culture purulent drainage, if present, as ordered.

9. Additional individualized interventions: _____
_____
_____

Rationales

1. This is an objective method of monitoring for bleeding and incisional drainage.

2. Reinforcement protects the incision and aids hemostasis while providing a protective barrier against infection. Removal of the primary dressing increases the risk of accidentally disrupting the incisional line and hemostasis.

3. These signs may reflect infection.

4. The pacemaker pocket is the most common entry site of infectious organisms, which can migrate along the pacing wires to the heart. A clean, dry incision promotes healing.

5. Antibiotics may be prescribed prophylactically, because pacemaker insertion is an invasive procedure that involves implanting a foreign object into the heart. Also, the disruption of the skin barrier provides a potential portal of entry for infectious organisms into the heart.

6. Commonly, elevated temperature is a systemic response to infection.

7. The WBC count increases in response to infectious organisms.

8. WBCs and cellular debris accumulate locally in response to infectious organisms. Proper treatment requires identifying the causative agent and its medication sensitivity.

9. Rationale: _____
_____
_____

Outcome criteria

Within 1 day postoperatively and throughout the period of hospitalization, the patient will:
• have a dry and intact incision
• experience no fever.

By the time of discharge, the patient will:
• have a WBC count within normal limits
• show no signs of infection.

Nursing diagnosis: *Self-care deficit: partial bathing, feeding, and toileting related to bed rest and activity limitations*

NURSING PRIORITY: Provide assistance for bathing, feeding, and toileting while bed rest is required.

Interventions

1. *Assist with bathing and oral hygiene* daily, as needed.

2. *Assist the patient at mealtime.* Elevate the head of the bed, as ordered.

3. *Supply a bedpan and urinal,* as needed.

4. Administer stool softeners and laxatives judiciously, as ordered, and document. Encourage alternatives or supplements to stool softeners and laxatives, such as increased dietary fiber (if possible) and prune juice.

5. After arm use is no longer restricted, encourage the patient to move the arm and resume self-care.

6. Additional individualized interventions: _____

_____

_____

Rationales

1. Bed rest and arm movement limitations mean that the patient will be unable to set up and use bathing and oral hygiene supplies.

2. The patient may be unable to reach the meal tray or manipulate items while on bed rest. Raising the head of the bed facilitates swallowing and minimizes the risk of aspiration.

3. The patient will be unable to use the bathroom.

4. Straining to defecate requires considerable energy and may produce vagal-mediated dysrhythmias. Overdependence on laxatives diminishes the urge for normal defecation.

5. The patient may be hesitant to use the arm initially for fear of dislodging the electrode.

6. Rationale: _____

_____

_____

Outcome criteria

While on bed rest, the patient will:
• accept self-care assistance
• observe activity restrictions.

Within 3 days postoperatively, the patient will:
• resume normal self-care activities
• perform normal bowel elimination without straining.

Nursing diagnosis: *Knowledge deficit: self-care after discharge related to unfamiliar therapeutic intervention*

NURSING PRIORITY: Teach the information and skills necessary for optimal self-care.

Interventions

1. *Explain potential signs and symptoms of decreased cardiac output* that should be reported to the doctor, such as shortness of breath, low or erratic pulse, light-headedness, chest pains, decreased exercise tolerance, prolonged fatigue or weakness, or recurrence of preimplant symptoms.

2. *Discuss signs and symptoms of extraneous stimulation that should be reported,* such as muscle, arm, or skin twitching near the generator box or prolonged and rapid hiccups.

3. *Teach the patient to recognize and report signs and symptoms of pocket infection,* such as fever or chills and incisional drainage, redness, swelling, or pain.

Rationales

1. These signs and symptoms may indicate pacemaker malfunction.

2. These signs and symptoms may result from electrode or lead malposition and adacent tissue stimulation.

3. Infection may not be apparent until after discharge from the hospital.

(continued)

Interventions *continued*

4. *Teach the patient to check his or her radial pulse* at the same time daily after resting for 5 minutes; reinforce guidelines for reporting significant changes, particularly a decrease of 3 to 5 beats/minute below the pacer setting or an erratic, persistent high rate.

5. *Emphasize the importance of compliance with the follow-up pacemaker monitoring regimen* (by in-person appointments or a phone monitoring device).

6. *Emphasize the need to inform health care providers about the pacemaker.* The patient can wear a Medic Alert bracelet and carry a wallet identification card with pacemaker specifications.

7. *Discuss potential environmental hazards,* such as power plants and radar stations, electromagnetic power fields, radio and television transmitters, and leaning over a running car engine.

8. *As specified by the doctor, provide instructions about activities and limitations* such as travel, exercise, bathing and showering, and sexual activity.

9. *Teach the purpose, dose, administration schedule, and side effects of all medications.*

10. Provide written material covering Interventions 1 through 9 above.

11. Additional individualized interventions: _____
_____
_____

Rationales *continued*

4. Changes in pacemaker function may be detected by regular assessment.

5. Pacemaker functioning can be evaluated most accurately by an EKG. Periodic checks using a donut-shaped magnet help determine when a new battery is needed.

6. Certain procedures, such as electrocautery, physical therapy, and nuclear magnetic resonance imagery, may be contraindicated.

7. Exposure to electromagnetic power sources may alter pacemaker functioning. Most home electric appliances, including microwave ovens, are not a problem if in proper working order.

8. Gradual resumption of activities according to patient tolerance is generally encouraged. Activities involving abrupt, forceful arm movement (such as tennis and golf) that may cause lead fracture may be limited for several weeks. Contact sports typically are not allowed.

9. Knowledge may increase compliance.

10. Written material reinforces and serves as a reference for this detailed information.

11. Rationale: _____
_____
_____

Outcome criteria
By the time of discharge, the patient will:
• demonstrate accurate pulse rate measurement
• list significant, reportable signs and symptoms
• verbalize activity expectations and limitations and environmental hazards

• explain initial follow-up arrangements or appointments
• state the purpose, dose, administration schedule, and side effects of medications
• verbalize understanding of the need to inform health care providers about the pacemaker.

Nursing diagnosis: *Potential disturbed self-concept: body image related to dependence on prosthetic device*

NURSING PRIORITY: Promote positive incorporation of the pacemaker into the patient's body image.

Interventions

1. *Assess the patient's adaptation to change, including perceptions and meaning of limitations.*

Rationales

1. The changes involved in pacemaker implantation may vary in significance among patients. Dependence on a prosthetic device may alter self-concept: many patients

Interventions *continued*

2. Encourage the patient to ask questions and verbalize feelings.

3. Encourage the patient to look at the incision and the pacemaker site.

4. Assess for maladaptive coping behaviors, such as manipulating the generator box, verbalizing inability to make life-style or health-promoting changes, crying or a flat affect, lack of participation and interest in activities, or anxiety.

5. If indicated, consult the "Grief and Grieving" and the "Ineffective Individual Coping" care plans, pages 41 and 51.

6. Additional individualized interventions: _____
_____
_____

Rationales *continued*

welcome the increased activity tolerance and show signs of improved self-image. For others, however, loss of a body function may trigger the grieving process.

2. Verbalization enables the nurse to critically listen, assess, and validate, thus facilitating the patient's adjustment to change.

3. Willingness to view the incision and site may reflect beginning acceptance and adjustment.

4. These behaviors may indicate difficulty adjusting to the physical change and to the need for pacemaker dependence.

5. These care plans contain generalized interventions related to these problems.

6. Rationale: _____
_____
_____

Outcome criteria
By the time of discharge, the patient will:
• participate actively in self-care
• ask appropriate questions and show interest in learning
• show no evidence of maladaptive coping.

Discharge planning
NURSING DISCHARGE CRITERIA
Upon discharge, documentation shows evidence of:
• absence of a fever
• absence of angina and dysrhythmias
• EKG within expected parameters, indicating appropriate pacemaker settings, sensing, firing, and capturing
• vital signs within acceptable parameters
• absence of pulmonary and cardiovascular complications
• absence of redness, swelling, and drainage at incision site
• WBC count within normal parameters
• ability to transfer, ambulate, and perform activities of daily living (ADLs) same as before hospitalization
• adequate home support system or referral to home care if indicated by inadequate support system and the patient's inability to perform ADLs.

PATIENT/FAMILY DISCHARGE TEACHING CHECKLIST
Document evidence that patient/family demonstrates understanding of:
__ symptoms of pacemaker failure or complications
__ symptoms of infection
__ type of pacemaker, set rate, and operating method

__ need for daily pulse rate measurement
__ method for obtaining wallet identification card and Medic Alert bracelet
__ need to inform other doctors, dentist, and physical therapists about pacemaker
__ plan for resuming activities
__ limitations and precautions
__ all discharge medications' purpose, dose, administration schedule, and side effects requiring medical attention (usual discharge medications may include oral analgesics and other medications based on individual patient's needs and underlying disorder)
__ follow-up routine
__ how to contact doctor.

DOCUMENTATION CHECKLIST
Using outcome criteria as a guide, document
Preoperatively:
__ clinical status on admission
__ 12-lead EKG reading
__ chest X-ray and results
__ urinalysis results
__ SMA and complete blood counts
__ preoperative teaching

___ telemetry strip documentation
___ surgical skin preparation
___ I.V. line patency and site condition
Postoperatively:
___ clinical status on return from postanesthesia recovery unit
___ significant status changes
___ telemetry strip documentation
___ 12-lead EKG reading
___ incision status and care
___ I.V. line patency and site condition
___ chest X-ray and results
___ pacemaker clinic check for correct functioning before discharge
___ patient/family teaching
___ discharge planning.

ASSOCIATED CARE PLANS
Acute Myocardial Infarction
Angina Pectoris
Congestive Heart Failure
Geriatric Considerations
Grief/Grieving
Ineffective Individual Coping
Pain
Surgical Intervention
Thrombophlebitis

REFERENCES

Carpenito, L.J. *Nursing Diagnosis: Application to Clinical Practice.* Philadelphia: J.B. Lippincott Co., 1983.

Duffin, E.G., Jr., and Zipes, D.P. "Artificial Cardiac Pacemakers," in *Comprehensive Cardiac Care,* 3rd ed. Edited by Andreoli, V.K., et al. St. Louis: C.V. Mosby Co., 1983.

Hastings, S.M. "Surgical Implants," *AORN Journal* 37:1324-40, June 1983.

Murdock, D.K., et al. "Pacemaker Malfunction: Fact or Artifact," *Heart & Lung* 15:150-54, March 1986.

Phibbs, B., and Marriott, H.J.L. "Complications of Permanent Transvenous Pacing," *New England Journal of Medicine* 1428-31, May 1985.

Potter, P.A. and Perry, A.G. *Fundamentals of Nursing.* St. Louis: C.V. Mosby Co., 1985.

Purcell, J.A., and Burrows, S.G. "A Pacemaker Primer," *American Journal of Nursing* 85(5):553-61, May 1985.

Ulrich, S.P., et al. *Nursing Care Planning Guides.* Philadelphia: W.B. Saunders Co., 1986.

Thrombophlebitis

DRG information
DRG 128 [Medical DRG] Deep Vein Thrombophlebitis.
  Mean LOS = 8.0 days
DRG 130 [Medical DRG] Peripheral Vascular Disorders.
  With Complication or Comorbidity (CC).
  Mean LOS = 5.6 days
DRG 131 [Medical DRG] Peripheral Vascular Disorders.
  Without CC.
  Mean LOS = 4.0 days

Introduction
DEFINITION AND TIME FOCUS
Thrombophlebitis is the severe, acute inflammatory process of small- and medium-sized veins associated with secondary thrombus formation. It can occur in superficial or deep veins: The most common site of superficial thrombophlebitis is the saphenous vein, and the most common sites of deep-vein thrombosis are the iliofemoral vein, popliteal veins, and small calf veins. This clinical plan focuses on the patient admitted for diagnosis and management of acute lower-extremity thrombophlebitis.

ETIOLOGY/PRECIPITATING FACTORS
• venous stasis resulting from prolonged bed rest, sitting, or standing; varicose veins; low cardiac output; obesity; or limb paralysis
• hypercoagulability resulting from dehydration or oral contraceptives
• vessel wall trauma resulting from venipunctures, leg injury, venous disease, infection, or chemical irritants, such as I.V. antibiotics or potassium chloride
• vascular narrowing or degeneration resulting from hypertension, hypercholesterolemia, diabetes, kidney disease, stroke, or smoking

Focused assessment guidelines
NURSING HISTORY (Functional health pattern findings)

Health perception–health management pattern
• may report *acute onset of local pain* (relieved by elevation of extremity), *tenderness, edema, erythema, warmth, induration, febrile reaction*
• may present with known risk factors

• may have a history of recent vessel cannulation or vessel trauma

Activity-exercise pattern
• may report a *sedentary life-style or occupation requiring standing*
• may report *recent prolonged bed rest or immobility*

Role-relationship pattern
• may report a family history of cardiac risk factors

PHYSICAL FINDINGS
Cardiovascular
• *local edema*
• *engorged vessel*
• positive Homans' sign

Integumentary
• *local erythema*
• *warmth*
• *local induration*
• ulceration

DIAGNOSTIC STUDIES
• complete blood count—inflammatory response and systemic infection reflected in evaluation of white blood cells
• blood clotting studies—may indicate defects or hypercoagulable state
• cholesterol levels—may be elevated, suggesting increased risk for atherosclerosis
• serum glucose levels—elevated, reflecting stress response or diabetes
• triglyceride levels—may be elevated, indicating increased risk of atherosclerosis
• Doppler ultrasound blood flow detector test—determines venous return, may identify thrombolic occlusion
• plethysmography—may determine segmental occlusion
• venography—may indicate loss of significant venous return
• ^{125}I fibrinogen leg scanning—may reflect vascular insufficiency

POTENTIAL COMPLICATIONS
• venous ulcer
• pulmonary embolus
• phlegmasia cerulea dolens (sudden, marked leg swelling and cyanosis related to ileofemoral venous thrombosis)

Collaborative problem: *Venous insufficiency related to obstruction and stasis*

NURSING PRIORITY: Promote venous flow.

Interventions

1. *Assess calves and thighs daily for signs and symptoms of thrombophlebitis:*
• Early signs include swelling, erythema, edema, tenderness, venous patterning, or engorgement along the path of the vein.
• Later signs include pain, cording, and a positive Homans' sign (not always present). Avoid deep palpation. If swelling is suspected or present, measure and record leg circumference, placing a reference mark on the leg. Repeat the measurement daily, comparing the latest measurement with previous values.

2. *Notify the doctor immediately if new signs and symptoms develop or existing ones worsen.*

3. *Implement activity restrictions:*
• Maintain complete bed rest, usually for 3 to 7 days.
• Elevate the extremity at least 30 degrees continuously unless contraindicated by other medical problems.
• Avoid using the knee gatch, pillows under the knees, and, when the patient is allowed out of bed, knee-crossing and prolonged sitting.

4. *Encourage hourly performance of gentle foot and leg exercises.* Consult the doctor about appropriate exercises, which may include isometric exercises (quadriceps setting or plantar flexion against a footboard) or isotonic exercises (active or passive foot and leg flexion and extension and ankle rotation).

5. *Increase fluid intake to 2,000 ml/day,* unless contraindicated.

6. Consult the doctor about using antiembolic stockings.

7. Teach the patient stress-control measures, as needed—for example, progressive relaxation techniques, breathing exercises, and visualization. Encourage the patient to stop smoking, if indicated, and provide a referral to appropriate resources for help in smoking cessation.

Rationales

1. The early signs and symptoms listed result from vessel wall inflammation; the later ones, from thrombus formation. Homans' sign (pain in the calf on dorsiflexion of the foot), commonly believed to indicate deep-vein thrombosis, actually is a relatively unreliable indicator. Absent in many cases of deep-vein thrombosis, Homans' sign can be produced in any painful calf condition. Deep palpation should be avoided because it may dislodge a clot. Leg circumference monitoring provides an objective method of evaluating swelling; using a reference mark ensures consistency among measurers.

2. New or worsening signs of thrombophlebitis require prompt medical attention. Superficial thrombophlebitis, although not dangerous, is painful. Untreated deep-vein thrombophlebitis, however, can progress to a life-threatening situation should the thrombus embolize to the lungs.

3. Bed rest and extremity elevation mechanically improve venous flow by using gravity to reduce the pressure gradient between the extremity and the heart. Also, bed rest reduces oxygen requirements, limits the risk of dislodging the thrombus, and promotes fibrinolytic breakdown and clot absorption. The remaining measures avoid increased popliteal pressure, which compresses veins, thereby impeding venous return.

4. Venous return is facilitated by the pumping effect of muscle action. Gentle exercises help minimize further thrombus formation, but overly vigorous exercise may dislodge clots. Isometric exercises, generally recommended for surgical patients, increase venous flow but also may increase blood pressure markedly. Because this effect may be detrimental, particularly to patients with cardiovascular disease, some doctors prefer isotonic exercises, which cause a more desirable cardiovascular response.

5. Increased fluid intake increases vascular volume, improving the velocity and viscosity of blood.

6. Superficial veins are often dilated and tortuous, particularly in elderly patients. Antiembolic stockings may support venous return by compressing superficial veins and redirecting the flow to deeper veins.

7. Stress-related catecholamine release and smoking induce vasoconstriction.

Interventions *continued*

8. *Administer medications,* as ordered: anti-inflammatory agents, such as ibuprofen, and anticoagulants, such as heparin, warfarin sodium (Coumadin), or aspirin.

9. *Monitor clotting studies,* as ordered: partial thromboplastin time (PTT) if the patient is receiving heparin, prothrombin time (PT) if the patient is receiving warfarin sodium. Report values outside the desired range to the doctor before the next scheduled anticoagulant dose.

10. *Observe for signs of bleeding,* such as oozing at I.V. or I.M. sites, epistaxis, ecchymoses, hematuria, or melena.

11. Increase the patient's activity level, as ordered.

12. Observe for signs of chronic venous insufficiency: dependent ankle edema, induration, shiny skin, varicosities, and stasis ulcers. Consult the doctor if these signs are present.

13. Additional individualized interventions: _____
_____
_____

Rationales *continued*

8. Anti-inflammatory agents, such as ibuprofen, are the primary mode of treatment for superficial thrombophlebitis. Anticoagulants, although usually unnecessary in superficial thrombophlebitis, may be used if the thrombosis extends or is located near the groin's deep venous system.

   Anticoagulants are the mainstay of treatment for deep venous thrombophlebitis. Heparin interferes with platelet aggregation, conversion of prothrombin to thrombin, and conversion of fibrinogen to fibrin, thereby minimizing further clot formation. Warfarin sodium interferes with vitamin K activity necessary for clot formation. Aspirin interferes with platelet aggregation.

9. Dosages are adjusted to maintain PT and PTT within a therapeutic range. The typical ranges desired are two to two and one half times control values.

10. Excessive dosages of anticoagulants increase bleeding tendencies.

11. Ambulation causes muscular compression of vessels, thereby improving venous return.

12. Chronic venous insufficiency from venous valvular destruction may follow repeated episodes of deep-vein thrombosis.

13. Rationale: _____
_____
_____

Outcome criteria
Within 3 days of admission, the patient will:
• show improved color and temperature of affected area
• have decreased edema

• perform leg exercises as instructed
• maintain fluid intake within desired range
• show no evidence of bleeding.

Nursing diagnosis: *Pain related to vessel inflammation, edema, and obstruction to flow*

NURSING PRIORITY: Relieve pain.

Interventions

1. See the "Pain" care plan, page 64.

2. *Promote venous flow,* as described in the previous problem.

Rationales

1. The "Pain" care plan contains multiple interventions for patients in pain.

2. The most effective pain-relief measure is elimination of the cause of pain.

(continued)

Interventions continued

3. *Use a bed cradle. Handle the extremity gently.*

4. Apply warm, moist heat to the affected area, as ordered.

5. Administer analgesics, as ordered, observing for therapeutic and adverse effects. Question the use of indomethacin or aspirin if the patient is receiving an anticoagulant.

6. Additional individualized interventions: _____
_____
_____

Rationales continued

3. The thrombophlebitic extremity is extremely sensitive; even slight pressure or movement may be painful. A bed cradle keeps the weight of linens off the affected extremity.

4. Heat is soothing and causes vasodilatation, improving flow to affected areas.

5. The selection of appropriate types and amounts of analgesics depends on the degree of pain and the presence of anticoagulant therapy. Indomethacin and aspirin, which may be used to control pain, increase anticoagulant activity and may be inappropriate for the patient on heparin or warfarin.

6. Rationale: _____
_____
_____

Outcome criterion
Within 1 hour of pain complaint, the patient:
• verbalizes relief of pain.

Collaborative problem: *Potential thromboembolic phenomena related to dislodged thrombus*

NURSING PRIORITY: Prevent or promptly detect thromboembolic phenomena.

Interventions

1. *Monitor for signs and symptoms of either a massive pulmonary embolism* (profound shock, cyanosis, diaphoresis, and a sense of impending doom) *or a submassive pulmonary embolism* (tachypnea, dyspnea, pleuritic chest pain [sharp, stabbing, and worse on inspiration or on coughing], and restlessness).

2. *Alert the doctor promptly* if any signs or symptoms of pulmonary embolism appear.
If signs of massive pulmonary embolism occur, place the patient in the high Fowler's position, administer oxygen at 6 liters/minute by nasal prongs, monitor vital signs, and summon immediate medical assistance.

3. During the acute stage of thrombophlebitis, maintain bed rest as ordered.

4. Caution the patient against rubbing the painful area.

5. Decrease the risk associated with a Valsalva maneuver. Teach the patient to exhale while moving; provide fluid, high-fiber foods, prune juice, or other measures to promote passage of soft stool.

Rationales

1. Pulmonary embolism is the most common pulmonary complication in hospitalized patients. Deep venous thrombophlebitis is the primary risk factor associated with emboli development.

2. Pulmonary emboli can cause local areas of pulmonary dysfunction and increase the risk of massive embolism development. Massive pulmonary embolism, in which 50% or more of the pulmonary vascular bed is occluded, is considered a medical emergency. Treatment may include full cardiopulmonary support, surgical intervention, I.V. streptokinase, and heparin.

3. Bed rest decreases the likelihood of a dislodged clot from muscular contraction.

4. Rubbing may cause the clot to break free and embolize.

5. The sudden surge of pressure caused by a Valsalva maneuver may dislodge the clot.

Interventions *continued*

6. *Observe for persistent or recurrent thrombophlebitis.* If present, consult with doctor about further treatment.

7. Additional individualized interventions: _____

_____

Outcome criteria

Within 24 hours of thrombophlebitis onset, the patient will:
• maintain activity restrictions
• exhale with movement
• show no signs of pulmonary embolism.

Rationales *continued*

6. Persistent or recurrent thrombophlebitis indicates continuing risk of pulmonary embolism. Treatment options may include prolonged anticoagulant therapy or insertion of an inferior vena caval umbrella to trap clots.

7. Rationale: _____

_____

By discharge, the patient will:
• show no signs of persistent or recurrent thrombophlebitis.

Nursing diagnosis: *Knowledge deficit related to postdischarge care*

NURSING PRIORITY: Educate patient/family about continuing therapy and preventing recurrence.

Interventions

1. *Teach the patient/family about factors that may increase the risk of recurrence.* Discuss measures that may reduce or eliminate risk factors, including dietary and exercise teaching for weight control/reduction, smoking cessation, pharmacologic control of hypertension, and careful monitoring and control of diabetes.

2. *Instruct about ways to improve venous flow:* foot and leg exercises hourly while awake; fluid intake > 2,000 ml/day (unless contraindicated); extremity elevation when sitting or lying down; active exercise program, as prescribed; avoidance of girdles, garters, knee-high stockings, and other constricting clothing; use of anti-embolism stockings; avoidance of crossing legs when sitting; and avoidance of oral contraceptives.

3. *Educate the patient/family to observe for recurrence of signs and symptoms.*

4. *Instruct about skin care* for extremities: maintaining clean, dry skin; carefully observing any skin lesions; and protecting skin from injury.

5. *Teach the patient/family about oral anticoagulation,* if prescribed. Also teach ways to minimize the risk of bleeding, such as using an electric shaver and avoiding aspirin. (See the "Cerebrovascular Accident" care plan, page 89, for further details.)

Rationales

1. Thrombophlebitis frequently recurs, particularly if risk factors are not eliminated. Teaching measures to eliminate or reduce modifiable risk factors may avert further problems.

2. The methods listed prevent one or more of the classic causative factors of thrombophlebitis: venous stasis, vessel trauma, and hypercoagulability.

3. Self-observation provides the earliest detection of the need for treatment.

4. Impaired circulation of the extremities predisposes the patient to developing stasis ulcers.

5. Patients with uncomplicated deep-venous thrombophlebitis are usually discharged on warfarin for 4 to 6 weeks. Those with complications may need lifetime anticoagulation therapy. The "Cerebrovascular Accident" care plan contains further details related to anticoagulant therapy.

(continued)

Interventions *continued*

6. *Emphasize the importance of regular medical follow-up,* including laboratory test monitoring, as recommended by the doctor. Also stress the value of wearing a Medic Alert bracelet or necklace, and provide the patient with information on how to obtain one.

7. Additional individualized interventions: _____

_____

_____

Rationales *continued*

6. Thrombophlebitis may recur or develop into chronic venous insufficiency. Conscientious medical follow-up provides the greatest protection against future life-threatening episodes or chronicity. Monitoring of laboratory parameters, such as PT for the patient discharged on warfarin sodium, helps the doctor maintain therapeutic dosage. Medic Alert bracelets or necklaces increase the likelihood of appropriate treatment should the patient suffer a medical emergency and be unable to communicate his health status.

7. Rationale: _____

_____

_____

Outcome criteria
By the time of discharge, the patient will:
• be able to list personal risk factors
• be able to list the signs and symptoms of thrombophlebitis
• be able to identify five ways to improve venous flow
• be able to correctly describe the details of administra-

tion and the ways to minimize bleeding risk, if discharged on an anticoagulant
• verbalize the importance of regular medical follow-up
• verbalize intent to obtain a Medic Alert bracelet or necklace.

Discharge planning
NURSING DISCHARGE CRITERIA
Upon discharge, documentation shows evidence of:
• absence of heat, pain, or swelling at affected site
• PTT or PT within acceptable parameters
• absence of pulmonary or cardiovascular complications
• absence of fever
• vital signs within normal parameters
• absence of bowel or bladder dysfunction
• heparin therapy discontinued for 24 hours
• anticoagulation controlled at an acceptable level with oral medication
• presence of bilateral pedal pulses
• absence of pain and pallor in the affected lower extremity
• ability to perform activities of daily living (ADLs), transfers, and ambulation at prehospitalization levels
• adequate home support system, or referral to home care or a nursing home if indicated by lack of home support system or inability to perform ADLs, transfers, and ambulation.

PATIENT/FAMILY DISCHARGE TEACHING CHECKLIST
Document evidence that patient/family demonstrates understanding of:
__ signs and symptoms of recurring thrombophlebitis
__ continued use of antiembolism stockings
__ all discharge medications' purpose, dosage, administration schedule, and adverse reactions requiring medical attention (usual discharge medications include oral anticoagulants)
__ allowable activity level

__ importance of wearing Medic Alert device if patient remains on anticoagulant therapy
__ need for modification of controllable risk factors
__ procedure for obtaining follow-up laboratory test, such as PT
__ date, time, and location of follow-up appointment
__ how to contact the doctor.

DOCUMENTATION CHECKLIST
Using outcome criteria as a guide, document:
__ clinical status on admission
__ significant changes in status
__ pertinent laboratory data and diagnostic test findings
__ pain-relief measures
__ position of comfort and effect of extremity elevation
__ application and effect of warm, moist compresses
__ anticoagulant administration
__ any change in clotting studies
__ any bleeding tendencies noted
__ administration of other pharmacologic agents, such as an anti-inflammatory or antibiotic
__ level of activity and patient response to progressive ambulation
__ patient/family teaching
__ discharge planning.

ASSOCIATED CARE PLANS
Cerebrovascular Accident
Ineffective Individual Coping
Knowledge Deficit
Pain
Surgical Intervention

REFERENCES

Alfaro, Rosalinda. *Application of Nursing Process*. Philadelphia: J.B. Lippincott Co., 1986.

Baum, Patricia L. "Heed the Warning Signs of Peripheral Vascular Disease (PVD)," *Nursing85* 15(3):50-57, March 1985.

Bullock, Barbara L., and Rosendahl, Pearl P. *Pathophysiology*. Boston: Little, Brown & Co., 1984.

Doenges, Marilynn, et al. *Nursing Care Plans*. Philadelphia: F.A. Davis Co., 1984.

Hurst, J. Willis, ed. *The Heart*, 6th ed. New York: McGraw-Hill Book Co., 1986.

Iyer, Patricia, et al. *Nursing Process and Nursing Diagnosis*. Philadelphia: W.B. Saunders Co., 1986.

Kenner, Cornelia, et al. *Critical Care Nursing: Body-Mind-Spirit*, 2nd ed. Boston: Little, Brown & Co., 1985.

Kneisl, Carol, and Ames, Sue Ann. *Adult Health Nursing*. Menlo Park, Calif.: Addison-Wesley Publishing Co., 1986.

Patrick, Maxine, et al. *Medical-Surgical Nursing*. Philadelphia: J.B. Lippincott Co., 1986.

Raffensperger, Ellen B., et al. *Clinical Nursing Handbook*. Philadelphia: J.B. Lippincott Co., 1986.

Colostomy

DRG information

DRG 148 [Surgical DRG] Major Small and Large
Bowel Procedure.
With Complication or Comorbidity (CC).
Mean LOS = 14.5 days

DRG 149 [Surgical DRG] Major Small and Large
Bowel Procedure.
Without CC.
Mean LOS = 10.7 days

Introduction

DEFINITION AND TIME FOCUS

A colostomy is a surgically created opening (stoma), between the abdominal wall and the colon, that provides for
fecal diversion. A colostomy may be created after a colectomy (colon excision), proctectomy (rectal excision), procto-
colectomy (colon and rectal excision), or abdominoperineal
(AP) resection (removal of the rectum and a wide area of
probably cancerous tissue, including muscle, fat, and skin).
Colostomies may be designated according to location, construction, or duration:
• location—Although a colostomy may be constructed any-
where in the large bowel, the two most common locations
are the transverse colon and the descending colon.
• construction—Common surgical construction methods
(see *Colostomy*) include:
 □ end colostomy (bowel is divided; proximal bowel is
 brought out as a stoma and distal bowel is either removed—as in abdominoperineal resection of the distal
 colon/rectum—or "oversewn" and left in place—as in
 Hartmann's procedure)
 □ double-barreled colostomy (bowel is divided and both
 ends are brought out as stomas; the proximal stoma
 drains stool and the distal stoma drains only mucus)
 □ loop colostomy (entire loop of bowel is brought out
 through the abdominal wall and stabilized over a
 rod, bridge, or catheter until granulation to abdominal wall occurs; the bowel's anterior wall is opened
 to provide fecal diversion; the posterior bowel wall
 remains continuous).
• duration—A colostomy is classified as permanent (no
potential for reversal) if the rectum and anus are removed or as temporary (potential for reversal) if the
rectum and anus remain.
 This clinical plan focuses on preoperative assessment
of teaching needs and on the postoperative phase, the
"active teaching" phase, between initial recovery or
stabilization and discharge.

ETIOLOGY/PRECIPITATING FACTORS

• disease conditions requiring removal of distal bowel
(for example, colorectal cancer or pelvic malignancies)
• infectious or inflammatory conditions of distal bowel
requiring fecal diversion (for example, diverticulitis or
Crohn's disease)

• obstruction of distal bowel requiring fecal diversion
(as in a gunshot or stab wound)
• extensive surgery of distal bowel requiring protective fecal
diversion (for example, low anterior colon resection)

Focused assessment guidelines

Note: Because a colostomy may be performed for widely
varied conditions, no typical presenting picture exists;
therefore, the nursing history and physical findings sections are omitted in this care plan. Presented instead
are guidelines for preoperative assessment.

Health perception–health management pattern

• Determine the diagnosis or reason for colostomy. Determine the planned procedure, prognosis, and potential
for independence as a basis for discharge planning and
patient teaching.
• Explore the patient's perceptions concerning colostomy
and its impact on health status and life-style. (Note:
Previous contact with a person with an ostomy will affect the patient's expectations and adaptation.)
• Identify any allergies, particularly to topical agents
such as tape; patients with such allergies may react to
colostomy products.

Nutritional-metabolic pattern

• Assess diet and fluid intake. Assess the home diet (as
a basis for patient teaching) for adequate fiber and fluid
intake and for consumption of gas-producing foods.
• Assess nutritional status (skin turgor, mucous membranes, hair condition, height and weight, and recent
weight loss). Be alert to signs of nutritional deficiency
that may predispose the patient to postoperative complications, such as wound infection or delayed healing.

Elimination pattern

• Determine usual bowel patterns. Assess the preoperative frequency and character of bowel movements as a
basis for colostomy management and patient teaching
(particularly important in selecting a management approach for descending/sigmoid colostomy).

Activity-exercise pattern

• Assess independence and any limitations in activities of
daily living. The amount of independence is significant in
planning for colostomy management and patient/family
teaching. The patient's manual dexterity and coordination
are particularly significant in selecting appropriate equipment, such as a pouching system or clip.

Cognitive-perceptual pattern

• As a basis for teaching, assess the patient's understanding of the diagnosis, prognosis, surgical procedure, and management of colostomy.

COLOSTOMY

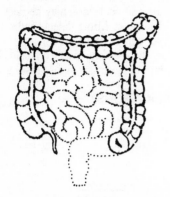

End colostomy: Sigmoid
colon

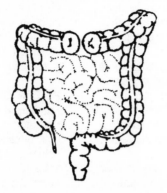

Double-barreled colostomy:
Transverse colon

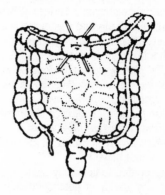

Loop colostomy: Transverse
colon

• Sensory deficits: Assess visual and auditory acuity as a basis for planning self-care instruction; most patients requiring colostomy are over age 60, so sensory loss is common.
• Learning style: Base teaching strategies on the patient's learning style and sensory strengths; for example, if a patient with diminished visual acuity says he learns best by doing, self-care instruction should involve much practice (with a magnifying mirror) but minimal reading.

Self-perception–self-concept pattern
• Self-concept and self-esteem correlate with adaptation potential; be alert to consistent self-derogatory statements or inappropriate affect, which may indicate low self-esteem.
• Emotional response is variable: It is common for a patient to have negative feelings regarding colostomy.
• Openness in expressing feelings is affected by the patient's personality and the nurse's communication skills.

Role-relationship pattern
• Assess areas of concern about roles and relationships. Patients commonly express concern about the impact of colostomy on relationships, with major concern relating to spouse or partner reaction.
• Young and middle-aged adults commonly express concern about their ability to resume preoperative roles and responsibilities.
• Older adults commonly express concern about their ability to maintain independence and to manage the cost of ostomy supplies.
• Assess family dynamics, particularly dependence-independence roles: Older patients may desire their spouse's or significant other's involvement in care, whereas younger adults may value independence and privacy.

Sexuality-reproductive pattern
• Assess the patient's and partner's openness with each other and in discussing sexuality, preoperative sexual patterns, and other major concerns.
• A common concern is the impact of colostomy on intimate relationships—that is, on sexual attractiveness and function.

Coping–stress tolerance pattern
• The patient's and family's responses to colostomy are highly variable and reflect coping patterns.
• Assess the patient's feelings about support groups, to determine the appropriateness of referral to the United Ostomy Association.

Value-belief pattern
• Response to colostomy is affected by cultural beliefs and familial response to illness, surgery, and elimination.

DIAGNOSTIC STUDIES
Studies vary according to the patient's condition and the underlying disorder creating the need for a colostomy; they may include:
• *complete blood count—may reveal low hemoglobin or hematocrit levels* indicative of continuing or unreplaced blood loss; *may also reveal elevated white blood cell count* indicative of infectious process, usually intraabdominal
• electrolyte panel—done to detect or rule out electrolyte abnormalities that affect fluid balance (for example, hyponatremia or hypernatremia) and GI tract function (for example, hypokalemia or hyperkalemia)
• chemistry panel—done to detect electrolyte imbalances and nutritional deficits that affect wound healing (for example, hypoproteinemia) and to monitor liver and kidney function, which may be affected by underlying disease, such as metastatic disease, or by treatment, such as antibiotic therapy

• serum drug levels—peak and trough levels may be done to detect toxic or subtherapeutic levels of prescribed antibiotics or other drugs
• carcinoembryonic antigen (CEA) levels—may be done preoperatively and postoperatively for comparison; if elevated preoperatively, effective surgical resection should result in decreased CEA level
• *flat plate/upright of abdomen—may be done preoperatively to rule out colon perforation (in trauma patient) or colon obstruction (in patient with suspected malignancy); done postoperatively as needed to differentiate postoperative ileus (visualized as air-filled loops of bowel) from mechanical obstruction* (visualized as air-fluid levels and dilated proximal bowel)
• computed tomography scan of abdomen—may be used preoperatively or postoperatively to rule out intraabdominal abscess or to detect metastatic lesions
• stool guaiac (Hemoccult) test—preliminary study to rule out GI bleeding; positive study requires further workup to rule out malignancy, hemorrhoidal bleeding, inflammatory bowel disease, or upper tract bleeding; negative study inconclusive because of high incidence of false-negative results
• barium enema with air and contrast—may be done to rule out diverticular disease or filling defects indicative of colon lesions (such as polyps and tumors)
• sigmoidoscopy or colonoscopy—done to rule out colon lesions and to remove polyps or biopsy suspicious lesions

POTENTIAL COMPLICATIONS
• prolonged ileus
• wound infection or dehiscence
• mechanical bowel obstruction
• stomal necrosis
• stomal retraction
• peritonitis or intraabdominal abscess
• thrombophlebitis or deep-vein thrombosis
• sexual dysfunction (if AP resection done)
• nonhealing perineal wound (if AP resection done)
• bladder dysfunction (if AP resection done)

Collaborative problem: *Potential stomal necrosis related to the surgical procedure, bowel wall edema, or traction on the mesentery*

NURSING PRIORITIES: (a) Optimize blood flow to bowel wall, and (b) prevent complications related to circulatory impairment.

Interventions

1. *Assess and document stoma color* every 8 hours, during the first 4 postoperative days (or until the stoma remains pink for 3 days).

2. *If the stoma is ischemic or necrotic, check the viability of the proximal bowel* by inserting a test tube into the stoma and using a flashlight to check for healthy versus ischemic mucosa. Document.

3. *Document and notify the doctor promptly if necrosis extends to the fascia level,* as indicated by necrosis extending to the end of the test tube (see Intervention 2 above).

4. *Implement measures to prevent or minimize abdominal distention:*
• If a nasogastric (NG) tube is present, irrigate as needed to maintain patency.
• Examine the abdomen for distention every 8 hours during the first 4 postoperative days.
• If distention is present, notify the doctor and request an order to insert an NG tube.
• If distention is present, monitor its degree by measuring abdominal girth at the umbilical level.

5. Additional individualized interventions: _____
_____
_____

Rationales

1. Healthy bowel tissue is pink; a dusky blue color indicates ischemia, and a brown or black color indicates necrosis. Ischemia may or may not progress to necrosis.

2. A distal stoma is most likely to necrose because it is farthest from the mesenteric blood supply. Stomal necrosis does not necessarily represent a surgical emergency (the stoma may be allowed to "slough" as long as the proximal bowel is viable).

3. Necrosis extending to the fascia level represents a surgical emergency because of the threat of perforation and peritonitis.

4. Severe abdominal distention may cause mesenteric "stretching," which places blood vessels under tension; this stress may result in decreased blood flow to the distal bowel and stoma. Using the umbilicus as the reference point for measuring abdominal girth provides a consistent measuring technique that increases the reliability of the data obtained.

5. Rationale: _____
_____
_____

Outcome criterion

Within first 4 days postoperatively, the patient will:
• display a pink and viable stoma.

Collaborative problem: *Potential stoma retraction related to mucocutaneous separation*

NURSING PRIORITIES: (a) Optimize wound healing and granulation of the stoma to the abdominal wall, and (b) prevent stomal retraction.

Interventions

1. *Assess and document the integrity of the mucocutaneous suture line at each pouch change.*

2. *Initiate and document nutritional support measures* for the patient at risk for nutritional deficiency, based on the recommendations of a nutritional resource nurse or dietitian.

3. Request vitamin A supplements for the patient receiving steroids.

4. *For the patient with a loop colostomy* stabilized by a rod or bridge, *anticipate delay in removing the loop support* until the stoma granulates to the abdominal wall.

5. *If mucocutaneous separation occurs, alter the pouching system* to prevent fecal contamination of exposed subcutaneous tissue. (Fill the separated area with absorptive powder or granules; cover with tape strips, then pectin-based paste. Apply a pouch sized to fit closely around the stoma.)

6. Additional individualized interventions: _____
_____
_____

Rationales

1. Breakdown of the stoma or skin suture line is a major contributing factor to stomal retraction.

2. Nutritional deficiency causes negative nitrogen balance, which compromises wound healing because wound repair depends on adequate protein stores; consequently, the suture line may break down.

3. Vitamin A partially compensates for corticosteroids' negative effects on wound healing; so, by supporting macrophage activity and wound repair, vitamin A helps prevent suture line breakdown.

4. Loop support removal before abdominal wall attachment may precipitate stomal retraction.

5. An optimal environment for healing includes protection from secondary infection, absorption of exudate, and maintenance of a clean, moist surface. The absorptive agent and tape strips prevent fecal contamination and absorb exudate. Using paste and a pouch sized for the stoma provides a secure pouch seal.

6. Rationale: _____
_____
_____

Outcome criteria

By the time of discharge, the patient will:
• display a stoma granulated to the abdominal wall

• exhibit a healed mucocutaneous suture line
• show no stomal retraction.

Nursing diagnosis: *Potential altered skin integrity: peristomal skin breakdown related to fecal material contact with skin*

NURSING PRIORITIES: (a) Maintain an intact pouch seal, and (b) prevent peristomal skin breakdown.

Interventions

1. *Have an enterostomal therapy nurse mark the optimal stoma site preoperatively,* if possible.

Rationales

1. For best results, the stoma should be located in an area free of creases or folds, within the patient's view, and within the rectus muscle. Site selection is best done preoperatively, when the patient can be evaluated lying down, sitting, and standing.

(continued)

Interventions continued

2. *Assess the patient's abdominal contours and select a pouching system that matches those contours* (for example, try an all-flexible system for a stoma in a crease or fold).

3. *Use the following principles in preparing and applying the pouch:*
• Use a drainable pouch.

• Remove peristomal hair.
• Use a skin sealant (such as Skin Prep) under the tape.
• Use a pouch with a barrier ring sized to fit closely around the stoma; use barrier paste (such as Stomahesive) to fill in the gaps.
• If an adhesive-only pouch is used, size it to clear the stoma by ⅛" (3.18 mm). (It should be used with a barrier ring and paste.)

4. Change the pouch routinely every 5 to 7 days and as needed if leakage or complaints of peristomal burning or itching occur.

5. Inspect the skin at each pouch change, and treat any denudation with absorptive powder (such as karaya) dusted onto the area and sealed by blotting with water or sealant.

6. Additional individualized interventions: _____
_____
_____

Outcome criteria
Throughout the postoperative phase, the patient will:
• display peristomal skin free of breakdown.

Rationales continued

2. Accurate matching of abdominal contours and the pouching system optimizes the pouch-to-skin seal and minimizes the leakage risk.

3. Good technique provides maximum security and skin protection:
• The pouch can be emptied as needed without being removed.
• Hair removal prevents folliculitis.
• The copolymer film prevents epidermal stripping with pouch removal.
• This procedure prevents fecal material from contacting skin (which can cause breakdown).

• Inadequate clearance of inflexible pouch edges can damage the stoma during peristalsis. Exposed skin must be protected.

4. Routine changes before leaks can occur protect skin and provide the patient with control. Burning or itching may indicate fecal contamination of skin.

5. Powder provides an absorptive protective layer next to the area of breakdown; sealing is necessary to provide a pouching surface.

6. Rationale: _____
_____
_____

By the time of discharge, the patient will:
• have an intact pouch for 5 days.

Nursing diagnosis: *Knowledge deficit related to unfamiliarity with management options for a descending/sigmoid colostomy**

NURSING PRIORITY: Help the patient select management options most appropriate for his or her physical status and life-style.

Interventions

1. *Assess the patient's candidacy for bowel function regulation* by irrigation. Consider the following factors: Is the colostomy permanent? Do stomal complications, such as hernia or prolapse, exist? Is the patient mentally and physically able to learn and perform the procedure? What were the preoperative bowel patterns? Is the patient to receive radiation? Does the patient have adequate home facilities?

Rationales

1. Irrigation is not usually the best option for the patient with a temporary colostomy (because of the time factor and potential for bowel dependence); the patient with a peristomal hernia (potential for perforation) or prolapse (potential for worsening of prolapse); the patient with coordination problems or learning difficulties; the patient with a preoperative history of diarrhea (less likely to achieve control than the patient with a preop-

---

*Note: The stoma's location in the GI tract determines stool consistency and frequency and affects selection of a management approach. With a descending/sigmoid colostomy, output is soft-to-solid, frequency is similar to preop-

erative patterns, and output may be regulated by irrigation. (With a transverse colostomy, output is mushy, occurs after meals and unpredictably, and cannot be regulated by irrigation.)

Interventions *continued*

2. If the patient meets feasibility criteria, *discuss management options*:
• continuous pouching with the pouch emptied as needed and changed every 5 to 7 days, or
• daily or every-other-day irrigations to stimulate bowel movements, using a security pouch or gauze between irrigations.

3. Help the patient explore the options based on personal priorities (for example, tolerance of the pouch vs. the time required for regular irrigations).

4. Establish a teaching plan based on the patient's decision.

5. Additional individualized interventions: _____
_____
_____

Rationales *continued*

erative history of regular stools or constipation); the patient receiving radiation therapy, because diarrhea is a usual side effect; the patient without running water or indoor plumbing in the home.

2. Colostomy irrigations are not necessary because peristalsis and bowel movements continue; however, regular irrigations induce evacuation and promote colonic "dependence" on their stimulating effects, providing increased control over bowel function. Thus, regulation by irrigation is a management option.

3. Exploring the pros and cons of various options and discussing the patient's concerns and priorities facilitates decision making by the patient and increases his or her sense of self-control.

4. The patient needs to be capable of self-care before discharge.

5. Rationale: _____
_____
_____

Outcome criterion
By 2 days before discharge, the patient will:
• describe options considered and select a preferred approach.

Nursing diagnosis: *Potential altered self-concept: body image related to loss of control of fecal elimination*

NURSING PRIORITIES: (a) Prevent or minimize alteration in self-concept, and (b) enhance the patient's sense of control over bowel functions.

Interventions

1. *Teach the patient measures for odor control* (for example, an odor-proof pouch; pouch hygiene; pouch deodorants, if desired; use of a room deodorant when the pouch is emptied; dietary alterations to reduce fecal odor; and over-the-counter internal deodorants such as bismuth subgallate).

2. *Teach the patient measures to reduce and control flatus* (for example, identifying gas-forming foods; social implications of "lag time" between ingestion and flatulence; measures to muffle sounds of flatus; and pouch filters that deodorize flatus).

Rationales

1. Odor control is a major concern of most patients; instruction in odor-control methods increases feelings of control and confidence and reduces feelings of embarrassment and shame. Onions, garlic, beans, and cabbage generally increase odor; orange juice, buttermilk, and yogurt may decrease odor. Bismuth reduces flatus and odor and thickens stool; it is contraindicated in patients with renal failure or on anticoagulant therapy.

2. Inability to control flatus may lead to social embarrassment and self-deprecation. The patient can time the intake of any gas-forming foods so that flatulence occurs during safe "at-home" periods. Filters keep the pouch flat by allowing flatus to escape and prevent odor by first deodorizing flatus.

(continued)

Interventions *continued*

3. *Teach the patient how to conceal the pouch* under clothing, using a knit or stretchy layer over the pouch and next to the body.

4. *Discuss the normal emotional response to colostomy* with the patient and significant others. Allow the patient and significant others to explore their feelings about colostomy. Assess the patient's usual coping strategies. Present helpful coping strategies, such as discussing feelings and seeking information.

5. Offer information on the United Ostomy Association; arrange for an "ostomy visitor" if the patient wishes.

6. Discuss colostomy management during occupational, social, and sexual activity. Help the patient to role-play situations that concern him (for example, whom to tell about the stoma, when to tell, and how to tell).

7. Additional individualized interventions: _____

Rationales *continued*

3. The ability to dress normally and "look the same" diminishes altered in body image and enhances self-concept.

4. Discussing the normal emotional response and accepting negative feelings gives the patient permission to explore feelings. Accepting feelings enhances self-concept and promotes adaptation. Discussing various coping strategies may provide the patient with new or more effective strategies.

5. Contact with others who have ostomies reduces isolation and increases perception of the colostomy as manageable, thus enhancing the patient's sense of control.

6. Discussion before encountering such activity increases coping skills and the likelihood that the patient will manage them successfully. Role playing helps the patient prepare for difficult situations, which increases the sense of control and enhances self-concept.

7. Rationale: _____

Outcome criteria
By 3 days before discharge, the patient will:
• observe and perform stoma care
• discuss feelings about the stoma with significant others.

By the time of discharge, the patient will:
• describe the colostomy as manageable
• achieve adequate self-care
• describe plans for resuming his or her preoperative life-style.

Nursing diagnosis: *Potential sexual dysfunction related to change in body image and/or damage to autonomic nerves**

NURSING PRIORITIES: (a) Facilitate the resumption and maintenance of intimate relationships, and (b) minimize alteration in sexual function.

Interventions

1. *Discuss with the patient (and spouse or partner, if possible) the importance of openness and honesty* as well as the fact that both must adapt to the change.

2. *Teach the patient measures for securing and concealing the pouch during sexual activity* (for example, pouch covers, a small pouch, a "tube top" or cummerbund around the midriff, or crotchless panties).

3. For a female with a wide rectal resection, discuss the possible need for artificial lubrication.

Rationales

1. Both patient and spouse (or partner) may have concerns and negative feelings that can affect their sexual relationship. Openness in discussing feelings may help resolve these.

2. The stoma and pouch affect overall body image and feelings of sexual attractiveness. Securing and concealing the pouch helps prevent leakage and allows focus on sexuality and sharing rather than on the pouch and stoma.

3. Wide rectal resection may damage parasympathetic nerves thought to mediate vaginal lubrication.

*Nerve damage applicable only to the patient with rectal resection, particularly wide resection for cancer.

Interventions continued

4. For a male with a wide rectal resection, explain potential interference with erection and ejaculation; explain that no loss of sensation or orgasmic potential will occur; explore alternatives to intercourse as indicated; and reinforce the importance of intimacy—whether or not it involves intercourse.

5. Additional individualized interventions: _____
_____
_____

Rationales continued

4. Wide rectal resection may damage parasympathetic nerves controlling erection and sympathetic nerves controlling ejaculation. Sensation and orgasm, mediated by the pudendal nerve, remain intact. Intimacy—emotional closeness—is a human need separate from the desire for sexual expression. It can be met in ways other than sexual behavior, such as sharing feelings and affectionate touching.

5. Rationale: _____
_____
_____

Outcome criteria

By the time of discharge, the patient will:
• share feelings about stoma with spouse or partner
• describe any alteration in sexual function (if applicable)

• describe measures for pouch management during sexual activity (if applicable).

Discharge planning

NURSING DISCHARGE CRITERIA

Upon discharge, documentation shows evidence of:
• absence of fever
• stable vital signs
• absence of pulmonary or cardiovascular complications
• healing wound with no signs of redness, swelling, or drainage
• ability to change and empty pouch using proper technique
• ability to tolerate diet
• absence of skin problems around stoma
• absence of bladder dysfunction
• absence of abdominal distention
• restored bowel function
• ability to perform activities of daily living and ambulate same as before surgery
• ability to control pain with oral medications
• adequate home support system or referral to home care if indicated by inadequate home support system or inability to manage colostomy care at home.

PATIENT/FAMILY DISCHARGE TEACHING CHECKLIST

Document evidence that patient/family demonstrates understanding of:
___ reason for colostomy
___ colostomy impact on bowel function
___ normal stoma characteristics and function
___ pouch-emptying procedure
___ pouch-changing procedure
___ peristomal skin care
___ colostomy irrigation procedure (if applicable)
___ management of mucous fistula stoma (if applicable)
___ flatus and odor control
___ management of diarrhea and constipation
___ normal adaptation process and feelings post-colostomy
___ community resources available for support

___ recommendations affecting resumption of preoperative life-style
___ potential alteration in sexual function (if applicable)
___ sources of colostomy supplies and reimbursement procedures for them
___ signs and symptoms requiring notification of doctor
___ need for follow-up appointment with doctor (and enterostomal therapy nurse, if available)
___ how to contact doctor.

DOCUMENTATION CHECKLIST

Using outcome criteria as a guide, document:
___ clinical status on admission
___ significant changes in clinical status
___ GI tract function (bowel sounds, NG tube output, and colostomy output)
___ stoma color and status of mucocutaneous suture line
___ oral intake and tolerance
___ episodes of abdominal distention, nausea, and vomiting
___ incision status (any signs of infection)
___ stoma location and abdominal contours
___ management plan, including pouching system selected (and decision about irrigation for patient with descending/sigmoid colostomy)
___ peristomal skin status
___ emotional response to colostomy and discussion of coping strategies
___ patient/family teaching
___ discharge planning.

ASSOCIATED CARE PLANS

Fluid and Electrolyte Imbalances
Grief/Grieving
Ineffective Family Coping
Ineffective Individual Coping
Knowledge Deficit
Pain
Surgical Intervention

REFERENCES

Alfaro, R. *Application of Nursing Process: A Step-by-Step Guide.* Philadelphia: J.B. Lippincott Co., 1986.

Broadwell, D., and Jackson, B. *Principles of Ostomy Care.* St. Louis: C.V. Mosby Co., 1982.

Dobkin, K., and Broadwell, D. "Nursing Considerations for the Patient Undergoing Colostomy Surgery," *Seminars in Oncology Nursing* 2(4):249-55, 1986.

Dudas, S. "Rehabilitation Concepts of Nursing," *Journal of Enterostomal Therapy* 11(1):6-15, 1984.

McGarity, W. "Complications Following Abdominoperineal Resection: Sexual and Bladder Dysfunction," *Ostomy Management* 3:4-8, 1980.

Maklebust, J. "United Ostomy Association Visits and Adjustment Following Ostomy Surgery," *Journal of Enterostomal Therapy* 12(3):84-92, May/June 1985.

Smith, D. "Colostomy Irrigations—So Simple?" *Journal of Enterostomal Therapy* 10(1):22-23, 1983.

Watson, P. "Meeting the Needs of Patients Undergoing Ostomy Surgery," *Journal of Enterostomal Therapy* 12(4):121-24, July/August 1985.

Duodenal Ulcer

DRG information

DRG 174 [Medical DRG] GI Hemorrhage. With
    Complication or Comorbidity (CC).
    Mean LOS = 5.6 days
    Principal diagnoses include:
    • duodenal ulcer
    – acute or chronic
    – with hemorrhage
    – with or without obstruction.
DRG 175 [Medical DRG] GI Hemorrhage. Without CC.
    Mean LOS = 4.4 days
DRG 176 [Medical DRG] Complicated Peptic Ulcer.
    Mean LOS = 6.1 days
    Principal diagnoses include:
    • acute or chronic duodenal ulcer
    – with or without perforation
    – with or without obstruction
      or hemorrhage.
DRG 177 [Medical DRG] Uncomplicated Peptic Ulcer.
    With CC.
    Mean LOS = 5.5 days
    Principal diagnoses include:
    • acute or chronic duodenal ulcer without
    hemorrhage, obstruction, or perforation.
DRG 178 [Medical DRG] Uncomplicated Peptic Ulcer.
    Without CC.
    Mean LOS = 4.3 days

Introduction

DEFINITION AND TIME FOCUS

Duodenal ulcer is the inflammatory and ulcerative process that affects the first portion of the duodenum within 1⅛″ (3 cm) of the gastroduodenal junction. This clinical plan focuses on the duodenal ulcer patient admitted to a medical-surgical unit with signs and symptoms that have not been controlled through outpatient management. Long-term maintenance medication therapy is generally recommended for duodenal ulcer patients rather than surgical treatment; therefore, the plan focuses on medical treatment.

ETIOLOGY/PRECIPITATING FACTORS

Gastric acid secretion is necessary for the development of duodenal ulcers. Pathophysiologic abnormalities that influence gastric acid secretion are:
• increased parietal cell and chief cell mass (related to gastrinoma [gastrin-secreting tumor] or familial or genetic factors)
• increased basal secretory or postprandial secretory drive (related to gastrinoma or antral G cell hyperfunction)
• rapid gastric emptying (related to familial or genetic factors)

• impaired mucosal defense (related to ingestion of aspirin, corticosteroids, or phenylbutazone and to other factors such as stress or infectious agents).

Focused assessment guidelines

NURSING HISTORY (Functional health pattern findings)

Health perception–health management pattern
• may report *steady, gnawing, burning, aching, or hunger-like discomfort high in the right epigastrium;* pain occurs 2 to 4 hours after meals, usually does not radiate, and is relieved by food or antacids
• *at increased risk if male, age 40 to 60,* with type O blood, a cigarette smoker, or exposed to chronic emotional stress
• may report *ingestion of certain drugs* that contribute to the development of duodenal ulceration, such as aspirin, corticosteroids, phenylbutazone, or indomethacin
• may report *family history of ulcer disease*

Nutritional-metabolic pattern
• diet history may include *excessive alcohol consumption*
• may report *nausea* (vomiting not common)
• appetite usually good

Elimination pattern
• may report *feeling of fullness, gaseous indigestion, or constipation*

Activity-exercise pattern
• may report *fatigue*
• may report exacerbation of pain following unusual physical exertion

Sleep-rest pattern
• may report *sleep disturbances from pain,* commonly occurring between 12:00 and 3:00 a.m.

Coping–stress tolerance pattern
• may report *stressful life events*—such as occupational, educational, or financial problems or family illness—preceding development or exacerbation of signs and symptoms
• may deny signs and symptoms during pain-free periods (symptoms commonly disappear for weeks or months and then recur)

PHYSICAL FINDINGS
Gastrointestinal
• *localized tenderness* in epigastrium over ulcer site

DIAGNOSTIC STUDIES

• routine laboratory studies—add little to the workup
• more sophisticated GI studies, such as serum pepsinogen I or fasting gastrin levels—may be ordered based on the suspected cause of the duodenal ulcer; a high serum pepsinogen I level and a high fasting gastrin level provide evidence for either a gastrinoma or antral G cell hyperfunction
• *endoscopy—reveals the ulcer* and allows for biopsy and cytology

• single- or double-contrast radiography—may be ordered along with endoscopy

POTENTIAL COMPLICATIONS

• duodenal obstruction
• perforation
• hemorrhage

Collaborative problem: *Potential GI hemorrhage related to extension of duodenal ulcer into the submucosal layer of the intestinal lining*

NURSING PRIORITY: Observe for, prevent, or promptly treat hemorrhage.

Interventions

1. *Observe for and report signs of GI hemorrhage.* Describe any hematemesis, melena, or other intestinal bleeding, including amount, consistency, and color. Test all stools and emesis with guaiac reagent strip (Hemoccult).

2. *Institute nasogastric (NG) intubation,* if ordered. Keep the tube patent by inserting 30 ml of saline solution every 2 to 4 hours, then removing the same amount by mechanical suction.

3. *Institute continuous saline lavage,* if ordered. Instill aliquots of fluid (500 to 1,000 ml), then remove the same amount by gentle suction and gravity drainage.

4. *If the patient is actively bleeding, check vital signs* hourly (more frequently if unstable). *Alert the doctor immediately to deterioration in status* as indicated by decreasing alertness, dropping systolic blood pressure, tachycardia, narrowing pulse pressure, or restlessness or agitation.

5. *Treat hypovolemia,* if present. Keep the patient warm, administer necessary I.V. fluids and blood transfusions, as ordered, and provide oxygen at 2 to 6 liters/minute via nasal cannula.

6. Prepare the patient for surgery, if indicated.

7. Maintain bed rest following the bleeding episode. Begin a medication regimen, as ordered.

Rationales

1. Hematemesis of frank red blood indicates active bleeding; coffee-ground emesis indicates old bleeding. Hemoccult unmasks occult bleeding.

2. NG intubation reveals the presence or absence of blood in the stomach, helps assess the rate of bleeding, and provides a route for saline lavage. If the tube is not patent, the patient may vomit stomach contents.

3. Continuous lavaging indicates the rapidity of bleeding and cleanses the stomach for possible endoscopy. Iced saline may impair coagulation. Experimental evidence suggests that room-temperature water lavage may be as effective as iced saline lavage.

4. Loss of blood volume leads rapidly to hypovolemic shock. Untreated, shock may progress to irreversible tissue ischemia; death follows rapidly. Early detection of active bleeding and aggressive fluid replacement therapy are essential to prevent shock.

5. Restoring intravascular volume and taking measures to supplement oxygen transport reduce the effects of blood loss on tissues until bleeding can be controlled.

6. Surgery may be indicated if bleeding continues beyond 48 hours, recurs, or is associated with perforation or obstruction. The preferred surgical treatment is parietal cell vagotomy.

7. Rest aids cessation of bleeding and decreases activity of the GI tract. A medication regimen (as in the following nursing diagnosis) is the usual therapy before surgery is considered.

Interventions *continued*

8. Additional individualized interventions: _____

_____

_____

Rationales *continued*

8. Rationale: _____

_____

_____

Outcome criteria

Within 24 hours of admission, the patient will:
• show evidence that bleeding has ceased, such as normal NG drainage and a negative Hemoccult
• have vital signs within normal limits for this patient.

Nursing diagnosis: *Pain related to increased hydrochloric acid secretion, and/or increased spasm, intragastric pressure, and motility of upper GI tract*

NURSING PRIORITIES: (a) Promote stomach and intestinal healing, and (b) teach risk factors and measures to prevent recurrence.

Interventions

1. *Administer and document ulcer-healing medications,* as ordered. Medications may include one or a combination of the following four types:
• histamine (H_2)-receptor antagonists (cimetidine [Tagamet], ranitidine [Zantac]), usually given with meals and at bedtime
• antacids, given after meals and at bedtime unless otherwise ordered
• anticholinergics
• sucralfate (Carafate).

2. *Provide bed rest and a quiet environment,* minimizing visitors and telephone calls. Help the patient identify specific personal stressors.

3. *Teach and reinforce the role of diet* in ulcer healing. Help the patient identify specific foods that may cause increased discomfort.

4. *Encourage intake of adequate calories* from basic foods at regular intervals. Encourage frequent small meals.

5. *Teach and reinforce required changes in life-style* for reduction of physical and emotional stress. Help the patient recognize the relationship between increased stress and occurrence of ulcer pain. Consider teaching related to relaxation techniques, exercise, priority-setting, time management/personal organization, building and nurturing relationships, "play" time, and assertiveness techniques.

6. *Discourage smoking.*

Rationales

1. Increased hydrochloric acid secretion results in edema and inflammation of gastric mucosa. H_2-receptor antagonists inhibit gastrin release, and antacids buffer hydrochloric acid; anticholinergics decrease hydrochloric acid secretion. Sucralfate binds to proteins at the base of the ulcer to form a protective barrier against acid and pepsin. Studies indicate ulcer healing occurs within 6 weeks of beginning a medication regimen.

2. Ulcer symptoms are usually reduced by rest, a quiet environment, and removal of stress factors.

3. Dietary restrictions other than avoidance of excessive alcohol and caffeine are not currently recommended. Promotion of specific diets is highly controversial; none has been scientifically proven to promote healing. Identification of personal food intolerances facilitates therapeutic dietary planning.

4. Food itself acts as an antacid, producing neutralization 30 to 60 minutes after ingestion.

5. Stressful life situations, such as occupational, financial, or family problems, have been reported to be more frequent in patients with duodenal ulcers that required longer than 6 weeks to heal. Identification of cause-and-effect relationships assists the patient to make necessary life-style changes.

6. Research indicates that patients who smoke have impaired ulcer healing and higher mortality compared with nonsmokers.

(continued)

Interventions *continued*

7. Teach the patient signs and symptoms indicating ulcer recurrence and bleeding including pain, hematemesis, dark or tarry stools, pallor, increasing weakness, dizziness, or faintness.

8. Additional individualized interventions: _____
_____
_____

Outcome criteria
Within 2 days of admission, the patient will:
• verbalize absence or relief of pain
• identify dietary intolerances
• observe dietary recommendations in menu selection

Rationales *continued*

7. Early identification and recognition of signs and symptoms of recurrence or bleeding may permit intervention before bleeding becomes severe.

8. Rationale: _____
_____
_____

• identify personal stressors
• demonstrate interest in stress-reduction measures
• list signs and symptoms of recurrence and bleeding.

Discharge planning

NURSING DISCHARGE CRITERIA
Upon discharge, documentation shows evidence of:
• stable vital signs
• absence of signs and symptoms of GI hemorrhage
• hemoglobin within expected parameters
• absence of pain
• ability to tolerate nutritional intake as ordered
• ability to verbalize diet and medication instructions
• ability to perform activities of daily living and ambulate as before hospitalization
• adequate home support system or referral to home care if indicated by inadequate home support system or inability to perform self-care.

**PATIENT/FAMILY DISCHARGE
TEACHING CHECKLIST**
Document evidence that patient/family demonstrates understanding of:
__ nature and implications of disease
__ relationship of ulcer pain and relief modalities
__ all discharge medications' purpose, dose, administration schedule, and side effects requiring medical attention (usual discharge medications include antacids or H_2-receptor antagonists, or both)
__ recommended dietary modifications
__ need for smoking cessation program (if applicable)
__ stress reduction measures
__ signs and symptoms of ulcer recurrence and GI bleeding
__ date, time, and location of follow-up appointment
__ how to contact doctor.

DOCUMENTATION CHECKLIST
Using outcome criteria as a guide, document:
__ clinical status on admission
__ significant changes in status
__ pain-relief measures
__ nutritional intake and intolerances
__ pertinent diagnostic test findings
__ medication administration
__ patient teaching
__ discharge planning.

ASSOCIATED CARE PLANS
Esophagitis and Gastroenteritis
Fluid and Electrolyte Imbalances
Ineffective Individual Coping
Knowledge Deficit
Pain

REFERENCES
Alspach, J., and Williams, S. *Core Curriculum for Critical Care Nursing.* Philadelphia: W.B. Saunders Co., 1985.
Gastrointestinal Disorders. Nurse's Clinical Library. Springhouse, Pa.: Springhouse Corp., 1985.
Given, B., and Simons, S. *Gastroenterology in Clinical Nursing.* St. Louis: C.V. Mosby Co., 1984.
Sleisinger, M., and Fordstran, J. *Gastrointestinal Disease: Pathophysiology, Diagnosis, Management.* Philadelphia: W.B. Saunders Co., 1983.

Esophagitis and Gastroenteritis

DRG information

DRG 182 [Medical DRG] Esophagitis, Gastroenteritis, and Miscellaneous Digestive Disorders.
Age greater than 17. With Complication or Comorbidity (CC).
Mean LOS = 4.9 days

DRG 183 [Medical DRG] Esophagitis, Gastroenteritis and Miscellaneous Digestive Disorders.
Age 0 to 17. Without CC.
Mean LOS = 3.7 days

DRG 184 [Medical DRG] Esophagitis, Gastroenteritis, and Miscellaneous Digestive Disorders.
Age 0 to 17.
Mean LOS = 2.4 days

Introduction

DEFINITION AND TIME FOCUS

Esophagitis and gastroenteritis are nonspecific inflammatory conditions of the mucosa of the esophagus and the stomach and small bowel, respectively. Esophagitis is usually related to inadequacy of the cardiac sphincter of the stomach, resulting in reflux of gastric contents and subsequent irritation. Gastroenteritis is most commonly caused by bacteria or viruses that produce severe vomiting, diarrhea, and abdominal cramping. Both conditions may cause temporary discomfort (which would not require hospitalization) or serious, even life-threatening, illness if the patient is elderly, debilitated, or otherwise at increased risk. This care plan focuses on the patient admitted for diagnosis and treatment of acute esophagitis or gastroenteritis.

ETIOLOGY/PRECIPITATING FACTORS

• infectious agents—fungal (moniliasis), viral (herpes simplex), and bacterial (staphylococcus)
• drugs and chemical agents—reflux of gastric acid; bile reflux; ingestion of caustic substances (such as lye); medications such as aspirin, steroids, indomethacin, antibiotics
• physical or traumatic factors—excessive ingestion of alcohol, spicy foods, coffee; cigarette smoking; ingestion of very hot or very cold substances; nasogastric (NG) intubation; radiation therapy; trauma due to severe physical stress from surgery, sepsis, burns, accidents, heavy weight lifting; excessive emotional stress

Focused assessment guidelines

NURSING HISTORY (Functional health pattern findings)

Health perception–health management pattern

• may present with a variety of nonspecific symptoms
• symptoms may be acute, as from infection or ingestion of a caustic substance, or gradual, as in reflux esophagitis

• may have delayed seeking medical attention because of vagueness of symptoms as in reflux esophagitis
• may report tendency to self-medicate with multiple over-the-counter remedies available for GI upset
• may be receiving radiation therapy treatment for diabetes, scleroderma, or other disease process that makes esophageal or gastric mucosa more susceptible to infection and inflammation
• may be receiving treatment for sepsis, trauma, burns, immunologic disorder, endocrine disorder, liver disease, pancreatitis, or pulmonary disease

Nutritional-metabolic pattern

• *with esophagitis,* may report *heartburn, dysphagia, or odynophagia* (pain on swallowing); *with gastroenteritis,* typically complains of *epigastric or abdominal discomfort, nausea, vomiting, diarrhea, and/or fever*
• may report hematemesis and food regurgitation
• may report eructation and epigastric fullness following meals
• may report anorexia or weight loss
• mouth may appear swollen and inflamed
• may report history of excessive alcohol consumption, aspirin ingestion, cigarette smoking, or ingestion of caustic substance
• may report habitually eating excessive amounts of spicy foods, consuming very hot or cold susbtances, and eating late at night

Elimination pattern

• may report cramping, abdominal distention, diarrhea, increased flatus, and/or melena.

Activity-exercise pattern

• may report sudden or chronic fatigue

Sleep-rest pattern

• may report restlessness
• may report awakening at night because of pain or with regurgitated food on pillow

Cognitive-perceptual pattern

• pain intensity and description depend on cause of problem (for example, acute gastritis may cause epigastric discomfort and abdominal cramping, and caustic chemical ingestion may cause immediate localized pain and odynophagia)
• may report morning hoarseness (laryngitis)
• may report salty salivary secretions (water brash)
• if symptoms from ingestion of caustic substance, may report alteration in taste (from damage of salivary glands)

Coping–stress tolerance pattern

• may report high levels of stress at work or home

PHYSICAL FINDINGS
Gastrointestinal
- esophagitis
  - □ *hematemesis*
  - □ eructation
  - □ dysphagia
- gastroenteritis
  - □ *vomiting*
  - □ *diarrhea*
  - □ eructation
  - □ hyperactive bowel sounds
  - □ flatulence
  - □ hematemesis
  - □ melena

Cardiovascular (if hypovolemia present)
- hypotension
- tachycardia

Neurologic (if hypovolemia present)
- *dizziness*
- restlessness
- irritability

Integumentary (if hypovolemia present)
- pallor
- cool, clammy skin
- poor skin turgor

Musculoskeletal (when in pain)
- tense posture
- facial grimacing

DIAGNOSTIC STUDIES
- for esophagitis and gastroenteritis:
  - □ complete blood count (CBC)—may show decreased hemoglobin or hematocrit, possibly indicating GI blood loss; elevated white blood cell (WBC) count, possibly indicating infection or inflammation
  - □ serum electrolyte levels—may be studied to detect signs of fluid imbalance due to blood loss, vomiting, or diarrhea (hypokalemia common with significant vomiting or diarrhea)
  - □ serum amylase and lipase levels—elevations indicate pancreatitis as cause of symptoms

- for esophagitis:
  - □ *barium swallow—frequently detects inflammation, ulceration, strictures of the esophagus, and reflux of gastric contents*
  - □ *esophagoscopy—allows direct visualization of the esophagus* to detect inflammation, ulceration, strictures, and hiatal hernia; biopsy of mucosa or brushing for cytology may be used for tissue diagnosis
  - □ esophageal manometry—may reveal decreased esophageal sphincter pressure, as seen with gastroesophageal reflux; may detect peristaltic abnormalities responsible for infections or inflammatory changes in the esophagus
  - □ acid perfusion test (Bernstein test)—if patient has pain or burning during perfusion of acid (via tube) into esophagus, may indicate esophagitis
  - □ pH reflux test—a pH < 4 may indicate gastroesophageal reflux (normal pH of esophagus is > 5).
- for gastroenteritis:
  - □ *esophagogastroduodenoscopy—allows direct visualization of esophagus, stomach, and duodenum;* biopsy of mucosa or brushing for cytology may be performed for tissue diagnosis
  - □ *upper GI series—radiographically visualizes lining of esophagus, stomach, and duodenum; may detect inflammation, ulcerations, or strictures*
  - □ occult blood in stool may detect blood loss

POTENTIAL COMPLICATIONS
- for esophagitis:
  - □ ulcerative esophagitis
  - □ hemorrhage
  - □ esophageal stricture
  - □ aspiration pneumonia
  - □ Barrett's epithelium—columnar (gastric) epithelium in the esophagus resulting from chronic gastroesophageal reflux; patient is at great risk for developing adenocarcinoma of the esophagus
  - □ carcinoma of esophagus
  - □ inflammatory polyps of vocal cords
  - □ lung abscess
- for gastroenteritis:
  - □ hemorrhage
  - □ gastric or duodenal ulcer
  - □ gastric outlet obstruction

Nursing diagnosis: *Potential fluid volume deficit related to vomiting, diarrhea, or GI hemorrhage*

NURSING PRIORITY: Reestablish and maintain fluid and electrolyte balance.

Interventions

1. *Monitor and record the patient's vital signs* every 15 minutes if actively bleeding or every 4 hours if stable. Record orthostatic blood pressure (BP) and pulses every 8 hours.

Rationales

1. Tachycardia and hypotension may indicate hypovolemia or shock. To test for hypovolemia, take the patient's BP and pulse while supine. Then have the patient sit up and measure BP and pulse rate again. A BP decrease of 20 mm or more or a pulse rate increase of 20 beats/minute or more may indicate hypovolemia.

Interventions *continued*

2. *Withhold oral foods and fluids until vomiting has subsided. Begin I.V. fluids*, as ordered. Monitor CBC count and serum electrolyte levels, as ordered, and report abnormalities. See the "Fluid and Electrolye Imbalances" care plan, page 21.

3. *Medicate with antiemetics, antidiarrheals, vasopressin, and anticholinergics, as ordered.*

4. Monitor and record the effectiveness of medications.

5. Assess the skin for signs of dehydration—poor skin turgor, dry skin and mucous membranes, and pallor. Also assess for thirst.

6. *Monitor and record intake and output* each shift. Include all vomitus, diarrhea, tube drainage, and blood loss in output, and all blood products and I.V. fluids in input. Record hourly urine outputs in the unstable patient. Record daily weights. Test all GI output with guaiac reagent strips (Hemoccult).

7. Assess and record level of consciousness, muscle strength, and coordination at least every 8 hours. Report changes promptly.

8. Additional individualized interventions: _____

_____

_____

Rationales *continued*

2. Allowing the patient to eat and drink may cause more vomiting and lead to metabolic alkalosis, hypokalemia, or hyponatremia. The "Fluid and Electrolyte Imbalances" care plan provides details related to specific abnormalities.

3. Antiemetics, such as prochlorperazine (Compazine), promethazine (Phenergan), and chlorpromazine (Thorazine), prevent activation of the vomiting center of the brain stem. Side effects include sedation, blurred vision, and restlessness.
    Antidiarrheals, such as diphenoxylate with atropine (Lomotil), loperamide (Imodium), and kaolin and pectin (Kaopectate), may be used to decrease fluid loss from diarrhea. Lomotil and Imodium are synthetic opium alkaloids that decrease intestinal motility, thereby decreasing diarrhea. They are contraindicated in patients with obstruction or diarrhea caused by infectious agents.
    Because Kaopectate acts by adsorbing liquids and bacteria, toxins, nutrients, and drugs, loss of essential nutrients may occur with prolonged use.
    Vasopressin (Pitressin) may be used to control severe GI hemorrhage by constricting the splanchnic vein.
    Anticholinergics, such as dicyclomine hydrochloride (Bentyl), and propantheline bromide (Pro-Banthine), decrease gastric acid secretion and GI tone and motility and effectively control nausea and vomiting in acute gastritis. Side effects include urinary retention, dryness of mucous membranes (including dry mouth), dizziness, flushing, and headache.

4. Lack of effectiveness may indicate the need to reevaluate the pharmacologic regimen.

5. Poor skin turgor, dry skin and mucous membranes, and increased thirst may indicate hypovolemia. They result from decreased extracellular fluid volume.

6. Accurate monitoring of intake and output alerts caregivers to imbalances that may cause hypovolemic shock. Oliguria (< 30 ml of urine/hour) indicates a decrease in the glomerular filtration rate; this may result from decreased blood flow, as in hypovolemia. Weight loss may reflect fluid loss. Checking GI output for occult blood may provide early detection of GI bleeding.

7. Confusion, dizziness, or stupor may indicate hypovolemia and electrolyte imbalance. Signs reflect cerebral hypoxemia due to decreased circulating blood volume. Vomiting and diarrhea can cause electrolyte loss. Sodium loss may cause confusion and delirium; potassium loss may cause muscle weakness.

8. Rationale: _____

_____

_____

Outcome criteria

Within 2 hours of admission, the patient will:
• display stable vital signs
• have ceased vomiting
• maintain adequate urine output (> 60 ml/hour).

Nursing diagnosis: *Pain related to inflammation of the esophagus, stomach, and duodenum*

NURSING PRIORITY: Relieve pain.

Interventions

1. See the "Pain" care plan, page 64.

2. *Assess and document the pain's characteristics:* onset, location, duration, and severity of pain; radiation to back, neck, or shoulder; relationship to activity or position changes; and relationship to eating patterns, bowel movements, and ingestion of spicy foods, coffee, alcohol, hot or cold liquids, or certain medications. Assess and document pain-relief measures.

3. *Medicate, as ordered, with antacids* (typically administered hourly and 1 hour after meals), *histamine- (H₂) receptor antagonists* (administered 1 hour before meals and at least 30 minutes before sucralfate administration), *and sucralfate (Carafate).*

4. Monitor and record the effectiveness of medications.

5. Assist and instruct the patient to rest, physically and emotionally. Help the patient to identify personal stressors and ways to minimize their effects. Limit the number of visitors. Coordinate patient care to minimize interruptions. Keep room lights low. Teach stress-relieving techniques such as deep-breathing and relaxation exercises.

6. Instruct the patient and family about pain-prevention measures. If the patient awakens at night or the pain is worse on awakening, instruct the patient to sleep with the head of the bed elevated and to avoid eating for 2 to 3 hours before bedtime. Advise the patient to avoid bending, lifting heavy objects, and wearing constrictive

Rationales

1. General interventions for pain are provided in this plan. Pain associated with esophagitis and gastroenteritis may be subtle, as in abdominal cramping or heartburn, or may be more acute—for example, sharp, substernal pain similiar to angina.

2. Accurate assessment is important to assist the doctor in determining the cause of the pain and formulating a medical diagnosis. Substernal burning pain (heartburn, or pyrosis) and odynophagia are commonly associated with esophagitis. Epigastric pain while eating and abdominal cramping and tenderness are associated with acute gastritis.

3. Antacids are most effective if given 1 hour after meals to neutralize increased gastric acid secretion stimulated by food ingestion. Antacids are effective for about 30 minutes in the fasting stomach and should be given hourly for optimum neutralization of gastric acid. In case of severe pain, antacids may be given every 30 to 60 minutes.

H₂-receptor antagonists decrease gastric acid secretions and lower gastric pH by blocking H₂. They lose effectiveness if given with meals, antacids, or sucralfate, because of poor absorption.

Sucralfate provides a protective coating for the gastric lining and is not absorbed. It may be ordered crushed and mixed with water to form a slush that will provide a protective coating for the esophagus.

4. Lack of effectiveness of medications may indicate improper administration, inadequate dosage, the need to change medications, or new or complicating factors.

5. Stress causes stimulation of the vagus nerve. Vagal stimulation increases gastric mucosal blood flow, gastric acid secretion, and gastric motility. These factors may result in increased pain and inhibit the healing process.

6. Eating stimulates gastric acid secretion. The patient with esophagitis should avoid eating for 3 hours before bedtime and elevate the head of the bed to prevent reflux of gastric contents into the esophagus during sleep. Bending, lifting, wearing constrictive clothing, and straining decrease esophageal pressure and in-

Interventions *continued*

clothing. Use stool softeners, if prescribed, to avoid straining during bowel movements. Assess the diet and habits to help the patient identify known pain-causing items, such as spicy foods, alcohol, caffeine-containing products, aspirin, and smoking.

7. Additional individualized interventions: _____

_____

Rationales *continued*

crease intraabdominal pressure. Spicy foods, alcohol, caffeine-containing products, and aspirin cause irritation of the gastric lining and are associated with increased discomfort and should be avoided. Cigarette smoking stimulates increased gastric secretion, which may contribute to further inflammation.

7. Rationale: _____

_____

Outcome criteria
Within 2 hours of admission, the patient will:
• verbalize pain relief

• rest comfortably in a relaxing environment
• have stable vital signs.

Nursing diagnosis: *Nutritional deficit related to nausea and vomiting, dysphagia, and mouth soreness*

NURSING PRIORITY: Reestablish nutritional balance.

Interventions

1. Assess the patient's ability to retain oral food and fluids. Is nausea, vomiting, or regurgitation present? Is there dysphagia for solids, liquids, or both? Does the patient complain of pain or soreness in the mouth? Record all observations.

2. Monitor intake and output. Withhold oral foods and fluids until vomiting subsides. If hyperalimentation is ordered, infuse total parenteral nutrition (TPN) at prescribed rate. (See the "Total Parenteral Nutrition" care plan, page 265.) Administer oral nutritional and vitamin supplements as ordered. Record daily weights and calorie counts.

3. Explain the dilatation procedure, if ordered, for dysphagia, and assist when needed.

4. Assist the dietitian in teaching a well-balanced, nutritious diet. The patient with esophageal strictures may be unable to eat solid food and must be taught to puree foods and to drink nutritional supplements. The patient with acute gastritis may need to eat frequent, smaller meals instead of three large meals per day. Spicy foods, alcohol, and caffeine-containing products may need to be restricted. Record all patient teaching.

Rationales

1. Careful assessment of symptoms is helpful for differential diagnosis. Pain or soreness in the mouth may indicate fungal infection or occur after ingestion of a caustic substance. Dysphagia may result from stricture formation from reflux esophagitis or ingestion of a caustic substance.

2. If not withheld, food and fluids may stimulate more vomiting and cause potential complications, such as Mallory-Weiss tear (tearing of the esophageal mucosa, usually following forceful or prolonged vomiting). TPN may be indicated for a patient unable to take oral fluids for an extended period of time. The TPN care plan contains details about this therapy. Nutritional supplements are indicated for the patient with esophageal strictures who is unable to swallow solid foods and the patient who is unable to maintain metabolic balance because of anorexia, nausea, or mouth soreness.

3. Esophageal strictures, a frequent cause of dysphagia, result from esophagitis from ingestion of a caustic substance, from gastric reflux, or from chronic infection (for example, moniliasis). Carefully explaining the dilatation procedure will help alleviate anxiety. (Because dilatation procedures vary widely, details are not discussed here.)

4. Dietary instruction is directed toward returning the patient's weight to normal and establishing a nutritionally balanced diet. Thorough dietary teaching may prevent subsequent problems and complications. Careful documentation of teaching provides a record for other caregivers so that reinforcement and review may be provided, as appropriate.

(continued)

Interventions *continued*

5. Additional individualized interventions: _____

_____

_____

Rationales *continued*

5. Rationale: _____

_____

_____

Outcome criteria

Within 2 hours of admission, the patient will:
• verbalize relief of nausea and vomiting.

Within 24 hours of admission, the patient will:
• discuss nutritional needs with dietitian.

Discharge planning

NURSING DISCHARGE CRITERIA

Upon discharge, documentation shows evidence of:
• stable vital signs
• absence of pulmonary or cardiovascular complications
• hemoglobin and hematocrit within expected parameters
• ability to tolerate adequate nutritional intake
• absence of signs and symptoms indicating dehydration
• absence of pain
• urinary output and bowel function same as before onset of acute illness
• stabilizing weight
• ability to follow diet restrictions
• ability to ambulate and perform activities of daily living same as before hospitalization treatments.

PATIENT/FAMILY DISCHARGE TEACHING CHECKLIST

Document evidence that patient/family demonstrates understanding of:
___ disease process and implications
___ all discharge medications' purpose, administration schedule, dosage, and side effects requiring medical attention (usual discharge medications include antacids, H_2 antagonists, anticholinergics, or antifungal medications)
___ recommended dietary modifications or TPN instruction
___ recommended life-style modifications, including smoking cessation and stress reduction
___ importance of medical follow-up, which may include weekly visits for dilatation
___ how to contact doctor
___ signs and symptoms of complications
___ community resource referrals such as to Alcoholics Anonymous, as indicated.

DOCUMENTATION CHECKLIST

Using outcome criteria as a guide, document:
___ clinical status on admission
___ significant changes in status
___ description of pain
___ pain-relief measures
___ episodes of nausea and vomiting
___ description of vomitus
___ description of stools
___ bleeding episodes
___ intake and output
___ stress-relief measures

___ pertinent laboratory/diagnostic test findings
___ nutritional status
___ patient teaching
___ discharge planning.

ASSOCIATED CARE PLANS

Fluid and Electrolyte Imbalances
Ineffective Individual Coping
Knowledge Deficit
Pain
Total Parenteral Nutrition

REFERENCES

Bellack, Janis P. *Nursing Assessment: A Multidimensional Approach*. Belmont, Calif.: Wadsworth Publishing Co., 1984.

Berk, J. Edward. *Bockus Gastroenterology*, vol. 2, 4th ed. Philadelphia: W.B. Saunders Co., 1985.

Cohen, Sidney, and Soloway, Roger D. *Disease of the Esophagus*. New York: Churchill Livingstone, Inc., 1982.

Gastrointestinal Disorders. Nurse's Clinical Library. Springhouse, Pa.: Springhouse Corp., 1985.

Given, Barbara A., and Simmons, Sandra J. *Gastroenterology in Clinical Nursing*, 4th ed. St Louis: C.V. Mosby Co., 1984.

Inflammatory Bowel Disease

DRG information

DRG 179 [Medical DRG] Inflammatory Bowel Disease.
　　Mean LOS = 7 days
　　Principal diagnoses: proctocolitis, regional en-
　　teritis.
DRG 182 [Medical DRG] Esophagitis, Gastroenteritis,
　　and Miscellaneous Digestive Disorders.
　　Age greater than 17. With Complication or
　　Comorbidity (CC).
　　Mean LOS = 4.9 days
　　Principal diagnosis: diverticulitis
　　infectious diarrhea.
DRG 183 [Medical DRG] Esophagitis, Gastroenteritis,
　　and Miscellaneous Digestive Disorders.
　　Age greater than 17. Without CC.
　　Mean LOS = 3.7 days
DRG 184 [Medical DRG] Esophagitis, Gastroenteritis,
　　and Miscellaneous Digestive Disorders.
　　Age 0 to 17.
　　Mean LOS = 2.4 days

Introduction

DEFINITION AND TIME FOCUS

Inflammatory bowel disease (IBD) is a broad diagnostic
category that includes ulcerative colitis, Crohn's disease
(regional enteritis), appendicitis, diverticulitis, infectious diarrhea, functional bowel disorders, and humor-
ally mediated diarrheal syndromes. Hospitalized IBD
patients may be acutely ill and may demonstrate similar management problems. This clinical plan focuses on
the management problems associated with acute exacerbations of ulcerative colitis and regional enteritis.
Ulcerative colitis and regional enteritis involve the formation of local defects characterized by excavation of
the bowel surface from sloughing of necrotic inflammatory tissue. The ulcerations in regional enteritis are
transmural, involving all layers of the bowel; those of
ulcerative colitis begin in the crypts of Lieberkühn and
usually involve the mucosa and submucosa. The lesions
in ulcerative colitis are usually confined to the descending large bowel and sigmoid colon; the defects in
regional enteritis occur predominantly in, but are not
confined to, the terminal ileum.

ETIOLOGY/PRECIPITATING FACTORS

• exact etiology unknown—infectious agents, genetic or
familial tendencies, immunologic mechanisms, and
stress-related psychological factors may be involved
• stressful event, possibly preceding an acute attack by
4 to 6 months
• bacterial infection, possibly occurring several weeks
before an acute attack

Focused assessment guidelines

NURSING HISTORY (Functional health pattern findings)

Health perception–health management pattern

• may report gradual or acute onset of *abdominal cramping, anorexia, and weight loss* related to fear of intake of
food and fluids that increase cramping; *low-grade fever*
(may be high-grade if perforation present); change in
bowel habits with *increasing frequency of stools* (typically
with ulcerative colitis, stools may exceed 15/day, be accompanied by urgency and tenesmus, and contain
blood, mucus, or pus)
• may report a history of previous acute exacerbations
• may report being on a drug regimen that includes corticosteroids or immunosuppressants
• may report other family members with the disorder
• typically white, but an unexplained increase in blacks
with regional enteritis has been observed
• may demonstrate growth retardation (seen in persons
who report childhood onset of IBD)

Nutritional-metabolic pattern

• typically reports *anorexia with weight loss*
• may present with signs and symptoms of *chronic
malnutrition*
• may report intake of fatty foods or other dietary in-
discretions; if disease is chronic, may report being on
a low-residue, low-fiber, bland diet

Elimination pattern

• reports increasing frequency of bowel movements (may
have been gradual or acute in onset)
• reports *abdominal pain* and possible audible bowel
sounds (borborygmi) before onset of discomfort
• may report bright-red rectal bleeding with fecal incontinence, particularly with ulcerative colitis
• may exhibit visible peristaltic waves over the abdomen

Activity-exercise pattern

• typically reports *malaise and fatigue*
• may report *muscle weakness*

Sleep-rest pattern

• may report sleep disturbance related to abdominal
discomfort and nocturnal defecation

Self-perception–self-concept pattern

• may have low self-esteem, compensated for by ambitious, hard-driving life-style

Role-relationship pattern
• may use dependent behavior to cope with feelings of anger, hostility, and anxiety
• may report other family members with similar GI problems

Sexuality-reproductive pattern
• may demonstrate altered ability to cope with all phases of human relationships if disease chronic
• typically demonstrates delayed development of secondary sex characteristics and sexual function if onset of IBD before puberty
• may experience decreased fertility

Coping–stress tolerance pattern
• may express feelings of hopelessness and despair
• may use somatization (recurrent, multiple physical complaints with no organic cause), expressions of helplessness, crying, excessive demands on staff time, and excessive praise as mechanisms for individual coping

PHYSICAL FINDINGS
Cardiovascular
• *hypotension*
• *tachycardia*
• dysrhythmias

Renal
• *decreased output*
• fecal material in urine (if bladder fistula present)

Gastrointestinal
• *diarrhea*
• weight loss
• hyperactive or hypoactive bowel sounds
• abdominal tenderness and mass
• abdominal distention and rigidity
• rectal bleeding
• liver tenderness

Neurologic
• restlessness
• irritability
• blurred vision (uncommon)
• iritis (uncommon)
• conjunctivitis (uncommon)
• uveitis (uncommon)

Integumentary
• poor skin turgor
• pallor
• pustules (uncommon)
• erythematous lesions (uncommon)
• pyoderma gangrenosum (uncommon skin infection)
• icterus (if hepatitis present)
• draining fistulas (particularly around umbilicus or surgical scars)
• ecchymoses

Musculoskeletal
• muscle weakness
• joint pain and tenderness
• rheumatoid spondylitis (uncommon)

DIAGNOSTIC STUDIES
• *complete blood count—may reveal moderate elevation in white blood cell (WBC) count,* unless perforation is present, when there is a major elevation above normal, hematocrit and hemoglobin levels are decreased if there is chronic blood loss; if blood loss is sudden and dramatic, hematocrit and hemoglobin levels may not immediately reflect the change in blood volume; the red blood cell (RBC) count may demonstrate a megaloblastic anemia if the part of the ileum responsible for vitamin B absorption is affected
• *electrolyte profile—sodium, potassium, and chloride may be deficient* if there has been a persistent or acute loss of fluids from the GI tract with inadequate replacement
• *total protein levels—decreased* because a significant amount of protein is lost in inflammatory exudate in the bowel and through bleeding of damaged tissues, which can lead to depletion of albumin and other plasma proteins
• *blood urea nitrogen (BUN) level—increased* because significant nutritional deficits cause the catabolism of body proteins; reflected in negative nitrogen balance
• *bleeding and clotting time—prolonged* because decreased synthesis of vitamin K occurs as bowel surfaces are destroyed; liver involvement may lead to altered clotting mechanisms as synthesis of clotting factors is disturbed
• stool studies—culture and sensitivity testing and a search for ova and parasites are usually ordered to rule out an infectious origin for the symptoms; a guaiac test is usually positive for occult blood; fat may also be found in stools (steatorrhea) if bile reabsorption is impaired by the destruction of bowel surfaces
• liver function tests—hepatitis is a complication of IBD: Elevation of bilirubin and liver enzyme levels may be observed
• alkaline phosphatase levels—increased if arthritic skeletal involvement or hepatitis is present
• urine studies—culture and sensitivity testing may be ordered if a fistula to the bladder is suspected; opportunistic infections may also occur in the genitourinary (GU) tract from overall immunosuppression
• tuberculin skin test—tuberculosis of the cecum may mimic symptoms associated with IBD
• antibody titers—anticolon antibodies are frequently demonstrated in patients with ulcerative colitis but not usually observed in other IBD patients
• carcinoembryonic antigen (CEA)—may be ordered particularly for patients with ulcerative colitis, because there is a tendency for these patients to develop cancer of the colon after 10 years with the disorder
• *barium enema—in ulcerative colitis, demonstrates the characteristic obliteration of haustral folds, blurring of*

bowel margins, and narrowing and stenosis of the large bowel; regional enteritis, usually found in the small bowel, sometimes may occur in the large bowel, so distinguishing between the two disorders on the basis of a barium enema is difficult; procedure may be omitted if abscess or fistula is suspected because the bowel preparation for the procedure, and the procedure itself, may aggravate the existing pathology
• *protoscopy or colonoscopy—demonstrates hyperemic, edematous, friable mucosa* of the bowel; if lesion site is past the ileocecal valve, narrowing and stenosis of the valve may be evident
• rectal biopsy—inflammation and abcesses of the crypts are evident in ulcerative colitis; biopsy will usually be noncontributory in regional enteritis
• computed tomography (CT) scan—used to demonstrate abdominal masses that could be fistulas or abcesses
• upper GI series—lesions in regional enteritis can occur at any point along the GI tract and tend to alter-

nate with segments of normal tissue; upper GI series is done to judge the extent of involvement and to observe for segments where scarring and stenosis may have produced obstructions to intestinal flow
• skeletal X-rays—used to demonstrate the presence and extent of arthritic changes and ankylosing spondylitis, which can occur with IBD

POTENTIAL COMPLICATIONS
• malnutrition
• bowel obstruction
• dysrhythmias
• peritonitis
• hepatitis
• toxic megacolon
• malabsorption syndrome
• gangrenous skin lesions
• ankylosing spondylitis
• exudative retinopathy

Collaborative problem: *Potential cardiac dysrhythmias related to electrolyte depletion*

NURSING PRIORITY: Maintain electrolyte levels within normal limits.

Interventions

1. *Monitor and record fluid losses. Evaluate serum electrolyte levels daily, as ordered. Monitor apical and radial pulses, changes in tendon reflexes, and muscle strength* every 4 hours or more frequently, depending on the severity of the patient's condition.

2. *Administer and document electrolyte replacement therapy.*

3. *Notify the doctor immediately if there is evidence of dysrhythmias,* for example, pulse irregularity, syncopal episodes, or altered level of consciousness. See the "Fluid and Electrolyte Imbalances" care plan, page 21.

4. Additional individualized interventions: _____
_____
_____

Rationales

1. Diarrhea and internal fluid sequestration can cause significant electrolyte loss. Frequent observations for signs of alterations in the cellular membrane potential are necessary. Reminders to the doctor to order electrolyte determinations may also be necessary.

2. Normal saline or Ringer's lactate solution and potassium supplements usually are ordered during the acute stage, when oral replacement may be contraindicated.

3. Cardiac arrest can occur without warning in severe hypokalemia (or hyperkalemia). The "Fluid and Electrolyte Imbalances" care plan provides more details on specific imbalances.

4. Rationale: _____
_____
_____

Outcome criteria
Within 24 hours of admission, the patient will:
• show vital signs within normal limits.

Within 3 days of admission, the patient will:
• have serum electrolyte levels within normal limits
• display normal cardiac rate and rhythm.

Nursing diagnosis: *Potential fluid volume deficit related to decreased fluid intake, increased fluid loss through diarrhea or internal sequestration of fluid, or hemorrhage*

NURSING PRIORITY: Maintain fluid balance or replace fluid loss to improve cellular perfusion.

Interventions

1. *Institute and document hourly urine outputs with specific gravity determinations* in acutely ill patients. Report urine output <30 ml/hour.

2. *Maintain accurate records* of the type and amount of fluid lost.

3. *Monitor and record skin color, turgor, and temperature; level of consciousness; body temperature; and vital signs* every 1 to 4 hours, depending on the severity of the patient's condition. Note trends.

4. Auscultate and palpate the abdomen, and observe for increasing pain. Document evidence of distention and changes in bowel sounds.

5. *Administer and document fluid replacement,* as ordered.

6. Additional individualized interventions: _____
_____
_____

Rationales

1. Urine output and specific gravity determinations provide immediate, objective indication of the need for volume replacement. Weight loss may indicate loss of fluid volume.

2. The type and amount of fluid lost will guide replacement therapy.

3. A persistent or dramatic change in the parameters listed indicates either sequestration of fluid or blood volume loss. Hypovolemia is indicated by hypotension, tachycardia, and signs of decreased peripheral perfusion.

4. Sudden, acute distention, increased pain, and loss of (or diminished) bowel sounds can be early indications of serious bowel injury. Increased bowel sound activity may also indicate early obstruction or increasing tissue damage and inflammation.

5. The preferable method of fluid replacement is by mouth. However, the IBD patient may be too ill for this, or oral replacement may increase distressing symptoms. The I.V. fluids ordered are usually volume expanders such as normal saline solution. Whole blood or packed RBCs may also be ordered if hypotension is related to blood loss.

6. Rationale: _____
_____
_____

Outcome criteria
Within 24 hours of admission, the patient will:
• display vital signs within normal limits
• maintain urine output of at least 30 ml/hour
• show good skin turgor.

Within 3 days of admission, the patient will:
• maintain urine output within normal limits.

Nursing diagnosis: *Nutritional deficit related to decreased nutrient intake, increased nutrient loss, and possible interference with the absorptive state of the bowel*

NURSING PRIORITIES: (a) Maintain or increase body weight, and (b) improve general nutritional condition.

Interventions

1. *Estimate and document the extent of the nutritional deficit* using body weight; character, color, and texture of hair and skin; and the presence or absence of changes in visual acuity, corneal plaques, cracked and bleeding gums and mucous membranes, muscle wasting and weakness, anemia, and decreased BUN level.

Rationales

1. Rapidly reproducing cells, such as those of hair, skin, mucous membranes, and retinas, tend to be the first to demonstrate the changes characteristic of nutritional deficits. Later manifestations of a severe deficit include muscle wasting, weakness, decreased BUN level, and anemia.

Interventions *continued*

2. Collaborate with the patient, family, and other health team members to set goals and plan for normal nutrition maintenance.

3. Administer medications, as ordered, to control peristalsis before meals.

4. Serve small, frequent feedings rather than three large meals a day. Assess patient response.

5. Administer I.V. nutritional supplements (total parenteral nutrition, Intralipid, vitamins), as ordered. See the "Total Parenteral Nutrition" care plan, page 265, for further details.

6. Additional individualized interventions: _____

_____

_____

Outcome criteria

Within 2 days of admission, the patient will:
• comply with the agreed-upon treatment plan.

By the time of discharge, the patient will:
• reach mutually agreed-upon weight gain

Rationales *continued*

2. The IBD patient has a tendency to ignore dietary recommendations and may eat irritating foods. The IBD patient also learns to associate food and fluid intake with unpleasant sensations and may voluntarily decrease intake to avoid distressing symptoms. The patient and the family must be involved to comply with the treatment plan.

3. The presence of food in the gut stimulates peristalsis and causes increased discomfort and diarrhea. Diphenoxylate hydrochloride with atropine sulfate (Lomotil) or opium tincture, camphorated (Paregoric), is commonly used.

4. Small, frequent feedings tend to be better accepted and cause fewer distressing symptoms.

5. I.V. nutritional supplements are indicated for the IBD patient who cannot take anything by mouth, to rest the gut and promote healing. They are also indicated for the patient who is too compromised nutritionally to tolerate surgery. Vitamin B_{12} is useful in reversing anemia associated with decreased blood cell formation and for treating immunosuppression associated with chronic inflammation. The "Total Parenteral Nutrition" care plan contains details about I.V. nutritional supplements.

6. Rationale: _____

_____

_____

• perform activities of daily living (ADLs)
• tolerate diet without undue distress.

Nursing diagnosis: *Potential infection related to perforation of the bowel, immunosuppression, and general debilitated condition*

NURSING PRIORITY: Prevent opportunistic infections.

Interventions

1. Monitor and record vital signs, body temperature, bowel sounds, breath sounds, urine character and odor, and the presence or absence of abdominal distention, joint pain, hepatic tenderness, icterus, increasing malaise, and exudative skin or eye lesions.

2. Administer antibiotics, as ordered. See the "Osteomyelitis" care plan, page 309, for discussion of selected antibiotics.

3. Obtain specimens for culture and sensitivity testing, as ordered, before beginning antibiotic therapy.

Rationales

1. Patients with IBD are susceptible to many types of opportunistic infections. Close observation is necessary, because they may not demonstrate the typically dramatic rise in body temperature and WBC count because of medication-related immunosuppression and the condition's chronicity.

2. Typically, broad-spectrum antibiotics are ordered as a prophylactic measure.

3. Culture and sensitivity testing tend to be inaccurate when performed after initiation of antibiotic therapy.

(continued)

Interventions *continued*

4. Utilize careful aseptic technique for nursing procedures.

5. Question the doctor's orders for extensive bowel preparation for the patient with observed abdominal tenderness, abdominal masses, decreased or absent bowel sounds, or abdominal distention or rigidity.

6. Additional individualized interventions: _____

_____

_____

Rationales *continued*

4. IBD patients tend to be immunosuppressed, as noted previously.

5. Enemas and purgatives are irritants that can precipitate or exacerbate detrimental changes in the patient with acute abdominal pathology.

6. Rationale: _____

_____

_____

Outcome criteria
By time of discharge, the patient will:
• have normal body temperature
• show no signs of infection.

Nursing diagnosis: *Pain related to abdominal and possible skeletal pathology*

NURSING PRIORITY: Prevent or control pain.

Interventions

1. Assess and document complaints of pain. Be especially alert for sudden and severe abdominal pain, guarding, rigidity, or distention, and for vomiting, and report their occurrence to the doctor immediately.

2. Administer appropriate analgesic medication, as ordered. Teach the patient about nonpharmacologic pain control measures. See the "Pain" care plan, page 64.

3. Administer anti-inflammatory medications, as ordered, and document their therapeutic effects and side effects.

4. Additional individualized interventions: _____

_____

_____

Rationales

1. Changes in the character and severity of abdominal pain in the IBD patient may indicate life-threatening abdominal pathology, such as perforation of the GI tract.

2. Narcotic analgesics are administered judiciously to IBD patients because of these medications' tendency to mask potentially life-threatening pathology. Medications that inhibit GI motility and abdominal cramping, such as Lomotil or Paregoric, may be ordered. Skeletal discomfort related to arthritis is best handled with gentle exercise, warm soaks, and frequent repositioning, because many of the oral anti-inflammatory medications used to control skeletal pain are GI irritants contraindicated in IBD. The "Pain" care plan contains general interventions for pain control.

3. Control of IBD reduces distressing and painful symptoms. Common medications used to suppress inflammation include hydrocortisone sodium succinate (Solu-Cortef), methylprednisolone sodium succinate (Solu-Medrol), and dexamethasone (Decadron).

4. Rationale: _____

_____

_____

Outcome criteria
Within 3 days of admission, the patient will:
• decrease complaints of pain.

By the time of discharge, the patient will:
• verbalize rationale for pain-control measures
• use nonpharmacologic pain-control methods, as appropriate.

Nursing diagnosis: *Sleep pattern disturbance related to uncomfortable sensations, possible anxiety related to hospitalization, nocturnal defecation, or change in usual sleeping environment*

NURSING PRIORITY: Promote adequate rest and sleep.

Interventions

1. Assess for and modify environmental factors that interfere with sleep.

2. Avoid performing prolonged or painful procedures during at least the last hour before bedtime.

3. Group all nursing procedures that must be done during sleep periods.

4. Encourage the patient to express fears. Offer reassurance as appropriate.

5. Allow the patient to follow rituals that promote sleep at home.

6. Reposition the patient for comfort, and offer soothing back rubs.

7. Provide a bedside commode for use at night. Administer antidiarrheal medication at bedtime.

8. Additional individualized interventions: _____

Rationales

1. An unfamiliar sleeping environment may inhibit sleep.

2. Autonomic nervous system stimulation, with increased catecholamine secretion, may interfere with sleep.

3. The sleep cycle is 90 to 120 minutes long. Grouping nursing procedures allows the patient to complete sleep cycles.

4. Some patients may equate sleep with death. They may need to be reassured that staff will be available to meet their needs.

5. At home, most individuals follow sleep rituals, such as reading, that help them fall asleep.

6. If the patient is on bed rest, immobility can increase discomfort.

7. These measures help minimize sleep disturbance related to nocturnal defecation.

8. Rationale: _____

Outcome criteria

Within 2 days of admission, the patient will:
• verbalize feelings of being at ease and rested.

Throughout period of hospitalization, the patient will:
• experience adequate rest and sleep.

Nursing diagnosis: *Impaired skin integrity (perianal) related to frequent stools and a propensity for skin breakdown associated with altered nutritional status*

NURSING PRIORITY: Prevent skin breakdown.

Interventions

1. Institute and document a regimen of perianal care after each bowel movement.

2. Institute and document a regimen of skin care, based on the general condition of the patient, to be performed every 2 to 4 hours.

Rationales

1. The acid secretions and digestive enzymes from diarrhea quickly excoriate the perianal area. A protective ointment (such as A&D) is commonly used because the skin is vulnerable to breakdown.

2. Anticipating and preventing skin breakdown on other body surfaces is important, because tissue damage will heal slowly, if at all, in the critically ill IBD patient.

(continued)

Interventions *continued*

3. Maintain and document food and fluid intake, paying special attention to protein comsumption.

4. Additional individualized interventions: _____

_____

_____

Rationales *continued*

3. Adequate intake of nutrients (especially protein) and fluids is necessary for tissue repair.

4. Rationale: _____

_____

_____

Outcome criterion
By time of discharge, the patient will
• show no evidence of skin breakdown.

Nursing diagnosis: *Social isolation related to nonfunctional behavior (dependency)*

NURSING PRIORITIES: (a) Decrease use of nonfunctional behavior, and (b) facilitate direct expression of feelings.

Interventions

1. Identify nonfunctional behavior for patient, self, staff, and family.

2. Collaborate with staff and family to set limits on unacceptable behavior. Ensure that all staff members agree to maintain the limits and to share mutual concerns with each other.

3. Avoid bargaining about or justifying limits. Enforce them without apology.

4. Discuss the patient's feelings concerning limits. Encourage expression of feelings of anxiety, hostility, and anger.

5. Investigate somatic complaints immediately and matter-of-factly.

6. If behavioral problems persist, arrange a referral for the patient to a psychiatric clinical nurse specialist or other mental health professional.

7. Additional individualized interventions: _____

_____

_____

Rationales

1. Dependent behavior may be manifested by crying, expressions of hopelessness, endless requests for staff attention, or excessive praise of staff. Although such behavior represents an attempt to control and manage underlying feelings of anger, hostility, and anxiety, it often provokes social isolation, which only reinforces negative feelings.

2. Specific limit setting and consistent enforcement allow the patient to know exactly what is expected and interrupts the cycle of dependency and isolation. Dependent patients may attempt to turn staff against each other by using manipulative behavior.

3. Engaging in dialogue concerning limits creates doubt about their enforcement.

4. The patient may have an impaired ability to identify feelings. A nonjudgmental atmosphere provides a way to recognize and discuss uncomfortable emotions.

5. Somatization is an attention-getting behavior used by people with inadequate coping skills. The seriousness of the illness warrants investigation of complaints; avoid prolonged discussions of physical complaints, however, and focus instead on the patient's feelings.

6. A mental health professional can offer expertise for dealing with manipulative behavior and the staff's negative response to such behavior.

7. Rationale: _____

_____

_____

Outcome criteria
By the time of discharge, the patient will:
• decrease use of ineffective coping behaviors
• express anger, hostility, and anxiety appropriately.

Nursing diagnosis: *Potential altered sexuality patterns related to diminished physical energy and persistence of uncomfortable physical symptoms*

NURSING PRIORITY: Encourage the discussion and expression of sexual desires.

Interventions

1. Initiate discussion about values, beliefs, and feelings concerning sexuality. Assess for sexual dysfunction. Include the patient's spouse or partner in discussions, if possible.

2. Allow the patient to discuss feelings, values, and beliefs concerning sexuality in a nonjudgmental atmosphere. It is important to be aware of one's own feelings about sexuality. If the nurse is too uncomfortable to counsel the patient and spouse or partner effectively, an appropriate referral should be made.

3. To the extent possible, allow the patient and spouse or partner uninterrupted private time together.

4. Construct a teaching plan for sexual expression. Address energy-conserving positions for intercourse, timing activity to coincide with peak energy, alternatives to intercourse, specific patient concerns, and potential interactions between contraceptives and medications used to treat IBD.

5. Additional individualized interventions: _____
_____
_____

Rationales

1. Discussions concerning sexuality are difficult for many patients to initiate, although the topic may be of considerable concern. It is the nurse's responsibility to anticipate that altered sexual function is common in patients with chronic or debilitating illnesses, who have diminished energy and persistent, uncomfortable physical sensations. The IBD patient may also be facing surgery for fecal diversion; thus, body image changes and altered sexual function should be anticipated.

  The patient may or may not have an open communication pattern with the spouse or partner. Both may welcome frank discussions of sexual matters.

2. The nurse's values and beliefs concerning sexual behavior may—but should not—interfere with the ability to provide professional care.

3. Sexuality can be expressed in many forms besides sexual intercourse, such as cuddling and fondling. The IBD patient may be hospitalized for prolonged periods of time; the need for privacy to express intimate feelings should not be overlooked.

4. The sexual intercourse guidelines for cardiac patients can be modified to meet the needs of the patient with chronic IBD who has diminished physical energy and uncomfortable physical sensations. Patient teaching should also cover the potential interactions between various types of contraceptives and the medications used to treat chronic IBD.

5. Rationale: _____
_____
_____

Outcome criteria
By time of discharge, the patient will:
• discuss sexual feelings openly with partner

• identify techniques for minimizing physical demands of sexual activity.

Discharge planning
NURSING DISCHARGE CRITERIA
Upon discharge, documentation shows evidence of:
• absence of fever
• absence of signs and symptoms of infection
• stable vital signs
• ability to tolerate oral nutritional intake
• I.V. lines discontinued for at least 24 hours before discharge
• stabilized weight

• ability to control pain using oral medications
• ability to perform perianal care
• controlled bowel movements
• absence of skin breakdown
• electrolyte levels within acceptable parameters
• ability to ambulate and perform ADLs
• adequate home support system, or referral to home care if indicated by inability to perform ADLs and perianal care independently, by inadequacy of the home support system, or by the need for reinforcement of teaching.

PATIENT/FAMILY DISCHARGE TEACHING CHECKLIST

Document evidence that the patient/family demonstrates understanding of:

___ extent of GI pathology

___ all discharge medications' purpose, dose, administration schedule, and side effects requiring medical attention. Usual discharge medications include steroids and immunosuppressants.

___ recommended dietary modifications. Usual diet is low fiber, low residue, and bland.

___ community support groups and resources, including an ostomy club, when appropriate

___ resumption of normal role activity

___ signs and symptoms indicating exacerbation of illness

___ date, time, and location of follow-up appointments

___ how to contact doctor.

DOCUMENTATION CHECKLIST

Using outcome criteria as a guide, document:

___ clinical status on admission

___ significant changes in status

___ pertinent laboratory and diagnostic findings

___ pain-relief measures

___ I.V. line patency

___ fluid intake

___ acute abdominal pain episodes

___ use of emergency protocols

___ nutritional intake

___ other therapies

___ patient/family teaching

___ discharge planning.

ASSOCIATED CARE PLANS

Colostomy
Fluid and Electrolyte Imbalances
Grief/Grieving
Ineffective Individual Coping
Pain
Total Parenteral Nutrition

REFERENCES

Beyers, M., and Dudas, S. *The Clinical Practice of Medical Surgical Nursing*. Boston: Little, Brown & Co., 1984.

Diagnostics, 2nd ed. Nurse's Reference Library. Springhouse, Pa.: Springhouse Corp., 1986.

Doenges, M., et al. *Nursing Care Plans: Nursing Diagnoses in Planning Patient Care*. Philadelphia: F.A. Davis Co., 1984.

Hui, Y. *Human Nutrition and Diet Therapy*. Belmont, Calif.: Wadsworth Publishing Co., 1983.

Keithly, J. "Nutritional Assessment of the Patient Undergoing Surgery," *Heart & Lung* 14(5):449-55, September 1985.

Long, B., and Phipps, W. *Essentials of Medical Surgical Nursing: A Nursing Process Approach*. St. Louis: C.V. Mosby Co., 1985.

Mathewson, M. *Pharmacotherapeutics*. Philadelphia: F.A. Davis Co., 1986.

Schultz, J., and Dark, S. *Manual of Psychiatric Nursing Care Plans*. Boston: Little, Brown & Co., 1986.

Total Parenteral Nutrition

DRG information

DRG 172 Digestive Malignancy.
With Complication or Comorbidity (CC).
Mean LOS = 6.9 days

DRG 173 Digestive Malignancy.
Without CC.
Mean LOS = 4.3 days

DRG 182 Esophagitis, Gastroenteritis, and Miscellaneous Digestive Disorders. Age greater than 17. With CC.
Mean LOS = 4.9 days
Principal diagnosis: ileus

DRG 188 Other Digestive System Diagnoses. Age greater than 17. With CC.
Mean LOS = 4.9 days
Principal diagnosis: intestinal fistula

DRG 205 Disorders of Liver Except Malignancy, Cirrhosis, and Alcoholic Hepatitis.
With CC.
Mean LOS = 6.7 days
Principal diagnosis: pancreatitis

Additional DRG information: Total parenteral nutrition (TPN) is used to treat numerous diagnoses. The diagnosis necessitating its use will determine the DRG assigned. Examples of diagnoses and DRGs that may indicate TPN are listed above. Several others associated with cancer could also require TPN but were omitted here for brevity.

Introduction

DEFINITION AND TIME FOCUS

TPN is the supplying of nutrients solely via the central venous system in sufficient quantities to maintain or replete body cell mass and promote anabolism. (The term central venous alimentation is also used for this method of providing nutrients.) The patient requiring TPN generally exhibits one of four problems:
• cannot eat—the patient may have an obstruction or ileus at any point along the GI tract or may be at risk for aspiration if fed orally
• will not eat—the geriatric, cancer, or anorexic patient may be unwilling to ingest food
• should not eat—the patient may have a disease or condition aggravated by oral intake, such as intestinal fistula, severe pancreatitis, small-bowel obstruction, or inflammatory bowel disease
• cannot eat enough—this condition is related to the severity of disease or degree of injury: Sufficient nutrients cannot be provided by the enteral route. Examples are short-bowel syndrome, multiple trauma, and major burns.
TPN is indicated when:
• The enteral route for nutritional support is unattainable.

• The patient has lost 10% to 15% of body weight.
• The patient is not permitted food or fluids for more than 7 days.
Safe delivery of TPN depends on four basic principles of care:
• aseptic technique in catheter placement
• aseptic technique in catheter care
• proper preparation and delivery of the TPN solution
• careful patient monitoring.
This clinical plan focuses on the patient who requires TPN to maintain nutritional status during hospitalization.

Focused assessment guidelines

NURSING HISTORY (Functional health pattern findings)

Health perception–health management pattern
• may be *chronically ill or have an acute condition that increases nutritional needs*

Activity-exercise pattern
• may report *decreased energy level*
• may report *generalized weakness* or weak extremities related to muscle wasting

Nutritional-metabolic pattern
• may report nausea, vomiting, diarrhea, or constipation
• may report lack of appetite
• may report recent weight loss
• may report lack of interest in food
• may have improperly fitting dentures
• may be chronically thirsty
• may prefer salty beverages

PHYSICAL FINDINGS

Note: The clinical signs of malnutrition are rarely observed and may not be recognized as clinically significant.

Musculoskeletal
• *generalized muscle wasting and weakness* (muscle mass and major organs are spared unless patient has moderate to severe malnutrition)
• edematous extremities

Integumentary
• skin—subcutaneous fat loss, scaly dermatitis (primarily on legs and feet), pellagrous dermatitis, seborrheic dermatitis of face, nasolabial seborrhea (greasy and scaly skin of the nasolabial folds of the nose, from riboflavin deficiency), follicular hyperodosis (thinning of the innermost layer of the epidermis, possibly from vitamin A deficiency), dilated veins, petechiae, purpura, poor skin turgor, dry mucous membranes

SIGNIFICANCE OF LABORATORY TESTS USED TO MONITOR TOTAL PARENTERAL NUTRITION

■ **glucose**—serum levels may be elevated above 200 mg/dl when TPN infusion is begun, decreasing to 150 to 200 mg/dl after 24 to 48 hours as body adjusts to increased glucose load. (Serum glucose levels > 200 mg/dl indicate glucose intolerance or hyperglycemia. Levels < 60 mg/dl indicate hypoglycemia, the more dangerous of the two states; without glucose, the brain cannot function and death is imminent if the hypoglycemic state continues.)

■ **electrolytes**—sodium, potassium, and chloride levels obtained for baseline and as guide for replacement therapy. (Fluid and electrolyte management is the most important aspect of TPN, because the patient requiring nutritional repletion typically has fluid and electrolyte abnormalities. Electrolytes are provided as needed to replace loss from fistulas, nasogastric [NG] drainage, diarrhea, or excessive output or—in an appropriate ratio—to promote lean muscle mass, nutritional repletion, and positive nitrogen balance.)

■ **magnesium**—low serum levels may occur in intestinal malabsorption syndrome, bowel resection, intestinal fistula, or in patients with extended NG suction. (Magnesium requirements increase with nutritional repletion related to new tissue synthesis: 0.35 to 0.45 mEq/kg/day is sufficient to prevent magnesium depletion in patients receiving TPN. Magnesium levels need to be monitored at least every week and twice a week for patients in renal failure. The normal range of magnesium is 1.4 to 2.2 mEq/liter.)

■ **phosphorus**—low serum levels occur in patients receiving TPN because of increased use of phosphorus for glucose metabolism. (For each kilocalorie of TPN administered, 2 mEq/dl of phosphorus is required. Serum levels should be measured once a week. Serum phosphorus levels below 1 mg/dl will produce clinical signs and symptoms of hypophosphatemia. The normal range is 2.5 to 4.5 mg/dl.)

■ **transferrin**—serum level of 150 to 200 mg/dl indicates mild, 100 to 149 mg/dl moderate, and < 100 mg/dl severe visceral protein depletion. (Serum transferrin is a protein synthesized by the liver. Serum concentrations fall rapidly with starvation and stress over approximately 8 days. Serial serum transferrin levels indicate response to nutritional therapy.)

■ **total iron-binding capacity** (TIBC)—followed serially, indicates if nutritional support is correcting the nutritional state. (Iron binds to transferrin transported in the blood.)

■ **albumin**—serum level < 3 gm/dl correlates with increased severity of illness. (2.8 to 3.5 gm/dl indicates mild, 2.1 to 2.7 gm/dl moderate, and < 2.1 gm/dl severe visceral protein depletion. Because the albumin level falls slowly, it is not considered a reliable early indicator of malnutrition.)

■ **24-hour urine urea excretion**—indicates the severity of protein catabolism. 4 to 10 gm/day is normal; > 10 gm/day in a patient with major injuries or sepsis indicates hypermetabolism and a need for increased calories or nitrogen for repair of tissues. In a patient who is stable, has no injuries, and is gaining weight, a 24-hour urine urea > 10 gm/day can be an indication of overfeeding. (To ensure a positive nitrogen balance in the catabolic patient, approximately 4 to 6 gm of nitrogen is given in excess of the amount excreted in the urine.)

■ **total lymphocyte count (TLC)**—helps evaluate immunocompetence; 1,200 to 2,000/mm³ indicates mild, 800 to 1,199/mm³ moderate, and < 800/mm³ severe lymphocyte depletion. (Severe depletion indicates inadequate antibody production and impairment of the ability to fight infection. Nutritional repletion is indicated to improve the body's defense mechanisms. TLC is not an accurate indicator of nutritional status in patients on immunosuppressive therapy.)

■ **creatinine height index**—indirectly measures depletion of muscle mass; 60% to 80% of normal represents moderate protein depletion; < 60% indicates severe depletion. (Creatinine excretion varies directly according to loss of skeletal muscle mass; creatinine height index is obtained by comparing creatinine and height/weight ratio with charts listing normal creatinine excretion for height and weight.)

■ **skin-test antigens**—evaluate cell-mediated immunity, which can decrease with severe malnutrition. (This may be assessed using skin-test antigens such as mumps, *Candida*, streptokinase, or streptodornase. If a negative reaction occurs, malnutrition may be the cause, and there are no defense mechanisms in the body to fight infection. A positive reaction is considered to be induration exceeding 5 mm or more, in response to at least two antigens, within 24 to 48 hours.)

• hair—pluckability, lack of luster, alopecia, sparsity, decreased pigmentation
• nails—brittleness, lines, rigidity, thinness, flattened or spoon-shaped

Eye
• xerosis (dryness) of conjunctivae
• keratomalacia (a condition linked to vitamin A deficiency that causes softening of the cornea; early signs include xerotic spots on conjunctivae and xerotic, insensitive, and hazy cornea)
• corneal vascularization
• blepharitis (scaling inflammation of eyelid edges)
• Bitot's spots (conjunctival spots which are gray and triangular, linked to vitamin A deficiency)

• "spectacle eye" (inflammation of the periorbital skin associated with deficiency in the vitamin B complex [biotin])

Neurologic
• *lethargy*
• hyporeflexia
• decreased proprioception
• disorientation
• confabulation
• paresthesias
• weakness of legs
• irritability
• convulsions

DIAGNOSTIC PROCEDURES IN TOTAL PARENTERAL NUTRITION

■ chest X-ray (following catheter placement)—verifies catheter placement in the superior vena cava before TPN is begun.

■ basal energy expenditure—provides data used to estimate the patient's daily caloric needs. There are several methods of determining basal expenditure (the number of calories required for maintenance of weight at rest). Among them, the Harris-Benedict equation uses height, weight, sex, and age to determine the required energy expenditure to maintain weight while at rest. The dietitian then adds a factor for the stress the patient is experiencing (sepsis, multiple trauma, surgery) to arrive at the number of calories needed to promote anabolism. Indirect calorimetry determines energy expenditure by measuring carbon dioxide production and oxygen consumption with a gas analyzer connected to a tube into which the patient breathes. The amount of oxygen consumed and the carbon dioxide produced indicate the number of calories being expended at the time—the resting energy expenditure. Measurement of energy expenditure by this method is time-consuming, and there are many potential sources of error. (For example, test results may be inaccurate if the face mask does not fit.) More studies are needed to determine the effectiveness and accuracy of this method of calculating energy expenditure.

■ height/weight ratio—85% or less of the expected value indicates significant protein-calorie malnutrition. (Height and weight are the most significant factors in determining malnutrition.) In the Harris-Benedict equation, the height/weight ratio of the patient is used to predict calorie expenditure. In the creatinine/height ratio, it is used to predict skeletal muscle loss. The height/weight ratio is compared with the historical height/weight ratio of the patient to determine the severity of malnutrition and the preferred method of refeeding the patient.

■ skin-fold measurements (such as triceps skin fold)—provide an estimation of body fat reserves. Measurements are compared with a standard table of values: 35% to 40% of normal indicates mild; 25% to 34%, moderate; and < 25%, severe fat depletion.

■ midarm circumference (MAC) and midarm muscle circumference (MAMC)—estimate fat and skeletal muscle mass; measurements are compared to a standard table: 35% to 40% of normal indicates mild depletion of muscle and fat; 25% to 34%, moderate depletion; and < 25%, severe depletion. MAMC is calculated using MAC and skin-fold measurements and evaluated in comparison with standard tables.

• flaccid paralysis
• confusion

Gastrointestinal
• tongue—baldness, glossitis, edema
• lips—cheilosis, angular stomatitis

Glandular
• parotid enlargement
• thyroid enlargement

DIAGNOSTIC STUDIES
See *Significance of Laboratory Tests Used to Monitor Total Parenteral Nutrition* and *Diagnostic Procedures in Total Parenteral Nutrition.*

POTENTIAL COMPLICATIONS
• sepsis
• mechanical injury from catheter
  □ pneumothorax, hemothorax
  □ arterial puncture
  □ air emboli
  □ catheter emboli
  □ catheter and venous thrombosis
• metabolic disorders
  □ hypoglycemia
  □ fluid and electrolyte abnormalities
  □ hyperglycemia
  □ essential fatty acid deficiency

Nursing diagnosis: *Potential for injury related to complications of TPN catheter insertion, displacement, use, or removal*

NURSING PRIORITY: Prevent or promptly treat complications that may result from TPN catheter.

Interventions

1. *Observe for signs and symptoms of respiratory distress and shock during insertion of the central venous catheter (CVC),* including tachypnea, tachycardia, dropping systolic blood pressure, dyspnea, use of accessory muscles for respiration, and decreased or absent breath sounds on side of insertion.

Rationales

1. The lungs or an artery may be punctured during subclavian venous cannulation. The artery may bleed to the point of compressing the trachea, precipitating life-threatening respiratory distress. A puncture of the lung creates a pneumothorax, causing respiratory compromise related to entry of air into the pleural space and collapse of all or part of the lung on the venipuncture side.

(continued)

Interventions *continued*

2. *Maintain the patient in Trendelenburg's position during CVC insertion.*

3. After CVC insertion, *assess for bilateral breath sounds in all lung fields* and *ensure that a chest X-ray is obtained.* Monitor the patient's respiratory status and breath sounds at least every 8 hours thereafter.

4. *Do not begin administering the TPN solution until the position of the catheter tip is confirmed by chest X-ray.*

5. *Use standardized Luer-Lok connections attached properly, or tape the connections securely.*

6. *Before opening the I.V. system to the air, instruct the patient to hold the breath and bear down* (Valsalva's maneuver). If the patient is unable to perform Valsalva's maneuver, change the tubing only during exhalation.

7. *Observe for signs and symptoms of large air emboli,* such as extreme anxiousness, sharp chest pain, cyanosis, or churning precordial murmur.

If air emboli are suspected, position the patient in Trendelenburg's position on the left side, administer oxygen, and notify the doctor immediately.

8. *During dressing changes, observe for a suture at the insertion site of a temporary CVC, a suture at the exit site of a permanent CVC, or increased external catheter length.*

9. *Observe for inability to withdraw blood; the patient's complaint of chest pain or burning; leaking fluid; and swelling around the insertion site, shoulder, clavicle, and upper extremity.*

10. *Observe for development of visible collateral circulation on the chest wall.*

11. *When the catheter is being removed, be sure that:*

• *the patient is supine*

Rationales *continued*

2. Trendelenburg's position causes increased venous pressure in the upper half of the body. This prevents air influx into the venous system through the insertion needle or I.V. catheters when their lumens are open to air.

3. Bilateral breath sounds and symmetrical pain-free chest movement indicate fully inflated lungs. Chest X-ray confirms placement of the catheter tip in the superior vena cava and rules out hemothorax, chylothorax (from puncture of a lymph vessel), and pneumothorax.

4. The hyperosmolar nature of TPN solution is irritating to veins smaller than the superior vena cava. Thrombophlebitis can result if the TPN solution is infused into the jugular, subclavian, or innominate vein.

5. Secure connections are essential to prevent accidental tubing disconnection. Accidental disconnection may cause bleeding, loss of catheter patency from clot formation, air emboli, hub contamination, and/or sepsis.

6. Valsalva's maneuver increases intrathoracic pressure, forcing blood through the area of least resistance (in this case, the catheter) and preventing inflow of air. Air will enter the catheter only as the patient inhales. (Negative intrathoracic pressure allows the lungs to fill with air. If the I.V. catheter is open to the air during inhalation, air also can be pulled into the bloodstream.)

7. Small amounts of air may be asymptomatic. Large amounts, however, may cause an air lock in the heart, in which case no blood can pass into or out of the heart. The patient may die from cardiac arrest related to blocked blood flow and resultant ischemia.

Trendelenburg's and the left lateral decubitus positions allow air to collect at the apex of the right ventricle. Small amounts of air may pass into the pulmonary circulation and be reabsorbed. Large amounts of air causing air lock in the heart may need to be aspirated through a catheter passed into the right atrium.

8. A suture at the insertion or exit site stabilizes the catheter. Increased external catheter length indicates movement and possible catheter displacement.

9. These may indicate catheter displacement and vein thrombosis.

10. Development of collateral circulation on the chest wall is a sign of vein thrombosis.

11. Conscientious attention to the removal technique is important for several reasons:

• The supine position allows a clear view while removing stitches and the catheter and applying a sealed dressing.

Interventions *continued*

• *the patient performs Valsalva's maneuver before the catheter is removed*

• *completely sealed airtight dressing is applied over the insertion site after the CVC is discontinued.*

12. *When the catheter is discontinued, measure its length and observe for jagged edges.*

13. Additional individualized interventions: _____
_____
_____

Rationales *continued*

• Air can be sucked in through the CVC sinus tract if the catheter is pulled out during inhalation, causing air emboli.

• The CVC sinus tract allows air to enter the venous system with each inhalation if an airtight dressing is not applied.

12. To ensure that the entire catheter was removed, the catheter should be measured and observed for integrity.

13. Rationale: _____
_____
_____

Outcome criteria
While the CVC is in place, the patient will:
• exhibit unrestricted, pain-free inhalation and exhalation
• exhibit symmetrical chest movement
• exhibit normal respiration

• present normal chest X-ray
• have a patent catheter
• show no fluid infiltration
• show no evidence of catheter emboli.

Nursing diagnosis: *Nutritional deficit related to inability to ingest nutrients orally, inability to digest nutrients optimally, and/or increased metabolic need for nutrients*

NURSING PRIORITY: Provide for adequate nutritional intake.

Interventions

1. *Keep TPN at a constant rate of infusion* with an infusion pump.

• Check the bag, rate, and patient every half hour.

• Do not interrupt the flow of TPN solution.

• Do not "catch up" if the I.V. is behind or "slow down" if it is ahead of schedule. Set the I.V. infusion to the ordered rate.

Rationales

1. The infusion pump regulates the flow rate with greater accuracy, decreasing the likelihood of accidentally infusing a bag of TPN solution over a short time.
• This prevents a hyperglycemic, hyperosmolar load. (The hyperosmolar state results in an osmotic diuresis that can lead to dehydration, lethargy, and coma.)
• Turning TPN on and off at intervals creates fluctuations in the serum glucose level. The body responds to the high or low serum glucose level by altering the secretion of glucagon and insulin from the pancreas. This system keeps the serum glucose level within the normal range; if the changes in rate are made too quickly, the body cannot adjust to the demand, so signs and symptoms of hypoglycemia or hyperglycemia may occur.
• If TPN on gravity drip has slowed from the accurate drip rate, there will be less glucose circulating in the blood and a decreased secretion of insulin to handle the glucose. A rapid infusion of TPN results in a rapid rise in serum glucose to above normal levels without a corresponding increase in insulin production. (The body takes ½ to 1 hour to sense the high serum glucose level and respond by increasing insulin production. Insulin decreases serum glucose levels by transporting glucose into the cell to be converted to glycogen for storage.)
  The physiologic effect of high serum glucose levels is dehydration. Water is drained out of the interstitial spaces into the vascular system in an attempt to equal-

(continued)

Interventions continued

• When discontinuing TPN, lower the rate to 50 ml/hour for 3 to 4 hours.

2. Ensure that the TPN does not stop suddenly or take appropriate corrective action:
• *From a clotted catheter, hang dextrose 10% in water* in another I.V. site to infuse at same rate TPN was infusing
• *during cardiopulmonary arrest, stop the TPN infusion and provide one or more boluses of dextrose 50%, as ordered.*

3. *Monitor urine glucose and acetone* every 6 hours.

4. *Monitor serum glucose levels,* as ordered.

5. *Observe for signs and symptoms of the following problems:*

• *hypoglycemia*—weakness; agitation; tremors; cold, clammy skin; urine tests negative for sugar and acetone; and serum glucose level < 60 mg/dl
• *hyperglycemia*—thirst, acetone breath, diuresis, dehydration; urine positive for glucose; serum glucose level above 200 mg/dl; and urine varying from negative to large amounts of acetone

Rationales continued

ize serum and interstitial glucose levels. This results in dehydrated interstitial spaces, causing excessive thirst and hunger. The increased vascular volume is sensed by the kidneys, which excrete the excess fluid and glucose. The dehydrated state, if not treated, will lead to lethargy, confusion, and coma.
• Slowing the TPN rate to 50 ml/hour for 3 to 4 hours allows the body to sense the lower serum glucose level and adjust to it. The pancreas responds by decreasing insulin production. These mechanisms prevent development of hypoglycemia, which can occur it TPN is discontinued too rapidly.

2. If the TPN infusion stops suddenly, another source of glucose must be supplied to prevent hypoglycemia. The high levels of insulin in the bloodstream will deplete the serum glucose level to <60 mg/dl within an hour.
• Brain cells cannot function without glucose as an energy source. Another source of I.V. glucose prevents a rapid drop in the serum glucose level.
• This precaution prevents accidentally giving a bolus of TPN during an emergency situation. One or more boluses of dextrose prevents hypoglycemia and allows more control. A rapidly decreasing serum glucose level in an emergency situation may otherwise go unnoticed.

3. Monitoring urine glucose and acetone evaluates the patient's tolerance of the glucose load being infused. Positive urine checks may indicate an excessive load or impending sepsis, among the most stressful of physiologic events. To handle the stress, the body increases the amount of glucose available for energy.

4. Monitoring serum glucose levels evaluates the patient's tolerance of the glucose load being infused. Levels >200 mg/dl may indicate that the body is not utilizing glucose, and additional insulin may be necessary to increase conversion of glucose to glycogen. Levels >200 mg/dl also may indicate new stressors. Medications, surgery, and sepsis are all stressors that may result in hyperglycemia.

5. The complex nature of TPN therapy is associated with a wide variety of potential complications:
• The brain cannot survive without glucose. Death may occur within an hour if glucose levels are not restored to normal.
• Monitoring signs and symptoms of hyperglycemia helps to identify glucose intolerance early and investigate the cause. This may be related to a new stress such as sepsis. Unchecked, hyperglycemia leads to osmolar diuresis, causing dehydration, thirst, confusion, lethargy, convulsions, and coma.

SIGNS AND SYMPTOMS OF VITAMIN AND TRACE MINERAL DEFICIENCIES

■ **Water-Soluble Vitamins***

B complex
blepharitis, periorbital fissures, cheilosis, glossitis, weakness, paresthesias of legs, dermatoses

vitamin C (ascorbic acid)
bleeding gums, joint and muscle aching

■ **Fat-Soluble Vitamins***

vitamin A
night blindness, Bitot's spots

vitamin D
bone tenderness

vitamin E
myopathy, creatinuria

vitamin K
prolonged blood clotting

■ **Trace Minerals†**

iodine
enlarged thyroid, impaired memory, hoarseness, hearing loss

copper
depigmentation of skin and hair within 2 to 4 weeks, kinky hair

zinc
hypogeusesthesia (abnormally diminished sense of taste); moist, excoriated rash in paranasal, anal, and groin areas

manganese
transient dermatitis

chromium
glucose intolerance, mental confusion

selenium
muscle pain and tenderness

molybdenum
night blindness, irritability

*Vitamin deficiencies are avoided by giving 1 unit of a multivitamin preparation every day in the TPN solution.
†Trace mineral deficiencies will usually not develop in patients until 2 to 4 weeks after oral intake has stopped.

Interventions *continued*

• *hyperosmolar overload*—thirst, headache, lethargy, convulsions, and urine positive for glucose and negative for acetone

• *electrolyte imbalances*—hypocalcemia (numbness and tingling), hypokalemia (muscle weakness, cramps, paresthesia, lethargy, confusion, ileus, and dysrhythmias), hypomagnesemia (confusion, positive Chvostek's sign, and tetany), hyponatremia (lethargy and confusion), and hypophosphatemia (weakness and signs of encephalopathy). (See the "Fluid and Electrolyte Imbalances" care plan, page 21.)

• *vitamin and trace mineral deficiencies* (see *Signs and Symptoms of Vitamin and Trace Mineral Deficiencies*).

Rationales *continued*

• Hyperglycemic hyperosmolar nonketosis (HHNK) coma may occur if TPN is infused over too short a time. A serum osmolar level above 300 mOsm/kg water pulls fluid into the vascular bed to dilute the osmolar load. The excess vascular fluid results in an osmotic diuresis. Also, HHNK may occur with simultaneous infusion of TPN and tube feeding. To prevent this problem, decrease the TPN rate as the tube feeding rate is increased.

• The "Fluid and Electrolyte Imbalances" care plan contains general information on these disorders. This section covers information specific to TPN. Fluid and electrolyte status requires careful monitoring for several reasons: (a) There is an increase in the use of potassium and phosphate for glucose metabolism and protein synthesis; if it is not replaced appropriately with TPN, a deficit may result. (b) The primary diagnosis may alter fluid and electrolyte balance. Fluid and electrolyte losses from fistulas, diarrhea, or nasogastric tubes can cause electrolyte and acid-base abnormalities. (c) To promote lean body mass repletion and positive nitrogen balance, electrolytes have to be supplied in a specific ratio: phosphorus 0.8 gm, sodium 3.9 mg, potassium 3 mEq, chloride 2.5 mEq, and calcium 1.2 mEq for every gram of nitrogen infused.

• Vitamins and trace minerals are necessary for vital processes. Vitamins may function as hormones and as catalysts in enzyme systems. Minerals serve as co-enzyme activators and as major factors in the regulation of acid-base and fluid and electrolyte balance.
 Deficiencies of vitamins and minerals result from inadequate intake, inability to digest and absorb, poor utilization of nutrients, excess losses, and increased requirements related to medication or severity of illness.

(continued)

Interventions *continued*

6. *Infuse I.V. fat emulsion* as ordered via one of three infusion methods:

• through a separate I.V., by itself

• connected into the TPN line through a Y-connector added between the TPN catheter and the I.V. tubing

• infused as a 3-in-1 solution.

7. *To prevent precipitate formation in a 3-in-1 solution, ensure that TPN is mixed in a ratio of calcium, ≤ 15 mEq/l; phosphorus, ≤ 30 mEq/l; and magnesium, ≤ 10 mEq/l.*

8. *Evaluate the 3-in-1 solution for correct volume* as infused by the infusion pump. Adjust the infusion rate as needed to ensure delivery of the desired volume.

9. *Observe for fat separation in the 3-in-1 solution* as indicated by a yellow ring around the edges of the solution. Stop TPN if this occurs, and replace the solution bag with a fresh one.

10. *Culture the 3-in-1 solution* if the patient develops sepsis.

11. *Administer a separate fat infusion slowly over the first 15 to 20 minutes* (1 ml/minute for a 10% fat infusion or 0.5 ml/minute for a 20% fat infusion). Observe for dyspnea, pain at the I.V. site, or chest or back pain. If any of these signs or symptoms is present, stop the infusion and notify the doctor. If none is present, increase the rate as ordered.

12. *If fat emulsion is to be infused in a second I.V., infuse it over 4 to 8 hours.*

Rationales *continued*

6. Fat emulsion is used as an adjunct to TPN therapy to prevent essential fatty acid deficiency. Fats also can be used as a caloric source if TPN cannot supply an adequate amount of calories. For example, if hyperglycemia is a consistent problem and insulin cannot control the serum glucose level, the glucose infusion is decreased, and the corresponding loss of calories is supplied as fat.

• Infusing fats separately prevents breakdown of the fat emulsion and decreases the risk of fat emboli.

• The Y-connector allows fats to infuse with minimal mixing with the TPN solution, preventing breakdown of the fat emulsion. This decreases the risk of fat emboli. Fats appear to float on top of TPN solution when administered through a Y-connector.

• Carbohydrates, protein, and fat are mixed in one bag. This is done only by the pharmacy, saving nursing time because there is no extra I.V. or Y-connector to add. There also is only one bag to hang over a 24-hour period: This saves time for the pharmacy, because only one bag must be mixed and dispensed. Less I.V. tubing and fewer I.V. catheters are used, making this method cost-effective. Most important, there is no additional pain for the patient from new I.V. starts for fat emulsion I.V.s.

7. Nurses cannot observe for particulate matter in 3-in-1 solutions because of the milky color of the mixture. The ratio listed prevents precipitate formation.

8. When fats are added to a TPN solution, the solution's increased viscosity may alter infusion pump delivery.

9. The 3-in-1 solution can separate if it is not mixed appropriately in the pharmacy or if it is left hanging more than 24 to 48 hours. Separation may cause fat emboli.

10. If it becomes contaminated, the 3-in-1 solution is more likely to support microbial growth than TPN solution without fat.

11. Allergic reactions to the fat emulsion may be local or systemic. Slow administration allows time for observation of an allergic reaction before a dangerous amount of antigen must be administered. Signs and symptoms listed indicate possible allergic reactions.

12. The addition of 500 ml of fluid 2 to 3 times/week may not be well tolerated in patients with renal failure or congestive heart failure (CHF). The slower rate allows the body to assimilate the emulsion and prevents hyperlipidemia.

Interventions *continued*

13. *Do not use I.V. filters with fat emulsion infusions.* When infusing fats on a long-term basis (longer than 3 months), ensure that thiosalicylate-free tubing is used.

14. *Encourage walking or mild exercise* to promote nitrogen retention and nutrient use.

15. *Weigh the patient* at the same time, with the same amount of clothing, on the same scale every day.

16. *When oral intake resumes, initiate a daily count of calories and measurement of fat intake.* Observe for nausea, vomiting, or diarrhea.

17. Observe for changes in muscle strength and energy level.

18. Additional individualized interventions: _____
_____
_____

Outcome criteria
Within 24 hours of starting TPN, and throughout TPN therapy, the patient will:
• maintain negative urine glucose level
• maintain serum glucose level of 100 to 200 mg/dl
• show no signs or symptoms of hypoglycemia, hyperglycemia, hyperosmolar nonketotic overload, electrolyte imbalance, or vitamin or trace metal deficiencies.

Rationales *continued*

13. The fat emulsion particle size exceeds the filter pore size, so the solution will not infuse through the filter. Fats leach thiosalicylate from ordinary tubing; it can accumulate in the body, with unknown effects.

14. Exercise improves use of nutrients and promotes lean muscle mass development rather than the storage of fatty acids. Exercise also prevents muscle wasting, which occurs with inactivity.

15. Weighing is necessary to determine if nutritional goals are being met. Weight is also used to assess the patient's fluid status. Weight gain of more than ½ lb/day may be an indication of fluid retention.

16. Daily monitoring of fat intake and calories provides guidelines for therapy. When the patient is taking 10 g of fat/day orally, I.V. fat emulsions can be discontinued. When 1,000 calories/day are consumed without nausea, vomiting, or diarrhea, TPN can be discontinued.

17. Increased strength, energy level, and sense of well-being indicate that TPN is replenishing the body.

18. Rationale: _____
_____
_____

Within 7 days of starting TPN, the patient will:
• exhibit weight gain less than ½ lb/day
• exhibit increased muscle strength
• exhibit increased energy level
• verbalize increased sense of well-being.

Nursing diagnosis: *Potential fluid volume excess or deficit related to fluid retention, altered oral intake, or osmotic diuresis*

NURSING PRIORITY: Maintain optimal fluid balance.

Interventions

1. See the "Fluid and Electrolyte Imbalances" care plan, page 21.

2. *Observe for edema, increased pulse rate, and increased blood pressure.* If any of these signs are present, consult with the doctor about decreasing the overall fluid load administered.

Rationales

1. The "Fluid and Electrolyte Imbalances" care plan contains further details related to fluid and electrolyte disorders.

2. Edema, increased pulse rate, and increased blood pressure may be signs of excess fluid volume. This situation may result from inability to tolerate the increased cardiac and renal work load imposed by TPN or from the underlying disease process itself (for example, CHF or renal failure). Edema in the malnourished patient is also often related to protein depletion, in

(continued)

Interventions *continued*

3. *Observe for thirst, dry mucous membranes, dry skin, decreased urine output, and increased urine specific gravity.*

4. *Assess breath sounds* each shift.

5. *Record intake and output* each shift.

6. *Weigh the patient* daily. (For every liter lost or gained, weight should change approximately 2 lb.)

7. Additional individualized interventions: _____
_____
_____

Outcome criteria
Throughout TPN therapy, the patient will:
• maintain intake that approximately equals output
• exhibit no signs or symptoms of fluid imbalance

Rationales *continued*

which circulating serum protein levels are lower than protein levels in the interstitial spaces. This inequality causes the shift of fluids into the interstitial spaces to equalize protein-to-fluid ratios in the blood and interstitial spaces.

3. These may be signs and symptoms of fluid deficit or dehydration. See the previous problem for further details.

4. Crackles or rhonchi may indicate fluid overload.

5. An intake consistently lower than output indicates a fluid deficit and the need for additional fluid to prevent dehydration and renal failure. An intake higher than output may reflect fluid overload and result in pulmonary complications.

6. The patient's daily weight is another way to determine whether the patient is being given too much fluid or too little. Weight gain over ½ lb/day is too rapid and reflects fluid retention.

7. Rationale: _____
_____
_____

• maintain urine output > 200 ml/8 hours
• exhibit weight gain < ½ lb/day.

Nursing diagnosis: *Knowledge deficit related to lack of prior experience with TPN*

NURSING PRIORITY: Teach patient and family about TPN.

Interventions

1. *Briefly explain the purpose and method of TPN therapy.*

• Explain that TPN is nutritional feeding into the bloodstream, providing nutritional intake until the patient can resume oral intake.
• Define the roles of the dietitian, nurses, pharmacist, doctor, and other health care team members.
• Explain that the TPN solution contains carbohydrate, protein, fat, vitamins, and electrolytes and will provide all the calories and protein needed until the patient can eat.
• Describe the route and equipment used, the length of time TPN may be infused, and the patient's responsibilities.
• Provide the patient/family with written material on TPN therapy.

Rationales

1. A general understanding of the purpose and methods provides a framework within which to understand the specific details of the therapy.
• This defines TPN in terms the patient can understand.

• Describing the roles of the health care team members ensures patient awareness of resources.
• Describing the TPN solution may reassure the patient and family.

• A thorough understanding of the TPN technique, clear expectations, and acceptance of responsibility for self-monitoring promote optimum therapeutic benefit.
• Written material reinforces the nurse's explanation.

Interventions *continued*

2. If the patient is to be discharged on home TPN, also do the following:

• Collaborate with the nutrition support service to determine appropriate teaching.

• Teach the signs, symptoms, and necessary actions for managing complications, such as infection, abnormal serum glucose levels, air emboli, clotted catheter, and displaced catheter. Ask the patient to report occurrence of any signs or symptoms to the nutritional support team.

• Review the information, and answer questions. Ask the patient "what if" questions.

• Provide written instructions on home TPN protocols.

3. See the "Knowledge Deficit" care plan, page 56, for further details.

4. Additional individualized interventions: _____
_____
_____

Rationales *continued*

2. TPN is a complex therapy requiring substantial expertise on the patient's part for successful home management.

• The service can provide expert advice on making teaching appropriate to the home setting. The patient on home TPN will need to be followed by the service (or by a home care agency specializing in home TPN management).

• Prompt reporting by the patient facilitates timely intervention.

• Reviewing, clarifying, and using practical "what if" examples promote understanding and boost problem-solving skills.

• Written information reinforces teaching and provides a future reference.

3. The "Knowledge Deficit" care plan contains interventions related to the process of patient teaching.

4. Rationale: _____
_____
_____

Outcome criteria
Within 24 to 48 hours of starting TPN, the patient or family will:
• describe TPN
• discuss medical reasons for TPN

• discuss the role of the nutrition support service staff
• utilize appropriate problem-solving skills
• list signs and symptoms of complications.

Nursing diagnosis: *Potential infection related to invasive CVC, leukopenia, or damp dressing*

NURSING PRIORITY: Prevent or detect and promptly treat infection.

Interventions

1. *Change the catheter dressing,* using sterile technique, according to hospital protocol. Apply a completely sealed dressing.

2. *Observe the dressing* every 8 hours, and change it any time it is unsealed or damp.

3. *Observe the insertion site* every 8 hours for signs of infection. Report any redness, swelling, pain, or purulent drainage.

4. *Follow hospital protocol for tubing changes* and antibacterial preparation at all connections before changing I.V. tubing.

Rationales

1. Good technique decreases the risk of infection. Dressing change frequency ranges from every day to once a week.

2. Moisture encourages microbial growth at the insertion site. Colonization at the insertion site may lead to sepsis.

3. These signs may indicate infection of the insertion site.

4. Good technique with tubing changes and antibacterial preparation before disconnecting tubing decreases TPN line contamination. Change tubing every 24 to 96 hours.

(continued)

Interventions *continued*

5. *Follow pharmacy or nutrition support services recommendations for I.V. filters.*

6. *Infuse only TPN solution through the TPN catheter.* Do not use the TPN line for injecting medications or drawing blood samples.

7. *Use only solutions prepared in the pharmacy* under a laminar flow hood. Do not make any additions on the unit. If additions are necessary, they should be added in the pharmacy under a laminar flow hood.

8. *Return cloudy or precipitated solution to the pharmacy.*

9. *Allow each bag or bottle to hang a maximum of 24 hours.*

10. *Monitor for signs of infection:*
• increased pulse and respiration rates
• temperature above 101° F. (38.3° C.)
• white blood cell (WBC) count over 10,000 mm³
• serum glucose level over 200 mg/dl
• glycosuria
• chills, diaphoresis, or lethargy

11. Additional individualized interventions: _____
_____
_____

Rationales *continued*

5. Controversy exists regarding filters for I.V. tubing. Some hospital pharmacies filter solutions rather than add filters to I.V. tubing on the unit.

6. Using the TPN catheter for other solutions provides another possible source of contamination and increases the risk of sepsis.

7. Preparing the solution in a sterile area decreases the risk of contamination. The laminar flow hood minimizes contamination from airborne microorganisms.

8. Cloudy solution indicates possible bacterial contamination. Precipitate may occlude the catheter or cause thrombus formation.

9. Infusing solutions over longer periods allows for rapid multiplication of any microorganisms inadvertently introduced during mixing of the TPN solution.

10. A change in vital signs or WBC count, hyperglycemia, glycosuria, chills, or diaphoresis may indicate that an infection is developing.

11. Rationale: _____
_____
_____

Outcome criteria

Throughout TPN therapy, the patient will:
• be afebrile
• present urine negative for glucose

• show no infection or inflammation at catheter site
• maintain serum glucose level < 200 gm/dl.

Discharge planning

NURSING DISCHARGE CRITERIA

Upon discharge, documentation shows evidence of:
• absence of fever
• stabilizing weight
• absence of pulmonary or cardiovascular complications
• electrolytes within acceptable parameters
• WBC counts within normal parameters
• absence of redness, swelling, pain, and drainage at catheter site
• absence of nausea and vomiting
• ability to perform activities of daily living (ADLs), transfer, and ambulate same as before hospitalization
• adequate home support system, or referral to home care or a nursing home if indicated by an inadequate home support system or the patient's inability to perform ADLs, transfers, and ambulation

• a plan for follow-up by nutrition support service or home care agency specializing in home TPN for the patient being discharged on TPN.

PATIENT/FAMILY DISCHARGE TEACHING CHECKLIST

(if the patient is being discharged on TPN)
Document evidence that patient/family demonstrates understanding of:
___ preventing complications of home TPN
___ actions to take if complications do occur
___ where and how to obtain supplies
___ catheter site care
___ procedure for TPN administration
___ community resources
___ date, time, and location of follow-up appointments
___ how to contact doctor.

DOCUMENTATION CHECKLIST

Using outcome criteria as a guide, document:
___ nutritional status on admission
___ any significant changes in status
___ CVC insertion—difficulties or complications; length of catheter; position and any change in position; signs of infection, thrombosis, emboli, or other post-insertion complication
___ dressing and tubing changes
___ TPN solution and fat emulsion—for each bag or bottle: date, time, name of nurse hanging solution; all ingredients; rate of infusion
___ patient/family teaching
___ discharge planning.

ASSOCIATED CARE PLANS

Fluid and Electrolyte Imbalances
Knowledge Deficit

REFERENCES

Bernard, M., et al. "Central Venous Alimentation," in *Nutritional & Metabolic Support of Hospitalized Patients*. Edited by Bernard, M., et al. Philadelphia: W.B. Saunders Co., 1986.

Cerrato, Paul L. "When You Think Your Patient Needs TPN," *RN* 48(5):79-83, May 1985.

Diagnostics, 2nd ed. Nurse's Reference Library. Springhouse, Pa.: Springhouse Corp., 1986.

Dobbins, D. "3 in 1 System of PN Solution Delivery," *Nutritional Support Service* 5(7):45-46, July 1985.

Dressler, D. "TPN" presented at proceedings of the 7th annual 1980 N.P.I. Irvine, Calif.: American Association of Critical Care Nurses, 1980.

Forlaw, L., et al. *Introduction to Nutritional and Physical Assessment of the Adult Patient for the Nurse*. American Society for Parenteral and Enteral Nutrition, 1983.

Fulton, J.S., et al. "Hyperalimentation Dressing and Skin Flora," *Journal of the National Intravenous Therapy Association* 4(5):354-57, September/October 1981.

Goldman, D., and Maki, D. "Infection Control in Total Parenteral Nutrition," *Journal of the American Medical Association* 223(12):1360-64, December 1973.

Guthrie, Peggy, and Turner, W. "Peripheral and Central Nutritional Support," *Journal of the National Intravenous Therapy Association* 9(5):393-98, September/October 1986.

Jarrard, M.M., et al. "Daily Dressing Changes' Effects on Skin Flora Beneath Subclavian Catheter Dressings During Total Parenteral Nutrition," *Journal of Parenteral and Enteral Nutrition* 4(4):391-92, July/August 1980.

Krey, S., and Murray, R. *Dynamics of Nutrition Support*. East Norwalk, Conn.: Appleton-Century-Crofts, 1986.

Louie, N., and Niemiee, P. "Parenteral Nutrition Solutions," in *Parenteral Nutrition*. Edited by Rombeau and Caldwell. Philadelphia: W.B. Saunders Co., 1986.

Mirtallo, J. "Advances in Parenteral Formulas," *Nutritional Support Service* 5(5):10-13, May 1985.

Mirtallo, J., and Fabri, P. "Assessment of Iron Requirements in Patients Receiving Parenteral Nutrition," *Nutritional Support Service* 5(10):45-50, October 1985.

Moghissi, K., and Boore, Jennifer. *Parenteral and Enteral Nutrition for Nurses*. Rockville, Md.: Aspen Pubs., Inc., 1983.

Powell, C., et al. "Op-Site Dressing Study: A Prospective Randomized Study Evaluating Povidone Iodine Ointment and Extension Set Changes with 7-Day Op-Site Dressing Applied to Total Parenteral Nutrition Subcalavian Sites," *Journal of Parenteral and Enteral Nutrition* 9(3):443-46, May/June 1985.

Silges-Serra, A., et al. "A Randomized Trial on the Effect of Tubing Changes on Hub Contamination and Catheter Sepsis During Parenteral Nutrition," *Journal of Parenteral and Enteral Nutrition* 9(3):322-25, May/June 1985.

"Standardized TPN Nursing Diagnosis," The Ohio State University Hospital's Nursing Service Department.

Traetow, M. "The Ohio State University Hospitals Patient Guide to Total Parenteral Nutrition (TPN) Therapy," Columbus, Ohio: Ohio State Patient Education, 1984.

Williams, W. "Infection Control During Parenteral Nutrition Therapy," *Journal of Parenteral and Enteral Nutrition* 9(6):735-44, 1985.

Cholecystectomy

DRG information

DRG 195* [Surgical DRG] Total Cholecystectomy with
    Common Duct Exploration (CDE)
    With Complications or Comorbidity (CC)
    for the following procedures:
    • exploration of duct to relieve obstruction
    • exploration of duct to remove stone.
    Mean LOS = 12.2 days

DRG 196 Total Cholecystectomy with CDE.
    Without CC.
    Mean LOS = 10.0 days

DRG 197* Total Cholecystectomy without CDE.
    With CC.
    Mean LOS = 9.5 days

DRG 198 Total Cholecystectomy. Without CDE.
    Without CC.
    Mean LOS = 6.9 days

PRO alert: In many states, these DRGs are being "focused
on" by professional review organizations [PROs] because of
the suspicion that these procedures too often are performed
unnecessarily. PROs are strictly reviewing admissions of
cases that fall into these DRGs. PROs also are focusing
their postoperative reviews on pulmonary symptoms because of the frequency of these complications. PRO review
guidelines include the following:
1. Documentation in the nursing admission history
must include a description of preoperative pulmonary
status.
2. High-risk patients, such as smokers and those who
are obese or have a history of pulmonary disease,
chronic cough, alcohol abuse, or insulin-dependent diabetes, must be identified.
3. Preoperative evaluation and education of high-risk
patients must include:
• incentive spirometry and documentation of teaching
• training in proper breathing and coughing techniques
• prophylactic antibiotics as ordered by the doctor
• a chest X-ray within 30 days of surgery.
4. Postoperative documentation should include:
• ambulation within 24 hours
• heparin ordered for high-risk patients
• use of compression stockings, when indicated
• monitoring of white blood cells
• chest X-ray.
    The nurse should be particularly attentive when doc-
umenting nursing activities involved with assessing
pulmonary status, preventing postoperative complications, obtaining diagnostic tests (as ordered by the doctor), and implementing medical treatments for
pulmonary symptoms.

Introduction

DEFINITION AND TIME FOCUS

Cholecystitis (inflammation of the gall bladder) is an
extremely common disorder usually associated with
cholelithiasis (gallstone formation), although cholelithiasis alone may be present without symptoms. Most
gallstones are composed of cholesterol and a matrix
substance to which the cholesterol adheres. The mechanism and etiology of stone formation are unknown, although infection, stasis, and genetic causes have been
suggested. Cholecystitis may be either acute or chronic.
Patients who require hospitalization usually present
with an acute attack of intense pain and nausea and
vomiting; for these patients, cholecystectomy (surgical
removal of the gallbladder) is the most common treatment. This procedure is usually performed with chole-
dochostomy (exploration of the common and hepatic bile
ducts) to remove stones that may be causing obstruction. This care plan focuses on the preoperative and
postoperative phases of care for the patient with acute
cholecystitis who requires cholecystectomy.

ETIOLOGY/PRECIPITATING FACTORS

• stones lodged in the neck of the gallbladder
• other causes unknown, but possibilities include kink-
ing of the neck of the gallbladder, adhesions, edema,
neoplasms, extensive fasting, anesthesia, narcotics, dehydration, pancreatic enzymes refluxing into the gallbladder, inadequate blood supply

Focused assessment guidelines

NURSING HISTORY (Functional health pattern findings)

Health perception–health management pattern

• may report *pain, initially situated in mid-epigastrium
that becomes pronounced in right upper quadrant* (RUQ):
pain is initially mild but persistent and intensifies as
inflammation spreads; pain may be referred to the right
scapula or right shoulder and is exacerbated by movement, coughing, and deep breathing
• may have history of diabetes, extensive bowel resec-
tions, hemolytic anemia
• if over age 50, is at increased risk

Nutritional-metabolic pattern

• may report *intolerance to heavy meals or fatty foods*
• may report indigestion leading to anorexia
• may report nausea, possibly with vomiting

Elimination pattern
• may report flatulence
• may report change in color of urine or stool (indicates obstruction of bile)
• may report pruritus

Activity-exercise pattern
• may report sedentary life-style; if so, is at increased risk for gallstones and therefore cholecystitis

Sleep-rest pattern
• may report pain that disturbs sleep

Sexuality-reproductive pattern
• women with more than one child are at increased risk for cholelithiasis
• women who use oral contraceptives are at increased risk for cholelithiasis

PHYSICAL FINDINGS
General
• *elevated temperature*
• obesity

Eyes
• icteric sclera

Mouth
• jaundiced mucous membranes

Cardiovascular
• rapid, irregular pulse
• hypertension

Pulmonary
• short and shallow respirations

Abdomen
• *pain in RUQ,* referred to right scapula, intensified by deep breathing or percussion above right costal margin

• localized rebound tenderness in RUQ
• distention
• light-colored stools

Urinary
• dark, frothy urine

Integumentary
• jaundice, especially on inner aspects of forearms
• bruising

DIAGNOSTIC STUDIES
• white blood cell count—often 10,000 to 15,000, although it may not be elevated
• bilirubin (direct and indirect)—may be elevated because gallstones are obstructing the bile duct
• prothrombin time—may be prolonged because bile is necessary for vitamin K absorption (prothrombin is dependent on vitamin K for synthesis)
• alkaline phosphatase—may be elevated because normal excretion of this enzyme through the biliary system may be impeded
• *oral cholecystogram—gallbladder may not visualize* because of obstruction of the biliary ducts or inability of the gallbladder to concentrate the dye; repetition may be ordered to rule out inadequate preparation
• cholangiogram—may show gallstones or strictures in biliary tree
• ultrasonography—may show gallstones

POTENTIAL COMPLICATIONS
• perforation of the gallbladder
• hemorrhage
• empyema of the gallbladder
• subphrenic or hepatic abscess
• fistulas
• pancreatitis
• cholangitis
• pneumonia

Collaborative problem: *Potential peritonitis related to possible perforation of the gallbladder preoperatively*

NURSING PRIORITIES: (a) Detect perforation and (b) minimize possible complications.

Interventions

1. *Monitor vital signs* every 2 hours for 12 hours, then every 4 hours if stable. Document and report abnormalities, especially noting fever, tachycardia, or dropping blood pressure.

2. *Assess the abdomen* during vital signs checks, particularly noting bowel sounds, distention, firmness, and presence or absence of a mass in the RUQ. Document and report any changes.

Rationales

1. Early detection of changes in vital signs will alert caregivers to possible perforation and the need for emergency surgery. Temperature changes indicate further inflammation or response to antibiotics.

2. Muscle rigidity and a palpable mass in the RUQ suggest peritonitis. In peritonitis, an initial period of hypermotility is followed by hypoactive or absent bowel sounds.

(continued)

Interventions continued

3. *Note the location and character of pain* during vital signs checks. Document and report any changes.

4. *Maintain antibiotic therapy*, as ordered.

5. Additional individualized interventions: _____
_____
_____

Rationales continued

3. RUQ pain that becomes generalized may indicate perforation.

4. Antibiotics excreted in the biliary tree are given to prevent or treat infection and to decrease the risk of perforation from a friable or necrotic gallbladder wall.

5. Rationale: _____
_____
_____

Outcome criteria
Within 24 hours of admission, the patient will:
• display vital signs within normal limits

• have reduction of pain
• show lessening of abnormal abdominal signs.

Collaborative problem: *Potential hemorrhage related to decreased absorption of vitamin K and decreased synthesis of prothrombin*

NURSING PRIORITIES: (a) Prevent hemorrhage and (b) detect clotting abnormalities so they can be corrected before surgery.

Interventions

1. *Monitor the prothrombin time* (PT), as ordered. Alert the doctor to an abnormally prolonged PT.

2. *Administer vitamin K*, as ordered.

3. *Observe for bleeding* from the gums, nose, or injection sites or for blood in the urine or stool. Document and report bleeding.

4. Give injections using small-gauge needles. If an increased bleeding tendency is noted, limit the number of injections or venipunctures as much as possible, and apply direct pressure for at least 5 minutes after such procedures.

5. Apply gentle pressure to injection sites instead of massaging them.

6. Additional individualized interventions: _____
_____
_____

Rationales

1. Prothrombin is manufactured in the liver and is dependent on vitamin K for synthesis. Bile is necessary for vitamin K absorption; thus, PT may be prolonged if an obstructive process has interfered with bile excretion.

2. Administration of vitamin K will correct any deficiency and promote the manufacture of prothrombin.

3. Observing for bleeding aids in detecting coagulation problems.

4. Small-gauge needles reduce the risk of bleeding at injection sites. Minimizing the number of punctures reduces the risk of significant blood loss. Direct pressure controls bleeding and allows clot formation.

5. Gentle pressure reduces the trauma at injection sites and ensures that bleeding has stopped.

6. Rationale: _____
_____
_____

Outcome criteria
Within 48 hours of admission, the patient will:
• have PT levels approaching normal
• show no evidence of bleeding.

Nursing diagnosis: *RUQ pain related to inflammation of the gallbladder*

NURSING PRIORITY: Relieve RUQ pain.

Interventions

1. *See the "Pain" care plan* on page 64.

2. *Administer specific medications*, as ordered, and document their effectiveness. Meperidine (the analgesic of choice), papaverine hydrochloride, amyl nitrite, or sublingual nitroglycerin may be ordered.

3. Additional individualized interventions: _____
_____
_____

Rationales

1. Generalized interventions regarding pain management are included in the "Pain" care plan.

2. Specific medications are most appropriate for pain from cholecystitis. Meperidine is less likely than morphine to cause spasm of the biliary tree. Papaverine hydrochloride exerts a nonspecific spasmolytic effect on smooth muscle. Amyl nitrite diminishes spasm of the biliary ducts and partially counteracts the spasmogenic effects of narcotics. (Other drugs with similar action may be ordered, depending on the doctor's preference.) Nitroglycerin relieves pain and relaxes smooth muscle.

3. Rationale: _____
_____
_____

Outcome criteria

Within 1 hour of admission, the patient will:
• verbalize pain relief
• display easy, deep, and regular respirations.

Collaborative problem: *Potential postoperative infection, obstruction, or dislodging of the tube related to external biliary drainage*

NURSING PRIORITIES: (a) Prevent or promptly detect complications and (b) maintain patency of the system.

Interventions

1. *Monitor vital signs* every 4 hours. Document and report abnormalities.

2. *Assess the abdomen* every shift, noting any abdominal pain or rigidity. Document and report any changes.

3. *Assess for signs of infection at the T-tube insertion site.* Document and report any redness, swelling, warmth, or purulent drainage. Teach the patient and family about signs of infection.

4. *Assess for signs of T-tube obstruction*: Document and report pain in the RUQ, bile drainage around the T-tube, nausea and vomiting, clay-colored stools, jaundice, or dark yellow urine.

5. *Assess for signs that the tube is dislodged*—decreased drainage or evidence that the tube has changed position.

Rationales

1. Elevated temperature may indicate infection (either wound infection or bile peritonitis).

2. The presence of generalized abdominal pain and rigidity, combined with an elevated temperature, may indicate bile peritonitis.

3. Early detection of infection facilitates prompt treatment.

4. The presence of signs of obstruction indicates lack of patency in the external biliary drainage system and backup of bile into the common bile duct and liver.

5. Prompt detection of a dislodged tube leads to prompt treatment and reduces the risk of complications (peritonitis) from bile leakage.

(continued)

Interventions *continued*

6. *Using sterile technique, connect the T tube to a closed-gravity system*, and attach sufficient tubing so it does not become kinked or pulled as the patient moves around.

7. *Monitor the amount and character of any T-tube drainage.* Measure and record the drainage once per shift.

8. *Monitor and record the patient's stool color.*

9. Place the patient in low Fowler's position upon return from surgery.

10. If the patient will be discharged with a T tube still in place, teach him the care of the external biliary drainage system, including expected amount of drainage, frequency of emptying bag and changing dressing, technique for site care and dressing change, and signs to report to doctor (excessive drainage, leakage, signs of obstruction).

11. Additional individualized interventions: _____
_____
_____

Rationales *continued*

6. A closed system ensures sterility. Providing enough tubing reduces the risk of obstructing or dislodging the T tube.

7. Initially, the entire output of bile (500 to 1,000 ml/day) may flow through the T tube. Within 7 to 10 days, however, most of the bile should flow into the duodenum. Monitoring the amount of drainage permits early detection of an obstructed or dislodged tube.

8. Stools will be light colored initially, when most of the bile is flowing out of the T tube. Stools gradually should become normal in color as bile passes into the duodenum. Persistence of light-colored stools for more than 7 days may indicate obstruction of the T tube.

9. Low Fowler's position facilitates T-tube drainage.

10. To successfully manage the T tube at home, the patient and family need to know about routine care, as well as what to do about potential complications.

11. Rationale: _____
_____
_____

Outcome criteria
Throughout the period of external biliary drainage, the patient will:
• display vital signs within normal limits

• show no signs of infection or peritonitis
• show no signs of T-tube obstruction
• show no signs of a dislodged T tube.

Nursing diagnosis: *Potential postoperative ineffective breathing pattern related to high abdominal incision and pain*

NURSING PRIORITY: Maintain optimal air exchange and prevent atelectasis.

Interventions

1. *Monitor respiratory rate and character* every 4 hours. Note the depth of respirations. Document and report abnormalities.

2. *Auscultate breath sounds* once per shift. Document and report changes.

3. *Instruct and coach the patient in diaphragmatic breathing.*

4. *Assist the patient to use the incentive spirometer*—10 breaths/hour when awake and every 2 hours at night.

Rationales

1. After cholecystectomy, the patient may breathe shallowly to avoid pain associated with deep breathing.

2. Breath sounds may be diminished at the bases, especially on the right side.

3. Diaphragmatic breathing increases lung expansion by allowing the diaphragm to descend fully.

4. Using the incentive spirometer promotes sustained maximal inspiration, which fully inflates alveoli.

Interventions *continued*

5. Turn the patient every 2 hours.

6. Assess pain and premedicate the patient, as needed, before starting breathing exercises and ambulation.

7. Assist the patient to splint the incision with a pillow or bath blanket while coughing.

8. Encourage the patient to increase ambulation progressively.

9. Additional individualized interventions: _____
_____
_____

Rationales *continued*

5. Position changes provide better ventilation of all lung lobes and promote drainage of secretions.

6. The pain-free patient is more likely to cooperate with pulmonary hygiene and is better able to take deep breaths.

7. Splinting the incision while coughing relieves incisional stress and pull.

8. Ambulation promotes adequate ventilation by increasing the depth of respirations.

9. Rationale: _____
_____
_____

Outcome criteria

Throughout the postoperative period, the patient will:
• maintain a respiratory rate of 12 to 24 breaths/minute

• display nonlabored, deep respirations
• have audible, clear breath sounds in all lobes.

Nursing diagnosis: *Potential nutritional deficit related to nausea and vomiting preoperatively, NPO status postoperatively, nasogastric suction, altered lipid metabolism, and increased nutritional needs during healing*

NURSING PRIORITIES: (a) Maintain optimal nutritional status and (b) tell the patient and family about postoperative recommendations.

Interventions

1. *Maintain I.V. fluid replacement*, as ordered. See the "Fluid and Electrolyte Imbalances" care plan, page 21.

2. *Once peristalsis returns, discontinue the NG tube and encourage a progressive dietary intake*, as ordered.

3. Clamp the T tube during meals, as ordered.

4. *Teach the patient and family about a fat-restricted diet*, as ordered. Involve a dietitian in meal planning and home care teaching.

Rationales

1. During the immediate postoperative period, the patient will be NPO until peristalsis returns. The patient may also have a nasogastric (NG) tube in place to reduce distention and minimize the pancreatic stimulation normally triggered by gastric juices. Gastric suction and an NPO status increase the risk of fluid and electrolyte disorders.

2. Patients usually are able to begin taking clear liquids 24 to 48 hours postoperatively and gradually increase to a full diet, including fat restrictions, as ordered.

3. Clamping the T tube during meals may aid fat absorption by allowing additional bile to flow into the duodenum.

4. After cholecystectomy, normal gallbladder functions related to lipid digestion (storage and release of bile) are dependent on the bile produced by the liver; thus, fat absorption may be altered, especially if postoperative edema limits bile excretion. Fat intake usually is limited for 1½ to 6 months, depending on the doctor's preference and the patient's response to gradual increases in fat intake. Involving a dietitian helps ensure that adequate intake of other nutrients (to replace calories lost by fat restriction) is considered in the diet plan.

(continued)

Interventions continued

5. Suggest small, frequent meals.

6. *Instruct the patient to minimize alcohol intake* during the postoperative recovery period.

7. Prepare the patient for the possibility of persistent flatulence.

8. Additional individualized interventions: _____

_____

_____

Rationales continued

5. Large meals may contribute to distention and increase discomfort.

6. Pancreatitis is a common complication after cholecystectomy. Alcohol intake often triggers acute pancreatic inflammation.

7. Flatulence is common postoperatively. Often these patients have other gastrointestinal disorders (hiatal hernia, ulcer) that may cause persistent symptoms, such as bloating and nausea. Dietary modifications and treatment of the underlying disorder may reduce symptoms.

8. Rationale: _____

_____

_____

Outcome criteria
Throughout the hospitalization period, the patient will:
• have normal fluid and electrolyte status.

By discharge the patient will:
• list three general dietary considerations
• identify specific foods in own diet that may need to be restricted.

Nursing diagnosis: *Potential alteration in the oral mucous membrane related to NPO status and possible NG suction*

NURSING PRIORITY: Maintain integrity of the oral mucous membrane.

Interventions

1. *Assess the oral mucous membrane* once per shift for dryness, cracks, coating, or lesions.

2. *Assist the patient with gentle oral hygiene* at least twice a day or as needed. Ensure that water and oral hygiene materials are within the patient's easy reach.

3. Apply lubricant to the lips every 2 hours while the patient is awake or more frequently as needed.

4. Additional individualized interventions: _____

_____

_____

Rationales

1. Early assessment for potential problems facilitates prompt treatment.

2. NPO status and NG suction (as well as any previously existing nutritional deficits) may contribute to fragility of the oral mucosa and increase the risk of infection or injury. Frequent oral hygiene reduces accumulation of bacteria in the mouth and decreases discomfort associated with NPO status.

3. Lubricant keeps lips smooth and moist.

4. Rationale: _____

_____

_____

Outcome criteria
Throughout the period of NPO status, the patient will:
• have an intact, moist oral mucous membrane
• display no evidence of inflamed oral mucosa.

Discharge planning
NURSING DISCHARGE CRITERIA
Upon discharge, documentation shows evidence of:
• absence of wound infection
• absence of fever
• stable vital signs
• absence of pulmonary and cardiovascular complications
• ability to tolerate diet as ordered
• ability to ambulate same as before surgery
• ability to perform activities of daily living (ADLs) independently
• adequate support system after discharge
• referral to home care if indicated by inadequate home support system or inability to perform ADLs.

PATIENT/FAMILY DISCHARGE TEACHING CHECKLIST
Document evidence that patient/family demonstrates understanding of:
__ signs and symptoms of wound infection
__ dietary modifications (patient may be on a low-fat diet for up to 6 months; a nonrestrictive diet is resumed as soon as tolerated)
__ resumption of normal activities
__ resumption of sexual activity
__ all discharge medications' purpose, dosage, administration schedule, and side effects (postoperative patients may be discharged with oral analgesics)
__ if discharged with a T tube: routine care and signs to report to doctor
__ date, time, and location of follow-up appointment
__ how to contact doctor.

DOCUMENTATION CHECKLIST
Using outcome criteria as a guide, document:
__ clinical status on admission
__ significant changes in status
__ pertinent laboratory and diagnostic test findings
__ wound assessment
__ amount and character of T-tube drainage
__ pain-relief measures
__ pulmonary hygiene measures
__ observations of oral mucous membrane
__ nutritional intake
__ gastrointestinal assessment
__ patient/family teaching
__ discharge planning.

ASSOCIATED CARE PLANS
Fluid and Electrolyte Imbalances
Knowledge Deficit
Pain
Surgical Intervention

REFERENCES
Carpenito, L.J. *Nursing Diagnosis: Application to Clinical Practice.* Philadelphia: J.B. Lippincott Co., 1983.
Given, B.J., and Simmons, S.J. *Gastroenterology in Clinical Nursing,* 4th ed. St. Louis: C.V. Mosby Co., 1984.
Govoni, L.E., and Hayes, J.E. *Drugs and Nursing Implications,* 5th ed. East Norwalk, Conn.: Appleton & Lange, 1985.
Kneisl, C.R., and Ames, S.W. *Adult Health Nursing: A Biopsychosocial Approach.* Reading, Mass.: Addison-Wesley Publishing Co., 1986.
Long, B.C., and Phipps, J.J. *Essentials of Medical-Surgical Nursing: A Nursing Process Approach.* St. Louis: C.V. Mosby Co., 1985.
Thompson, J.M., et al. *Clinical Nursing.* St. Louis: C.V. Mosby Co., 1986.

Amputation

DRG information
DRG 213 [Surgical DRG] Amputation for Musculoskeletal System and Connective Tissue Disorders.
Mean LOS = 10.4 days

Introduction
DEFINITION AND TIME FOCUS
Amputation is the surgical removal of an irreparably damaged or diseased limb. An amputation may be immediate because of the nature of an injury (such as from a motor vehicle accident or thermal injury), or offered together with use of a prosthesis as an option to improve function. The residual limb is closed with sutures or staples unless massive infection was present preoperatively, in which case a guillotinelike surgery is performed and the wound is left unsutured. Traction may be applied to prevent skin retraction and to allow healing.

This clinical plan focuses on the postoperative period of care after amputation of an upper or lower extremity.

ETIOLOGY/PRECIPITATING FACTORS
• advanced peripheral vascular disease (especially when associated with diabetes mellitus, infection, and smoking)
• trauma (such as that from crushing injuries, motor vehicle accidents, or industrial accidents)
• thermal injury (such as that from frostbite, chemical exposure, or burns)
• tumors
• congenital anomalies

Focused assessment guidelines
NURSING HISTORY (Functional health pattern findings)

Health perception–health management pattern
• *may be under treatment for diabetes mellitus, atherosclerotic arterial occlusive disease, or osteomyelitis*
• if a smoker with peripheral vascular disease, amputation risk is significantly increased

Activity-exercise pattern
• if lower limb is involved, may experience difficulty in ambulation, leading to an altered exercise pattern
• may report severe pain associated with exercise in lower limbs if peripheral vascular disease is present

Sleep-rest pattern
• may report interrupted sleep pattern associated with discomfort

Cognitive-perceptual pattern
• *may report tingling or burning sensation or paresthesia*

Self-perception–self-concept pattern
• may experience difficulty with accepting body image change
• may verbalize concern about returning to present occupation

Role-relationship pattern
• may voice concern about relationships and rejection by others
• may verbalize fear of role change

Coping–stress tolerance pattern
• may have failed to seek or follow medical treatment for problem, necessitating amputation
• may use denial to deal with current experience

PHYSICAL FINDINGS
Integumentary (in affected extremity)
• shiny skin
• skin atrophy
• *skin cool to touch*
• *cyanosis or rubor of extremities* when in dependent position
• *thickened nails*
• *stasis ulcer*
• *edema*
• *nonhealing wound*
• palpable mass

Cardiovascular
• *capillary refill time > 3 seconds*
• *severe, cramping pain with exercise,* usually relieved by rest
• *decreased pulse amplitude*
• *diminished or absent peripheral pulses*

Musculoskeletal
• *limited limb movement*
• *limited ambulation*
• pain
• contractures
• protective holding of affected extremity

DIAGNOSTIC STUDIES
• wound culture and sensitivity—if infection is present, may identify causative microorganism and identify appropriate antibiotics(s)
• complete blood count—elevated white blood cell count demonstrates presence of infection
• erythrocyte sedimentation rate—elevation indicates presence of an inflammatory response

• X-rays—may demonstrate skeletal trauma, anomalies, or presence of a mass
• computed tomography scan—may reveal primary and metastatic tumors, infection, or trauma
• arteriography and Doppler flow studies—may confirm circulatory inadequacy in major arteries or veins
• biopsy—confirms presence of a malignant or benign mass
• evaluation by physical therapy and occupational ther-apy for gross or fine motor function—determines potential use of assistive devices (such as prosthesis, crutches, or walker)

POTENTIAL COMPLICATIONS
• hemorrhage
• infection
• flexion contracture
• psychopathologic adaptation to limb loss

Collaborative problem: *Potential hemorrhage related to major surgical intervention (amputation)*

NURSING PRIORITY: Maintain circulatory volume.

Interventions

1. *Document assessment of the surgical site* immediately upon arrival in unit postoperatively. Include the type of dressing and a description of any drainage and drain devices, such as a Hemovac.

2. *Observe and document signs of oozing on the dressing.* Reinforce the dressing as required. Do not remove the dressing until ordered. Document the amount of supplies used and the frequency of reinforcement.

3. *Maintain I.V. line.* Document its site, appearance, and patency.

4. *Keep a tourniquet at the bedside.* Apply it to the limb or apply direct pressure to the artery if significant bleeding occurs. Notify the doctor immediately, document the events, and remain with the patient until the doctor arrives.

5. Additional individualized interventions: _____
_____
_____

Rationales

1. Baseline assessment permits comparison of data, assisting in ongoing status evaluation. A drain or portable wound suction device (such as Hemovac or Jackson-Pratt) may be in place to remove fluid or blood postoperatively to keep it from interfering with granulation. Observed drainage will be minimal and serosanguineous. Increased amounts and bright red drainage may indicate hemorrhage.

2. A small amount of oozing from the incision is normal. Documenting the supplies used and drainage characteristics helps other caregivers assess status changes. Initially, most postamputation dressings are pressure or pressure/cast dressings; premature removal may permit development of undesirable edema, bleeding, or both.

3. Loss of circulating blood volume results in vessel constriction, increasing the difficulty of establishing an I.V. access. An already established line provides a route for rapid fluid replacement if necessary.

4. If hemorrhage occurs, immediate tourniquet application to the residual limb prevents significant blood loss and shock. If bleeding is severe, direct arterial pressure may be necessary. The patient may be frightened by the amount of blood lost; the nurse's presence is reassuring.

5. Rationale: _____
_____
_____

Outcome criteria
Within 1 day postoperatively, the patient will:
• have vital signs that are stable and within normal limits.
• have decreased drainage.

Within 3 days postoperatively, the patient will:
• have no hemorrhage.

Nursing diagnosis: *Pain related to postoperative tissue, nerve, and bone trauma*

NURSING PRIORITIES: (a) Relieve pain and (b) provide reassurance and teach about phantom limb phenomena.

Interventions

1. See the "Pain" care plan, page 64.

2. *Monitor for pain continuously*. Listen to complaints of discomfort and observe for tense posture, tightening fists, diaphoresis, and increased pulse rate.

3. *Document pain episodes*, noting location, characteristics, radiation, frequency, severity, and associated findings.

4. *When pain occurs, medicate promptly*, as ordered. Evaluate and document the patient's response. Taper the frequency of intramuscular medication administration after the 3rd or 4th postoperative day, as ordered; substitute oral medication, as ordered and as needed.

5. *Evaluate the dressing or cast for tightness* each time the patient complains of pain and every 3 to 4 hours. Document the findings. If circulation, sensation, or movement is impaired, notify the doctor and reapply the dressing more loosely.

6. *Reposition the patient or the residual limb* every 2 to 3 hours. Document repositionings.

7. *Gently massage the stump* every 4 hours after the surgeon removes the dressing. Avoid using emollients. Evaluate and document the patient's response.

8. *Explain the cause of phantom limb sensation and pain*. Inform the patient that this may last as long as 6 months (rarely longer), although phantom limb pain may arise again even years later.

9. *Use nonpharmacologic pain-relief measures* between times of medication administration and when the patient has not had pain relief. Consider diversion, activity, backrub, relaxation techniques, imagery, or cutaneous stimulation (such as counterirritation with oil of wintergreen). Consider consulting the doctor about a transcutaneous electrical nerve stimulation (TENS) device.

10. Additional individualized interventions: _____
_____
_____

Rationales

1. The "Pain" care plan provides general guidelines and interventions for pain.

2. Early detection and intervention promote patient comfort. Pain is what the patient states it is to him or her. Pain stimulates the sympathetic nervous system, resulting in the physical symptoms.

3. Documentation provides a baseline to help others interpret pain-related behaviors.

4. Early administration of pain medication is more effective in controlling pain than waiting until the pain is severe enough to warrant analgesics. Pain normally begins to diminish in intensity after the 3rd or 4th postoperative day.

5. Decreased circulation causes tissue hypoxia and increases the pain response.

6. Pain increases with external pressure or fatigue. Changing position decreases the area of pressure and the risk of complications from immobility.

7. Massage increases circulation to the traumatized area. Skin maceration may develop if emollients are used.

8. Phantom limb sensation is the feeling or perception of the amputated limb's continued presence. Phantom limb pain, a separate clinical event, is the awareness of pain in the amputated body part. The pathogenesis of this relatively uncommon phenomenon is unknown. Unfortunately, treatment methods for persistent phantom limb pain are of limited value. Knowing this is a normal phenomenon may reassure the patient.

9. Alternative methods decrease awareness of painful stimuli.

10. Rationale: _____
_____
_____

Outcome criteria

Within 4 hours postoperatively, the patient will:
• verbalize pain relief
• show no associated pain behaviors.

Within 1 day postoperatively, the patient will:
• verbalize understanding of phantom limb pain and sensation.

Within 3 days postoperatively, the patient will:
• decrease requests for medication.

Nursing diagnosis: *Potential infection related to interrupted skin integrity*

NURSING PRIORITY: Promote wound healing.

Interventions

1. *Observe the incision line* during each dressing change for redness, edema, or exudate. Document all findings. If a plaster cast is in place, check for signs of tissue necrosis: "hot" spots, drainage on the cast, unrelieved pain, or foul odor.

2. *Protect the residual limb from contamination and trauma.* If the patient is incontinent, protect the limb with a plastic covering. Always use sterile technique during dressing changes.

3. Always rewrap dressings securely but not tightly. Do not apply tape to skin.

4. *Encourage intake of the prescribed diet.* Document the patient's likes and dislikes, and assist with menu selection. Promote intake of foods high in protein, vitamins, calories, and minerals.

5. *Bathe the stump daily* with mild soap and water after a dressing is no longer necessary. Dry it thoroughly and leave it exposed to air twice a day for at least 20 minutes.

6. *Teach the signs and symptoms of stump breakdown.* Examine the residual limb daily for edema, redness, and breaks in the skin. Teach the patient to examine the stump regularly during exercise or cleansing after discharge.

7. *Teach stump-toughening exercises.* Have the patient push the stump against a soft pillow four to six times each day. Increase resistance gradually. Document progress.

8. Additional individualized interventions: _____
_____
_____

Rationales

1. Assessment of the incision line during the first dressing change provides baseline data for future comparison. Release of histamine causes the classic signs of inflammation. Diminished tissue perfusion, resulting from decreased circulation secondary to external pressure, causes cell death. Tissue necrosis results in pain, a sensation of local heat, drainage, and odor.

2. The introduction of microorganisms predisposes the patient to infection. Trauma causes tissue death and slows healing.

3. Tight dressings may inhibit blood flow to the healing wound, reducing the availability of oxygen and essential nutrients.

4. Preexisting diseases, such as diabetes, may require that the patient follow a specific diet. Additional amounts of protein, calories, vitamins, and minerals are needed for wound healing.

5. Hygiene is essential to maintaining healthy skin in preparation for a prosthesis. Moist skin allows maceration to occur.

6. Early detection of complications in the residual limb allows prompt treatment. Undetected complications jeopardize the rehabilitation program and may necessitate further amputation.

7. Fragile, delicate skin will not withstand the pressure applied while wearing a prosthesis. Toughening the skin prepares the patient for use of the prosthesis and reduces the chance of infection related to skin breakdown.

8. Rationale: _____
_____
_____

Outcome criteria

By the time of discharge, the patient will:
• show no signs or symptoms of infection

• list signs of stump breakdown
• demonstrate stump-toughening exercises.

Nursing diagnosis: *Potential loss of joint function related to impaired physical mobility**

NURSING PRIORITY: Maintain range of motion (ROM) in joint(s).

Interventions

1. *Promote joint extension.* Do not use pillows under a lower-extremity stump; raise the foot of the bed instead. Use slings and pillows under an upper-extremity stump.

2. *Place the patient in the prone position* for 30 minutes four times daily and for sleep (for lower-limb amputation), if not contraindicated.

3. *Do not allow the knee to bend over the edge of the chair or bed* if the patient had a below-the-knee amputation.

4. *Institute ROM exercises of the residual limb* two to three times daily, beginning on the 1st postoperative day. Gradually increase the frequency on subsequent days. Evaluate and document the patient's response.

5. Provide a trapeze bar over the patient's bed.

6. Plan activities around the time of pain medication administration. Be alert for side effects of medications that can decrease alertness or increase the patient's potential for injury.

7. Position personal belongings, water, the telephone, and the call light within the patient's reach at all times, particularly if an arm was amputated.

8. Instruct a patient with a lower-extremity amputation to call for assistance when getting out of bed. Keep the bed in the low position at all times.

9. *Teach transfer techniques* appropriate to the type of amputation (for example, repositioning in bed, or bed-to-chair or bed-to-wheelchair transfer). Document the teaching and the patient's use of the techniques.

10. *Teach muscle-strengthening exercises* specific to the limb amputated. Gluteal-setting exercises for above-the-knee amputation, hamstring-setting exercises for below-the-knee amputation, and straightening the flexed proximal joint against resistance are examples of valuable exercises. Include exercises for increasing triceps strength, such as pushing against the bed with the fists and raising the buttocks off the bed. Begin the regimen twice a day and gradually increase as muscle strength increases.

Rationales

1. Proper positioning promotes venous return and decreases edema without causing flexion contracture.

2. The prone position facilitates normal joint alignment in extension.

3. Allowing the stump to hang in a dependent position decreases venous return and increases edema. Flexion contracture may occur if the stump is allowed to remain in a bent position.

4. ROM exercises are directed toward maintaining normal joint mobility. Permanent shortening of the muscles results from disuse, thereby creating contractures.

5. A trapeze increases mobility in bed, allows the patient to be more independent, and prevents exclusive use of the heel or elbow when the patient pushes up in bed (this may contribute to skin breakdown).

6. Pain prevents full participation in physical and psychological activities. Narcotics may cause orthostatic hypotension and fainting from vascular dilation.

7. Being able to reach needed items promotes independence and increases self-confidence in a patient with an altered self-concept.

8. Muscle weakness and impaired balance after a lower-limb amputation may result in an injury.

9. Learning transfer techniques reestablishes the patient's independence and promotes a feeling of security when moving in and out of bed.

10. Optimal muscle strength is required to maintain balance while using assistive devices, such as crutches or a walker or prosthesis.

*Non-NANDA diagnosis

Interventions *continued*

11. *Explain that stance will be altered.* Teach abdominal and gluteal muscle-tightening exercises to be done while standing. Have the patient practice balancing on the toes, and bending the knee and hopping while holding onto a chair. Remain with the patient during this practice.

12. *Consult the doctor concerning physical therapy or occupational therapy referrals.*

13. For lower-extremity amputees, reinforce skills of ambulation, crutch walking, or use of assistive devices learned during physical therapy. Encourage the patient to use these techniques whenever ambulating.

14. *Ensure appropriate referral for home care* if self-care ability or motivation is a problem. Emphasize the importance of ongoing rehabilitative follow-up.

15. Additional individualized interventions: _____
_____
_____

Rationales *continued*

11. Alteration in the center of gravity requires increased muscle strength, balance, and coordination to compensate for the amputated extremity. Remaining with the patient during practice provides reassurance and helps prevent injury related to loss of balance.

12. Early intervention by physical and occupational therapy specialists increases rehabilitation potential.

13. Consistent use of learned methods increases the patient's skill, self-confidence, and awareness of their importance.

14. Inadequate follow-up may lead to functional limitations or further limb compromise. Ongoing follow-up allows early detection of problems.

15. Rationale: _____
_____
_____

Outcome criteria

By the time of discharge, the patient will:
• display no signs of joint contracture
• demonstrate independent use of transfer techniques

• use assistive devices independently
• demonstrate muscle-strengthening exercises
• initiate discussion of follow-up plans.

Nursing diagnosis: *Disturbed self-concept: body image related to loss of a body part*

NURSING PRIORITY: Promote acceptance of the loss of a body part.

Interventions

1. *Show an accepting attitude toward the patient.* Anticipate a period of mourning for the lost limb. See the "Grief/Grieving" care plan, page 41.

2. Spend time with the patient each shift. *Encourage verbalization of feelings about the amputation.* Provide clarification in areas of misunderstanding and reassurance that the patient's feelings are normal.

3. *Encourage family and friends to interact with the patient.* Explain the patient's response, if necessary. Refer family members to a counseling resource person, as needed.

4. *Encourage the patient to look at the residual limb and to begin participating in its care* during the early postoperative period. Do not force this, however, if the patient is hesitant.

Rationales

1. The patient needs to feel valued as an individual. Various manifestations of the grieving process may be experienced. For example, the patient may direct anger and frustration toward staff and family members. The "Grief/Grieving" care plan contains detailed information on assisting with the grieving process.

2. Clarifying knowledge and encouraging ventilation of feelings assists passage through the grieving stages.

3. The demonstration of acceptance and love by significant others is essential to completing the grieving process.

4. Acknowledging the stump results in recognizing reality and promotes movement toward accepting an altered body image. Each patient works through the acceptance process individually. Forcing may provoke undue distress.

(continued)

Interventions *continued*

5. Introduce the patient to others with similar amputations who have adapted successfully.

6. *Provide information about an appropriate prosthesis and its use,* reinforcing the teaching of the prosthetist or physical therapist.

7. *Consult a minister, psychiatric clinician, or social worker if the patient is unable to progress through the grieving process.* See the "Ineffective Individual Coping" care plan, page 51.

8. Additional individualized interventions: _____
_____
_____

Rationales *continued*

5. Seeing someone who has adapted successfully demonstrates that the amputation does not have to interfere with a normal life-style. Peers may provide realistic encouragement and practical help in adapting to the change.

6. Replacement of the amputated body part with a prosthesis gives the body a more normal appearance and increases the patient's participation in daily activities. Knowledge of the availability of the prosthesis provides the patient with a goal to work toward.
   A prosthesis may be applied in the immediate postoperative period. This reduces residual limb edema, loss of muscle strength, and complications of immobility and also promotes healing through increased tissue perfusion at the operative site as a result of early ambulation. More importantly, immediate application of a prosthesis improves the psychological outlook of the patient.
   A prosthesis may also be applied 1 to 6 months postoperatively. This occurs when wound healing is delayed because of infection, peripheral vascular disease, or the patient's debilitated status.

7. Specialized assistance with the grieving process may be necessary to help the patient accept the amputation. Maladaptation to amputation may result in severe depression or suicidal behavior.

8. Rationale: _____
_____
_____

Outcome criteria
By the time of discharge, the patient will:
• verbalize feelings regarding amputation

• participate in care of the residual limb
• express knowledge about the availability of a prosthesis (if appropriate).

Discharge planning
NURSING DISCHARGE CRITERIA
Upon discharge, documentation shows evidence of:
• stable vital signs
• absence of pulmonary or cardiovascular complications
• a healing incision with no signs of swelling, redness, inflammation, or drainage
• absence of fever
• absence of contractures
• pain controlled by oral medication
• ability to tolerate diet
• ability to perform stump care independently or with minimal assistance
• ability to perform activities of daily living (ADLs) independently or with minimal assistance
• completion of initial physical therapy program with appropriate assistive devices
• ability to transfer and ambulate independently or with minimal assistance (with a lower-extremity amputation)

• adequate home support, or referral to a home care or rehabilitation setting if indicated by lack of availability of a home support system; inability to perform ADLs, stump care, and safe transfers; or continued need for physical therapy.

PATIENT/FAMILY DISCHARGE TEACHING CHECKLIST
Document evidence that patient/family demonstrates understanding of:
__ disease process and implications
__ all discharge medications' purpose, dosage, administration schedule, and side effects requiring medical attention (there are no usual discharge medications unless the patient has an infection or a preexisting condition, such as diabetes mellitus; patient may be given a pain medication prescription, to be taken as needed)
__ prescribed diet

___ necessary equipment and supplies
___ care of residual limb and prosthesis
___ phantom limb sensation and pain
___ signs of wound inflammation and infection that require medical attention
___ prescribed exercises for the residual limb
___ need for smoking cessation program (if appropriate)
___ name and telephone number of contact person for additional information or answers to questions
___ date, time, and location of follow-up appointments
___ how to contact doctor
___ available community resources.

DOCUMENTATION CHECKLIST
Using outcome criteria as a guide, document:
___ clinical status on return from surgery
___ significant changes in status
___ pertinent laboratory and diagnostic test findings
___ pain at surgical site
___ phantom limb pain
___ phantom limb sensation
___ pain-relief measures
___ mobility and positioning
___ dressing changes
___ appearance of wound
___ drainage device(s)
___ I.V. line patency
___ oxygen therapy
___ nutritional intake
___ psychological status
___ physical therapy, occupational therapy, or both
___ assistive devices, such as a walker, crutches, or prosthesis
___ patient and family teaching
___ discharge planning.

ASSOCIATED CARE PLANS
Diabetes Mellitus
Grief/Grieving
Ineffective Individual Coping
Knowledge Deficit
Pain
Surgical Intervention

REFERENCES
Guyton, A.C. *Textbook of Medical Physiology,* 7th ed. Philadelphia: W.B. Saunders Co., 1986.
Lewis, S.M., and Collier, I.C. *Medical Surgical Nursing: Assessment and Management of Clinical Problems.* New York: McGraw-Hill Book Co., 1983.
Long, B.C., and Phipps, W.J. *Essentials of Medical Surgical Nursing.* St. Louis: C.V. Mosby Co., 1985.
Pinnell, N.N., and deMenesses, M. *The Nursing Process: Theory, Application, and Related Processes.* East Norwalk, Conn.: Appleton & Lange, 1986.
Price, S.A., and Wilson, L.M. *Pathophysiology: Clinical Concepts of Disease Processes.* New York: McGraw-Hill Book Co., 1986.

Fractured Femur

DRG information

DRG 210 [Surgical DRG] Hip and Femur Procedures, Except Major Joint. Age >17 with Complication or Comorbidity (CC).
Mean LOS = 13.5 days
Principal diagnoses for DRGs 210, 211, 212 include:
• fixation of bone without fracture reduction
• closed and open reduction with internal fixation
• open reduction without internal fixation.

DRG 211 [Surgical DRG] Hip and Femur Procedures, Except Major Joint. Age >17 without CC.
Mean LOS = 12.7 days

DRG 212 [Surgical DRG] Hip and Femur Procedures, Except Major Joint. Ages 0 to 17.
Mean LOS = 8.3 days

PRO alert: DRG 210 is a frequently occurring DRG. Professional review organizations (PROs) are scrutinizing this category for discharge planning criteria closely because patients in this DRG have frequently complained of premature discharge. Therefore, daily nursing documentation must describe the patient's progress with activities of daily living (ADLs), transfers, and ambulation, and the patient's status on discharge in regard to ADLs and transfers must be documented carefully before patient discharge.

Introduction

DEFINITION AND TIME FOCUS

The femur, which connects the hip joint and the knee joint, is the longest and strongest bone in the body. It follows, therefore, that most fractures of the femur are the result of traumatic accidents involving considerable force.

The two primary classifications of femur fractures are:
• proximal end fractures, involving the portion of the femur that engages with the acetabulum. These fractures may be further classified into two subtypes: intracapsular, involving the head and neck of the femur within the hip joint, and extracapsular, involving the area from the femoral neck distally to about 2″ (5 cm) below the lesser trochanteric portion of the femur.
• femoral shaft fractures, involving the distal portion of the femur.

This clinical plan focuses on preoperative and postoperative care of the patient admitted to the hospital for treatment of a femur fracture. The reader is referred to the "Total Joint Replacement in the Lower Extremity" care plan, page 315, for more information on fractures involving the hip joint.

ETIOLOGY/PRECIPITATING FACTORS

• Proximal end fractures—fall injuries most common, with osteoporosis a significant contributing factor in elderly patients
• femoral shaft fractures—high-impact traumatic accidents, most often in younger patients

Focused assessment guidelines

NURSING HISTORY (Functional health pattern findings)

Health perception–health management pattern
• if elderly, may have history of coexisting medical conditions (such as heart disease, diabetes, or hypertension) that contributed to the fall or caused it
• if younger, may be the first contact with an inpatient medical setting

Activity-exercise pattern
• in proximal end fractures, may be able to walk but, more typically, *cannot bear weight*
• in femoral shaft fractures, usually unable to bear weight

Cognitive-perceptual pattern
• *typically complains of severe, localized pain in the affected limb*
• may complain of numbness or tingling in the affected limb

Value-belief pattern
• in proximal end fractures, commonly expresses disbelief that injury is severe; an elderly patient may insist he or she will be "fine" if only pain can be relieved; may deny need for surgical intervention

PHYSICAL FINDINGS
Cardiovascular
• *edema* at injury site or distally
• tachycardia
• hypotension
• if severe vascular involvement, reduced pulse rate or amplitude in the affected limb

Pulmonary
• hyperventilation

Musculoskeletal
• *deformity at injury site* (for example, external rotation or shortening)
• *severe pain with movement of affected limb*
• ecchymosis
• crepitus

Integumentary
• *diaphoresis*
• pallor (if significant blood is lost)

DIAGNOSTIC STUDIES
(may reveal no significant abnormalities initially, unless related to coexisting condition)
• *complete blood count—performed preoperatively for baseline;* may reveal extent of blood loss associated with the injury (decreased hemoglobin and hematocrit levels are late signs). White blood cell count may be elevated in response to injury.
• *type and cross match—performed in preparation for blood replacement* if significant blood loss is present or incurred during surgery
• *chemistry panel—obtained preoperatively for baseline* to assess for underlying imbalances that may have contributed to the cause of injury or that may be significant for intraoperative care (for example, potassium imbalances, which can cause increased cardiac irritability during anesthesia). Blood urea nitrogen and creatinine levels evaluate renal function.
• prothrombin time and partial thromboplastin time—performed preoperatively for baseline; usually are normal unless an underlying bleeding disorder is present. Elderly patients may be started on anticoagulant therapy during postoperative period to minimize possibility of thromboembolic complications.

• urinalysis—performed for baseline evaluation of renal function
• serum drug levels—performed if medication overdose or noncompliance is suspected as contributing factor to injury
• *femur X-ray—identifies location and type of fracture*
• *chest X-ray—routinely obtained preoperatively* to rule out associated injuries or preexisting conditions affecting surgical care (such as cardiomegaly or congestive heart failure)
• *12-lead EKG—obtained preoperatively for baseline* and to identify preexisting cardiac abnormalities, if any; may be especially significant in elderly patients or in those with blunt trauma to the chest (possible cardiac contusion) besides the leg injury

POTENTIAL COMPLICATIONS
• shock
• hemorrhage
• pulmonary embolism
• fat embolism
• thrombophlebitis
• aseptic necrosis of the femoral head
• nonunion of the affected portions
• osteomyelitis
• pneumonia
• arthritic deformities

Collaborative problem: *Potential preoperative complications related to nature of traumatic injury*

NURSING PRIORITIES: (a) Prepare the patient to undergo surgery in optimal physical condition and (b) prevent, or identify and promptly treat, preoperative complications.

Interventions

1. *Ensure adequacy of respirations.* Auscultate the lungs and note any evidence of unequal chest excursion, unequal or diminished breath sounds, pain with respiration, cyanosis, restlessness, or dyspnea. Report any respiratory difficulty to the doctor immediately, and prepare to support ventilation, if indicated.

2. *Assess for signs of bleeding, and maintain circulatory volume.* Report increasing pulse rate, decreasing blood pressure, pallor, diaphoresis, or decreasing alertness. Establish and maintain an I.V. fluid line, usually with Ringer's lactate solution initially, as ordered. If an open fracture is actively bleeding, apply direct, continuous pressure to the area and notify the doctor.

Rationales

1. High-impact accidents, such as those which cause femoral fractures, have a high incidence of multisystems injuries, including chest trauma. Pulmonary or chest abnormalities may indicate tracheal injury, pneumothorax, rib fractures, or other complications. In elderly patients, preexisting medical conditions may involve cardiac or central nervous system functions, affecting respiratory capability and adequacy.

2. Femoral fractures are associated with significant blood loss because of the vascularity of long bones and the proximity of large vessels. The parameters noted are signs of shock and require immediate intervention. Intravenous infusions help replace fluids lost from bleeding; Ringer's lactate expands blood volume and replaces electrolyte losses. Direct pressure controls active bleeding until surgical intervention is initiated.

(continued)

Interventions *continued*

3. *Assess the limb's neurovascular status.* Note weakened or absent pulses, mottling, cyanosis, paresthesias, or loss of sensation. Compare pulse rates bilaterally. Avoid moving the limb unnecessarily. Report deficits to the doctor immediately.

4. *Control pain.* Administer analgesics as ordered during the preoperative period, making sure all medications are noted on the surgical checklist. Apply cold packs to the fracture area. Maintain traction or splinting as ordered.

5. If an open fracture is present, ensure that tetanus and infection prophylaxis are considered preoperatively. Cover the wound site with a sterile dressing.

6. Prepare the patient for surgical intervention, if indicated. See the "Surgical Intervention" care plan, page 71, for details.

7. Additional individualized interventions: _____
_____
_____

Outcome criteria
Before surgery, the patient will:
• have normal respirations or, if abnormal, respiratory problems treated
• show stable vital signs
• have no uncontrolled bleeding
• have neurovascular findings within expected limits, with doctor aware of the current status

Rationales *continued*

3. Blood vessels and nerves in the fracture area may be displaced or severed by bone fragments or by post-fracture edema and deformity. Movement may cause further injury. Inadequate perfusion of the limb may result in permanent functional impairment or loss of the affected portion.

4. Pain contributes to increasing anxiety, stresses the cardiovascular system, and may contribute to increased muscle tension and associated displacement at the injury site. Noting medications on the checklist ensures that their effect is considered in the administration of anesthesia. Cold packs help minimize edema by causing local vasoconstriction. Traction and splints may help reduce muscle spasms and pain.

5. Tetanus immunization, if not current, should be updated, because open wounds associated with trauma are considered tetanus-prone. Any break in skin integrity predisposes the patient to infection. Covering the wound minimizes further contamination from airborne bacteria.

6. Depending on the location and type of fracture, a femoral fracture may be treated with traction or a cast; usually, however, surgery is the treatment of choice. A variety of surgical procedures is used to repair these fractures, including placement of a prosthesis, pins, or nails and bone grafts. Proper preoperative preparation helps minimize postoperative problems. General interventions for the surgical patient are included in the "Surgical Intervention" care plan.

7. Rationale:_____
_____
_____

• verbalize reduction in the severity of pain
• have had tetanus and infection prophylaxis begun, if indicated
• have had preoperative teaching and preparation.

Collaborative problem: *Potential postoperative complications related to the nature of the traumatic injury, surgical intervention, or immobility*

NURSING PRIORITIES: (a) Prevent, or identify and promptly treat, postoperative complications and (b) promote healing.

Interventions

1. See the "Pain" and "Surgical Intervention" care plans, pages 64 and 71, respectively.

Rationales

1. General guidelines for care of the surgical patient and for pain management are included in these care plans.

Interventions *continued*

2. *Assess vital signs* according to postoperative protocol or more often if unstable. Check dressings and drains for bleeding. Report any abnormalities in vital signs; excessive bleeding, if any, from the wound or from surgical sites, drains, or graft sites; increasing edema; or ecchymosis. Assess for associated injuries if a high-impact trauma was involved.

3. *Assess neurovascular status* at least once every hour or more often if compromised. Note weakened or absent pulses, mottling, cyanosis, paresthesias, loss of sensation, or a significant increase in edema postoperatively. Be especially alert for signs of compartment syndrome: progressive pain that is exacerbated by stretching, sensory deficits, paralysis, tense or hard swelling, or decreasing distal pulses. Notify the doctor immediately if the patient's status becomes impaired.

4. *Maintain the patency of the I.V. infusion and administer fluids* as ordered, usually for at least 24 hours postoperatively.

5. *Administer antibiotic medications, if ordered. Observe the wound site carefully* and report any increase in erythema or swelling or any fever, purulent drainage, or other signs of infection.

6. *Prevent complications associated with immobility.*

• Encourage performance of gentle range-of-motion exercises for unaffected extremities; encourage dorsiplantar flexion, or quadriceps-setting exercises for affected limb, as permitted. Increase activity level as permitted and as tolerated.

• Apply antiembolic stockings as recommended by physician.

• Provide a trapeze to assist movement.

• Encourage coughing and deep breathing hourly while the patient is awake.

• Urge adequate fluid intake, when allowed, forcing fluids unless contraindicated. Document intake and output.

Rationales *continued*

2. As noted previously, femoral fractures may cause massive bleeding. Tachycardia and hypotension may indicate inadequate fluid replacement, excessive blood loss related to injury and repair, or other undetected injuries.

3. Careful neurovascular assessment ensures prompt intervention should the status of the limb become compromised postoperatively. Increasing edema may put pressure on surrounding vascular structures, impairing oxygenation of tissue. Immediate intervention is needed to restore circulation. Compartment syndrome is a complication caused by muscle swelling in which increased tissue pressure causes circulatory impairment and ischemia. This condition may occur immediately after injury or may develop over several days. Immediate treatment (fasciotomy) may avert permanent damage.

4. I.V. infusions replace fluid losses related to bleeding, NPO status, preexisting dehydration, or tissue loss during surgery. Also, maintaining venous access allows administration of I.V. medication.

5. I.V. antibiotics are usually ordered during the initial postoperative period, particularly for patients with open fractures or increased susceptibility to infections. Infection related to bone wounds can be particularly serious; untreated, it may lead to osteomyelitis and bone disintegration. If the patient is already on antibiotic therapy when the infection develops, a change in antibiotic agent may be indicated because the causative organism may be resistant to current therapy.

6. Immobility predisposes patients to a variety of complications.

• Exercises, as allowed, decrease venous stasis and help maintain muscle tone.

• Antiembolic stockings increase venous return and may help prevent thrombus formation.

• A trapeze allows the patient to assist with repositioning.

• Pulmonary hygiene measures help prevent postoperative lung infections related to immobility, anesthesia, decreased respiratory effort, and accumulation of secretions.

• Forcing fluids helps maintain hydration, liquefy secretions, maintain renal function, and minimize risk of urinary infection related to stasis. Documentation of intake and output identifies fluid imbalances.

(continued)

Interventions *continued*

• Provide clean, dry bedding and a special bed or mattress as needed; reposition the patient at least every 2 hours, and provide skin care, with special attention to bony prominences.

• Encourage verbalization of feelings. Provide diversionary activities.

7. *Observe for signs and symptoms of thromboembolic complications,* as follows:

• fat embolism—tachycardia, dyspnea, pleuritic pain, pallor and cyanosis, petechiae, crackles, wheezing, nausea, syncope, weakness, altered mentation, EKG changes, or fever; in the affected limb, pallor, numbness, or coldness to touch

• pulmonary embolism—sudden chest pain, dyspnea, tachycardia, cough, hemoptysis, anxiety, syncope, EKG changes, hypotension, or fever

• thrombophlebitis—positive Homans' sign, pain in calf, swelling, or redness locally in the limb.

   Report any signs to the doctor immediately, and initiate treatment, as ordered.

8. *Maintain proper immobilization of the affected limb,* depending on the fracture site and the type of repair. Commonly, adduction, external rotation, and acute hip flexion should be avoided in a patient with a proximal end fracture; lateral pressure or overpulling with traction must be avoided in a patient with a femoral shaft fracture. Verify specific positioning orders with the doctor.

9. *Observe for and report immediately any sudden, sharp pain, shortening or rotation of the affected limb, or persistent muscle spasm.*

10. *Encourage adequate nutritional intake,* especially of protein-rich foods and foods high in vitamins and minerals.

11. Additional individualized interventions: _____
_____
_____

Rationales *continued*

• The immobilized patient is at increased risk for skin breakdown from constant pressure. A warm, moist environment encourages bacterial growth. Special beds and careful skin care prevent pressure sore development.

• Prolonged immobilization contributes to depression, anxiety, and frustration. Verbalizing feelings to an accepting caregiver may help decrease stress. Diversionary activities decrease boredom and give the patient some sense of self-control.

7. The nature of the injury and the period of postoperative immobility predispose the patient to such complications.

• Fat embolism occurs most often in association with long-bone fractures, usually within the first 3 days after injury. The exact physiologic mechanism is unknown. Fat emboli may lodge in the lungs, heart, brain, or extremities, and associated lipase release may cause tissue irritation besides occlusion.

• Pulmonary embolism is usually a later complication, occurring 10 to 24 days after injury. Signs may be related to obstruction from a blood clot that travels to the lungs and from reflex vasoconstriction.

• Thrombophlebitis usually occurs in the lower extremities as the result of clot formation and obstruction of superficial veins, although thrombi can occlude major vessels as well.

   Immediate intervention is required, because these complications may be life-threatening. Treatment may include ventilatory support, corticosteroids, anticoagulants, or thrombolytic agents.

8. Movement of the fracture site may displace bone fragments and interfere with the healing process. Positioning of the affected limb depends on the fracture location and the surgical approach; common rules do not hold true for all patients. Verification of positioning recommendations and careful positioning avert dislocation during turning.

9. These signs may indicate dislocation of the joint or necrosis of the femoral head in a patient with a proximal end fracture. Immediate intervention is needed to prevent permanent damage.

10. The healing process requires additional calories and protein. Deficits in vitamins and minerals (particularly vitamins B and C and calcium) retard healing and can contribute to long-term bone disorders, such as osteomalacia.

11. Rationale: _____
_____
_____

Outcome criteria

Within 2 hours of arrival on the unit postoperatively, the patient will:
• have vital signs within normal limits
• have no signs of excessive bleeding, neurovascular impairment, or infection
• have no uncontrolled pain
• manage coughing and deep breathing well
• maintain proper positioning.

Within 24 hours postoperatively, the patient will:
• perform exercises as permitted
• show no signs of skin breakdown
• show no signs of thromboembolic phenomena
• verbalize awareness of positioning restrictions
• take adequate food and fluids orally, if permitted.

Nursing diagnosis: *Knowledge deficit related to changes in allowable activity level and ongoing care of injury after discharge*

NURSING PRIORITIES: (a) Reinforce the doctor's recommendations for home care, and (b) identify potential problems related to home care and intervene as appropriate.

Interventions

1. See the "Knowledge Deficit" care plan, page 56.

2. *Provide patient and family teaching* related to positioning, activity restrictions, cast care, crutch walking, use of a cane or walker, diet, complications, and medications. Verify recommendations with the doctor, and incorporate teaching throughout the hospitalization period.

3. *Assess resources for home care, and make appropriate referrals.*

4. Additional individualized interventions: _____
_____
_____

Rationales

1. General interventions for patient and family teaching are included in this plan.

2. Home care recommendations vary widely, depending on the nature of the fracture and repair, the age and condition of the patient, and any associated or preexisting conditions. The patient may be more responsive to continuous, repetitive instruction during inpatient care routines than to provision of a large amount of information at one time.

3. Depending on the factors mentioned above and on the family support structure, the patient may require home medical or nursing assistance or other follow-up care to ensure an uncomplicated recovery.

4. Rationale: _____
_____
_____

Outcome criteria

By time of discharge, the patient and family will:
• verbalize and demonstrate understanding of positioning and activity restrictions or recommendations and care of the injury

• verbalize understanding of the recommended diet and medication regimen
• identify signs and symptoms of complications
• receive appropriate referrals for home care and follow-up.

Discharge planning
NURSING DISCHARGE CRITERIA

Upon discharge, documentation shows evidence of:
• stable vital signs
• absence of pulmonary or cardiovascular complications
• healing incision with no signs of swelling, redness, inflammation, or drainage
• ability to control pain using oral medication
• absence of fever

• hemoglobin levels within expected parameters
• ability to perform activities of daily living (ADLs) independently or with minimal assistance
• ability to transfer independently or with minimal assistance
• ability to demonstrate weight-bearing restrictions when transferring
• ability to verbalize activity restrictions

• completion of initial ambulation training with the appropriate assistive device
• ability to tolerate diet
• normal voiding and bowel movements
• referral to home care if indicated by inability to perform ADLs and safe transfer technique or by continued need for physical therapy
• adequate home support, or if home support is *not* adequate:
• ability to verbalize agreement with nursing home transfer
• ability to verbalize understanding of the time frame for remaining in a nursing home to convalesce and continue physical therapy.

PATIENT/FAMILY DISCHARGE TEACHING CHECKLIST
Document evidence that patient/family demonstrates understanding of:
___ site and nature of injury and repair
___ implications of injury
___ all discharge medications' purpose, dosage, administration schedule, and side effects requiring medical attention (discharge medications may include antibiotics, analgesics, anticoagulants, and antispasmodics)
___ signs and symptoms of complications
___ activity and positioning restrictions and recommendations
___ care of cast(s), if present
___ dietary recommendations
___ when and how to access the emergency medical system
___ home care and follow-up referrals
___ date, time, and location of follow-up appointments; transportation availability, if indicated
___ how to contact doctor.

DOCUMENTATION CHECKLIST
Using outcome criteria as a guide, document:
___ clinical status on admission
___ preoperative assessment and treatment
___ postoperative assessment and treatment
___ significant changes in status
___ pertinent laboratory and diagnostic findings
___ pain-relief measures
___ activity and positioning and tolerance of same
___ nutritional intake
___ fluid intake and output
___ bowel status
___ patient/family teaching
___ discharge planning.

ASSOCIATED CARE PLANS
Fluid and Electrolyte Imbalances
Geriatric Considerations
Knowledge Deficit
Pain
Surgical Intervention
Total Joint Replacement in the Lower Extremity

REFERENCES
Emergencies. Nurse's Reference Library. Springhouse, Pa.: Springhouse Corp., 1985.
Holloway, N. *Nursing the Critically Ill Adult: Applying Nursing Diagnosis,* 3rd ed. Reading, Mass.: Addison-Wesley Publishing Co., 1988.
Luckmann, J., and Sorensen, K. *Medical-Surgical Nursing: A Psychophysiological Approach,* 3rd ed. Philadelphia: W.B. Saunders Co., 1987.

Low Back Pain—Conservative Medical Management

DRG information

DRG 243 [Medical DRG] Medical Back Problems.
Mean LOS = 5.6 days

PRO alert: Low back pain is usually treated on an outpatient basis. In fact, one of the criteria professional review organizations (PROs) look at is whether conservative outpatient management was tried before hospitalization. (This documentation would be found in the doctor's history and physical notes or in the discharge summary.) Therefore, the care plan, once the patient is hospitalized, must include frequent monitoring of pain and pain management—for example, every 4 hours. For a back pain case to be covered in an acute-care setting, the following would need to be documented:

• onset of sudden, acute pain or, if chronic pain is present, failure of outpatient management
• severe, debilitating pain needing pain relief administered intramuscularly
• the patient's inability to undergo outpatient radiology testing
• bed rest ordered and complied with.

In many cases, if myelography or magnetic resonance imaging (MRI) is positive, the patient will need a laminectomy, and documentation will need to address the future plans and potential timing for this surgery. If a patient with a positive myelogram or MRI test is discharged and subsequently readmitted within 15 days (soon to be 30 days), the PRO would consider the case "fragmented care"—"care that could have or should have been performed during the first admission." In such a case, the hospital would not be paid for the second admission. Thus, documentation at the time of the first discharge must address the future plans for treating the back pain if conservative management proves unsuccessful. The patient's understanding of future treatment plans should also be documented, especially when a myelogram or MRI test is positive. This is important because, if the patient decides to be discharged for conservative treatment, the PRO will not consider this to be "fragmented care." This necessary documentation would be the doctor's responsibility. Nurses should be aware of the necessity for this type of documentation, however, and document related nursing care, such as pain-relief attempts and discharge teaching.

Introduction

DEFINITION AND TIME FOCUS

Low back pain requiring medical management results from localized injury such as muscle strain or sprain, from degenerative changes in the vertebral facets or from abrupt dislocation of an intervertebral disk of the lumbar spine. Usually a disabling condition, it is one of the most common health problems reported. This clini-cal plan focuses on the patient admitted for diagnosis and conservative management during an episode of acute or chronic pain and limited mobility.

Note: This care plan does not address back pain from visceral conditions, such as pancreatitis, renal calculi, gynecologic diseases, spinal cord infections, or spinal tumors.

ETIOLOGY/PRECIPITATING FACTORS

• poor posture, scoliosis, or exaggerated lordotic curve
• congenital malformation, spondylolisthesis, or spondylosis
• degenerative changes in the vertebrae from osteoarthritis or osteoporosis
• muscle or ligament tears, or degenerative disk
• muscle deconditioning, or unaccustomed physical activity
• history of stooping, bending, improper body mechanics, heavy lifting, or sudden movement
• obesity

Focused assessment guidelines

NURSING HISTORY (Functional health pattern findings)

Health perception–health management pattern

• if outpatient management was tried, *may report failure to follow previous medical recommendations for back pain control* because of personal and family attitudes about the condition that conflict with therapeutic regimen for back pain
• *may report occupation that requires manual labor,* leading to mechanical stress to the back muscles, *or sedentary work,* leading to deconditioning of muscles
• may describe present health status as a threat to job security
• may describe self-care activities, including use of over-the-counter medication and visits to chiropractor

Nutritional-metabolic pattern

• may report pretrauma and present dietary intake that exceeds therapeutic recommendations

Elimination pattern

• *may describe alteration in bowel or bladder elimination,* such as difficulty urinating or constipation

Activity-exercise pattern

• *commonly describes a recent change in normal activity level,* including activities of daily living (ADLs) and work-related activities
• commonly reports emotional intolerance to bed rest confinement

Sleep-rest pattern
- *may report sleep often interrupted by low back pain or referred pain*
- may report "bed rest fatigue"

Cognitive-perceptual pattern
- *generally reports disabling acute or chronic pain, or both*
- usually does not understand, or is misinformed about, diagnosis and treatment
- may report decreased tactile sensation in body area distal to injury site
- may have experienced a significant decrease in sensory-perceptual stimulation because of bed rest

Self-perception–self-concept pattern
- *may express concern about loss of independence*
- may describe feelings of low self-esteem

Role-relationship pattern
- *may report decreased ability to maintain social, occupational, and family roles,* leading to a sense of isolation
- may report family resentment concerning inability to perform roles

Sexuality-reproductive pattern
- *commonly describes altered sexual functioning*

Coping–stress tolerance pattern
- may report concern about financial security
- *may describe frustration with bed rest routine*
- may express anxiety about long-term implications of condition

Value-belief pattern
- may express values or beliefs that conflict with long-term therapeutic regimen and life-style changes

PHYSICAL FINDINGS
Musculosketal
- *sprains or strains*
  - □ *painful and limited spinal motion*
  - □ *paravertebral muscle tenderness*
  - □ weak abdominal muscles
  - □ no increase in pain with dorsiflexion of foot

- *disk problems* (abrupt and degenerative)
  - □ *painful, limited spinal motion*
  - □ *pain in low back region*
  - □ *increased sciatic pain with movement, activity, or straight-leg raising* (associated with L2-3 or L3-4 disk herniation)
  - □ *pain or numbness in neck, shoulders, or arms* (associated with cervical disk herniation)
  - □ *pain radiating down one or both lower extremities*
- *vertebral problems* (degenerative conditions)
  - □ *painful, limited spinal motion*
  - □ *pain in the low back*

Neurologic
- sprains or strains
  - □ no abnormal findings—for example, deep tendon reflexes are present
- disk problems (abrupt and degenerative)
  - □ *positive neurologic signs, such as absent deep tendon reflexes*
  - □ sensory deficit noted on one or both extremities corresponding to level of lesion

DIAGNOSTIC STUDIES
- no specific laboratory data apply to lower back pain
- lumbar spine X-ray—usually unrevealing
- *computed tomography scan and MRI—performed to demonstrate the spinal canal diameter, showing disk displacement*
- *myelography—may be normal or may show narrowing of the disk space*
- electromyography—done to test the electrical potential of skeletal muscles; helpful in localizing the site of nerve root pressure related to ruptured disk
- epidural phlebography (injection of contrast medium into anterior internal vertebral blood vessel)—may reveal altered venous flow over area of disk herniation

POTENTIAL COMPLICATIONS
- herniation of intervertebral disk
- major neurologic deficits distal to lesion
  - □ paralysis
  - □ nerve damage
  - □ loss of urinary bladder and bowel control
  - □ muscle atrophy

Nursing diagnosis: *Impaired physical mobility related to acute pain and limitations of the therapeutic regimen*

NURSING PRIORITIES: (a) Promote healing, (b) prevent complications associated with immobility, and (c) prepare the patient for participation in a long-term rehabilitation program.

Interventions

1. *Maintain strict and complete bed rest* for 1 to 6 weeks, using a firm mattress or a bed board. Supervise bathroom privileges if ordered.

Rationales

1. "Bed rest with bathroom privileges only" is the essential ingredient in the conservative treatment of low back pain. Bed rest allows inflammation to subside so the affected disk shrinks back away from the spinal nerve on which it has impinged.

Interventions *continued*

2. *Evaluate neurologic function in the lower extremities daily, and report new or increasingly abnormal findings to the doctor.* Assess the following parameters: deep tendon reflexes, sensation (presence in both extremities, sharp and dull differentiation, position and temperature awareness), muscle strength (bilateral symmetry of muscle groups, dorsiflexion against resistance, and plantar flexion against resistance).

3. *Supervise maintenance of body alignment,* observing the following guidelines:
• During side-lying, keep the bed flat and one or both lower extremities flexed.
• When the patient is supine, elevate the head of the bed 20 degrees to 45 degrees and flex the knees at least 45 degrees.
• Do not allow the patient to lie prone.

4. *Administer medications,* as ordered, observing for therapeutic effectiveness and monitoring as follows:

• muscle relaxants—observe for excessive drowsiness, and alert the patient to use caution when beginning ambulation
• anti-inflammatory drugs—if nonsteroidal drugs are used, observe for GI irritation or bleeding, and monitor for signs of hepatotoxicity; if steroids are used, watch for development of infection
• analgesics—observe for side effects according to the particular medications used, and encourage discussion of long-term pain-control plans and alternative therapies.

5. *Assess lung sounds* at least every 8 hours and report any abnormal findings. Supervise 10 deep breaths every 2 hours while the patient is awake. Encourage hourly use of the incentive spirometer, as ordered.

6. *Supervise quad sets, calf pumping, and circle motions of the ankle* 10 times each, four times per day.

7. Apply elastic stockings, as ordered, until the patient is ambulatory. Remove them twice daily, then provide skin care:
• Bathe patient once daily.
• Apply lotion without massaging the muscle.
• Inspect for and report any reddened areas.
• Keep the stockings wrinkle-free.

8. *Supervise repositioning* at least every 2 hours, using the logrolling method to turn the patient. Use caution to prevent shearing of delicate skin.

Rationales *continued*

2. Development or extension of abnormal neurologic signs indicates the need for reevaluating the therapeutic regimen.

3. Positioning should not stress the back muscles or the vertebral column. Improper alignment may impair healing or extend injury.

4. Medication protocols may vary significantly, depending on the doctor's preference and on underlying conditions affecting patient status:
• Muscle relaxants reduce painful spasm and promote rest.

• Anti-inflammatory medications decrease edema and pressure on adjacent tissues and structures.

• Analgesics control pain and promote relaxation. Dependence may be a problem with long-term analgesic use, so early planning for alternatives is essential.

5. The bed acts as a splint, restricting thoracic movement. Reduced chest expansion contributes to the development of atelectasis, pneumonia, and other respiratory complications. Full expansion promotes optimal lung function.

6. Immobility may cause thrombophlebitis or embolus formation from poor venous return. Exercise decreases venous stasis.

7. Elastic stockings are thought to assist venous return by exerting support on affected muscle groups.

8. Skin breakdown is prevented by periodically relieving pressure over bony prominences. Logrolling prevents twisting and strain on back muscles.

(continued)

Interventions *continued*

9. While the patient is on bed rest, *maintain dietary intake high in bulk, fluids, and roughage and lower than usual in calories.* Consult with the dietitian to develop a diet plan that incorporates patient preferences as much as possible.

10. *Coordinate and supervise implementation of a progressive activities schedule,* incorporating the doctor's medical recommendations and the physical therapist's expertise. Ensure that the patient participates in the planning process.

11. *Instruct about movements that may stretch or strain back muscles and the vertebral column*—for example, poor body mechanics when lifting, bending, pulling, or pushing; quick, jerky motions; and improper use of such implements as a broom, rake, or shovel.

12. Instruct about the effects of straining at stool, coughing, or sneezing. Advise splinting the abdomen with arms or pillows and assuming a recumbent position (if possible) during coughing or sneezing episodes.

13. If ordered, apply pelvic traction, 1 hour on and 3 to 4 hours off. Ensure that the belt fits snugly over the iliac crests and that the patient's torso aligns with the pull of traction. Avoid pressure on ropes or pulleys from bedding or equipment. Elevate the patient's knees and the head of the bed slightly, avoiding extreme angles. If traction increases pain, notify the doctor.

14. As ordered, apply moist heat for 20 minutes, four times daily.

15. As ordered, instruct the patient in the correct application and use of a back brace or corset, emphasizing that such devices should be worn only for the prescribed amount of time.
   Teach the patient to apply the brace or corset while lying supine, to fasten it snugly and ensure that the belts or ties are not twisted, to inspect the skin for pressure points daily and report areas of discomfort, to wear low-heeled shoes with no-slip soles, and to remain cautious about avoiding falls.

16. Additional individualized interventions: _____
_____
_____

Rationales *continued*

9. Immobility reduces peristaltic movement. Dietary requirements may need alteration to maintain the patient's normal bowel habits. Metabolic needs are lower when the patient is on bed rest; undesired weight gain can occur if the diet is not adjusted. Incorporating preferred foods may increase compliance with restrictions.

10. A gradually progressive activities schedule reduces the risk of reinjury during the healing phase and allows muscle strength to increase to meet demands.

11. These activities are under the patient's control. Exercising precautionary measures may help reduce or prevent stress to the injured back.

12. These activities increase muscle stress and pain. Splinting the abdomen provides added back support.

13. Short-term pelvic traction may relieve pressure on the affected nerve by counteracting muscle spasm. Long-term traction, however, tends to aggravate the condition. Proper application and positioning are essential for therapeutic benefit. Increased pain with traction indicates the need to reevaluate the therapy.

14. Moist heat is more effective than dry heat in promoting muscle relaxation.

15. A back brace or corset usually is used for only a short period of time. Extended use may cause the muscles to weaken, thereby reducing the support and strength needed to maintain a healthy back. Proper teaching prevents complications.

16. Rationale: _____
_____
_____

Outcome criteria

Because the degree of injury and response to therapy vary widely among patients with low back injury, expectations for outcome criteria must be evaluated on an individual basis.

Within 7 to 10 days of admission, the patient will:
• verbalize absence of pain at rest
• engage in prescribed movement without pain
• assume only recommended positions
• perform pulmonary hygiene measures regularly as taught
• perform leg exercises regularly as taught
• have neurologic findings at the preinjury level.

By the time of discharge, the patient will:
• have clear lungs
• have intact skin without signs of breakdown
• have no signs or symptoms of thromboembolic phenomena
• have normal bowel elimination
• have weight at or slightly below the preinjury level
• list precautions to observe regarding medication therapy
• list movements to avoid
• apply corset or brace (if ordered) appropriately.

Nursing diagnosis: *Disturbed self-concept: role performance related to bed rest, effects of medications, prolonged discomfort, and required alterations in activity*

NURSING PRIORITY: Promote a positive self-concept.

Interventions

1. *Include the patient as a participant in care-planning conferences.* Allow as many choices as possible within therapeutic guidelines. Encourage the patient's active participation in designing and implementing goals and activities.

2. Discuss positive and negative feelings the patient may experience during various phases of care—for example, about the sick role, the recovery or rehabilitation role, role expectations when well, the potential for being accused of malingering, and life-style changes for preventing further injury.

3. *Help the patient identify coping resources and refocus negative feelings*—for example, seeing difficulties as challenges rather than obstacles.

4. Avoid authoritarian attitudes.

5. As appropriate, facilitate referral to the occupational therapy department for diversionary activities while patient activity is limited.

6. *Identify, with the patient, strategies to maintain motivation* during rehabilitation. Consider using a reward system, breaking down long-term goals into short-term goals, and varying activity routines to maintain the patient's interest.

7. Additional individualized interventions: _____
_____
_____

Rationales

1. Participation in planning and implementing health management activities helps reduce frustration from loss of usual roles and fosters an increased sense of independence and self-control.

2. Exploration of feelings experienced during phases of long-term disability helps prepare the patient for potential problems and facilitates adjustment to life-style alterations. For example, sick and recovery roles may actually provide the patient with certain rewards, such as increased time for hobbies and more time to spend with the family. Identifying such factors early in care planning may help the patient plan other ways to meet such needs when well again.

3. Identifying resources and positive focusing promote a full commitment to recovery.

4. "Taking over" by caregivers diminishes the patient's self-esteem.

5. Suitable diversionary activities provide opportunities to meet goals and feel productive despite the disability. Such activities also may help promote relaxation and reduce boredom during periods of prolonged bed rest.

6. Maintaining motivation is a key factor in successful rehabilitation. The ability to plan motivation strategies reflects the patient's level of self-esteem and acceptance of responsibility.

7. Rationale: _____
_____
_____

Outcome criteria

Throughout the period of hospitalization, the patient will:
• participate actively in care planning
• participate in diversionary activities
• identify coping resources
• plan and use strategies to maintain motivation.

Nursing diagnosis: *Knowledge deficit related to recovery, rehabilitation, and long-term management of low back injury*

NURSING PRIORITY: Teach the patient and family about back care, assisting with adaptation to necessary changes.

Interventions

1. *Provide information about the anatomy and physiology of the following structures:* vertebrae, including their articulation; disks and how their positions relate to pressure; spinal cord and nerve branches and their sensory and motor functions; and the spinal canal and fluid.

2. *Provide information about changes that need to be made in the patient's life-style.*
Sitting recommendations include:
• Don't sit for more than 20 minutes at a time without changing position.

• Keep the knees higher than the hips. A footstool is an ideal way to accomplish this.

• Sit in a firm chair with a straight back.

Driving recommendations include:
• Always wear seat belts.

• Tilt the front seat to allow the knees to be higher than the hips.
• Change position frequently, keeping the buttocks tilted forward.
• Allow for frequent rest stops that include walking, standing, or lying down.
Standing and walking recommendations include:
• Stand to perform as many tasks as possible, being careful not to stand in one position too long. If prolonged standing is required, shift body weight from one foot to the other, or elevate one foot on a stool.
• When turning, turn the feet first, avoiding a quick jerk with the body.
• Avoid shoes with heels higher than ½".

Lifting recommendations include:
• Use principles of body mechanics when lifting, such as squatting directly in front of the object to be lifted, holding it close to the body, and then rising to a standing position without bending the back. Do not keep legs straight while lifting and do not reach over furniture to perform such tasks as closing windows.

• Do not lift heavy objects.

Rationales

1. Knowledge of anatomy and physiology lays the groundwork for further teaching about the therapeutic regimen.

2. Teaching the patient about these activities promotes health and reduces or eliminates the possibility of reinjury.
• Sitting greatly increases intervertebral pressure.

• This position reduces stress on the spinal column.

• Soft or overstuffed chairs and sofas do not firmly support the spinal column.

• Seat belts help prevent serious trauma to the spinal column should a motor vehicle accident occur.
• This position decreases strain on back and shoulder muscles.
• This position decreases lumbar lordosis and reduces strain on the low back muscles and spinal column.
• Frequent rest stops relieve stress caused by sitting.

• Next to lying down, standing best reduces intervertebral pressure.

• The low back is vulnerable to injury from twisting movements.
• High heels shift the center of gravity and cause strain on the vertebral column and back musculature.

• Bending from a forward position with the legs straight places unnecessary strain on the vertebral column and back musculature.

• Lifting heavy objects strains the back muscles.

Interventions *continued*

Exercise recommendations include:
• Perform the following exercises as prescribed, beginning with 5 repetitions once a day and increasing to 20 repetitions twice a day within a 4-week period: pelvic tilt, knee-chest exercises, gluteal setting, and modified sit-ups (keeping the knees bent, as prescribed).

Begin and end all exercise sessions by applying heat to the low back for at least 10 minutes. If any of these exercises causes pain, or if pain is present before beginning exercise, omit the exercise program and notify the doctor.

3. *Teach about correct posture.* Have the patient stand against the wall with head, shoulders, and buttocks touching it and with one hand placed in the lumbar lordotic space between the back and the wall. Then demonstrate how contraction of the rectus abdominis and gluteus maximus muscles rotates the pelvis and decreases this space. Explain that the patient should use this posture for walking, standing, and sitting.

4. *Discuss the most common causes of pain in the low back,* particularly muscle spasm and pressure on the nerve root, causing pain (associated with the low back) to radiate down the sciatic nerve.

5. *Discuss how nerve pressure damage may affect the lower extremities' structure and function.* Emphasize the importance of reporting muscle atrophy, lost or decreased reflexes, lost or decreased function, and sensory loss.

6. Discuss with the family or significant others their ideas and feelings concerning the patient's current and long-term health status.

7. Additional individualized interventions: _____
_____
_____

Rationales *continued*

• A regular prescribed exercise program will strengthen abdominal and back muscles. Heat application allows for maximum muscle extension and contraction and reduces the incidence of muscle spasm.

3. Correct posture reduces stress on the lumbosacral spine and musculature.

4. Knowing the causes of pain in the low back may help the patient identify the origin of pain and may help determine relief strategies.

5. Early reporting of changes in lower-extremity function, sensation, or appearance may facilitate corrective intervention.

6. Support from family members or significant others is essential to recovery and rehabilitation.

7. Rationale: _____
_____
_____

Outcome criteria
By the time of discharge, the patient will:
• demonstrate understanding of the back's structure and function
• demonstrate knowledge of and strategies for implementing specific life-style changes, as prescribed

• select appropriate pain-relief strategies
• list specific significant neurologic changes to report
• perform an exercise regimen as taught
• list precautionary measures for activities.

Discharge planning
NURSING DISCHARGE CRITERIA
Upon discharge, documentation shows evidence of:
• absence of severe debilitating pain
• ability to control pain using oral medications
• initiation of physical therapy exercise program or plans for outpatient treatment program
• completion of diagnostic radiology work-up

• ability to perform ADLs independently or with minimal assistance
• ability to transfer and ambulate with minimal difficulty
• absence of pulmonary or cardiovascular complications
• absence of skin problems or breakdown
• adequate home support system or referral to home care if indicated by inadequate home support system or the patient's inability to care for self.

PATIENT/FAMILY DISCHARGE TEACHING CHECKLIST

Document evidence that patient/family demonstrates understanding of:

__ nature of low back injury
__ signs and symptoms indicating delayed healing or reinjury
__ recommended daily exercise program
__ common feelings about life-style changes
__ plan for resuming activity
__ resources for support of life-style modification
__ role of family members or significant others in rehabilitation program
__ proper posture, lifting techniques, and positioning to prevent reinjury
__ all discharge medications' purpose, dosage, administration schedule, and side effects requiring medical attention (usual discharge medications include analgesics and muscle relaxants)
__ date, time, and location of follow-up appointments
__ how to contact doctor.

DOCUMENTATION CHECKLIST

Using outcome criteria as a guide, document:

__ clinical status on admission
__ significant changes in clinical status
__ pertinent diagnostic findings
__ pain-relief measures
__ nutritional intake
__ elimination status
__ progressive activities schedule and progress
__ complications of immobility, if any
__ patient/family teaching
__ discharge planning.

ASSOCIATE CARE PLANS

Ineffective Individual Coping
Knowledge Deficit
Laminectomy
Pain

REFERENCES

Carpenito, Lynda. *Handbook of Nursing Diagnosis*. Philadelphia: J.B. Lippincott Co., 1985.

Carpenito, Lynda. *Nursing Diagnosis: Application to Clinical Practice*. Philadelphia: J.B. Lippincott Co., 1984.

Gordon, M. *Nursing Diagnosis: Process and Application*. New York: McGraw-Hill Book Co., 1982.

Luckmann, Joan, and Sorensen, Karen. *Medical-Surgical Nursing: A Psychophysiologic Approach*, 3rd ed. Philadelphia: W.B. Saunders Co., 1987.

Ziegler, Shirley, et al. *Nursing Process, Nursing Diagnosis, and Nursing Knowledge*. East Norwalk, Conn.: Appleton & Lange, 1986.

Osteomyelitis

DRG information

DRG 238 [Medical DRG] Osteomyelitis.
    Mean LOS = 10.7 days
    Principal diagnoses include:
      • acute osteomyelitis
      • chronic osteomyelitis
      • unspecified osteomyelitis.

Introduction

DEFINITION AND TIME FOCUS

Osteomyelitis is a bone infection that may be classified as primary, secondary, or chronic. *Primary osteomyelitis* occurs from compound fractures, penetrating wounds, or surgery. *Secondary osteomyelitis* may be hematogenous (blood-borne) or may represent extension of nearby infections (especially pressure sores). *Chronic osteomyelitis,* a persistent bone infection manifested by draining sinus tracts, is rare.

This clinical plan focuses on the person hospitalized for nonsurgical treatment of osteomyelitis for which postdischarge I.V. antibiotic therapy is anticipated.

ETIOLOGY/PRECIPITATING FACTORS

• infection of bone (either blood-borne or from an open wound) with sufficient numbers of pathogenic bacteria, most commonly *Staphylococcus aureus*
• sufficient bone and soft-tissue trauma and hematoma to provide growth media for the infecting agent
• implantation of foreign material (joint replacements, methyl methacrylate, or metallic internal fixation devices) that may impair the body's ability to control bacterial growth
• infection near bone or joints

Focused assessment guidelines

NURSING HISTORY (Functional health pattern findings)

Health perception–health management pattern

• may display lack of knowledge about basic health care practices, especially hand washing and signs and symptoms of infection
• commonly has a history of unreported local infection
• *may have unreported systemic indicators of infection,* such as fever, malaise, weakness, irritability, anorexia, and generalized sepsis (rare)
• may report a recent upper respiratory tract infection, urinary tract infection, otitis media, tonsillitis, or dental procedure
• may have a history of disinterest in learning about care of an immobilization device or devices (for example, cast, splint, external fixator, or brace) needed previously

Activity-exercise pattern

• may complain of weakness and fatigue

Cognitive-perceptual pattern

• *may report pain in affected limb,* increasing with movement

Sleep-rest pattern

• may report night sweats

PHYSICAL FINDINGS
General

• *emotional irritability*

Cardiovascular

• tachycardia

Integumentary

• *localized edema and erythema* in infection area
• *localized tenderness* in infection area
• *draining wound,* with either serous or gross purulent drainage (may not be present in all patients)
• diaphoresis and flushing with fever
• chronically draining sinus tracts (rare)

Musculoskeletal

• pseudoparalysis (inability to move joints adjacent to area of osteomyelitis because of anticipatory pain)
• muscle spasm in infected extremity

DIAGNOSTIC STUDIES

• *wound aspirate or bone biopsy of sequestrum (involved bone)—demonstrates the infecting organism*
• *complete blood count (CBC)—reveals leukocytosis and, after prolonged infection, anemia related to associated decrease in erythropoietin production and reduced red blood cell lifespan*
• *erythrocyte sedimentation rate—elevated;* degree of elevation relates to amount of infection
• *blood cultures—may reveal infecting organism* when shaking chills and temperature spikes are associated with osteomyelitis
• *X-rays of involved bones—may eventually show evidence of osteonecrosis and new bone formation*
• *radioisotope scanning—may reveal areas of increased vascularity, indicating infection*
• sinograms of draining sinus tracts—may outline involved areas of chronic osteomyelitis
• computed tomography scan—may reveal changes indicating osteonecrosis

POTENTIAL COMPLICATIONS

• chronic osteomyelitis
• sepsis
• dysfunctional limb
• refractory, life-threatening infection requiring amputation
• pathologic fractures
• nonunion of existing fractures

Nursing diagnosis: *Pain related to inflammation*

NURSING PRIORITY: Relieve pain.

Interventions

1. *See the "Pain" care plan,* page 64.

2. *Clearly identify and document the source and degree of pain.* Aid the patient in rating pain, using a scale of 1 to 10 (1 = minor pain, 10 = severe pain).

3. *Medicate the patient with narcotics and nonsteroidal anti-inflammatory drugs (NSAIDs),* as ordered, and carefully document their effectiveness. Monitor for side effects.

4. *Instruct the patient in nonpharmacologic pain-control methods,* including relaxation, enhanced relaxation, guided imagery, distraction (verbal, auditory, visual, or tactile), rhythmic breathing, cutaneous stimulation (for example, with oil of wintergreen), massage, a transcutaneous electrical nerve stimulation device, use of heat and cold, and biofeedback. Document methods that the patient finds helpful.

5. Elevate and support the affected extremity.

6. Schedule necessary activity of the involved extremity to coincide with the peak effectiveness of analgesics or anti-inflammatory agents.

7. Instruct the patient to report increasing or uncontrolled pain. Explain the rationale.

8. Use adjunctive devices (such as bed cradle, antirotation boots, or a mechanical bed) to aid in pain control.

9. Maintain traction and support devices (such as a cast, a splint, or internal fixators), as ordered.

10. Additional individualized interventions: _____
_____
_____

Rationales

1. General interventions for pain are detailed in this plan.

2. Continuing or increasing severe pain may indicate increasing inflammation.

3. Bone pain is usually severe.

4. Nonpharmacologic pain control allows self-control of pain without medication's side effects. Use of ice, for example, not only acts as a tactile distraction and stimulates large-diameter cutaneous sensory neurons, decreasing deeper pain sensation (the gate control theory), but also causes vasoconstriction, thus reducing edema that contributes to pain.

5. Elevation enhances venous return to reduce inflammatory edema; supportive positioning protects against muscle strain and spasm.

6. Timing activity with the peak of medication action decreases discomfort while allowing necessary mobility.

7. Increasing or uncontrolled pain may indicate worsening of the osteomyelitis, ineffective therapy, or both.

8. Reducing direct pressure, rotational force, and discomfort from turning may help control pain in some circumstances.

9. Immobilization and external support devices aid fracture healing, protect the infected bone from excessive stress, and decrease pain.

10. Rationale: _____
_____
_____

Outcome criteria
Within 1 day of admission, the patient will:
• show no indications of uncontrolled pain, such as facial grimacing, tachycardia, increased blood pressure, or groaning
• verbalize pain control
• rate pain severity, on a scale of 1 to 10, as decreased since admission.

Within 2 days of admission, the patient will:
• verbalize or demonstrate an understanding of at least two personally effective nonpharmacologic methods of pain control
• verbalize an understanding of the need to report increasing or uncontrolled pain.

Nursing diagnosis: *Knowledge deficit related to infectious process*

NURSING PRIORITY: Teach the patient to recognize local and systemic indicators of infection.

Interventions

1. *Instruct about signs of infection:* local (erythema, edema, localized tenderness, serous or purulent discharge, and local warmth) and systemic (fever, malaise, weakness, and irritability). Stress the need to report these findings promptly.

2. Evaluate learning by having the patient list the signs and symptoms of infection, preferably in writing. Document learning. See the "Knowledge Deficit" care plan, page 56.

3. Provide the patient with a written list of local and systemic signs and symptoms of infection for periodic review. Document the material provided.

4. When necessary, establish continuity through community health nurse referrals for continued education or evaluation of learning.

5. Additional individualized interventions: _____
_____
_____

Rationales

1. Patient knowledge of these signs and symptoms and of the importance of prompt reporting ensures early identification and treatment of infection.

2. Having the patient list signs and symptoms provides feedback about learning and an opportunity to identify omissions and correct misconceptions. The "Knowledge Deficit" care plan contains further details related to patient teaching.

3. Readily accessible review materials help the patient retain new knowledge.

4. Some patients will not be able to use the patient education provided and will require continued instruction or appropriate follow-up care.

5. Rationale: _____
_____
_____

Outcome criteria

Within 2 days of admission, the patient will:
• be able to list local and systemic signs and symptoms of infection
• verbalize an understanding of the need to alert health care providers promptly if infection occurs.

By the time of discharge, the patient will:
• have arrangements for appropriate follow-up care by a public health or visiting nurse (if appropriate).

Nursing diagnosis: *Potential for injury related to use of antibiotics with high potential for toxic side effects*

NURSING PRIORITY: Prevent or minimize toxic effects of antibiotic therapy.

Interventions

1. *Teach the patient about antibiotic administration, especially monitoring for significant antibiotic side effects.* See *Side Effects of Antibiotic Therapy: What to Monitor, What to Teach*, page 312, for details.

2. Instruct the patient to report any untoward findings promptly.

3. Additional individualized interventions: _____
_____
_____

Rationales

1. A patient's knowledgeable participation in self-care while hospitalized improves the quality of care, allows for rapid identification of complications, and prepares the patient for self-care after discharge.

2. Prompt identification and notification reduce potential long-term complications.

3. Rationale: _____
_____
_____

SIDE EFFECTS OF ANTIBIOTIC THERAPY: WHAT TO MONITOR, WHAT TO TEACH

For aminoglycosides (gentamicin, neomycin, streptomycin, and tobramycin):

Teach the potential for ototoxicity (as shown by high-frequency hearing loss [for example, decreased ability to hear a ticking wristwatch], tinnitus, vertigo, and dizziness); superimposed infections (especially fungal infections of mucous membranes or from indwelling vascular access catheters); and nephrotoxicity (as shown by oliguria, polyuria, abnormal specific gravity, and rapid weight gain).

Explain the rationale for baseline and weekly audiograms and serum creatinine and blood urea nitrogen (BUN) studies.

Monitor and document intake and output and urine specific gravity while the patient is hospitalized. Report oliguria, polyuria, and specific gravity extremes (<1.010 and >1.030). When appropriate, instruct the patient about continuing this monitoring after discharge.

Weigh the patient twice a week and document. Instruct about twice-weekly weight measurement after discharge. Report weight gain exceeding 3 lb between weighings.

Teach close monitoring of mucous membranes for indications of fungal infection (redness, tenderness, cheesy-white discharge, black or furry tongue, fever, nausea, and diarrhea) and the need to report any that occur.

For penicillin antibiotics (ampicillin, carbenicillin, cyclacillin, methacillin, and oxacillin):

Teach the potential for anemia (as shown by weakness, paleness, and malaise), hypersensitivity reactions (as shown by asthmatic reactions, erythematous-maculopapular rash, urticaria, and anaphylaxis), and overgrowth of nonsusceptible organisms leading to opportunistic infection (as shown by fever, chills, and continuing or increasing indications of infection or inflammation).

For cephalosporin antibiotics (cefamandole, cefazolin, cefoxitin, cephalothin, cephapirin, and cephradine):

Teach the potential for opportunistic infections (as shown by fever, chills, and continuing or increasing indications of infection or inflammation), photosensitivity (unusual sensitivity to sunlight), and, in patients with suspected renal or hepatic disease, nephrotoxicity (as shown by oliguria, pyuria, abnormal specific gravity, and rapid weight gain) and hepatotoxicity (as shown by jaundice, icteric sclera, dark brown urine, and pale, pasty stools).

Explain the rationale for baseline and weekly measurement of serum creatinine, BUN, lactic dehydrogenase, serum glutamic-oxaloacetic transaminase, and serum glutamic-pyruvic transaminase levels.

Monitor and instruct the patient about nephrotoxicity and weight gain, as discussed under "For aminoglycosides" above.

When oral medications are used, teach the patient to avoid concurrent intake of iron products or dairy foods, because they decrease cephalosporin absorption.

Instruct the patient to avoid direct sunlight and to use sunblocking agents when sun exposure is unavoidable.

For sulfonamide antibiotics (sulfadiazine, sulfamethoxazole, sulfamethoxydiazine, sulfamethoxypyridazine, sulfapyridine, and sulfisoxazole):

Teach the potential for nephrotoxicity (as shown by polyuria, oliguria, abnormal specific gravity, and rapid weight gain), agranulocytosis (as shown by fever and lesions of the mucous membranes, gastrointestinal tract, and skin), crystalluria (as shown by evidence of renal calculi—hematuria, pyuria, frequency, urgency, retention, and pain in the flank, lower back, perineum, thighs, groin, labia, or scrotum), and hemorrhagic tendencies (as shown by epistaxis, bleeding gums, prolonged bleeding from wounds, ecchymoses, melena, hematuria, hemoptysis, and hematemesis from disruption of intestinal flora and synthesis of vitamin K).

Explain the rationale for baseline and weekly measurement of serum creatinine, BUN, and granulocyte levels.

Monitor and instruct the patient about nephrotoxicity and weight gain, as discussed under "For aminoglycosides" above.

Instruct the patient taking oral sulfonamides to drink 8 oz of fluid with each dose. Encourage total fluid intake of at least 2 liters daily.

For I.V. antibiotic therapy:

When indwelling vascular access catheters are used for antibiotic administration, closely monitor the insertion sites for inflammation or irritation that does not respond to treatment with topical antibiotics. Teach patients discharged with these catheters to monitor for this complication and promptly report it to the health care provider.

Teach close monitoring of wounds for indications of unresolving or increasing inflammation or infection (which are evidence of opportunistic infection).

Outcome criteria

Within 2 days after initiation of therapy, the patient will:
• (with aminoglycoside therapy) list signs and symptoms of ototoxicity, nephrotoxicity, and superimposed infections
• (with penicillin therapy) list signs and symptoms of anemia, hypersensitivity reaction, and opportunistic infections
• (with cephalosporin therapy) list signs and symptoms of photosensitivity, hepatotoxicity, nephrotoxicity, and opportunistic infections

• (with sulfonamide therapy) list signs and symptoms of nephrotoxicity, agranulocytosis, crystalluria, and hemorrhagic tendencies
• verbalize the importance of rapidly reporting signs and symptoms of untoward effects.

By the time of discharge, the patient will:
• demonstrate the ability to perform monitoring procedures as needed for specific antibiotics
• have arrangements for appropriate follow-up care (if appropriate).

Nursing diagnosis: *Activity intolerance related to prolonged infection, pain, and immobilization*

NURSING PRIORITY: Help the patient regain or exceed his or her preadmission activity level.

Interventions

1. Assess and document the patient's baseline activity level, including muscle strength and ability to perform activities of daily living (ADLs).

2. Document activity goals set in collaboration with the patient.

3. Teach the patient about the need to maintain muscle strength and endurance while immobilized. Provide instruction in isotonic and isometric exercises that can be accomplished within the patient's activity limitations.

4. Have the patient demonstrate the exercises, and document evaluation of the patient's learning. Establish and monitor an exercise regimen during hospitalization. Help the patient establish a home exercise program as well, and ensure community health care follow-up after discharge, when needed.

5. Provide abundant positive reinforcement. Develop goals of increasing strength (increasing increments of resistance or weight) and endurance (increased numbers or repetitions or longer exercise periods), when feasible.

6. Provide written materials on exercises for review as needed. Document the materials provided.

7. Additional individualized interventions: _____
_____
_____

Rationales

1. Adequate baseline information allows determination of individualized goals.

2. Involving the patient in planning increases the potential for success. Goals provide focus.

3. Maintenance exercise programs decrease loss of muscle strength and endurance during immobilization by maintaining adequate blood flow to muscle and by stressing bone to ensure continued balance in bone remodeling.

4. Return demonstration of exercises allows effective evaluation of patient learning. Monitoring the exercise regimen ensures that the patient will maintain strength and endurance.

5. Positive reinforcement helps establish health-promoting behaviors. Isometric and isotonic exercises performed with restricted activity may increase strength and endurance in unaffected body areas.

6. Written materials increase understanding of exercises and the potential for doing exercises as required.

7. Rationale: _____
_____
_____

Outcome criteria

Within 2 days of admission, the patient will:
• verbalize an understanding of the need for exercise, list exercise goals, and return-demonstrate the exercise regimen.

By the time of discharge, the patient will:
• independently perform exercises and verbalize an understanding of their necessity while activities are restricted.

Discharge planning
NURSING DISCHARGE CRITERIA
Upon discharge, documentation shows evidence of:
• wound drainage within expected parameters, with little or no purulent or bloody drainage
• stable vital signs
• absence of fever
• absence of pulmonary or cardiovascular complications
• no erythema, edema, or tenderness at wound site
• ability to control pain using oral medications
• stabilizing weight and adequate nutritional intake
• ability to perform ADLs at prehospitalization level
• ability to transfer, ambulate, and perform prescribed exercise regimen at prehospitalization level or with minimal assistance
• ability to perform wound care and dressing changes as prescribed, with minimal assistance
• hemoglobin and blood cultures within normal parameters
• white blood cell count within expected parameters
• normal bowel and bladder function
• adequate home support system or referral to home care if indicated by inadequate home support system or inability to care for self.

If patient is discharged with an indwelling vascular access catheter, documentation also shows:
• evidence of automatic referral to home care or arrangements for short-term stay in a nursing home (dependent upon the patient's home support system and ability to care for catheter and administer medications independently)
• knowledge of where to obtain additional supplies
• knowledge of signs and symptoms indicating catheter dysfunction or infection
• ability to follow prescribed medication regimen and I.V. administration technique
• ability to monitor weight and follow instructions for oral intake, as directed
• knowledge of signs and symptoms indicating fungal or other systemic infection.

PATIENT/FAMILY DISCHARGE TEACHING CHECKLIST
Document evidence that patient/family demonstrates understanding of:
___ disease process and implications
___ hand washing techniques
___ dressing changes, pin site care, cast care, or care of braces or splints, as appropriate
___ nonpharmacologic pain-control interventions
___ use of elevation and supportive positioning
___ range-of-motion exercise of the affected extremity, as appropriate
___ dietary requirements
___ all discharge medications' purpose, dosage, administration schedule, precautions, and side effects requiring medical attention (usual discharge medications include antibiotics, analgesics, and NSAIDs)
___ need to report increasing or uncontrolled pain

___ care of indwelling vascular access catheters
___ self-administration of I.V. antibiotics
___ vascular access complications
___ patient exercise regimen
___ how to obtain clarification or further information
___ date, time, and place of follow-up appointments
___ referral agencies and medical supply resources
___ how to contact doctor.

DOCUMENTATION CHECKLIST
Using outcome criteria as a guide, document:
___ clinical status on admission
___ significant changes in status
___ pertinent laboratory and diagnostic test findings
___ baseline information on muscle strength, ADLs performed, endurance, and collaborative goals established with the patient
___ source and degree of pain, especially if persistent or increasing
___ effective pain-relief measures
___ daily or biweekly measurement of weight, intake, output, and urinary specific gravity, when appropriate
___ appearance of indwelling vascular access catheter site, and care and patency maintenance of the catheter
___ patient/family teaching
___ discharge planning.

ASSOCIATED CARE PLANS
Chronic Renal Failure
Ineffective Individual Coping
Pain
Surgical Intervention
Urolithiasis

REFERENCES
Carpenito, L. *Handbook of Nursing Diagnosis*. Philadelphia: J.B. Lippincott Co., 1984.
Gordon, M. *Manual of Nursing Diagnosis 1984-1985*. New York: McGraw-Hill Book Co., 1985.
Hoyt, N.J. "Infections Following Orthopaedic Injury," *Orthopaedic Nursing* 5(5):15-24, September/October 1986.
Kneisl, C.R., and Ames, S.A. *Adult Health Nursing: A Biopsychosocial Approach*. Reading, Mass.: Addison-Wesley Publishing Co., 1986.
Pagliaro, A.M., and Pagliaro, L.A. *Pharmacologic Aspects of Nursing*. St. Louis: C.V. Mosby Co., 1986.
Pozzi, M., and Peck, N. "An Option for the Patient with Chronic Osteomyelitis: Home Intravenous Antibiotic Therapy," *Orthopaedic Nursing* 5(5):9-14, September/October 1986.
Swearingen, P.L. *Manual of Nursing Therapeutics*. Reading, Mass.: Addison-Wesley Publishing Co., 1986.
Vick, R.L. *Contemporary Medical Physiology*. Reading, Mass.: Addison-Wesley Publishing Co., 1984.

Total Joint Replacement in the Lower Extremity

DRG information

DRG 209 [Surgical DRG] Major Joint and Limb Reattachment Procedure.
Mean LOS = 12.3 days

DRG 471 [Surgical DRG] Bilateral or Multiple Major Joint Procedures of the Lower Extremity.
Mean LOS = 18.0 days

Additional DRG information: One of the PRO criteria used when reviewing total joint replacement is, "Did the patient receive maximum hospital benefit?" The major criteria are, "Did the patient get a physical therapy evaluation?" and "Is there evidence that discharge planning was appropriate?" The discharge would be deemed premature if a rehabilitation program had not been designed and if the patient showed evidence of medical instability.

Discharge planning for a patient who undergoes joint replacement of a lower extremity should include automatic referral to the social services department. Most patients cannot perform at their prehospitalization functioning level after this procedure, especially if it is bilateral. Documentation should indicate the posthospitalization rehabilitation plan. This documentation will not necessarily be done by the nurse; it could be done by the physical therapist, occupational therapist, or discharge planner–social worker.

In many cases, patients are eligible for nursing home or extended care facility (ECF) care after discharge until they can ambulate 50' to 80' independently or with minimal assistance. Because the discharge plan commonly includes early discharge with a transfer to an ECF, early referral to the social services department is essential for this diagnosis to allow adequate time for finding appropriate posthospitalization placement.

These DRGs have been significant money losers because of the cost of surgical components and the rehabilitation time. Although the surgeon may inform the patient before surgery about a nursing home or ECF transfer, most patients want to stay in the hospital until they feel ready to go home. Nurses can help prepare the patient for an early discharge and transfer.

Introduction
DEFINITION AND TIME FOCUS
Total joint replacement involves the surgical implantation of a prosthesis, which replaces the damaged articulating surfaces of the joint. Joint damage may be from debilitating arthritis or from traumatic degenerative bone disease. In the lower extremity, total joint replacement entails removing the damaged tissues,

including bone, synovium, and cartilage. An acrylic cement may be used to cement a metallic prosthesis, which replaces the femoral head or the femoral condyle, or a polyethylene prosthesis, which replaces the acetabulum or tibial plateau. Porous, coated metal implants have been developed that allow bone to grow into the joint area; this method may be used instead of the acrylic cement.

This clinical plan focuses on preoperative and postoperative care of the patient admitted for total hip or knee replacement.

ETIOLOGY/PRECIPITATING FACTORS
• factors contributing to joint debilitation, including arthritis, infection, trauma, and obesity
• causes of degenerative joint incongruity, including hormonal imbalance, instability related to dysplasia, calcium deficiency from menopause, and physiologic changes from aging
• femoral head irregularities from Legg-Calvé-Perthes disease or avascular necrosis

Focused assessment guidelines
NURSING HISTORY (Functional health pattern findings)

Health perception–health management pattern
• *may demonstrate decreased motivation to carry out a previously prescribed rehabilitation program* for injured or painful joint(s)
• *may report a history of misconceptions about care of injured or painful joint(s)*—for example, may report exercise during acute pain episodes, or inappropriate use of mobility aids
• *may have accompanying problems, such as obesity, excessive involvement in sports, neurologic deficits, arthritis, or evidence of osteoporosis*
• *may have a history of problems with, or surgical procedures involving, this or other joints*
• may report need for specific aids (such as a knee immobilizer) to prevent falls or further damage
• may report short- or long-term use of prescribed corticosteroids

Nutritional-metabolic pattern
• may report inadequate nutrient intake before admission, indicating poor tissue state for wound healing

Elimination pattern
• may report constipation (related to decreased mobility)

Activity-exercise pattern
• *may report inability to ambulate, sit up, change position, move extremities, or get in and out of bed*
• *may report inability to tolerate an exercise program because of unusual fatigue and weakness before or after exercise*
• *may report some soreness over bony prominences*
• *may report a history of unusual swelling around affected joint(s)*
• may report decreased ability to perform activities of daily living (ADLs)
• may report decreased leisure activity related to joint problems

Sleep-rest pattern
• may report ineffective rest and sleep patterns, with frequent waking because of pain or stiffness
• may report stiffness after sleep or periods of rest

Cognitive-perceptual pattern
• *reports pain or stiffness,* or both, usually chronic and associated with movement or weight bearing
• *may report lack of knowledge about the specific joint condition, causes of the condition, aggravating factors, ways this procedure will change the condition, stages of recovery and rehabilitation, and personal responsibility during recovery and rehabilitation*
• may display poor recognition of needs related to healing of affected joint, especially concerning nutrition needed for healing and limitations on ADLs and planned exercise

Role-relationship pattern
• *may describe inadequate support system* in relation to needs during planned rehabilitation program

Coping–stress tolerance pattern
• *may report concern about recovery of full function in affected joint*

PHYSICAL FINDINGS
Note: Physical findings vary, depending on the joint involved and the nature and extent of the injury or disease process.

Cardiovascular
• normal peripheral pulses in affected extremity

Neurologic
• *decreased bilateral patellar and Achilles reflexes*

Musculoskeletal
• *pain on active or passive range-of-motion (ROM) exercise of affected joint*
• *limited ROM or contracture of affected joint*
• *varus, valgus, or flexion deformity of knees*
• *decreased leg strength*
• *shortening of affected limb*
• *impaired gait*
• *joint enlargement, inflammation, or tenderness*
• *distorted posture* from pain or effort to maintain balance
• *crepitation* on movement

Integumentary
• ischemic blanching or redness over bony prominences

DIAGNOSTIC STUDIES*
• electrolytes—may show hypokalemia from corticosteroid use
• fasting blood sugar—may show hyperglycemia from corticosteroid use
• bilateral X-ray of hip or knee joints—demonstrates extent of degenerative changes
• chest X-ray—demonstrates presence of lung disease

POTENTIAL COMPLICATIONS
• hemorrhage
• thrombophlebitis
• infection (systemic or wound- or joint-related)
• disarticulation of prosthesis
• pulmonary embolus
• atelectasis
• pneumonia
• neurovascular damage in the extremity
• fat embolism
• osteomyelitis

Collaborative problem: *Potential postoperative complications (hypovolemic shock, neurovascular damage, or thromboembolic phenomena) related to surgical trauma, bleeding, edema, improper positioning, or immobility*

NURSING PRIORITY: Prevent or promptly detect complications.

Interventions
1. For hypovolemic shock, implement these measures:

Rationales
1. Both usual postoperative factors and the unique nature of joint replacement place the patient at risk for hypovolemic shock.

---

*Laboratory findings are usually nonspecific for the disease process.

Interventions *continued*

• *See the "Surgical Intervention" care plan,* page 71.

• *Maintain patency of the wound drainage device. Assess, measure, and record the amount of Hemovac drainage* every 8 hours or as needed to maintain continuous suction. Monitor the amount of bleeding, and report unusual increases.

2. For neurovascular damage, implement these measures:

• *Perform neurovascular checks* every hour for the first 4 hours after the patient's return from surgery, then every 2 hours for 12 hours, and then every 4 hours until ambulatory. Assess pedal pulses, capillary refill time, toe temperature, skin color, foot sensation, and ability to move the toes and dorsiflex the ankle. Compare findings to the other extremity as well as to earlier findings. Once the patient is ambulatory, reassess at least daily.

• *Notify the doctor immediately if pedal pulses are absent or unequal bilaterally; if capillary refill time > 3 seconds; if the patient has cold toes, pale skin, foot numbness, tingling, or pain; or if the patient cannot move the toes.*

• *Maintain positioning as recommended.* See the "Impaired physical mobility" nursing diagnosis in this care plan for further details.

• Apply ice packs to the affected joint for 24 to 48 hours postoperatively.

• Maintain patency of the drainage device as previously described.

3. For thromboembolic phenomena, implement these measures:

• Instruct and coach preoperative exercises for calves, quadriceps, gluteals, and ankles. Postoperatively, supervise performance of exercises 5 to 10 times hourly while the patient is awake.

• Monitor for signs of thromboembolism, assessing daily for calf pain, a positive Homans' sign, redness, and swelling. See the "Surgical Intervention" and "Thrombophlebitis" care plans, pages 71 and 229, respectively, for details.

• Apply elastic stockings to both legs (to the affected extremity only after the dressing is removed). Remove twice daily for 1 hour. Check the skin for signs of pressure.

Rationales *continued*

• The "Surgical Intervention" care plan contains general interventions related to postoperative shock. This plan presents information particularly pertinent to hip or knee replacement patients.

• The hip area is highly vascular. Also, the patient may be on an anticoagulant to prevent thromboembolism. Initial drainage may be frank blood but should become serosanguineous within a few hours. A typical amount is 300 to 500 ml in the first 24 hours postoperatively, decreasing to 100 ml within 48 hours. The drainage device usually is removed by the 5th postoperative day.

2. Alterations in neurovascular status may be associated with trauma to the nerves or blood vessels as a result of surgical intervention, joint dislocation, edema, improper positioning, or excessive tightness of abduction pillow straps.

• Early detection of neurovascular damage facilitates prompt intervention to correct the underlying cause and minimize the chance of permanent damage.

• Early medical intervention can prevent permanent damage in the affected extremity.

• Proper positioning is critical to prevent prosthesis dislocation, which can trap and irreparably damage nerves or blood vessels.

• Ice packs promote vasoconstriction, thereby decreasing inflammation, edema, and bleeding at the operative site.

• Drainage must be maintained because fluid accumulation could exert pressure on nearby nerves and vessels.

3. Patients undergoing total joint replacement are at particular risk for thrombophlebitis, embolism, and fat embolism because of immobility-induced venous stasis and possible surgical trauma to veins.

• Practice during the preoperative period enhances the patient's ability to perform exercises postoperatively. These exercises are designed to promote venous return, minimizing the risk of thromboembolic phenomena.

• Calf pain, redness, or swelling may indicate thrombus formation. The "Surgical Intervention" care plan contains general interventions related to various thrombotic and embolic phenomena. The "Thrombophlebitis" care plan provides additional details on assessing for this complication.

• Elastic support stockings may promote venous return by redirecting flow from superficial veins to deeper veins.

(continued)

Interventions *continued*

• Monitor for signs of fat embolism daily. Immediately report sudden onset of dyspnea, tachycardia, pallor or cyanosis, or pleuritic pain. See the "Surgical Intervention" care plan for details.

• Administer prophylactic anticoagulants (aspirin, heparin, or warfarin), as ordered. Monitor clotting studies and report findings outside the recommended therapeutic range. Observe for (and advise the patient and family to report) melena, petechiae, epistaxis, hematuria, ecchymoses, or other unusual bleeding.

4. Additional individualized interventions: _____

_____

_____

Outcome criteria for hypovolemic shock
Within 2 hours postoperatively, the patient will:
• exhibit blood pressure and pulse within normal limits for this patient
• exhibit drainage lightening in color from frank bleeding.

Outcome criteria for neurovascular damage
Throughout the period of hospitalization, the patient will:
• exhibit bilaterally equal pedal pulses and toe temperature

Outcome criteria for thromboembolic phenomena
Within 3 days postoperatively, the patient will:
• exhibit no signs or symptoms of fat embolism
  □ alert and oriented
  □ no respiratory distress
  □ no petechiae
  □ PO₂ level of 80 to 100 mm Hg.

Rationales *continued*

• Patients undergoing total joint replacement are at particular risk for fat embolism because of bone marrow release from surgical disruption of flat (pelvic) or long bones.

• Prophylactic anticoagulants may reduce the risk of thrombophlebitis or thromboembolism. However, the patient must be monitored carefully, because anticoagulant use may cause uncontrolled bleeding.

4. Rationale: _____

_____

_____

Within 1 day postoperatively, the patient will:
• exhibit drainage < 500 ml/24 hours
• exhibit serosanguineous drainage

Within 2 days postoperatively, the patient will:
• exhibit drainage < 100 ml/24 hours.

• exhibit capillary refill time < 3 seconds
• have no foot numbness or tingling
• be able to move the toes spontaneously and dorsiflex the ankle.

Throughout the period of hospitalization, the patient will:
• exhibit no signs or symptoms of thromboembolism
  □ breath sounds clear bilaterally
  □ vital signs within normal limits for this patient
  □ no calf pain on foot dorsiflexion (Homans' sign).

Nursing diagnosis: *Impaired physical mobility related to hip or knee surgery*

NURSING PRIORITIES: (a) Maintain proper alignment of the affected extremity to prevent dislocation of the prosthesis, (b) increase mobility in the extremity through implementation of the rehabilitation plan, and (c) educate the patient concerning rehabilitation needs.

Interventions

1. *Preoperatively, instruct the patient about the correct postoperative positioning of the affected extremity:*
• hip—maintain flexion of the hip joint at a 45-degree angle or less. Do not rotate the hip joint externally. Do not adduct the hip joint (do not cross the legs).
• knee—do not flex or hyperextend the leg. Maintain a position with the leg slightly elevated from the hip, using a pillow or continuous passive motion machine, as ordered—typically, for 48 to 72 hours.

Rationales

1. Preoperative teaching provides information that helps the patient maintain proper positioning of the joint postoperatively. The positioning identified helps prevent prosthesis dislocation.

Interventions *continued*

2. Preoperatively, teach the patient how to use the walking device (walker or crutches) he or she will use postoperatively. Provide practice with the device, if possible.

3. *Postoperatively, maintain bed rest as ordered, usually 24 to 72 hours. Place the affected joint in position, as ordered* (usually in the neutral position), using traction, rolls, splints, pillows, or derotation boots, as ordered and appropriate. Observe position and activity precautions, as noted above.

4. *At least every 8 hours, observe for shortening of the extremity, a sudden increase in pain, a bulge over the femoral head on the affected side (in hip replacement), and decreased neurovascular status of the affected extremity. Report any such findings to the doctor immediately.*

5. Supervise position changes at least every 2 hours. Have the patient use a trapeze and either shift weight in bed or turn to the unaffected side. Assist only as necessary.

6. Implement a planned and progressive daily ambulation schedule, as ordered, 24 to 72 hours postoperatively. Use either crutches or a walker to allow weight bearing as recommended. Coordinate this activity with the physical therapy program.

7. Ensure that unaffected joints are put through full ROM exercises at least 10 times, 3 to 4 times daily.

8. Help the patient maintain preferred rest and sleep routines. Use back rubs, other skin care measures, positioning, and ordered medications, as necessary.

9. *Collaborate with the health care team to design an appropriate rehabilitation plan* that includes:
• muscle-strengthening activities until maximum potential strength is reached
• increasing ROM of the affected joint until full ROM is attained
• return to occupational and leisure activities.

10. *Identify, with the patient, the specific methods that will be used to implement the plan.*

11. Additional individualized interventions: ⎯⎯⎯⎯⎯⎯⎯

⎯⎯⎯⎯⎯⎯⎯⎯⎯⎯⎯⎯⎯⎯⎯⎯⎯⎯⎯⎯⎯⎯⎯⎯⎯⎯⎯⎯⎯⎯⎯

Rationales *continued*

2. Preoperative instruction, and practice if possible, allow the patient to feel more secure when using the device.

3. The affected joint must be stabilized to prevent dislocation. Excessive flexion, internal rotation, or adduction will cause postoperative hip dislocation. Knee elevation helps reduce swelling and pain.

4. These signs indicate prosthesis dislocation, a common occurrence in hip replacement that requires immediate attention.

5. Self-propelled movement helps the patient maintain muscle tone and reduces the risk of skin breakdown.

6. Progressive daily ambulation promotes the patient's return to increased physical activity and self-care.

7. ROM exercises of unaffected joints must be maintained during periods of decreased activity. Arthritic joints lose function more rapidly when activity is restricted.

8. Uninterrupted periods of full relaxation and deep sleep help maintain the energy needed for remobilization of the affected joint.

9. An effective rehabilitation plan requires input from the doctor, physical therapist, occupational therapist, and members of other appropriate disciplines to maximize rehabilitation potential.

10. For a rehabilitation program to be successful, the patient must agree to the plan and must be able to describe implementation in his unique environment.

11. Rationale: ⎯⎯⎯⎯⎯⎯⎯⎯⎯⎯⎯⎯⎯⎯⎯⎯⎯⎯⎯

⎯⎯⎯⎯⎯⎯⎯⎯⎯⎯⎯⎯⎯⎯⎯⎯⎯⎯⎯⎯⎯⎯⎯⎯⎯⎯⎯⎯⎯⎯⎯

Outcome criteria

By the time of discharge, the patient will:
• maintain mobility of other joints equal to or greater than preoperative mobility
• perform self-care activities at or above the preoperative level
• verbalize an understanding of the rehabilitation plan.

By the time of discharge, the patient with a hip replacement will:
• walk with an assistive device and partial weight bearing on affected side, as tolerated

• observe ROM restrictions—flexion of the affected joint limited to 90 degrees during the rehabilitation phase.

By the time of discharge, the patient with a knee replacement will:
• ambulate with an assistive device and light weight bearing, as tolerated
• wear a knee immobilizer until independent straight leg-raising is demonstrated.

Nursing diagnosis: *Impaired skin integrity related to surgical intervention*

NURSING PRIORITIES: (a) Promote wound healing and (b) prevent infection.

Interventions

1. *Maintain the patency and cleanliness of the drainage device*, as previously described. Avoid contaminating the drainage port when emptying the device.

2. Do not administer injections in the affected extremity. Teach the patient to exercise protective precautions to minimize the risk of injury.

3. *Assess daily for signs of infection:* fever, chills, purulent drainage, incisional swelling, redness, and increasing tenderness. Teach the patient about signs and symptoms that should be reported.

4. Additional individualized interventions: _____
_____
_____

Rationales

1. Adequate suction with a self-controlled vacuum must be maintained to prevent blood collection in the joint—an excellent medium for bacterial growth. Contamination of the device may lead to wound infection.

2. Any break in the skin may predispose the patient to infection.

3. Infection is devastating to a patient with total joint replacement because the joint cannot be saved once infection and prosthetic loss occur.

4. Rationale: _____
_____
_____

Outcome criteria

By the time of discharge, the patient will:
• exhibit no bleeding
• exhibit no signs of infection

• exhibit warm and dry skin
• exhibit wound healing
• list signs and symptoms to report.

Discharge planning
NURSING DISCHARGE CRITERIA

Upon discharge, documentation shows evidence of:
• absence of fever
• vital signs within acceptable limits
• absence of infection signs and symptoms at operative site
• absence of contractures or skin breakdown
• oral anticoagulant medication for at least the previous 48 to 72 hours and partial thromboplastin time within acceptable parameters
• ability to control pain using oral medications
• absence of bowel or bladder dysfunction
• absence of pulmonary or cardiovascular complications
• ability to perform ADLs independently or with minimal assistance

• adherence to hip flexion and adduction restrictions when transferring and ambulating
• adherence to weight-bearing restrictions when transferring or ambulating
• ability to transfer and ambulate independently or with minimal assistance, using appropriate assistive devices
• ability to tolerate adequate nutritional intake
• absence of signs and symptoms of prosthesis dislocation
• adequate home support system or referral to home care or nursing home if indicated by an inadequate home support system; inability to perform ADLs, transfers, and ambulation independently; or inability to adhere to flexion or weight-bearing restrictions
• demonstration of maximum hospital rehabilitation benefit.

PATIENT/FAMILY DISCHARGE TEACHING CHECKLIST

Document evidence that patient/family demonstrates understanding of:
___ implications of joint replacement
___ rationale for continued use of antiembolism stockings
___ all discharge medications' purpose, dosage, administration schedule, and side effects requiring medical attention (discharge medications typically include analgesics, antibiotics, anti-inflammatories, and anticoagulants)
___ need for laboratory and medical follow-up if discharged on warfarin
___ schedule for progressive ambulation and weight bearing
___ additional activity restrictions
___ signs and symptoms of infection, bleeding, and dislocation
___ use of self-help devices such as raised toilet seat
___ appropriate resources for posthospitalization care
___ diet to promote healing
___ wound care
___ date, time, and location of follow-up appointments
___ how to contact doctor.

DOCUMENTATION CHECKLIST

Using outcome criteria as a guide, document:
___ clinical status on admission
___ significant changes in status
___ preoperative and postoperative teaching
___ position of affected extremity
___ exercises and ROM achieved
___ neurovascular checks
___ calf pain
___ Hemovac drainage
___ progressive ambulation
___ pain-relief measures
___ patient/family teaching
___ discharge planning and referrals
___ presence or absence of disabling fatigue
___ nutritional intake.

ASSOCIATED CARE PLANS

Ineffective Individual Coping
Knowledge Deficit
Pain
Surgical Intervention

REFERENCES

Carpenito, Lynda. *Nursing Diagnosis: Application to Clinical Practice*. Philadelphia: J.B. Lippincott Co., 1983.

Doenges, M., et al. *Nursing Care Plans*. Philadelphia: F.A. Davis Co., 1984.

Farrell, J. *Illustrated Guide to Orthopedic Nursing*, 2nd ed. Philadelphia: J.B. Lippincott Co., 1982.

Gordon, M. *Nursing Diagnosis: Process and Application*. New York: McGraw-Hill Book Co., 1982.

Phipps, Wilma, et al. *Medical Surgical Nursing*. St. Louis: C.V. Mosby Co., 1987.

Thompson, June, et al. *Clinical Nursing*. St. Louis: C.V. Mosby Co., 1986.

Ulrich, S., et al. *Nursing Care Planning Guides*. Philadelphia: W.B. Saunders Co., 1986.

Ziegler, Shirely, et al. *Nursing Process, Nursing Diagnosis, and Nursing Knowledge*. East Norwalk, Conn.: Appleton & Lange, 1986.

Skin Grafts

DRG information

DRG 263 [Surgical DRG] Skin Grafts and/or Debridement for Skin Ulcer or Cellulitis. With Complication or Comorbidity (CC).
Mean LOS = 15.2 days

DRG 264 [Surgical DRG] Skin Grafts and/or Debridement for Skin Ulcer or Cellulitis. Without CC.
Mean LOS = 10.7 days

DRG 439 [Surgical DRG] Skin Grafts for Injuries.
Mean LOS = 7.2 days

Additional DRG information: The patient undergoing skin grafts for decubitus ulcers is commonly disabled, not independently mobile, and dependent on others for care. Because of this, the patient is considered a "vulnerable adult." Any patient who presents with decubitus ulcers should automatically be referred to the social services department so that the ulcers' cause can be investigated. Most states have an automatic reporting mechanism for vulnerable adults, and nurses should be aware of this.

The patient with this diagnosis often lives in a nursing home, in which case the nursing home staff should be contacted to ascertain their ability to care for the patient in the convalescence period after discharge. Important questions to be considered include: Does the nursing home have adequate staff to care for the patient? Does the nursing home have access to a special mattress or bed that promotes healing? What is the charge for such equipment? Will an alternative nursing home be needed if the current nursing home cannot adequately care for the patient or supply needed equipment?

Under Medicare, the cost of special equipment—such as a Clinitron bed—is covered in an acute-care setting but is not covered in a nursing home at the per diem rate charged. This causes difficulty when it is discovered after patient discharge that the nursing home cannot supply the necessary equipment. Another issue to be considered is whether the patient will meet the eligibility criteria for extended care benefits under Medicare. Many patients who have undergone skin grafting will be eligible for care in extended care facilities upon discharge. All of these issues must be considered early in the hospitalization in order to prevent a delay in discharge. These are all nursing considerations, but they will probably be addressed by the social services department. This is why a referral to social services should be automatic in all cases. If a patient lives at home with a capable, willing caregiver, the issue of equipment and supplies and how they will be paid for will also need to be addressed.

Introduction

DEFINITION AND TIME FOCUS

Skin grafting is the process of covering damaged tissue, such as burned areas or decubitus ulcers, with healthy skin transplants. The skin transplants may be autografts from the patient's body, homografts from another person, or heterografts from a different species—such as porcine grafts. Grafts of varying thicknesses may be used, depending on the extent of the wound to be covered, the availability of donor sites, the mobility and vascularity of the area to be covered, and the desired cosmetic results. The usual types of grafts are:
• split-thickness—epidermis and a dermis layer varying from thin to thick, the thinner graft used for large, hidden areas and the thicker layers for large, visible areas
• full-thickness—epidermis and dermis layers, used for visible, mobile areas such as the eyelids and hands
• flap grafts—autografts of skin and subcutaneous layers, with part of the flap still attached to the donor site, used for large areas with a poor blood supply.

This clinical plan focuses on the patient who has a large, open skin wound from any cause and is admitted for preoperative wound preparation and skin grafting with a split-thickness autograft.

ETIOLOGY/PRECIPITATING FACTORS

• burns of sufficient extent or depth to require coverage by grafting to achieve protective function and healing
• large decubitus ulcers, particularly over bony, avascular areas, that cannot heal effectively by the normal processes of epithelialization and granulation from the outside wound edges, progressing inward
• major trauma, such as avulsion of an extremity, that may require grafting for protective coverage and preservation of function

Focused assessment guidelines

NURSING HISTORY (Functional health pattern findings)

Note: Because skin grafts are performed for a number of disparate reasons, such as burns, decubitus ulcers, and trauma, a typical presenting picture does not exist. However, a common need does exist to assess preoperative preparedness to ensure optimal graft success; therefore, a preoperative assessment guideline is provided instead of a description of a typical presenting picture.

Health perception–health management pattern

• Determine the purpose for grafting, including the cause and extent of the injury; the type of grafting procedure; expectations for successful graft adherence; and the potential for return of function as the basis for hospitalization care, patient teaching, and discharge planning.

• Determine the patient's perceptions regarding potential disfigurement and its impact on health status and life-style.

Nutritional-metabolic pattern
• Assess typical nutritional intake for adequate fluids, calories, proteins, and vitamins.
• Assess nutritional status for signs of nutritional deficiency, such as weight loss and poor skin and hair condition, that may contribute to nonadherence of the graft and may increase the infection risk.
• Assess for general conditions that may contribute to poor healing, such as general debilitation, immobility, age, prolonged bed rest, skin and circulatory problems, and inability to perform activities of daily living (ADLs).
• Assess the graft site for the presence of healthy granulation tissue and the absence of necrotic areas, drainage, and odor. Grafts will adhere only to healthy granulated tissue.

Elimination pattern
• Assess for elimination problems, such as frequent bowel and bladder incontinence, that may contribute to skin breakdown and poor healing.

Activity-exercise pattern
• Assess normal activity and exercise habits to determine the patient's potential for adjusting to position and activity limitations.
• Establish a baseline assessment of present musculoskeletal and neurologic functions for comparision to potential postoperative changes in function and sensation.

Sleep-rest pattern
• Assess normal sleep patterns to provide guidelines for postoperative management of pain and rest.

Cognitive-perceptual pattern
• Assess the patient's understanding of the injury's extent, the prognosis for return of function, the surgical procedure, and rehabilitation phases during hospitalization and home care, to determine the patient's readiness for treatment.

Self-perception–self-concept pattern
• Assess the patient's usual self-perception–self-concept pattern to determine his or her ability to adapt positively during the hospitalization and recovery phases.
• Assess the impact of body changes on the patient's feelings of self-worth.

Role-relationship pattern
• Assess the patient's concerns regarding the impact of current or potential disfigurement on relationships with family and others.
• Assess family members' and friends' ability to support the patient.

Sexuality-reproductive pattern
• Assess the patient's concerns regarding alterations in physical attractiveness, ability to feel sensations, and ability to perform sexually. (Note: Grafted tissue may have decreased touch sensation.)

Coping–stress tolerance pattern
• Assess for anxiety, anger, and depression related to changes in body image and potentially permanent disfigurement. (Note: Regression is a common coping pattern for patients with large wounds needing grafting.)

Value-belief pattern
• Assess the effect of cultural and value-belief systems on the patient's response to illness.

PHYSICAL FINDINGS*
Cardiovascular
• poor capillary refill

Neurologic
• diminished sensation, including pain response, over ulcerated area
• increased pain response around wound edges

Integumentary
• fragile skin
• poor skin turgor
• ulcerated area (damage may extend to subcutaneous tissue, underlying fat, and muscle; tissue may be reddened, draining, and necrotic)

Musculoskeletal
• limited mobility
• limited range of motion (ROM)

DIAGNOSTIC STUDIES
• *culture and sensitivity testing of wound drainage—may indicate infecting organism* and help determine the most desirable antibiotic treatment
• *white blood cell (WBC) count—may be elevated* in presence of inflammation and infection
• complete blood count—may show a low hematocrit level, which may affect tissue healing
• clotting time—may be prolonged, affecting tissue healing
• serum protein (albumin and globulin) and fat (cholesterol and triglycerides) levels—may be depressed in presence of poor nutritional status
• *postoperative tissue biopsy—may show infection or indicate degree of graft success*
• ultrasound—may determine size of wound, particularly if deep

POTENTIAL COMPLICATIONS
• nonadherence of graft
• infection
• contractures
• hypertrophic scar formation of donor or recipient site

---

*The physical findings listed here are related to the wound area.

Collaborative problem: *Potential nonadherence of graft related to inadequate pregrafting preparation of wound*

NURSING PRIORITY: Prepare the wound properly for grafting.

Interventions

1. *Assess and document the condition of the wound* on admission and at least every shift: size, color, depth, and the presence or absence of odor, drainage, necrotic tissue, and swelling around the wound.

2. *Change dressings* every shift, as ordered, using good hand washing and sterile technique. Use wet-to-dry dressings.

3. Cleanse the wound and surrounding skin with soap and water, as ordered, every shift. Apply topical agents such as povidone-iodine (Betadine), as ordered, according to recommended guidelines.

4. Irrigate the wound with sterile water every shift, as ordered.

5. Apply hydrophilic agents such as dextranomer (Debrisan) every shift, as ordered.

6. Apply enzymes such as Elase to the wound every shift, as ordered. Apply only to the wound, protecting healthy tissue with ointments such as zinc oxide.

7. Assist the doctor, as needed, with surgical debridement of necrotic tissue.

8. Apply barrier dressings such as Op-Site, if ordered, every 3 to 4 days or as needed for leakage.

9. Change the patient's position every 2 hours, protecting the affected area from pressure by using rubber rings, extra padding, or special positioning.

10. Additional individualized interventions: _____

_____

_____

Rationales

1. Initial documentation provides baseline data concerning wound condition. Regular assessment and documentation provide data on the pattern of tissue healing.

2. Conscientious attention to technique helps prevent infection. Wet-to-dry dressings aid healing by debriding the wound, keeping the tissue moist, and applying antiseptics to the wound.

3. Skin cleansing prevents bacterial colonization and spread. Topical microbicidal agents such as povidone-iodine may help prevent infections.

4. Wound irrigation with large amounts of sterile water removes drainage, debriding agents, and contaminants.

5. Hydrophilic agents absorb drainage and aid in wound debridement.

6. Enzymes soften necrotic tissue by fibrinolytic action, breaking up clots and exudates. Although enzymes act primarily on necrotic tissue, healthy tissue may be irritated unless protected.

7. Surgical debridement to remove necrotic tissue speeds healing and granulation tissue development.

8. Barrier dressings maintain a moist environment, which promotes granulation tissue formation.

9. Position changes promote circulation and prevent tissue damage caused by prolonged pressure on one area.

10. Rationale: _____

_____

_____

Outcome criteria
Within 2 days of admission, the patient will:
• exhibit signs of wound healing
• exhibit no redness over pressure points.

Collaborative problem: *Potential nonadherence of graft related to postoperative exudate or blood accumulation, movement, or infection*

NURSING PRIORITIES: (a) Maintain graft integrity and (b) promote graft healing.

Interventions

1. *Maintain movement restrictions* for 3 days or as ordered. Use splints, restraints, pillows, or other devices to maintain the desired position.

2. *Elevate the grafted area,* if possible, for 1 week after surgery.

3. *Continuously protect the graft site from injury,* using splints or bed cradles.

4. Assist the doctor during initial postoperative removal of inner dressings and during graft site inspection, usually done 1 to 2 days after surgery. Document. Thereafter, *carefully assess the graft site every 8 hours and document. Report immediately any swelling, redness, and exudate or blood between the graft and the underlying tissue.*

5. Maintain dressings continuously, as ordered. Report unusual drainage or dislodged dressings.

6. Apply moist, warm compresses for 20 to 30 minutes q.i.d., as ordered.

7. Medicate with topical or systemic antibiotics, or both, as ordered.

8. Additional individualized interventions: _____
_____
_____

Rationales

1. Movement of the tissue under the graft may dislodge it. Graft adherence will be evident several days after surgery, although 2 to 3 weeks are needed for graft vascularization.

2. Elevation prevents swelling, which could cause graft separation.

3. Jarring or pressure may dislodge the graft.

4. Initial dressing removal must be done with utmost care to prevent separating the graft from the underlying tissue. Regular inspections provide timely assessment data concerning the need to treat complications. Any substance, such as exudate or blood, coming between the graft and underlying tissue may cause graft separation. Swelling or redness may indicate infection, which can dislodge the graft. The doctor must carefully remove any drainage by aspiration or by rolling an applicator toward a nicked area.

5. Various dressings—including petroleum gauze, nonadhesive gauze, coarse mesh gauze, and moist saline solution—are used to maintain gentle pressure on the graft site. Drainage or dislodged dressings may prevent graft adherence.

6. Warmth and moisture increase circulation and enhance epithelial tissue formation and blood supply to the graft.

7. Antibiotics may be used prophylactically or for suspected graft infection.

8. Rationale: _____
_____
_____

Outcome criteria

Within 2 days postoperatively, the patient will:
• exhibit an intact graft
• exhibit a graft free of injury
• maintain position
• maintain activity limitations
• keep the dressing intact.

Within 2 weeks postoperatively, the patient will:
• exhibit a graft free of infection, swelling, and exudate or blood accumulation
• exhibit graft adherence and blood supply formation.

Nursing diagnosis: *Potential infection of donor site related to increased susceptibility secondary to surgical excision of half of the skin layer*

NURSING PRIORITY: Promote healing of the donor site.

Interventions

1. *Maintain dressings over the donor site* for 1 to 2 days. Document. Then replace the outer layers or remove them and leave the inner layer exposed, as ordered. Leave the inner dressing in place until it falls off spontaneously.

2. *Promote donor site drying* by leaving the wound open continuously or by cautiously applying heat from a heat lamp or hair dryer for 15 to 30 minutes q.i.d. or as ordered.

3. Promote air circulation to the donor site by using a cradle to keep bedding and clothing away from the site.

4. If infection occurs, apply wet antiseptic dressings such as acetic acid q.i.d., as ordered.

5. After healing (usually in 2 to 3 weeks), apply lotion to the site q.i.d. or as ordered.

6. Additional individualized interventions: _____
_____
_____

Rationales

1. Dressings are left over the site until serum dries. The first layer of dressing is either a nonadherent dressing, such as Xeroform, or fine mesh gauze; it is left in place until it falls off (usually 2 to 3 weeks).

2. Drying enhances dry serum formation and helps prevent infection. Heat dries the area. (Note: Skin at the donor site is sensitive to excess heat.)

3. Air circulation aids drying and healing.

4. Antiseptic dressings decrease microorganism growth and aid healing.

5. Lotions keep the skin soft and help prevent scarring.

6. Rationale: _____
_____
_____

Outcome criteria

Within 2 days postoperatively, the patient will:
• exhibit a dry, infection-free donor site.

Within 2 weeks postoperatively, the patient will:
• exhibit a reepithelialized donor site
• exhibit soft and unscarred skin.

Nursing diagnosis: *Impaired physical mobility related to position and movement limitations*

NURSING PRIORITY: Promote muscle tone and skin integrity.

Interventions

1. *Provide active and passive ROM exercises* of unaffected areas every 2 hours, as ordered.

2. Promote self-care as tolerated by the patient and ordered by the doctor.

3. *Provide splints and other devices,* as ordered, either continuously or as needed during activities or ambulation.

4. Provide relief as needed for discomfort or pain. See the "Pain" care plan, page 64.

Rationales

1. ROM exercises promote muscle tone, circulation, and a feeling of well-being; they also help prevent contractures.

2. Allowing the patient to participate in self-care enhances feelings of independence and control over the course of recovery.

3. Protective devices allow some mobility while protecting the graft site.

4. The patient will experience pain from the graft and donor sites and discomfort from immobility. Relief from pain or discomfort encourages movement, as allowed, and aids healing by promoting a sense of well-being. General interventions related to pain are contained in the "Pain" care plan.

Interventions *continued*

5. Additional individualized interventions: _____

_____

_____

Outcome criteria

Within 8 hours postoperatively, the patient will:
• have no pain or discomfort
• exhibit an intact graft

Rationales *continued*

5. Rationale: _____

_____

_____

• perform allowable ADLs, position changes, ROM exercises, and other activities.

Nursing diagnosis: *Nutritional deficit related to increased metabolic needs secondary to tissue healing*

NURSING PRIORITY: Provide adequate calories and protein to promote tissue healing.

Interventions

1. *Assess and document nutritional status daily,* including weight; skin, hair, and mucous membrane condition; and wound healing. Note baseline serum total protein findings.

2. *Provide a high-calorie, high-protein diet* along with vitamin supplements. Document calorie intake and fluid intake and output daily.

3. Additional individualized interventions: _____

_____

_____

Rationales

1. Baseline and continuous assessment data will help in planning dietary intake.

2. A diet high in calories, protein, and vitamins aids tissue healing. Maintaining an adequate fluid balance is necessary for supple skin.

3. Rationale: _____

_____

_____

Outcome criteria

Within 1 week postoperatively, the patient will:
• exhibit no signs or symptoms of inadequate nutritional intake
• exhibit a healed wound.

Nursing diagnosis: *Disturbed self-concept: body image related to wound and potential scarring*

NURSING PRIORITY: Optimize adjustment to body changes.

Interventions

1. *Allow expression of fears and concerns* related to wounds and scarring. Document patient concerns. Encourage continuity of discussion by all health team members on all shifts by documenting the patient's current psychological status on the written nursing care plan.

2. *Provide information about the expected stages of graft site healing* during nursing procedures and as needed.

Rationales

1. Sharing concerns releases tension and opens discussion, which may lead to more realistic self-appraisal of body changes.

2. Knowledge of the expected recovery stages decreases fear of the unknown and allows the patient to participate in assessment of the healing process. Initially, the area will be reddened, swollen, and different in appearance from surrounding tissue. After 6 months, the area will be more normal in appearance as swelling decreases and color matches other tissue.

(continued)

Interventions *continued*

3. Additional individualized interventions: _____

_____

_____

Rationales *continued*

3. Rationale: _____

_____

_____

Outcome criteria

Within 8 hours postoperatively, the patient will:
• be free of anxiety about the wound and the healing process

• express appropriate expectations regarding the healing process.

Nursing diagnosis: *Knowledge deficit related to home care of donor and graft sites*

NURSING PRIORITY: Provide information to optimize long-term healing of donor and graft sites.

Interventions

1. See the "Knowledge Deficit" care plan, page 56.

2. Teach the patient and family the following care measures:

• Apply topical ointments such as corticosteroids (as ordered) and skin softeners (lanolin and mineral oil) to the donor and graft sites.

• Maintain pressure and protective dressings as ordered by the doctor.

• Avoid sun exposure by wearing protective clothing and using sunscreen lotions until the tissue heals completely (usually in 6 to 12 months).

• Maintain activity and position limitations as ordered by the doctor.

• Perform ROM exercises and maintain a positioning program, as ordered, until the tissue heals and matures in 6 to 12 months.

• Maintain a diet high in calories, protein, and vitamins.

• Avoid smoking. (Refer the patient to a smoking cessation program, as indicated.)

• Assess the donor and graft sites daily for healing progress and absence of such complications as redness or other discolorations, swelling, drainage, bad odor, pain, and excessive warmth.

3. Additional individualized interventions: _____

_____

_____

Rationales

1. General interventions related to knowledge deficits are contained in the "Knowledge Deficit" care plan.

2. These measures provide the following benefits:

• Corticosteroids prevent inflammation, which can compromise circulation and healing. Grafted tissue may lack the normal lubricating glands and may dry more readily.

• Pressure dressings inhibit excessive scar formation. Protective dressings may be necessary because new tissue is very sensitive and may be easily injured.

• New tissue lacks melanin-producing cells and is more susceptible to sunburn. Melanin-producing cells may regenerate in 6 to 12 months.

• Premature or excessive activity may dislodge the graft.

• ROM exercises and positioning are necessary to extend the affected area and to prevent contractures.

• Additional calories, protein, and vitamins are necessary to promote tissue healing during the catabolic state caused by the stresses of an open wound, surgery, and hospitalization.

• Smoking decreases blood flow and oxygen supply to peripheral tissues, thus inhibiting healing.

• Tissue that is healing well should be warm, flat, only slightly more reddened than the surrounding tissue, and flexible, and it should have a capillary refill time of less than 3 seconds. Such signs and symptoms as redness, swelling, and pain may indicate an infection, which could prevent permanent graft adherence.

3. Rationale: _____

_____

_____

Outcome criteria

By the time of discharge, the patient will:
• demonstrate ointment and dressing application
• describe specific activity and position limitations
• explain skin protection methods

• identify diet requirements
• describe appropriate graft and donor site appearance
• list two risk factors for poor healing
• list four signs of complications.

Discharge planning
NURSING DISCHARGE CRITERIA
Upon discharge, documentation shows evidence of:
• healing and intact donor and graft sites with no evidence of abnormal drainage or swelling
• ability to control pain using oral medications
• stable vital signs
• absence of fever
• absence of pulmonary or cardiovascular complications
• hemoglobin and WBC count within normal parameters
• ability to perform proper graft- and donor-site care independently or with minimal assistance
• ability to tolerate adequate nutritional intake
• absence of hospital-acquired contractures
• ability to verbalize and demonstrate activity and position limitations
• absence of bowel and bladder dysfunction
• ability to perform ADLs, transfers, and ambulation with minimal assistance at prehospitalization level
• an adequate home support system or referral to home care or a nursing home if indicated by an inadequate home support system, inability to perform ADLs, or inability to independently care for graft and donor sites.

PATIENT/FAMILY DISCHARGE TEACHING CHECKLIST
Document evidence that patient/family demonstrates understanding of:
___ care of the graft and donor sites
___ complication signs and symptoms
___ activity and position limitations
___ all discharge medications' purpose, dosage, administration schedule, and side effects requiring medical attention (usual discharge medications include topical ointments, such as corticosteroids, and skin softeners, such as lanolin or mineral oil)
___ recommended dietary modifications
___ date, time, and location of follow-up appointments
___ how to contact doctor.

DOCUMENTATION CHECKLIST
Using outcome criteria as a guide, document:
___ clinical status on admission
___ significant changes in status
___ pertinent laboratory and diagnostic test findings
___ wound condition (donor and graft sites)
___ pain episodes
___ pain-relief measures
___ activity and position limitations
___ resumption of ADLs

___ nutritional intake
___ psychological adjustment
___ patient/family teaching
___ discharge planning.

ASSOCIATED CARE PLANS
Grief/Grieving
Ineffective Family Coping
Ineffective Individual Coping
Knowledge Deficit
Pain
Surgical Intervention

REFERENCES
Brodt, D.E. *Medical-Surgical Nursing and the Nursing Process.* Boston: Little, Brown & Co., 1986.

Brunner, L., and Suddarth, D. *Lippincott Manual of Nursing Practice,* 4th ed. Philadelphia: J.B. Lippincott Co., 1986.

Cassell, B.L. "Treating Pressure Sores Stage by Stage," *RN* 49(1):36-40, January 1986.

Jacobs, M.M., ed. *Signs and Symptoms in Nursing.* Philadelphia: J.B. Lippincott Co., 1984.

Kenner, C.V., et al. *Critical Care Nursing: Body-Mind-Spirit.* Boston: Little, Brown & Co., 1985.

Lewis, S.M., and Collier, I.C. *Medical-Surgical Nursing.* New York: McGraw-Hill Book Co., 1983.

Long, B.C., and Phipps, W.J. *Essentials of Medical-Surgical Nursing.* St. Louis: C.V. Mosby Co., 1985.

Phipps, M., et al. "Staging Care for Pressure Sores," *American Journal of Nursing* 8:999-1003, 1984.

Swearingen, P.L. *Manual of Nursing Therapeutics: Applying Nursing Diagnoses to Medical Disorders.* Reading, Mass.: Addison-Wesley Publishing Co., 1986.

Diabetes Mellitus

DRG information

DRG 294 Diabetes. Age >35.
     Mean LOS = 6.0 days
DRG 295 Diabetes. Ages 0 to 35.
     Mean LOS = 4.5 days
     Principal diagnoses for DRGs 294 and
     295 include:
     • diabetes mellitus (DM) without complication
     • DM with coma
     • DM with ketoacidosis
     • DM with other manifestations
     • DM with unspecified complications
     • glycosuria.

Introduction

DEFINITION AND TIME FOCUS

DM is a chronic metabolic disorder in which the absolute or relative lack of endogenous insulin or insulin resistance causes abnormal metabolism of carbohydrates, proteins, and fats, typically manifested as diabetic ketoacidosis. In turn, the alteration in metabolism provokes a pattern of associated short- and long-term complications. This clinical plan focuses on the two most common types of DM, Type I (insulin-dependent) and Type II (non-insulin-dependent), during hospitalization for initial diagnosis and initiation of a treatment and management regimen.

Note: Although Type II DM is commonly called non-insulin-dependent, these patients may require insulin as part of their management plan, either initially or later in the course of the disease.

ETIOLOGY/PRECIPITATING FACTORS

Type I (10% to 15% of cases)
• genetic predisposition, probably related to genes of human leukocyte antigen affecting immune system
• destruction of beta (insulin-producing) cells in pancreas, possibly related to the body's autoimmune response
• islet-cell antibodies
• viral infections.
(Primary defect: inadequate or absent insulin)
Type II (approximately 80% of cases)
• genetic predisposition, not yet as clearly implicated as in Type I, leading to diminished endogenous insulin secretion and action
• obesity
• decreased activity
• possibly other environmental factors.
(Primary defect: inadequate insulin and insulin resistance)

Note: Many medications may be associated with impaired glucose tolerance, including some diuretics, oral contraceptives, anticonvulsants, psychoactive medications, and others. The clinician involved with a patient suspected of having diabetes should ensure that medication-related factors are identified and ruled out before making the diagnosis.

Focused assessment guidelines

NURSING HISTORY (Functional health pattern findings)

Note: Type I DM is commonly diagnosed when the patient presents in ketoacidotic coma; Type II is commonly diagnosed on routine examination or when the patient seeks treatment for one of the many associated symptoms.

Health perception–health management pattern

Type I
• *history of diabetes in family*
• weight loss
• *usually under age 30*
• acute onset of symptoms
Type II
• *history of diabetes in family*
• *may be obese*
• *usually over age 30*
• gradual onset of symptoms
• may complain of multiple minor symptoms (flulike syndrome)

Nutritional-metabolic pattern

Type I
• *increased thirst* (polydipsia)
• *increased appetite* (polyphagia)
• (occasionally) nausea
Type II
• may have polydipsia and polyphagia
• may give history of high–refined-carbohydrate, high-calorie diet

Elimination pattern

Type I
• *typically complains of polyuria*
• may have constipation or diarrhea
Type II
• may complain of polyuria
• may have constipation or diarrhea
• may be taking diuretics for another condition

Activity-exercise pattern

Type I
• *may complain of sudden weakness*
Type II
• *may complain of gradually increasing weakness* and fatigability
• may give history of lack of regular exercise

Sleep-rest pattern

Type I
• *sleep disturbance related to nocturia*

Type II
• may complain of nocturia
• may complain of drowsiness following meals

Cognitive-perceptual pattern
Type I
• may report dizziness or orthostatic hypotension
Type II
• may complain of pruritus, acute or recurrent urinary tract infections (UTIs), or recurrent vaginitis
• may observe poorly healing skin infections
• may complain of myopia or blurred vision
• may complain of muscle cramping
• may complain of abdominal pain
• may complain of numbness, pain, or tingling in extremities

PHYSICAL FINDINGS
Cardiovascular
• tachycardia
• postural hypotension
• syncope

Pulmonary
• deep, rapid (Kussmaul's) respirations (if ketoacidosis is present)

Gastrointestinal
• abdominal distention
• decreased bowel sounds
• abdominal tenderness

Integumentary
• poorly healing skin wounds
• skin infections
• warm, flushed, dry skin (if ketoacidosis is present)

Neurologic
• irritability
• drowsiness
• confusion
• coma (if ketoacidosis is present)

Genitourinary
• vaginal discharge
• vaginal infections
• perineal irritation

DIAGNOSTIC STUDIES*
• *random serum glucose test—a level $\geq$ 200 mg/dl plus classic signs and symptoms is diagnostic of DM*
• *fasting serum glucose test—elevation > 140 mg/dl on more than one occasion is diagnostic of DM*
• *urinalysis—reveals glycosuria and (in Type I) ketonuria.*
• *glucose tolerance test—is diagnostic of DM if levels $\geq$ 200 mg/dl for at least two sample values* (at 2 hours and at one other time between 0 and 2 hours after glucose load)
• blood insulin level—Type I, absent or minimal; Type II, normal to high
• plasma proinsulin level—normal to elevated in Type II
• plasma C-peptide level—Type I, absent; Type II, normal to elevated
• arterial blood gas levels—may reveal metabolic acidosis, particularly common in Type I, with compensatory respiratory alkalosis
• electrolyte panel—may be normal or may reveal hyponatremia or hyperkalemia associated with ketoacidosis; needed for baseline
• blood urea nitrogen level—may be normal or elevated (if ketoacidosis present)
• thyroid function studies—may be ordered to rule out coexisting thyroid dysfunction, which could increase need for insulin and contribute to hyperglycemia
• EKG—commonly ordered as baseline and to rule out underlying cardiac disorders
• chest X-ray—needed for baseline

POTENTIAL COMPLICATIONS
• coma related to ketoacidosis, hypoglycemia, or hyperglycemic hyperosmolar nonketosis (HHNK)
• renal failure
• degenerative vascular disease–related complications: accelerated atherosclerosis, cerebrovascular accident, myocardial infarction, thrombophlebitis
• retinopathy or blindness
• neuropathies, especially peripheral
• microangiopathies
• cataracts

Collaborative problem: *Hyperglycemia related to inadequate endogenous insulin (Type I) or inadequate endogenous insulin and insulin resistance (Type II)*

NURSING PRIORITY: Prevent or minimize complications when establishing treatment regimen for control of altered glucose metabolism.

Interventions

1. Administer insulin (I.V., I.M., or S.C.) or oral hypoglycemics.

Rationales

1. Insulin increases cellular glucose uptake and decreases gluconeogenesis. Exogenous insulin is essential for controlling Type I DM. In initial treatment of Type

(continued)

*Laboratory values listed apply to nonpregnant adults; for values in children and pregnant women, see Kneisl and Ames (1986).

Interventions *continued*

• Check the glucose level before giving hypoglycemic medications. Follow unit or hospital protocol for withholding the dose based on serum values.

• Be aware of differences in peak action and in duration of action for various types of hypoglycemic medications:

□ rapid-acting insulins (Regular, Semilente) peak between 2 and 8 hours; intermediate-acting insulins (NPH, Lente) peak between 6 and 12 hours; long-acting insulins (Ultralente, PZI) peak between 10 and 30 hours; and other human and semisynthetic insulins peak between 2 and 15 hours.

□ oral hypoglycemics peak on the average between 3 and 4 hours.

2. *Establish and maintain an I.V. fluid infusion* (usually normal saline solution). Monitor for dry mucous membranes, poor skin turgor, cracked lips, abdominal pain, elevated urine specific gravity, elevated hematocrit, and other signs of dehydration. Keep an accurate intake and output record.

3. *Monitor fingerstick blood glucose levels and urine sugar and acetone levels.* Document weight daily.

4. *Observe for signs of medication-induced hypoglycemia:* pallor, confusion, diaphoresis, headache, weakness, shallow respirations, irritability, and restlessness or stupor. Insulin reactions are most likely to coincide with the peak effect of insulin, which varies depending on type of insulin and individual patient response. If reaction occurs, notify the doctor, obtain a blood glucose level measurement immediately, and treat immedi-

Rationales *continued*

I or II, especially if ketoacidosis is present, I.V. injections of regular insulin may be ordered concurrently with aggressive fluid replacement. The I.V. route is preferred because of action, but too-rapid lowering of blood glucose without adequate fluid replacement may precipitate vascular collapse or cerebral edema. Alternatively, the slower-acting I.M. route may be used, because circulatory insufficiency can make uptake from S.C. sites unpredictable. The S.C. route is, however, the route of choice for ongoing therapy. Oral hypoglycemics are indicated to treat Type II DM only because their effectiveness depends on an endogenous source of insulin.

• Checking the glucose level and withholding the dose if the level is acceptable prevent medication-induced hypoglycemia. Protocols for withholding doses vary depending on the type of hypoglycemic ordered and patient status.

• Awareness of these characteristics helps the nurse correlate signs and symptoms with peaks and troughs in serum drug levels.

□ Insulins differ according to onset and duration of action. The type of insulin, timing of injections, and individual response influence when a reaction is most likely to occur. With insulins given in the morning, a reaction from a short-acting insulin is most likely before lunch; an intermediate-acting insulin, in midafternoon; and a long-acting insulin, between 2 and 7 a.m.

□ Because duration of action is more prolonged with oral agents, a single daily dose usually is sufficient for control. Reactions are most likely to coincide with peak action.

2. Hyperglycemia causes dehydration related to hyperosmolar effect: Water is drawn from the cells into the vascular system and then into the urine in an attempt to maintain homeostasis. Normal saline is the preferred solution to prevent further elevation of the blood sugar (and to replace sodium in ketoacidosis). Accurate intake and output documentation is essential for assessing fluid status and for early detection of inadequate renal function.

3. In the initial diagnosis and establishment of a treatment plan, frequent assessment of glucose levels is essential in monitoring the individual patient's response. Pharmacologic doses are based on laboratory findings. Daily weight is a gross indicator of general fluid and nutritional status.

4. Insulin reactions can occur with relative suddenness. If the newly diagnosed diabetic patient is unaware of the symptoms' significance and goes untreated, such a hypoglycemic reaction may be fatal.

Interventions *continued*

ately with I.V. glucose, glucagon, or oral glucose, depending upon protocol and the patient's responsiveness. Once the patient is stable, use the episode as an example for teaching.

5. *Observe for signs of ketoacidosis:*
• early—nausea; fatigue; polyuria; dry, flushed skin; dry mucous membranes; thirst; and tachycardia
• late—vomiting, poor skin turgor, lethargy, Kussmaul's respirations, acetone breath, hypotension, and abdominal pain.

If you suspect ketoacidosis, notify the doctor immediately. Immediately obtain a blood glucose level measurement (usually over 200 mg/dl), and check urine ketones (typically positive). Treat according to protocol (usually rapid hypotonic or isotonic I.V. fluid replacement, I.V. insulin, bicarbonate, and—as hyperglycemia and dehydration resolve—potassium replacement). Once the patient is stable, use the episode as an example for teaching.

6. *Observe for signs of HHNK:* confusion, seizures, coma, intense thirst, and very dry mucous membranes. If you suspect HHNK, notify the doctor immediately. Immediately obtain a blood glucose level measurement (typically over 600 mg/dl), check urine ketones (usually negative), and obtain a serum osmolality level, as ordered (characteristically over 330 mOsm/kg). Treat according to protocol: typically, vigorous hypotonic fluid replacement, low-dose insulin, and potassium repletion. Once the patient is stable, use the episode as an example for teaching.

7. Additional individualized interventions: _____
_____
_____

Outcome criteria
Within 2 hours of admission, the patient will:
• have an improved blood glucose level
• be awake and alert
• present vital signs within normal limits.

Rationales *continued*

5. Inadequate pharmacologic control, increased dietary intake, infection, stress, or the interaction of other factors may precipitate ketoacidosis in Type I DM. Hyperglycemia causes osmotic diuresis, which provokes compensatory mechanisms to maintain blood volume and pressure. In ketoacidosis, incomplete breakdown of fatty acids leads to accumulation of ketones in the bloodstream in addition to high (unutilizable) glucose levels. This leads to a state of metabolic acidosis, usually with a compensatory respiratory alkalosis. I.V. fluids correct dehydration, insulin facilitates glucose metabolism, and bicarbonate helps restore acid-base balance. As hyperglycemia and dehydration resolve, potassium shifting from the plasma back into the cells may unmask hypokalemia related to urinary potassium loss.

6. HHNK, a complication that occurs over a period of days to weeks, develops most often in the elderly and infirm Type II diabetic patient, who does not recognize (or does not react to) fluid loss. It usually is precipitated by prolonged use of oral hypoglycemics, by infection, or by massive fluid loss. The pathophysiology includes severe hyperglycemia and profound dehydration in the absence of ketosis. Perhaps because of pancreatic exhaustion, not enough insulin is produced to metabolize glucose, so glucose accumulates. However, enough insulin is produced to prevent adipose tissue breakdown, so ketosis does not occur. Blood glucose and osmolality levels are much more elevated in HHNK than in ketoacidosis.

Hypotonic fluids help reverse high serum osmolality; vigorous replacement is necessary because of the extent of dehydration. The HHNK patient may be more sensitive to insulin than the ketoacidotic patient. Urinary potassium loss may require earlier potassium replacement in HHNK treatment than in ketoacidosis.

7. Rationale: _____
_____
_____

Within 24 to 48 hours of admission, the patient will:
• show no signs of dehydration
• have controlled blood glucose levels
• have no hypoglycemia, or have promptly treated hypoglycemic episodes with no associated complications.

Nursing diagnosis: Knowledge deficit related to the newly diagnosed complex and chronic disease process

NURSING PRIORITY: Coordinate the teaching of diabetic self-care with inpatient establishment of a disease control regimen.

Interventions

1. See the "Knowledge Deficit" care plan, page 56.

2. *Teach management, including the significance of insulin or oral hypoglycemics for disease control.* Demonstrate injection techniques, and observe patient performance. Initiate documentation of rotating sites for S.C. injections; include the abdomen. Link medication needs to other factors, such as diet and exercise. Ensure that patient and family are aware of signs and treatment of hypoglycemia as well as the protocol for managing persistent hyperglycemia, ketoacidosis, and HHNK. Involve family members in all teaching. Use the patient's symptomatic episodes as teaching tools.

3. *Coordinate involvement of the patient, family, and dietitian in planning a therapeutic diet for disease control.* Reinforce nutritional guidelines. Encourage supervised weight loss if the patient is overweight. Ensure the patient has written exchange lists and diet guidelines prior to discharge. Provide referral for further questions.

4. *Teach blood and urine glucose testing methods for home use.* Observe patient demonstrations for accuracy of testing, interpretation of results, and documentation. Be aware that some patients may think "the lower the better" regarding blood glucose measurement; ensure that the patient understands the body's need for glucose in regulated amounts. Encourage the patient to keep a daily record of glucose monitoring.

5. *Emphasize the importance of regular activity and exercise and of maintaining an approximately equivalent level of activity from day to day.*

6. *Tell the patient to be aware of increased susceptibility to infections;* discuss ways to avoid exposure. Review signs of infection: redness, swelling, exudate, and fever. Emphasize the importance of prompt, appropriate treatment of even minor injuries to avoid serious complications.

Rationales

1. This care plan provides guidelines for patient teaching.

2. Patient understanding is essential for management of DM at home. Observing the patient's injection technique and providing opportunities for supervised practice help ensure accuracy. Rotating injection sites minimizes lipodystrophy and helps prevent scar tissue formation; documentation serves as a reminder. Insulin absorption is faster from abdominal sites and minimally affected by exercise. The need for medication increases with stress, infection, and higher caloric intake but may decrease with excessive activity, decreased caloric intake, or vomiting. Awareness of signs of hyperglycemia and hypoglycemia decreases patient anxiety and increases sense of self-control; using the patient's personal experiences with symptoms as teaching tools helps the patient identify and recognize personal responses to the disease.

3. Involving the patient and family with dietary planning helps ensure compliance at home. Dietary control is specific for each patient; however, for some Type II DM patients, diet alone or diet with weight loss may be sufficient to control hyperglycemia. Written materials help minimize misunderstanding. Referral ensures an ongoing source of information related to diet.

4. Successful management of DM at home requires self-monitoring by the patient to ensure that the prescribed regimen of medication, diet, and exercise remains appropriate to needs. Stressors (or disease progression) may precipitate changes in body requirements; blood and urine testing alerts the patient to alterations and helps avert complications. Misconceptions about the disease process may have disastrous consequences if uncorrected. Keeping a record of glucose levels helps identify trends.

5. Exercise stimulates carbohydrate metabolism, lowers blood pressure, aids in weight control, and may help avert or minimize circulatory complications by increasing levels of high-density lipoproteins. Increases or decreases in activity may necessitate dietary or medication changes.

6. Diabetic patients may be more susceptible to some types of infections because of their general state of health; also, healing may be impaired or prolonged because of associated vascular insufficiency. Awareness of signs may help ensure prompt treatment. Because of DM-related impairment of healing, even minor cuts or scratches may develop into gangrenous lesions. Infection also affects medication and dietary needs.

Interventions *continued*

7. *Discuss vascular complications* of the disease process:

• Teach foot care, skin care, leg exercises, and assessment of circulatory status; observe patient demonstrations of all techniques. If the patient smokes, emphasize the importance of quitting. Ensure that the patient and family receive a written foot care protocol.

• Discuss the eye disorders associated with DM. Help the patient understand the significance of careful disease control in preventing or slowing development of diabetic retinopathy. Emphasize the importance of early reporting of vision changes.

• Teach the symptoms of UTI and renal impairment—flank pain, fever, dysuria, pyuria, frequency, urgency, and oliguria—and emphasize the importance of prompt treatment.

8. *Discuss the implications of diabetic neuropathy.* Explain peripheral symptoms, such as paresthesias, pain, and sensory loss. Emphasize foot care routines as noted in Intervention 7. Alert the patient and family to report urinary retention or incontinence, orthostatic hypotension, decreased perspiration, diarrhea, or impotence.

9. Additional individualized interventions: _____

_____

_____

Rationales *continued*

7. DM is characterized by degenerative vascular changes that predispose the patient to infections, ulcerations, and gangrene, particularly of the legs and feet.
• Careful skin care may help avert serious problems. Leg exercises may help develop collateral circulation and promote venous return. Nicotine causes vasoconstriction and contributes to circulatory impairment; additionally, smoking greatly increases the risk of significant heart disease. Written instructions help ensure full compliance.
• The retina has a higher rate of oxygen consumption than other body tissues; thus, it is sensitive to the effects of vascular degeneration (microangiopathy) associated with DM. These effects may eventually lead to retinal detachment and blindness. Although some treatment is available, the most effective deterrent to blindness as a complication of DM is careful disease control. Early reporting of vision changes may permit palliative treatment.
• Glycosuria from DM predisposes the patient to UTIs; recurrent severe UTIs or pyelonephritis may increase the likelihood of renal failure. Renal failure is a long-term complication related to vascular degeneration of the small vessels in the glomerulus.

8. Gradual degeneration of peripheral nerves associated with DM may cause paresthesias and pain, followed by loss of sensation, particularly in the legs and feet; the patient may thus be unaware of injuries. These symptoms may indicate autonomic nervous system involvement; if so, the patient may not exhibit the usual signs of hypoglycemia.

9. Rationale: _____

_____

_____

Outcome criteria
Within 48 hours of diagnosis, the patient will:
• initiate diet planning with dietitian
• observe and practice injection technique (if insulin ordered)
• practice testing of blood and urine for glucose levels.

By the time of discharge, the patient will:
• demonstrate proficiency in injection technique
• produce evidence of site rotation documentation
• discuss disease management in relation to medication, diet, exercise, and stress

• list signs of infection
• demonstrate proper foot care
• list signs of hypoglycemia and appropriate treatment
• list signs of hyperglycemia and appropriate treatment
• plan adequate diet for 3-day period
• perform and interpret blood and urine glucose tests accurately.

Nursing diagnosis: *Health maintenance alteration related to the necessity for disease control*

NURSING PRIORITY: Optimize health maintenance ability.

Interventions

1. *Emphasize that DM control involves coordinating many aspects of daily living with medically prescribed interventions.* Where possible, link alterations in habits to prevention of complications.

2. *Assess the patient's resources, including financial management capabilities and family support system.*

3. *Involve significant others in all teaching and planning.*

4. *Arrange appropriate follow-up home health visits prior to patient discharge.*

5. Link the patient and family with community resources and mutual support groups.

6. Encourage verbalization of feelings, and support healthy coping behaviors. (See also the "Ineffective Individual Coping" care plan, page 51.)

7. Additional individualized interventions: _____
_____
_____

Rationales

1. A patient may mistakenly believe that attention to a single factor (for example, medication) will control the disorder. Compliance may increase if the patient links control with personal preventive efforts.

2. Independent home management of DM requires the ability to organize activities in a relatively stable setting. Patients are commonly admitted to the hospital "out of control" because of poor financial management and lack of a support system.

3. Significant others may help reinforce teaching and encourage compliance.

4. Transferring new knowledge and skills for disease management from the hospital to the home setting may be difficult for some patients. A home visit allows assessment of environmental factors that may contribute to noncompliance.

5. Diagnosis of DM often necessitates major patient reeducation and alterations in life-style. Community or mutual support groups can offer ongoing education and support.

6. As with the diagnosis of any serious, chronic disease, patients who discover they have DM may experience denial, anger, grief, and other emotions as part of a normal response. Expression of feelings is a necessary prelude to acceptance of the disease and active, responsible management. Supporting healthy coping behaviors helps maintain the patient's independence and sense of self-control—both essential for compliance. (The "Ineffective Individual Coping" care plan contains detailed interventions related to this problem.)

7. Rationale: _____
_____
_____

Outcome criteria

By the time of discharge, the patient will:
• verbalize understanding of need for life-style changes
• ask appropriate questions
• verbalize feelings about diagnosis

• participate actively in disease control planning
• have resource deficits resolved or appropriate referrals completed
• have a home visit scheduled.

Discharge planning
NURSING DISCHARGE CRITERIA

Upon discharge, documentation shows evidence of:
• blood glucose level controlled for at least 48 hours
• ability to manage medication administration

• ability to understand and follow dietary regimen
• ability to follow and perform exercise regimen
• ability to perform foot and skin care
• ability to perform and interpret results of urine and blood testing

• adequate home support system
• referral to home care if reinforcement of teaching is needed or if home support is unavailable*
• no signs of infection
• stable vital signs
• ability to understand emergency measures for managing hyperglycemia and hypoglycemia.

PATIENT/FAMILY DISCHARGE TEACHING CHECKLIST
Document evidence that patient/family demonstrates understanding of:
___ disease process and implications
___ for all medications: purpose, dosage, administration schedule, and side effects requiring medical attention (usual discharge medications include insulin or oral hypoglycemics)
___ blood and urine glucose testing
___ interrelationship of diet, exercise, and other factors in disease management
___ signs of hypoglycemia and appropriate treatment
___ signs of hyperglycemia and appropriate treatment
___ diet management
___ exercise regimen
___ foot care
___ signs of infection and appropriate treatment
___ signs and implications of neuropathy
___ symptoms of retinopathy and need to report them
___ signs and symptoms of urinary and renal complications and need to report them
___ community resources
___ when and how to access emergency medical treatment
___ date, time, and location of follow-up appointments
___ how to contact doctor
___ written materials, insulin, and syringes, as provided.

DOCUMENTATION CHECKLIST
Using outcome criteria as a guide, document:
___ clinical status on admission
___ significant changes in status
___ pertinent laboratory and diagnostic test findings
___ episodes of hyperglycemia and hypoglycemia
___ dietary intake and planning
___ activity and exercise regimen
___ medication therapy
___ I.V. line patency
___ patient/family teaching
___ discharge planning.

ASSOCIATED CARE PLANS
Chronic Renal Failure
Fluid and Electrolyte Imbalances
Grief/Grieving
Ineffective Individual Coping
Knowledge Deficit
Retinal Detachment
Thrombophlebitis

REFERENCES
Berkow, R. *The Merck Manual of Diagnosis and Therapy,* 14th ed. Merck Sharp & Dohme, 1982.
Cooper, K. "Making the Diabetes Connection," *American Journal of Nursing* 86(9):1009-10, September 1986.
Haire-Joshu, D., et al. "Contrasting Type I and Type II Diabetes," *American Journal of Nursing* 86(9):1240-43, November 1986.
Hudak, C., et al. *Critical Care Nursing: A Holistic Approach,* 4th ed. Philadelphia: J.B. Lippincott Co., 1986.
Kneisl, C., and Ames, S. *Adult Health Nursing: A Biopsychosocial Approach.* Reading, Mass.: Addison-Wesley Publishing Co., 1986.
Luckmann, J., and Sorensen, K. *Medical-Surgical Nursing: A Psychophysiologic Approach,* 3rd ed. Philadelphia: W.B. Saunders Co., 1987.
Thompson, J., et al. *Clinical Nursing.* St. Louis: C.V. Mosby Co., 1986.

*Because patients with DM are rarely admitted to an acute care setting unless the disease is out of control or is causing complications, always consider a referral to home care to reinforce hospital teaching and to allow further observation.

Chronic Renal Failure

DRG information

DRG 316 [Medical DRG] Renal Failure without
    Dialysis
        Mean LOS = 6.2 days
        Principal diagnoses include:
        • chronic renal failure.

DRG 317 [Medical DRG] Renal Failure with Dialysis.
        Mean LOS = 1.8 days

DRG 315 [Surgical DRG] Other Kidney and Urinary
    Tract Operating Room Procedures.
        Mean LOS = 9.8 days
        Prinicpal diagnoses include:
        • arteriovenostomy for renal dialysis.

Introduction

DEFINITION AND TIME FOCUS

Chronic renal failure (CRF) is a progressive, irreversible
decrease in kidney function to the point when homeostasis can no longer be maintained. Usually a slow, insidious decrease in kidney function, CRF eventually
causes consequences in all organ systems and physiologic processes. The final stage of CRF, when more
than 90% of kidney function is permanently lost, is
called end-stage renal disease (ESRD). During ESRD,
chronic abnormalities occur, and patient survival depends on maintenance dialysis or a kidney transplant.
This care plan focuses on the ESRD patient receiving
maintenance hemodialysis or peritoneal dialysis, who
has been admitted for an evaluation of the systemic
consequences of CRF and for an assessment of the therapeutic regimen.

CREATININE RANGES IN RENAL FAILURE

Renal function	Serum creatinine (approximate mg/100 ml)	Creatinine clearance (ml/min)
Normal	1.0–1.4	85–150
Mild failure	1.5–2.0	50–84
Moderate failure	2.1–6.5	10–49
Severe failure	>6.5	<10
End-stage	>12	0

Data from Lancaster (1984)

ETIOLOGY/PRECIPITATING FACTORS

• untreated acute renal failure or poor response to treatment (for example, acute tubular necrosis)
• diabetes mellitus (DM) leading to diabetic nephropathy
• severe hypertension leading to hypertensive nephropathy
• lupus erythematosus leading to lupus nephritis
• recurrent glomerulonephritis, often precipitated by
chronic streptococcal infection
• pyelonephritis
• polycystic kidney disease
• chronic use of nephrotoxic drugs
• frequent lower urinary tract infections (UTIs) with
eventual kidney involvement
• neoplasms (metastatic or primary)
• developmental and congenital disorders
• complications of pregnancy (for example, eclampsia,
UTI, hemorrhage, abruptio placentae)
• sarcoidosis
• amyloidosis
• Goodpasture's syndrome (autoimmune disease involving basement membrane of glomerular capillaries)

Focused assessment guidelines

NURSING HISTORY (Functional health pattern findings)

Health perception–health management pattern
• signs and symptoms that cause the patient to seek
health care vary widely and may include decreased urinary output, edema, extreme fatigue, depression, loss
of interest in environment, impotence, and flank pain
• frequently has a history of previous episode(s) of
acute or chronic renal problems and may be receiving
treatment for acute renal failure, chronic renal insufficiency, hypertension, DM, generalized arteriosclerosis
and atherosclerosis, lupus erythematosus, or other systemic diseases involving the kidneys

Nutritional-metabolic pattern
• *typically reports anorexia, nausea, and vomiting*
• may report weight loss related to decreased intake of
nutrients or weight gain related to retention of fluid
• may report unpleasant taste in mouth

Elimination pattern
• if in an early stage of CRF, may report polyuria and
nocturia
• if in advanced stage of CRF, may report oliguria (but
with polycystic kidney disease, urinary output may be
normal, or polyuria may occur)
• may report diarrhea alternating with constipation

Activity-exercise pattern
• typically reports fatigue, malaise, and decreased energy level

Sleep-rest pattern
• may report extreme somnolence or insomnia and restlessness
• may report sleep often interrupted by muscle cramps and leg pain

Cognitive-perceptual pattern
• may report shortened attention span
• may report memory loss
• may report decreased ability to perform abstract reasoning or mathematical calculations
• may report loss of interest in environment

Self-perception–self-concept pattern
• may report depression or frequent mood swings
• may report altered self-concept and body image
• may report decreased self-esteem
• may report reduced level of independence and self-care
• may report sense of powerlessness and hopelessness

Role-relationship pattern
• may be unable to work
• may be unable to maintain spousal and parental roles
• may report decrease in social contacts and activities

Sexuality-reproductive pattern
• females may report amenorrhea, infertility, decreased libido, and decreased or absent sexual expression
• males may report impotence, decreased libido, and decreased or absent sexual expression

Coping–stress tolerance pattern
• may describe ineffective individual and family coping patterns in response to changes caused by chronic catastrophic disease and its treatment
• may exhibit defense mechanisms (for example, denial, projection, displacement, or rationalization)

Value-belief pattern
• may express loss of confidence in health care providers
• may question lifelong religious and philosophical values and beliefs or may intensify beliefs and derive support from them

PHYSICAL FINDINGS
Integumentary
• *rough, dry skin*
• *bronze-gray, pallid skin color*
• *pruritus*
• ecchymoses
• poor skin mobility and turgor (skin mobility is the ease with which it can be lifted between the fingers; turgor is the speed with which it returns into place)
• excoriation
• signs and symptoms of inflammation
• thin, brittle nails
• coarse and thinning hair

Cardiovascular
• *hypertension,* or hypotension (uncommon)
• orthostatic hypotension

• *pitting edema of feet, legs, fingers, and hands*
• periorbital edema
• sacral edema
• engorged neck veins
• dysrhythmias
• pericardial friction rub (with pericarditis)
• paradoxical pulse (with pericardial effusion or tamponade)
• palpitations

Pulmonary
• *crackles*
• *shortness of breath*
• *coughing*
• *thick, tenacious sputum*
• deep, rapid respirations (with acidosis)

Gastrointestinal
• *smell of urine and ammonia on the breath*
• *gum ulcerations and bleeding*
• *dry, cracked, bleeding mucous membranes and tongue*
• *vomiting*
• bleeding from GI tract
• constipation or diarrhea
• weight loss related to decreased intake of nutrients masked by fluid retention (peripheral edema), leading to increase in overall body weight; after the patient is receiving appropriate treatment (that is, fluid restriction and dialysis), excess fluid is decreased and weight loss becomes especially evident
• liver enlargement
• ascites

Neurologic
• *malaise, weakness, fatigue*
• *confusion and disorientation*
• *memory loss*
• *slowing of thought processes*
• *changes in sensorium* (somnolence, stupor, or coma)
• *convulsions*
• *changes in behavior* (irritability, withdrawal, depression, psychosis, or delusions)
• *numbness and burning of soles of feet*
• *decreased sensory perception*
• *muscle cramps*
• *restlessness of legs*
• diminished deep tendon reflexes
• positive Chvostek's and Trousseau's signs

Musculoskeletal
• *muscle cramps* (especially in the legs)
• *loss of muscle strength*
• *limited range of motion of joints*
• *bone fractures*
• *lumps (calcium-phosphate deposits) in skin, soft tissues, and joints*
• footdrop with motor nerve involvement

Reproductive
• amenorrhea (in females)

- atrophy of testicles (in males)
- gynecomastia

DIAGNOSTIC STUDIES

- *blood urea nitrogen (BUN) levels—elevated*
- *serum creatinine levels—elevated* (see *Creatinine Ranges in Renal Failure*, page 338)
- *creatinine clearance—decreased by 90% in ESRD* (see *Creatinine Ranges in Renal Failure*, page 338)
- *serum electrolyte levels—hypernatremia (common), hyperkalemia, hyperphosphatemia, hypocalcemia, elevated calcium-phosphate product, hypermagnesemia*
- *venous CO_2 (comparable to arterial HCO_3) levels—decreased*
- *arterial blood gas levels—acid-base imbalance,* typically metabolic acidosis
- *hemoglobin and hematocrit levels—decreased (hemoglobin usually 6 to 8 mg, hematocrit usually 20% to 25%)*
- *red blood cell (RBC) count—decreased*
- serum albumin and total protein levels—commonly decreased
- alkaline phosphatase levels—may be elevated
- white blood cell (WBC) count—may be elevated
- urinalysis—of minimal diagnostic value in ESRD
- renal biopsy—indicates the nature and extent of the renal disease; necessary to diagnose CRF cause
- radionuclide tests (renal scan and renogram)—may show abnormal renal structure and function
- renal arteriogram—may identify narrowed, stenosed, missing, or misplaced blood vessels
- plain X-ray of kidneys, ureters, and bladder—may indicate gross structural abnormalities
- ultrasonography—may indicate gross structural abnormalities
- computed tomography scan—may show renal masses, abnormal filling of the collecting system, or vascular disorders

Note: Because CRF commonly coexists with other systemic diseases and because it affects all organ systems and physiologic processes, numerous additional laboratory tests and diagnostic procedures are commonly required to assess the other systemic disease(s) and systemic consequences of CRF.

POTENTIAL COMPLICATIONS

- uncontrollable hypertension
- hyperkalemia and related cardiac electrical conduction deficits
- pericarditis, pericardial effusion, or pericardial tamponade
- pulmonary edema
- congestive heart failure
- osteodystrophy
- metastatic calcium-phosphate calcifications
- aluminum intoxication
- profound neurologic impairment
- profound psychosocial disequilibrium
- abnormal protein, lipid, and carbohydrate metabolism
- accelerated atherosclerosis

Collaborative problem: *Potential hyperkalemia related to decreased renal excretion, metabolic acidosis, excessive dietary intake, blood transfusion, catabolism, and noncompliance with therapeutic regimen*

NURSING PRIORITY: Implement measures to prevent or treat hyperkalemia, and monitor their effectiveness.

Interventions

1. *Monitor serum potassium daily, and notify the doctor if the level exceeds 5.5 mEq/liter.*

2. *Assess and report signs and symptoms of hyperkalemia*—slow, irregular pulse; muscle weakness and flaccidity; diarrhea; and EKG changes (tall, tented T wave; ST segment depression; prolonged PR interval; wide QRS complex; or cardiac standstill, indicating extreme hyperkalemia).

3. Implement measures to prevent or treat metabolic acidosis, as ordered, such as alkaline medications (for example, sodium bicarbonate) and maintenance dialysis therapy.

4. If blood transfusions are necessary, administer fresh-packed RBCs during dialysis, as ordered.

Rationales

1. Hyperkalemia causes adverse and even lethal physiologic effects.

2. Cardiovascular signs and symptoms are the most important physiologic indicators of the effects of hyperkalemia.

3. In the acidotic state, hydrogen ions move into the cell to compensate for the acidosis; potassium ions move out of the cell and into the plasma to maintain electrochemical neutrality.

4. In fresh blood, fewer RBCs have hemolyzed and released potassium as compared with stored blood. Dialysis removes excess potassium.

Interventions *continued*

5. Decrease catabolism by encouraging the patient to consume prescribed amounts of dietary protein and carbohydrates, by treating infections, and by decreasing fever.

6. *Encourage compliance with the therapeutic regimen.*

7. Implement and evaluate therapy for hyperkalemia, as ordered, and evaluate:

• sodium bicarbonate I.V.

• hypertonic glucose and insulin I.V.

• calcium lactate or calcium gluconate I.V.

• cation-exchange resin (such as Kayexalate)

• dialysis therapy.

8. Assess serial serum potassium determinations and EKG monitoring for hypokalemia during treatment.

9. Additional individualized interventions: _____

_____

_____

Outcome criteria
Within 2 hours after treatment is initiated, the patient will:
• maintain serum potassium levels within a range of 3.5 to 5.5 mEq/liter
• exhibit EKG without evidence of hyperkalemia

Rationales *continued*

5. Catabolism causes release of intracellular potassium into the plasma. Appropriate intake of dietary protein mitigates breakdown of the body's cells. Infections and fever increase the metabolic rate and can lead to a catabolic state.

6. Dietary noncompliance can result in excessive potassium intake; noncompliance with the dialysis regimen causes hyperkalemia because of decreased removal of potassium.

7. Rationales for hyperkalemia therapy include the following:
• Sodium bicarbonate helps correct acidosis and causes potassium to shift from the plasma back into the cells.
• Hypertonic glucose and insulin cause potassium to move from the extracellular to the intracellular space.
• Calcium antagonizes potentially deleterious effects of potassium on the conduction system of the heart.
• This medication exchanges sodium for potassium and increases excretion of potassium through the intestines.
• Dialysis rapidly and efficiently removes potassium from the body.

8. Overtreatment of hyperkalemia may result in hypokalemia.

9. Rationale: _____

_____

_____

• have arterial pH of 7.35 to 7.45; venous CO_2 of 22 to 25 mEq/liter (or as defined as acceptable for the patient).

By time of discharge, the patient will:
• demonstrate ability to plan a 3-day diet incorporating potassium restrictions and other dietary requirements.

Collaborative problem: *Potential pericarditis, pericardial effusion, and pericardial tamponade related to uremia or inadequate dialytic therapy*

NURSING PRIORITY: Maximize cardiac output and cellular perfusion.

Interventions

1. *Daily, assess for, and report to the physician, signs and symptoms of pericarditis:* fever, chest pain, and pericardial friction rub.

2. *If signs and symptoms of pericarditis are present, collaborate with the nephrology team to assess the adequacy of dialysis and increase frequency as necessary and as ordered.*

Rationales

1. Of CRF patients on dialysis, 30% to 50% develop uremic pericarditis; the classic triad of fever, chest pain, and pericardial friction rub is the hallmark of this condition.

2. *Inadequate dialysis therapy and uremic toxic accumulation are one cause of pericarditis; intense dialysis therapy is the usual treatment.*

(continued)

Interventions *continued*

3. *If signs and symptoms of pericarditis are present, assess for signs and symptoms of pericardial effusion and tamponade* every 4 hours, as follows:
• Palpate peripheral pulses for rate, quality, waxing, and waning.
• Assess for paradoxical pulse greater than 10 mm Hg.
• Assess for peripheral edema.
• Assess for decrease in sensorium.
• Rapidly occurring large tamponade is manifested by profound hypotension, narrow pulse pressure, weak or absent peripheral pulses, cold and poorly perfused extremities, rapid decrease in sensorium, and bulging neck veins.

4. If tamponade develops, prepare the patient for emergency pericardial aspiration.

5. Encourage compliance with the therapeutic regimen.

6. Additional individualized interventions: _____
_____
_____

Rationales *continued*

3. Pericardial effusion is a common complication of pericarditis that can lead to tamponade, a life-threatening condition. Signs and symptoms vary from mild compromise of cardiac output with small effusion to severely compromised hemodynamic status in tamponade.

To assess paradoxical pulse, place a blood pressure cuff on the patient's arm and instruct the patient to breathe normally. Inflate the cuff above the systolic level. Slowly deflate the cuff and note the systolic pressure on expiration. Wait, reinflate the cuff, and deflate it again, this time noting the systolic pressure on inspiration. The difference between the two points is the paradoxical pulse. A paradoxical pulse of 10 mm Hg or less indicates a normal blood pressure response to inspiration. A value greater than 10 mm Hg indicates an exaggerated response to inspiration, noted in many cases of cardiac tamponade.

4. Mortality in tamponade is 95%. Immediate aspiration of blood from the pericardial cavity is essential to restore cardiac function and hemodynamic status.

5. Dialysis removes uremic toxins, which may be a cause of pericarditis. Dialysis combined with fluid restriction mitigates formation of effusion.

6. Rationale: _____
_____
_____

Outcome criteria
Ongoing (with adequate therapeutic regimen), the patient will exhibit amelioration of pericarditis, maintenance of hemodynamic status, and prevention of complications as evidenced by:
• normal blood pressure (as defined for the patient)
• strong, regular peripheral pulses
• normal heart sounds (strong, readily audible apical impulse without friction rub)

• normal temperature
• alert and oriented (or maintenance of usual mental status)
• maintenance of usual respiratory status
• absent or decreased peripheral edema
• EKG without evidence of pericarditis
• maintenance of usual energy level.

Collaborative problem: *Hypertension related to sodium and water retention and malfunction of the renin-angiotensin-aldosterone system*

NURSING PRIORITY: Implement and assess the therapeutic regimen and patient teaching to control hypertension.

Interventions

1. *Administer antihypertensive medications, as ordered, and assess for desired and adverse effects.* Reassure the patient that some side effects may decrease once the body adjusts to the medication.

Rationales

1. Antihypertensive medications are an essential part of the regimen of patients with CRF. Antihypertensives act by vasodilatation, beta-adrenergic blocking, or angiotensin blocking. Reassurance helps prevent noncompliance from medications' initial adverse effects.

Interventions *continued*

2. *Measure blood pressure at various times of day with the patient in supine, sitting, and standing positions.* Record blood pressure readings on a flow sheet to correlate the influence of time of day, positioning, medications, diet, and weight. Teach the patient to measure his or her own blood pressure and pulse.

3. Teach the patient how to avoid orthostatic hypotension by changing position slowly, especially from lying to sitting, for 5 minutes before standing.

4. Encourage compliance with the therapeutic regimen.

5. Instruct the patient to report any changes in status that may indicate fluid overload, hypertensive encephalopathy, or vision changes. These include periorbital, sacral, or peripheral edema; headaches; seizures; and blurred vision.

6. Recognize the significance of funduscopic changes reported on medical or nursing examination: arteriovenous nicking, exudates, hemorrhages, and papilledema.

7. Additional individualized interventions: _____
_____
_____

Rationales *continued*

2. Blood pressure measurements commonly vary throughout the day and in relation to medication administration, diet, weight, and positioning. Orthostatic hypotension may occur with too much medication or with fluid deficit.

3. Orthostatic hypotension may cause falls and injuries. Medication noncompliance may result if the patient is unable to prevent occurrence of orthostatic hypotension.

4. Dialysis removes sodium and water and controls vascular volume; diet control prevents excessive sodium and fluid intake.

5. Presence of listed signs and symptoms may indicate poor control of hypertension and the need for alteration in the therapeutic regimen.

6. Same as Rationale 5.

7. Rationale: _____
_____
_____

Outcome criteria

Ongoing, the patient will:
• exhibit acceptable blood pressure level as defined for the patient
• show no hypertensive complications.

By the time of discharge, the patient will:
• demonstrate ability to measure blood pressure and pulse.

Collaborative problem: *Anemia related to decreased life span of RBCs in CRF, bleeding, decreased production of erythropoietin and RBCs, and blood loss during hemodialysis*

NURSING PRIORITY: Stabilize the RBC count and maximize tissue perfusion.

Interventions

1. *Assess daily the degree of anemia and its physiologic effects:* low hemoglobin, hematocrit, and RBC count; fatigue; pallor; dyspnea; palpitations; ecchymoses; and tachycardia.

2. *Administer medications as ordered, and assess for desired and adverse effects:* iron and folic acid supplements, androgens, and vitamin B complex with C.

Rationales

1. The severity of anemia and its physiologic effects vary from patient to patient. The therapeutic plan is based on anemia's effects on the individual patient.

2. Iron, folic acid, and vitamins are required for RBC production. These are commonly deficient in the CRF patient's diet and also may be removed by dialysis, thus necessitating supplements. Do not administer folic acid and vitamins during dialysis because they are removed by the treatment. Do not administer iron along with phosphate binders because iron absorption is decreased. Androgens help stabilize the RBC count.

(continued)

Interventions *continued*

3. *Assist the patient to develop an activity and exercise schedule to avoid undue fatigue.*

4. Avoid unnecessary collection of laboratory specimens.

5. Instruct the patient in measures to prevent bleeding: using a soft toothbrush, avoiding vigorous nose blowing, preventing constipation, and avoiding contact sports.

6. Administer blood transfusions as indicated and ordered.

7. Additional individualized interventions: _____

_____

_____

Rationales *continued*

3. Decreased hemoglobin decreases tissue oxygenation and causes increased fatigability. A carefully developed activity and exercise plan can lessen fatigue and allow the patient to perform activities of daily living (ADLs).

4. Frequent collection of blood specimens worsens anemia.

5. Bleeding from any site worsens anemia.

6. Blood transfusions are administered only when the patient becomes symptomatic with low hematocrit; frequent blood transfusions cause the body to decrease RBC production even further. Fresh-packed RBCs are administered during dialysis, as noted previously.

7. Rationale: _____

_____

_____

Outcome criteria
Ongoing, the patient will:
• maintain hematocrit in a stable range as defined for the patient, usually about 20% to 25%

• exhibit symptomatic relief of the effects of anemia
• verbalize ways to protect himself from trauma
• perform ADLs without undue fatigue.

Collaborative problem: *Potential osteodystrophy and metastatic calcifications related to hyperphosphatemia, hypocalcemia, abnormal vitamin D metabolism, hyperparathyroidism, and elevated aluminum levels*

NURSING PRIORITY: Minimize bone demineralization and metastatic calcifications.

Interventions

1. *Administer phosphate binding medications, calcium supplements, and vitamin D supplements, as ordered, and assess their effects.*
• Weekly, monitor levels of serum calcium, phosphate, alkaline phosphatase, aluminum, and calcium-phosphate product; report abnormal findings to the doctor.
• Monitor X-rays for bone fractures and joint deposits.
• Weekly, palpate joints for enlargement, swelling, and tenderness.
• Weekly, inspect the patient's gait, joint range of motion, and muscle strength.

Rationales

1. In renal failure, the decreased glomerular filtration rate causes phosphate retention and hyperphosphatemia; plasma calcium levels decrease to compensate. Decreased vitamin D metabolism by the kidneys causes decreased calcium absorption from the GI tract, worsening the problems. A decrease in plasma calcium levels stimulates production of parathormone, which causes reabsorption of calcium and phosphate from the bones and eventual bone demineralization.

As plasma calcium and phosphate levels rise concurrently, the plasma calcium-phosphate product level also rises; the excess calcium phosphate is deposited as metastatic calcifications in joints, soft tissue, eyes, heart, and brain. These metastatic calcifications cause decreased function of the involved organ(s). The problems are ameliorated by administering phosphate binders, such as Amphojel, Basaljel, or Alu-Caps, with meals to bind phosphate in the GI tract and decrease its absorption. Calcium and vitamin D supplements help support normal plasma calcium levels.

Interventions *continued*

2. With the patient, develop an activity and exercise schedule to avoid immobilization.

3. Daily, question the patient about signs and symptoms of hypocalcemia: numbness, tingling, and twitching of fingertips and toes; carpopedal spasms; seizures; and confusion.

4. Monitor each EKG (or EKG report) for prolonged QT interval, irritable dysrhythmias, and atrioventricular conduction defects.

5. Daily, assess for Chvostek's and Trousseau's signs. See the "Fluid and Electrolyte Imbalances" care plan, page 21, for details.

6. Encourage compliance with the therapeutic regimen.

7. Additional individualized interventions: _____
_____
_____

Rationales *continued*

Excess aluminum (absorbed from the aluminum hydroxide gels used as phosphate binders and from high levels of aluminum in water used to prepare dialysate) is deposited into the bones and exacerbates osteodystrophy.

2. Immobilization increases bone demineralization.

3. Hypocalcemia causes irritability of the nervous system and alters nerve conduction. The signs and symptoms listed indicate tetany, hypocalcemia's most obvious manifestation.

4. Hypocalcemia can alter normal cardiac electrical conduction.

5. Positive Chvostek's and Trousseau's signs indicate hypocalcemia.

6. Dialysis, medications, and diet work together to maintain acceptable calcium-phosphate balance.

7. Rationale: _____
_____
_____

Outcome criteria
Ongoing, the patient will:
• exhibit serum calcium, phosphorus, alkaline phosphatase, aluminum, and calcium-phosphate product levels within an acceptable range

• present minimal bone demineralization as seen on bone scan
• present minimal calcium-phosphate deposits
• show no signs or symptoms of hypocalcemia
• maintain a safe, painless level of activity.

Nursing diagnosis: *Potential nutritional deficit related to anorexia, nausea, vomiting, diarrhea, restricted dietary intake of nutrients, GI inflammation with poor absorption, and altered metabolism of proteins, lipids, and carbohydrates*

NURSING PRIORITY: Maintain acceptable nutritional status.

Interventions

1. Assess nutritional status on admission by determining weight in relation to height and body build; serum albumin, protein, cholesterol, and transferrin values; triceps skin-fold thickness; weakness and fatigue; dietary intake; and history of anorexia, nausea, vomiting, and diarrhea.

2. Weigh daily, and compare the patient's actual and ideal body weights. Be sure to consider the effect of excess fluid on actual weight by comparing the current weight with nonedematous weight (500 ml = 1 lb). Teach the patient to weigh him- or herself under consistent conditions, to maintain a weight record, and to maintain an intake and output record.

Rationales

1. A baseline assessment is necessary to monitor progress and the need for modification of the dietary prescription.

2. Achieving ideal body weight is the goal. If the patient is at less than ideal body weight additional calories may be added to the diet; if above ideal body weight, caloric restrictions may be necessary.

(continued)

Interventions *continued*

3. Encourage the patient to eat the maximum amount of nutrients allowed. Encourage compliance with the dialysis regimen.

4. Encourage foods high in calories from carbohydrates and low in protein, potassium, sodium, and water content. Provide related teaching, including planning of food and fluid intake.

5. As necessary, consult with a dietitian to include the patient's preferences in daily diet.

6. Implement interventions to reduce nausea and vomiting, diarrhea or constipation, and stomatitis.

7. Monitor BUN, serum creatinine, sodium, potassium, serum albumin, and total protein levels as indicators of dietary adequacy and compliance with dietary restrictions. (Consult with the doctor regarding appropriate laboratory values for the patient.)

8. Additional individualized interventions: _____
_____
_____

Rationales *continued*

3. The diet prescription and dialysis regimen are planned to complement each other to minimize toxins and maintain fluid and electrolyte and acid-base balance.

4. High-carbohydrate foods provide calories for energy and allow storage of dietary proteins. Restriction of potassium, sodium, and water is necessasry to prevent electrolyte imbalances and volume overload. Protein is restricted to control the levels of uremic toxins and the degree of uremia.

5. Including food preferences makes the diet more palatable and increases dietary compliance.

6. These conditions often result in anorexia or decreased GI absorption of nutrients.

7. BUN levels may be elevated from too much dietary protein intake; serum creatinine levels may be elevated from inadequate dietary protein intake and subsequent muscle breakdown; serum albumin levels are decreased in malnourished patients; serum sodium and potassium levels are elevated by excessive intake and noncompliance. Appropriate ranges of laboratory values must be determined for each patient, because they vary depending on the type of dialysis and other therapeutic measures.

8. Rationale: _____
_____
_____

Outcome criteria
During hospitalization, the patient will:
• maintain weight within 2 lb of ideal body weight
• exhibit BUN, serum sodium, potassium, albumin and total protein levels within acceptable limits
• maintain pre-illness pattern of elimination.

By the time of discharge, the patient will:
• plan a 3-day dietary intake (including fluid)
• demonstrate ability to weigh self and to maintain weight record and intake and output record.

Nursing diagnosis: *Potential alteration in oral mucous membrane and unpleasant taste in mouth, related to the effects of urea and ammonia*

NURSING PRIORITY: Maintain intact oral mucous membrane and relieve unpleasant taste.

Interventions

1. On admission, inspect oral mucous membrane for ulcerations and bleeding.

Rationales

1. Early detection and treatment can lessen consequences of severe stomatitis. (Stomatitis is caused by effects of excessive uremic toxins on the oral mucosa.)

Interventions *continued*

2. *Teach the patient an appropriate mouth care regimen* that includes rinsing with a pleasant-tasting or dilute-vinegar mouthwash as needed, using a soft toothbrush to clean teeth at least twice a day, sucking sour candies or lemons as needed, and drinking cool liquids (within fluid restrictions).

3. Encourage compliance with the therapeutic regimen.

4. Additional individualized interventions: _____
_____
_____

Rationales *continued*

2. Mouthwash improves bad taste in the mouth and halitosis. Vinegar neutralizes ammonia, thus improving taste in the mouth and decreasing halitosis. A soft toothbrush prevents bleeding, and frequent mouth care decreases bacteria and chance of infection. Sour candies or lemons improve taste in the mouth while decreasing thirst.

3. Dialysis removes uremic toxins, which are partly responsible for stomatitis.

4. Rationale: _____
_____
_____

Outcome criteria
Throughout the period of hospitalization, the patient will:
• present clean, moist, mucous membrane without ulcerations, bleeding, or signs of infection
• report pleasant taste and sensation in mouth.

Collaborative problem: *Potential peripheral neuropathy related to effects of uremia, fluid and electrolyte imbalances, and acid-base imbalances on the peripheral nervous system*

NURSING PRIORITY: Mitigate effects of peripheral neuropathy.

Interventions

1. On admission, consult a physical therapist for assessment of muscle strength, gait, and degree of neuromuscular impairment.

2. *In collaboration with a physical therapist, help the patient develop an activity and exercise regimen.*

3. Guard against leg and foot trauma.

4. Administer analgesics as ordered and indicated; observe for desired effects.

5. Encourage compliance with the therapeutic regimen.

6. Additional individualized interventions: _____
_____
_____

Rationales

1. A baseline assessment is essential for devising an individualized activity and exercise schedule.

2. Regular activity and exercise prevent the hazards of immobility.

3. With decreased peripheral sensation, the patient may be unaware of impending trauma.

4. Analgesics may be necessary for severe pain; if the medication ordered is excreted by the kidneys, observe for toxic effects.

5. Dialysis lowers the level of uremic toxins and improves fluid and electrolyte and acid-base balance.

6. Rationale: _____
_____
_____

Outcome criterion
Ongoing, the patient will:
• ambulate and carry out ADLs safely and comfortably.

Nursing diagnosis: *Potential impairment of skin integrity related to decreased activity of oil and sweat glands, scratching, capillary fragility, abnormal blood clotting, anemia, retention of pigments, and deposition of calcium phosphate on the skin*

NURSING PRIORITY: Maintain intact skin, and relieve dryness and itching.

Interventions

1. On admission and twice a day, assess skin for color, turgor, ecchymoses, texture, and edema.

2. *Keep the skin clean while relieving dryness and itching* using superfatted soap, oatmeal bath, bath oils; daily and as needed, apply lotion, especially while the skin is still moist after bathing.

3. Keep the nails trim.

4. Monitor serum calcium and phosphorus levels weekly.

5. Administer phosphate-binding medications, as ordered.

6. Administer antipruritic medications as indicated and ordered; assess effects.

7. Encourage compliance with the therapeutic regimen.

8. Additional individualized interventions: _____
_____
_____

Rationales

1. A baseline assessment is essential for development of an individualized plan. Regular follow-up assessments allow modification as necessary.

2. These measures help relieve dry skin. Lotion is more readily absorbed while the skin is moist. Itching decreases when the skin is kept moist; decreased itching prevents scratching and skin excoriation.

3. Trimming prevents excoriation from scratching.

4. Excess calcium phosphate deposited in the skin causes dryness and itching.

5. These medications decrease serum phosphate and thus lessen deposits in the skin.

6. See Rationale 4. These medications are indicated in severe pruritus when other measures are not effective.

7. Dialysis removes uremic toxins that dry and irritate the skin and helps normalize serum calcium and phosphorus levels.

8. Rationale: _____
_____
_____

Outcome criteria
Throughout the period of hospitalization, the patient will:
• present intact, clean, infection-free skin
• exhibit relief from dryness and itching.

Nursing diagnosis: *Potential alteration in thought processes related to the effects of uremic toxins, acidosis, fluid and electrolyte imbalances, and hypoxia on the central nervous system*

NURSING PRIORITY: Protect the patient from neurologic complications.

Interventions

1. On admission and daily, assess the patient's thought processes. With assistance from the family, compare current findings with premorbid intellectual status.

2. Alter methods of communication with the patient as needed.

Rationales

1. In general, alterations in thought processes reflect an exacerbation of premorbid problems. The premorbid status provides guidelines for establishing realistic outcomes. Ongoing assessment allows modification of the approach as needed.

2. The patient will typically require short periods of simple communication, responding best to direct questioning.

Interventions *continued*

3. Minimize environmental stimuli. Alter the environment as needed to ensure the patient's safety.

4. Do not administer opiates or barbiturates.

5. Encourage compliance with the therapeutic regimen.

6. Additional individualized interventions: _____
_____
_____

Rationales *continued*

3. Excessive environmental stimuli may cause sensory overload and disorientation. The patient usually functions best in a consistently quiet, organized environment that is free of hazards.

4. Opiates and barbiturates have an increased half-life in renal failure. Mental status worsens as a result.

5. Dietary control and dialysis are essential to control uremic toxins and fluid and electrolyte and acid-base balance. Imbalances of these parameters have adverse effects on the central nervous system.

6. Rationale: _____
_____
_____

Outcome criteria
By the time of discharge, the patient will:
• show improved memory and reasoning ability
• show an increased interest in ADLs

• present no neurologic complications such as seizures and encephalopathy.

Nursing diagnosis: *Potential noncompliance related to knowledge deficit; lack of resources; side effects of diet, dialysis, and medications; denial; and poor relationships with health care providers*

NURSING PRIORITY: Help the patient make informed choices about compliance and noncompliance.

Interventions

1. Clarify the patient's understanding of the therapeutic regimen and the consequences of noncompliance.

2. Assess for physiologic, psychological, social, and cultural factors that could contribute to noncompliance. Explore ways to alter the treatment regimen to fit the patient's social and cultural beliefs.

3. Provide instruction about the therapeutic regimen, including medications, common problems related to CRF and their management, and plan for follow-up care. Clarify areas of misunderstanding in relation to the disease process and therapeutic regimen. Allow the patient to make as many informed decisions and choices from as many alternatives as possible.

4. Additional individualized interventions: _____
_____
_____

Rationales

1. In many cases, noncompliance results from the patient's lack of understanding about the nature of the disease process and the objectives of the therapeutic regimen.

2. Many patients deny that they have a chronic, irreversible illness. Often the regimen is incongruent with the patient's social and cultural life-style.

3. Patients are generally more likely to comply if they are encouraged to participate in decision making and allowed maximum independence. Thus, each patient requires an individualized plan of care that considers physiologic, psychosocial, and cultural factors and the patient's own desires.

4. Rationale: _____
_____
_____

Outcome criteria

Ongoing, the patient will:
• verbalize knowledge of therapeutic regimen
• verbalize willingness to follow therapeutic regimen or follow suggestions for realistic alternatives to the therapeutic regimen that are more acceptable to his or her life-style.

By the time of discharge, the patient will:
• explain the cause and implications of the disease
• name each medication, its dosage amount and interval, and its desired effects and side effects
• describe associated problems, how to manage them, and when to report them
• explain the plan for follow-up care.

Nursing diagnosis: *Potential sexual dysfunction related to the effects of uremia on the endocrine and nervous systems and to the psychosocial impact of CRF and its treatment*

NURSING PRIORITY: Help the patient and spouse (or partner) achieve a satisfying method of sexual expression.

Interventions

1. Discuss with the patient and spouse (or partner) the meaning of sexuality and reproduction to them, ways changes in sexual functioning affect masculine and feminine roles, and mutual goals for their sexual functioning.

2. Evaluate the couple's receptiveness to learning, and discuss alternative methods of sexual expression.

3. Emphasize the importance of giving and receiving love and affection as alternatives to performing intercourse.

4. Consider (with the doctor) a penile prosthesis for a male patient, as indicated.

5. Additional individualized interventions: _____
_____
_____

Rationales

1. Sexuality and reproduction assume different levels of significance at various stages of maturity and at various times during the period of CRF. The sex drive itself varies from person to person; therefore, sexuality and reproduction are very personal experiences. Sexual dysfunction will affect one's sex role in many ways, based on past experiences and future expectations. Thus, the nurse must explore sexuality with the patient and spouse or partner to establish baseline data and to determine their mutual goals.

2. If impotence or decreased libido is present, or if intercourse causes fatigue, and if the couple is receptive to experimentation with alternative methods, then fellatio, cunnilingus, or mutual masturbation may provide sexual gratification.

3. Sexual intercourse and orgasm are not necessarily the goal of all meaningful intimate interactions: love and affection are also important in strengthening a relationship.

4. If a male patient cannot achieve or maintain an erection, a penile prosthesis may provide a means for successful intercourse.

5. Rationale: _____
_____
_____

Outcome criteria

Ongoing, the patient will:
• express concerns about sexual and reproductive functioning with spouse or partner
• express satisfaction with sexual relationship with spouse or partner.

Nursing diagnosis: *Knowledge deficit related to vascular access care*

NURSING PRIORITY: Teach the patient about care and precautions related to vascular access.

Interventions

1. *Emphasize the patient's crucial role in protecting the vascular access.*

2. *Whether the patient has an AV shunt or an AV fistula, explain these activity restrictions for the extremity with the access:*
• Do not wear constrictive clothing or jewelry.
• Do not carry heavy objects.
• Do not allow blood pressure measurements.
• Do not allow venipunctures for I.V. fluids or laboratory blood specimens.
• Do not lie on the access.

3. *In addition to Intervention 2, if the patient has an external shunt, teach these measures:*
• Check shunt patency every 4 hours by examining the shunt for the presence of bright red blood and feeling above the venous side of the shunt for a thrill.

• If blood has separated into serum and fibrin strands or if a thrill is absent, contact a nephrology nurse or nephrologist immediately.

• Perform daily AV-shunt care according to the dialysis unit protocol.

• At the time of AV-shunt care, check insertion sites for redness, swelling, or drainage. Report any of these signs to the doctor.

• After AV-shunt care, apply a sterile dressing and wrap gauze securely (but not tightly) around the extremity. Clip two bulldog clamps to the edge of the gauze dressing.

• Do not pull on the tubing.

Rationales

1. The vascular access is essential for hemodialysis treatment. Loss of access may disrupt the dialysis schedule and necessitate surgical intervention.

A variety of vascular access methods may be used. Most common are the external arteriovenous (AV) shunt (or cannula) and the internal AV fistula.

An AV shunt is the connection of an artery and vein using two pieces of Silastic tubing and a Teflon connector to form an external loop. Although immediately available for use, it is considered temporary. An AV shunt may be used while an internal fistula matures.

An AV fistula, an internal surgical anastomosis of an artery and vein, usually is preferred for vascular access in the patient with CRF. It usually is placed in the nondominant forearm and requires 2 to 3 months for the venous wall to thicken and the fistula to distend.

The major complications of the external AV shunt are clotting, infection, and accidental separation. The major complications of the AV fistula are occlusion and post-dialysis bleeding.

2. Some interventions apply to both types of access, whereas others are specific to an AV shunt or AV fistula. These activities threaten the integrity of the vascular access and may cause occlusion, dislodgement, or infection.

3. These interventions apply only to an external shunt.

• The shunt is wrapped with a gauze dressing between dialyses, with a small loop left accessible under the edge of the dressing. The presence of bright red blood and a thrill confirm shunt patency.

• The shunt must be declotted immediately to salvage the vascular access. Declotting may be done by a doctor or a specially educated nephrology nurse.

• Details of recommended protocols for care vary among institutions. Follow your institution's recommended protocol.

• These are signs of infection, a common problem. Unless treated promptly, site infection may lead to septicemia and the loss of the AV shunt.

• Dressing protects the tubing from separating or becoming dislodged. Bulldog clamps must be immediately accessible at all times in case of shunt separation.

• Pulling on the tubing can cause skin erosion and accidental separation or dislodgement of the shunt. If a shunt separates, the patient can bleed to death within a few minutes.

(continued)

Interventions *continued*

• If the shunt separates, use bulldog clamps to clamp the arterial side of the shunt first and then the venous side; reconnect the tubing and remove the clamps. Notify the doctor.

• If the shunt dislodges, apply firm pressure about 2 cm above the exit site. If bleeding is minimal and stops, notify nephrologist about dislodgment. If bleeding is profuse or continues, go immediately to the emergency department.

4. *In addition to Intervention 2, if the patient has an internal AV fistula, teach these measures:*

• Assess patency daily by feeling for pulsation at the anastomosis site.

• If pulsation is absent, contact a nephrology professional immediately.

• If pressure dressing is applied after dialysis, remove after 4 hours.

• Check needle insertion sites for bleeding for 4 hours after dialysis, or longer if bleeding occurs.

5. Additional individualized interventions: _____
_____
_____

Rationales *continued*

• Because arterial pressure is higher than venous pressure, more blood can be lost from the arterial side of the shunt. Immediately clamping both lines minimizes blood loss and facilitates reconnection.

• Usually, the elasticity of blood vessels allows them to seal the openings remaining after shunt dislodgement. If bleeding is profuse or continues, however, suturing may be required.

4. These interventions apply only to an internal fistula.

• Because the fistula is internal, patency cannot be determined visually. Pulsation is caused by the surge of arterial blood into the vein to which the artery has been anastomosed.

• Loss of pulsation implies impending loss of patency of the fistula. A clotted fistula may require surgical intervention.

• Direct pressure on the venipuncture sites is necessary to control bleeding. Usually 10 minutes of firm finger pressure is sufficient, but at times a pressure dressing may be applied. If the pressure dressing is left on too long, occlusion may occur.

• Because patients are heparinized during hemodialysis, bleeding may occur after dialysis.

5. Rationale: _____
_____
_____

Outcome criteria
Ongoing, the patient will:
• describe all protective measures appropriate to the particular type of vascular access
• correctly demonstrate the procedure for checking shunt or fistula patency

• describe specific measures to control bleeding
• state correctly how to reach a nephrology professional
• demonstrate performance of daily care for an external AV shunt, if appropriate
• state three signs of infection related to an AV shunt.

Discharge planning
NURSING DISCHARGE CRITERIA
Upon discharge, documentation shows evidence of:
• ability to perform care of the shunt, fistula, or peritoneal catheter
• vital signs within expected parameters
• stable nutritional status
• unimpaired skin integrity
• ability to control pain using oral medications
• acceptable hemoglobin levels
• absence of pulmonary complications
• absence of cardiovascular complications
• ability to comply with and tolerate diet and fluid restrictions
• weight within expected parameters
• home support adequate to ensure compliance to therapeutic regimen or appropriate referrals made

• appropriate activity tolerance
• absence of fever and other signs of infection
• ability to manage ADLs.

PATIENT/FAMILY DISCHARGE TEACHING CHECKLIST
Document evidence that patient/family demonstrates understanding of:
___ cause and implications of renal failure
___ purpose of dialysis regimen
___ for all discharge medications: purpose, dosage, administration schedule, and desired effects and side effects (usual discharge medications include antihypertensives, phosphate binders, calcium supplement, vitamin D, folic acid, iron, vitamins B and C, and others, depending on patient's response to the disease process)

___ recommended diet and fluid modifications

___ common problems related to CRF and their management

___ care of the shunt or fistula (if receiving hemodialysis) or of the peritoneal catheter (if receiving peritoneal dialysis)

___ how to obtain and record weights

___ how to measure and record blood pressure and pulse

___ how to maintain an intake and output record

___ problems to report to health care provider

___ financial and community resources to assist with treatment of CRF

___ dialysis schedule, location of dialysis facility, and day and time of appointments

___ resources for counseling

___ how to contact doctor or nephrology nurse.

DOCUMENTATION CHECKLIST
Using outcome criteria as a guide, document:

___ clinical status on admission

___ significant changes in status

___ pertinent laboratory and diagnostic test findings

___ response to medication regimen

___ physical and psychological response to dialysis therapy

___ nutritional intake

___ activity and exercise ability

___ ability to perform self-care measures

___ compliance with therapeutic regimen

___ patient/family teaching

___ postdischarge referrals and long-term care and follow-up plans.

ASSOCIATED CARE PLANS
Anemia
Death and Dying
Fluid and Electrolyte Imbalances
Grief/Grieving
Ineffective Individual Coping
Knowledge Deficit
Pain
Peritoneal Dialysis

REFERENCES
Eknoyan, G., and Knochel, J.P., eds. *The Systemic Consequences of Renal Failure.* New York: Grune & Stratton, 1984.

Hekelman, F.P., and Ostendarp, C.A. *Nephrology Nursing: Perspectives of Care.* New York: McGraw-Hill Book Co., 1979.

Kneisl, C.R., and Ames, S.A. *Adult Health Nursing: A Biopsychosocial Approach.* Reading, Mass.: Addison-Wesley Publishing Co., 1986.

Lancaster, L.E. "Renal Failure: Pathophysiology, Assessment, and Intervention," *Critical Care Nursing* 2(1):38-40, January/February 1982.

Lancaster, L.E., ed. *The Patient With End Stage Renal Disease*, 2nd ed. New York: John Wiley & Sons, 1984.

Renal and Urologic Disorders. Nurse's Clinical Library. Springhouse, Pa.: Springhouse Corp., 1984.

Richard, C.J. *Comprehensive Nephrology Nursing.* Boston: Little, Brown & Co., 1986.

Schoengrund, L., and Balzar, P., eds. *Renal Problems in Critical Care.* New York: John Wiley & Sons, 1984.

Ulrich, S.P., et al. *Nursing Care Planning Guide: A Nursing Diagnosis Approach.* Philadelphia: W.B. Saunders Co., 1986.

Peritoneal Dialysis

DRG information

DRG 316 [Medical DRG] Renal Failure.
  Mean LOS = 6.2 days
  Principal diagnoses include:
  • acute renal failure
  • chronic renal failure.
DRG 449 [Medical DRG] Poisoning and Toxic Effects of Drugs. Age > 17 with Complication or Comorbidity (CC).
  Mean LOS = 4.5 days
  Principal diagnoses include:
  • drug overdose.
DRG 450 [Medical DRG] Poisoning and Toxic Effects of Drugs. Age > 17 without CC.
  Mean LOS = 3.0 days
DRG 451 [Medical DRG] Poisoning and Toxic Effects of Drugs. Ages 0 to 17.
  Mean LOS = 3.1 days
DRG 205 [Medical DRG] Disorders of the Liver except Malignancy, Cirrhosis, and Alcoholic Hepatitis. With CC.
  Mean LOS = 6.7 days
  Principal diagnoses include:
  • hepatic coma.
DRG 206 [Medical DRG] Disorders of the Liver except Malignancy, Cirrhosis, and Alcoholic Hepatitis. Without CC.
  Mean LOS = 4.2 days

Additional DRG information: Peritoneal dialysis is used as a treatment for numerous diagnoses. Therefore, the diagnosis necessitating its use will determine the DRG assigned. Examples of diagnoses for peritoneal dialysis are listed above.

Introduction

DEFINITION AND TIME FOCUS
Peritoneal dialysis (PD) is a treatment that removes excess water, solutes, and toxins from the blood indirectly by using the peritoneal membrane as a dialyzing membrane.

Solution (dialysate) is instilled into the peritoneal cavity via a catheter, where it remains for a prescribed period of time, usually 30 to 45 minutes. During that time (dwell time), substances in the blood and in the dialysate equalize across the membrane, moving from areas of higher concentration of the substance to areas of lower concentration. The solution is then allowed to flow out (drain time), removing with it excess water and waste products. PD is contraindicated with:
• recent abdominal, retroperitoneal, or chest surgery
• abdominal drains
• preexisting peritonitis
• diaphragmatic tears
• paralytic ileus

• diffuse bowel disease
• respiratory insufficiency.
  This clinical plan focuses on the patient receiving PD for the first time and on a regular basis, normally at least three times per week.

ETIOLOGY/PRECIPITATING FACTORS
PD is indicated in patients with chronic renal failure, acute renal failure, drug overdose, and hepatic coma. Patients awaiting hemodialysis whose vascular devices are not operable may also be treated with PD temporarily. Because peritoneal dialysis is not a diagnosis but a procedure, this care plan does not address specific illnesses necessitating PD. See care plans related to specific disorders for more information: "Chronic Renal Failure" in this book, and "Acute Renal Failure," "Drug Overdose," and "Liver Failure" in the author's forthcoming *Critical Care Care Plans* (Springhouse Corp., 1989).

Focused assessment guidelines
NURSING HISTORY (Functional health pattern findings)

Health perception—health management pattern
• *may have a history of chronic or acute renal failure*
• may have inadequate or exhausted venous access
• may be under treatment for diabetes
• may have a history of drug overdose or drug intolerance
• may have a history of a clotting disorder or cardiovascular disease

Nutritional-metabolic pattern
• may report anorexia, nausea, vomiting
• may report weight loss or intolerance to diet

Elimination pattern
• *may report diminished urinary output*
• may report constipation

Role-relationship pattern
• may report inability to work or maintain usual roles related to chronic, disabling illness or treatment regimen or both

Self-perception—self-concept pattern
• may verbalize decreased sense of self-worth

Coping—stress tolerance pattern
• may express denial, anger, or depression over condition and needed treatment

Activity-exercise pattern
• may report fatigue
• may report shortness of breath or other signs of exercise intolerance

Value-belief pattern
• may report religious or personal beliefs that do not allow blood transfusions

PHYSICAL FINDINGS*
Cardiovascular
• *hypertension*
• *edema* (periorbital, ankle, sacral)

Pulmonary
• *crackles*
• dyspnea

Gastrointestinal
• *nausea*
• *anorexia*
• hiccoughs
• *constipation*
• stomatitis

Neurologic
• lethargy
• confusion
• shortened attention span
• restlessness

Integumentary
• *fragile skin*
• *dry, flaky skin*
• yellow-gray skin hue
• ecchymoses or purpura
• poor skin turgor

Musculoskeletal
• *impaired mobility*
• bone deformities

DIAGNOSTIC STUDIES
• creatinine clearance—used as a guide to determine the glomerular filtration rate, which is a direct reflection of renal function

□ normal, 85 to 150 ml/minute
□ mild renal failure, 50 to 84 ml/minute
□ moderate renal failure, 10 to 49 ml/minute
□ severe renal failure, <10 ml/minute
□ end-stage renal failure, 0 ml/minute

• serum creatinine levels—used to determine renal function (normal is 0.6 to 1.2 mg/dl; elevation indicates renal impairment; see "Chronic Renal Failure" care plan, page 338)
• arterial blood gas (ABG) measurements—used to determine acid-base abnormalities (normal pH is 7.35 to 7.45; renal failure patients are usually acidotic)
• serum electrolyte levels—usually show hyperkalemia (> 5 mEq/liter)
• sodium level—may be low (<120 mEq/liter) because of kidney's inability to conserve sodium
• phosphate and calcium levels—commonly show hypocalcemia and hyperphosphatemia
• blood urea nitrogen (BUN) levels—elevated in renal failure, reduced in severe liver damage
• complete blood count—hemoglobin may be lower from decreased erythropoietin production
• erythrocyte sedimentation rate—increased if infection present
• serum drug levels—obtained to determine degree of drug overdose
• culture and sensitivity of PD drainage—obtained if peritoneal infection suspected; identifies causative organism and appropriate antibiotic
• chest X-ray—obtained to rule out congestive heart failure

POTENTIAL COMPLICATIONS
• peritonitis
• respiratory distress
• cardiac dysrhythmias
• hypovolemia and hypervolemia
• hyperglycemia
• electrolyte imbalance
• perforation of bowel or bladder

Nursing diagnosis: *Potential for injury: bleeding, perforation, or ileus related to catheter insertion procedure or irritation from dialysate*

NURSING PRIORITY: Prevent or promptly detect and report injuries related to procedure.

Interventions

1. *Have the patient void before catheter insertion.*

2. *During dialysate infusion, observe for indications of bladder or bowel perforation,* such as extreme urgency to urinate or defecate, large urinary output, fecal color or odor in returned dialysate, visible fecal material in dialysate, and liquid or watery stools. If any of these occurs, stop the dialysate infusion and notify the doctor immediately.

Rationales

1. The catheter is inserted using a trocar. Bladder distention increases the risk of bladder perforation related to proximity of the insertion site.

2. Bowel or bladder perforation during insertion may lead to severe peritonitis unless detected. Surgical repair and prompt initiation of antibiotic therapy are indicated. The signs listed appear because of dialysate leakage into affected organs.

(continued)

*Physical findings listed here are related to renal failure.

Interventions *continued*

3. *Report persistently blood-tinged dialysate return.*

4. *Auscultate bowel sounds* every 8 hours.

5. Inspect and palpate the abdomen every 8 hours and between dialysate infusions.

6. Monitor the patient's appetite and sense of well-being.

7. Encourage ambulation.

8. Apply warm compresses to the abdomen.

9. Additional individualized interventions: _____
_____
_____

Rationales *continued*

3. Slight bleeding may be normal initially following catheter insertion, but the fluid should clear rapidly. Persistent bleeding or gross blood in the return flow indicates the need for prompt reevaluation.

4. Diminished or absent bowel sounds are a clue to possible ileus or bowel obstruction, which may result from bowel injury or irritation from catheter placement or dialysate.

5. Abdominal distention and tenderness may indicate ileus.

6. Anorexia, nausea, vomiting, and malaise are signs of ileus.

7. Ambulation stimulates peristalsis.

8. Heat increases peristaltic activity.

9. Rationale: _____
_____
_____

Outcome criteria
Following catheter insertion, the patient will:
• have no unusual urgency to void or defecate
• present the usual amount of urine and stool
• have dialysate returns without evidence of fecal material or persistent bleeding.

Throughout the period of hospitalization, the patient will:
• have normal bowel sounds
• maintain a normal bowel elimination pattern
• show no abdominal distention and tenderness.

Nursing diagnosis: *Potential ineffective breathing pattern related to elevation of diaphragm during exchanges and reduced mobility*

NURSING PRIORITIES: (a) Prevent respiratory distress during exchanges and (b) prevent development of pulmonary complications.

Interventions

1. *Elevate the head of the bed* during exchanges.

2. *Administer oxygen,* as ordered.

3. *Assess for possible causes if pain or discomfort is present.* Medicate with analgesics, as ordered.

4. Encourage deep-breathing and coughing exercises during PD treatment, every 2 hours while awake. Teach and promote hourly use of the incentive spirometer, as ordered.

Rationales

1. Use of gravity minimizes pressure on the diaphragm and allows fuller chest expansion.

2. Hypoventilation related to pressure on the diaphragm causes reduced arterial PO_2 levels.

3. Pain may prevent effective breathing. It may be related to an excessively rapid inflow of dialysate, to patient positioning, to air in the system, or to other causes and should be investigated before treatment with analgesics is instituted.

4. Good pulmonary hygiene measures help prevent fluid accumulation in the lungs and air passages by promoting full chest expansion and preventing collapse of alveoli.

Interventions *continued*

5. Auscultate the patient's lungs every 2 hours, assessing for and reporting crackles or other abnormal findings.

6. Turn and reposition the patient at least every 2 hours.

7. Perform chest percussion every 2 hours.

8. Additional individualized interventions: _____
_____
_____

Rationales *continued*

5. Crackles indicate development of pulmonary complications related to fluid retention.

6. Changing position promotes full chest excursion and facilitates optimal drainage of dialysate.

7. Percussion helps loosen secretions.

8. Rationale: _____
_____
_____

Outcome criteria
During PD treatment, the patient will:
• show no dyspnea

• have no or minimal crackles
• perform pulmonary hygiene measures effectively.

Collaborative problem: *Potential alteration in fluid and electrolyte balance* related to dialysis and underlying disease or disorder*

NURSING PRIORITY: Maintain normal fluid and electrolyte balance.

Interventions

1. See the "Fluid and Electrolyte Imbalances" general care plan, page 21. Particularly monitor vital signs, observing for tachycardia or orthostatic changes.

2. Monitor serum potassium levels, as ordered, to help determine appropriate additions to the dialysate.

3. *Maintain accurate intake and output records,* and notify the doctor if the fluid return deficit exceeds 500 ml.

4. Additional individualized interventions: _____
_____
_____

Rationales

1. The "Fluid and Electrolyte Imbalances" care plan provides interventions related to the range of fluid and electrolyte disturbances seen in patients receiving PD.

2. Dialysate normally contains no potassium. This is desirable for the hyperkalemic patient, but it may provoke hypokalemia in others.

3. Normally, return should be equal to or slightly greater than the amount infused. A persistent deficit that is not corrected by position changes may indicate undesirable fluid retention.

4. Rationale: _____
_____
_____

Outcome criteria
During PD treatment, the patient will:
• show no distended neck veins
• have a decrease in peripheral edema

• have blood pressure within the patient's normal range
• have a dialysate deficit less than 500 ml.

Nursing diagnosis: *Potential infection related to invasiveness of procedure*

NURSING PRIORITY: Prevent infection.

Interventions

1. *Use strict aseptic technique* in all aspects of PD, including daily dressing changes.

Rationales

1. Introduction of pathogens into the patient's system may cause peritonitis.

(continued)

Interventions continued

2. *Maintain a sterile, closed system during exchanges.*

3. *Observe for and report leakage around the catheter.*

4. *Observe the catheter site for redness, exudate, and edema.*

5. *Observe the outflow for cloudiness, sediment, and odor.* Observe the patient for signs of peritonitis, such as abdominal pain, guarding, rigidity, and rebound tenderness.

6. Take and record the patient's temperature at least every 8 hours.

7. Administer systemic or local antibiotics, as ordered. Add the antibiotics to the dialysate using the two-needle technique (one needle used to draw up the medication, another to inject it into the dialysate).

8. Additional individualized interventions: _____

_____

_____

Rationales continued

2. Bacteria present in air can also cause infection if introduced into the peritoneal cavity.

3. Further securing the catheter at the entry site and reducing the amount or rapidity of the infusion may control leakage. A moist dressing around the catheter provides a pathway for microorganisms and increases the risk of infection.

4. These are signs of infection.

5. Appearance or odor of fluid indicates peritonitis. Physical signs result from peritoneal inflammation.

6. Temperature elevation is a sign of infection.

7. Antibiotics prevent the growth and reproduction of bacteria. The two-needle technique reduces the risk of contamination.

8. Rationale: _____

_____

_____

Outcome criteria

By the time of discharge, the patient will:
• be afebrile for 24 hours
• have no exudate, edema, redness, or leakage around the catheter site

• show no signs of peritonitis
• have clear return drainage.

Nursing diagnosis: *Pain related to dialysate temperature or to rapid filling of the abdomen with dialysate*

NURSING PRIORITY: Minimize discomfort during fluid exchanges.

Interventions

1. *Warm the dialysate to body temperature* before beginning the infusion.

2. Change the patient's body position at least every 1 to 2 hours.

3. Slow the infusion rate by lowering the height of the bottle and by clamping the tubing as needed.

4. Avoid allowing air into the tubing that enters the abdominal cavity.

Rationales

1. Cold dialysate causes vasoconstriction (which interferes with circulation to the peritoneal membrane) and discomfort.

2. Frequent position changes improve dialysate drainage.

3. Lowering the bottle height decreases the infusion rate and reduces pressure during fill time.

4. Air introduced into the abdominal cavity causes distention and produces discomfort, sometimes manifested as pain referred to the shoulder area. Air in the tubing may also create air lock, inhibiting adequate dialysate flow.

Interventions *continued*

5. Notify the doctor if pain persists.

6. See the "Pain" care plan, page 64.

7. Additional individualized interventions: _____
_____
_____

Rationales *continued*

5. Persistent pain may indicate peritonitis.

6. The "Pain" care plan contains further details related to care of the patient experiencing pain.

7. Rationale: _____
_____
_____

Outcome criterion
During PD treatment, the patient will:
• verbalize absence or minimal amount of abdominal discomfort.

Nursing diagnosis: *Nutritional deficit related to anorexia, abdominal distention, stomatitis, or nausea*

NURSING PRIORITY: Promote adequate nutritional intake.

Interventions

1. *Facilitate a dietary consultation* to plan, with the patient, a menu that incorporates personal preferences, increased nutrient needs, and any restrictions related to the underlying disorder.

2. *Offer snacks and supplements* between meals, providing plenty of high-protein foods unless contraindicated. Avoid foods high in potassium if hyperkalemia is a problem. See the "Chronic Renal Failure" care plan, page 338, for more information about nutritional needs.

3. Encourage frequent oral hygiene.

4. Offer small, frequent meals.

5. Avoid manipulating equipment or emptying drainage bags at mealtime.

6. Drain the peritoneal cavity before offering a meal. If possible, allow 1 to 2 hours between a meal and the next dialysate infusion.

7. If the patient is cannot tolerate adequate oral intake, discuss enteral or parenteral options with both patient and doctor.

8. Additional individualized interventions: _____
_____
_____

Rationales

1. The dietitian's expertise may be helpful in selection of food for optimal nutritional value. When the patient's appetite is decreased, consideration of individual preferences is essential to promote adequate intake.

2. PD can cause loss of 30 to 70 g of protein weekly. Adult dialysis patients require 45 to 50 kcal/kg daily. Hyperkalemia is common in patients with renal failure. The "Chronic Renal Failure" care plan contains specific interventions related to dietary planning for these patients.

3. Good oral hygiene decreases unpleasant odors and tastes in the mouth.

4. Large amounts of food may seem overwhelming and unappetizing. Patients frequently complain of being too full to eat due to pressure from peritoneal fluid.

5. Unpleasant sights and odors may cause nausea and vomiting.

6. Draining peritoneal fluid decreases intraabdominal pressure and may enable the patient to eat and retain food more easily.

7. During acute illness, enteral or parenteral nutritional repletion may be indicated.

8. Rationale: _____
_____
_____

Outcome criteria
During PD treatment, the patient will:
• participate in dietary planning
• perform oral hygiene before and after meals
• take adequate amounts of protein-rich foods.

By the time of discharge, the patient will:
• not vomit for at least 12 hours
• tolerate oral intake of at least 1.5 g/kg and 45 to 50 kcal/kg/day.

Discharge planning
NURSING DISCHARGE CRITERIA
Upon discharge, documentation shows evidence of:
• vital signs stable and within expected parameters
• electrolyte, ABG, and hemoglobin levels within acceptable parameters
• absence of drainage, redness, and edema at catheter site
• absence of cardiovascular and pulmonary complications
• absent or minimal peripheral edema
• ability to tolerate adequate nutritional intake, as ordered
• absence of abdominal distention and tenderness
• absence of nausea and vomiting
• normal bowel and bladder function
• stabilizing weight
• ability to control pain using oral medications
• ability to ambulate and perform ADLs independently or with minimal assistance
• adequate home support system or referral to home care or a nursing home as indicated by inadequate home support system, frequency and tolerance of PD treatments, and inability to care for self.

Additional information: For long-term PD, patients often receive treatments at home with the assistance of home-care nurses. The number of treatments needed and the patient's ability to perform treatments at home are the essential factors in determining where the patient will go upon discharge. Long-term PD treatments are a financial problem for most patients. For this reason, an automatic referral to the social services department should be an essential part of discharge planning.

PATIENT/FAMILY DISCHARGE TEACHING CHECKLIST
Document evidence that patient/family demonstrates understanding of:
__ renal failure—disease process, signs and symptoms, and implications
__ concepts of PD treatment
__ importance of aseptic technique during treatment
__ dietary modifications (sodium restrictions and high protein intake)
__ all discharge medications' purpose, dosage, administration schedule, and side effects requiring medical attention (discharge medications vary, depending on underlying disorder)
__ care of catheter between treatments
__ activity restrictions (only contact sports and swimming are generally prohibited)

__ importance of a daily weight record
__ changes in condition to report to doctor
__ date, time, and location of next treatment
__ community resources
__ how to access help in emergencies.

DOCUMENTATION CHECKLIST
Using outcome criteria as a guide, document:
__ clinical status at beginning of treatment, including vital signs and weight
__ significant changes in clinical status
__ appearance of catheter site
__ time each exchange begins and ends
__ intake and output
__ color, odor, and character of dialysate return
__ care of catheter site
__ weight at end of treatment
__ nutritional intake
__ pertinent laboratory and diagnostic test findings
__ bowel status
__ patient/family teaching
__ discharge planning.

ASSOCIATED CARE PLANS
Chronic Renal Failure
Fluid and Electrolyte Imbalances
Knowledge Deficit
Pain
Total Parenteral Nutrition

REFERENCES
Alfaro, Rosalinda. *Application of Nursing Process.* Philadelphia: J.B. Lippincott Co., 1986.
Carpenito, Lynda. *Nursing Diagnosis: Application to Clinical Practice.* Philadelphia: J.B. Lippincott Co., 1983.
Richard, Cleo J. *Comprehensive Nephrology Nursing.* Boston: Little, Brown & Co., 1986.

Ileal Conduit Urinary Diversion

DRG information

DRG 303 [Surgical DRG] Kidney, Ureter, and Major
    Bladder Procedure for Neoplasm.
    Mean LOS = 12.7 days

DRG 304 [Surgical DRG] Kidney, Ureter, and Major
    Bladder Procedure for Non-Neoplasm.
    With Complication or Comorbidity (CC).
    Mean LOS = 9.9 days

DRG 305 [Surgical DRG] Kidney, Ureter, and Major
    Bladder Procedure for Non-Neoplasm.
    Without CC.
    Mean LOS = 5.6 days

Introduction

DEFINITION AND TIME FOCUS

An ileal conduit, usually performed in conjunction with
a cystectomy, is the most common urinary diversion
procedure for adults. It involves first isolating a 15- to
20-cm segment of the terminal ileum, with its mesentery intact, then reanastomosing the gastrointestinal
tract. The proximal end of this isolated ileal segment is
sutured closed, and the distal end of the ileal segment
is brought out through the right lower abdominal quadrant and everted to form a stoma. The ureters are implanted into the body of this ileal segment, which then
becomes a conduit for urine. It is possible to isolate and
use other segments of small or large bowel as conduits
for urinary diversion, especially if the ileum has been
damaged by radiation. Ileal conduit urinary diversion is
most often performed for transitional cell cancer of the
bladder; however, it should be noted that in rare instances, it may also be done for other conditions requiring total cystectomy, such as severe trauma to the
bladder or persistent, severe urinary tract infections.
This clinical plan focuses on the immediate preoperative and postoperative care of a patient undergoing an
ileal conduit diversion procedure for transitional cell
cancer of the bladder.

ETIOLOGY/PRECIPITATING FACTORS

• transitional cell carcinoma of the bladder necessitating cystectomy—that is, lesions unresponsive to conservative treatment, lesions at or near the bladder neck in
the female, or deep infiltrating tumors that may involve
the lymphatic system.

Focused assessment guidelines

NURSING HISTORY (Functional health pattern findings)

Health perception–health management pattern

• *may report sudden onset of gross painless hematuria;*
may be intermittent

• may have been under treatment for transitional cell
carcinoma of the bladder (being followed by cystoscopy
every 3 to 6 months)

• may have history of intravesical instillations of chemotherapeutic agents like thiotepa or mitomycin C after
transurethral resection of a bladder tumor, or may have
received intravesical Bacillus Calmette-Guérin (BCG) as
prophylactic treatment against tumor recurrence

• may have received limited information from physician
about upcoming urinary diversion surgery and its effects on activities of daily living (ADLs)

• if 50 to 70 years old and male, at increased risk

• may be cigarette smoker (increases risk of bladder
cancer)

Elimination pattern

• may have a history of urinary urgency or frequency
for 3 to 8 months before diagnosis of transitional cell
carcinoma of bladder

• may currently have cystitis as a side effect of intravesical chemotherapy

Sleep-rest pattern

• may report sleep disturbances from nocturia

Self-perception–self-concept pattern

• typically expresses negative feelings about self along
with anger; disappointment; fear of pain, mutilation,
loss of control; distaste for alteration of bodily functions

Role-relationship pattern

• may have job involving exposure to dust and fumes
from dyes, rubber, leather, leather products, paint, or
organic chemicals (increases risk of bladder cancer)

• usually concerned about spouse's or partner's adjustment to ostomy and possibility that presence of ostomy
may change that person's feelings toward the patient

Coping–stress tolerance pattern

• if diagnosis of bladder cancer is recent, patient may
focus concerns on cancer treatment, and not on the creation of an ostomy

Value-belief pattern

• may have delayed seeking medical attention due to
fear combined with embarrassment over the intimate
nature of this problem

PHYSICAL FINDINGS

Note: Transitional cell carcinoma may be asymptomatic
except for the following genitourinary symptoms.

Genitourinary

• gross hematuria

• urgency, frequency, and dysuria unrelieved by
antibiotics

DIAGNOSTIC STUDIES

• complete blood count (CBC)—drop in hematocrit and hemoglobin may indicate internal bleeding. Elevated white blood cell (WBC) count may signify beginning of infection or abscess
• electrolyte panel—used to monitor patient's fluid status and acid-base balance
• serum creatinine, and blood urea nitrogen levels— used to monitor renal function
• *preoperative intravenous pyelogram (IVP)—helpful in evaluating upper urinary tract functioning:* size and location of kidneys, filling of the renal pelvis, and outline of ureters
• *postoperative conduitogram or loopogram—assesses length and emptying ability of the conduit* along with the presence or absence of stricture, reflux, angulation, or obstruction
• *X-ray of kidneys, ureter, and bladder—indicates structural changes in the urinary tract* along with presence or absence of stool or gas in gastrointestinal tract

POTENTIAL COMPLICATIONS

• peritonitis
• leakage at point of gastrointestinal anastomosis
• leakage at proximal end of the conduit
• ureteral leakage
• abscess formation
• thrombophlebitis
• stoma necrosis
• ureteral obstruction from edema or mucus
• wound dehiscence
• small-bowel obstruction
• pneumonia
• ileus
• atelectasis
• wound infection
• mucocutaneous separation around stoma

Nursing diagnosis: *Preoperative knowledge deficit related to impending creation of an ileal conduit*

NURSING PRIORITY: Prepare the patient physically and emotionally for upcoming urinary tract alterations.

Interventions

1. *Assess what the patient already knows about the upcoming cystectomy and creation of an ileal conduit* from information the doctor has provided or from acquaintance with someone who has had an ostomy.

2. *Assess the patient's ability to learn.* Check occupation, level of education, and hobbies, and note if the patient may have difficulty learning.

3. *Assess the patient's manual dexterity, and determine if any sensory deficits are present.* Enlist the help of a family member, if possible and appropriate.

4. Inquire about the patient's past and recent hydration habits, especially quantity and preferred types of fluids.

5. *Describe construction of the conduit, the rationale for bowel preparation, and normal stoma characteristics.*

6. Anticipate postoperative problems with pouching: Is the patient allergic or sensitive to tape or adhesives?

Rationales

1. Patient may have limited or confusing information from the doctor. If the patient has known anyone with an ostomy, impressions from knowing that person will strongly influence personal expectations of surgery and adaptation to the ostomy.

2. Learning difficulties, especially reduced reading ability, will impact on the nurse's choice of strategy and literature used to teach ostomy care.

3. Degree of dexterity will affect the patient's ability to care for stoma and apply pouch effectively. If the patient cannot care for the stoma, a family member is the best substitute.

4. Inadequate hydration may contribute to problems with urine odor, because of concentration, and postoperative condition of peristomal skin (because of dehydration).

5. The patient should know that an ileal conduit is not a substitute bladder. Bowel preparation usually consists of 2 to 3 days of clear liquids by mouth only, enemas until clear daily, and erythromycin and neomycin every 4 hours.

6. Any allergy to these products suggests a need to patch-test the patient for sensitivity to products before selection of ostomy equipment.

Interventions *continued*

7. *Mark the stoma site in the right lower quadrant preoperatively.* This mark should place stoma away from old scars, dimples, umbilicus, belt line, fat folds, and skin creases, and within the rectus muscle in a spot the patient can see.

8. *If the patient is male, discuss effects the cystectomy may have on his sexual functioning.*

9. Additional individualized interventions: _____
_____
_____

Rationales *continued*

7. The stoma should be marked on the surface where the pouch will have optimal seal. This gives the patient some control over the stoma. Placing the stoma within the rectus muscle reduces the risk of hernia or prolapse.

8. Informed legal consent includes male patient's preoperative understanding that erectile dysfunction can be expected along with ejaculatory incompetence. It is important to give the patient "permission" to discuss sex. Also, promise future help in this area if the patient needs it.

9. Rationale: _____
_____
_____

Outcome criterion
Before surgery, the patient will:
• verbalize understanding of upcoming surgery and its expected effects on ADLs.

Collaborative problem: *Potential postoperative peritonitis related to gastrointestinal (GI) or genitourinary (GU) anastomosis breakdown or leakage*

NURSING PRIORITY: Prevent and assess for signs of peritonitis.

Interventions

1. *Monitor and document patency of the nasogastric (NG) tube, NG output, abdominal pain and distention, bowel sounds, appearance and drainage of the abdominal incision.*

2. *Evaluate for signs of GI anastomosis leakage and peritonitis,* such as paralytic ileus and abdominal pain with muscle rigidity, vomiting, and leukocytosis.

3. *Monitor for signs of urine leakage.* Document characteristics of urine output, presence of ureteral stents or catheters, abdominal wound drainage, such abdominal characteristics as tenderness or distention, bowel sounds, and temperature.

4. Additional individualized interventions: _____
_____

Rationales

1. Adynamic ileus usually resolves within 72 hours after surgery. Changes in NG output, rapid abdominal distention, and crampy pain with hyperactive and tinkling bowel sounds may indicate small bowel obstruction. Obstruction increases pressure on newly anastomosed sites.

2. A GI anastomosis is weakest until the fourth postoperative day. Leakage of intestinal secretions may result in peritonitis. I.V. fluids, electrolyte replacement, intestinal decompression, and massive doses of antibiotics are indicated if peritonitis is present.

3. Urine should be blood-tinged for only 1 to 2 days postoperatively. Ureteral stents prevent ureteral obstruction from edema or mucus; it is normal to see urine flowing out around the stents. Signs of urine leakage may include sudden decrease in urine output with corresponding increase in wound drainage or Penrose drain output. Abdominal distention, an increase in abdominal pain, prolonged ileus, and fever may also indicate urine leakage. Small leaks may seal themselves within 8 to 12 hours; otherwise, surgical intervention is needed.

4. Rationale: _____
_____

Outcome criteria

Within 1 to 2 days postoperatively, the patient will:
• have stabilized urine output
• have no gross hematuria.

Within 4 to 5 days postoperatively, the patient will:
• pass flatus

• have normal bowel sounds
• be afebrile
• show no signs of peritonitis.

Collaborative problem: *Potential stomal ischemia and stomal necrosis related to vascular compromise of conduit*

NURSING PRIORITY: Monitor stoma viability.

Interventions

1. *Apply disposable transparent urinary pouch*, as ordered, and attach the pouch to a bedside drainage bag.

2. *Observe the stoma for color changes* every 4 hours and as needed.

3. *Report color change of stoma* (to purple, brown, or black) *immediately to the doctor.*

4. To differentiate superficial ischemia from necrosis, insert a small, lubricated test tube about one-half inch into the stoma, then shine a flashlight into the lumen of the test tube. Observe the inner lumen of the conduit for red, moist mucosa indicating body of conduit is viable.

5. Additional individualized interventions: _____

_____

Rationales

1. Transparent pouch with use of continual bedside drainage allows visualization of stoma.

2. Color changes reflect adequacy of perfusion. Stoma should stay red or pink.

3. Color changes may imply ischemia leading to a necrotic, nonviable stoma. A necrotic stoma can develop from tension on the mesentery, possibly from abdominal distention; from twisting of the conduit during surgery; or from arterial or venous insufficiency. A necrotic stoma requires surgical intervention.

4. If the inner lumen of conduit is viable, the stoma may be showing only minimal ischemia from edema. The stoma may then change color and appear viable, or a dusky stoma may slough its outer layer during the next 5 to 7 days.

5. Rationale: _____

_____

Outcome criterion

Within 12 to 24 hours after surgery, the patient will have:
• viable stoma with red, moist mucosa or dusky stoma but viable conduit.

Collaborative problem: *Potential stoma retraction and mucocutaneous separation related to peristomal trauma or tension on the intestinal mesentery*

NURSING PRIORITIES: (a) Monitor the mucocutaneous border, (b) minimize the risk of separation, and (c) encourage healing.

Interventions

1. *Apply a pouch with an antireflux valve*, as ordered.

Rationales

1. An antireflux valve promotes healing by preventing urine from pooling on the stoma and mucocutaneous border.

Interventions *continued*

2. *Always use a skin sealant under the pouch* to protect and waterproof peristomal skin.

3. If mucocutaneous separation occurs, protect the area of separation and take measures to encourage granulation: Fill the mucocutaneous separation with karaya powder, then cover it with criss-crossed Steri-Strips and the pouch using a skin-barrier wafer and paste.

4. Additional individualized interventions: _____
_____
_____

Rationales *continued*

2. Protection and waterproofing of peristomal skin by routine use of a skin sealant encourages healing of the mucocutaneous border and minimizes trauma to this area when removing the pouch.

3. Mucocutaneous separation does not usually require surgical intervention. Measures described promote increased rate of healing, thus providing additional support for the stoma. If, however, the stoma retracts through the fascia into the peritoneum, peritonitis may develop and surgical intervention is essential.

4. Rationale: _____
_____
_____

Outcome criterion
By 5 to 7 days after surgery, the patient will:
• have a healed mucocutaneous border around budded stoma.

Nursing diagnosis: *Total urinary incontinence related to creation of an ileal conduit*

NURSING PRIORITIES: (a) Protect peristomal skin and contain urine, and (b) teach the functioning and purpose of the conduit.

Interventions

1. *Maintain a good pouch seal, and protect peristomal skin with sealants.*

2. *Review the construction and function of the conduit,* assuring the patient of GI tract continuity. Use diagrams and pictures.

3. *Emphasize and demonstrate normal urine and stoma characteristics.* Explain the following: The conduit and stoma are made from the GI tract, so they have the same lining as the inside of the mouth, i.e., red and moist. The stoma is without sensory nerve endings, so it is insensitive to pain. There is no sphincter, so voluntary control of urine is gone. The stoma is very vascular and may bleed when cleaned and cause blood in the urine. The GI tract makes mucus, so mucus in the urine is to be expected.

4. Additional individualized interventions: _____
_____
_____

Rationales

1. Urine in prolonged contact with skin can irritate and macerate.

2. It is appropriate to review preoperative teaching postoperatively. The patient should understand the nature of the surgery and its anatomical effects. The patient may mistakenly expect the ileal conduit to act as a substitute bladder.

3. The patient needs to know what is now normal for him or her. The vascular, insensitive stoma may cause blood in the urine that the patient should recognize as stomal bleeding. Urine will flow fairly frequently from the stoma. There will be a greater amount of mucus in the urine normally during the early postoperative period, when oral intake is low, or when a urinary infection is present. The mucus should not be interpreted as pus by the patient.

4. Rationale: _____
_____
_____

Outcome criteria
Within 3 days postoperatively, the patient will:
• have nonmacerated skin around the stoma
• describe normal stoma and urine characteristics.

Nursing diagnosis: *Disturbed self-concept: body image related to urinary diversion*

NURSING PRIORITY: Minimize damage to self-concept and promote a healthy body image.

Interventions

1. *Encourage the patient to express feelings and beliefs* about the diagnosis, surgery, and stoma.

2. *Allow for privacy when teaching ostomy care.*

3. *Have the patient empty the pouch in the bathroom.*

4. Suggest a visit from the United Ostomy Association (UOA) (may also be helpful preoperatively).

5. Show an accepting, tolerant attitude when doing or teaching ostomy care.

6. Additional individualized interventions: _____
_____
_____

Rationales

1. The patient may feel fear or isolation or may harbor misconceptions. Expression of feelings is the first step in the coping process.

2. A private environment encourages the patient to ask questions and facilitates learning.

3. Mimicking normal bathroom behavior minimizes feelings of being handicapped or "different."

4. The UOA provides patients with fellowship, information, and support from other rehabilitated patients. Seeing someone else with an ostomy who is well adjusted can encourage hope and provide a positive role model for the patient.

5. The nurse's acceptance and tolerance reassure the patient and facilitate advancement to complete self-care.

6. Rationale: _____
_____
_____

Outcome criteria
Within 2 to 4 days postoperatively, the patient will:
• verbalize feelings about presence of ostomy

• demonstrate ability to empty pouch in bathroom
• express confidence about ability to care for self.

Nursing diagnosis: *Postoperative knowledge deficit related to care of the ileal conduit*

NURSING PRIORITY: Encourage independence in caring for ileal conduit.

Interventions

1. *Instruct the patient in the procedure for emptying the pouch* when it is one-third to one-half full. Demonstrate the emptying procedure using a pouch the patient is not wearing. (A female can sit on the toilet to empty; a male can stand.)

2. *Demonstrate the use and care of the nighttime bedside drainage bag (BDB).* Run tubing from the BDB down the patient's pajama leg, or attach it to the leg by a Velcro strap. Attach the pouch, with urine in it, to the BDB. Explain that cleaning the BDB is easy using white vinegar and water or a commercial cleaner.

Rationales

1. This is usually taught first, because it is done most often. A too-full pouch may pull away and have to be changed. The patient can get a better look at a pouch he or she is not wearing during practice in opening and closing its spout. Mimicking normal bathroom behavior facilitates patient adjustment.

2. Use of a BDB at night prevents pouch overfilling and leakage. Attaching a partially filled pouch prevents suction vacuum, which can lead to overfilling and leakage. Cleaning keeps the BDB free of odor and urine sediment or crystals.

Interventions *continued*

3. *Encourage the patient to change the pouch* by giving step-by-step written instructions, teaching the use of wicks, having the patient practice on a model of a stoma, explaining that the patient should clean urine and mucus from stoma and skin with warm water only, using a mirror if necessary to help the patient see the underside of the stoma, and having the patient apply the pouch while standing.

4. *Teach the patient treatment of minor peristomal skin irritations* using karaya powder and a skin sealant. Explain that momentary stinging may result if karaya powder or skin sealant is applied to denuded skin, but they should be used to prevent more serious peristomal skin complications.

5. Explain fluid intake requirements. Demonstrate pH testing of urine. Check pH routinely on the first few drops of urine in a freshly changed pouch. Warn against touching the Nitrazine paper to skin or stoma. Explain the wisdom of not drinking more than 3 or 4 glasses of citrus juices or milk per day.

6. List recommended dietary considerations to control urine odor. Explain that pouches are odorproof except during emptying and changing.

7. Define routine follow-up care, and explain the rationale for it.

8. Address any special concerns the patient has about living with an ostomy. Consult an enterostomal therapy (ET) nurse for specialized ostomy care.

9. Additional individualized concerns: _____
_____
_____

Rationales *continued*

3. Written instructions help provide continuity of care. Wicks (rolled-up gauze or paper towels) are placed on the stoma to absorb urine and keep the peristomal skin dry, so the pouch can seal. Practicing on a model of a stoma can decrease fear and allow for repetition. Water is used for cleaning because soap can leave a film on skin and disrupt the pouch seal. The patient needs to monitor the condition of the peristomal skin during each pouch change. Standing minimizes abdominal creases, which predispose pouch to leakage.

4. Routine use of a skin sealant prior to pouch application protects skin from adhesives and urine. Treating skin irritations with karaya powder and sealant while they are still minor minimizes risk of serious complications requiring surgery. Intact, healthy skin increases pouch's wearing time and prevents unexpected leaks.

5. Healthy urine is acidic in a well-hydrated adult. Touching the Nitrazine paper to the skin or stoma will yield inaccurate results. It may take 10 to 12 glasses of fluid every day to keep urine acidic; drinking large amounts of citrus juices or milk will negate this effect and make urine alkaline. Alkaline urine predisposes the patient to foul-smelling urine, urine infections, peristomal skin irritations, stomal stenosis, increased mucus production from conduit, urine crystals and calculi, and pyelonephritis.

6. Increased urine odor is associated with eating fish, eggs, asparagus, onions, and spicy foods.

7. The patient will see the urologist routinely every 6 to 12 months. Routine follow-up includes urine culture and sensitivity testing to rule out or detect infection plus IVP or a renal scan to check function of upper urinary tract and evaluate for recurrent tumor. The stoma and skin should be checked and pouching problems evaluated.

8. ET nurses are specially trained to teach, counsel, and help rehabilitate the ostomy patient. They are knowledgeable about the newest pouching supplies and can assist the patient in coping with problems of daily living.

9. Rationale: _____
_____
_____

Outcome criteria
Within 5 days postoperatively, the patient will:
• display learning readiness cues, such as looking at the stoma or helping hold wicks.

By the time of discharge, the patient will:
• have changed the pouch two or three times with minimal standby assistance from the nurse.

Nursing diagnosis: *Potential sexual dysfunction: male erectile dysfunction related to cystectomy, possible ejaculatory incompetence if prostate removed*

NURSING PRIORITIES: (a) Help the patient maximize sexual functions left intact and (b) provide information on sexual matters or referrals as needed.

Interventions

1. *Assess the patient's readiness to discuss sexual matters.* If the patient is not ready, refer him for outpatient follow-up.

2. Describe the separate nerve pathways for sexual excitement, erection, ejaculation, and orgasm. Explain which ones may be affected by surgery and why.

3. If indicated, mention sexual alternatives such as penile prosthesis or external devices to aid in achieving erections. Refer the patient to the urologist or ET nurse for details.

4. Additional individualized interventions: _____
_____

Rationales

1. The patient may deny interest in resumption of sexual activity at first, while learning to cope with the ostomy and his diagnosis of cancer.

2. Cystectomy may only affect the patient's ability to experience erection or ejaculation.

3. The patient may need specific suggestions for resumption of fulfilling sexual activity. A urologist may implant a penile prosthesis surgically. The ET nurse can counsel the patient on sexual alternatives, help him obtain information on external devices to aid in achieving an erection, and make suggestions on how to minimize the presence of the ostomy during sex.

4. Rationale: _____
_____

Outcome criterion

During the postoperative teaching phase, the patient will:
• ask questions about sexual matters or agree to appropriate referrals.

Discharge planning
NURSING DISCHARGE CRITERIA
Upon discharge, documentation shows evidence of:
• a viable stoma
• stable vital signs
• stable nutritional status
• absence of pulmonary or cardiovascular complications
• adequate support system for postdischarge assistance and ability to perform stoma care
• referral to home care if indicated by lack of a home support system or inability to perform ADLs and stoma care
• absence of fever
• ability to control pain using oral analgesics
• no need for I.V. support (discontinued for at least 24 hours before discharge)
• bowel sounds
• healing incision with no redness or other sign of infection
• ability to ambulate same as before surgery.

PATIENT/FAMILY DISCHARGE TEACHING CHECKLIST
Document evidence that patient/family demonstrates understanding of:
___ extent of tumor and resection
___ nature of urinary diversion done and its construction
___ incision care (if not healed)
___ procedure for emptying and changing pouch
___ use and cleaning of bedside drainage system
___ treatment of minor peristomal skin irritations
___ written list of supplies and suppliers, with doctor's prescription to facilitate insurance payment
___ chemotherapy (if needed) and its expected side effects
___ availability of support groups like UOA and American Cancer Society
___ amount and types of fluids preferred, along with any dietary considerations, such as avoiding odor-causing foods
___ signs and symptoms to call doctor about—such as, fever, flank pain, or hematuria

___ concerns to call ET nurse about—such as pouch problems and skin or stoma problems

___ signs and symptoms of urinary tract infection

___ considerations in resuming sexual activity

___ date and time of follow-up appointments

___ how to contact doctor.

DOCUMENTATION CHECKLIST

Using outcome criteria as a guide, document:

___ clinical status on admission

___ significant changes in status

___ pertinent laboratory and diagnostic test findings

___ preoperative marking of stoma site

___ preoperative teaching done

___ bowel preparation

___ UOA visitor recommendation (if appropriate)

___ stoma viability

___ mucocutaneous border, sutures

___ urine characteristics

___ patient's response to ostomy

___ fluid intake and output

___ presence of stents

___ GI status

___ incision status

___ patient's progress in learning ostomy care

___ patient/family teaching

___ discharge planning.

ASSOCIATED CARE PLANS

Fluid and Electrolyte Imbalances
Grief/Grieving
Ineffective Family Coping
Ineffective Individual Coping
Knowledge Deficit
Surgical Intervention

REFERENCES

Alfaro, Rosalinda. *Applications of Nursing Process: A Step-by-Step Guide.* Philadelphia: J.B. Lippincott Co., 1986.

Dobkin, Kathleen A. "Nursing Care of a Patient with Urinary Diversion," *Journal of Urological Nursing* 4:4, October/November/December 1985.

Dudas, Susan. "Postoperative Considerations," in *Principles of Ostomy Care.* Broadwell, D.C., and Jackson, B.S., eds. St. Louis: C.V. Mosby Co., 1982.

Gray, Mikel. "Treatment Modalities for Bladder Cancer," *Seminars in Oncology Nursing* 2(4):260-64, November 1986.

King, Ann W. "Nursing Management of Stomas of the Genitourinary System," in *Principles of Ostomy Care.* Broadwell, D.C., and Jackson, B.S., eds. St. Louis: C.V. Mosby Co., 1982.

Watt, Rosemary C. "Bladder Cancer: Etiology and Pathophysiology," *Seminars in Oncology Nursing* 2(4):256-59, November 1986.

Urolithiasis

DRG information

DRG 323 [Medical DRG] Urinary Stones. With Complication or Comorbidity (CC) and/or Treatment with Extracorporeal Shock-wave Lithotripsy [ESWL].
Mean LOS = 3.6 days

DRG 324 [Medical DRG] Urinary Stones. Without CC.
Mean LOS = 2.3 days

DRG 304 [Surgical DRG] Kidney, Ureter, and Bladder Procedures for Non-Neoplasm. With CC.
Mean LOS = 9.9 days

DRG 305 [Surgical DRG] Kidney, Ureter, and Bladder Procedures for Non-Neoplasm. Without CC.
Mean LOS = 5.6 days

DRG 310 [Surgical DRG] Transurethral Procedures. With CC.
Mean LOS = 4.5 days

Additional DRG information: The diagnosis used in the following care plan would fall under DRG 323, even though it is a *medical*, not a *surgical*, DRG.

Introduction

DEFINITION AND TIME FOCUS

Urolithiasis is the formation of mineral crystals (renal calculi, or stones) around organic matter in the urinary tract. Calcium oxalate and calcium phosphate stones are the most common. Renal calculi that remain in the kidney pelvis may remain asymptomatic until passed into a ureter, where they commonly cause severe pain, obstruction of urine flow, and complications such as bleeding and infection. This clinical plan focuses on the patient admitted for treatment of upper urinary tract calculi by percutaneous nephrolithotomy (opening into the kidney) with ultrasonic lithotripsy (crushing of the calculi using ultrasonic energy). In this procedure, a nephroscope is passed through a small incision into the kidney to provide access through which the calculi are fragmented by ultrasonic waves, flushed, and aspirated by suction or grasped and removed by forceps or special baskets.

ETIOLOGY/PRECIPITATING FACTORS

• urinary tract infection (UTI), which increases the alkalinity of the urine and causes precipitation of calcium and other substances that form renal calculi
• immobility, dehydration, and obstruction or stasis of urine, increasing risk of precipitation of calculus-forming substances
• metabolic or dietary changes, such as hyperthyroidism; bone disease; use of corticosteroids; excessive vitamin A and D intake; diet high in calcium or purine; or other factors increasing calcium, phosphorus, uric acid, and other calculus-forming substances in blood or urine

Focused assessment guidelines

NURSING HISTORY (Functional health pattern findings)

Health perception–health management pattern
• typically complains of severe pain. Location depends on calculus location: If pelvic, reports dull constant pain, usually over costovertebral angle; if in a ureter, reports *intermittent, excruciating pain radiating anteriorly down to vulva (female) or testes (male)*; in some cases, may not report pain or may report abdominal pain.
• *may have history of UTI or previous calculus formation* and treatment. A history of calculi increases risk of recurrence.
• Risk greater in males 30 to 50 years old

Nutritional-metabolic pattern
• may report *nausea and vomiting*, diarrhea, abdominal discomfort
• may report diet high in calcium (milk, cheese, beans, nuts, cocoa), purine (fish, fowl, meat, including organ meats), oxalate (spinach, parsley, rhubarb, cocoa, instant coffee, tea), or vitamins A and D
• *may report decreased fluid intake*

Elimination pattern
• may report history of UTI or urinary tract obstruction
• may report blood in urine (*hematuria*)
• *may report changes in urinary elimination* such as cloudy, odorous urine (indicates infection); painful, urgent, and frequent urination; and decreasing urine output

Activity-exercise pattern
• may report sedentary occupation or recent increased need for bed rest

Cognitive-perceptual pattern
• may report difficulty understanding metabolic influences on calculus formation and the new treatment options available (percutaneous ultrasonic lithotripsy and ESWL)

Role-relationship pattern
• may report family history of renal calculi, gout, or other renal problems

Sexuality-reproductive pattern
• may describe sexual dysfunction related to UTI and pain

Coping–stress tolerance pattern
• may appear anxious and in obvious distress

PHYSICAL FINDINGS
Genitourinary
• *presence of stones in urine*
• *costovertebral tenderness*
• *hematuria*
• pyuria
• oliguria
• urinary frequency

Gastrointestinal
• *vomiting*
• abdominal tenderness
• diarrhea
• abdominal distention
• absent bowel sounds

Integumentary
• warm, flushed skin or chills and fever
• pallor
• diaphoresis

DIAGNOSTIC STUDIES
• *urinalysis—commonly shows red blood cells, white blood cells (WBCs), crystals, casts, minerals, and changes in pH; urine culture commonly shows presence of bacteria*
• *24-hour urine study—commonly shows high levels of calcium, phosphorus, uric acid, creatinine, oxalate, or cystine*

• nitroprusside urine test—may show cystine levels
• blood studies—may show high serum levels of calcium, protein, electrolytes, uric acid, phosphates, blood urea nitrogen, creatinine, or WBCs
• serum and urine creatinine tests—may show renal dysfunction (creatinine levels high in serum, low in urine)
• *kidney, ureter, bladder X-ray—commonly shows presence of calcium calculi and gross anatomical changes,* such as distortions or enlargement (uric acid calculi cannot be visualized)
• *intravenous urography (intravenous pyelogram, or IVP)— commonly shows abnormalities in anatomical structures, areas of obstruction, and outlines of radiopaque calculi*
• computed tomography scan with or without dye—commonly shows calculi, masses, or other abnormalities
• cystoscopy—commonly shows calculi obstruction or other problems

POTENTIAL COMPLICATIONS*
• bleeding (may be acute or delayed for 1 to 2 weeks)
• sepsis
• renal pelvic perforation and loss of irrigating fluid into retroperitoneal area
• nonremovable calculi
• loss of calculus fragments outside kidneys (into retroperitoneum)

Nursing diagnosis: *Pain related to procedural manipulation, incision, and passage of calculus fragments*

NURSING PRIORITY: Relieve pain.

Interventions

1. See the "Pain" care plan, page 64.

2. *Assess and document pain episodes.*

3. *Medicate with analgesics and antispasmodics,* as ordered. Narcotic analgesics are usually necessary.

4. Apply heat to painful area(s), as ordered, for 15 to 20 minutes every 2 hours as needed.

5. Medicate, as ordered, with antiemetics as needed.

Rationales

1. General interventions for pain are included in this plan.

2. Pain may indicate calculus movement. Persistent pain may indicate obstruction or perforation. Sudden absence of pain may indicate calculus passage. Increased ureteral pressure may cause abdominal pain from extravasation of urine into perirenal spaces.

3. These medications reduce pain, relax tense muscles, and reduce reflex spasms. Narcotic analgesics are warranted because of pain severity.

4. Heat relaxes tense muscles and diminishes reflex spasms.

5. Nausea and vomiting are commonly associated with renal pain from shared nerve pathways.

(continued)

*Potential complications listed here rarely occur after percutaneous ultrasonic lithotripsy.

Interventions *continued*

6. Encourage activity, as allowed. (The patient with an indwelling ureteral catheter may be on bed rest to prevent dislodging the catheter.)

7. Additional individualized interventions: _____

_____

_____

Outcome criteria
Within 1 to 2 hours of the procedure, the patient will:
• have relief of pain or no pain

Rationales *continued*

6. Activity prevents stasis of urine, helps retard formation of calculi, and aids in passage of calculus fragments and return of urinary tract function.

7. Rationale: _____

_____

_____

• show a relaxed expression and posture
• have no nausea or vomiting.

Nursing diagnosis: *Potential altered urinary elimination patterns: dysuria, oliguria, pyuria, or frequency related to calculus fragment passage, obstruction, hematuria, or infection*

NURSING PRIORITIES: (a) Prevent urinary tract complications and (b) optimize return of normal urinary function.

Interventions

1. *Measure each voiding and note urine characteristics. Monitor intake and output* every 4 to 8 hours or more frequently if the patient is oliguric. Alert the doctor if urinary output <30 ml/hour.

2. *Monitor the patency of an indwelling ureteral catheter or Foley catheter* every hour.

3. *Strain all urine for calculi and calculus fragments.* Send any calculi for laboratory analysis. Notify the doctor of calculi passage and document.

4. Observe for signs of ureteral obstruction (increased flank pain, oliguria) or urethral obstruction (bladder distention, suprapubic pain), and report any that occur.

5. Observe for signs of dehydration, such as dry skin and mucous membranes, thirst, poor skin turgor, low urine output, decreased blood pressure, tachycardia, and weight loss.

6. *Encourage fluid intake* of 3 to 4 liters/day. Document.

Rationales

1. Assessing the character of the urine provides data indicating such complications as infection (cloudy, odorous urine) and hemorrhage. Some hematuria is expected for 1 to 2 days because of the surgical manipulation, but the presence of bright red blood may indicate hemorrhage. Adequate intake is necessary to flush calculi through the kidneys, prevent further calculus formation, and prevent tissue damage. Adequate output indicates proper kidney function. Calculi may increase frequency and urgency of urination as they near the ureterovesical junction.

2. If present, a ureteral catheter aids in passage of calculus fragments and prevents obstruction of urine flow. A patent Foley catheter aids in monitoring fluid output and assessing calculus passage. Calculus fragments can easily obstruct catheters.

3. The type and amount of calculi passed may influence the type of prophylactic treatment used to prevent recurrence.

4. As the calculus moves through the renal system, it is most likely to lodge in a ureter or the urethra.

5. Dehydration concentrates urine, increasing the risk of calculus formation and infection.

6. Fluids enhance passage of calculus fragments and help prevent obstruction and infection.

Interventions *continued*

7. Give antibiotics every 4 to 8 hours, as ordered.

8. Monitor and document vital signs every 2 to 4 hours, as ordered.

9. As ordered, irrigate the catheter with acid or alkaline solutions, depending on the type of calculus.

10. Additional individualized interventions: _____
_____
_____

Rationales *continued*

7. UTI and renal calculi are commonly associated (UTI is a major predisposing factor for the formation of renal calculi). UTI provides organic material and alkalizes urine, precipitating minerals and causing formation of calculi. Antibiotics are commonly given prophylactically to prevent infection and recurrence.

8. Changes in vital signs may indicate infection or other complications. Fever is common.

9. Catheter irrigations with acid or alkaline solutions promote acidification or alkalinization of the urine and help prevent further calculus formation.

10. Rationale: _____
_____
_____

Outcome criteria
Within 3 days of the procedure, the patient will:
• have urine that is normal in appearance and quantity
• have no infection
• have no hematuria

• show reduced amount of calculus fragments in urine
• have catheters removed without problems
• show adequate hydration
• have normal vital signs.

Nursing diagnosis: *Knowledge deficit related to potential causes of calculus formation*

NURSING PRIORITY: Optimize knowledge of medical regimen to prevent calculi recurrence.

Interventions

1. See the "Knowledge Deficit" care plan, page 56.

2. *Provide information and reinforce as necessary, and document teaching* regarding:
• dietary limitations for calcium calculi (dairy products and green leafy vegetables), uric acid calculi (meats, legumes, and whole grains), and oxalate calculi (chocolate, caffeine drinks, beets, and spinach). Consult a dietitian.

• need for activity on regular basis

• need for 3 to 4 liters of fluid daily

• need for maintenance of desired urine pH with medications and regular urine pH testing, in accordance with the doctor's recommendations

• need for monitoring and treating metabolic and other conditions (such as gout) that predispose the patient to calculus formation
• signs and symptoms of calculus recurrence such as pain, hematuria, oliguria.

Rationales

1. The "Knowledge Deficit" care plan contains general information on patient teaching.

2. Patients need accurate information to comply with their preventive regimen.

• Depending on the type of calculus, limiting foods rich in calculus-forming substances may inhibit recurrence. The dietitian can provide details of specific diets, which vary considerably.

• Activity decreases stasis and risk of calculus formation.
• Fluids flush calculus fragments and help prevent recurrence.
• Depending on their composition, calculi may form in either acid or alkaline urine. The goal of treatment is to prevent calculus formation by maintaining the urine pH at the desired level using appropriate medications.
• Treating underlying conditions such as gout (uric acid accumulation) is necessary for prevention of calculus formation.
• The incidence of recurrence is high.

(continued)

Interventions *continued*

3. Additional individualized interventions: _____

_____

_____

Rationales *continued*

3. Rationale: _____

_____

_____

Outcome criteria
By the time of discharge, the patient will:
• verbalize diet restrictions related to foods contributing to calculus formation, the need for increased fluid requirements, the recommended activity level, the need

for monitoring of such metabolic problems as gout, and the signs and symptoms of calculus recurrence
• demonstrate accurate testing and interpretation of urine pH.

Discharge planning

NURSING DISCHARGE CRITERIA
Upon discharge, documentation shows evidence of:
• absence of gross hematuria
• absence of fever
• healing incision with no redness or other signs of infection
• absence of pulmonary or cardiovascular complications
• ability to tolerate and follow dietary and fluid regimen
• ability to perform activities of daily living independently
• ability to ambulate same as before hospitalization
• ability to perform pH monitoring
• ability to control pain using oral medications
• absence of infection (or regimen including appropriate antibiotic)
• stable vital signs
• absence of indwelling ureteral or Foley catheter or, if Foley catheter is present, ability to perform appropriate catheter care
• referral to home care if catheter is in place or if the patient's home support system is inadequate.

PATIENT/FAMILY DISCHARGE TEACHING CHECKLIST
Document evidence that patient/family demonstrates understanding of:
___ postoperative care of incisions, drains, or catheters
___ activity precautions
___ dietary modifications
___ desired fluid intake
___ all discharge medications' purpose, dosage, administration schedule, and side effects requiring medical attention; usual medications include ascorbic acid (to increase urine acidity), ammonium chloride (if phosphate calculi present), sodium or potassium phosphate (to decrease urinary calcium if calcium calculi present), sodium bicarbonate, acetazolamide and allopurinol (if uric acid calculi present), and antibiotics
___ signs and symptoms of recurring calculi
___ urine pH testing
___ need for laboratory follow-up
___ need for follow-up visits with doctor
___ need for follow-up diagnostic tests
___ date, time, and location of next appointment
___ how to contact doctor.

DOCUMENTATION CHECKLIST
Using outcome criteria as a guide, document:
___ clinical status on admission
___ significant changes in status
___ pertinent laboratory and diagnostic test findings
___ renal pain episodes
___ pain-relief measures
___ passage of renal calculi fragments
___ fluid intake
___ output and characteristics of urine
___ other therapies
___ nutritional intake
___ patient/family teaching
___ discharge planning.

ASSOCIATED CARE PLANS
Fluid and Electrolyte Imbalances
Knowledge Deficit
Pain
Surgical Intervention

REFERENCES
Cain, Harvey D. *Flint's Emergency Treatment and Management*. Philadelphia: W.B. Saunders Co., 1985
Charig, C.R., et al. "Comparison of Treatment of Renal Calculi by Open Surgery, Percutaneous Nephrolithotomy, and Extracorporeal Shockwave Lithotripsy," *British Medical Journal* 292:879-82, March 29, 1986.
Crowley, Arthur R., and Smith, Arthur D. "Percutaneous Ultrasonic Lithotripsy," *Postgraduate Medicine* 79(8):57-60, June 1986.
Harwood, Charlotte T. "Pulverizing Kidney Stones: What You Should Know about Lithotripsy," *RN* July 1985, pp 32-37.
Lewis, Sharon M., and Collier, Idolia C. *Medical-Surgical Nursing: Assessment and Management of Clinical Problems*. New York: McGraw-Hill Book Co., 1983.
The Lippincott Manual of Nursing Practice. Philadelphia: J.B. Lippincott Co., 1986.
Long, Barbara C., and Phipps, Wilma J. *Essentials of Medical-Surgical Nursing: A Nursing Process Approach*. St. Louis: C.V. Mosby Co., 1985.
Metheny, Norma. "Renal Stones and Urinary pH," *American Journal of Nursing* 82:1372-75, 1982.
Pawlowski, Jacqueline. "Percutaneous Nephrolithotripsy," *APRN Journal* 39(5):779-81, 1984.

Reddy, P.K., et al. "Percutaneous Removal of Renal and Ureteral Calculi: Experience with 400 Cases," *Journal of Urology* 134:662-65, October 1985.

Schulze, Harold, et al. "Combined Treatment of Branched Calculi by Percutaneous Nephrolithotomy and Extracorporeal Shock Wave Lithotripsy," *Journal of Urology* 135:1138-41, June 1985.

Stone, Linda. "Percutaneous Nephrolithotripsy," *AORN Journal* 39(5):773-778, April 1984.

Swearingen, Pamela L. *Manual of Nursing Therapeutics: Applying Nursing Diagnoses to Medical Disorders.* Reading, Mass.: Addison-Wesley Publishing Co., 1986.

Volkmann-Jones, Sheila. "A New Method of Kidney Stone Retrieval," *Today's OR Nurse* 6(8):8-10, August 1984.

Hysterectomy

DRG information
DRG 354 [Surgical DRG] Uterine, Adnexa Procedure for Non-Ovarian, Adnexal Malignancy with Complication or Comorbidity (CC).
Mean LOS = 9.1 days

DRG 355 [Surgical DRG] Uterine, Adnexa Procedure for Non-Ovarian, Adnexal Malignancy. Without CC.
Mean LOS = 6.7 days

DRG 357 [Surgical DRG] Uterine and Adnexa Procedures for Ovarian or Adnexal Malignancy.
Mean LOS = 11.3 days

DRG 358 [Surgical DRG] Uterine and Adnexa Procedures for Non-Malignancy. With CC.
Mean LOS = 8.1 days

DRG 359 [Surgical DRG] Uterine and Adnexa Procedures for Non-Malignancy. Without CC.
Mean LOS = 6.3 days

Introduction
DEFINITION AND TIME FOCUS
Hysterectomy is the surgical removal of the uterus. Several surgical variations exist. Subtotal hysterectomy, seldom performed, is the surgical removal of the corpus (body) of the uterus, leaving the cervical stump in place. Total hysterectomy is the surgical removal of the uterus and cervix. Total hysterectomy with bilateral salpingo-oophorectomy is the surgical removal of the uterus, cervix, uterine (Fallopian) tubes, and ovaries. (Salpingectomy is the surgical removal of the uterine tube or tubes; oophorectomy is the removal of an ovary or ovaries.) Radical hysterectomy is the surgical removal of the uterus, cervix, upper portion of the vagina, connective tissue, and lymph nodes.

All hysterectomy procedures result in permanent sterilization. If performed in conjunction with bilateral oophorectomy in the premenopausal woman, abrupt menopause results.

The surgical approach for a hysterectomy may be vaginal or abdominal. The vaginal approach is used for cervical cancer and uterine prolapse. The abdominal approach is commonly used for pelvic exploration for cancer or infection, removal of an enlarged uterus, or removal of tubes and ovaries.

This clinical plan focuses on assessment of the preoperative patient and postoperative care for a patient who has undergone total abdominal hysterectomy.

ETIOLOGY/PRECIPITATING FACTORS
• recent diagnosis of cervical, endometrial, or ovarian cancer
• irreparable rupture or perforation of the uterus
• severe (life-threatening) pelvic infection
• myoma or nonmalignant tumor of the uterus
• history of endometriosis
• hemorrhage, metrorrhagia (dysfunctional uterine bleeding [DUB]), postmenopausal bleeding, perimenopausal menometrorrhagia (excessive prolonged vaginal bleeding at irregular intervals), menorrhagia (excessive uterine bleeding occurring at the regular intervals of menstruation), or postcoital bleeding with pelvic pain

Focused assessment guidelines
NURSING HISTORY (Functional health pattern findings)

Health perception–health management pattern
• *may be postmenopausal with sudden uterine bleeding*
• may have had abnormal Papanicolaou (Pap) smear results (if cervical or endometrial cancer present)
• may have a history of prolonged postmenopausal estrogen replacement therapy (if endometrial cancer present)
• may have a history of prolonged, heavy, or painful menstruation (if uterine myoma, DUB, or endometrial cancer present)
• may report a history of fibroids in the uterus (if uterine myoma present)

Nutritional-metabolic pattern
• may be obese

Elimination pattern
• may report a pattern of frequent urination related to presence and proximity of tumor

Activity-exercise pattern
• may report fatigue-related decrease in activity level if excessive vaginal bleeding has caused anemia

Sleep-rest pattern
• may report sleep disturbance related to nocturia
• may report sleep disturbance related to emotional stress of planned hospitalization and surgery

Cognitive-perceptual pattern
• may report a history of abdominal, pelvic, back, or leg pain
• may report fear of anticipated discomfort and pain from abdominal incision

Self-perception–self-concept pattern
• may express *concerns about abdominal scar and removal of uterus*
• may express concerns about femininity
• may express concerns about infertility

Role-relationship pattern
• may express concerns about spouse's or partner's acceptance of surgical infertility

Sexuality-reproductive pattern
• may express concerns about resuming sexual intercourse postoperatively

Value-belief pattern
• may have delayed seeking medical attention if perimenopausal (because irregular menses are normal during early menopause)

PHYSICAL FINDINGS
Gastrointestinal
• lower abdominal distention (with ovarian cancer)
• abdominal discomfort (with uterine myoma)
• adnexal mass (with ovarian cancer)

Genitourinary
• leukorrhea (with infection)
• vaginal bleeding (with uterine myoma)

Musculoskeletal
• leg edema (less common)

DIAGNOSTIC STUDIES
• hemoglobin level—may reveal decreased hemoglobin concentration, indicating anemia
• hematocrit—may reveal a decrease in volume percentage of red blood cells in whole blood, indicating blood loss
• white blood cell (WBC) count—may be elevated because of severe pelvic infection

• *D & C* (cervical dilatation and fractional curettage) *and four-quadrant endometrial biopsy*—performed to remove endometrial tissue for a histopathologic study, which *may reveal endometrial cancer*
• *wedge biopsy or conization biopsy of the cervix* (removal of tissue for microscopic examination)—*may reveal cervical cancer*
• Pap smear (removal of exfoliated cervical cells)—may reveal cellular dysplasia
• colposcopy (visualization of the cervix with a colposcope)—may identify abnormal cell growth
• Schiller's test (staining of the cervix with iodine)—used to identify abnormal cells
• ultrasound or computed tomography (CT) scan—may reveal size and location of mass

POTENTIAL COMPLICATIONS
• hemorrhagic shock
• peritonitis
• emboli
• pneumonia
• perforated bladder
• ligation of ureter
• wound infection
• atelectasis
• thrombophlebitis
• urinary retention
• urinary tract infection

Collaborative problem: *Potential thromboembolic and hemorrhagic complications related to immobility, venous stasis, pelvic congestion, or possible predisposing factors*

NURSING PRIORITY: Prevent or promptly treat thromboembolic and hemorrhagic complications.

Interventions	Rationales
1. *Monitor for signs of bleeding.* Check vital signs and the surgical site according to standard postoperative protocol (see the "Surgical Intervention" care plan, page 71, for details), and report tachycardia, dropping blood pressure, increasing drainage, restlessness, pallor, diaphoresis, or any other sign of hemorrhage immediately. Institute fluid replacement therapy, as ordered.	1. Proximity of the operative surgical site to large vessels may increase the risk of significant bleeding postoperatively. Additionally, a patient with a presurgical diagnosis of cancer may have alterations in clotting factors that predispose to hemorrhage. Untreated, such bleeding rapidly progresses to hypovolemic shock; death may rapidly ensue. The "Surgical Intervention" care plan provides further details about standard postoperative monitoring.
2. *Institute measures to prevent and assess for thromboembolic phenomena,* including frequent position changes, avoidance of knee gatch, avoidance of prolonged sitting, antiembolic hose, and range-of-motion exercises. See the "Surgical Intervention" and "Thrombophlebitis" care plans, pages 71 and 229, respectively, for further details.	2. Postoperative patients are always at increased risk for thromboembolic complications because of circulatory disruption, immobility, and edema. Posthysterectomy patients may be especially at risk because of pelvic congestion. The "Surgical Intervention" and "Thrombophlebitis" care plans contain further details regarding this common postoperative problem.

(continued)

Interventions *continued*

3. Before discharge, instruct the patient to promptly report any bleeding, avoid heavy lifting, avoid prolonged sitting, and avoid wearing constrictive clothes.

4. Additional individualized interventions: _____

_____

Rationales *continued*

3. Postoperative hemorrhage may occur as late as 14 days following surgery. Avoiding activities that put stress on the operative site or cause venous stasis or pelvic congestion helps minimize the risk of bleeding or thromboembolic phenomena after discharge.

4. Rationale: _____

_____

Outcome criteria
Throughout the period of hospitalization, the patient will:
• show no significant postoperative bleeding
• show no signs or symptoms of thromboembolic complications.

Nursing diagnosis: *Potential postoperative infection related to abdominal incision, urinary tract proximity, contamination of peritoneal cavity, hypoventilation, anesthesia, or preoperative infection*

NURSING PRIORITY: Prevent or promptly detect and treat infection.

Interventions

1. *Monitor for signs and symptoms of peritonitis,* such as significant increase in abdominal pain or a change in pain quality, abdominal rigidity or tenderness, nausea and vomiting, absent bowel sounds, or tachycardia. Report abnormal findings to the doctor immediately.

2. Implement standard postoperative nursing measures to prevent or detect:

• atelectasis/pneumonia

• urinary tract infection (UTI)

• incisional infection.

See the "Surgical Intervention" care plan, page 71, for further details.

Rationales

1. The uterus is a peritoneal organ, so tissue oozing after its removal drains into the peritoneal cavity. Significant contamination from tissue, bleeding, or infection may result in potentially life-threatening peritonitis if not promptly treated.

2. The hysterectomy patient may be at increased risk for infection compared to other surgical patients because of the site of the surgery and the predisposing factors that may be involved.
• Anesthetic ciliary depression, decreased mobility, and hypoventilation from pain from the abdominal incision contribute to stasis of pulmonary secretions, thus increasing the risk of infection.
• The urinary tract's proximity to the surgical area makes it prone to surgical trauma, edema, and resultant urinary retention, which may predispose the patient to infection.
• Wound infection can be a complication of any surgery, but if the hysterectomy is performed because of cancer, the patient's immune response may be impaired, further increasing the risk.

Nursing measures related to these problems are standard postoperative interventions, detailed in the "Surgical Intervention" care plan.

Interventions *continued*

3. Before discharge, teach the patient about signs and symptoms indicating infection, such as cough or respiratory congestion; urinary pain or burning, or cloudy urine; or redness, swelling, or purulent wound drainage. Emphasize the importance of promptly reporting such findings to the doctor.

4. Additional individualized interventions: _____

_____

_____

Rationales *continued*

3. Prompt detection facilitates early treatment.

4. Rationale: _____

_____

_____

Outcome criteria
Throughout the postoperative course, the patient will:
• show no signs of peritonitis
• perform pulmonary hygiene measures regularly

• show no signs of UTI
• have normal wound healing without evidence of infection.

Nursing diagnosis: *Potential urinary retention related to decreased bladder and urethral muscle tone from anesthesia and mechanical trauma*

NURSING PRIORITY: Promote optimal urinary elimination.

Interventions

1. *Monitor for signs of urinary retention,* such as small, frequent voidings; bladder distention; intake greater than output; or restless behavior.

2. Implement measures to deal with retention, if it occurs. Encourage voiding. Obtain an order to catheterize if no voiding occurs within 8 hours postoperatively. See the "Surgical Intervention" care plan, page 71, for details.

3. Additional individualized interventions: _____

_____

_____

Rationales

1. Small, frequent voidings (<100 ml) may indicate urinary retention, possibly related to edema, decreased muscle tone, or nerve damage to the bladder or urethra from mechanical trauma during surgery. Urinary retention occurs most often during the first 24 hours after surgery.

2. The "Surgical Intervention" care plan contains specific information about this common postoperative problem.

3. Rationale: _____

_____

_____

Outcome criteria
Within 8 hours postoperatively, the patient will:
• void at least once
• empty the bladder with adequate output: at least 100 ml per voiding
• evidence clear, yellow urine.

Nursing diagnosis: *Pain related to abdominal incision and distention*

NURSING PRIORITY: Minimize and relieve abdominal pain.

Interventions

1. *Implement measures for pain control.* See the "Pain" and "Surgical Intervention" care plans, pages 64 and 71, respectively.

Rationales

1. These plans contain measures applicable to any patient in pain.

(continued)

Interventions *continued*

2. Offer application of heat to the abdomen after 48 hours postoperatively.

3. Additional individualized interventions: _____

_____

_____

Rationales *continued*

2. Heat increases the elasticity of collagen tissue; lessens pain; relieves muscle spasms; helps resolve inflammatory infiltration, edema, and exudates; and increases blood flow. Heat applied less than 48 hours postoperatively may cause undesirable edema.

3. Rationale: _____

_____

_____

Outcome criteria

Within 1 hour of pain onset, the patient will:
• verbalize reduction or relief of abdominal pain.

Within 3 days postoperatively, the patient will:
• need analgesics less frequently or in lower doses than on admission
• pass flatus.

Nursing diagnosis: *Potential altered self-concept related to changes in body appearance and function as a result of surgery*

NURSING PRIORITY: Assist the patient in recognizing and accepting alteration in body appearance and function.

Interventions

1. *Assess the patient's level of understanding regarding hysterectomy and the recovery period.*

2. *Acknowledge the patient's feelings of loss* and dependency and her fears of complications. Provide reassurance that these concerns are normal.

3. Provide opportunities, every shift, for the patient to discuss concerns about symptoms associated with posthysterectomy recovery. Encourage discussion of fatigue, wound problems, discomfort, urinary problems, and weight gain. Clarify misconceptions of such posthysterectomy myths as growing fat and flabby, developing facial hair, becoming wrinkled or masculine in appearance, or becoming depressed and nervous.

4. Encourage the patient to discuss plans for posthysterectomy recovery at home.

5. Additional individualized interventions: _____

_____

_____

Rationales

1. Evaluation of the patient's level of understanding allows the caregiver to individualize patient teaching according to the preexisting knowledge base.

2. Loss of the uterus frequently triggers grief over lost childbearing capacity in young women and concerns about loss of femininity. Acknowledgment validates the patient's feelings and encourages continuation of communication to alleviate fears and anxieties.

3. Frequent, short teaching sessions enhance learning through repetition and through prevention of content overload. Factual discussion prepares the patient for acceptance of common symptoms. The literature supports the fact that such information does not act as a self-fulfilling prophecy. Clarification of misconceptions and myths reduces fears and anxiety during the recovery period.

4. Such discussion allows the patient to make future plans incorporating appropriate limitations in physical activities. It also demonstrates her acceptance and understanding of her physical condition.

5. Rationale: _____

_____

_____

Outcome criteria

By the time of discharge, the patient will:
• verbalize understanding of body changes

• verbalize acceptance of the alterations in body appearance and function.

Nursing diagnosis: *Potential sexual dysfunction: decreased libido or dyspareunia related to fatigue, pain, grieving, altered body image, decreased estrogen levels, loss of vaginal sensations, sexual activity restrictions, or concerns about acceptance by spouse or partner*

NURSING PRIORITY: Facilitate healthy coping with sexual alterations.

Interventions

1. Encourage the patient to explore perceptions of how surgery will affect her sexual function. Listen sensitively.

2. Discuss the potential impact of surgery on sexuality by explaining:
• the predictability of temporarily decreased libido

• the temporary nature of loss of vaginal sensations and of activity restrictions (sexual intercourse is discouraged for 4 to 6 weeks, then may be resumed gradually); also explain that return to full function is likely in approximately 4 months

• the rationale for avoiding douching during the recovery period.

3. Explain that decreased libido and vaginal dryness may result from hormonal loss and that hormonal replacements are available.

4. Suggest ways to ease sexual adjustment during the immediate postoperative period, such as holding hands, kissing, massage, and other alternative methods of expressing love and sexuality.

5. Provide information and discuss options for conserving the patient's energy and preventing discomfort during her return to sexual functioning, such as using a vaginal lubricant, scheduling sex for the time when she has the most energy, and using positions that avoid pressure on the incision.

6. Encourage the patient and spouse or partner, if present, to share concerns and feelings with each other.

7. Additional individualized interventions: _____
_____
_____

Rationales

1. Identifying current perceptions is the first step in coping with concerns. Sensitive listening allows the caregiver to identify appropriate and inappropriate perceptions.

2. Providing factual information clarifies misconceptions and reduces fears of sexual loss.
• Abdominal hysterectomy is major surgery that can have profound emotional implications. Fatigue, pain, and grieving may require so much coping energy that little remains for dealing with sexuality. The patient may need gentle "permission" to allow time to recover.
• Vaginal sensory loss from surgical trauma resolves typically over a period of weeks to months. Activity restrictions allow time for tissues to heal.

• Douching may increase the risk of infection or bleeding.

3. The patient may not recognize that changes in sexual feelings and function can have a physiologic basis.

4. Continued physical affection provides reassurance that a spouse's or partner's sexual interest continues after the hysterectomy.

5. Sexual activity during the recovery period may be modified temporarily, but return to full sexual function is expected.

6. Mutual loving support is a positive factor in both the patient's and the spouse's or partner's adjustment to sexual alterations.

7. Rationale: _____
_____
_____

Outcome criterion

By the time of discharge, the patient will:
• verbalize strategies to manage temporary alteration in sexual functioning.

Discharge planning

NURSING DISCHARGE CRITERIA

Upon discharge, documentation shows evidence of:
• stable vital signs
• hemoglobin level and WBC count within normal parameters
• absence of cardiovascular and pulmonary complications
• bowel function same as before surgery
• absence of dysuria, hematuria, pyuria, burning, frequency, or urgency
• absence of fever
• absence of signs and symptoms of infection
• ability to control pain using oral medications
• ability to ambulate and perform activities of daily living (ADLs) same as before surgery
• healing surgical incision without redness, inflammation, or drainage
• ability to perform wound care independently or with minimal assistance
• ability to tolerate adequate nutritional intake
• adequate home support, or referral to home care if indicated by inadequate home support system or inability to perform ADLs and wound care.

PATIENT/FAMILY DISCHARGE TEACHING CHECKLIST

Document evidence that patient/family demonstrates understanding of:
___ implications of total abdominal hysterectomy
___ all discharge medications' purpose, dosage, administration schedule, and side effects requiring medical attention
___ incision care (aseptic technique, dressing changes, irrigations, cleansing procedures, hand-washing technique, and proper disposal of soiled dressings)
___ signs and symptoms of possible infection
___ dietary requirements and restrictions, if any
___ activity and exercise restrictions
___ date, time, and location of follow-up appointment
___ how to contact doctor.

DOCUMENTATION CHECKLIST

Using outcome criteria as a guide, document:
___ clinical status on admission
___ postoperative clinical assessment
___ significant changes in status
___ appearance of incision and wound drainage
___ I.V. line patency and condition of site
___ assessment of pain, and relief measures
___ nutritional intake
___ fluid intake and output
___ patient/family teaching
___ discharge planning.

ASSOCIATED CARE PLANS

Grief/Grieving
Ineffective Individual Coping
Knowledge Deficit
Pain
Surgical Intervention
Thrombophlebitis

REFERENCES

Brunner, L., and Suddarth, D. *Manual of Nursing Practice*, 4th ed. Philadelphia: J.B. Lippincott Co., 1986.

Carpenito, L. *Nursing Diagnosis: Application to Clinical Practice*. Philadelphia: J.B. Lippincott Co., 1983.

Dugan, K. "The Bleak Outlook on Ovarian Cancer," *American Journal of Nursing* 85(2):144-147, 1985.

Gordon, M. *Manual of Nursing Diagnosis*. New York: McGraw-Hill Book Co., 1985.

Gould, D. "Hidden Problems After a Hysterectomy," *Nursing Times* 82(23):43-46, 1986.

Howe, J., et al. *The Handbook of Nursing*. New York: John Wiley & Sons, 1984.

Kniesl, C., and Ames, S. *Adult Health Nursing: A Biopsychosocial Approach*. Reading, Mass.: Addison-Wesley Publishing Co., 1986.

McNally, J., et al. *Guidelines for Cancer Nursing Practice*. New York: Grune & Stratton, 1985.

Snyder, M. *Independent Nursing Interventions*. New York: John Wiley & Sons, 1985.

Tucker, S., et al. *Patient Care Standards*, 3rd ed. St. Louis: C.V. Mosby Co., 1984.

Prostatectomy

DRG information

DRG 334 [Surgical DRG] Major Male Pelvic Procedure.
  With Complication or Comorbidity (CC).
  Mean LOS = 11 days

DRG 335 [Surgical DRG] Major Male Pelvic Procedure.
  Without CC.
  Mean LOS = 9.3 days

DRG 336 [Surgical DRG] Transurethral Prostatectomy.
  With CC.
  Mean LOS = 6.1 days

DRG 337 [Surgical DRG] Transurethral Prostatectomy.
  Without CC.
  Mean LOS = 4.9 days

Introduction

DEFINITION AND TIME FOCUS

Prostatectomy is the surgical removal of the prostate, a gland (in males) located in line with the urethra and positioned between the bladder and rectum. There are three types of prostatectomies: partial resection, simple, and radical. A partial resection removes only enlarged tissue. A simple prostatectomy removes the prostate and its capsule. A radical prostatectomy removes the prostate (and its capsule), the seminal vesicles, and a portion of the bladder neck.

Four surgical approaches are used for prostatectomies: transurethral, suprapubic, retropubic, and perineal (see figure below). The surgeon's selection of a type of surgery and an approach depends on the patient's general condition and the specific problem necessitating the surgery. The transurethral approach is suitable for a partial resection; the suprapubic for a simple prostatectomy; and the retropubic and the perineal for simple and radical prostatectomies.

The transurethral resection of the prostate (TURP), in which prostatic tissue is removed via the urethra, is performed most frequently. It is indicated for benign prostatic hypertrophy that can no longer be managed medically and for small cancerous lesions. Because the surgery requires a lithotomy position, it is not suitable for patients with hip problems or prior surgery of the hip joint.

The suprapubic approach involves making a lower abdominal suprapubic incision and then a bladder incision. It is indicated for prostatic obstruction and removal of bladder calculi or diverticula.

In the retropubic approach, an abdominal incision is made and the gland is entered directly, without an incision into the bladder. It is used for removal of a gland too large for a TURP, for removal of large cancerous lesions, and for the patient who cannot tolerate a lithotomy position.

With the perineal approach, an incision is made in the perineum, the area between the scrotum and anus. This approach is used for removal of a large gland when an abdominal approach is contraindicated, such as in an obese patient.

TURP usually has the shortest recovery period; the suprapubic approach, somewhat longer; and the retropubic and perineal approaches, the longest.

This clinical plan focuses on the prostatectomy patient during the preoperative and postoperative phases for any of these types of surgery.

ETIOLOGY/PRECIPITATING FACTORS

• age—men 50 and over usually experience some prostate enlargement
• benign prostatic hypertrophy or hyperplasia—usually associated with hormonal changes of aging
• prostate cancer—unknown etiology, most common tumor is adenocarcinoma. Risk factors include:
  □ age (peak incidence averages at age 65)
  □ race (progresses at a faster rate in black men)
  □ marital status (lowest incidence in single men)
  □ occupation (increased incidence among workers employed in the rubber and cadmium industries)
  □ hormonal factors (altered androgen and estrogen metabolite levels may contribute).

Focused assessment guidelines

NURSING HISTORY (Functional health pattern findings)

Health perception—health management pattern
• may report preexisting cardiac, pulmonary, or diabetic disorders

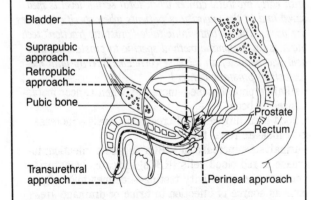

TYPES OF PROSTATECTOMIES

Bladder

Suprapubic approach

Retropubic approach

Pubic bone

Prostate

Rectum

Transurethral approach

Perineal approach

Transurethral approach: Instrument inserted into urethra for prostate resection—no visible scar
Suprapubic approach: Incision made into lower abdomen and bladder neck
Retropubic approach: Incision made into lower abdomen; bladder neck not resected
Perineal approach: Incision made anterior to rectum

• may report preoperative urinary tract infection (UTI) and bladder outlet obstruction
• may report medication with antibiotics for UTIs

Nutritional–metabolic pattern
• may report weight loss, nausea and vomiting, or anorexia (from impaired renal function because of obstruction or chronic UTI)

Elimination pattern
• *may report urinary retention, dysuria, frequency, hesitancy, nocturia, urgency, decreased stream, postvoid dribbling, urinary incontinence,* or hematuria (rare)
• may report constipation or epigastric discomfort (from pressure of the bladder on the gastrointestinal tract)

Activity-exercise pattern
• may report decreased activity coinciding with pain
• may report fatigue and weakness from anorexia or nocturia, with associated sleep deprivation
• may report preexisting age-related cardiopulmonary disorders influencing exercise tolerance

Sleep-rest pattern
• may report sleep pattern disturbances from pain, nocturia, frequency, or urinary incontinence

Cognitive-perceptual pattern
• may report lack of knowledge about disease (benign prostatic hypertrophy or cancer) or surgical procedure and expected outcomes

Self-perception–self-concept pattern
• may express fears and anxieties about alterations in body image, retrograde ejaculation, or impotence from nerve transection or injury
• may express feelings of hopelessness, powerlessness, and lowered self-esteem associated with diagnosis of cancer

Role-relationship pattern
• may report disturbed role performance
• may express fear of social isolation associated with diagnosis of cancer
• may report experiences of family or friends who died from cancer or during surgery

Sexuality-reproductive pattern
• may report preexisting impotence as side effect of cardiac medications
• may discuss concerns about impotence that surgery may cause
• spouse or sexual partner may express concerns about postoperative sexual performance

Coping–stress tolerance pattern
• may report fears and anxieties associated with diagnosis of cancer
• may appear depressed

*Preoperative values from the laboratory tests listed here should be within normal limits.

Value–belief system
• may express disbelief (denial) about diagnosis of cancer
• may report increased reliance on spiritual support system as coping mechanism

PHYSICAL FINDINGS
Patients with localized prostatic cancer commonly have no symptoms; symptoms indicate advanced disease.

Genitourinary
• *enlarged prostate* on rectal examination:
  □ smooth, elastic, nonfixed gland suggests benign prostatic hypertrophy
  □ hard, irregular, fixed nodule suggests cancer
• *postvoid dribbling or incontinence*
• *urinary retention*
• hematuria (rare)

Cardiovascular
• peripheral edema (in renal failure or in hydroureteronephrosis from obstruction)

Pulmonary
• pulmonary edema (in renal failure or in hydroureteronephrosis from obstruction)

Musculoskeletal
• costovertebral angle tenderness (in renal failure)
• back pain or stiffness (with bony metastasis)

DIAGNOSTIC STUDIES
• white blood cell (WBC) count and sedimentation rate—increase with inflammation and infection*
• hemoglobin level, hematocrit, platelets—decrease with hemorrhage*
• prothrombin time (PT), partial thromboplastin time (PTT)—increase with hemorrhage*
• blood typing and cross matching—may be done in case transfusion is needed*
• *acid phosphatase—increases in about 25% of patients with early prostatic cancer when total serum level is measured and in the majority of patients when specific enzymes are used. (The tartrate inhibitable "prostatic fraction" technique is an enzymatic method specific to prostate-secreted acid phosphatase; an increase correlates directly with metastasis of prostatic cancer.)*
• alkaline phosphatase—increases when cancer metastasizes to bone
• blood urea nitrogen and creatinine levels—increase may indicate renal failure
• urinalysis—increase in WBCs suggests infection; increase in red blood cells (RBCs) indicates hematuria
• culture and sensitivity testing— defines microorganisms as source of infection in urine or drainage areas
• *cystoscopy—evaluates degree of fixation of prostate gland, especially when cancerous; evaluates bladder problems and allows direct assessment of obstruction*

- *prostatic biopsy—provides differential diagnosis of cancer*
- *intravenous pyelogram—aids in determining presence and severity of kidney obstruction*
- chest X-ray—indicates lung status preoperatively, may reveal lung metastasis
- EKG—indicates preoperative cardiac status; used as baseline for comparison if changes occur
- bone scan—aids in detecting bony metastasis

POTENTIAL COMPLICATIONS
- hemorrhage
- shock (hypovolemic or septic)
- infection
- epididymitis
- rectal perforation intraoperatively
- pulmonary embolism
- atelectasis
- bowel incontinence (with perineal prostatectomy, rare)

Collaborative problem: *Potential hypovolemia related to prostatic or incisional bleeding postoperatively**

NURSING PRIORITY: Prevent or promptly detect internal or external bleeding.

Interventions

1. *Monitor and document the amount of blood* lost from incisional dressings and the urinary drainage system hourly for the first 12 to 24 hours postoperatively, then every 4 hours. Typical drains and catheters include the following:
- for TURP, a urethral catheter
- for the suprapubic approach, a urethral catheter, a suprapubic tube, and an abdominal drain
- for the retropubic approach, a urethral catheter and an abdominal drain
- for the perineal approach, a urethral catheter and a perineal drain.
Observe the frequency of clots in the urine. Consult the surgeon concerning the amount of bleeding anticipated. Alert the surgeon if any of the following occur:
- bright red drainage
- persistent burgundy-colored drainage
- persistent clot formation.

2. *Evaluate and document pulse rate, blood pressure, respirations, skin color, and level of consciousness* according to unit protocol—typically every 4 hours for 24 hours or until stable, then every 8 hours.

3. *Monitor hemoglobin level, hematocrit, platelet count, and coagulation values daily.* Compare current values with preoperative values. Alert the doctor about abnormal values. Administer blood transfusions as ordered.

Rationales

1. The amount of bleeding expected after surgery varies with the cause and extent of the surgery. Usually heavy bleeding for the first 24 hours is expected for a TURP or a suprapubic or retropubic prostatectomy. Minimal bleeding is expected with the perineal approach.

Blood volume loss from incisional drainage usually is minimal, whereas blood volume loss via the urinary catheter may range from minimal to life-threatening. Bright red blood indicates arterial bleeding; dark blood suggests venous bleeding.

Hemorrhage may occur with any surgical approach, but it is a particular problem with TURP. Venous bleeding during the early postoperative period is very common. If necessary, it may be treated with traction placed on the catheter for 6 to 8 hours.

Hemorrhage may occur with a suprapubic or perineal approach, but usually it is not a major problem. With the retropubic approach, hemorrhage usually is minimal, because this approach affords better control of bleeding than the others do.

Blood volume loss may decrease cardiac output, arterial and venous blood pressure, and hemoglobin level, leading to decreased oxygen-carrying capacity. A blood volume loss of 20% or more can precipitate hypovolemic shock.

Expected removal times for urinary catheters are discussed later in this plan; abdominal drains are usually removed in 4 to 7 days, and occasionally in 10 days with a radical perineal prostatectomy.

2. An increased pulse rate; decrease in blood pressure of 20 mm Hg below normal or a blood pressure of 80 mm Hg or less; rapid and deep respirations; cold, clammy skin; pallor; and restlessness indicate shock.

3. A sudden decrease in hemoglobin level, hematocrit, and platelet count or an increase in PT or PTT may indicate the need for transfusion.

(continued)

---

*Although this and the following collaborative problems and nursing diagnoses apply to all types of prostatectomies, their relative importance varies with the specific surgical approach, as indicated in each problem.

Interventions *continued*

4. *Consult the surgeon about applying traction to the catheter or preparing the patient for surgery if bleeding persists.*

5. *Teach the patient to avoid straining for bowel elimination. Avoid using rectal thermometers or tubes or giving enemas.*

6. *Administer and document stool softeners and laxatives, as ordered.* Use alternatives such as increased fiber, fluids, and prune juice in the diet. Monitor the frequency and consistency of bowel movements.

7. *Teach the patient to avoid lifting heavy objects postoperatively* for 6 to 8 weeks, to allow time for internal and external wound healing.

8. Additional individualized interventions: _____
_____
_____

Outcome criteria
Within 24 hours postoperatively, the patient will:
• show normal vital signs
• have normal laboratory values.

Rationales *continued*

4. Applying traction pulls the balloon against the bladder neck. The resulting pressure tamponades bleeding vessels in the prostatic fossa. For prolonged or excessive bleeding, suturing or cauterizing may be necessary.

5. Straining to defecate or introducing objects into the rectum may precipitate bleeding, especially following the retropubic or perineal incision used for radical prostatectomy.

6. Preventing constipation is important to decrease the risk of bleeding or rectal tearing.

7. Undue strain on the abdominal and perineal muscles places stress on the bladder and prostate and may precipitate bleeding.

8. Rationale: _____
_____
_____

Within 3 days postoperatively, the patient will:
• have regular bowel elimination
• have no muscle straining.

Nursing diagnosis: *Potential postoperative infection related to preoperative status, urinary catheter, or drainage placement*

NURSING PRIORITY: Prevent or promptly detect infection.

Interventions

1. *Monitor and record vital signs* according to unit protocol, typically every 4 hours for 24 hours or until stable, then every 8 hours. Notify the doctor of significant changes from the patient's baseline values.

2. *Monitor the surgical incision site daily for induration, erythema, and purulent or odorous drainage.* Document all findings. Send drainage samples for culture and sensitivity testing, as ordered.

3. *Monitor drains and catheters for patency, and irrigate as ordered.*

4. *Provide and document meticulous urinary catheter care* at least once daily. Send urine samples for culture and sensitivity testing, as ordered.

Rationales

1. The risk of infection varies with the procedure used. It is a major problem with the suprapubic approach, which involves a bladder incision that allows urine to leak into surrounding tissues. Infection can develop with other approaches, but is particularly a problem with the presence of catheters or drains. Sudden fever, chills, hypotension, and tachycardia are signs of septic shock, a particular risk after prostatectomy.

2. The skin is the first line of defense against infection. Testing drainage samples will identify the causative microorganism.

3. Catheter obstruction commonly occurs from blood clots at the tip of the indwelling (Foley) catheter. This may cause urinary retention, stasis, and infection. Irrigation usually relieves obstruction.

4. Although questioned by some, most authors believe that cleansing with soap and water is essential to prevent microbial growth. Analysis of urinary samples will identify the causative microorganisms.

Interventions continued

5. *Administer I.V. fluids, as ordered.* Beginning on the first postoperative day, *encourage oral fluid intake of 2 to 3 liters daily* (unless contraindicated) to maintain urinary output of at least 1,500 ml daily. Record intake and output.

6. *Encourage ambulation* the day after surgery.

7. *Administer and document prophylactic antibiotics,* as ordered.

8. Additional individualized interventions: _____

_____

Rationales continued

5. Adequate hydration promotes renal blood flow and flushes out bacteria in the urinary tract. The I.V. line is usually removed on the first postoperative day if the patient is tolerating oral fluids.

6. Immobility contributes to urinary stasis and creates a reservoir for microorganisms.

7. Antibiotics combat and control microbial growth. They are ordered prophylactically because of the high risk of infection with prostatectomy.

8. Rationale: _____

_____

Outcome criteria

Within 24 hours postoperatively, the patient will:
• have no fever
• have no urinary clots
• ambulate.

Within 3 days postoperatively, the patient will:
• present an incision free from inflammation, induration, bleeding, or purulent drainage
• have no cloudiness in urine.

Nursing diagnosis: *Pain related to urethral stricture, catheter obstruction, bladder spasms, or surgical intervention*

NURSING PRIORITY: Relieve pain.

Interventions

1. See the "Pain" care plan, page 64.

2. *Observe for signs of bladder spasms,* such as sharp, intermittent pain, a sense of urgency, or urine around the catheter.

3. *Irrigate and check the urinary catheter and tubing for kinks, blood clots, and mucus plugs,* as needed.

4. Assess for incisional pain.

5. *For severe or persistent pain, medicate with analgesics or antispasmodics,* such as oxybutynin chloride (Ditropan). Medicate at the onset of pain. Monitor vital signs before and after administering medication, and evaluate pain relief after 30 minutes.

Rationales

1. Generalized interventions regarding pain management are included in the "Pain" care plan. Measures specific to prostatectomy patients are covered below.

2. Bladder spasms are caused by irritation of bladder stretch receptors from catheter placement or surgical manipulation.
     Pain from bladder spasms can be severe in TURP and suprapubic approaches, in which the bladder is entered surgically. Spasm-induced pain is minimal with the retropubic and perineal approaches, because they do not involve a bladder incision.

3. Urinary retention from catheter obstruction causes abdominal distention and pain, and may trigger bladder spasms. When the patient complains of suprapubic pain, this intervention often is all that is needed.

4. Incisional pain with the suprapubic and retropubic approaches usually is moderate; with the perineal approach, it usually is mild.

5. Medicating at the onset of pain prevents severe pain. Ditropan directly relaxes smooth muscle and inhibits acetylcholine's parasympathetic-stimulating action on smooth muscle.

(continued)

Interventions *continued*

6. *Provide alternative pain relief measures and teach them to the patient.* Encourage sitz baths and application of heat to the rectal area with a heat lamp after a perineal prostatectomy. Position the patient comfortably.

7. Additional individualized interventions: _____
_____
_____

Rationales *continued*

6. Alternative pain relief measures may enhance relief in conjunction with pharmacologic analgesia. Heat application reduces inflammation. Proper positioning may decrease discomfort from the urinary catheter.

7. Rationale: _____
_____
_____

Outcome criteria
Within 30 minutes postoperatively, the patient will:
• have vital signs within normal limits
• have no urinary obstruction.

Within 1 hour postoperatively, the patient will:
• have absence or relief of pain
• find a relaxed position in bed.

Nursing diagnosis: *Potential urinary retention related to urinary catheter obstruction*

NURSING PRIORITY: Prevent or minimize urinary retention.

Interventions

1. *Monitor and record continuous bladder irrigation,* as ordered. Adjust the rate of the irrigating solution, as ordered, to maintain pink-tinged urine.

2. *If the patient is not on continuous irrigation, irrigate the urinary catheter* with 30 to 60 ml of normal saline every 3 to 4 hours or as needed and as ordered, using gentle pressure. Use aseptic technique.

3. *Monitor and document intake and output.* Encourage fluid intake of 2 to 3 liters daily.

4. Weigh the patient daily. Compare with preoperative weight, and document.

5. Observe for suprapubic distention and discomfort every 4 hours while the patient is awake. If a suprapubic catheter is in place, monitor and record urinary outflow from it.

6. Additional individualized interventions: _____
_____
_____

Rationales

1. Continuous irrigation dilutes blood clots and decreases obstruction. Urine normally remains pink-tinged for 3 to 4 days.

2. Blood clots or mucus plugs may adhere to the tip of the catheter and cause obstruction. This occurs most commonly when continuous irrigation is not used.

3. Hydration increases urinary flow. Urinary output less than 60 ml/hour suggests obstruction or decreased renal perfusion.

4. Increasing weight suggests urinary retention.

5. Increased distention may signal urinary retention. A suprapubic catheter is commonly placed after suprapubic prostatectomy or injuries to the urethra caused by trauma or stricture.

6. Rationale: _____
_____
_____

Outcome criteria
Within 24 hours postoperatively, the patient will:
• have no urinary clots
• show approximately equal intake and output
• have no suprapubic distention.

Within 48 hours postoperatively, the patient will:
• have stable weight.

Nursing diagnosis: *Urge incontinence related to urinary catheter removal, trauma to the bladder neck, and/or decrease in detrusor muscle or sphincter tone, or both*

NURSING PRIORITY: Relieve or minimize incontinence.

Interventions

1. *Preoperatively, teach the patient to tighten buttock and perineal muscles* for 5 to 10 seconds, then relax them, repeating 10 to 20 times/hour. Instruct the patient to perform this exercise before and after surgery.

2. *Monitor and document the patient's urinary pattern after catheter removal.* Instruct the patient to void with each urge but no more frequently than every 2 hours during the first 24-hour postoperative period and no more than every 4 hours subsequently.

3. *If a suprapubic catheter is present after the urethral catheter is removed, measure residual volume after each voiding.* Alert the doctor if the postvoid residual volume exceeds 50 ml.

4. *Obtain one urine sample with each voiding during the first 24 hours after catheter removal, and note its color, amount, and specific gravity.*

5. *Provide absorbent incontinence pads. Keep the perineal area clean and dry.*

6. Additional individualized interventions: _____
_____
_____

Rationales

1. Urinary incontinence is a major problem with the perineal approach. Compared to the other approaches, it is more common and takes longer to resolve. Temporary incontinence after TURP results from trauma to the urinary sphincter. Temporary incontinence may result from the bladder neck incision with the suprapubic approach, although permanent urinary continence is unaltered.

   Strengthening the bladder sphincter promotes bladder control after urinary catheter removal. Normal urinary function usually returns in 2 to 3 weeks, although complete urinary control may take as long as 6 months to return with the perineal approach.

2. Catheter removal occurs 3 to 5 days after TURP and as long as 12 days after other prostatectomies. Voiding with each urge prevents urinary retention, and spacing voidings aids in bladder retraining.

3. When urethral and suprapubic catheters are present, the urethral catheter usually is removed on the first postoperative day to minimize the risk of stricture formation. The suprapubic catheter usually is clamped for 24 hours before removal on the 7th to the 10th postoperative day. If the residual volume exceeds 50 ml per voiding, the catheter may be left in until complete emptying is achieved urethrally.

4. Analysis of a urine specimen provides an indication of renal function. Hematuria should gradually decrease, and volume should increase. Specific gravity reflects urine concentration.

5. Keeping the perineal area clean and dry promotes comfort and reduces the risk of infection.

6. Rationale: _____
_____
_____

Outcome criteria

Within 24 hours postoperatively, the patient will:
• exercise perineal muscles
• void less frequently than every 2 hours

• have no postvoid residual volume
• present clean, dry perineal area.

Nursing diagnosis: *Potential altered sexuality patterns: decreased libido related to fear of incontinence and decreased self-esteem; infertility related to retrograde ejaculation (from TURP and suprapubic prostatectomy); or impotence related to parasympathetic nerve damage (from radical prostatectomy)*

NURSING PRIORITY: Prevent or minimize impact of altered sexuality patterns.

Interventions

1. *Teach the patient preoperatively, and reinforce postoperatively the expected effects of prostatectomy regarding impotence and ejaculation.* Include the patient's spouse or partner in the discussion.

2. *Encourage the patient and spouse or partner to verbalize feelings of loss, grief, anxiety, and fear.*

3. *Encourage discussion between the patient and spouse or partner with regard to feelings and expectations in the sexual relationship.*

4. *Provide information about a penile prosthesis,* if appropriate, which may be implanted after a radical prostatectomy wound heals.

5. *Provide information and initiate referral for sexual counseling,* as needed postoperatively.

6. Additional individualized interventions: _____
_____
_____

Rationales

1. Providing correct information may decrease threats to the patient's sexual self-esteem and body image by clarifying misconceptions. A patient having TURP or a suprapubic prostatectomy will have some degree of retrograde ejaculation secondary to opening of the bladder neck during surgery: seminal fluid flows into the bladder and is excreted in the urine. Retrograde ejaculation does not interfere with sexual activity but does cause infertility. This pattern should return to normal within a few months. Sexual function is unaffected by suprapubic prostatectomy; a patient with erectile capability can usually resume intercourse in 4 to 6 weeks. Impotence always results from a radical prostatectomy when perineal nerves are cut.

2. Loss of the prostate gland often causes feelings of loss and grief similar to those experienced by a woman after a hysterectomy. The patient with prostate cancer may also express feelings of fear of transmitting cancer to his sexual partner during intercourse. This, however, is a myth—sexual activity will not precipitate tumor growth.
   Some men feel that impotence and sterility make them less manly. Verbalizing these feelings decreases anxiety and may assist in identifying ways to deal with the changes.

3. Promoting open communication between sexual partners may prevent misunderstandings, enhance the relationship, and increase the patient's feelings of self-worth.

4. A penile prosthesis reinstitutes erectile capacity and may increase the patient's feelings of self-worth and sexual self-esteem. A prosthesis is used after radical prostatectomy, which causes impotence. It is recommended that the patient be totally healed (2 to 3 months after prostatectomy) before pursuing prosthetic surgery.

5. The patient may have preexisting sexual problems that are exacerbated by the prostatectomy and require a sexual counselor. Follow-up after discharge may be needed.

6. Rationale: _____
_____
_____

Outcome criteria

Within 24 hours before discharge, the patient will:
• identify impact of surgery or disease on sexuality
• express feelings about masculinity and changes in sexuality
• verbalize understanding of anticipated sexual capacity
• identify available community resources.

Nursing diagnosis: *Disturbed self-concept: self-esteem related to incontinence, potential impotence, or sexual alterations*

NURSING PRIORITY: Maximize feelings of self-esteem.

Interventions

1. *Encourage the patient to verbalize feelings about postoperative changes in body functioning and the meaning these changes will have for his life-style.*

2. *Assist the patient in identifying and using effective coping behaviors.* If problems arise, see the "Ineffective Individual Coping" care plan, page 51.

3. Encourage the patient to continue perineal and buttock exercises to decrease incontinence. Provide reassurance that this is temporary. Instruct the patient to use absorbent pads to prevent embarrassment.

4. Compliment the patient on his personal appearance. Instruct his spouse or partner and family to provide compliments and positive feedback to the patient.

5. Encourage the patient to participate in activities of daily living (ADLs) and in decisions affecting his care.

6. Additional individualized interventions: _____

Rationales

1. As with sexual alterations discussed in the previous problem, verbalizing feelings about other changes in body function is the first step in identifying healthy coping modes.

2. Promoting positive coping behavior increases adaptation to change and also increases self-esteem.

3. Incontinence may cause decreased social activities and self-neglect. See the "Urge incontinence" nursing diagnosis in this entry.

4. Knowledge that a person is perceived by others as attractive and sexually desirable fosters self-esteem. Positive feedback reinforces a positive self-image.

5. Participating in care activities fosters independence. Decision making increases self-control and self-confidence.

6. Rationale: _____

Outcome criteria

By the time of discharge, the patient will:
• identify changes in social relationships
• identify effective coping behaviors
• express satisfaction with personal appearance
• express positive feelings of self-worth
• participate in daily care.

Discharge planning
NURSING DISCHARGE CRITERIA

Upon discharge, documentation shows evidence of:
• absence of urinary obstruction
• absence of urinary retention
• urinary output of at least 800 ml for past 24 hours
• absence of gross hematuria or large clots
• absence of infection
• absence of pulmonary complications
• absence of cardiovascular complications (including thrombophlebitis)
• stable vital signs (temperature below 100° F. [37.8° C.] orally for past 24 hours without antipyretics, and blood pressure within preoperative limits)
• ability to control pain using oral medications
• ability to perform ADLs independently
• ability to perform catheter care
• ability to tolerate diet
• adequate home support or referral to home health agency or extended care facility.

PATIENT/FAMILY DISCHARGE TEACHING CHECKLIST

Document evidence that patient/family demonstrates understanding of:
___ surgical outcome and disease process
___ all discharge medications' purpose, dosage, administration schedule, and side effects requiring medical attention (usual discharge medications include analgesics, antispasmotics if a urinary catheter is present, and antibiotics)
___ urinary catheter care techniques and supplies
___ signs and symptoms indicating obstruction, bleeding, or infection
___ supplies to manage incontinence
___ exercises to regain urinary control
___ common postoperative feelings
___ the appropriate activity level to prevent muscle straining
___ resumption of sexual activity and community resources for sexual counseling
___ community or interagency referral
___ need for consultation with an oncology specialist (if the diagnosis of cancer is confirmed)
___ availability of cancer support groups
___ date, time, and location of follow-up appointments
___ how to contact doctor.

DOCUMENTATION CHECKLIST

Using outcome criteria as a guide, document:
___ clinical status on admission
___ significant changes in status postoperatively
___ pertinent laboratory and diagnostic test findings
___ episodes of hemorrhage
___ transfusion with blood products
___ infection and treatment
___ intake and output
___ urinary obstruction episodes
___ urinary retention
___ urinary incontinence
___ patient/family teaching
___ discharge planning
___ community or interagency referral.

ASSOCIATED CARE PLANS

Grief/Grieving
Ineffective Family Coping
Ineffective Individual Coping
Pain
Surgical Intervention
Thrombophlebitis

REFERENCES

Bachers, Eileen S. "Sexual Dysfunction After Treatment for Genitourinary Cancers," *Seminars in Oncology Nursing* 1(1):18-24, February 1985.

Casciato, Dennis, and Lowitz, Barry. *Manual of Bedside Oncology*. Boston: Little, Brown & Co., 1983.

Clark, Nancy, and O'Connell, Paulette. "Prostatectomy: A Guide to Answering Your Patient's Unspoken Questions," *Nursing* 14(4):48-51, April 1984.

Datta, Pradip K. "The Post-Prostatectomy Patient," *Nursing Times* 77(41):1759-61, October 7, 1981.

Hogan, Rosemarie. *Human Sexuality: A Nursing Prospective*, 2nd ed. East Norwalk, Conn.: Appleton & Lange, 1985.

Kneisl, Carol, and Ames, Sue Ann. *Adult Health Nursing: A Biopsychosocial Approach*. Reading, Mass.: Addison-Wesley Publishing Co., 1986.

Lawler, Patricia E. "Benign Prostatic Hyperplasia: Knowing Pathophysiology Aids Assessment," *AORN Journal* 40(5):745-50, November 1984.

Long, Pamela Peters. "Prostatic Cancer," *Nursing81* 11(12):22-23, December 1981.

McNally, Joan C., et al. *Guidelines for Cancer Nursing Practice*. New York: Grune & Stratton, 1985.

Paulson, David F. "Prostatic Malignancy," *Journal d' Urologie* 91(7):401-07, 1985.

Shaw, Linda M. "A Teaching Plan for TURP," *AORN Journal* 33(2):240-45, February 1981.

Radioactive Implant for Cervical Cancer

DRG information

DRG 357 [Surgical DRG] Uterine and Adnexa Procedures for Ovarian or Adnexa Malignancy.
Mean LOS = 11.3 days

DRG 363 [Surgical DRG] Dilation and Curettage
(D&C), Conization and Radio-Implant for
Malignancy.
Mean LOS = 3.5 days

Additional DRG information: Many patients now receive
radioactive implants on an outpatient basis, although in the
past such patients were routinely hospitalized. A patient
who receives an implant during admission for removal of the
malignant neoplasm is always hospitalized.

Introduction

DEFINITION AND TIME FOCUS

The primary treatment for cervical cancer, radiation
therapy, usually combines internal irradiation (given as
inpatient therapy) with external irradiation (generally
given as outpatient therapy). This clinical plan focuses
on inpatient management of the patient receiving a radioactive implant for cervical cancer. Cancers of the vagina and endometrium may also be treated in this
manner with a similar nursing care plan.

Insertion of the implant may take place before, during, or after external radiation therapy.

With the patient in the operating room (OR) and
anesthetized, an applicator is inserted into the vagina.
The stainless steel applicator consists of a central hollow tube, passed through the cervical os into the uterine cavity, and two hollow ovoids, placed in the vagina
next to the cervix. After correct placement is confirmed by X-ray, the patient is brought back to her room
and the physician threads the radioactive material (rad-
ium or cesium is most commonly used) into the central
cylinder and ovoids to radiate the cervix and the para-
cervical tissue, the usual area into which cervical cancer spreads.

The implant stays in place from 2 to 5 days. Computer calculations determine the radiation dose to the
tumor and the dose absorbed by normal tissues such as
the bladder and rectum. After the dose has been delivered, the doctor removes the radioactive material and
then the applicator. Occasionally an analgesic or sedative may be required before removal.

ETIOLOGY/PRECIPITATING FACTORS

Risk factors associated with the development of squamous cell carcinoma of the cervix include:
• early age of first intercourse
• multiple sexual partners
• multiparity
• history of herpes simplex virus II or human papilloma
virus infection (condyloma, genital warts)

• cigarette smoking
• history of an abnormal Papanicolaou (Pap) smear.
Most of these risk factors are related to early or repeated exposure of the cervix to an oncogenic virus
that is probably transmitted sexually.

Focused assessment guidelines

NURSING HISTORY (Functional health pattern findings)

Health perception–health management pattern
• *reports abnormal vaginal bleeding*, often occurring after
intercourse or douching
• may have history of an *abnormal Pap smear* that was
never adequately evaluated

Nutritional-metabolic pattern
• may report unexplained weight loss (not usually seen
with early cancers)

Elimination pattern
• may report feelings of pelvic pressure with resulting
constipation or frequent urination
• may report decreased urine output if the tumor has
caused ureteral obstruction
• may report incontinence of stool or urine if rectova-
ginal or vesicovaginal fistulae are present

Activity-exercise pattern
• *may report weakness* or fatigue, especially if anemic
from vaginal blood loss

Cognitive-perceptual pattern
• *may report pelvic pain or pressure*, sometimes experienced as low back pain
• may report leg or hip pain as the tumor encroaches on
nerve roots

Self-perception–self-concept pattern
• may report *anxiety or depression* over the diagnosis of
cancer and perceived threat of death

Role-relationship pattern
• may report *isolation* from family, friends, or co-workers

Sexuality-reproductive pattern
• may express fear of sexual intercourse because of bleeding
or concern about transmitting cancer to partner
• may express grieving related to loss of reproductive
function

Coping–stress tolerance pattern
• may express feeling powerless and less able to cope
with other stresses
• may express need for education and support from
community resources

Value-belief pattern
• may express guilt over delaying early detection behaviors (regular Pap smears) or evaluation of early symptoms

PHYSICAL FINDINGS
Reproductive
• *vaginal bleeding*
• *cervical tumor* that may:
  ☐ be exophytic (growing outward on the cervix) or endophytic (growing inside the endocervical canal, making the cervix "barrel-shaped")
  ☐ extend down the vagina
  ☐ extend to the pelvic side wall
  ☐ invade the bladder or rectum

Gastrointestinal
• constipation
• passage of stool through vagina (rare)

Urinary
• frequent urination
• decreased urine output or anuria (rare)
• passage of urine through vagina (rare)

DIAGNOSTIC STUDIES*
• blood urea nitrogen and creatinine levels—may be elevated, indicating ureteral obstruction and diminished renal function
• hemoglobin and hematocrit—may be lowered if vaginal bleeding has been heavy
• intravenous pyelogram—may show ureteral obstruction by pelvic tumor
• cystoscopy—may show bladder wall invasion by tumor
• barium enema or proctoscopy—may show extrinsic pressure by pelvic tumor or invasion into rectal wall
• lymphangiogram or computed tomography scan—may indicate spread of tumor outside the pelvis to para-aortic lymph nodes or other organs

POTENTIAL COMPLICATIONS
• deep-vein thrombosis or pulmonary embolus
• peritoneal perforation by the implant apparatus
• hemorrhage
• atelectasis or pneumonia

Nursing diagnosis: *Potential for injury related to dislodging of implant*

NURSING PRIORITY: Minimize risk of dislodging and resulting perforation and peritonitis.

Interventions

1. *Administer and document laxatives or enemas* the night before the implant insertion.

2. *Encourage a low-residue diet* with adequate fluid intake.

3. *Administer medications* as ordered to decrease peristalsis (for example, diphenoxylate hydrochloride [Lomotil], loperamide hydrochloride [Imodium], or codeine).

4. *Document the presence and position of the implant.* When the patient returns from the OR, place a small ink mark on her leg at the bottom of the applicator as a baseline indicator in case the applicator is dislodged. Also note the position of the handles on the applicator (vertical, horizontal, oblique) to assess for changes.

5. *Assess for signs and symptoms of perforation*, including vaginal bleeding, abdominal pain or distention, fever, nausea, and vomiting. Notify the doctor immediately.

Rationales

1. Evacuating the lower colon minimizes the likelihood of stool contamination of the field during the insertion procedure. Occurrence of a bowel movement or bedpan placement during the time the implant is in place may dislodge it or cause perforation by radioactive implant apparatus.

2. Low-residue foods minimize bulk formation in the colon. Adequate oral fluid intake lessens the need for I.V. hydration.

3. Medications that slow bowel function will induce constipation necessary for optimal placement and effectiveness of the implant.

4. Accurate ongoing assessment of the implant position detects dislodgment, which may lead to uterine perforation.

5. The uterine cavity may be perforated at the time of insertion or if there is considerable pelvic movement. Prompt medical intervention is required because perforation can lead to peritonitis.

---

*Initial laboratory data may reflect no significant abnormalities.

Interventions continued

6. *Document placement of an indwelling (Foley) catheter* (may be done in the OR at the time of implant insertion) and connection to bedside drainage; record output.

7. *Raise the head of the bed slightly* (usually no more than 45 degrees); place a trapeze bar over the bed. Limit side-to-side movement.

8. Encourage self-care for personal hygiene. Do not change bed linen unless necessary.

9. After removal of the implant, administer (and document use of) laxatives or enemas, begin regular diet, and discontinue constipating medications.

10. Additional individualized interventions: _____
_____
_____

Rationales continued

6. Continuous urinary drainage allows the patient to keep her hips positioned as recommended and avoids movement necessary for bedpan use. The catheter also helps decrease the potential for bladder injury during the procedure.

7. Because the implant apparatus may protrude slightly from the vagina, raising the patient's head more than 45 degrees may change the angle of her hips and could dislodge the implant. Changing the angle of her head will allow the patient to sleep, eat, or read more comfortably. A trapeze bar may allow the patient to move her upper body more easily. Side-to-side movement may dislodge the implant.

8. Self-care increases patient involvement and decreases the caregiver's radiation exposure. Changing linens may cause pelvic movement that could dislodge the implant.

9. Normal bowel function is restored after the implant is removed so that the patient can be discharged with normal functions intact.

10. Rationale: _____
_____
_____

Outcome criteria

While the implant is in place, the patient will:
• have no bowel movement
• show no signs or symptoms of perforation.

After the implant is removed, the patient will:
• have normal bowel movements.

Nursing diagnosis: *Impaired physical mobility related to imposed bed rest*

NURSING PRIORITY: Minimize risks of bed rest.

Interventions

1. *Attach a footboard to the foot of the bed; teach and encourage foot and leg exercises,* to be done every 2 hours to increase blood flow; and *apply antithromboembolic stockings.*

2. *Assess for signs and symptoms of thromboembolic phenomena,* including calf pain, redness, and warmth; positive Homans' sign; sudden onset of chest pain and dyspnea. See the "Thrombophlebitis" care plan, page 229, for details. Report abnormalities promptly.

3. *Administer anticoagulants* as prescribed by the doctor; monitor for excessive bleeding around the implant.

Rationales

1. Deep-vein thrombophlebitis or pulmonary embolus may occur in the patient on bed rest. Patients with gynecologic cancer face increased risk from the pressure of the pelvic tumor on large vessels. Measures to decrease venous pooling lessen this risk.

2. Signs and symptoms reflect inflammation of the vein wall and clot formation. The "Thrombophlebitis" care plan contains detailed information on thromboembolic phenomena.

3. Anticoagulants (heparin, warfarin) inhibit reactions that lead to blood clotting, thus decreasing the risk of a thromboembolic event but increasing the risk of hemorrhage.

(continued)

Interventions *continued*

4. *Teach and encourage the use of deep-breathing exercises,* to be done every 2 hours.

5. *Assess for signs and symptoms of lung infection* every shift, such as crackles, bronchial breath sounds, fever, productive cough, and pleuritic chest pain. Report abnormalities.

6. Additional individualized interventions: _____
_____
_____

Rationales *continued*

4. Bed rest contributes to poor lung expansion. Stasis of secretions leads to airway obstruction and atelectasis and provides a medium for bacterial growth. Deep-breathing exercises prevent pooling of secretions.

5. Systematic assessment improves likelihood of prompt detection and treatment of developing infection.

6. Rationale: _____
_____
_____

Outcome criteria

While the implant is in place, the patient will:
• exercise lower extremities every 2 hours
• perform deep-breathing exercises every 2 hours.

Throughout the period of hospitalization, the patient will:
• show no signs of pulmonary or vascular complications of bed rest.

Nursing diagnosis: *Social isolation related to the radioactivity of the implant*

NURSING PRIORITY: Minimize feelings of social isolation while radioactive implant is in place.

Interventions

1. *Explain to the patient and family the reasons for her isolation* from other patients and the nursing staff. Limit time spent with the patient and remind the family to remain behind the lead shields as much as possible. (Usually, the areas of lowest radiation levels are at the foot and the head of the bed, and the lead shields are placed at the patient's sides where the radiation dose is higher.) Limit the number of visitors, and do not allow children or pregnant women into the room.

2. *Organize patient care around multiple short interactions* instead of spending a lot of time in the room. Arrange the room so that items are within the patient's reach. Make frequent patient checks from the door.

3. Encourage diversional activities such as reading, handwork, talking on the phone, or watching television.

4. Additional individualized interventions: _____
_____
_____

Rationales

1. Time, distance, and lead shielding are the three components of safe care of a patient with a radioactive implant.

2. Time is one of the three components of radiation safety. Because of the limited number of visitors permitted, the patient will welcome frequent contact with the nurse.

3. Patients often experience social isolation simply from the diagnosis of cancer. Add to this their physical isolation because of the radioactive implant, and they may feel disoriented, with lowered self-esteem. Performing activities that are meaningful to them will help pass the time and lend some sense of normalcy to the situation. Support and encouragement from the nurse may boost the patient's spirits.

4. Rationale: _____
_____
_____

Outcome criteria

While the implant is in place, the patient will:
• encourage visitors' compliance with radiation safety principles

• verbalize understanding of why nursing time must be limited
• pass time with diversional activities.

Nursing diagnosis: *Altered sexuality patterns related to vaginal tissue changes or fear of radioactivity*

NURSING PRIORITY: Minimize the physical and psychosexual effects of a vaginal implant.

Interventions

1. *Allow the patient to explore her concerns and fears about the radioactive implant and resumption of sexual activity.* Reassure her that once the implant has been removed, the tissues do not retain any radioactivity and, therefore, cannot "pass" it to anyone else.

2. *Encourage intercourse* (if the patient has a partner) *or use of vaginal dilators* when the postimplant discomfort has abated (usually 2 to 4 weeks).

3. Discuss with the patient and spouse or partner (if present) fears and concerns related to pain and bleeding during intercourse. Encourage use of lubrication with intercourse.

4. Additional individualized interventions: _____
_____
_____

Rationales

1. Many patients (and their partners) will be concerned with the potential for "passing" radioactivity from one person to another during intercourse.

2. Radiation can cause scarring, narrowing, or fibrosis of the vaginal tissues. Regular dilatation of the vagina through intercourse, or the use of dilators, will help minimize these effects. Vaginal flexibility facilitates vaginal examination and the taking of Pap smears to monitor the disease.

3. Atrophy and resulting dryness of the vaginal tissues can occur after insertion of a radioactive implant. Tissues may be thin and easily traumatized, leading to pain or bleeding. Lubrication with water-soluble jellies may make the patient and partner more comfortable. Do not recommend petrolatum products; they are too thick and may cause greater irritation.

4. Rationale: _____
_____
_____

Outcome criteria

By the time of discharge, the patient will:
• verbalize understanding concerning potential problems after radioactive implant

• verbalize purpose and methods concerning maintenance of vaginal patency.

Discharge planning

NURSING DISCHARGE CRITERIA

Upon discharge, documentation shows evidence of:
• ability to perform activities of daily living (ADLs) independently
• ability to ambulate same as before surgery
• absence of dysuria
• stable vital signs
• absence of pulmonary or cardiovascular complications
• ability to have a bowel movement
• absence of infection
• ability to control pain with oral medications
• no need for I.V. support (preferably discontinued for at least 24 hours)
• hemoglobin level within expected parameters
• minimal vaginal discharge and absence of gross bleeding
• knowledge of how to contact a cancer support group
• adequate home support, or referral to home care if indicated by the inadequacy of home support system or inability to perform ADLs.

PATIENT/FAMILY DISCHARGE TEACHING CHECKLIST

Document evidence that the patient/family demonstrates understanding of:
___ type of cancer and implications
___ type of treatment administered
___ all discharge medications' purpose, dosage, administration schedule, and side effects requiring medical attention. Generally, no routine medications are used, but the patient may be on pain medication, antibiotics, or bowel medications (for constipation or diarrhea), depending on special problems
___ need to call the doctor if abdominal pain or fever above 100° F. (37.8° C.) develops
___ the possibility she may feel weak or fatigued for 7 to 10 days after discharge
___ likelihood of vulvovaginal discomfort for a few days
___ the fact that she may have some discharge (possibly bloody), for up to 2 weeks. Tell her to call the doctor if bleeding becomes heavy (requiring one or more

pads every hour). Tampons are usually discouraged due to the increased risk of toxic shock syndrome.
___ permission to resume intercourse after tenderness and discharge decrease
___ community resources for cancer education and support
___ date, time, and location of follow-up appointments
___ how to contact doctor.

DOCUMENTATION CHECKLIST
Using outcome criteria as a guide, document:
___ clinical status on admission
___ significant changes in clinical status
___ pertinent laboratory and diagnostic test findings
___ preimplant patient teaching
___ results of preimplant laxatives or enemas
___ antiembolic hose applied; lower extremity exercises taught
___ Foley catheter functional
___ head of bed elevated no more than 45 degrees
___ correct placement of radioactive implant
___ nutritional intake
___ pulmonary toilet
___ results of postimplant laxatives or enemas
___ patient/family teaching
___ discharge planning.

ASSOCIATED CARE PLANS
Grief/Grieving
Ineffective Family Coping
Ineffective Individual Coping
Knowledge Deficit
Pain

REFERENCES
Burns, Nancy. *Nursing and Cancer*. Philadelphia: W.B. Saunders Co., 1982.
Edlund, Barbara, J. "The Needs of Women with Gynecologic Malignancies," *The Nursing Clinics of North America* 17:1, 1982.
Leahy, Irene M., et al. *The Nurse and Radiotherapy: A Manual for Daily Care*. St Louis: C.V. Mosby Co., 1979.
NAACOG. "Irradiation Therapy for Gynecology Patients," *The Organization for Obstetric, Gynecologic and Neonatal Nurses Technical Bulletin* 8, September 1980.
Wood, Hilary A. "Radiation Therapy Impants," in *Handbook of Oncology Nursing*. Johnson, Bonny L., ed. New York: John Wiley & Sons, 1985.

Acquired Immune Deficiency Syndrome

DRG information

DRG 398 Reticuloendothelial and Immunity Disorders.
With Complication or Comorbidity (CC).
Mean LOS = 6.3 days
Principal diagnoses include:
• acquired immune deficiency syndrome
with other conditions
• related complex with other conditions.

DRG 399 Reticuloendothelial and Immunity Disorders.
Without CC.
Mean LOS = 3.9 days

Additional DRG information: The data on AIDS are based on statistics from 1986. Because of ongoing research, the reader is urged to consult the latest AIDS information from the Centers for Disease Control (CDC) and other reputable sources besides this care plan.

Introduction

DEFINITION AND TIME FOCUS

Acquired immune deficiency syndrome (AIDS) is a disorder of cell-mediated and humoral immunity caused by a virus known as the human immunodeficiency virus (HIV), previously referred to as the human T-lymphotropic virus type III (HTLV-III) or the lymphadenopathy-associated virus (LAV). The virus causes destructive changes in the immune system, specifically believed to affect the T_4 (helper or inducer) lymphocytes by altering their genetic makeup so that they reproduce the HIV virus instead of themselves. This alteration contributes to further disruption of the immune system, as B-cell and monocyte function are affected by T_4 activity. The infected person is thus rendered immunodeficient and susceptible to characteristic opportunistic infections, cancers, and other complications. Diagnosis is based on clinical finding of an opportunistic infection or cancer associated with AIDS, wasting syndrome, or AIDS-related dementia, along with laboratory evidence of HIV infection or immunodeficiency not attributable to another cause (such as steroid use or another disease process).

Two disorders commonly linked with AIDS are *Pneumocystis carinii* pneumonia (PCP) and Kaposi's sarcoma (KS). PCP, the most common opportunistic infection present in patients with AIDS at diagnosis, is a protozoal type of pneumonia usually observed only in immunocompromised persons. KS is a malignant neoplasm that begins as reddish or purplish skin lesions in variable distribution and may gradually spread, involving internal organs, mucous membranes, and lymph nodes.

A wide variety of other conditions may present in association with AIDS, including infections related to cytomegalovirus (CMV), *Mycobacterium avium, M. intracellulare, Cryptococcus, Candida,* herpesvirus, and *Salmonella.*

Although a diagnosis of AIDS is commonly viewed as a "death sentence," the prognosis for AIDS patients presenting with one of these conditions is actually quite variable. It depends on the patient's overall status, the availability of effective treatment for the specific organism, the patient's response to treatment, the presence or absence of other conditions, and the promptness with which treatment is started. Early detection appears to facilitate more favorable outcomes (in first episodes of PCP, for example). This care plan focuses on the patient admitted to a medical-surgical unit for diagnosis and treatment of one or more of the conditions associated with AIDS.

ETIOLOGY/PRECIPITATING FACTORS

Identified *risk factors*
• multiple sexual partners, anal intercourse, and other situations that may increase the risk of sexual transmission of the virus
• I.V. drug abuse, multiple blood transfusions, and other conditions that may allow exposure to blood infected with the virus

High-risk groups include male homosexuals or bisexuals, I.V. drug abusers, hemophiliacs, and sexual partners of persons at high risk.

Focused assessment guidelines

NURSING HISTORY (Functional health pattern findings)

Health perception–health management pattern
• *may report weeks to months of fatigue, malaise, low-grade fever, drenching night sweats,* anorexia, sore throat, *upper respiratory disorder that lingers,* cough, or shortness of breath
• may have a history of recurrent infections, amebiasis, or herpes simplex infections
• *may have known exposure to AIDS*
• *may identify self as belonging to one of the high-risk groups*—such as male homosexual or bisexual, I.V. drug abuser, or hemophiliac
• may have a history of multiple blood transfusions
• may be the sexual partner of someone in a high-risk group

Nutritional-metabolic pattern
• *may report anorexia or dysphagia*
• *may report weight loss* > 10 lb in 1 month
• may report episodes of oral *Candida albicans* (thrush) infection

Elimination pattern
• *may report persistent diarrhea* despite treatment of infections
• may report incontinence (related to myelopathy)

Activity-exercise pattern
• *may report progressive shortness of breath*
• *may report dry cough*
• *may report general malaise* and lack of energy
• may report leg weakness (related to myelopathy)

Sleep-rest pattern
• *may report drenching night sweats*

Cognitive-perceptual pattern
• may report headache
• may report or exhibit forgetfulness, depression, mental dullness, difficulty concentrating, or other changes in mental status

Self-perception–self-concept pattern
• may describe self as previously healthy, active, and "successful"
• may report increasing general clumsiness

Role-relationship pattern
• may report close friends or sexual partners who have died from AIDS

Sexuality-reproductive pattern
• may report active sexual activity with multiple partners
• may report previous infection with sexually transmitted diseases

Coping–stress tolerance pattern
• typically a young to middle-age, previously healthy person; patient may report little experience coping with illness and death
• may report *extreme anxiety* regarding fear of diagnosis and its repercussions in personal and social relationships
• may exhibit denial ("not me" syndrome) as a necessary coping behavior initially

Value-belief pattern
• may have delayed seeking medical attention because of fear, lack of information, or lack of sense of self-worth

PHYSICAL FINDINGS
Pulmonary
• *shortness of breath*
• dry cough
• crackles

Gastrointestinal
• *diarrhea*
• hepatomegaly
• splenomegaly
• diffuse abdominal tenderness
• thrush
• mucosal lesions
• hairy leukoplakia on tongue

Neurologic
• *anxiety*

• decreased intellectual acuity (as shown by slowed speech or impaired memory)
• tendency not to initiate conversation
• impaired sense of position or vibration
• weakness
• paresthesias or paralysis
• hyperreflexia
• retinal abnormalities
• diffuse retinal hemorrhage or exudates
• positive Babinski's sign

Integumentary
• *drenching night sweats*
• red or purple lesions (in KS) varying in size from a few millimeters to a few centimeters across; may be macules or papules, usually appearing first on head and neck or mucous membranes
• dermatitis
• *lymphadenopathy*
• herpes zoster or simplex
• anal warts
• diffuse dry skin
• butterfly rash on nose or cheeks
• tinea
• edema (with advanced KS)
• hypersensitivity to light touch

Musculoskeletal
• *weakness*
• pain
• stiff neck

DIAGNOSTIC STUDIES
• *enzyme-linked immunosorbent assay (ELISA)—identifies antibody to HIV.* In the asymptomatic person, the ELISA is not diagnostic for AIDS: An individual may have a positive ELISA without subsequently developing signs or symptoms of the disease. In addition, the ELISA may be negative if performed too soon after exposure to the virus, falsely negative, or falsely positive if the person has had recent influenza or another viral illness. *A positive ELISA in a patient who exhibits one of the conditions specifically linked with AIDS (PCP, KS, emaciation, or dementia) can be considered diagnostic.*
• *Western blot—uses electrophoretically marked proteins to distinguish and differentiate antibodies; used with ELISA to confirm diagnosis.*
   The following laboratory findings represent characteristic values in patients with AIDS but are not specific or diagnostic AIDS indicators:
• *complete blood count (CBC)—reveals leukocytopenia and anemia*
• *total T-cell count—reduced;* T_4 cell count often <400/mm³
• T_4 *positive (helper or inducer) T-cell to* T_8 *positive (cytotoxic or suppressor) T-cell (*T_4 *to* T_8*) ratio—low;* decrease depends on patient status, usually <1.0
• *immunoglobulin levels—usually elevated,* especially IgG and IgA

- *platelet count—shows thrombocytopenia*
- sedimentation rate—elevated
- skin test antigen studies—anergy
- aspartate aminotransferase [or SGOT] level—may be elevated (associated with hepatitis)
- lactic dehydrogenase level—may be elevated in PCP
- serum cholesterol level—may be low
- serum iron level—may be low
- hepatitis screen—may demonstrate carrier state or active disease (positive hepatitis-B surface antigen in serum)
- stool examination for ova and parasites—may reveal parasites or infections (such as cryptosporidiosis or salmonellosis)
- serum albumin and protein levels—may be low in emaciation
- blood urea nitrogen (BUN) level—may be elevated in emaciation.

The following diagnostic procedures may be ordered for patients with AIDS:

- *bronchoscopy—to diagnose PCP or other disorders,* by transbronchial lung biopsy (to examine tissue) or by use of bronchoalveolar lavage to obtain a specimen containing PCP cysts
- *chest X-ray—may reveal diffuse interstitial infiltrates (associated with PCP);* however, may be nondiagnostic even in active PCP
- open-lung biopsy—may provide definitive diagnosis of KS-related pulmonary symptoms or evidence of CMV infection
- culture of lesions—may demonstrate *Candida* or other organisms
- biopsy of lesions—may demonstrate KS, toxoplasmosis, or other complications
- *gallium scan—may show radio-labeled gallium accumula-*

tion in white blood cells of infected areas; used to help establish early diagnosis of PCP, although test is non-specific
- blood cultures—may identify pathogen if bacteremia is present
- lumbar puncture—results vary; may reveal cryptococcal meningitis; culture of spinal fluid may reveal HIV; results may be inconclusive for CMV infection
- sputum test for acid-fast bacillus—may indicate *Mycobacterium*
- computed tomography scan or magnetic resonance imaging (MRI)—may identify areas of lesions for later biopsy; MRI may be only means of detecting progressive multifocal leukoencephalopathy
- bone marrow aspiration—may reveal hypoplasia

POTENTIAL COMPLICATIONS
- Burkitt's lymphoma
- primary lymphoma
- toxoplasmosis
- multifocal leukoencephalopathy
- cryptococcal meningitis
- *Candida* esophagitis
- herpes simplex
- cryptosporidiosis
- CMV infection
- diffuse organ infection
- disseminated bacterial infection
- hemorrhage
- encephalopathy
- tuberculosis
- *Mycobacterium avium or M. intracellulare*
- dementia

Collaborative problem: *Immunosuppression related to low number of T_4 lymphocytes and/or low T_4 to T_8 ratio*

NURSING PRIORITIES: (a) Prevent or promptly treat new infections, and (b) minimize effects of associated hyperthermia.

Interventions

1. *Wash your hands upon entering and leaving the patient's room. Screen visitors and care providers for signs and symptoms of infection.* Institute other protective measures according to the patient's status and unit protocol, such as providing only cooked foods (no raw fruit or vegetables), avoiding standing water in the room (such as in flower vases), and preventing the patient from handling live flowers or plants.

2. *Monitor vital signs,* including temperature, at least every 4 hours. Report any new fever onset or temperature spikes immediately.

Rationales

1. Handwashing helps prevent transmission of infective organisms to the patient and also protects persons coming in contact with the patient. Gloves are recommended only if coming in direct contact with blood or body fluids (such as sputum, urine, feces, or wound drainage). Screening persons reduces the risk of infection transmission to the already-compromised patient. Raw fruit and vegetables are a source of gram-negative bacilli; live plants and soil may be sources of fungi. Standing water may provide a medium for the growth of microorganisms, particularly *Pseudomonas.*

2. Fever indicates that the body is responding to new infection as pyrogens are released from invading microorganisms. To compensate for increased metabolism,

(continued)

Interventions *continued*

3. *Monitor the CBC daily, and report increasing leukopenia or neutropenia.*

4. *Assess for signs and symptoms of neurologic infection,* including increased confusion, headache, stiff neck, visual or motor abnormalities, short-term memory loss, and flat affect. Compare new findings with baseline neurologic-mental status findings; report new or changed abnormalities to the doctor immediately. Consult with the doctor regarding possible lumbar puncture or MRI.

5. *Monitor potential infection sites daily.* Check I.V. and injection sites, mucous membranes, the rectum, the vagina, and any breaks in the skin for changes in color, texture, or sensation and for development of swelling, pain, purulent drainage, or other abnormalities. *Teach the patient to observe for new findings and to report them promptly.*

6. *Assess lung sounds* at least every 8 hours. Report crackles, decreased breath sounds, or other (new) abnormalities promptly.

7. *Obtain cultures, as ordered* (for example, blood, stool, urine, sputum, or wound drainage). Check sensitivity results and notify the doctor about the results.

8. *Administer antibiotics, as ordered.* The following medications are commonly used in protocols for AIDS-related infections, but others may be used, depending on the infective organism:

Rationales *continued*

the patient's heart rate and respiratory rate increase in an attempt to restore homeostasis. If hyperthermia persists and significant septicemia occurs, these compensatory mechanisms may begin to fail, and septic shock may rapidly result.

3. These changes indicate further reduction in the body's ability to resist or fight infection.

4. Neurologic abnormalities are common in patients with AIDS. These may be related to the HIV infection itself or to a secondary infection. For this reason, a thorough baseline assessment is essential. Encephalitis, the most common neurologic complication, may be caused by various microorganisms, including CMV and *Toxoplasma gondii.* Progressive multifocal leukoencephalopathy, another common finding, is usually detectable only by MRI scanning. HIV infection involving the white matter of the brain may cause dementia, seizures, or paralysis. Early detection and timely treatment of neurologic symptoms may result in improvement; once such involvement is advanced, however, the prognosis is poor. Examination of spinal fluid may or may not prove diagnostic.

5. The skin forms an important protective barrier; any break in it provides a potential port of entry for infectious microorganisms. Classic signs and symptoms of infection may be masked or delayed in the immunocompromised patient, so careful observation for subtle changes is essential. Oral candidal infections (such as thrush) are very common in patients with AIDS: They appear as white patches in the mouth. Dysphagia may indicate esophagitis. Any area of possible infection must be investigated promptly, because infections that are relatively benign in normal persons may be life-threatening in the patient with AIDS.

6. Respiratory infections are common in patients with AIDS. The most devastating of these is PCP, but other infectious processes—including tuberculosis—may occur. Early detection of pulmonary complications allows prompt initiation of appropriate therapy, although current pharmacologic treatment measures for PCP have limited effectiveness and may cause severe side effects.

7. Cultures may identify causative organisms if new infections are suspected. Sensitivity results guide antibiotic therapy.

8. Depending on the opportunistic organism, antibiotic therapy may be instituted on an inpatient or outpatient basis; antibiotics may also be prescribed prophylactically for patients with AIDS. Effectiveness is variable, especially in second episodes of PCP, which are associated with a mortality as high as 75%. Mortality may be higher if CMV or KS is also involved.

Interventions *continued*

• trimethoprim-sulfamethoxazole (Bactrim, Septra)—observe for and report side effects, such as rash, leukopenia, sore throat, purpura, jaundice, or signs of renal failure. Discontinue use if a rash occurs. Advise the patient to avoid using antacids while taking this medication.

• pentamidine isethionate (Pentam)—observe for and report any side effects, such as leukopenia, hypotension, hypoglycemia, or formation of sterile abscesses at injection sites. (Hypotension may be reduced if the medication is given slowly I.V. over 45 to 90 minutes.)

• sulfadoxine and pyrimethamine (Fansidar), pyrimethamine (Daraprim)—observe for and report leukopenia, rash, purpura, or pruritus. Administer folic acid supplements, as ordered, and observe for glossitis, an indicator of folic acid deficiency.

9. *If zidovudine (Retrovir) therapy is ordered, provide appropriate patient teaching as follows* (consult current guidelines, because recommendations may change with further studies):

• Do not use acetaminophen (Tylenol), aspirin, indomethacin (Indocin), probenecid (Benemid), cimetidine (Tagamet), lorazepam (Ativan), or ranitidine (Zantac) while taking zidovudine. Consult the doctor before taking any other medications, including over-the-counter medications, while taking zidovudine.

• Obtain laboratory tests, as ordered (usually T-cell count, liver and renal function tests, and CBC initially and at least every 2 weeks for several months). Transfusions may be required if toxicity develops.

• Observe for and report any side effects, such as headache, abdominal discomfort, anxiety, rash, or itching.

10. If fever is present, administer acetaminophen, as ordered. Consult with the doctor regarding alternating doses of acetaminophen with aspirin or ibuprofen for persistent fever. Check platelet count and bleeding time before giving aspirin or ibuprofen, and withhold medication if clotting is prolonged. Avoid use of these medications if the patient is taking zidovudine.

Rationales *continued*

• Trimethoprim-sulfamethoxazole is the antibiotic of choice to treat PCP and may also be used in infections related to *Shigella, Proteus, Klebsiella,* and *Enterobacter,* among others. Skin rash may be an early sign of a severe, even life-threatening reaction.

• Pentamidine is used to treat PCP and is administered I.M., I.V., or by aerosol.

• Sulfadoxine and pyrimethamine are indicated for infections related to toxoplasmosis. Because pyrimethamine is a folic acid inhibitor, folic acid supplementation is recommended. Rash may be an early sign of severe reaction.

9. Zidovudine is an antiviral agent that has shown promising results against the HIV virus in early studies. It is made from thymidine, a component of deoxyribonucleic acid, and appears to block reproduction of the HIV virus, probably by interfering with reverse transcriptase. Early studies also revealed increases in T_4 cell counts, restored sensitivity to skin test antigens, reduction in fever, and improvement in neurologic status. Zidovudine may inhibit HIV reproduction and cause improvement in overall status; it does *not* kill the virus, cure AIDS, or prevent transmission.

• These medications may impair metabolism of zidovudine and result in toxicity.

• To qualify for the use of zidovudine, patients must exhibit PCP or T-cell count < 200/mm³. Because the use of zidovudine may result in severe neutropenia, anemia, and/or other blood dyscrasias, periodic monitoring is essential. Neutrophil counts of 1,000 mm³ or less may indicate the need for dosage reduction or for temporary discontinuation of therapy.

• Because no long-term studies have been completed, the side effects listed are based on results from a small, controlled trial group. Any new symptom, or worsening of an existing symptom, should be promptly investigated to determine the cause.

10. Acetaminophen, aspirin, and ibuprofen inhibit the effects of pyrogens on the thermoregulatory center, thereby reducing fever. Aspirin and ibuprofen may decrease platelet adhesion, thus prolonging clotting time. Aspirin and acetaminophen may impair zidovudine metabolism, resulting in toxicity.

(continued)

Interventions *continued*

11. If fever persists, monitor for signs of dehydration, such as dry mucous membranes, decreased skin turgor, increased hematocrit, and increased urine specific gravity. Report findings and institute appropriate fluid replacement therapy, as ordered. See the "Fluid and Electrolyte Imbalances" care plan, page 21, for details.

12. Consider using a hypothermia blanket to treat persistent hyperthermia, as ordered, if other cooling measures (such as tepid sponges or antipyretic medication) are ineffective.

13. Additional individualized interventions: _____
_____

Rationales *continued*

11. Prolonged fever causes dehydration from an increased metabolic rate and diaphoresis.

12. A cooling blanket assists in reducing temperature if hyperthermia produces deleterious effects.

13. Rationale: _____
_____
_____

Outcome criteria
Throughout the period of hospitalization, the patient will:
• have new infections detected and treated promptly

• have fever controlled by medication
• show no signs of dehydration.

Nursing diagnosis: *Potential ineffective coping related to diagnosis of life-threatening illness, potential loss of ability to maintain usual roles, decisions regarding treatment options, and/or poor prognosis for long-term survival*

NURSING PRIORITY: Promote healthful coping behaviors.

Interventions

1. *Assess for excessive anxiety.* Note signs and symptoms such as poor eye contact, agitation, or restlessness.

2. *Introduce yourself and other staff members. Attempt to provide continuity of caregivers,* minimizing use of "new" staff whenever possible. Demonstrate acceptance: Use touch, make eye contact, and use active listening skills.

3. *Implement measures to promote physical relaxation,* as indicated, including progressive relaxation or controlled breathing techniques, therapeutic use of heat, massage, environmental modifications (reduction of noise, heat, light, and other stimuli), physical therapy, and familiar articles brought from home.

4. *Encourage verbalization of feelings. Anticipate fear, guilt, and anger, and accept such expressions as normal responses.* If uncomfortable discussing explicit issues, arrange for another professional to care for the patient. Whenever possible, make an initial referral at the time of diagnosis to a mental health professional who can follow the patient on an ongoing basis.

Rationales

1. Prolonged or excessive anxiety may have negative psychological and physiologic effects. Anxiety interferes with the ability to learn, make decisions, and mobilize resources. Anxiety also contributes to increased sympathetic nervous system activity, increasing metabolic and cardiac demands and placing further stress on the body.

2. Development of trust is facilitated by consistency in staffing. The need to readjust routines for "new" staff increases anxiety. Demonstrating acceptance promotes establishment of a therapeutic relationship. Patients with AIDS often verbalize "feeling like lepers"; use of touch reduces this sense of isolation.

3. The patient may be unaware of physical tension and its contribution to anxiety level. Physical relaxation promotes restoration of psychological equilibrium.

4. The diagnosis of AIDS carries an enormous psychosocial impact that may be initially overwhelming. The patient is often unable to make use of usual defenses and resources; for example, denial may be made impossible by media coverage, and friends or family may abandon the patient once the diagnosis is confirmed. If the disease was contracted through sexual contact, the

Interventions *continued*

Rationales *continued*

patient may experience guilt over unresolved issues, anxiety or anger in relation to previous partners, or ambivalence about past or future desires or behaviors. The diagnosis necessitates an immediate rethinking of relationships and often involves a loss of intimacy at a time when the patient most needs support. Multiple referrals may lead to fragmentation of care; consistency in follow-up promotes optimal utilization of resources.

5. *Identify and discuss any unhealthy coping behaviors observed.* Teach the patient about the effects of alcohol or drug abuse on immune function.

5. Patients may use alcohol or illegal drugs in attempts to avoid the painful realities of their condition. If the disease was contracted through I.V. drug use, the underlying dependency must be addressed in planning care. Alcohol and drug abuse have been linked to compromised immune activity.

6. Help the patient identify and list specific fears and concerns contributing to anxiety. Focus on modifiable factors.

6. Characteristically, anxiety is increased when fears seem overwhelming and all-encompassing. Identifying specific concerns helps quantify feelings and allows the patient to begin planning a coping strategy. Focusing on modifiable factors may increase the patient's sense of control.

7. *Help the patient identify and activate resources,* considering inner strengths, coping ability, and such external supports as friends, family, and a spiritual advisor. See the "Ineffective Individual Coping" care plan, page 51.

7. Anxiety may initially be so overwhelming that the patient is unable to mobilize the usual coping methods. The "Ineffective Individual Coping" care plan provides specific interventions helpful for the patient experiencing anxiety.

8. Acknowledge the "unknowns" of AIDS. Provide honest and accurate responses to questions. Validate the normality of the patient's responses to losses. See the "Death and Dying" and "Grief/Grieving" care plans, pages 10 and 41, respectively.

8. Acknowledging "unknowns" provides reassurance that the caregiver understands and is sensitive to the profound changes AIDS implies for the patient. Reminding the patient that a variety of emotional reactions is a normal and healthy response to a realistic threat may reduce anxiety and facilitate initiation of healthy coping. The "Grief/Grieving" and "Death and Dying" care plans provide further interventions related to psychosocial adjustment to illness and the losses illness entails.

9. Additional individualized interventions: _____

9. Rationale: _____

Outcome criteria
Within 1 day of admission, the patient will:
• show reduced signs of anxiety.

Within 3 days of admission, the patient will:
• identify specific personal stressors
• identify resources and begin mobilizing them.

Collaborative problem: *Potential hypoxemia related to ventilation/perfusion imbalance, pneumonia, and weakness*

NURSING PRIORITY: Optimize oxygenation.

Interventions

1. *Assess continuously for signs of hypoxemia,* such as tachycardia, restlessness, anxiety, tachypnea, irritability, and pallor or cyanosis. Monitor arterial blood gas

Rationales

1. PCP causes hard cysts to form in the interstitial spaces of the lungs, displacing surfactant and decreasing diffusion across the alveolar-capillary membrane.

(continued)

Interventions *continued*

(ABG) measurements as ordered and as needed for increasing dyspnea or inadequate respiratory effort. Report abnormal findings immediately, and prepare the patient for possible ventilatory support, as indicated by condition.

2. Administer oxygen therapy, as ordered.

3. *Perform airway clearance measures,* as needed:
• If the patient is cooperative, teach coughing and deep-breathing exercises, and encourage hourly use of the incentive spirometer, as ordered.
• If the patient is uncooperative, perform artificial sighing and coughing with the Ambu bag hourly. Suction as needed if the patient is unable to cough effectively, as indicated by noisy respirations or rhonchi auscultated over the large airways. Use supplemental oxygen before, during, and after airway clearance procedures.

4. Observe for postbronchoscopy complications; report any bleeding, anxiety, or unusual findings.

5. Evaluate and document at least every 8 hours and as needed the presence or absence of an effective cough, sputum character and color, respiratory effort, skin color, breath sounds, and activity tolerance. Be alert for changes in level of consciousness, and report promptly any that occur.

6. If narcotic analgesics are used to control pain, be alert for signs of respiratory depression after analgesic administration. Report an excessively slowed respiratory rate, frequent sighing, decreased alertness, or any other indications of inadequate respiratory effort.

7. Assist with self-care activities as needed (see the "Activity intolerance" nursing diagnosis in this care plan). Teach energy conservation measures, such as using a shower chair, organizing activities and grouping procedures, using large muscles, avoiding activities involving raising the arms over the head, and scheduling frequent rest periods between activities.

8. Additional individualized interventions: _____
_____
_____

Rationales *continued*

As arterial PO_2 levels decrease, the sympathetic nervous system responds (in an attempt to compensate) by increasing the heart rate. Progressive deterioration in ventilatory status may lead to respiratory failure—a frequent cause of death in AIDS-related illness; ventilatory support may be required to maintain oxygenation. However, it has been noted that arterial PO_2 levels in AIDS patients with PCP tend to be less decreased than in non-AIDS PCP patients and are sometimes even within normal range.

2. Supplemental oxygen elevates arterial oxygen content and decreases hypoxia.

3. The patient may be unable to clear the airway effectively because of general debilitation and weakness. Deep-breathing helps to expand the lungs fully and prevents areas of atelectasis associated with pneumonia and bed rest. Incentive spirometry and coughing also promote lung expansion; however, caution must be used with PCP patients, because coughing and positive-pressure breathing may cause alveolar rupture secondary to decreased surfactant. All airway clearance procedures may cause reduced PO_2 levels. Supplemental oxygen may be provided with nasal prongs during suctioning.

4. Irritation from the bronchoscope may cause bleeding, further decreasing oxygenation and threatening airway patency.

5. Careful serial observation of respiratory status is essential to detect subtle changes that may indicate the need to reevaluate therapy. Patients with PCP may require multiple antibiotics if other infections occur simultaneously. Changes in level of consciousness may signal impending respiratory failure.

6. Narcotics cause central nervous system depression and may impair function of the respiratory center.

7. Because energy required for activity increases oxygen demand, hypoxemia may worsen with exertion. Sitting requires less energy than standing. Organizing and grouping procedures reduce unnecessary exertion. Raising the arms over the head rapidly causes fatigue; large-muscle groups are more efficient.

8. Rationale: _____
_____
_____

Outcome criteria
Within 2 days of admission, the patient will:
• exhibit decreased dyspnea
• exhibit ABG measurements improved from baseline

• cough and deep-breathe effectively
• initiate a plan for energy conservation.

Nursing diagnosis: *Sensory-perceptual alteration related to disease-related neurologic involvement*

NURSING PRIORITY: Minimize effects of neurologic changes.

Interventions

1. *Assess the patient's mental and neurologic status* on admission and daily, including level of consciousness; orientation; memory; ability to follow directions, speak, and abstract; judgment; strength and sensation of extremities; and pupillary responses.

2. Consider the effects of emotional depression, grieving, and adverse reactions from medications when evaluating the patient's mental and neurologic status.

3. Assess for vision changes with the eye chart. Institute precautions to prevent injury if significant visual deficit is present, placing items within easy reach, ensuring that side rails are up, and assisting with activity as needed.

4. If confusion is present, provide cues for reorientation, such as identifying yourself when entering the room, putting signs on doors, providing a large calendar and clock, discussing the day's events, and encouraging frequent visits, if possible, from significant others.

5. Explain neurologic symptoms to the patient and to family and friends. Emphasize supportive behaviors, such as using humor, changing the subject if repetitive or irrational behaviors are present, gentle reminders of appropriate behavior, and active listening.

6. Provide a safe and supportive environment, instituting safety measures according to the deficits present.

7. Observe for involuntary movements, paresthesias, numbness, pain, weakness, and atrophy of extremities. Consult with the doctor regarding treatment, if needed, and institute measures to protect the extremities if sensation is impaired.

8. Additional individualized interventions: _____
_____
_____

Rationales

1. Baseline and ongoing mental and neurologic assessments allow early detection of neurologic involvement, a common and usually ominous finding in patients with AIDS. Neurologic manifestations occur in 30% to 60% of patients with AIDS and include confusion, emotional lability, memory loss, and mental dullness.

2. Emotional responses and medication side effects and/ or reactions may contribute to reduced alertness, confusion, withdrawal, hyperactivity, or anxiety.

3. CMV infection involving the optic nerve can cause blindness. Vision changes may be particularly frightening and difficult for the patient to accept. Precautionary interventions, particularly if confusion is also a factor, reduce the risk of injury.

4. Reorientation may help decrease anxiety, reduce the risk of injury, and facilitate coping.

5. Explanations may help the patient feel less isolated and anxious about mentation changes. Family members and friends may be more supportive if they understand that mentation changes may be related to disease progression.

6. Confusion, disorientation, and loss of function are emotionally devastating for many patients. Because the disoriented patient is at increased risk for injury, safety measures must be instituted.

7. Distal symmetrical sensorimotor neuropathy is a common peripheral nerve complication in patients with AIDS, manifested by the signs and symptoms listed. The cause is unknown. Although it is a relatively benign condition, it may cause significant discomfort. Treatment may include heat, range-of-motion exercises, and electrical stimulation.

8. Rationale: _____
_____
_____

Outcome criteria

Throughout the period of hospitalization, the patient will:
• use cues for self-reorientation

• take appropriate precautions to prevent injury
• acknowledge limitations appropriate to any neurologic deficit.

Nursing diagnosis: *Social isolation related to communicable disease, associated social stigma, and fear of infection from social contact*

NURSING PRIORITY: Minimize feelings of social isolation.

Interventions

1. *Assess the patient's support system,* such as family, spouse (or partner), and significant others. Ask the patient and others in the support system about any recent loss of their significant others, any recent change in the patient's living situation, and attitudes of family and friends toward the disease.

2. *Provide opportunities for the patient and family to express feelings.*

3. *Provide an atmosphere of acceptance.* Encourage staff, family, and significant others to touch and hug the patient.

4. *Teach significant others about ways the AIDS virus is not transmitted,* including the following: toilet seats and bathroom fixtures, swimming pools, dishes, furniture, handshakes, hugging, social (dry) kissing and other nonsexual physical gestures of affection, pets (though pets may carry microorganisms threatening to the patient), doorknobs, or casual social contact.

   Saliva, tears, and coughing are currently considered relatively unlikely sources of possible transmission to others. If an opportunistic infection is present, family members should observe the precautions they usually would, including handwashing, good health habits, and avoidance of contact with contaminated secretions.

   Provide literature covering these points.

5. *Provide the patient and family with telephone numbers of available resources for counseling, support, and information.* Check with the local public health department for resources in your area. The following numbers may also be helpful:
• Centers for Disease Control (CDC), Atlanta: 1-800-342-AIDS
• CDC Information: 1-800-342-7514
• AIDS Foundation, San Francisco: 415-864-4376
• National Gay Task Force, New York: 1-800-221-7044.
Provide referral to a social services professional to assist with financial planning.

6. Additional individualized interventions: _____
_____
_____

Rationales

1. The patient's and others' lack of accurate knowledge, as well as the social stigma associated with AIDS, may diminish the patient's social contacts. In addition, the patient may become isolated from fear of catching infections from others. Assessing the patient's social support system helps identify resources and may allow for correction of misconceptions about the disease.

2. Expressing feelings helps decrease sense of isolation.

3. Physical contact decreases feelings of isolation and demonstrates caring. Family and friends may need gentle reminders that such contact does not transmit the virus to others. The nurse can be a good role model for family and friends.

4. The "worried well" (those who are healthy but worried about catching AIDS) may be torn between their desire to support the patient and concerns for their own health. Specific education may help reduce their conflicts and encourage normal interaction with the patient. The AIDS virus does not survive on inanimate objects and is killed by soap and hot water. Opportunistic infections are a source of possible illness for others, but healthy individuals are at no greater risk than usual. Literature reinforces oral education and provides a source for future reference.

5. Ongoing support is essential for patients with AIDS and their families. Anxiety at the time of the initial diagnosis may reduce information retention. A referral to the social services department is essential because most patients cannot afford expensive treatments and special housing and care arrangements.

6. Rationale: _____
_____
_____

Outcome criteria

Throughout the period of hospitalization, the patient will:
• verbalize feelings related to social losses
• express and receive affection
• contact support and resource persons, as appropriate.

Nursing diagnosis: *Activity intolerance related to fatigue and weakness, hypoxemia, depression, alterations in sleep patterns, side effects of medications, and orthostatic hypotension*

NURSING PRIORITIES: (a) Achieve optimal balance between rest and activity, and (b) prevent injury.

Interventions

1. *Assess for signs of activity intolerance*—increased fatigue, tachypnea, tachycardia, or cyanosis—and adjust the patient's activity level to minimize hypoxemia.

2. *Provide an environment that supports the patient's need for sleep, rest, or activity,* suggesting limitations on telephone calls or visitors as appropriate. Encourage the patient to prioritize activities as needed, using energy conservation techniques.

3. Assess the need for pharmacologic support of sleep, administer medications as ordered, and monitor their effects.

4. Space care activities, such as administering medications, blood samples, and diagnostic tests.

5. For patients with weakness or orthostasis, encourage use of the call light, assist with standing and walking, and leave belongings within reach.

6. Assist with activities of daily living (ADLs) as necessary. Anticipate the patient's needs.

7. Additional individualized interventions: _____
_____
_____

Rationales

1. The effort required for even minimal activities may overtax the patient's ventilatory capabilities. Fatigue further contributes to hypoxemia.

2. Needs for rest and activity vary tremendously among patients. Patients may need assistance prioritizing energy expenditure, because significant fatigue usually accompanies the disease.

3. Anxiety and worry often interrupt sleep in patients with AIDS. Rest is essential for healing.

4. A continual flow of hospital activity interferes with rest.

5. Often these patients have never been this weak or dizzy; they may be surprised by how weak they are. For this reason, they need reminders to ask for assistance.

6. These patients often have never been sick or hospitalized before. They may need assistance but feel uncomfortable asking for help.

7. Rationale: _____
_____
_____

Outcome criteria
Throughout the period of hospitalization, the patient will:
• appear rested
• verbalize adequacy of rest times

• call for assistance as appropriate
• experience no falls or other injuries related to weakness.

Nursing diagnosis: *Nutritional deficit related to nausea, vomiting, diarrhea, anorexia, medication side effects, or decreased nutrient absorption secondary to disease process*

NURSING PRIORITY: Promote adequate nutritional intake.

Interventions

1. *On admission, assess nutritional status,* documenting height, weight, skin turgor, fatigue, and any history of weight loss. Monitor intake and output, maintaining a 3-day record of dietary intake. Note serum protein, blood urea nitrogen (BUN), and albumin levels, and report abnormal findings.

Rationales

1. Baseline assessment provides a guide for planning a therapeutic diet. Immunosuppressed patients have an increased need for nutrients to help repair tissue and decrease muscle wasting. Serum albumin and protein levels are decreased in malnutrition. BUN levels may be elevated, reflecting increased protein breakdown and insufficient intake.

(continued)

Interventions *continued*

2. *Involve the dietitian and patient in planning for nutritional replenishment* that incorporates patient preferences.

3. Encourage family and friends to bring favorite foods from home.

4. Offer frequent, small meals of high-calorie, high-protein foods, or supplement regular meals with milkshakes, custard, or other snack foods.

5. Avoid giving liquids with meals.

6. Provide soft, nonirritating foods if the patient has oral mucosal lesions.

7. Administer antiemetics, as ordered, if nausea and vomiting are present.

8. Remove noxious stimuli, such as secretions and vomitus, from the environment before meals.

9. Consult with the doctor regarding nutritional support via nasogastric (NG) feedings or total parenteral nutrition (TPN) if the patient is unable to tolerate adequate oral intake or if severe chronic diarrhea is present. See the "Total Parenteral Nutrition" care plan, page 265, for further information.

10. Additional individualized interventions: _____

_____

_____

Rationales *continued*

2. The dietitian may offer specific suggestions relevant to the patient's nutritional needs. Considering preferences is essential for maximum dietary compliance.

3. The patient may be more willing to eat "home" favorites.

4. Small meals may be better tolerated if anorexia is a problem. Increased calories provide energy; protein facilitates tissue repair and regeneration.

5. Liquids stimulate volume receptors, causing early satiety that reduces solid food intake.

6. Soft foods may be easier to swallow and may minimize further irritation to mucous membranes.

7. Chemotherapeutic agents administered for infections commonly cause nausea and vomiting. Antiemetics block stimulation of the vomiting center.

8. Noxious stimuli may provoke nausea and vomiting.

9. NG feedings provide nutrients without as many associated complications as TPN. However, severe diarrhea from cryptosporidiosis or salmonellosis or from the presence of intestinal KS lesions may reduce GI absorption so that TPN is necessary.

10. Rationale: _____

_____

_____

Outcome criteria

Within 2 days of admission, the patient will:
• participate in dietary planning.

Throughout the period of hospitalization, the patient will:
• maintain adequate oral intake of food *or*
• tolerate enteral or parenteral feedings without complications.

By the time of discharge, the patient will:
• exhibit BUN values decreased since admission
• take food orally without excessive nausea or vomiting *or* verbalize and demonstrate understanding of outpatient or home TPN therapy, if appropriate (see the "Total Parenteral Nutrition" and "Lymphoma" care plans, pages 265 and 437, respectively, for details on catheter care).

Nursing diagnosis: *Potential fluid volume deficit related to chronic, persistent diarrhea associated with opportunistic infection*

NURSING PRIORITY: Maintain optimal fluid status.

Interventions

1. See the "Fluid and Electrolyte Imbalances" care plan, page 21.

Rationales

1. Diarrhea is common in patients with AIDS because of opportunistic infections from various microorganisms. The "Fluid and Electrolyte Imbalances" care plan provides detailed interventions related to caring for patients with such disorders.

Interventions *continued*

2. Additional individualized interventions: _____
_____
_____

Rationales *continued*

2. Rationale: _____
_____
_____

Outcome criterion

Throughout the period of hospitalization, the
patient will:
• exhibit normal fluid and electrolyte status.

Nursing diagnosis: *Altered oral mucous membrane related to oral infections and/or masses*

NURSING PRIORITY: Reduce discomfort and avert further damage to the mucous membrane.

Interventions

1. Assess the patient's mouth at least twice daily for
signs and symptoms of thrush, lesions, or bleeding.

2. Ensure that the patient receives or completes oral
care after meals and at bedtime. Provide the following
instructions:
• Use a soft toothbrush or swabs.
• Use dilute hydrogen peroxide or toothpaste.

3. Apply lubricant to the lips as needed.

4. Obtain cultures from suspicious oral lesions, as ordered.

5. Avoid using alcohol, lemon-glycerin swabs, and commercial mouthwashes.

6. Assess for and report any inflammation or ulceration
of the oral mucosa and any leukoplakia, pain, dysphagia, or voice change.

7. Additional individualized interventions: _____
_____
_____

Rationales

1. The patient with AIDS is at risk for new opportunistic infections. Lesions may occur as side effects of medications or as a result of altered normal flora. Candidiasis is extremely common and has even been considered a harbinger of the disease.

2. Oral care helps reduce the risk of new infections by
maintaining circulation to the mucous membranes and
by decreasing bacteria in the mouth. Vigorous brushing
is discouraged, because it may cause bleeding and injury to the mucous membrane, thus providing a new
entrance for pathogens.

3. Lubricant helps prevent dry and cracked lips.

4. Culture results guide therapeutic intervention.

5. These products contain alcohol, which may dry and
irritate mucous membranes.

6. Stomatitis, pharyngitis, and esophagitis are common
AIDS-associated infections. Initial symptoms include inflammation of the mucous membranes, voice changes,
and difficulty swallowing if the inflammation involves
the esophagus or larynx.

7. Rationale: _____
_____
_____

Outcome criteria

Throughout the period of hospitalization, the
patient will:
• perform or receive oral care at least four times daily
• have oral mucous membrane lesions (if present)
treated promptly.

Nursing diagnosis: *Potential altered skin integrity related to effects of immobility, disease process, medications, and/or poor nutritional status*

NURSING PRIORITY: Prevent skin breakdown.

Interventions

1. *Assess the skin* at least every 8 hours for areas of redness, breakdown, excessive moisture, or lesions.

2. *Implement preventive skin care measures*, such as the following:

• Perform position changes at least every 2 hours, encouraging maximum mobility and using care in turning.

• Keep the skin clean and dry.
• Provide frequent gentle massage to bony prominences or other pressure-susceptible areas.
• Consider using an egg-crate mattress or other special bedding.

• Use lotion if the skin is dry, massaging well for maximum absorption.

3. If a pressure sore develops, institute therapeutic treatment, as ordered. This may include:
• cleansing or debridement agents per hospital protocol or the doctor's recommendations

• topical antibiotics

• blow-drying after bathing or treatments

• positioning to avoid pressure on the area of the lesion, using foam or other padding as needed.

4. If the patient is receiving I.V. or I.M. pentamidine isethionate for PCP, rotate injection sites and observe them carefully for development of sterile abscesses.

5. Observe for urticaria, maculopapular rash, or pruritus.

6. Provide appropriate patient teaching related to the above measures.

7. Additional individualized interventions: _____
_____
_____

Rationales

1. Redness is usually the first sign of impaired skin integrity. Prompt identification of areas at risk for breakdown allows preventive measures to be instituted.

2. Because of the immunosuppression associated with AIDS, effective treatment of pressure sores may be difficult. Preventive care is essential.

• Position changes help maintain circulation to all areas and reduce the effects of pressure on bony prominences. Overly vigorous turning may cause delicate skin to shear.
• Moisture promotes bacterial growth.
• Massage stimulates skin circulation.

• Special bedding may minimize pressure effects by redistributing pressure more evenly or by padding sensitive areas.
• Dry skin is prone to breaks and cracks. Excessive moisture may lead to maceration, however.

3. Prompt treatment is essential to prevent further complications.
• Agent selection depends on patient status and doctor's preference. Half-strength povidone-iodine solution is commonly used.
• The choice of prophylactic antibiotic (which varies) should be reevaluated if infection develops.
• A blow dryer may be useful for certain areas, such as rectal lesions.
• Additional pressure will lead to further tissue breakdown.

4. Pentamidine is a very irritating drug, and sterile abscesses are a common side effect.

5. Medications commonly used to treat AIDS patients (such as trimethoprim-sulfamethoxazole, ethambutol, and pyrimethamine) may cause skin irritation. Additionally, HIV infection itself may result in skin abnormalities.

6. For able patients, such knowledge promotes self-care and a sense of increased control and self-esteem. For patients unable to care for themselves, such knowledge promotes understanding of the frequent interventions by the staff.

7. Rationale: _____
_____
_____

Outcome criterion
Throughout the period of hospitalization, the patient will:
• present clean, dry, and intact skin.

Nursing diagnosis: *Potential sexual dysfunction related to fatigue, depression, fear of rejection, and fear of disease transmission*

NURSING PRIORITIES: (a) Promote a positive sexual self-concept, and (b) teach "safer sex" practices.

Interventions

1. *Assess the current status of the patient's sexual relationships* by asking direct questions in a nonjudgmental manner. If you are uncomfortable discussing sexuality, refer the patient to another professional or an AIDS counselor who can provide this information.

2. *Encourage open discussion and sharing of feelings between the patient and spouse (or partner).* Provide accurate information.

3. *Encourage expression of affection* and nonsexual touching—such as hugging, massage, and holding hands.

4. *Discuss "safer sex" practices. Refer to current CDC guidelines for detailed, up-to-date recommendations.* Teach the patient and spouse or partner to observe the following guidelines:
• Engage in mutually monogamous relationships.

• Avoid exchange of blood or body fluids, including swallowing semen.
• Practice sexual techniques that do not involve exchange of body fluids, such as mutual masturbation and fantasy.
• Avoid sex practices classified as "unsafe"—for example, intercourse without a condom, oral sex without a condom, and insertion of objects into the rectum.

5. Additional individualized interventions: _____
_____
_____

Rationales

1. Because the disease may be transmitted via sexual contact, assessing sexual relationships is essential. Many patients with AIDS experience abandonment by partners after diagnosis. If the patient is a homosexual, the high incidence of AIDS among homosexual males may add to the anxiety of both patient and spouse or partner. This is especially true if the patient's sexual orientation is not known or not accepted by his family or co-workers.

2. Sharing of feelings may help the couple maintain closeness and offer mutual support. Accurate information helps dispel fears based on misunderstandings about AIDS.

3. Liberal use of touch reduces feelings of shame and abandonment.

4. "Safer sex" guidelines may help reduce the likelihood of disease transmission. CDC guidelines are revised frequently, so nurses should consult current information before providing specific teaching.
• Multiple sexual contacts are associated with increased risk of AIDS transmission.
• The disease is transmitted through such exchanges.

• Alternative techniques may help provide sexual satisfaction without risk of disease transmission.

• Unsafe practices are associated with disease transmission.

5. Rationale: _____
_____
_____

Outcome criteria
By the time of discharge, the patient will:
• list "safer sex" measures

• exchange affection with significant others
• share sexual concerns with spouse or partner, if present.

Nursing diagnosis: *Knowledge deficit related to symptoms of disease progression, risk factors, transmission of disease, home care, and treatment options*

NURSING PRIORITY: Provide patient and family with complete and accurate information.

Interventions

1. See the "Knowledge Deficit" care plan, page 56.

2. *Teach the patient and family about precautionary measures for infection prevention,* including:
• regular cleaning of bathrooms and kitchen

• avoiding crowds and persons with known or suspected infections; good handwashing techniques

• avoiding touching fish tanks, animal waste, or birdcages

• consulting with the doctor before obtaining pets
• avoiding raw fruits and vegetables and unpasteurized milk

• smoking cessation, as indicated

• consulting with the doctor about vaccines

• maintaining dietary recommendations, including high-protein, high-calorie intake
• avoiding of standing water
• adhering to healthy habits, such as adequate rest and regular exercise, and avoiding steroids or recreational drugs that may further decrease immune function.

3. *Discuss symptoms that may indicate AIDS-related complications.* These include night sweats, chest pain, shortness of breath, swollen glands, persistent fever, weight loss, diarrhea, weakness, purplish blotches on the skin, white patches or ulcerations in the mouth, difficulty swallowing, dry cough, headache, confusion, easy bruising, and skin lesions. Emphasize the importance of prompt reporting of symptoms to health care providers.

4. *Review recommendations for home care and waste disposal,* such as the following:
• Family members should use thorough handwashing before touching the patient and after contact with blood or secretions.
• Use 1:10 bleach-in-water solution for cleaning blood spills and washing soiled bedding, medical equipment, bedpans or commodes, and soiled surfaces.
• Dispose of contaminated waste carefully: Such items as body fluids, blood, and used tissues should be flushed down the toilet. Needles should be placed in puncture-proof containers, which should be sealed and disposed of in the trash. Nonflushable items soiled with secretions should be double-bagged in plastic bags, tied closed, and disposed of in the trash.

Rationales

1. This care plan contains detailed interventions useful in patient and family teaching.

2. Infection control is essential to minimize the risk of further complications.
• Moisture in bathrooms and kitchen may facilitate fungal growth.
• Immunosuppression renders the patient extremely susceptible to new infections.
• Animal waste harbors microorganisms.

• Pets may carry intestinal protozoa.
• These may be sources of microorganisms.

• Smoking increases the incidence of respiratory infections.
• Immunosuppressed persons may not be able to manufacture appropriate antibodies and may thus be susceptible to actually developing the vaccine disease.
• Malnutrition predisposes the patient to development of infection.
• Standing water provides a medium for microbial growth.
• Overall health maintenance maximizes immune response.

3. Early reporting of new symptoms, and prompt treatment of complications, may prolong active life.

4. Thorough, specific teaching reduces anxiety for family members and promotes safe and effective care. Current evidence does not suggest any danger of transmission from casual contact. Blood and body fluids precautions are recommended.

Interventions *continued*

• Use masks only when suctioning or performing other measures that may allow direct contact with secretions, or to protect the patient from the caregiver's infection.
• Gloves should be worn only when handling body fluids or blood.
• Wash dishes and utensils in hot, soapy water. Avoid sharing utensils or glassware.

5. *Teach the patient and significant others about how the AIDS virus may be spread:* by sexual activity or by direct contact of an infected person's blood or body fluids with broken skin or mucous membrane of an uninfected person. Discuss such precautionary measures as:

• notifying other health care providers (such as the dentist) of the patient's AIDS status

• avoiding sharing needles and personal toiletry items (such as razors and toothbrushes)

• avoiding donating blood or organs

• birth control methods to prevent pregnancy
• "safer sex" practices (see the "Sexual dysfunction" nursing diagnosis in this care plan for details).

6. *Provide information regarding the legal rights of patients with AIDS,* including privacy and confidentiality of medical records, laws protecting the patient from discrimination in housing and employment, and the right to choose treatment options and participation in research studies.
    Provide referral to an AIDS support group or to other resources as appropriate.

7. Encourage the patient to explore treatment options with the doctor, including new or experimental medications and alternatives to traditional medicine (such as acupuncture, visualization, nutritional therapy, and stress control).

8. Additional individualized interventions: _____
_____
_____

Rationales *continued*

5. Awareness of transmission factors may help the patient avoid spreading the disease to others.

• This allows health care providers to observe appropriate precautions to protect both the patient and themselves.
• Sharing items may contribute to transmission of the virus.

• The disease has been transmitted through blood transfusions and transplanted organs.
• The disease is likely to be transmitted to the fetus.
• Sexual activity is a primary method of transmission of the virus.

6. Because of the widespread fear of AIDS, patients may encounter discriminatory practices. Knowledge of legal rights and options may help avert further losses.

7. At this time no known cure for AIDS exists; however, new or alternative therapies may offer as-yet-undocumented effectiveness. In addition, such therapies may offer an individual hope, energy, and an increased sense of wellness.

8. Rationale: _____
_____
_____

Outcome criteria

By the time of discharge, the patient will:
• list precautionary measures to avoid new infections
• list symptoms that may indicate new infections or other complications

• discuss appropriate home care and waste disposal guidelines
• list precautions to avert transmission of disease
• verbalize awareness of legal rights.

Discharge planning
NURSING DISCHARGE CRITERIA

Upon discharge, documentation ideally shows evidence of:
• stable vital signs
• absence of cardiovascular and pulmonary symptoms
• absence of skin breakdown
• stabilizing weight
• ability to tolerate adequate nutritional intake

• ability to control pain and nausea using oral medications
• ability to transfer, ambulate, and perform ADLs independently or with minimal assistance
• absence of bowel or bladder dysfunction
• mentation indicating an ability to remain independent with ADLs
• adequate home support system *or* referral to home care or hospice if indicated by stage of disease, inadequate home support system, or inability to manage ADLs and care independently.

PATIENT/FAMILY DISCHARGE TEACHING CHECKLIST

Document evidence that patient/family demonstrates understanding of:
___ disease process and implications
___ all discharge medications (may include antibiotics or other chemotherapeutics)
___ community resources available for emotional support, financial counseling, grief counseling, and individual and family counseling
___ treatment options, including investigational areas
___ resources for long-term care or terminal care, such as a hospice
___ signs and symptoms of new opportunistic infection or of reinfection
___ ways to prevent the spread of AIDS during sexual activity
___ ways to decrease risk of new infection
___ symptoms to report to the health care provider
___ importance of keeping follow-up appointments with the healthcare provider
___ how to contact doctor.

DOCUMENTATION CHECKLIST

Using outcome criteria as a guide, document:
___ clinical status on admission
___ significant changes in status
___ pertinent laboratory and diagnostic test findings
___ occurrence and type(s) of opportunistic infection(s)
___ treatment decisions
___ nutritional program and support
___ breathing patterns
___ sleep patterns
___ emotional coping
___ family and significant other support
___ patient/family teaching
___ discharge planning.

ASSOCIATED CARE PLANS

Death and Dying
Fluid and Electrolyte Imbalances
Grief/Grieving
Ineffective Family Coping
Ineffective Individual Coping
Lymphoma
Pain
Pneumonia
Total Parenteral Nutrition

REFERENCES

Abbott Diagnostics HTLV-III Education Series Monographs. Abbott Laboratories, 1986.

Abrams, D. "AIDS: In Search of Hope," *California Nursing Review* 9(1):5-40, January 1986.

Bennett, J. "HTLV-III AIDS Link," *American Journal of Nursing* 85:1086-89, 1985.

Bennett J. "What We Know About AIDS," *American Journal of Nursing* 86:1016-21, 1986.

Berger, J. "Neurologic Complications of HIV Infection," *Postgraduate Medicine* 81(1):73-79, 1987.

Car G.S., and Gee, C. "AIDS and AIDS-Related Conditions: Screening for Populations at Risk," *Nurse Practitioner* 11:25-48, 1986.

Centers for Disease Control Morbidity and Mortality Weekly Report. "Recommendations for Preventing Transmission of Infection with Human T-Lymphotropic Virus Type III/Lymphadenopathy-Associated Virus During Invasive Procedures," *Journal of the American Medical Association* 256:1257-58, 1986.

Devita, V.T., et al. *AIDS: Etiology, Diagnosis, Treatment and Prevention.* Philadelphia: J.B. Lippincott Co., 1985.

Fischinger, P.J., and Bolognesi, D.P. "Prospects for Diagnostic Tests, Intervention and Vaccine Development in AIDS," in *AIDS Etiology, Diagnosis, Treatment and Prevention.* Edited by DeVita V.T., et al. Philadelphia: J.B. Lippincott Co., 1985.

Friedland, G.H., et al. "Lack of Transmission of HTLV II/LAV Infection to Household Contacts of Patients with AIDS or AIDS-Related Complex with Oral Candidiasis," *New England Journal of Medicine* 314:344-49, 1986.

Griffin, J.P. "Nursing Care of the Immunosuppressed Patient in an Intensive Care Unit," *Heart & Lung* 15:179-87, 1986.

Guyton, A. *Textbook of Medical Physiology,* 7th ed. Philadelphia: W.B. Saunders Co., 1986.

Halliburton, P. "Impaired Immunocompetence," in *Pathophysiological Phenomena in Nursing.* Edited by Carrieri, V.K., et al. Philadelphia: W.B. Saunders Co., 1986.

Holloway, N.M. "AIDS Awareness in the Emergency Department." *Critical Care Nurse* 6:2, 90-94, 1986.

LaCamera, D.J., et al. "The Acquired Immunodeficiency Syndrome," *Nursing Clinics of North America,* 20:241-56, 1985.

Lotze, M.T. "Treatment of Immunologic Disorders in AIDS," in *AIDS Etiology, Diagnosis, Treatment, and Prevention.* Edited by DeVita, V.T., et al. Philadelphia: J.B. Lippincott Co., 1985.

Peabody, B. "Living with AIDS: A Mother's Perspective," *American Journal of Nursing* 86:45-46, 1986.

Porth, C.M. *Pathophysiology Concepts of Altered Health States,* 2nd ed. Philadelphia: J.B. Lippincott Co., 1986.

Schietinger, H. "A Home Care Plan for AIDS," *American Journal of Nursing* 86:1021-28, 1986.

Shaw, G.M., et al. "HTLV-III Infection in Brains of Children and Adults with AIDS Encephalopathy." *Science* 227:177-82, 1985.

Turner, J.G., and Williamson, K.M. "AIDS: A Challenge for Contemporary Nursing," *Focus on Critical Care* Part I, 13(3):53-61; Part II, 13(4):41-50, 1986.

Wolff, P.H., and Colletti, M. "AIDS: Getting Past the Diagnosis and on to Discharge Planning," *Critical Care Nurse* 6(4):76-82, 1986.

Wollschlager, C.M., et al. "Pulmonary Manifestations of the Acquired Immunodeficiency Syndrome," *Chest* 85:197-202, 1984.

Anemia

DRG information
DRG 395 Red Blood Cell Disorder. Age > 17.
      Mean LOS = 4.4 days
      Principal diagnoses include:
      • acquired hemolytic anemia
      • iron-deficiency anemia
      • aplastic anemia
      • other.
DRG 396 Red Blood Cell Disorder. Age 0 to 17.
      Mean LOS = 1.7 days

Introduction
DEFINITION AND TIME FOCUS
Anemia is not a disease but a laboratory diagnosis comprising a constellation of physiologic symptoms. These symptoms result from an inadequate number of circulating red blood cells (RBCs) or from a decreased hemoglobin level. The primary function of the RBC is to carry oxygen from the lungs to the tissues; anemia reduces RBCs' oxygen-carrying capacity and produces signs and symptoms of tissue hypoxia.

Anemia is encountered on the acute care unit in one of three settings:
• life-threatening manifestations such as massive hemorrhage or bone marrow depression requiring strict isolation
• life-threatening complications such as dysrhythmias, angina, or pulmonary edema
• as a complication of another disease, such as lymphoma.

Anemia may be classified by etiology or by RBC morphology; both are discussed in the appropriate sections below. This care plan focuses on the newly diagnosed anemic patient with hemorrhagic or dietary-deficiency anemia, the most common types. The principles of care can be generalized to other types of anemia but would need supplementation with condition-specific care—for example, cessation of the offending medications (in toxic hemolytic reactions) or genetic counseling (in sickle-cell disease).

ETIOLOGY/PRECIPITATING FACTORS
• excessive bleeding (acute or chronic)
• decreased RBC production, caused by:
    □ dietary deficiencies of iron, folic acid, or vitamin B_{12}
    □ damaged bone marrow (aplastic anemia) from medications, such as chloramphenicol or sulfonamides; from chemotherapy with alkylating and antimetabolite agents; or from radiation
    □ impaired production of erythropoietin (in kidney disease)
    □ defective hemoglobin synthesis, as in sickle-cell disease and thalassemia
    □ decreased metabolic oxygen demand, as in hypothyroidism
• increased RBC destruction (hemolytic anemia), caused by:
    □ hereditary disorders such as sprue, sickle-cell disease, or thalassemia
    □ autoimmune hemolytic reactions (for example, from transfusions or lupus erythematosus)
    □ toxic drug reactions, such as from penicillin, methyldopa, quinine, quinidine, sulfonamides, or phenacetin
    □ trauma, such as burns and crush injuries
    □ systemic diseases, such as Hodgkin's disease and lymphomas

Focused assessment guidelines
NURSING HISTORY (Functional health pattern findings)
Note: Not all of the following signs and symptoms are present in all anemias. Because of the many types of anemias, the symptoms reported by patients vary widely. The symptoms also vary according to the severity of the anemia: Patients with mild anemia (hemoglobin >10 g) are usually asymptomatic at rest but become symptomatic with exertion. Those with moderate anemia (hemoglobin 6 to 10 g) are chronically fatigued as well as symptomatic on exertion. Patients with severe anemia (hemoglobin <6 g) are exhausted, cold, and symptomatic even at rest.

Health perception–health management pattern
• typically reports fatigue, headaches, dizziness, irritability, or sensation of being cold
• may report history of bleeding (for example, from ulcers or hemorrhoids), renal disease, liver disease, cancer, chronic infections, or (especially in the elderly) angina
• may report current or recent use of medications (see list above) that affect RBC production (rare)
• may report recent exposure to a chemical or a myelotoxic substance (such as benzene or a benzene derivative) or to large doses of radiation (rare)
• may report family history of a disease such as sickle-cell anemia, thalassemia major, or hereditary spherocytosis (all rare)

Activity-exercise pattern
• reports fatigue, decreasing activity tolerance, weakness, shortness of breath, palpitations, or claudication

Cognitive-perceptual pattern
• may report dizziness, headache, numbness, or tingling of fingers and toes

Nutritional-metabolic pattern
• may report weight loss, anorexia, nausea, indigestion, pruritus, or soreness of mouth, esophagus, or tongue (all rare)

Elimination pattern
• may report tarry stools, constipation, diarrhea, or flatulence (all rare)
• may report brown, hazy urine (rare)
• may report gross blood in excretions (rare)

Sexuality-reproductive pattern
• may report loss of libido, irregular menstruation or amenorrhea (if female), or impotence (if male)

PHYSICAL FINDINGS
Cardiovascular
• tachycardia
• cardiac enlargement (less common)
• murmurs (less common)
• dependent edema (less common)
• vascular bruits (less common)
• bounding arterial pulses (less common)

Pulmonary
• *dyspnea on exertion*
• tachypnea
• orthopnea (less common than other signs)

Integumentary
• *pallor* of skin and mucous membranes
• *diaphoresis*
• delayed wound healing
• purpura (less common than other signs)
• jaundice (less common than other signs)
• spider angiomas (less common than other signs)

DIAGNOSTIC STUDIES
• *hemoglobin level—may be decreased* with iron-deficiency, pernicious, hemolytic, and hemorrhagic anemias
• *hematocrit level—may be low*
• RBC count—may be below normal
• *microscopic evaluation of peripheral blood by hematologist—reveals size, shape, color, and number of RBCs; useful in diagnosing the specific type of anemia*
  Note: The morphologic classification of anemias is based on structural changes seen in RBCs, which are classified by size and hemoglobin content:
  □ Normocytic (normal size) and normochromic (normal color) RBCs are associated with anemias of sudden blood loss; pregnancy; chronic disease such as cancer, kidney disease, or chronic infection; and some hemolytic anemias.
  □ Macrocytic (abnormally large) and normochromic RBCs are associated with pernicious anemia, folic acid anemia, vitamin B_{12} deficiency, and some hemolytic anemias.

□ Microcytic (abnormally small) and normochromic RBCs are associated with anemias of chronic disease.
□ Microcytic and hypochromic (pale-colored) RBCs are associated with iron-deficiency anemia and thalassemia.
• *erythrocyte indices—use the RBC count and hematocrit and hemoglobin levels to define the size, hemoglobin weight, and hemoglobin concentration of a typical RBC;* mean corpuscular volume (MCV) gives the average cell size; mean corpuscular hemoglobin (MCH) gives the average hemoglobin weight; and mean corpuscular hemoglobin concentration (MCHC) identifies the average hemoglobin volume in a RBC. Low MCV and MCHC indicate microcytic, hypochromic anemia (for example, iron-deficiency anemia and thalassemia); a high MCV suggests macrocytic anemia (for example, folic acid anemia or vitamin B_{12} deficiency).
• reticulocyte count—if low, may indicate hypoplastic or pernicious anemia; if high, may indicate bone marrow response to anemia resulting from blood loss or hemolysis
• erythrocyte fragility test—if low, may indicate thalassemia, iron-deficiency anemia, or sickle-cell disease; if high, may indicate spherocytosis (hereditary and associated with autoimmune hemolytic anemia)
• direct Coombs' test—positive response may indicate autoimmune hemolytic anemia (idiopathic, drug-induced, or caused by underlying disease such as cancer or lupus erythematosus)
• hemoglobin electrophoresis—used to identify hemoglobin types by measuring the degree of negative charge
• sickle-cell test—used to identify sickle-cell disease and trait (a hemoglobin electrophoresis is then needed to differentiate the two disorders)
• serum iron and total iron-binding capacity (TIBC) levels—serum iron level decrease and TIBC increase indicate iron-deficiency anemia
• serum folic acid—low levels may indicate megaloblastic anemia
• serum vitamin B_{12} levels—low levels could indicate inadequate dietary intake of vitamin B_{12} or a malabsorption disorder
• bone marrow aspiration and biopsy—histologic examination and differential count with erythroid-to-myeloid ratio useful for differential diagnosis of aplastic, hypoplastic, or pernicious anemia
• liver-spleen scan—can be used to detect splenomegaly associated with hereditary spherocytosis
• chest X-ray—may show cardiac enlargement

POTENTIAL COMPLICATIONS
• hemorrhagic shock
• angina pectoris
• congestive heart failure
• pulmonary edema
• renal damage
• dysrhythmias

Collaborative problem: *Hypoxemia related to decreased oxygen-carrying capacity of RBCs*

NURSING PRIORITY: Prevent or promptly relieve hypoxemia.

Interventions

1. *Elevate the head of the bed.*

2. *Monitor for and report signs of hypoxemia,* such as restlessness, irritability, and confusion. Observe oral mucosa, fingernail beds, palmar creases, and conjunctivae for pallor or cyanosis.

3. *Monitor respirations before and after activity.* Assess lung sounds at least every 8 hours and report crackles, rhonchi, or decreased breath sounds to the doctor promptly.

4. *Monitor the patient's pulse,* noting strength and rate. Report if not within normal limits for the patient.

5. *Note and chest pain or palpations.*

6. Monitor arterial blood gas (ABG) measurements as ordered, and report results to the doctor.

7. *Administer oxygen, as ordered.*

8. *Administer whole blood or packed RBCs, as ordered.*

9. Monitor hemoglobin and hematocrit levels.

10. Maintain a warm room temperature. Provide extra blankets if desired.

Rationales

1. This position allows for greater lung expansion, thus promoting alveolar gas exchange.

2. Baseline and serial assessments of these signs of hypoxemia help provide a basis for individualizing the care plan. Neurologic signs reflect cerebral ischemia. Skin color changes unaffected by skin pigmentation are observed best in the sites specified. Because cyanosis indicates the presence of 5 g or more of desaturated hemoglobin, and anemic patients may have such depressed hemoglobin levels that they cannot accumulate 5 g of desaturated hemoglobin without decompensating, cyanosis may be an absent or very late sign.

3. Dyspnea and tachypnea may be present in mild to moderate anemia. The exact mechanism causing the dyspnea is unclear: One hypothesis is that the decreased oxygen pressure may play an important role. Congestive heart failure may develop with severe anemia, because the heart may be unable to handle the increased cardiac output necessary to compensate for the lower oxygen saturation of the blood.

4. To compensate for the decreased hemoglobin, the cardiac rate and output increase. Pulse weakness, threadiness, and rapidity become more pronounced as anemia becomes more severe.

5. Angina pectoris may develop with severe anemia from ischemia of the heart muscle. Palpitations reflect increased myocardial irritability secondary to hypoxemia.

6. ABG measurements document the degree of hypoxemia. Inadequate hemoglobin saturation decreases the oxygen-carrying capacity of the blood.

7. Supplemental oxygen helps prevent tissue hypoxia by elevating the arterial oxygen content.

8. Transfusions elevate the RBC count, hemoglobin level, and hematocrit value. An increased hemoglobin level improves arterial oxygen content, lessening signs and symptoms of hypoxemia.

9. These tests provide objective evidence of the degree of anemia and the efficacy of therapeutic interventions.

10. The body compensates for chronic hypoxemia by lowering the metabolic rate and shunting blood to vital organs, making the patient more sensitive to cold. A cold room temperature induces vasoconstriction, which further impairs the hemoglobin's release of oxygen to tissues.

(continued)

Interventions *continued*

11. Additional individualized interventions: _____
_____
_____

Rationales *continued*

11. Rationale: _____
_____
_____

Outcome criteria

Note: The expected outcomes for a patient newly diagnosed as being anemic vary, depending upon the type of anemia, its severity, its chronicity, the treatment selected, and concurrent disease processes. Therefore, these outcome criteria are general; more specific outcomes may need to be determined for each patient.

Throughout the period of hospitalization, the patient will:
• display vital signs within normal limits for this patient
• have no palpitations or chest pain

• maintain usual mental status
• have ABG meaurements within normal limits
• show normal skin color
• have clear lung sounds
• maintain hemoglobin and hematocrit within acceptable levels for this patient (as determined by the doctor)
• have no complaints of feeling cold.

Nursing diagnosis: *Nutritional deficit related to stomatitis, glossitis, anorexia, fatigue, inadequate nutritional education, and/or sociocultural factors*

NURSING PRIORITY: Maintain adequate nutritional intake.

Interventions

1. *Provide oral hygiene before and after meals,* or assist the patient in performing oral hygiene measures. (Using of a soft toothbrush or sponge applicator minimizes trauma to the gums.)

2. *Observe for soreness of the tongue, mouth, and esophagus.*

3. *Recommend a bland diet* (avoidance of hot, spicy, or acidic foods).

4. *Serve six small meals a day,* providing foods that appeal to the patient and meet specific dietary needs. Consult the dietitian for a specific dietary prescription. Specific needs vary with the type of anemia and may include the following:
• for iron deficiency—red meat, organ meats, green vegetables, and enriched breads and cereals
• for vitamin B_{12} deficiency—organ meats, milk, eggs
• for folic acid deficiency—green and leafy vegetables, meats, and whole-grain breads and cereals
• for vitamin C deficiency—citrus fruits and fruit juices.

5. *Administer vitamins and minerals, as ordered* (for example, iron preparations, vitamin B_{12}, folic acid, and vitamin C). Use the Z-track method to administer parenteral iron. If oral iron is prescribed, observe the patient and teach these precautions:
• Take the prescribed iron with meals.

Rationales

1. A patient with pernicious anemia or severe iron-deficiency anemia may have a sore mouth, tongue, or esophagus. Oral hygiene can be comforting and refreshing and can also stimulate the patient's appetite. Frequent oral hygiene also decreases the bacterial count, thereby decreasing the risk of infection.

2. Stomatitis and glossitis may be present in pernicious anemia.

3. The patient with a sore mouth, tongue, or esophagus may tolerate only bland foods because of irritation from spicy and acidic foods. Cold foods also have weaker odors and therefore may be less offensive and better tolerated than hot foods.

4. Small portions require less energy expenditure for consumption and digestion. Large meals require shunting of blood to the GI tract, further contributing to fatigue. Foods that appeal to the patient are more likely to be eaten.
   The dietitian is the expert on nutrition, so collaboration on dietary planning results in a diet most suitable for the patient's needs.

5. Iron, vitamin B_{12}, and folic acid are needed to synthesize hemoglobin. Vitamin C promotes iron absorption and influences folic acid metabolism. The Z-track method minimizes leakage of the medication into surrounding tissues (thus minimizing pain) or out through the injection site (thus minimizing medication loss and

Interventions *continued*

• Avoid taking it with milk or antacids.
• Increase vitamin C intake.
• If it is a liquid, dilute it, drink it through a straw, and rinse the mouth afterward.

6. Teach the patient the importance of a well-balanced diet including specific dietary needs. Emphasize the importance of adequate intake. Relate dietary recommendations to reversal of signs and symptoms experienced by the patient.

7. *Document what the patient actually eats.*

8. *Weigh the patient daily or as ordered.*

9. If the patient's nutritional needs are not met by dietary intake, consult the doctor about enteral or parenteral feeding.

10. Before discharge:
• assess the patient's understanding of the importance of proper nutrition
• evaluate the patient's ability to obtain the prescribed diet and medications
• make referrals to social or community agencies as indicated.

11. Additional individualized interventions: _____
_____
_____

Rationales *continued*

tissue staining). Precautions for taking oral iron maximize absorption and minimize gastric distress and tooth staining.

6. Teaching removes lack of knowledge as a contributor to poor dietary intake. Stressing the importance of diet may enlist the patient's cooperation in the nutritional plan despite fatigue or discomfort. Using personal examples makes recommendations more meaningful.

7. Accurate documentation of the patient's food intake assists with daily caloric calculations.

8. The patient's weight can be used as part of the ongoing nutritional assessment and can be helpful in monitoring fluid status.

9. Tube feedings or total parenteral nutrition may be indicated to improve nutritional status.

10. Poor nutrition may result from ignorance, poverty, or limited ability to shop for food, as in the debilitated elderly person dependent on public transportation.

11. Rationale: _____
_____
_____

Outcome criteria

By the time of discharge, the patient will:
• show signs of improving nutritional deficiencies (manifested by improved levels of hemoglobin, hematocrit, serum albumin, folic acid, and other parameters)
• have less tongue, mouth, and esophagus soreness

• increase weight toward normal for age, height, and body type
• have increased energy level
• follow recommended diet
• verbalize ability to obtain recommended diet after discharge or have appropriate referral(s) made.

Nursing diagnosis: *Potential impaired skin integrity related to tissue hypoxia, decreased mobility, and bed rest*

NURSING PRIORITY: Maintain skin integrity.

Interventions

1. *Assess the patient's skin, including anatomical pressure points,* for redness and induration. Assess during every position change.

Rationales

1. Mechanical pressure and decreased hemoglobin availability increase the risk of tissue hypoxia and cell damage. Abnormally red skin, especially over a pressure point, may indicate reactive hyperemia after relief of pressure-induced ischemia. Induration is the result of cellular changes that occur with ischemia.

(continued)

Interventions *continued*

2. Keep the skin clean and dry; keep the bed linen dry and wrinkle-free.

3. *Reposition the patient* at least every 2 hours. Apply lotion and massage pressure points. Increase the frequency of position changes if redness or induration occurs. Avoid weight-bearing on reddened areas.

4. Teach active range-of-motion (ROM) exercises, and instruct the patient to do them hourly while awake, if tolerated. (If the patient cannot tolerate active ROM exercises, substitute passive ones.)

5. *Assess for the need for a pressure-relieving device* such as a foam mattress or alternating pressure mattress, and initiate obtaining the device if indicated. (A doctor's order may be required to ensure insurance reimbursement.)

6. Additional individualized interventions: _____
_____
_____

Rationales *continued*

2. The skin is the first line of defense against infection. Moisture provides a good medium for bacterial growth and can lead to maceration.

3. Hypoxemia increases susceptibility to tissue breakdown. Frequent turning allows relief of pressure and reestablishment of nutritional blood flow. Massaging pressure points with lotion keeps the skin soft and increases circulation. Redness results from reactive hyperemia when pressure is relieved. Weight-bearing on reddened areas may further worsen ischemia.

4. Movement stimulates circulation and maintains muscle tone and joint mobility.

5. Pressure-relieving devices eliminate, change, or decrease the amount of pressure on the skin and thus improve or maintain circulation.

6. Rationale: _____
_____
_____

Outcome criterion

Throughout the period of hospitalization, the patient will:
• maintain skin integrity.

Nursing diagnosis: *Self-care deficit related to weakness and fatigue*
(from decreased oxygen-carrying capacity of the blood)

NURSING PRIORITY: Increase the patient's independence in activities of daily living (ADLs) while minimizing weakness and fatigue.

Interventions

1. *Provide rest periods between activities and an environment that promotes rest.* Ask the patient to describe the environment when he or she is resting at home, and try to simulate it if possible. Teach the importance of rest.

2. Assess the patient's normal ADLs, and offer help in prioritizing them.

3. Provide assistance with ambulation. Observe for and teach signs of activity intolerance, such as dizziness, fainting, shortness of breath, chest pain, and worsened fatigue. Monitor orthostatic vital signs.

4. Allow as much self-care as possible, and assist as needed.

Rationales

1. Rest decreases oxygen demand. Simulating features of the home environment contributes to relaxation.

2. Initially, the patient may need to limit activities. Involving the patient in selecting these activities gives a sense of control.

3. Orthostatic hypotension may aggravate cerebral ischemia or cardiac ischemia. The patient may need encouragement to change position slowly and to pace activities according to tolerance.

4. Self-care encourages patient independence and is helpful in promoting and maintaining self-esteem.

Interventions *continued*

5. Place personal items (such as a water pitcher, and tissues) within the patient's reach.

6. Additional individualized interventions: _____
_____
_____

Rationales *continued*

5. Placing personal items within the patient's reach encourages independence while conserving energy.

6. Rationale: _____
_____
_____

Outcome criteria
By the time of discharge, the patient will:
• be independent in simple ADLs, such as eating, washing face and hands, and eliminating, without complaints of fatigue
• verbalize priority tasks on which to expend energy.

Nursing diagnosis: *Hopelessness related to chronic fatigue, activity intolerance and lack of independence*

NURSING PRIORITY: Provide emotional support and guidance in solving practical problems.

Interventions

1. *Spend time actively listening* while the patient expresses personal feelings and frustrations.

2. *Identify and assess the patient's personal resources.* Assist with problem solving.

3. Provide information about available community agencies and the services provided by each. With the patient's consent, make appropriate referrals.

4. Additional individualized interventions: _____
_____
_____

Rationales

1. Active listening provides empathic support.

2. The patient's participation in identifying personal resources represents a significant step in actively coping with problems.

3. The patient may require assistance from the community to meet basic needs. Community assistance may be available for preparing meals, performing light household duties, assisting with ADLs, and counseling.

4. Rationale: _____
_____
_____

Outcome criteria
By the time of discharge, the patient will:
• identify support systems within family and friends
• identify community resources.

Discharge planning
NURSING DISCHARGE CRITERIA
Upon discharge, documentation shows evidence of:
• stable vital signs
• absence of fever
• hemoglobin and hematocrit levels within acceptable parameters
• ABG measurements within normal parameters
• absence of cardiovascular and pulmonary complications, such as dyspnea and angina
• ability to tolerate adequate nutritional intake
• stabilizing weight
• verbalized ability to obtain recommended diet
• ability to perform ADLs and ambulate the same as or better than before hospitalization

• adequate home support system, *or* referral to home care as indicated by lack of home support system, inability to follow diet and medication regimen, or inability to perform ADLs and tolerate moderate activities.
   Note: State professional review organizations (PROs) have specific parameters for acceptable hemoglobin levels upon discharge. Parameters vary depending on each state's PRO guidelines. It is not unusual to see a quality occurrence citation for discharging a patient whose hemoglobin is < 10 g, especially if the patient is readmitted within 15 days of a previous discharge. Therefore, the patient's blood work results upon discharge should be monitored closely, and any abnormal findings should be indicated in the discharge summary.

PATIENT/FAMILY DISCHARGE TEACHING CHECKLIST

Document evidence that patient/family demonstrated understanding of:
___ type of anemia and implications
___ all discharge medications' purpose, dosage, administration schedule, and side effects requiring medical attention
___ special dietary needs
___ community resources
___ signs and symptoms indicating need to seek further medical attention
___ dates, times, and location of follow-up appointments
___ how to contact doctor.

DOCUMENTATION CHECKLIST

Using outcome criteria as a guide, document:
___ clinical status on admission
___ significant changes in clinical status
___ pertinent laboratory and diagnostic test findings
___ nutritional intake
___ activity tolerance
___ patient/family teaching
___ discharge planning.

ASSOCIATED CARE PLANS

Geriatric Considerations
Ineffective Individual Coping
Knowledge Deficit
Pain

REFERENCES

Carpenito, Lynda. *Nursing Diagnosis: Application to Clinical Practice.* Philadelphia: J.B. Lippincott Co., 1983.

Carrieri, Virginia, et al. *Pathophysiological Phenomena in Nursing.* Philadelphia: W.B. Saunders Co., 1986.

Diagnostics, 2nd ed. Nurse's Reference Library. Springhouse, Pa.: Springhouse Corp., 1986.

Doenges, Marilynn, et al. *Nursing Care Plans: Nursing Diagnoses in Planning Patient Care.* Philadelphia: F.A. Davis Co., 1984.

Griffin, Joyce. *Hematology and Immunology: Concepts for Nursing.* East Norwalk, Conn.: Apple-Century-Crofts, 1986.

Luckmann, Joan, and Sorensen, Karen. *Medical-Surgical Nursing: A Psychophysiological Approach.* Philadelphia: W.B. Saunders Co., 1987.

Thompson, June, et al. *Clinical Nursing.* St. Louis: C.V. Mosby Co., 1986.

Ulrich, Susan, et al. *Nursing Care Planning Guides.* Philadelphia: W.B. Saunders Co., 1986.

Leukemia

DRG information

DRG 403 [Medical DRG] Lymphoma or Non-acute Leukemia. With Complications or Comorbidity (CC).
Mean LOS = 7.8 days

DRG 404 [Medical DRG] Lymphoma or Non-acute Leukemia. Without CC.
Mean LOS = 4.8 days

DRG 405 [Medical DRG] Acute Leukemia without Major Operating Room (OR) Procedure. Age 0 to 17.
Mean LOS = 4.9 days

DRG 473 [Medical DRG] Acute Leukemia without Major OR Procedure. Age over 17.
Mean LOS = 8.2 days

DRG 409* [Medical DRG] Radiotherapy.
Mean LOS = 7.0 days

DRG 410* [Medical DRG] Chemotherapy.
Mean LOS = 2.4 days

Introduction

DEFINITION AND TIME FOCUS

Leukemia is a disease characterized by proliferation and accumulation of abnormal blood cells in the bone marrow or lymph tissue. The malignant cells accumulate in the bone marrow, preventing normal hematopoiesis, and migrate out of the bone marrow to invade other organs and tissues, giving rise to the symptomatology of the disease.

Leukemia is classified as *acute* if the bone marrow is infiltrated with undifferentiated, immature cells (blasts) and as *chronic* if the cells are primarily differentiated and mature. The most common types of leukemia involve abnormalities of white blood cells (WBCs), specifically granulocytes and lymphocytes. Four major classifications of leukemia exist:

Acute myeloblastic (granulocytic) leukemia (AML) is characterized by uncontrolled proliferation of myeloblasts, the precursors of granulocytes. The incidence of AML increases with advancing age. The overall prognosis is poor, with high mortality from infection and hemorrhage.

In *acute lymphoblastic leukemia* (ALL), immature lymphocytes proliferate in the bone marrow. ALL is primarily a disease of children, with peak incidence at age 2 to 4. The prognosis is optimistic, with 50% to 60% of patients achieving 5-year survival.

Chronic granulocytic leukemia is caused by excessive development of neoplastic granulocytes in the bone marrow. It occurs most commonly in patients age 30 to 50. Patients survive 2 to 4 years after diagnosis, with death resulting from infection and hemorrhage.

Chronic lymphocytic leukemia is characterized by the production and accumulation of functionally inactive

*These DRGs would be used for patients with leukemia if admitted for either radiation or chemotherapy treatment.

but long-lived and mature-appearing lymphocytes. Patients (usually age 50 to 70) can live well with this leukemia, surviving 2 to 10 years.

This clinical plan focuses on the adult patient admitted for diagnosis of leukemia and for medical treatment on the medical-surgical unit.

ETIOLOGY/PRECIPITATING FACTORS

The exact etiology of leukemia is unknown. Possible etiologies include:
• exposure to carcinogenic chemical agents such as benzene and alkylating agents, ionizing radiation, or viruses (such as Epstein-Barr virus)
• familial tendency, congenital disorders such as Down's syndrome, or chromosomal abnormalities

Focused assessment guidelines

NURSING HISTORY (Functional health pattern findings)

Health perception–health management pattern
• *usually reports gradual or sudden onset of fever, fatigue, weakness and lassitude, or headache*
• *may relate evidence of bleeding tendencies,* such as gingival bleeding, purpura, petechiae, ecchymoses and easy bruising, epistaxis, and prolonged menstruation
• may report being a monozygotic (identical) twin
• may relate a positive family history for leukemia or chromosomal abnormalities
• may relate exposure to carcinogenic agents or ionizing radiation

Nutritional-metabolic pattern
• *reports nausea, anorexia, or weight loss*
• may complain of sore throat or dysphagia

Elimination pattern
• may report blood in urine
• may report tarry stools

Activity-exercise pattern
• *reports fatigue and weakness*
• *may report dyspnea and palpitations on exertion*
• may report diminished activity because of bone and joint pain
• may report abnormal bruising after minor trauma

Sleep-rest pattern
• reports increased desire or need for sleep and rest

Cognitive-perceptual pattern
• may complain of discomfort from mouth ulcers; abdominal, bone, and joint pain; and chills

Role-relationship pattern
• *may verbalize difficulty in maintaining role function* because of fatigue

Sexuality-reproductive pattern
• may have decreased libido secondary to extreme fatigue
• may report menorrhagia, if female

Coping–stress tolerance pattern
• *may initially express denial of diagnosis*

Value-belief system
• may view diagnosis of cancer as punishment
• may have a passive, fatalistic philosophy of life and death

PHYSICAL FINDINGS
General
• *elevated temperature*
• fatigued appearance

Cardiovascular
• *tachycardia*
• systolic ejection murmur

Respiratory
• *labored breathing*
• rapid breathing
• wheezing
• rhonchi
• decreased breath sounds
• nosebleeds

Gastrointestinal
• *gingival hypertrophy or bleeding*
• *mouth ulcers*
• *hepatosplenomegaly*
• increased abdominal girth
• *vomiting*
• oral or rectal mucosal ulceration

Neurologic
• confusion
• visual changes

Integumentary
• *pallor*
• *purpura*
• *petechiae*
• pale mucous membranes
• *ecchymoses*
• erythema
• rash
• poor turgor

Genitourinary
• hematuria

Lymphoreticular
• lymphadenopathy

Musculoskeletal
• joint swelling
• decreased exercise tolerance

DIAGNOSTIC STUDIES
• *complete blood count (CBC)—reflects bone marrow suppression by WBC infiltration*
  □ WBC count usually > 50,000/mm³ but may be low
  □ differential shows increased number of lymphocytes or increased number of polymorphonuclear cells
  □ red blood cell (RBC), hemoglobin, and hematocrit levels below normal; platelet count very low, may be < 50,000/mm³
• prothrombin time and partial thromboplastin time — may be prolonged
• histochemistry—specific chemistry tests for leukemia show Sudan black, peroxidase, or muramidase positive
• uric acid and lactic dehydrogenase levels—elevated in acute leukemia; may indicate extensive bone marrow infiltration
• liver enzyme levels—may be elevated, showing hepatic infiltration
• leukocyte alkaline phosphatase levels —may be decreased
• blood cultures—may show general sepsis
• urinalysis—may show bacteria and WBCs (indicating infection) or RBCs (indicating bleeding)
• blood urea nitrogen (BUN) and creatinine levels—may be elevated in renal infiltration and failure
• *bone marrow aspiration—shows domination of marrow by leukemia blast cells of the affected cell line*, may show abnormalities specific to leukemia, such as Auer bodies, Philadelphia chromosome; shows decreased RBC levels and decreased platelet formation
• *lumbar puncture—may detect central nervous system (CNS) infiltration and meningeal irritation*
• *liver-spleen scan—shows hepatosplenomegaly and enlarged abdominal lymph nodes*
• *chest X-ray—may show lung infiltration, infection, or mediastinal adenopathy*
• *computed tomography scan—may show enlarged lymph nodes or areas of consolidation*

POTENTIAL COMPLICATIONS
• infection, including sepsis
• hemorrhage, especially of CNS
• immunosuppression
• meningeal irritation
• cardiotoxicity secondary to chemotherapy
• hyperuricemia
• mouth ulcers
• constipation or diarrhea secondary to chemotherapy
• dysrhythmias secondary to electrolyte imbalance
• malnutrition, including protein-calorie imbalances

Nursing diagnosis: *Potential for infection related to incompetent bone marrow and immunosuppressive effects of chemotherapy treatment*

NURSING PRIORITIES: (a) Recognize early signs of infection, and (b) minimize local and systemic infection.

Interventions

1. *Assess the CBC*, noting if the WBC count falls below 2,000/mm³ and if any sudden rise or fall in neutrophil level occurs.

2. *Place the patient in a private room or in protective isolation*, according to hospital protocol and patient condition. Maintain the immediate environment free of bacterial contamination; disinfect or sterilize equipment; keep equipment at the bedside; and do not use such items for other patients.
   Prohibit contact with visitors or staff with known infections, such as a cold or influenza.

3. *Monitor, report, and document any sign or symptom of infection:* temperature above 100.4° F. (38° C.) lasting longer than 24 hours; chills; pulse above 100 beats/minute (bpm); crackles or rhonchi; cloudy, foul-smelling urine; urgency or burning upon urination; redness; swelling; drainage from any orifice; perineal, rectal, or vaginal pain or discharge; and painful skin lesions.

4. *Monitor and record intake and output.* Encourage fluids up to 3,000 ml/day, unless contraindicated.

5. Use only steel I.V. needles. Change the I.V. site every 48 hours and tubing every 24 hours.

6. *Provide a low-bacteria diet:* Avoid raw fruits and vegetables, and use only cooked and processed or pasteurized foods.

7. *Perform actions to prevent respiratory tract infections:* Instruct the patient to turn, cough, deep-breathe, and use the incentive spirometer every 2 hours. Document respiratory assessment every 4 hours.

8. *Avoid, if possible, invasive procedures* such as urinary catheterization, injections, and venipunctures. Examine the sites of earlier or unavoidable invasive procedures (such as bone marrow aspirations, or old venipuncture sites) for signs of inflammation.

9. *Provide meticulous skin care,* paying close attention to any alteration in skin integrity. Cleanse the skin at least twice a day with antibacterial solutions. Monitor and document skin condition every shift.

Rationales

1. A WBC count decrease places the patient at increased risk of developing an infection. Such a decrease results from both the disease and from chemotherapy. A suddenly changed neutrophil level indicates impending infection. Infection is a major cause of morbidity and mortality in the immunosuppressed patient.

2. The patient must be protected from potential sources of infection. Avoiding contact with others helps minimize contamination with pathogens.

3. An elevated temperature unrelated to drugs or blood products indicates infection in about 80% of patients with leukemia. Immunosuppressed patients are unable to mount a normal response to infection, so an infection that would be harmless in a patient with a normal WBC count can and commonly does develop into septicemia in leukopenic patients. Prevention and early treatment of any infection is essential to prevent complications and death.

4. Adequate fluid balance is essential to prevent dehydration from fever and fluid shift in septic shock.

5. Steel needles are less likely to cause inflammation if neutropenia is present. Frequent site and tubing changes minimize the risk of bacterial contamination.

6. These measures minimize potential sources of bacterial contamination from food.

7. Immobility promotes stasis of respiratory secretions, potentiating development of pneumonia and atelectasis.

8. Any invasive procedure is a potential source of bacterial invasion. Care should be taken to minimize trauma to the skin because of impaired healing abilities.

9. The skin is the body's first line of defense against infection. Any break in skin integrity is a source of potentially lethal bacterial contamination. The leukemic patient is as much at risk of infection from *normal* flora as from outside contamination. Frequent skin cleansing minimizes the possibility of superficial skin breakdown and resultant infection.

(continued)

Interventions *continued*

10. *Avoid trauma to rectal mucosa;* take the patient's temperature orally, and prevent constipation by ensuring adequate hydration and administering stool softeners, as ordered.

11. *Observe for and report clinical signs of septicemia,* such as tachycardia, hyperventilation, hypotension, or subtle mental changes. Obtain cultures and institute I.V. antibiotic therapy with cephalosporins (as ordered) within 1 hour of initial development of signs and symptoms. Monitor fibrin degradation products (FDP) levels if the patient is septicemic.

12. *Implement measures to reduce fever higher than 100° F. (38° C.).* Administer acetaminophen (Tylenol) 650 mg every 4 hours, as ordered. Use tepid sponge baths, only the necessary amount of clothing, and hypothermia, as ordered. Prevent chilling and encourage oral fluids.

13. *Prepare the patient for granulocyte transfusion if the WBC count is consistently below 500/mm³ and the patient has signs of infection.* Infuse granulocytes slowly over 2 to 4 hours, as ordered. Observe for and document signs of a serious transfusion reaction, such as hypotension, allergic response, or wheezing. Discontinue the transfusion and notify the doctor immediately if a reaction occurs.

14. Additional individualized interventions: _____
_____
_____

Rationales *continued*

10. Damage to rectal mucosa from frequent rectal temperatures or hard, dry stools may result in the formation of rectal abscesses.

11. Septicemia may occur without fever. Symptoms reflect initial stages of insufficient tissue perfusion. Prompt recognition of septic shock and equally prompt intervention are mandatory before irreversible hypovolemia and decreased cardiac output result. The septicemic patient is at increased risk of developing disseminated intravascular coagulation (DIC). Elevated FDP levels are seen in DIC.

12. Several measures may be necessary to reduce fever to a manageable level in the immunosuppressed patient. Untreated, high temperatures contribute to fluid imbalance, discomfort, and CNS complications.

13. Granulocyte transfusions are usually effective in patients who have granulocytopenia and progressive infections that are nonresponsive to antibiotics or in leukemia patients who do not develop bone marrow recovery after chemotherapy.
   Shaking chills and temperature elevations are not serious reactions to a WBC transfusion and should not be considered a cause for discontinuation of this critically important transfusion.

14. Rationale: _____
_____
_____

Outcome criteria
Within 8 hours of admission, the patient will:
• have potential sites of infection identified and monitored
• present a temperature ≤ 100° F.
• exhibit pulse and respirations within normal limits for this patient.
Within 3 days of admission, the patient will:
• exhibit no septicemia

• exhibit no dysuria
• have normal lung sounds.

Within 7 days of admission, the patient will:
• have intact oral mucous membranes
• have no skin or rectal abscesses
• exhibit a WBC count stable for this patient
• maintain normal temperature
• display negative urine, vaginal, blood, and sputum cultures.

Collaborative problem: *Potential hemorrhage related to incompetent bone marrow and the immunosuppressive effects of chemotherapy treatment*

NURSING PRIORITY: Minimize the potential for life-threatening hemorrhage.

Interventions

1. *Monitor, report, and document signs and symptoms of bleeding problems:*
• platelet count less than 50,000/mm³
• petechiae, especially on distal portions of upper and lower extremities

Rationales

1. Normal platelet levels are required for maintaining vascular integrity, platelet plug formation, and stabilizing clotting. A decrease leads to local or systemic hemorrhage. With a platelet count of less than 20,000/mm³, the patient is prone to spontaneous life-threatening

Interventions *continued*

- ecchymotic areas
- bleeding gums
- prolonged oozing from minor cuts or scratches
- frank or occult blood in urine, stool, emesis, or sputum
- prolonged heavy menstruation
- decline in hematocrit and hemoglobin levels
- narrowing pulse pressure with increased pulse rate
- restlessness, confusion, or lethargy.

2. *Implement measures to prevent bleeding during invasive procedures:*

- Use the smallest-gauge needle possible when performing venipuncture or giving injections. Apply firm, direct pressure to the injection site for 3 to 5 minutes after the injection. If bleeding does not stop after 5 minutes, apply a sandbag to the site and notify the doctor.
- Monitor and document the condition of old puncture sites (for example, venipuncture, lumbar puncture, or I.V. sites).

3. *Provide a soft, bland diet*, avoiding foods that are thermally, mechanically, or chemically irritating. Use only a soft-bristle or sponge toothbrush and nonalcohol mouthwash (such as normal saline) every 4 to 8 hours.

4. *Administer docusate sodium (Colace) or another stool softener* daily, as ordered. Monitor and document the frequency of bowel movements. Avoid using enemas, suppositories, harsh laxatives, and rectal thermometers.

5. Instruct the patient to avoid activities that may cause bleeding, such as forcefully blowing the nose; using a straight-edged razor; wearing tight, restrictive clothing; and cutting nails.

6. *Prepare for platelet transfusion, as ordered, when platelet counts drop below 20,000/mm³.* Obtain baseline vital signs before initiating the transfusion. Use a 19-G butterfly needle, infusing each unit over approximately 10 minutes. Observe, report, and document signs of transfusion reactions: nausea, vomiting, fever, chills, urticaria, or wheezing. Discontinue the transfusion immediately if symptoms develop, keep the vein open with normal saline, and notify the doctor. Be prepared to administer diphenhydramine (Benadryl), hydrocortisone (SoluCortef), or acetaminophen.

7. Monitor hemoglobin and hematocrit levels and test stools, urine, and sputum for occult blood, noting and reporting positive findings.

Rationales *continued*

bleeding. Patients with leukemia are prone to platelet deficiency because of the proliferation of WBCs, which interfere with normal platelet production, and because of the immunosuppressive effects of drug treatment.

2. Even minor invasive procedures can cause excessive bleeding, especially when the platelet count falls below 50,000/mm³.
- Patients with thrombocytopenia may continue to bleed excessively even after minor invasive procedures. Firm pressure minimizes further blood loss and hematoma formation. Firm pressure dressings may be necessary if bleeding continues.
- Spontaneous bleeding from old puncture sites may occur at platelet levels below 20,000/mm³.

3. The oral mucous membrane is very delicate in the leukemic patient and very prone to hemorrhage with even minor irritation. Minimizing irritation decreases bleeding and improves the patient's comfort level.

4. Rectal bleeding may develop with minimal trauma. Constipation and straining during defecation must be avoided to prevent trauma to the rectal mucosa as well as increased intracranial pressure, which could precipitate spontaneous CNS bleeding.

5. Many patients are unaware that minor habits in their daily routine can become dangerous when platelet counts are severely decreased.

6. Platelet transfusions are usually administered for counts below 20,000/mm³ to lessen the possibility of hemorrhage. Although small-gauge needles are preferred for most venipunctures to minimize trauma, a 19-G needle is preferable for blood transfusions to prevent clogging of the needle lumen by cells. Although platelet transfusions are compatible with regard to Rh and ABO factors, it is not always possible to remove all RBCs and antibodies from the serum. Therefore, the possibility of transfusion reaction always exists, especially for a patient receiving multiple transfusions. If a transfusion reaction occurs, the doctor must evaluate the patient. If the signs and symptoms are adequately controlled by diphenhydramine and acetaminophen, the remaining platelets can be transfused.

7. Decreasing hemoglobin and hematocrit values indicate hemorrhage. Occult bleeding must be detected and monitored to prevent hypovolemia.

(continued)

Interventions *continued*

8. Avoid administration of aspirin, anticoagulants, indomethacin (Indocin), and medications containing alcohol. Give phenothiazines only with caution.

9. *Force fluids to 2 to 3 liters/day* (if tolerated). Check uric acid levels for elevation and urine pH for acidity. Administer acetazolamide, sodium bicarbonate, and allopurinol, as ordered. Monitor and record intake and output. Provide appropriate patient teaching for measures to be continued after discharge.

10. Additional individualized interventions: _____

_____

Rationales *continued*

8. These medications induce or prolong bleeding.

9. Hyperuricemia is a possible result of rapid chemotherapy-induced leukemic cell lysis. Proper hydration and medication therapy are essential to prevent obstruction of the renal pelvis and ducts and subsequent renal failure. Acetazolamide acts as a diuretic, sodium bicarbonate maintains alkaline urine pH, and allopurinol inhibits synthesis of uric acid.

10. Rationale: _____

_____

Outcome criteria
Within 1 day of admission, the patient will:
• exhibit platelet count above 50,000/mm^3
• exhibit normal blood pressure and pulse.

Within 3 days of admission, the patient will:
• exhibit no frank bleeding in stool, urine, emesis, or sputum
• present minimal extension of ecchymoses

• present minimal bleeding from puncture sites, gums, and nose
• have stable or improved hemoglobin, hematocrit, and platelet levels
• exhibit minimal or no restlessness, confusion, lethargy, or other CNS symptoms.

Nursing diagnosis: *Activity intolerance related to fatigue secondary to rapid destruction of leukemic cells from chemotherapy; tissue hypoxia secondary to anemia; and depressed nutritional status*

NURSING PRIORITIES: (a) Minimize energy-depleting activities, (b) maximize energy resources, and (c) decrease tissue hypoxia.

Interventions

1. *Assess, monitor, and document the etiology, pattern, and impact of fatigue on the patient's ability to engage in routine activities of daily living (ADLs).*

2. *Monitor and document the degree of anemia present.* Assess for pallor, weakness, dizziness, headache, and dyspnea. Evaluate and report hemoglobin, hematocrit, and RBC values, especially a significant or consistent drop in hemoglobin (below 8 g/dl) or hematocrit (below 25%). Prepare for blood transfusion, as ordered.

3. Monitor and document vital signs before, during, and after blood transfusion. Use a 19-G or larger needle and tubing with a standard blood filter. Use standard Y tubing with normal saline solution.

Rationales

1. Causes of fatigue in the patient with leukemia commonly have an additive effect. To treat the problem effectively, the nurse must have a holistic approach to the patient.

2. The degree of anemia significantly affects the level of fatigue resulting from the RBCs' decreased oxygen-carrying capacity. The decreased RBC levels cause severe weakness, exhaustion, and inability to mobilize energy for ADLs. The values given indicate severe anemia and necessitate therapy with blood transfusions.

3. Knowledge of baseline and ongoing vital signs is imperative in order to monitor signs and symptoms of transfusion reaction. A large needle allows a suitable flow rate and prevents clumping and destruction of RBCs. The filter screens fibrin clots and particulate matter. Normal saline is the only solution suitable for use with RBCs, because dextrose solutions cause cell hemolysis.

Interventions *continued*

4. *Infuse blood slowly (20 drops/minute) for 15 minutes.* Complete the transfusion within 1½ to 2 hours if the patient's condition remains stable.

5. *Stop the transfusion at the first sign of transfusion reaction:* fever, chills, headache, low back pain, urticaria, wheezing, or hypotension. Keep the vein open with normal saline, and notify the doctor.

6. Implement measures to improve activity tolerance, such as the following:
• Provide uninterrupted rest periods before and after meals, procedures, and diagnostic tests.
• Instruct the patient to sit rather than stand when performing hygiene and daily care.
• Limit the number of visitors.
• Minimize environmental activity and noise.
• Assist the patient with activities.
• Keep supplies and personal articles within easy reach.

7. *Assess, report, and document tolerance for progressive activity.* Stop activity if the patient's pulse rate increases more than 20 beats/minute above the resting rate, if the blood pressure increases more than 40 mm Hg systolic or 20 mm Hg diastolic, or if dyspnea, chest pain, dizziness, or syncope occurs.

8. Reassure the patient that fatigue is an expected effect of chemotherapy.

9. Additional individualized interventions: _____
_____
_____

Outcome criteria

Within 1 day of admission, the patient will:
• exhibit no side effects or toxic effects of blood transfusion, such as elevated temperature, or urticaria.

Within 3 days of admission, the patient will:
• show improved ability to participate in self-care, bathing, and hygiene measures
• sleep 1 hour before and after treatments

Rationales *continued*

4. Blood is administered slowly during the first 15 minutes of the transfusion because transfusion reactions typically occur during this time. A slow rate minimizes the volume of cells transfused.
   However, blood should be transfused within 4 hours after leaving the blood bank, to prevent bacterial proliferation and RBC hemolysis.

5. Transfusion reactions are potentially lethal and must be recognized immediately to prevent death or organ damage.

6. Quiet, restful periods before and after meals, procedures such as chemotherapy, and diagnostic procedures help increase activity tolerance and promote a rested feeling. Conserving energy and improving activity tolerance usually help the patient participate more actively in care and treatment.

7. The patient's response should be the guideline for any plan of progressive activity. Changes in baseline vital signs indicate that the patient is being pushed beyond therapeutic levels and activity should be stopped.

8. The patient may fear that fatigue is related to extension of the disease process. The patient should be reassured that fatigue is common after chemotherapy and is not necessarily an extension of the disease.

9. Rationale: _____
_____
_____

• sleep 8 hours at night
• ambulate 20% farther distance each day
• participate in diversional activities, such as reading, doing puzzles, and watching television
• maintain hemoglobin level at 8 g/dl or higher
• maintain hematocrit level at 25% or higher.

Nursing diagnosis: *Nutritional deficit related to anorexia, nausea, vomiting, taste perception changes, and alterations in cellular metabolism secondary to disease process and chemotherapy treatment*

NURSING PRIORITIES: (a) Maximize oral intake of foods and fluids, and (b) minimize catabolism and protein and vitamin deficiencies.

Interventions

1. *Assess nutritional status.* Monitor and document height, weight, skin turgor, and intake and output, and compile a 3-day oral intake record. Note serum laboratory values for BUN, albumin, protein, cholesterol, and transferrin.

2. *Provide high-calorie, high-protein, food snacks that are sweetened,* such as milk shakes, puddings, and eggnog.

3. Avoid serving liquids with meals.

4. *Serve only small portions of nutritious, high-calorie foods.* Remove all unpleasant stimuli from the environment, especially noxious odors.

5. *Encourage rest periods before and after meals.*

6. *Provide nutritional supplements between meals,* as ordered. Serve them cold in a glass or other container, not in the can. Observe for and document undesirable side effects such as gastric distention, cramping, or diarrhea.

7. Encourage significant others to bring appropriate favorite foods from home and to provide company during meals whenever possible.

8. If nausea and vomiting occur:
• Serve foods cold rather than warm or hot.
• Use clear-liquid and bland diets until nausea subsides.
• Avoid serving sweet, fatty, or spicy foods and foods with strong odors.
• Monitor, report, and document the frequency of vomiting and the amount of emesis; serum electrolyte levels; and urinary output.

Rationales

1. Baseline assessments of nutritional status enable the nurse to assess calorie, protein, and fluid depletion. This information will be used to develop an appropriately individualized nutritional plan. Laboratory values reflect decreased nutritional status and can be used to monitor improvement. The BUN level is monitored to reflect the rate of protein catabolism and nitrogen balance. A negative nitrogen balance indicates protein breakdown that exceeds protein intake.

Albumin, protein, and transferrin levels, decreased in malnourished persons, assess protein status by evaluating the liver's production and transport of proteins. Decreased cholesterol levels reflect decreased fat metabolism in the malnourished patient.

2. Protein-calorie malnutrition is common in leukemic patients. Increased protein intake facilitates repair and regeneration of cells, and increased calories help fight the body's tendency toward cancer-induced catabolism.

3. Liquids promote nausea and, because they stimulate volume receptors, early satiety.

4. The anorexic patient may be overwhelmed by large amounts of food and commonly will not eat at all when presented with large quantities at once. Unpleasant stimuli such as noxious odors will stimulate nausea and vomiting.

5. Fatigue commonly impairs the desire and ability to eat. Planned rest periods improve appetite and the ability to consume appropriate amounts of nutrients.

6. Oral supplements are high in protein and serve as a valuable supplement to nutritious food. Many patients experience a metallic taste secondary to disease pathology, and the sight of the can may aggravate this feeling. The side effects listed result from the high osmolality of supplemental liquids.

7. The patient may eat more when the food is familiar and appetizing. Visitors make meals a more enjoyable experience, so the patient may eat more.

8. Cold foods are better tolerated, because the odor of hot foods usually intensifies nausea. Clear liquids and bland foods are usually better tolerated and are easily digested. Food with a strong taste or smell commonly aggravates nausea.

Vomiting and fluid loss cause electrolyte depletion, which should be replaced parenterally.

Interventions *continued*

9. When nausea or vomiting is present, *administer anti-emetics and drugs with antiemetic properties* (such as phenothiazines, sedatives, or antihistamines), as ordered, 1 to 12 hours before chemotherapy and every 4 to 6 hours thereafter, for at least 12 to 24 hours.

Monitor, report, and document the effectiveness of medications.

10. Consult the doctor if weight loss, dehydration, or electrolyte imbalance persists.

11. Additional individualized interventions: _____

_____

_____

Outcome criteria

Within 1 day of admission, the patient will:
• increase oral intake to 2,000 ml.
Within 3 days of admission, the patient will:
• exhibit no weight loss
• maintain serum electrolyte levels within normal limits

Rationales *continued*

9. Antiemetic medications block stimulation of the true vomiting center and the chemoreceptor trigger zone in the brain, thus decreasing nausea and vomiting and promoting relaxation.

In order to maintain a therapeutic blood level, antiemetic medications must be administered around the clock rather than as needed.

10. Parenteral nutrition, such as central I.V., hyperalimentation, or tube feedings, may be necessary if catabolism persists.

11. Rationale: _____

_____

_____

• tolerate nutritional supplements between meals
• maintain intake equal to output
• have no nausea or vomiting
• retain 75% of food intake.

Nursing diagnosis: *Altered oral mucous membrane: stomatitis, related to decreased nutrition and immunosuppression secondary to disease process and cytotoxic effects of chemotherapy treatment*

NURSING PRIORITIES: (a) Minimize pain and discomfort from stomatitis, and (b) prevent further trauma and infection of the oral mucous membrane.

Interventions

1. *Assess for signs and symptoms of stomatitis,* such as dry, ulcerated oral mucosa, pain, viscous saliva, or difficulty in swallowing.

Document and report the condition of the oral mucous membrane—including the lips, tongue, and gums—on a scale of 1 to 4, with 1 being normal and 4 being ulcerated, bleeding, irritated, and infected. Also observe the amount and viscosity of saliva.

Obtain a culture of suspicious lesions, noting the results.

2. Teach an appropriate mouth care regimen.

• If platelet levels are above 40,000/mm³ and leukocyte levels above 1,500/mm³, recommend the following: brush the teeth with a soft, nylon-bristle toothbrush 30 minutes after meals and every 4 hours while awake. Place the brush at a 45-degree angle between the gums and the teeth, and move it in short horizontal strokes. Floss between teeth twice daily.

Rationales

1. Stomatitis is both a sign of leukemia secondary to decreased immunocompetence and a side effect of chemotherapy that develops 7 to 10 days after treatment begins.

Objective assessment is imperative for early identification of developing stomatitis so that appropriate therapy can be instituted.

2. Preventing accumulation of food debris and bacteria is essential to preventing breakdown of the oral mucous membrane.

• Take care to observe specified laboratory values, because if platelet counts are low, even this regimen will cause severe bleeding. If the WBC count is low, mouth care could cause local areas of infections.

(continued)

Interventions *continued*

• If platelet or leukocyte levels are below the parameters specified, recommend rinsing only (using water or saline) until the values return to safer levels.

3. Provide hydrogen peroxide and water solution (1:2 or 1:4), baking soda and water (1 tsp to 500 ml), or normal saline, to rinse the mouth during and after brushing.

4. Administer lidocaine (Xylocaine) viscous solution as needed, 1 tsp swished in the mouth every 3 to 4 hours, or acetaminophen with codeine elixir as needed, as ordered.

5. Lubricate lips with petrolatum or K-Y Lubricating Jelly, ChapStick, Blistex, or mineral oil. Use gauze lubricated with petrolatum for lip protection when the patient drinks from a cup or glass.

6. Encourage use of Ora-Lub, Salivart, Xero-Lube, or another artificial saliva product.

7. *Monitor, report, and document the appearance of white patches on the tongue and oral mucosa.* Administer nystatin (Mycostatin) oral suspension or a gentian violet preparation, as ordered. Document the patient's reponse to this therapy.

8. Apply substrate of milk of magnesia or a kaolin preparation with a swab or a gauze-covered tongue blade. To prepare the substrate, allow the bottle of milk of magnesia to stand for several hours, then pour off the supernatant liquid. Leave the substrate in contact with the oral mucosa for 15 minutes, then rinse with normal saline.

9. Additional individualized interventions: _____
_____
_____

Outcome criteria
Within 3 days of admission, the patient will:
• have no frank bleeding from gums
• show improved ability to swallow
• have decreased viscosity and improved amount of saliva.

Rationales *continued*

• For patients with low platelet or leukocyte levels, this regimen removes debris while minimizing the risks of bleeding or infection.

3. Commercial mouthwashes contain alcohol, which is drying and irritating to the oral mucosa.

4. Lidocaine is a topical anesthetic that relieves pain from mouth ulcers.
    Acetaminophen with codeine works systemically to control pain, and the elixir is easily swallowed.

5. Severe dryness, sores, and ulcerations on the lips cause pain when the patient drinks from a cup or glass. This pain further discourages the patient from drinking adequate fluids and maintaining an adequate fluid balance.

6. Severe dryness of the oral mucous membrane predisposes to tissue breakdown and impairs optimal nutritional intake. Artificial saliva supplements ease dryness, buffer acidity, and lubricate and soothe the mucous membrane.

7. These white patches indicate yeast infection. (The immunosuppressed patient is prone to opportunistic infections such as candidiasis.) Prompt treatment of oral infection will prevent undue discomfort.

8. Use of topical protective agents soothes irritated areas and promotes healing of mucosa.

9. Rationale: _____
_____
_____

Within 5 days of admission, the patient will:
• exhibit decreased number of open ulcers
• present negative cultures
• exhibit decreased areas of white patches.

Nursing diagnosis: *Potential ineffective coping related to uncertain prognosis and multiple disease- and treatment-induced losses*

NURSING PRIORITY: Promote healthy coping behavior.

Interventions

1. See the care plans "Death and Dying," "Grief/Grieving," and "Ineffective Individual Coping," pages 10, 41, and 51, respectively.

2. Additional individualized interventions: _____
_____
_____

Rationales

1. Patients with leukemia suffer multiple losses, and self-care ability, social contact, and energy level are reduced. Additionally, side effects from chemotherapy may cause body image changes that are difficult to accept. Weakness, dependence on others, and an uncertain prognosis may create anxiety or contribute to depression. The care plans listed provide specific interventions helpful in dealing with the psychosocial aspects of the care of the leukemic patient.

2. Rationale: _____
_____
_____

Outcome criteria
Throughout the period of hospitalization, the patient will:
• use healthy coping behaviors
• verbalize feelings.

Discharge planning

NURSING DISCHARGE CRITERIA
Upon discharge, documentation shows evidence of:
• absence of fever
• absence of cardiovascular or pulmonary complications such as rhonchi, crackles, dysrhythmias, or atelectasis
• stabilizing weight
• WBC count greater than 2,000/mm³
• platelet count greater than 50,000/mm³
• hemoglobin level above 8 g/dl
• hematocrit level above 25%
• absence of signs and symptoms of infection
• ability to tolerate adequate nutritional intake
• absence of gingival bleeding and sores
• absence of hematuria or other bladder or bowel dysfunction
• ability to control pain using oral medications
• ability to perform ADLs, transfers, and ambulation independently or with minimal assistance
• adequate home support system *or* referral to home care or nursing home if indicated by an inadequate home support system or the patient's inability to perform ADLs, transfer, ambulate, and follow medication regimen.
   Note: All patients with leukemia must be referred to the social service department. A check on financial considerations is always needed, because leukemia is a financially draining disease, commonly requiring long-term and expensive treatment. If the patient has terminal leukemia, he or she should be referred to a hospice.

PATIENT/FAMILY DISCHARGE TEACHING CHECKLIST
Document evidence that patient/family demonstrates understanding of:
__ diagnosis and course of treatment
__ all discharge medications' purpose, dosage, administration schedule, and side effects requiring medical attention (usual chemotherapy medications include alkylating agents, such as busulfan [Myleran] and chlorambucil [Leukeran], antibiotics such as daunorubicin and doxorubicin [Adriamycin], antimetabolites such as methotrexate and 6-mercaptopurine, and plant alkaloids such as vincristine and vinblastine)
__ ways of preventing and identifying infections
__ appropriate modifications of activity-rest patterns
__ ways of preventing, identifying, and reporting abnormal bleeding tendencies
__ techniques to control nausea, vomiting, and anorexia
__ recommended dietary modifications
__ techniques to prevent urinary calculi formation
__ appropriate oral hygiene techniques and procedures
__ signs and symptoms indicating relapse or exacerbation of disease
__ frequency of follow-up laboratory tests (patient's values compared with normal ones)
__ schedule for future diagnostic tests, chemotherapy administration, and appointments with health care providers
__ how to contact doctor

___ community resources for home management and life-style modifications; support groups
___ emotional response to chronic or terminal illness
___ changes in family role patterns.

DOCUMENTATION CHECKLIST
Using outcome criteria as a guide, document:
___ clinical status on admission
___ significant changes in status, especially development of CNS symptoms and septicemia
___ pertinent laboratory and diagnostic test findings
___ response to chemotherapy treatments
___ management of chemotherapy side effects
___ response to transfusions of RBCs, WBCs, or platelets
___ nutritional intake
___ fluid-electrolyte balance
___ activity-rest pattern
___ emotional coping patterns
___ condition of skin and mucous membranes
___ signs and symptoms of infection or bleeding tendencies
___ I.V. line patency and condition of veins
___ tolerance of diagnostic procedures
___ response to anti-infection measures.

ASSOCIATED CARE PLANS
Anemia
Death and Dying
Fluid and Electrolye Imbalances
Grief/Grieving
Ineffective Individual Coping
Total Parenteral Nutrition

REFERENCES
Becker, T. *Cancer Chemotherapy: A Manual for Nurses.* Boston: Little, Brown & Co., 1981.

Diseases, 2nd ed. Nurse's Reference Library. Springhouse, Pa.: Springhouse Corp., 1987.

Gordon, M. *Manual of Nursing Diagnoses: 1984-1985.* New York: McGraw-Hill Book Co., 1985.

Griffin, J. *Hematology and Immunology Concepts of Nursing.* East Norwalk, Conn.: Appleton-Century-Crofts, 1986.

Kneisl, C., and Ames, S. *Adult Health Nursing.* Reading, Mass.: Addison-Wesley Publishing Co., 1986.

Lewis, S., and Collier, I. *Medical-Surgical Nursing.* New York: McGraw-Hill Book Co., 1983.

McIntirl, S., and Cioppa, A. *Cancer Nursing: A Developmental Approach.* New York: John Wiley & Sons, 1986.

Marino, L. *Cancer Nursing.* St. Louis: C.V. Mosby Co., 1981.

Neoplastic Disorders. Nurse's Clinical Library. Springhouse, Pa.: Springhouse Corp., 1985.

Ulrich, S., et al. *Nursing Care Planning Guides: A Nursing Diagnosis Approach.* Philadelphia: W.B. Saunders Co., 1986.

Yasko, J. *Guidelines for Cancer Care: Symptom Management.* Reston, Va.: Reston Publishing Co., 1983.

Lymphoma

DRG information

DRG 400 [Surgical DRG] Lymphoma or Leukemia
    with Major Operating Room (OR) Procedure.
    Mean LOS = 11.2 days
    Major OR Procedures: Biopsy, Excision,
    or Incision.

DRG 401 [Surgical DRG] Lymphoma or Non-Acute
    Leukemia with Other OR
    Procedure. With Complication or
    Comorbidity (CC).
    Mean LOS = 9.8 days

DRG 402 [Surgical DRG] Lymphoma or Non-Acute
    Leukemia with Other OR Procedure.
    Without CC.
    Mean LOS = 4.6 days

DRG 403 [Medical DRG] Lymphoma or Non-Acute
    Leukemia. With CC.
    Mean LOS = 7.8 days

DRG 404 [Medical DRG] Lymphoma or Non-Acute
    Leukemia. Without CC.
    Mean LOS = 4.8 days

Additional DRG information: After hospitalization for
the staging workup and initial course of therapy, the
patient would most likely be treated as an outpatient
when receiving ongoing chemotherapy treatments.

Introduction
DEFINITION AND TIME FOCUS

Lymphoma is the abnormal, malignant proliferation and
enlargement of lymph nodes, spleen, and other lym-
phoid tissue, resulting in impaired cellular and humoral
immunity, obstruction and infiltration of adjacent structures, and systemic involvement. Lymphomas are classified as Hodgkin's (commonly called Hodgkin's
disease) or non-Hodgkin's.

Hodgkin's disease is characterized by contiguous
node involvement and, uncommonly, extranodal spread
at the time of diagnosis. Staging is important in Hodgkin's disease, as in other cancers, because it is used as
a basis for determining treatment and estimating prognosis. (See *Hodgkin's Disease*, page 438, for staging and
treatment guidelines for Hodgkin's disease.) Commonly,
the disease is only localized; fever, weight loss, and
night sweats (termed "B" symptoms in staging classification) are common (seen in about 40% of patients) at
presentation. Hodgkin's disease occurs most commonly
between age 15 and 35, with a second peak in occurrence between age 50 and 59.

Non-Hodgkin's lymphomas comprise many histologic
variations. They are characterized by noncontiguous
nodal spread, commonly with extranodal involvement,
usually in the GI tract, testes, central nervous system
(CNS), or bone marrow. The disease is usually disseminated; "B" symptoms occur in only about 20% of patients. Non-Hodgkin's lymphoma is three times more

common than Hodgkin's lymphoma in the United States
and can occur at any age, although peak incidence is
between age 50 and 60.

Both types of lymphoma are more common in males than
in females, and males tend to have a worse prognosis.

Hodgkin's and non-Hodgkin's lymphomas are considered together here because clinical presentation, diagnostic workup, treatment, and nursing management are
similar for both types. This care plan focuses on the
undiagnosed, symptomatic patient with lymphoma who
is admitted for a staging workup and initial course of
therapy.

ETIOLOGY/PRECIPITATING FACTORS

• viral etiology (suggested for some lymphomas. May involve a herpeslike virus related to Epstein-Barr virus)
• family history (increased incidence among family
members suggests genetic and environmental factors)
• environmental exposure to certain herbicides (such as
phenoxyacetic acid) linked to increased risk of non-
Hodgkin's lymphoma

Focused assessment guidelines
NURSING HISTORY (Functional health pattern findings)

Health perception–health management pattern
• *may report fever*—highest in the afternoon, often
twice-daily peaks greater than 101° F. (38.3° C.)
• *may report drenching night sweats*
• may report pruritus—more intense at night, worse
with bathing
• may report general malaise and fatigue
• *may report painless, swollen lymph nodes* (typically in
the cervical chain)

Nutritional-metabolic pattern
• *may report unexplained weight loss*
• may report anorexia
• may report pain in nodes immediately after drinking
alcohol (cause unknown)

Activity-exercise pattern
• *may report general fatigue:* "unable to do the things I
want to do"
• may report shortness of breath if ascites, pleural effusion, or anemia present

Sleep-rest pattern
• may report sleep disturbances from night sweats

Self-perception–self-concept pattern
• may report fear regarding prognosis and progression
of disease
• may report difficulty coping with changes in life-style,
self-esteem, and body image

HODGKIN'S DISEASE

STAGING CLASSIFICATION (ANN ARBOR)

Stage

I	Nodal involvement within one region
I E	Single extralymphatic organ or site
II	Nodal involvement within two or more regions, limited by the diaphragm
II E	Localized extranodal site and nodal involvement within one or more regions limited by the diaphragm
III	Nodal involvement of regions above and below the diaphragm
III E	With localized extralymphatic site
III S	With spleen involvement
III ES	Or both
IV	Diffuse or disseminated involvement of one or more extralymphatic organs or tissues, with or without lymph node involvement

DETERMINATION OF TREATMENT

Stage

I A	Radiation therapy
I B	Radiation therapy
II A	Radiation therapy
II B	Radiation therapy
III A	Radiation and chemotherapy (determined by presence of high-risk factors, which include bulky disease, large mediastinal mass, extranodal lesions, and hilar adenopathy)
III B	Chemotherapy
IV A	Chemotherapy
IV B	Chemotherapy

A = without fever, weight loss, and night sweats
B = with fever, weight loss, and night sweats

E = extralymphatic involvement
S = spleen involvement
ES = both extralymphatic and spleen involvement

Data from: Carbone, P., et al. "Report of the Committee on Hodgkin's Disease Staging," *Cancer Research* 31:1860, 1971.

Cognitive-perceptual pattern
• may or may not want to know prognosis and expected progression of disease

Role-relationship pattern
• may report concern regarding role reversals at home and inability to fullfill previous roles

Sexuality-reproductive pattern
• may express concern regarding side effects of chemotherapy on fertility and sexual performance
• may report decreased libido from chemotherapy, radiation, or general fatigue

Coping–stress tolerance pattern
• may report increased anxiety

PHYSICAL FINDINGS

Integumentary
• *lymphadenopathy*

Lymphoreticular
• tonsillar enlargement
• edema and cyanosis of face and neck (rare)

Pulmonary
• shortness of breath (rare)
• cough (rare)
• stridor (rare)
• signs of pleural effusion (rare)

*Extensive testing is necessary to diagnose and stage lymphoma.

Gastrointestinal
• splenomegaly
• hepatomegaly
• ascites (uncommon)
• jaundice (rare)

DIAGNOSTIC STUDIES*
• complete blood count (CBC) and platelet count—may reveal neutrophilic leukocytosis and mild normochromic anemia, lymphopenia, or increased sedimentation rate
• serum alkaline phosphatase values—increased values indicate liver or bone involvement
• direct Coombs' (antiglobulin) test—detects autoimmune hemolytic anemia (more common in non-Hodgkin's lymphoma)
• immunoglobulin studies—may show overproduction of immunoglobulin by proliferating B-cell lymphocytes
• *lymph node biopsy*—performed using the most central node of the involved group for biopsy. Hodgkin's disease shows *Reed-Sternberg cells*, non-Hodgkin's lymphoma reveals destruction of lymph node architecture; normal cellular elements are replaced by *increased lymphocytes and lymphoblasts.*
• *intravenous pyelogram*—used to detect unsuspected renal involvement and ureteral deviation and obstruction by involved nodes
• *chest X-ray*—with computed tomography (CT) scan, may reveal hilar lymphadenopathy; mediastinal masses in lymphoma usually appear as a dense rounded mass (oc-

curring as commonly in the anterior mediastinum as in the middle mediastinum)

• *lymphangiography—may show enlarged, foamy-looking nodes* (number of nodes affected, unilateral or bilateral involvement, and extent of extranodal involvement help determine stage); less useful in non-Hodgkin's lymphoma because does not visualize mesenteric nodes, which are usually involved; occasionally, nodes are so enlarged they cannot be visualized

• *abdominal (CT) scan—may detect intraabdominal intrapelvic nodal involvement as well as liver involvement*

• *bone scan—used to detect bone involvement*

• *bone marrow aspirate and biopsy—elevated lymphocyte values indicate bone marrow involvement* more common in non-Hodgkin's lymphoma

• bilateral bone marrow biopsies—commonly performed because of spotty bone marrow involvement chances of identifying bone marrow involvement are increased by 15% to 20% if bilateral procedure is performed

• lapanotomy and splenectomy—undertaken only if outcome will affect a therapeutic decision; may detect splenic involvement

POTENTIAL COMPLICATIONS
• intestinal obstruction and perforation
• ureteral obstruction
• sepsis (treatment-related)
• anemia
• thrombocytopenia (treatment-related)
• hyperuricemia (treatment-related)
• superior vena cava syndrome (airway occlusion related to edema from impaired superior vena cava drainage)
• spinal cord compression (rare)
• hypercalcemia (rare)
• sterility (treatment-related)
• secondary cancers (treatment-related)
• effusions—pleural, pericardial, or abdominal

Collaborative problem: *Potential respiratory compromise related to enlarged mediastinal nodes, pulmonary compression, and, for non-Hodgkin's lymphoma only, superior vena cava syndrome*

NURSING PRIORITY: Optimize alveolar ventilation.

Interventions

1. *Position the patient comfortably when short of breath,* usually with a 45 degree or greater elevation of the upper torso, shoulders tilted forward, arms supported away from sides, and feet supported.

2. *Teach and supervise use of therapeutic breathing techniques:*

• pursed-lip breathing

• abdominal diaphragmatic breathing.

3. *Limit activity* in accordance with respiratory capabilities.

4. Plan activities to allow minimal energy expenditure and adequate rest periods: provide bed baths, assist the patient with meals as needed, and limit visitors.

5. Decrease anxiety associated with dyspnea: explain all procedures in a calm, supportive manner; provide a quiet environment to promote adequate rest; and use relaxation techniques, music, and other diversionary activities.

Rationales

1. The position described promotes maximum aeration, because weight is taken off the shoulders and arms and all accessory muscles can be used solely for breathing.

2. Use of breathing exercises minimizes respiratory impairment.

• Pursed-lip breathing has two benefits: it creates a back pressure to the lungs, holding the airways open, and the prolonged expiration time slows the flow of air. Premature closure of the airways is prevented, allowing more complete emptying of the lungs.

• Use of the abdominal muscles aids the diaphragm during expiration. As the patient inhales, the abdominal muscles relax. During expiration, they contract and help the diaphragm to move upward to expel air.

3. Decreased activity decreases the need for oxygen.

4. Fatigue is both a symptom of hypoxemia and a cause of increased dyspnea. As respiratory muscles tire, respiratory excursion and alveolar ventilation drop, worsening hypoxemia and reinforcing the vicious circle of fatigue and dyspnea.

5. Anxiety and fear increase the heart rate, increasing the need for oxygen—already at a premium.

(continued)

Interventions continued

6. Control pain with analgesics, as ordered. Use non-pharmacologic pain control techniques also. See the "Pain" care plan, page 64.

7. *Monitor for signs and symptoms of suspected superior vena cava syndrome,* as follows:
• early—neck vein distention (especially on arising), change in collar size, headache
• advanced—progressive periorbital and facial edema, dizziness, cough, stridor, dysphagia, dyspnea
   Report such findings to the doctor immediately, and expedite transportation of the patient to the radiation therapy department, as ordered, if superior vena cava syndrome is identified.
   After radiation therapy, assess for indications of improvement: reduced edema, increased ease in swallowing, and improved respiratory parameters.

8. Administer tranquilizers, as ordered.

9. Additional individualized interventions: _____
_____
_____

Outcome criteria
Within 48 hours of admission, the patient will:
• demonstrate effective, regular use of breathing techniques
• verbalize pain relief

Rationales continued

6. Pain may be present if enlarged nodes are causing pressure on adjacent structures or compressing nerve roots. Pain control will help decrease anxiety, thereby allaying associated shortness of breath. The "Pain" care plan contains specific information and detailed interventions.

7. In superior vena cava syndrome, enlarged nodes put pressure on the superior vena cava, impairing normal venous drainage from the head and neck. The resulting progressive edema may lead to tracheal deviation and airway occlusion. Superior vena cava syndrome is considered an oncologic emergency. Radiation therapy is the treatment of choice: immediate therapy of 300 to 400 rads daily for 3 to 4 days, then completion of a full course of 3,000 to 6,000 rads. In most patients, symptoms should decrease rapidly, usually within 48 to 72 hours.

8. Physiologic reactions to anxiety include reactions of the autonomic nervous system, such as increased heart rate and respirations. Tranquilizers relieve anxiety without inducing sleep. The benzodiazepines appear to depress the CNS at the limbic and subcortical levels of the brain, producing sedation and relaxing skeletal muscles.

9. Rationale: _____
_____
_____

• tolerate increased activity level
• show relaxed posture and facial expression
• exhibit no head or neck cyanosis.

Collaborative problem: *Potential sepsis related to leukopenia, lymphopenia from bone marrow involvement, chemotherapy, and radiation therapy side effects*

NURSING PRIORITIES: (a) Maximize immunocompetence, and (b) prevent or promptly detect and treat suprainfection.

Interventions

1. *Prioritize patient care.* Care for neutropenic patients first.

2. *Observe good hand-washing technique.*

3. *Monitor daily white blood cell (WBC) counts and differentials.* Inform the patient and doctor of results daily.

Rationales

1. This minimizes risk of cross-contamination by caregiver.

2. The most important act for protection against infection is meticulous hand washing. Improper or infrequent hand washing is a well-known contributor to cross-contamination.

3. The degree of granulocytopenia indicates the degree of resistance of the host and is the most important factor in determining the risk of sepsis.

Interventions *continued*

4. *Use protective precautions protocol when the absolute granulocyte count is dangerously depressed,* typically when < 1,000/mm³. Protective measures should include:
• eating only cooked foods
• avoiding raw fruits and vegetables
• avoiding standing water (such as vases of flowers and fishbowls)
• not handling live flowers or plants.
Institute further protective measures according to hospital protocol, as indicated by the patient's condition.

5. *Assess actual and potential infection sites* at least every 8 hours, including the lungs, mouth, rectum, I.V. site, urine, vagina, and surgical incisions. Observe carefully for subtle changes in skin and mucous membrane color, texture, or sensation.

6. Screen and limit visitors. Prohibit visits by those with recent or current infections.

7. Institute the hospital's oral hygiene protocol. Monitor for oral herpes lesions and *Candida* stomatitis.

8. Avoid invasive measures, such as I.M. injections, enemas, rectal temperatures, suppositories, and indwelling urinary (Foley) catheters, whenever possible.

9. *Monitor temperature at least every 4 hours; if it is higher than 101.3° F. (38.5° C.) and the patient develops signs and symptoms of septic shock* (tachycardia, tachypnea, restlessness, confusion, cough, decreased pulse pressure, and cool extremities), *notify the doctor.*

10. Obtain blood, urine, throat, and sputum cultures, using correct technique, as ordered. Ensure that cultures are obtained before beginning antibiotic therapy.

11. *Report all positive blood cultures,* even if the patient is already taking antibiotics.

Rationales *continued*

4. The risk of infection increases significantly when the absolute granulocyte count ranges from 500 to 1,000/mm³ and persists for more than a few days. The absolute granulocyte count provides an indication of the number of mature WBCs, the ones most effective in fighting infection. To calculate it, add the percentage of polys (mature neurophils) reported and the percentage of bands (slightly immature neutrophils) reported; multiply the result by the WBC count. Protective precautions may decrease the amount of pathogenic organisms coming in contact with the immunosuppressed patient. Raw fruits and vegetables are sources of gram-negative bacilli; live plants and soil are sources of fungi. Standing water may provide a medium for growth of microorganisms, particularly *Pseudomonas.*

5. Early detection of infection may prevent serious complications and spread of infection. Early detection in the immunocompromised patient, however, is complicated by an altered inflammatory response. Classic signs and symptoms of infection (such as erythema, pus, and fever) may be masked in a neutropenic patient or in a patient taking steroids (a factor in many lymphoma protocols).

6. Minimizing exposure to microorganisms may help avert sepsis.

7. Patients with lymphoma are at increased risk for viral and fungal infections because of their impaired cell-mediated immunity. (T lymphocytes provide protection against viruses, fungi, and parasites.)

8. Intact skin is the body's first line of defense. Sweat glands and sebaceous glands keep bacterial flora under control. Lysozymes, secreted by the sweat glands, are antimicrobial enzymes that attack the cell walls of bacteria. Sebum, secreted by the sebaceous glands, has antifungal and antibacterial properties. Infections of the skin and blood may occur when invasive measures damage the integrity of the skin.

9. Septic shock (a medical emergency) is reversible in its early stages. Massive infection, usually from gram-negative bacteria, is the cause of septic shock. As the body fights the infection, the bacteria die, releasing endotoxins that in turn impair cell metabolism and damage surrounding tissue. Lysozomal enzymes, bradykinin, and histamine cause peripheral vasodilation and increased capillary permeability, resulting in peripheral pooling, inadequate venous return, and severely reduced cardiac output.

10. Cultures must be uncontaminated to reflect accurate diagnosis. Antibiotic therapy depends on current culture results.

11. When particular organisms are identified, antibiotic therapy should be modified based on antibiotic sensitivity.

(continued)

Interventions continued

12. *Administer antibiotics* only after obtaining blood and urine cultures, ideally within 60 minutes of detection of suspected sepsis. Give subsequent doses on time.

13. Additional individualized interventions: _____
_____
_____

Rationales continued

12. Prompt, timely administration of antibiotics is related to an increased survival rate in neutropenic patients. Therapeutic blood levels of medication must be maintained for effective treatment of sepsis.

13. Rationale: _____
_____
_____

Outcome criteria

After a full course of antibiotic therapy (5 to 10 days) and return to immune status, or 14 days after completion of chemotherapy cycle, the patient will:
• be afebrile
• show no signs of systemic or localized infection.

Collaborative problem: *Pruritus related to histamine and/or leukopeptidase release from WBCs and to side effects of radiation therapy*

NURSING PRIORITIES: (a) Relieve discomfort, and (b) prevent or minimize skin injury.

Interventions

1. *Promote adequate hydration:* 3,000 ml/day oral intake, unless contraindicated.

2. *Use emollient creams for skin.*

3. *Provide tepid, cooling baths.*

4. *Keep the patient's fingernails short.* Provide clean cotton gloves at night.

5. Use soap for sensitive skin.

6. Administer antihistamines, antibiotics, tar extracts, or chemotherapeutic agents, as ordered. Add urea to steroid creams to enhance absorption.

7. Instruct the patient to avoid harsh cold and wind.

8. Reduce excessive clothing or bedding; instruct the patient not to wear restrictive clothing.

Rationales

1. Adequate hydration is essential to minimize dryness.

2. Emollient creams are oil-in-water emulsions. Water keeps the skin moist while the oil creates an oily film, which helps skin hold the moisture by slowing normal evaporation.

3. Immunosuppressed individuals need the hygienic protection of bathing. Additionally, tepid water promotes vasoconstriction. Proteases are sensitive to heat, and the cutaneous nerve endings that mediate the scratch impulse are made more sensitive by vasodilation.

4. These measures may prevent damage to the skin if the patient cannot control scratching.

5. Soaps for sensitive skin have a large proportion of emollient oils and contain no detergents or dyes to strip the skin. They liquefy instantly and leave no residue on the skin to cause irritation.

6. Antihistamines will help if the underlying cause of pruritus is increased histamine release. Tar extracts and steroid topical creams may inhibit protease release. If infection is the underlying cause, antibiotics are indicated. If the tumor is releasing enzymes, chemotherapy may reduce its bulk and proportionately reduce the amount of enzyme being released.

7. Exposure decreases skin lubrication.

8. A cool environment promotes vasoconstriction. Restrictive clothing may physically irritate the skin.

9. Launder the patient's clothing using nondetergent cleanser, and rinse thoroughly.

9. These precautions remove sources of chemical irritation to the skin.

10. Additional individualized interventions: _____ _____ _____

10. Rationale: _____ _____ _____

Outcome criteria

Throughout the period of hospitalization, the patient will:
• present intact skin

• verbalize reduced discomfort
• list three self-care measures to minimize pruritus.

Collaborative problem: *Potential hemorrhage related to decreased platelets secondary to chemotherapy or radiation therapy side effects*

NURSING PRIORITY: Maximize the patient's available protective mechanisms.

Interventions

1. *Do not administer aspirin or aspirin-containing products.*

2. *Administer stool softeners*, as ordered, and monitor the frequency of stools to detect constipation.

3. Avoid such invasive measures as I.M. injections, enemas, and rectal suppositories.

4. Use an electric razor when shaving the patient. Avoid activities with potential for physical injury.

5. Administer steroids, as ordered, with milk products or antacids.

6. Maintain optimal nutritional status, encouraging high-protein intake.

7. Test all stool, emesis, and urine for occult blood.

8. Apply direct pressure to venipuncture sites for at least 5 minutes.

9. Administer platelet infusions, as ordered.

10. Use a soft-bristle toothbrush, and avoid flossing the patient's teeth.

11. Instruct the patient to avoid strenuous activity, Valsalva's maneuver, and lifting heavy objects.

Rationales

1. The acetyl group in the aspirin compound inhibits platelet aggregation, thereby impairing the process of fibrin strand formation. A single dose of aspirin produces an effect that remains for days, long after the aspirin has been metabolized and excreted.

2. Straining at stool produces excessive pressure on the anal orifice; the rectal area is highly vascular and has potential for hemorrhage.

3. Intact skin reduces the risk of bleeding episodes. A decreased platelet count means that even minor trauma may result in significant bleeding.

4. These measures minimize the risk of skin trauma.

5. This helps avoid gastric irritation by coating the stomach.

6. Protein is needed for production of megakaryocytes, precursors of platelets.

7. Early detection of bleeding sites can result in early and effective treatment.

8. Decreased availability of platelets prolongs clot formation time.

9. A platelet count below 20,000/mm³ increases the risk of a spontaneous hemorrhage. Active bleeding is an indication for platelet administration.

10. These measures decrease the risk of physical irritation to oral mucous membranes.

11. These activities increase intracranial pressure and may precipitate cerebrovascular hemorrhage.

(continued)

Interventions *continued*

12. Teach the patient self-protection measures related to the above interventions—for example, avoiding aspirin, taking stool softeners, and using an electric razor.

13. Additional individualized interventions: _____

_____

Rationales *continued*

12. The knowledgeable patient's active involvement in self-care minimizes the risk of hemorrhage, especially after hospital discharge.

13. Rationale: _____

_____

Outcome criteria
Throughout the hospitalization period, the patient will:
• have regular, soft, formed stools
• exhibit no uncontrolled bleeding.

Nursing diagnosis: *Nutritional deficit related to anorexia, taste alterations, fatigue, nausea and vomiting, and stomatitis*

NURSING PRIORITY: Promote adequate nutrition to enhance response to therapy and prevent complications.

Interventions

1. *Arrange for a dietary consultation* to address appropriate caloric and protein needs. Explore the patient's food preferences and attempt to obtain the foods requested. Explain prescribed dietary recommendations and help the patient set goals for meeting them.

2. Offer sandwiches and other cold foods.

3. *Avoid giving liquids with meals.*

4. *Avoid offering favorite foods during peak periods of nausea and vomiting* or while the patient is receiving chemotherapy.

5. Offer salty foods (such as broth or crackers) and tart foods (such as lemons or dill pickles) unless the patient has stomatitis.

6. *Offer small, frequent meals,* and encourage the patient to eat and drink slowly.

7. Avoid offering greasy foods.

8. Provide oral hygiene before mealtime and after vomiting episodes.

9. If taste alterations are present, consult with the dietary department and advise the patient to:
• Use plastic utensils instead of metallic silverware.
• Use meat substitutes (such as eggs, cheese, dried beans, and peanut butter).

Rationales

1. The dietitian's expertise may be helpful in planning a therapeutic diet that incorporates patient preferences. Including the patient in planning and goal-setting enhances compliance and promotes a sense of self-control.

2. The odor of hot foods commonly aggravates nausea.

3. Excessive intake of fluids with meals contributes to gastric distention and may reduce intake of solid foods.

4. Serving favorite foods during periods of nausea and vomiting may contribute to the development of aversion. During anorexic periods, favorite foods may supply the patient's only intake, so maintaining positive associations is essential.

5. These foods increase salivation and stimulate the taste buds. In patients with stomatitis, however, salt and acidity will further irritate open mucous membranes.

6. Small meals and slow eating minimize gastric distention, which leads to early satiety.

7. High-fat foods decrease gastric emptying time, causing feelings of overfullness and distention.

8. Oral hygiene refreshes the mouth and enhances the flavor of foods.

9. The presence of actively dividing cells that excrete amino acidlike substances enhances the bitter taste sensation. Large tumor load also increases the degree and duration of any taste sensation. Beef and pork have high amino acid levels. The presence of a negative ni-

Interventions *continued*

• Experiment with spices and flavorings to enhance taste sensation (such as mint, vanilla, lemon, and basil), unless contraindicated by the presence of stomatitis.

10. Advise the patient to use increased amounts of sugar and sweet foods.

11. Teach the patient how to use viscous lidocaine (Xylocaine) ("swish and swallow") 15 minutes before meals for stomatitis pain (15 ml/dose). If ineffective, try dyclonine (Dyclone).

12. Offer soft, moist foods, such as custards, ice cream, gelatins, cottage cheese, and ground meats with sauces and gravies.

13. Explore and experiment with various liquid and pudding supplements (such as Ensure, Isocal, and Enrich).

14. Consult with the doctor regarding temporary enteral or parenteral feedings if other interventions are ineffective.

15. Additional individualized interventions: _____
_____
_____

Rationales *continued*

trogen balance also decreases the threshold for the bitter taste sensation. Certain chemotherapy agents, specifically nitrogen mustard, cyclophosphamide, vincristine, and dacarbazine (DTIC) (all used in lymphoma protocols) contribute further to taste alterations.

10. Taste alterations associated with the disease process and chemotherapy commonly include decreased sensitivity to sweetness, although this is sometimes accompanied by an aversion to sweet foods. Increased sugar also boosts caloric intake.

11. A topical anesthetic, decreases the sensitivity of nerves, enabling the patient to eat without discomfort.

12. Soft foods minimize physical irritation to the oral mucous membrane and are easier to swallow.

13. High-calorie supplements may compensate for overall decreased intake.

14. The patient may need a temporary alternate route of nutrition to prevent severe malnutrition, which may alter response to an otherwise effective course of therapy.

15. Rationale: _____
_____
_____

Outcome criteria

Throughout the period of hospitalization, the patient will:
• participate in planning and implementing a dietary regimen
• maintain nutritional status adequate to facilitate therapy.

Nursing diagnosis: *Knowledge deficit related to self-care of central venous catheter or subcutaneous port*

NURSING PRIORITY: Teach self-care techniques and measures for home management of the central venous catheter or port.

Interventions

1. *Review with the patient the name of the catheter or port and its purpose and anatomical placement.*

Rationales

1. Central venous catheters or subcutaneous ports may be inserted to facilitate administration of chemotherapy. Patients who are knowledgeable about all aspects of their care are better prepared to make decisions based on good judgment and to teach others about their care. As the patient assumes greater responsibility for the device, an increased sense of control should result, easing incorporation of the device into the patient's body image.

(continued)

Interventions *continued*

2. *If the patient has a catheter, teach the patient the technique for dressing changes at home* (usually a clean, occlusive dressing changed when wet or soiled, or per protocol). Observe a patient demonstration and arrange for home care follow-up. If the patient has a subcutaneous port, explain that a dressing is not necessary at home because the device is completely under the skin.

3. *Teach the patient to identify early signs and symptoms of local or generalized infection,* such as redness, swelling, purulent drainage, fever, increased fatigue, and malaise.

4. *Teach the patient the appropriate irrigation technique,* the required frequency, the type of solution used, and the purpose of irrigation, as follows:
• for Hickman/Raaf types of catheters—Irrigate daily with 2 ml of heparin solution, whether or not the catheter is in use.
• for Groshong-type catheters—Irrigate with 5 ml normal saline once a week when not in use.
• for subcutaneous ports—Irrigate with 5 ml of heparin solution once a month when not in use.

5. *Inform the patient of potential complications and appropriate interventions,* as follows:

• clot formation (catheter will not irrigate): Avoid forcing irrigation if resistance is felt. Contact the doctor.
• catheter damage (break or cut in catheter): For the Hickman/Raaf types of catheter, clamp immediately with a toothless hemostat (send one home with the patient) and notify the doctor. For the Groshong type, wipe the proximal end clean and use a repair kit (send one home with the patient) to mend the distal portion or port.

• catheter displacement (catheter pulled out): Apply a pressure dressing and call the doctor. If bleeding is present, apply direct manual pressure until it stops.

6. *Give the patient appropriate names and telephone numbers of resource persons,* such as doctor, nutritional support services staff, emergency services, and the resource nurse.

7. Additional individualized interventions: _____

_____

_____

Rationales *continued*

2. Because the catheter exit site is a break in skin integrity, an increased risk exists for entry of opportunistic organisms. A clean occlusive dressing can decrease the potential for microbial contamination. The frequency of dressing changes varies among institutions.
    Anxiety may interfere with learning by decreasing the patient's ability to concentrate. Written materials and home care follow-up reinforce earlier learning and can be used in a less-threatening environment.

3. Early detection of infection results in more timely and effective treatment.

4. Although catheters and subcutaneous ports are in place continuously, they are used only intermittently for chemotherapy administration. Catheter or port patency must be maintained for the device to remain functional. Proper technique must be used to decrease the risk of contamination.

5. Recognizing complications may prevent a potentially hazardous situation—such as infection, tissue damage, catheter migration, or loss of device.
• Forcing irrigation may push a clot out the end of the catheter and into the circulatory system.
• Hickman/Raaf types of catheters may allow air to enter the vein when damaged. Immediate clamping stops any bleeding and prevents air influx. Groshong types of catheters have valvelike devices to prevent air influx and may be repaired by the patient using the kit provided.

• Pressure controls bleeding if the catheter is accidentally removed.

6. Notifying a health team member speeds resolution of a patient problem or concern. Knowing how and where to contact resource persons may help decrease anxiety and promote a sense of control.

7. Rationale: _____

_____

_____

Outcome criteria
By the time of discharge, the patient will:
• list signs of infection
• demonstrate dressing change and irrigation techniques as taught, if catheter is present

• list three possible complications and identify appropriate interventions for each if catheter is present.

Nursing diagnosis: *Disturbed self-concept: body image and/or self-esteem related to side effects of chemotherapy or radiation therapy*

NURSING PRIORITIES: (a) Prepare the patient for therapy, and (b) promote a positive self-concept.

Interventions

1. *Inform the patient of anticipated side effects of chemotherapy or radiation that will affect body image and role performance. Suggest measures to prevent or lessen their impact, as shown in table below.*

2. Inform male patients of the availability of sperm banking before beginning chemotherapy.

3. *Provide adequate time to discuss the patient's concerns and feelings.* Strive to maintain a nonjudgmental attitude. See the "Grief/Grieving," "Ineffective Family Coping," and "Ineffective Individual Coping" care plans, pages 41, 47, and 51, respectively.

4. *Include the patient in decision making.* Allow the patient to plan a schedule of the day's events (within hospital limitations).

Rationales

1. Chemotherapy protocols for lymphoma are aggressive combinations of agents that cause numerous side effects. Radiation therapy may also cause severe side effects. Teaching the patient about specific preventive or palliative measures before therapy begins increases the patient's sense of control, decreases powerlessness, and promotes self-image.

2. Because males are affected more commonly than females, and the peak incidence of Hodgkin's disease corresponds with peak childbearing years, fertility is a major concern. Chemotherapy may result in permanent sterility. Well-informed patients are able to make decisions based on sound judgment after considering available options.

3. Patients will be more likely to discuss their personal concerns if a trusting relationship is developed. Judgmental responses that reflect the caregiver's personal biases may inhibit open discussion. These care plans provide interventions helpful in addressing emotional needs.

4. Promoting maximum patient participation in care planning conveys respect and increases the patient's sense of control.

(continued)

SUGGESTIONS FOR MINIMIZING CHEMOTHERAPEUTIC SIDE EFFECTS

Alopecia
- Shampoo only one or two times weekly.
- Use a mild, protein shampoo.
- Avoid using an electric hair dryer or electric curlers.
- Avoid using hair spray or other drying products.
- Try a satin pillowcase to minimize tangling.
- Avoid excessive hair brushing or combing.
- Use a wide-toothed comb.
- Avoid using scalp hypothermia devices, which may reduce flow of medication to the head.

Weight gain
- Exercise regularly.
- Follow prescribed dietary guidelines.
- Select flattering, loose-fitting clothing.

Nausea/vomiting
- Avoid fatty, salty, or spicy foods.
- Use diversionary activities.
- Avoid eating or drinking for at least 1 hour before and after chemotherapy.
- Use a sedative that has amnesic effect (for example, lorazepam) before chemotherapy, if prescribed.
- Suggest that family members avoid perfumes, aftershaves, and other aromatic toiletries.

Constipation
- Maintain a diet high in fiber, bulk, and fluids.
- Exercise regularly.
- Use stool softeners.

Diarrhea
- Try adding nutmeg to foods.
- Avoid milk or milk products (except yogurt, which may be helpful).
- Ensure adequate replacement of fluid and potassium.

Depression
- Understand that this is normal and usually temporary.
- Identify and use resources for emotional support.

Sore throat/dysphagia
- Observe self closely while eating for sore throat or difficulty swallowing.
- Eat soft foods.
- Use topical anesthetics as prescribed.

Dermatitis
- Avoid using deodorants, cosmetics, or creams, unless prescribed.

Interventions continued

5. Instruct the patient and spouse (or partner) on specific sexual side effects of chemotherapy and radiation therapy—for example, decreased libido, decreased vaginal lubrication, and temporary impotence. Provide written material for specific interventions related to each. Encourage the couple to share concerns and ask questions.

6. Additional individualized interventions: _____
_____
_____

Rationales continued

5. Many side effects related to lymphoma therapy are temporary and will resolve with time. Fatigue, fear, anxiety, and lack of privacy may also contribute to problems. Many patients (and many health care professionals) are not well educated about sex or are uncomfortable discussing sexuality problems. Written information is a less threatening but effective means of providing this information. Sharing concerns may reduce anxiety for both patient and spouse (or partner).

6. Rationale: _____
_____
_____

Outcome criteria
Throughout the period of hospitalization, the patient will:
• verbalize feelings freely
• participate in decision making related to care.

By the time of discharge, the patient will:
• identify personal concerns that may affect self-concept

• identify personal or external resources to deal with concerns
• list measures to minimize effects of chemotherapy or radiation therapy.

Discharge planning
NURSING DISCHARGE CRITERIA
Upon discharge, documentation shows evidence of:
• stable vital signs
• absence of fever
• absence of cardiovascular or pulmonary complications
• ability to control pain using oral medications
• absence of bowel or bladder dysfunction
• WBC count within expected parameters
• absence of signs and symptoms of infection
• absence of supplemental oxygen and I.V. lines for at least 48 hours
• ability to tolerate adequate nutritional intake
• ability to perform activities of daily living and to ambulate independently or with minimal assistance
• ability to care appropriately for central venous catheter, if present
• adequate home support system or referral to home care or a nursing home if indicated by inadequate home support system or patient's inability to care for self.

PATIENT/FAMILY DISCHARGE TEACHING CHECKLIST
Document evidence that patient/family demonstrates understanding of:
__ disease process and progression
__ signs and symptoms of infection and preventive measures
__ all discharge medications' purpose, dosage, administration schedule, and side effects requiring medical attention (usual discharge medications may include antineoplastics, analgesics, stool softeners, antiemetics, and others, depending on symptoms)

__ purpose and results of radiation therapy, schedule for future treatments, and management of anticipated side effects
__ maintenance of indwelling central venous catheter
__ indications for seeking emergency medical care
__ services available from local American Cancer Society chapter
__ availability of home health services and ancillary support services
__ date, time, and location of next scheduled appointment
__ how to contact doctor.

DOCUMENTATION CHECKLIST
Using outcome criteria as a guide, document:
__ clinical status on admission
__ significant changes in clinical status
__ teaching about and response to diagnostic and staging workups
__ chemotherapy administration—I.V. line patency and site status, name of medication, dosage, and response (include teaching about protocol and patient's response)
__ skin integrity over irradiated areas
__ transfusion therapy and response or allergic reactions
__ nutritional status
__ status and maintenance of central venous catheter
__ referrals initiated
__ patient/family teaching
__ discharge planning.

ASSOCIATED CARE PLANS
Death and Dying
Fluid and Electrolyte Imbalances
Grief/Grieving
Ineffective Family Coping
Ineffective Individual Coping
Knowledge Deficit

REFERENCES
Brunner, L., and Suddarth, D. *The Lippincott Manual of Nursing Practice* 3rd ed. Philadelphia: J.B. Lippincott Co., 1982.

Burns, K., and Johnson, P. *Health Assessment in Clinical Practice.* East Brunswick, N.J.: Prentice-Hall, 1980.

Chernecky, C., and Ramsey, P. *Critical Nursing Care of the Client with Cancer.* East Norwalk, Conn.: Appleton-Century-Crofts, 1984.

Gordon, M. *Nursing Diagnosis: Process and Application.* New York: McGraw-Hill Book Co., 1982.

Hoar, S., et al. "Agricultural Herbicide Use and Risk of Lymphoma and Soft-Tissue Sarcoma," *Journal of the American Medical Association* 256(9): 1141-47, September 5, 1986.

Reheis, C. "Neutropenia: Causes, Complications, Treatment and Resulting Nursing Care," *Nursing Clinics of North America* 20(1), March 1985.

Rubin, P., ed. *Clinical Oncology: A Multidisciplinary Approach,* 3rd ed. New York: American Cancer Society, 1983.

Sheppard, K. "Care of the Patient with Superior Vena Cava Syndrome," *Heart & Lung* 636-43, November 15, 1986.

Terry, B. "Hodgkin's Disease and Non-Hodgkin's Lymphoma," *Nursing Clinics of North America* 20(1), March 1985.

Yasko, J. *Guidelines for Cancer Care: Symptom Management.* Reston, Va.: Reston Publishing Co., 1983.

Anorexia Nervosa and Bulimia

DRG information

Anorexia Nervosa
DRG 428 Disorders of Personality and Impulse Control.
    Mean LOS = 6.1 days

Bulimia
DRG 432 Other Diagnoses of Mental Disorders.
    Mean LOS = 4.2 days

Introduction
DEFINITION AND TIME FOCUS
Anorexia nervosa and bulimia are complex psychiatric disorders primarily affecting young women and characterized by abnormal eating patterns and eating-related behaviors. Anorexia nervosa is dramatic weight loss unrelated to organic causes: Intentional starvation, ritualistic or compulsive eating behaviors, and bizarre delusional disturbances in body image are part of the typical picture. Bulimia was once diagnostically associated with anorexia nervosa but is now viewed as a separate disorder. It is characterized by binge-purge cycles in which the patient consumes large quantities of usually high-calorie food, then uses laxatives or purgatives, fasts excessively, or induces vomiting, to rid the body of the calories consumed.

Anorexia patients may have associated binge-purge behaviors similar to those seen in bulimia, but the two disorders are distinguished from one another by several features. The body image–body concept distortion typical in anorexia nervosa is not usually present in bulimia; in fact, the bulimic patient may maintain normal or even above-normal weight with frequent, sometimes abrupt fluctuations. Usually, the bulimic patient displays more insight into the abnormal character of the eating behaviors, whereas the anorectic patient may be more secretive about them and less able to recognize them as potentially harmful.

In persons with either disorder, life-threatening physical complications related to the physiologic effects of malnutrition may occur. Estimates of the mortality for patients with these disorders vary but range as high as 21% in anorexia nervosa.

Treatment recommendations also vary widely. Some clinicians advocate rigorous behavior modification techniques; other use in-depth psychotherapy, psychoanalysis, family therapy, or a combination of approaches. When these patients present on an inpatient medical-surgical unit, the immediate primary focus is likely to be controlled nutritional replenishment, prevention of further complications, restoration of physiologic equilibrium, and concurrent initiation of appropriate psychiatric treatment.

This clinical plan focuses on the anorectic or bulimic patient admitted for diagnosis and management of severely disruptive and potentially dangerous eating patterns.

ETIOLOGY/PRECIPITATING FACTORS
No clear-cut or consistent factors have been identified as causing these disorders. Instead, a combination of complex psychodynamic, familial, and societal factors appears to be involved.
- psychodynamic
    □ developmental deficits related to issues of loss, separation, sexuality, autonomy, and power
    □ sense of ineffectiveness
- familial
    Anorexia nervosa:
    □ perfectionistic or overprotective families
    □ pattern of avoiding family conflicts
    □ lack of conflict-resolution skills
    Bulimia:
    □ perfectionistic or overprotective families, *or* families lacking clear interpersonal boundaries or roles
- societal
    □ emphasis on being thin and exercising as a basis for peer acceptance
    □ thin societal image of beauty for females
- cultural
    □ seen in all economic, cultural, and religious groups
    □ less common among blacks and southern Europeans
- gender-linked
    □ predominantly adolescent girls and young women affected, with a small percentage of males

Focused assessment guidelines
NURSING HISTORY (Functional health pattern findings)

Health perception–health management pattern
Anorexia nervosa:
- *onset may have followed a successful diet taken to extremes* (a typical finding in adolescent girls)
- may report pleading, punitive measures, or arguments by others to eat, with no effect on eating patterns
- may report frequent pressure to seek treatment

Bulimia:
- *onset may have followed actual or impending separation from home* (a typical finding in young adult women age 18 to 25)
- may have begun as a quick weight-loss attempt and escalated to a compulsive need to binge, followed by vomiting
- may have a history of an undiagnosed anorectic episode in adolescence
- may report a history of drug or alcohol abuse

Nutritional-metabolic pattern
Anorexia nervosa:
- likely to report absence of hunger

• may report a variety of reasons for restricting food intake, such as GI discomfort, food allergies, or dislike for certain foods
• may urge foods on others—for example, brothers or sisters
• *may report rituals occurring at mealtimes, with an excessive amount of time spent over each meal*
• may express interest in recipes and cooking
• likely to eat low-calorie, low-fat, low-carbohydrate, and "diet" foods
• family may report patient hiding or hoarding food

Bulimia:
• may complain of difficulty breathing after bingeing
• likely to report planning of, or preoccupation with, bingeing and purging
• typically reports secretive binge eating but may binge with others (a group binge)
• may report a history of hiatal hernia
• may report esophageal or GI discomfort
• *likely to report eating high-carbohydrate foods during a binge but eating balanced meals or "diet" food at regular meals*

Elimination pattern
Anorexia nervosa:
• likely to report chronic constipation
• may report vomiting, self-induced or spontaneous

Bulimia:
• may report constipation or diarrhea
• likely to report constipation if abuse of laxatives has been relinquished
• may report permanent loss of bowel reactivity once laxatives are discontinued (rare)
• *may report vomiting, most commonly self-induced and less commonly accompanied by nausea*
• *may also report spontaneous regurgitation*

Activity-exercise pattern
Anorexia nervosa:
• *may report a high level of energy*
• may report exercising secretly after meals
• *may report a history of rigidly scheduled and compulsive exercise*
• may report emotional distress when exercise is not possible or is interrupted
• may report an extremely structured and active life-style

Bulimia:
• *all of the above,* plus may report lethargy after bingeing

Sleep-rest pattern
Anorexia nervosa and bulimia:
• may report sleep disturbances
• may report dreams about food or eating
• may report nocturnal binges after delaying food intake during the day

Cognitive-perceptual pattern
Anorexia nervosa:
• *may exhibit dichotomous thinking,* that is, an all-or-nothing attitude toward many issues
• *may report preoccupation with food, weight, and diets*
• *typically denies feelings of hunger, along with denial of any other needs*
• *typically denies seriousness of weight loss, weight loss itself, and body image distortion*
• may report blurred vision
• may report difficulty concentrating
• may report auditory disturbances
• may report dizziness or headaches

Bulimia:
• may exhibit dichotomous thinking
• may report preoccupation with food, weight, or diets
• *may acknowledge need for treatment and report distress over bingeing; less commonly, reports distress about purging behavior*

Self-perception–self-concept pattern
Anorexia nervosa and bulimia:
• may report guilt over "worrying" others or "being a burden" because of disorder
• *may exhibit body-image distortion—for example, may report "feeling fat" despite being at normal or below-normal weight*
• may report feelings of low self-esteem or self-loathing alternating with feelings of superiority

Role-relationship pattern
Anorexia nervosa:
• may describe self as compliant and introverted or shy with others
• *commonly reported by others as being "a good girl" who had no problems before the onset of the eating disorder*

Bulimia:
• *same as above,* or may report temper outbursts followed by guilt

Sexuality-reproductive pattern
Anorexia nervosa:
• commonly reports sexual inactivity
• commonly denies use of masturbation
• reports feelings of shame, guilt, or disgust regarding sexuality or sexual functioning
• *denies having any sexual desires*
• may report amenorrhea

Bulimia:
• same as above, *or* reports episodes of sexual promiscuity that are impulsive or compulsive in nature
• *may report a history of sexual abuse* by others

Coping–stress tolerance pattern
Anorexia nervosa:
• *may exhibit a perfectionistic, obsessive, and compulsive personality*
• may report a feeling of well-being from control of body size through food restriction and exercise

Bulimia:
• same as above, *or may exhibit a pattern of losing control through impulsive behaviors, then regaining control through purging, exercise, or (less commonly) self-mutilation*

Value-belief pattern
Anorexia nervosa:
• may express belief that to negate needs and desires is "good," to "give in" to needs and desires is "bad"
• *may equate being thin with being happy*

Bulimia:
• same as above
• may wish to be anorectic, expressing shame over loss of control
• more commonly than the anorectic, may express distress over symptoms and behaviors

PHYSICAL FINDINGS
General appearance
Anorexia nervosa:
• *commonly 20% to 25% below normal weight for height and frame*

Bulimia:
• *commonly low-normal to high-normal weight range*
• less commonly obese

Cardiovascular
Anorexia nervosa:
• *hypotension*
• *bradycardia*
• *hypothermia*
• *edema*, possibly generalized

Bulimia:
• *dysrhythmias*
• finger clubbing
• dehydration
• *rebound water retention* (on cessation of purging)

Gastrointestinal
Anorexia nervosa:
• vomiting
• *constipation or diarrhea*

Bulimia:
• erosion of dental enamel
• irritation of esophagus or chronic hoarseness
• reddened throat
• swollen salivary glands, especially parotids
• steatorrhea
• constipation or diarrhea

Neurologic
Anorexia nervosa:
• *hyperactivity*
• poor motor control
• paresthesias
• hypersensitivity to noise and light

Bulimia
• seizures
• weakness and lethargy

Integumentary
Anorexia nervosa:
• *cyanotic or yellow-tinged skin*
• *hair loss*
• *growth of lanugo*
• redness of extremities
• poor skin turgor

Bulimia:
• dry skin and hair
• pale color

Musculoskeletal
Anorexia nervosa:
• *emaciated appearance*
• loss of muscle mass

Bulimia:
• tetany (rare)

Genitourinary
Anorexia nervosa:
• chronic or persistent infection in the vaginal and urinary tracts

DIAGNOSTIC STUDIES*
• complete blood count (CBC) with differential—may indicate anemias or blood dyscrasias associated with malnutrition
• urinalysis and culture and sensitivity testing—may indicate renal dysfunction, dehydration, or infection related to malnourished state
• chemistry panel—may indicate electrolyte imbalances, such as hypokalemia or hypocalcemia
• growth hormone—may be overactive
• luteinizing hormone—may be low because of decreased body fat
• follicle-stimulating hormone—may be low
• thyroid (T_3, T_4, renal uptake, and plasma T_3 levels)—may be low
• fasting plasma cortisol levels—may be high
• testosterone levels (in males)—may be low
• dexamethasone suppression test (if indicated)—may show nonsuppression of adrenal response
• chest X-ray—may indicate pulmonary edema or congestive heart failure
• EKG—may indicate dysrhythmias

POTENTIAL COMPLICATIONS
Anorexia nervosa and bulimia:
• cardiac arrest (from hypokalemia)
• dysrhythmias
• starvation
• amenorrhea or irregular menses (exact etiology unknown)
• dental caries (from vomiting)
• peripheral myopathy and cardiomyopathy (with ipecac syrup use)

*Initial laboratory data may reflect no abnormalities.

- gastric dilatation and perforation (from refeeding)
- congestive heart failure
- blood disorders (from malnutrition)
- osteoporosis (from hypocalcemia)

- insulin-dependent (Type I) diabetes (relationship to eating disorders is not clearly understood)
- liver damage
- renal damage

Nursing diagnosis: *Nutritional deficit related to inadequate food intake and/or purging behavior*

NURSING PRIORITY: Establish and monitor safe and controlled refeeding.

Interventions

1. *On admission, perform a baseline nutritional assessment,* noting weight in relation to height, body protein stores, skin and hair condition, and fluid and electrolyte status. See the "Total Parenteral Nutrition" care plan, page 265, for further details.

2. *With the doctor and dietitian, plan the type, amount, and route of refeeding* based on the individual's nutritional needs and ability to comply with the refeeding plan. *Discuss the plan in advance with the patient,* including a clear explanation of the alternative procedures for feeding (tube feeding or hyperalimentation) if the patient does not comply with the plan for oral food intake. If a nasogastric (NG) tube is used, remove it after each feeding.

3. *Provide emotional support while closely monitoring intake and output of both food and fluids.* Avoid authoritative attitudes. Convey an attitude of warm yet firm support and consistent expectations.

4. *Set and maintain specific limits* regarding the amount of time allowed for meals or tube feedings, the amount of intake, and the privileges linked to compliance. Ensure that the patient and all personnel working with or around the patient are aware of the limits.

5. *Provide one-to-one supervision during meals.*

6. *Monitor weight* at the same time daily, ensuring that the patient is wearing only a hospital gown. Reward meeting weight goals by increasing privileges.

7. *Monitor vital signs* at least every 8 hours.

Rationales

1. Baseline assessment of nutritional status is essential for development of a refeeding plan. The "Total Parenteral Nutrition" care plan contains more detailed information on nutritional assessment.

2. Refeeding must be carefully controlled in order to avoid too-rapid weight gain with subsequent psychological and physiologic trauma. Resistance to taking any nutrition may be so strong that tube feeding or hyperalimentation must be instituted. A clear understanding, in advance, of alternative methods if the patient refuses to eat provides choices and may minimize manipulative behavior. If the patient does not take food orally, an NG tube may be inserted for feeding of a previously specified amount of liquid nutrients. Use of this method is controversial. If it is used, a matter-of-fact, nonpunitive attitude is essential to minimize feelings of powerlessness. The patient may try to siphon food back out of the stomach if the tube is left in place.

3. Feelings of powerlessness are increased as refeeding begins. A careful tally of intake and output is essential in assessing the adequacy of the feeding plan. Consistency reduces manipulative behavior.

4. Limit-setting conveys caring and clear expectations, helping to minimize manipulative behavior. If all personnel (including nonnursing staff such as housekeepers and laboratory technicians) are not made aware of the limits, the patient may be able to circumvent the diet plan by manipulating others.

5. Refusal to eat and hiding or hoarding food may occur as a means of controlling weight gain.

6. Weight gain provides objective measurement of nutritional status improvement. Weighing at the same time daily ensures consistency. The patient may try to hide objects in clothing in order to increase weight if weighed in street clothes.

7. Hypotension and bradycardia may be present on admission from malnourishment and dehydration. Vital signs should reflect improvement as refeeding is instituted.

(continued)

Interventions *continued*

8. *Observe for signs and symptoms of hypokalemia and hypovolemia:* weakness, irregular pulse, paresthesias, and hypotension. Maintain a normal fluid and electrolyte balance, including administering I.V. electrolyte replacements, as ordered by the doctor. See the "Fluid and Electrolyte Imbalances" care plan, page 21, for details.

9. When the patient refuses to eat, avoid excessive attentiveness while carrying out alternative feeding measures.

10. *Ensure that the patient is referred to a psychiatric specialist in eating disorders.*

11. Additional individualized interventions: _____
_____
_____

Rationales *continued*

8. Hypokalemia-induced dysrhythmias may be fatal, and severe hypovolemia can provoke cardiovascular collapse. Specific signs, symptoms, and interventions associated with hypokalemia and hypovolemia are contained in the "Fluid and Electrolyte Imbalances" care plan.

9. Providing extra attention, even if negative, when the patient refuses food may be perceived as an indirect reward for such behavior, contributing to the self-destructive cycle.

10. Treating the nutritional deficit and other life-threatening manifestations is essential, but ongoing psychiatric therapy is also necessary for definitive treatment of these complex disorders.

11. Rationale: _____
_____
_____

Outcome criteria
Throughout the period of hospitalization, the patient will:
• verbalize understanding of the diet plan and alternatives

• gain weight according to preestablished goals
• show improving vital signs as refeeding progresses
• show no evidence of dysrhythmias.

Nursing diagnosis: *Powerlessness related to inability to identify and meet emotional, physical, sexual, and social needs resulting from conflict between familial and societal expectation of focus on others' needs and negation of own needs*

NURSING PRIORITIES: (a) Help the patient identify emotional, physical, sexual, and social needs, and (b) explore ways in which identified needs can be met.

Interventions

1. *Be aware that the issue of control permeates all aspects of the patient's personal life.*

2. *Encourage activities on the unit that foster socialization and mutual sharing.*

3. *Encourage self-nurturing behaviors* while discouraging self-destructive behaviors. Observe for signs of depression, anxiety, or suicide potential, such as withdrawal, lack of eye contact, agitation, frequent references to death or self-destructive activities, or sudden improvement in a previously depressed patient.

Rationales

1. Fear of losing control may relate to anxiety over eating or sexual issues. Fear of becoming "fat" commonly correlates with anxiety over potential for promiscuous behavior.

2. Patients with eating disorders tend to be isolated because of feelings of shame or fear of "not measuring up" to others. If these feelings are explored in a group setting, as they occur, the patient will learn to seek feedback from others. This learning process increases the patient's sense of power and control.

3. Once needs are identified and attempts are made to meet them, the patient may sabotage or "spoil" her progress. The patient with an eating disorder believes that her needs are "bad" and that *she* is bad for "wanting." She may become so uncomfortable with her needs that suicide appears an acceptable option. Sudden improvement of mood in a previously depressed patient may indicate reduction in anxiety over suicidal thoughts because the patient has decided to kill herself.

Interventions continued

4. *Give positive reinforcement for expressing and meeting personal needs* in spite of fears of losing control.
• Encourage expression of anger, and help the patient learn assertive conflict-resolution skills, especially in interactions with family.
• Help the patient identify non-food-related goals.
• Provide opportunities for creative expression.

5. Additional individualized interventions: _____
_____
_____

Outcome criteria
Within 1 week of admission, the patient will:
• establish a regular pattern of socialization and sharing with others, if only on a superficial level, without undue anxiety
• identify one non-food-related goal.

Rationales continued

4. Once needs are identified and met and the patient's worst fears are not realized, she will be able to achieve a sense of satisfaction from being self-nurturing. Families may need guidance in learning to react supportively to expressions of anger instead of withdrawing affection. Identifying goals promotes a sense of self-control. Creative expression may facilitate recognition of previously "unacceptable" feelings.

5. Rationale: _____
_____
_____

Several weeks to months after discharge, the patient will:*
• engage spontaneously in self-nurturing behaviors without self-sabotage
• respond to familial and societal expectations in ways that do not negate personal goals
• participate in creative activity.

Nursing diagnosis: *Disturbed self-concept: self-esteem related to perfectionism, sense of inadequacy, or possible dysfunctional family dynamics*

NURSING PRIORITY: Promote a healthy self-image.

Interventions

1. *Provide a positive role model* for the patient by displaying a consistent, caring, truthful attitude and realistic self-acceptance.

2. *Promote activities that have a high probability of resulting in success,* beginning with simple tasks and gradually increasing the amount of effort required. Making the bed, cleaning the room, and helping another patient with room-cleaning are examples of tasks that are related but that require increasing effort. Praise and recognize successes.

3. Initiate referrals to an occupational or physical therapist as appropriate. Link these privileges to continued compliance with the dietary plan and make sure the patient is aware of this linkage. Consult with other therapists to ensure consistency in carrying out the treatment plan.

4. *If family dysfunction is identified, encourage family members to consider family therapy.*

Rationales

1. If the family unit is dysfunctional, the patient may have had limited opportunity for role or behavior testing. A "safe" setting such as the hospital may encourage healthful identification and experimentation.

2. Successful achievement, even in small activities, provides a sense of satisfaction and helps decrease depression and feelings of inadequacy. Helping others involves increased effort and promotes realistic self-appraisal as the patient receives positive feedback from others.

3. Diversionary activity decreases boredom and improves the patient's general feeling of well-being. Adjunctive therapies may also provide avenues for demonstrating success in terms of goal achievement.

4. The "identified patient's" behavior usually reflects underlying family psychopathology.

(continued)

*Because of their long-term nature, these criteria will not be met during any one hospitalization. They are included here so the nurse is aware of them and can recognize and reward steps toward meeting them.

Interventions *continued*

5. Observe the patient's interactions with others, and provide support and positive reinforcement when the patient is able to identify emotions and express them clearly—particularly "negative" feelings such as anger. Encourage assertiveness.

6. Additional individualized interventions: _____

_____

_____

Rationales *continued*

5. Patients with eating disorders may be using eating behaviors as a means of self-assertion, even though this is self-destructive. Learning that it is acceptable to express feelings more directly and forcefully may decrease attachment to eating behavior as a coping device and promote a more positive self-image.

6. Rationale: _____

_____

_____

Outcome criterion
By the time of discharge, the patient will:
• express feelings assertively.

Nursing diagnosis: *Disturbed self-concept: body image related to intense fear of becoming fat secondary to unrealistic and perfectionistic expectations concerning physical appearance*

NURSING PRIORITY: Create greater, more-accurate awareness of body image in order to decrease body loathing.

Interventions

1. *Provide experiential exercises that depict the patient's body-image distortion.* Use photographs, videotapes, body tracings, or measurements as appropriate.

2. Encourage the patient to explore family beliefs and attitudes (especially her mother's) regarding food, eating, and body image.

3. Additional individualized interventions: _____

_____

_____

Rationales

1. Providing an objective measure such as body tracings or videotapes can highlight discrepancies between the perceived and actual body images.

2. Unrealistic and perfectionistic attitudes about one's body are taught by the family as well as by society. Such attitudes need to be questioned in a supportive manner. The mother's attitudes are important because she is the primary and earliest object of identification.

3. Rationale: _____

_____

_____

Outcome criteria
Within 1 week of admission, the patient will:
• make fewer statements indicating body loathing
• increasingly verbalize doubt about unrealistic beliefs and attitudes.

Several weeks to months after discharge, the patient will:
• exhibit decreased boundary diffusion, that is, show

greater understanding of differentiation between her own and her mother's body
• demonstrate increased awareness of body image distortion and how it relates to disordered eating.

Discharge planning
NURSING DISCHARGE CRITERIA
Upon discharge, documentation shows evidence of:
• stable vital signs
• stabilizing weight
• electrolytes and CBC within normal parameters
• I.V. lines or hyperalimentation feedings, if used, discontinued for at least 48 hours
• adequate oral nutritional intake

• ability to comply with refeeding regimen
• absence of cardiovascular or pulmonary complications
• motivation to continue psychotherapy on outpatient basis
• referral for ongoing psychiatric follow-up.

PATIENT/FAMILY DISCHARGE TEACHING CHECKLIST
Document evidence that patient/family demonstrates understanding of:
___ physical status at time of discharge

___ warning signs of hypokalemia, dehydration, or any other physical complications of fasting, bingeing, or purging

___ all discharge medications' purpose, dosage, administration schedule, and side effects requiring medical attention

___ dietary plan

___ community resources for support

___ helpful attitudes and behaviors family members can exhibit toward the patient

___ attitudes and behaviors to avoid

___ reminder that treatment for persons with eating disorders is long-term and involves the family as well as the patient

___ date, time, and location of follow-up appointments

___ emergency telephone numbers to use when the patient or family is in crisis.

DOCUMENTATION CHECKLIST
Using outcome criteria as a guide, document:

___ clinical status on admission and discharge

___ significant changes in clinical status

___ completion of all diagnostic studies and laboratory tests indicated by clinical status on admission, with repeat testing of all abnormal findings

___ eating pattern before and at discharge

___ exercise pattern

___ daily weights

___ any occurrence of vomiting, prohibited exercise, or unprescribed use of laxatives or diuretics

___ daily mental status, including assessment for depression, suicide potential, and body-image distortion

___ sleep patterns

___ complete intake and output records, especially use of I.V., hyperalimentation, or tube feeding

___ patient/family teaching, including medication teaching

___ discharge planning.

ASSOCIATED CARE PLANS
Chronic Renal Failure
Fluid and Electrolyte Imbalances
Ineffective Family Coping
Ineffective Individual Coping

REFERENCES
Garner, D., and Garfinkel, R. eds. *Handbook of Psychotherapy for Anorexia Nervosa and Bulimia.* New York: Guilford Press, 1985.

Kneisl, C.R., and Ames, S.W. *Adult Health Nursing: A Biopsychosocial Approach.* Menlo Park, Calif.: Addison-Wesley Publishing Co., 1986.

Schultz, J.M., and Dark, S.R. *Manual of Psychiatric Care Plans.* Boston: Little, Brown & Co., 1982.

Section III

Selected condensed care plans, arranged alphabetically, provide a database for quick review of problems, interventions, teaching, and documentation.

Acquired Immune Deficiency Syndrome

COLLABORATIVE PROBLEM: *Immunosuppression related to low number of T_4 lymphocytes and/or low T_4-to-T_8 ratio*
Interventions
1. Wash your hands upon entering and leaving the patient's room. Screen visitors and care providers for signs and symptoms of infection. Institute appropriate protective measures.
2. Monitor vital signs at least every 4 hours, and report abnormalities.
3. Monitor the complete blood count daily, and report increasing leukopenia or neutropenia.
4. Assess for signs and symptoms of neurologic infection.
5. Monitor potential infection sites daily. Teach the patient to observe for new findings and report them promptly.
6. Assess lung sounds at least every 8 hours, and report abnormalities.
7. Obtain cultures, as ordered. Check and report sensitivity results.
8. Administer antibiotics, as ordered, observing for untoward side effects.
9. Provide patient teaching if the patient is on zidovudine (Retrovir) therapy.
10. Medicate for fever, as ordered.
11. Monitor for dehydration signs. Institute fluid replacement therapy as indicated and ordered.
12. Institute cooling measures as indicated for fever.
13. Additional individualized interventions:_____
_____

NURSING DIAGNOSIS: *Potential ineffective coping related to diagnosis of life-threatening illness, potential loss of ability to maintain usual roles, decisions regarding treatment options, and/or poor prognosis for long-term survival*
Interventions
1. Assess for signs of excessive anxiety.
2. Introduce yourself and other caregivers, and ensure continuity of caregivers. Demonstrate acceptance by use of touch, eye contact, and active listening.
3. Implement measures to promote physical relaxation.
4. Encourage verbalization of feelings. Anticipate and accept normal responses of fear, guilt, and anger. Provide for ongoing mental health intervention.
5. Identify and discuss any unhealthy coping behaviors, if observed.
6. Help the patient identify and list specific anxiety-related fears and concerns, focusing on modifiable factors.
7. Help the patient identify and activate resources.
8. Acknowledge "unknowns" of acquired immune deficiency syndrome (AIDS); provide accurate responses to questions, and validate the normality of the patient's responses to loss.

See the "Death and Dying" and "Grief/Grieving" care plans, pages 10 and 41, respectively.
9. Additional individualized interventions: _____
_____
_____

COLLABORATIVE PROBLEM: *Potential hypoxemia related to ventilation/perfusion imbalance, pneumonia, and weakness*
Interventions
1. Assess continuously for signs of hypoxemia. Monitor arterial blood gas measurements and report findings. Prepare the patient for possible ventilatory support, as needed.
2. Administer oxygen therapy, as ordered.
3. Perform airway clearance measures as needed.
4. Observe for postbronchoscopy complications.
5. Evaluate and document respiratory parameters—cough, sputum, respiratory effort, skin color, breath sounds, and activity tolerance—at least every 8 hours and as needed. Be alert for changes in level of consciousness.
6. Watch for respiratory depression if narcotic analgesics are used.
7. Help with self-care as needed, and teach energy conservation measures.
8. Additional individualized interventions: _____
_____
_____

NURSING DIAGNOSIS: *Sensory-perceptual alteration related to disease-related neurologic involvement*
Interventions
1. Assess the patient's mental and neurologic status on admission and daily.
2. Consider depression, grieving, and medication side effects when assessing the patient's mental and neurologic status.
3. Assess for vision changes, and institute protective measures as needed.
4. If confusion occurs, provide cues for reorientation.
5. Explain neurologic symptoms to the patient and to significant others, emphasizing supportive behaviors.
6. Ensure environmental safety according to the deficits present.
7. Observe for indications of distal symmetrical sensorimotor neuropathy.
8. Additional individualized interventions: _____
_____

NURSING DIAGNOSIS: *Social isolation related to communicable disease, associated social stigma, and fear of infection from social contact*
Interventions
1. Assess the patient's support systems.
2. Provide opportunities for the patient and family to express feelings.

3. Provide an atmosphere of acceptance.

4. Teach significant others about ways the AIDS virus is *not* transmitted.

5. Provide the patient and family with telephone numbers of available resources.

6. Additional individualized interventions: _____

_____

_____

NURSING DIAGNOSIS: *Activity intolerance related to fatigue and weakness, hypoxemia, depression, alterations in sleep patterns, side effects of medications, and orthostatic hypotension*

Interventions

1. Assess for signs of activity intolerance, and adjust activities to minimize hypoxemia.

2. Help the patient prioritize activities and set limits.

3. Assess the need for pharmacologic sleep aids.

4. Space care activities.

5. Institute precautions for weakness or orthostasis.

6. Assist with activities of daily living as needed.

7. Additional individualized interventions: _____

_____

_____

NURSING DIAGNOSIS: *Nutritional deficit related to nausea, vomiting, diarrhea, anorexia, medication side effects, or decreased nutrient absorption secondary to disease process*

Interventions

1. On admission, assess nutritional status. Monitor intake and output. Assess serum protein, blood urea nitrogen, and albumin levels, and report abnormal findings.

2. Involve the dietitian and patient in planning for nutritional replenishment.

3. Encourage family members and friends to bring favorite foods from home.

4. Offer frequent, small meals of high-nutrient foods.

5. Avoid giving liquids with meals.

6. Provide soft foods if oral mucosal lesions are present.

7. Administer antiemetics as ordered.

8. Remove noxious stimuli from the environment before meals.

9. Consult with the doctor regarding the need for enteral or parenteral nutritional replenishment.

10. Additional individualized interventions: _____

_____

_____

NURSING DIAGNOSIS: *Potential fluid volume deficit related to chronic, persistent diarrhea associated with opportunistic infection*

Interventions

1. See the "Fluid and Electrolyte Imbalances" care plan, page 21.

2. Additional individualized interventions: _____

_____

_____

NURSING DIAGNOSIS: *Altered oral mucous membrane related to oral infections and/or masses*

Interventions

1. Assess the patient's mouth at least twice daily for thrush, lesions, or bleeding.

2. Ensure meticulous oral care after meals and at bedtime.

3. Apply lubricant to the lips as needed.

4. Obtain cultures from suspicious oral lesions, as ordered.

5. Avoid using alcohol, mouthwashes, or lemon-glycerine swabs.

6. Assess for indications of stomatitis, pharyngitis, or esophagitis.

7. Additional individualized interventions: _____

_____

_____

NURSING DIAGNOSIS: *Potential altered skin integrity related to effects of immobility, disease process, medications, and/or poor nutritional status*

Interventions

1. Assess the skin at least every 8 hours for evidence of breakdown.

2. Implement preventive skin care measures.

3. If a pressure sore develops, institute therapeutic treatment, as ordered.

4. If the patient is receiving I.V. or I.M. pentamidine isethionate for *Pneumocystis carinii* pneumonia, rotate injection sites and observe them carefully for development of sterile abcesses.

5. Observe for urticaria, maculopapular rash, or pruritus.

6. Additional individualized interventions: _____

_____

_____

NURSING DIAGNOSIS: *Potential sexual dysfunction related to fatigue, depression, fear of rejection, and fear of disease transmission*

Interventions

1. Assess the current status of the patient's sexual relationships.

2. Encourage open discussion of sexual issues between the patient and spouse (or partner).

3. Encourage expressions of affection and nonsexual touching.

4. Discuss "safer sex" practices. Teach specific guidelines as detailed in the latest Centers for Disease Control recommendations.

5. Additional individualized interventions: _____

_____

_____

NURSING DIAGNOSIS: *Knowledge deficit related to symptoms of disease progression, risk factors, transmission of disease, home care, and treatment options*

Interventions

1. See the "Knowledge Deficit" care plan, page 56.

2. Teach infection-prevention measures.

3. Discuss symptoms of AIDS-related complications.

4. Review recommendations for home care and waste disposal.

5. Teach ways in which the virus may be spread.

6. Provide information regarding the legal rights of AIDS patients. Also provide referral to AIDS support groups.

7. Encourage the patient to explore treatment options with the doctor.

8. Additional individualized interventions: _____

_____

_____

PATIENT/FAMILY DISCHARGE TEACHING CHECKLIST

___ disease process and implications

___ all discharge medications (discharge medications may include antibiotics or other chemotherapeutics)

___ community resources for emotional support, financial counseling, grief counseling, and individual and family counseling

___ treatment options, including investigational areas

___ resources for long-term or terminal care, such as a hospice

___ signs and symptoms of and ways to prevent new opportunistic infection or reinfection

___ ways to prevent the spread of AIDS

___ symptoms to report to the health care provider

___ importance of keeping follow-up appointments with the health care provider

___ how to contact doctor

DOCUMENTATION CHECKLIST

___ clinical status on admission

___ significant changes in status

___ pertinent laboratory and diagnostic test findings

___ occurrence and type(s) of opportunistic infection(s)

___ treatment decisions

___ nutritional program and support

___ breathing patterns

___ sleep patterns

___ emotional coping

___ family and significant other support

___ patient/family teaching

___ discharge planning

ASSOCIATED CARE PLANS

Death and Dying
Fluid and Electrolyte Imbalances
Grief/Grieving
Ineffective Family Coping
Ineffective Individual Coping
Lymphoma
Pain
Pneumonia
Total Parenteral Nutrition

Acute Myocardial Infarction*

NURSING DIAGNOSIS: *Activity intolerance related to myocardial ischemia, decreased contractility, and/or dysrhythmias*
Interventions

1. Using telemetry, continuously monitor heart rate, rhythm, and conduction.

2. Promote physical comfort and rest.

3. Prohibit smoking and intake of stimulants, such as coffee.

4. Encourage performance of activities of daily living and diversional activities.

5. Implement the prescribed activity and exercise program.

6. Assess and document intolerance to activity or exercise, monitoring vital signs before, during, and after each session.

7. Stress the importance of avoiding Valsalva's maneuver and isometric exercises.

8. Provide supplemental oxygen, as ordered, using nursing judgment.

9. Administer vasodilators, as ordered, monitoring patient response and side effects, particularly hypotension.

10. Teach the patient to monitor pulse rate before and after activity or exercise.

11. Stress the importance of compliance with the activity and exercise program and with rest requirements.

12. Encourage the family and significant others to support the patient in appropriately instituting changes in activity or exercise.

13. Additional individualized interventions: _____

_____

_____

NURSING DIAGNOSIS: *Potential ineffective coping related to anxiety, denial and/or depression*
Interventions

1. Encourage verbalization of feelings.

2. Anticipate feelings of denial, shock, anger, anxiety, and depression.

3. Explain the grieving process to the patient and family.

4. Evaluate the meaning of the person's altered body image and role responsibilities.

5. Additional individualized interventions: _____

_____

_____

Anxiety (from fear of unknown, unfamiliar surroundings and unfinished business)

1. Assess daily for indicators of anxiety.

2. Introduce yourself and other caregivers to the patient and family.

3. Assign a primary care nurse, and limit the number of other nurses caring for the patient.

4. Care for the patient calmly and confidently.

5. Explain the purpose and routine nature of frequent assessments.

*This clinical plan focuses on the patient with a diagnosis of acute myocardial infarction who has been transferred from the coronary care unit to an intermediate care unit.

6. Repeat explanations as necessary.
7. Orient the patient to the unit environment.
8. Administer minor tranquilizers, as ordered, using nursing judgment.
9. Help the patient explore alternatives for resolving unfinished business.
10. Additional individualized interventions: _____

_____

_____

Denial (associated with grieving process or previous coping pattern)
1. Assess daily for indicators of denial.
2. Evaluate the impact of denial on health.
3. If the patient verbalizes denial, listen nonjudgmentally.
4. If denial is being expressed through acting-out behavior, document, express concern, and promote greater control over the environment.
5. Be alert for topics the patient consistently fails to raise or refuses to discuss when prompted.
6. Encourage the patient to focus on remaining abilities.
7. Encourage the patient to resume full self-care as physical abilities allow.
8. Consult psychiatric resources for further assistance if needed.
9. Additional individualized interventions: _____

_____

_____

Depression (about changed body image and altered role performance)
1. Assess daily for indicators of depression.
2. Assess for and document specific causes of depression.
3. Assess and document the patient's sleep pattern, and take measures to promote restful sleep—such as providing relaxation measures at bedtime.
4. Encourage verbalization of feelings and crying.
5. Assist with realistic problem solving.
6. When pessimism is expressed, point out hopeful aspects of the situation.
7. Encourage physical activity, as appropriate, and document responses.
8. Help the patient identify and implement enjoyable diversions.
9. Share updated information on the patient's status, as appropriate, emphasizing even small signs of progress.
10. Additional individualized interventions: _____

_____

_____

NURSING DIAGNOSIS: *Altered sexuality patterns related to physical limitations secondary to tissue ischemia and medications*
Interventions
1. Obtain a sexual history, including the incidence of chest pain during or after foreplay and intercourse.
2. Encourage the patient and spouse (or partner) to verbalize fears and anxieties. Provide time for joint and individual discussion.

3. Be aware of personal feelings about sexuality, making an appropriate referral if too uncomfortable to counsel effectively.
4. Provide printed material about acute myocardial infarction (AMI) and resumption of sexual activities.
5. Inform the patient that some medications can cause impotence or decrease libido.
6. Discuss ways to decrease the effects of sexual activity on the cardiovascular system—for example, medications and positioning.
7. Emphasize that sexual activity should be avoided after large meals or excessive alcohol intake, in extreme temperatures, and under conditions of fatigue or increased stress.
8. As ordered, evaluate activity tolerance.
9. Teach symptoms that should be reported to the doctor if they occur during foreplay or intercourse.
10. Additional individualized interventions: _____

_____

_____

NURSING DIAGNOSIS: *Knowledge deficit related to newly diagnosed, complex disease process and to therapy*
Interventions
Disease process
1. Describe the basic anatomy and physiology of the heart, the atherosclerotic process, and the pathophysiology of chest pain and AMI.
2. Discuss angina symptoms and what to do if they occur.
3. Instruct the patient about medication therapy.
4. Additional individualized interventions: _____

_____

_____

Dietary modifications
1. Explain the rationale for a diet low in calories (if the patient is obese), saturated fats, and salt.
2. Take a dietary history, and help the patient identify eating patterns.
3. Have the dietitian help the patient plan a reduced-calorie, -fat, and -salt diet that fits his or her life-style, culture, and socioeconomic status.
4. Discuss the role of exercise in reducing weight, blood pressure, and serum lipid levels.
5. Stress the need for the entire family to follow the modified diet.
6. Give information about antilipid medications (if prescribed), including action, dosage, scheduling, and side effects.
7. Provide a list of programs available for weight reduction, if appropriate.
8. Give printed diet information for home use.
9. Additional individualized interventions: _____

_____

_____

Management of hypertension
1. Explain the risks of hypertension.

2. Discuss medication therapy, including action, dosage, scheduling, and side effects.
3. Describe ways to reduce salt intake, based on the diet history.
4. Emphasize the need for follow-up visits.
5. Provide printed information about antihypertensive medications.
6. Stress the importance of contacting the doctor if symptoms occur.
7. Additional individualized interventions: _____

_____

Smoking cessation
1. Explain the rationale for smoking cessation.
2. Discuss the benefits of not smoking.
3. Help the patient to identify needs currently met by smoking and to explore substitute options.
4. Discuss with the patient's spouse (or partner) and significant others the need to assist and support the patient's efforts to stop smoking.
5. Provide a list of community stop-smoking programs.
6. Additional individualized interventions: _____

_____

Stress reduction
1. Discuss stress and its effect on the cardiovascular system.
2. Help the patient to identify stressors and learn health-promoting behaviors.
3. Identify the characteristics of Type A behavior exhibited by the patient, and review their relationship to AMI.
4. Teach stress-reduction techniques. Provide outpatient referral(s), as appropriate.
5. Additional individualized interventions: _____

_____

PATIENT/FAMILY DISCHARGE TEACHING CHECKLIST
__ AMI disease process and implications
__ accuracy in taking radial pulse
__ all discharge medications' purpose, dosage, administration schedule, and side effects requiring medical attention (usual discharge medications include nitrates, beta blockers, antiarrhythmics, calcium antagonists, antihypertensives, and inotropic agents)
__ need for risk factor modification
__ prescribed diet
__ prescribed activity and exercise program
__ need for regularly scheduled rest periods
__ signs and symptoms to report to health care provider
__ need for follow-up care
__ when to resume sexual activity
__ availability of community resources
__ how to contact doctor

DOCUMENTATION CHECKLIST
__ status on admission to intermediate care unit
__ significant changes in status
__ pertinent laboratory and diagnostic test findings
__ telemetry monitoring
__ chest pain episodes
__ interventions for pain relief
__ diet and intake and output
__ medical management therapies, including medications
__ emotional status
__ patient/family teaching
__ activity tolerance

ASSOCIATED CARE PLANS
Death and Dying
Fluid and Electrolyte Imbalances
Geriatric Considerations
Grief/Grieving
Ineffective Family Coping
Ineffective Individual Coping
Knowledge Deficit
Pain

Alzheimer's Disease

COLLABORATIVE PROBLEM: *Impaired cognitive function related to degenerative loss of cerebral tissue*
Interventions
1. Assess the patient's present level of cognitive functioning.
2. Assign the patient to a room close to the nursing station.
3. Minimize hazards in the environment.
4. Maintain consistency in nursing routines.
5. Promote self-care independence.
6. Establish a therapeutic relationship.
7. Give simple, specific instructions for accomplishing tasks.
8. Orient the patient to reality frequently and repetitively.
9. Administer medications, as ordered.
10. Use aids to improve language skills.
11. Minimize communication barriers.
12. Encourage social interaction.
13. Prevent excessive stimulation.
14. Communicate attentively.
15. Encourage reminiscence.
16. Prepare a patient identification card, bracelet, or name tag.
17. Additional individualized interventions: _____

_____

NURSING DIAGNOSIS: *Nutritional deficit related to memory loss and inadequate food intake*
Interventions
1. Assess present nutritional status.

2. Offer a balanced diet, with small quantities of food given at regular and frequent intervals.
3. Prepare the food tray in advance, so that the patient may eat unassisted.
4. Provide time and privacy for eating.
5. Monitor and record daily weight.
6. Provide dietary information to the home caregiver.
7. Additional individualized interventions: _____
_____
_____

NURSING DIAGNOSIS: *Potential for injury related to wandering behavior, aphasia, agnosia, and/or hyperorality*
Interventions
1. Consider use of a bell to alert caregivers when the patient is wandering.
2. Ensure that the patient is dressed appropriately for the temperature, including shoes that fit well.
3. Avoid using restraints.
4. Recommend safety measures to the family for home care.
5. Encourage a regular exercise program as tolerated by the patient.
6. Observe for nonverbal cues to potential injury. Note repeated words or seemingly inappropriate statements. Alert the family to cues observed.
7. Additional individualized interventions: _____
_____
_____

NURSING DIAGNOSIS: *Constipation related to memory loss about toileting behaviors and to inadequate diet*
Interventions
1. Identify the bathroom location clearly.
2. Promote toileting at regular intervals.
3. Encourage a therapeutic diet with ample fluids and fiber.
4. Observe for nonverbal cues signaling the need for elimination.
5. Administer elimination aids, as ordered, and document.
6. Monitor and document elimination frequency.
7. Additional individualized interventions: _____
_____
_____

NURSING DIAGNOSIS: *Altered family processes related to progressive mental deterioration of the family member with Alzheimer's disease (AD)*
Interventions
1. Involve the family in all teaching. Use teaching as an opportunity to assess family roles, resources, and coping behavior.
2. Offer support, understanding, and reassurance to the family.
3. Involve a social worker or discharge planner in decisions regarding home care or nursing home placement.

4. Provide information regarding community resources, such as home care, financial and legal assistance, and an Alzheimer's support group. Encourage use of all available resources.
5. Additional individualized interventions: _____
_____
_____

PATIENT/FAMILY DISCHARGE TEACHING CHECKLIST
__ diagnosis and disease process—for example, through literature from the John Douglas French Foundation for Alzheimer's Disease (Los Angeles) and the *American Journal on Alzheimer's Care and Related Disorders*
__ preparatory plans for adequate supervision and behavior management
__ approaches recommended to minimize environmental hazards
__ instructions for promoting self-care independence
__ recommended procedure for reorientation to home environment
__ need for identification bracelet or other medical alert device
__ all discharge medications' purpose, dosage, administration schedule, and side effects requiring medical attention (discharge medications may include antianxiety agents)
__ techniques for continually improving language skills
__ specific suggestions for meeting nutritional and elimination needs
__ knowledge of available community resources
__ need to restore family equilibrium
__ awareness of probable total patient regression
__ how to contact doctor

DOCUMENTATION CHECKLIST
__ clinical status on admission, including level of cognitive function
__ planned approach to maintain patient safety, security, and orientation
__ laboratory and diagnostic test findings
__ any change in the patient's behavioral responses
__ level of communication and social interaction
__ dietary and elimination patterns
__ patient/family teaching
__ discharge planning

ASSOCIATED CARE PLANS
Fluid and Electrolyte Imbalances
Geriatric Considerations
Grief/Grieving
Ineffective Family Coping
Ineffective Individual Coping
Knowledge Deficit

Angina Pectoris

NURSING DIAGNOSIS: *Chest pain related to myocardial ischemia*
Interventions
1. Assess for and document chest pain episodes.
2. Assess the patient for nonverbal signs of chest pain.
3. Obtain a 12-lead EKG immediately during acute pain.
4. Medicate the patient with sublingual nitroglycerin (according to protocol) and document results.
5. Implement measures to improve myocardial oxygenation such as oxygen therapy, bed rest, semi- to high-Fowler's position, and minimal noise and distractions.
6. Stay with the patient during the chest pain episode.
7. Monitor and document the effects of beta blockers and calcium channel blockers.
8. Establish and maintain I.V. access.
9. Additional individualized interventions: _____
_____
_____

COLLABORATIVE PROBLEM: *Potential dysrhythmias or myocardial infarction related to myocardial hypoxia and ischemia*
Interventions
1. Monitor, report, and document signs and symptoms of dysrhythmias.
2. Administer antiarrhythmic medications as ordered, noting and documenting their effectiveness and side effects.
3. Decrease myocardial oxygen demands.
4. Monitor, report, and document signs and symptoms of inadequate tissue perfusion.
5. Monitor and report signs and symptoms of developing myocardial infarction.
6. Additional individualized interventions: _____
_____
_____

NURSING DIAGNOSIS: *Activity intolerance related to development of chest pain upon exertion*
Interventions
1. Instruct the patient to immediately cease any activity that precipitates chest pain.
2. Instruct the patient to avoid Valsalva's maneuver.
3. Instruct the patient to increase activities gradually.
4. Promote physical rest and emotional comfort.
5. Additional individualized interventions: _____
_____
_____

NURSING DIAGNOSIS: *Altered health maintenance related to presence of cardiovascular risk factors*
Interventions
1. Teach the patient about factors that may precipitate anginal attacks.
2. Instruct the patient on required nutritional modifications. Document current height and weight.
3. Provide six small meals per day.

4. Encourage eliminating high-caffeine foods and beverages from the diet.
5. Discourage cigarette smoking.
6. Teach stress-reduction techniques.
7. With the doctor's approval, start the patient on a cardiovascular fitness regimen.
8. Additional individualized interventions: _____
_____
_____

PATIENT/FAMILY DISCHARGE TEACHING CHECKLIST
___ pathophysiology and implications of the clinical condition
___ recommended modification of risk factors, such as smoking, stress, obesity, lack of exercise, and a high-fat, high-cholesterol diet
___ prescribed dietary modifications
___ plan for resuming daily activities
___ plan for resuming sexual activity
___ all discharge medications' purpose, dosage, administration schedule, side effects, and toxic effects (usual discharge medications include nitrates, beta blockers, calcium channel blockers, and antilipid drugs)
___ common emotional adjustments
___ community resources for life-style and risk factor modification: stress- and weight-reduction groups, cardiac exercise programs, and stop-smoking programs
___ signs and symptoms indicating need for medical attention, such as chest pain unrelieved by three nitroglycerin tablets within 20 minutes, onset of new pattern of anginal attacks, palpitations or skipped beats, syncope, dyspnea, or diaphoresis
___ date, time, and location of follow-up appointments
___ how to contact doctor

DOCUMENTATION CHECKLIST
___ clinical status on admission
___ significant changes in status
___ pertinent laboratory and diagnostic test results
___ chest pain episodes
___ pain-relief measures
___ oxygen therapy
___ I.V. therapy
___ use of protocols
___ nutritional intake
___ response to medications
___ emotional response to illness; coping skills
___ activity tolerance
___ patient/family teaching
___ discharge planning

ASSOCIATED CARE PLANS
Acute Myocardial Infarction
Ineffective Individual Coping
Knowledge Deficit
Pain

Cerebrovascular Accident

NURSING DIAGNOSIS: *Potential ineffective airway clearance related to hemiplegic effects of cerebrovascular accident (CVA)*
Interventions
1. Position the patient to keep the airway open.
2. Provide supplemental oxygen, as ordered.
3. If hemiplegia is present, position the patient on the affected side for shorter periods (1 to 1½ hours) than on the unaffected side (2 hours). Avoid positioning the hemiplegic arm over the abdomen.
4. Encourage coughing (except in patients with hemorrhagic CVAs) and deep breathing. Suction as necessary. Note respiration adequacy.
5. Assess lung sounds at least every 4 hours.
6. Assist and observe the patient while eating, as needed.
7. Additional individualized interventions: _____

_____

COLLABORATIVE PROBLEM: *Potential extension of cerebrovascular injury related to continued occlusion or further bleeding*
Interventions
1. Assess neurologic status at least every 4 hours. Promptly report any abnormalities or changes.
2. If CVA is occlusive:
• Administer anticoagulant therapy, as ordered. Monitor prothrombin time and partial thromboplastin time, and check current results before giving each dose. Observe carefully for unusual bleeding, and report any that occurs.
• Administer antiplatelet aggregation medications, as ordered. Observe for gastric irritation.
• Administer medications to control blood pressure, as ordered. Be alert for signs of decreased cerebral perfusion and report immediately any that occur. Check blood pressure at least every 4 hours while the patient is awake.
3. If CVA is hemorrhagic:
• Maintain the patient on complete bed rest for the first 24 hours to 1 week, as ordered. Minimize stress and external stimulation. Administer stool softeners or laxatives, as ordered.
• Administer medications to control blood pressure, as ordered. Report any sign of neurologic deterioration.
• Administer I.V. aminocaproic acid, as ordered. Observe for and report hypotension, bradycardia, or any sign of thrombus formation.
• Monitor to maintain optimal fluid status, observing fluid restrictions, as ordered. Administer osmotic diuretics, as ordered. Monitor intake and output.
4. Additional individualized interventions: _____

_____

NURSING DIAGNOSIS: *Impaired physical mobility related to impaired cerebral function*
Interventions
1. Maintain the patient's body in a position of functional alignment while at rest. Support the affected arm when out of bed.

2. Provide passive (and active, as permitted) range-of-motion exercises to all extremities at least four times a day. Collaborate with the physical therapist to maintain a maximum activity level within restrictions.
3. When permitted, encourage the patient to do as much self-care as possible.
4. Apply antiembolism stockings, as ordered. Assess for signs of thromboembolic complications, and immediately report any that occur.
5. Protect the patient's skin.
6. Maintain adequate elimination. If the patient is catheterized, begin bladder retraining as soon as possible. If the patient is not catheterized, offer the bedpan every 2 hours. Observe urine and report any sign of infection. Monitor bowel movements. Reassure the patient that bowel and bladder control usually returns.
7. Additional individualized interventions: _____

_____

NURSING DIAGNOSIS: *Potential sensory-perceptual alteration and impaired verbal communication related to cerebral injury*
Interventions
1. Establish closeness. Call the patient by name. Approach the unaffected side.
2. Assess communication ability.
3. Speak slowly and clearly. Use simple explanations and gestures, but not "baby talk." Allow ample time for responses. Provide an alternate means of communication if needed.
4. Arrange a speech therapy referral if indicated.
5. Reassure the patient that functional recovery is possible. Help with practice of verbal and physical exercises. Involve family members in practice.
6. Protect the affected side from injury.
7. Teach precautions concerning visual deficits.
8. Additional individualized interventions: _____

_____

NURSING DIAGNOSIS: *Potential alteration in family processes related to emotional lability associated with cerebral injury*
Interventions
1. Maintain an attitude of acceptance and understanding. Encourage normal expression of feelings related to lost abilities.
2. Explain emotional lability to the patient's family.
3. Additional individualized interventions: _____

_____

NURSING DIAGNOSIS: *Knowledge deficit related to the rehabilitation process and ongoing home care*
Interventions
1. See the "Knowledge Deficit" care plan, page 56.
2. Instruct the patient and family about all medications to be taken at home.

3. If the patient is to be discharged home on anticoagulant therapy, instruct thoroughly about:
• medications' action, dosage, and schedule
• need for frequent laboratory testing follow-up
• signs of bleeding problems and need to report them
• measures to control bleeding
• dietary considerations
• avoiding aspirin and over-the-counter medications
• avoiding trauma
• the importance of wearing a Medic Alert tag and of notifying other health professionals about anticoagulant therapy.
4. Teach the importance of life-style modifications to minimize the risk of recurrence.
5. Teach the patient and family to recognize and report symptoms associated with transient ischemic attacks.
6. Teach the patient and family about:
• activity and positioning recommendations
• use of mobility aids such as slings, braces, and walkers
• airway maintenance and feeding considerations
• the bowel and bladder control program
• safety considerations
• signs and symptoms of complications
• dietary and fluid intake recommendations
• skin care
• communication techniques and considerations
• coping methods to deal with emotional lability
• home care follow-up arrangements.
7. Additional individualized interventions: _____
_____
_____

PATIENT/FAMILY DISCHARGE TEACHING CHECKLIST
__ injury or disease process and implications
__ all discharge medications' purpose, dosage, administration schedule, and side effects requiring medical attention (discharge medications may include anticoagulants, antiplatelet aggregation medications, and antihypertensives)
__ need for laboratory test follow-up (if indicated)
__ signs of cerebral impairment
__ signs of infection
__ signs of thromboembolic or other complications
__ activity and positioning recommendations and mobility aids
__ dietary and fluid intake recommendations
__ bowel and bladder control program
__ risk factors
__ safety measures
__ use of Medic Alert tag
__ advisability of cardiopulmonary resuscitation classes for family
__ skin care
__ communication measures
__ verbal practice exercises
__ expectation of and coping methods for emotional lability
__ community resources

__ when and how to access emergency medical system
__ date, time, and location of follow-up appointment
__ home care arrangements

DOCUMENTATION CHECKLIST
__ clinical status on admission
__ significant changes in status
__ neurologic assessments
__ pertinent laboratory and diagnostic test findings
__ medication therapy
__ activity and positioning
__ dietary intake
__ fluid intake and output
__ bowel and bladder control measures
__ communication measures
__ patient/family teaching
__ follow-up and home care arrangements

ASSOCIATED CARE PLANS
Fluid and Electrolyte Imbalances
Geriatric Considerations
Grief/Grieving
Ineffective Family Coping
Ineffective Individual Coping
Knowledge Deficit
Thrombophlebitis

Cholecystectomy

COLLABORATIVE PROBLEM: *Potential peritonitis related to possible perforation of the gallbladder preoperatively*
Interventions
1. Monitor vital signs every 2 hours for 12 hours, then every 4 hours if they are stable. Document and report abnormalities.
2. Assess the abdomen during vital sign checks, noting bowel sounds, distention, firmness, and presence of a right upper quadrant (RUQ) mass.
3. Note the location and character of pain during vital sign checks.
4. Maintain ordered antibiotic therapy.
5. Additional individualized interventions: _____
_____
_____

COLLABORATIVE PROBLEM: *Potential hemorrhage related to decreased vitamin K absorption and decreased prothrombin synthesis*
Interventions
1. Monitor prothrombin time.
2. Administer vitamin K as ordered.
3. Observe for bleeding.
4. Give injections using small-gauge needles.
5. Apply gentle pressure to injection sites instead of massaging them.
6. Additional individualized interventions: _____
_____
_____

NURSING DIAGNOSIS: *Alteration in comfort: RUQ pain related to gallbladder inflammation*
Interventions
1. See the "Pain" care plan, page 64.
2. Administer specific medications, as ordered. These may include meperidine, papaverine hydrochloride, amyl nitrite, and nitroglycerin.
3. Additional individualized interventions: _____

_____

_____

COLLABORATIVE PROBLEM: *Potential postoperative infection, obstruction, or tube dislodgment related to external biliary drainage*
Interventions
1. Monitor vital signs.
2. Assess the abdomen every shift for pain and rigidity.
3. Assess for signs of infection at the T-tube insertion site.
4. Assess for signs of T-tube obstruction.
5. Assess for signs that the T tube is dislodged.
6. Connect the T tube to closed gravity drainage, using sterile technique, and attach sufficient tubing.
7. Monitor the amount and character of any T-tube drainage.
8. Monitor stool color.
9. Place the patient in low Fowler's position upon return from surgery.
10. If discharged with T tube, teach care related to external biliary drainage system.
11. Additional individualized interventions: _____

_____

_____

NURSING DIAGNOSIS: *Potential ineffective breathing pattern related to high abdominal incision and pain*
Interventions
1. Monitor respiratory rate and character every 4 hours.
2. Auscultate breath sounds once per shift.
3. Instruct and coach the patient about diaphragmatic breathing.
4. Help the patient use the incentive spirometer every hour when awake and every 2 hours at night.
5. Turn the patient every 2 hours.
6. Assess pain and premedicate as needed before activity.
7. Help the patient splint the incision while coughing.
8. Encourage the patient to progressively increase ambulation.
9. Additional individualized interventions: _____

_____

_____

NURSING DIAGNOSIS: *Potential nutritional deficit related to nausea and vomiting preoperatively, NPO status postoperatively, nasogastric suction, altered lipid metabolism, and increased nutritional needs during healing*
Interventions
1. Maintain I.V. fluid replacement, as ordered. See the "Fluid and Electrolyte Imbalances" care plan, page 21.

2. Once peristalsis returns, discontinue the nasogastric (NG) tube and encourage progressive resumption of dietary intake.
3. Clamp the T tube during meals, as ordered.
4. Teach about a fat-restricted diet, as ordered. Involve a dietitian.
5. Suggest small, frequent meals.
6. Instruct the patient to minimize alcohol intake.
7. Prepare the patient for the possibility of persistent flatulence.
8. Additional individualized interventions: _____

_____

_____

NURSING DIAGNOSIS: *Potential alteration in oral mucous membrane related to NPO status and possible NG tube suction*
Interventions
1. Assess the oral mucous membrane once per shift.
2. Assist with oral hygiene twice a day and as needed.
3. Apply lubricant to the lips at least every 2 hours while the patient is awake.
4. Additional individualized interventions: _____

_____

_____

PATIENT/FAMILY DISCHARGE TEACHING CHECKLIST
___ signs and symptoms of wound infection
___ dietary modifications (patient may be on a low-fat diet for up to 6 months; a nonrestrictive diet is resumed as soon as tolerated)
___ resumption of normal activities
___ resumption of sexual activity
___ all discharge medications' purpose, dosage, administration schedule, and side effects (postoperative patients may be discharged with oral analgesics)
___ if discharged home with a T tube: care of the external biliary drainage system, including expected amount of drainage, frequency of emptying bag and changing dressing, technique for site care and dressing change, and signs to report to doctor (excessive drainage, leakage, and signs of obstruction)
___ how to contact doctor
___ date, time, and location of follow-up appointment

DOCUMENTATION CHECKLIST
___ clinical status on admission
___ significant changes in status
___ pertinent laboratory and diagnostic test findings
___ wound assessment
___ amount and character of T-tube drainage
___ pain-relief measures
___ pulmonary hygiene measures
___ observations of oral mucous membrane
___ nutritional intake
___ GI assessment
___ patient/family teaching
___ discharge planning

ASSOCIATED CARE PLANS
Fluid and Electrolyte Imbalances
Knowledge Deficit
Pain
Surgical Intervention

Chronic Obstructive Pulmonary Disease

COLLABORATIVE PROBLEM: *Respiratory failure (PO$_2$ less than 50 mm Hg, with or without PCO$_2$ greater than 50 mm Hg) related to ventilation-perfusion imbalance*
Interventions
1. Obtain and report arterial blood gas (ABG) measurements.
2. Administer oxygen, as ordered.
3. Administer pharmacologic agents (bronchodilators, antibiotics, corticosteroids, and expectorants), as ordered. Monitor therapeutic levels, as indicated.
4. Perform bronchial hygiene measures, as ordered. Assess lung sounds. Report and document treatment effectiveness.
5. Maintain fluid intake at 2 to 3 quarts of water per day.
6. Monitor, document, and report signs of infection or further deterioration in respiratory status.
7. If possible, reduce or eliminate environmental irritants.
8. Additional individualized interventions: _____
_____
_____

NURSING DIAGNOSIS: *Ineffective breathing pattern related to emotional stimulation, fatigue, and blunting of respiratory drive*
Interventions
1. Reduce the work of breathing and lessen depletion of oxygen reserves.
2. Assist the patient to perform breathing exercises and coordinate breathing with activity.
3. Pace all activities.
4. Instruct the patient in breathing techniques to use when expression of feelings creates shortness of breath.
5. Avoid use of sedatives and hypnotics.
6. Additional individualized interventions: _____
_____
_____

NURSING DIAGNOSIS: *Nutritional deficit related to shortness of breath during and after meals and to the side effects of medications*
Interventions
1. Use supplemental oxygen during mealtimes, as ordered.
2. Arrange to perform bronchial hygiene measures before meals. Maintain good oral hygiene. Remove secretions from the eating area.

3. Provide small, frequent meals.
4. Monitor weight and nutritional intake daily.
5. Obtain a dietary consultation as soon as the patient can take foods or fluids.
6. Additional individualized interventions: _____
_____
_____

NURSING DIAGNOSIS: *Impaired mobility related to shortness of breath, avoidance of physical activity with resultant muscle weakness, deconditioning, depression, and (possibly) exercise-related hypoxemia*
Interventions
1. Instruct the patient in breathing techniques to use when performing activities of daily living.
2. Administer oxygen during activity, as ordered.
3. Before recommending an activity level, determine ABG levels (should be stable), fitness level, and factors contributing to inactivity.
4. Instruct the patient in ways to control shortness of breath when walking.
5. Develop and implement a daily walking schedule, increasing time and distance as tolerated.
6. Before, during, and after walking, monitor the patient's response to the exercise.
7. Additional individualized interventions: _____
_____
_____

NURSING DIAGNOSIS: *Sleep pattern disturbance related to bronchodilator medications (stimulant effect), bouts of nocturnal shortness of breath, depression, and anxiety*
Interventions
1. Identify the patient's normal sleep pattern and the abnormal pattern being experienced.
2. Consult the doctor about adjusting medications to optimize bronchodilation while minimizing stimulant effects.
3. Instruct the patient in performing the nocturnal bronchial hygiene regimen.
4. Administer oxygen therapy during the night, as ordered.
5. Monitor the patient's bouts of sleeplessness, including degree of shortness of breath, pulse rate and rhythm, respiratory rate, and breath sounds.
6. Instruct the patient in relaxation techniques to be used at bedtime.
7. Additional individualized interventions: _____
_____
_____

NURSING DIAGNOSIS: *Potential for injury related to failure to recognize signs and symptoms indicating impending exacerbation*
Interventions
1. Teach the signs and symptoms of impending exacerbation.
2. Emphasize the need to notify the doctor promptly, rather than adjust medication regimen by self, if signs and symptoms of exacerbation occur.

3. Caution the patient to avoid overmedication.
4. Additional individualized interventions: _____
_____
_____

NURSING DIAGNOSIS: *Altered sexuality patterns related to shortness of breath, change in body image, deconditioning, change in relationship with spouse (or partner), and side effects of medications*
Interventions
1. Establish rapport. Discuss with the patient and spouse (or partner) their feelings concerning changes in sexual functioning.
2. Help the patient learn or arrange therapeutic modalities to optimize sexual function.
3. Additional individualized interventions: _____
_____
_____

PATIENT/FAMILY DISCHARGE TEACHING CHECKLIST
___ practical energy conservation and breathing techniques
___ signs and symptoms of infection or exacerbation
___ all discharge medications' purpose, dosage, administration schedule, and side effects requiring medical attention (usual discharge medications include bronchodilators, corticosteroids, antibiotics, and expectorants)
___ bronchial hygiene measures
___ use, care, and cleaning of needed respiratory equipment
___ need to drink 2 to 3 quarts of water per day
___ dietary restrictions
___ daily weight monitoring
___ avoiding exposure to infections; need for flu vaccination
___ avoiding lung irritants
___ exercise prescription
___ referrals to community agencies, as appropriate
___ date, time, and location of next appointment
___ how to contact doctor

DOCUMENTATION CHECKLIST
___ clinical status on admission
___ significant changes in status
___ pertinent laboratory and diagnostic test findings, such as ABG levels
___ shortness of breath episodes, including physical assessment parameters during each episode, treatment modality administered, and treatment outcome
___ respiratory status per shift
___ administration and outcome of therapeutic modalities given
___ nutritional intake
___ fluid intake
___ exercise and activity ability
___ patient/family teaching
___ discharge planning

ASSOCIATED CARE PLANS
Death and Dying
Fluid and Electrolyte Imbalances
Grief/Grieving
Ineffective Individual Coping
Knowledge Deficit
Pneumonia

Chronic Renal Failure

COLLABORATIVE PROBLEM: *Potential hyperkalemia related to decreased renal excretion, metabolic acidosis, excessive dietary intake, blood transfusions, catabolism, and noncompliance with therapeutic regimen*
Interventions
1. Monitor serum potassium levels.
2. Assess for and report signs and symptoms of hyperkalemia.
3. Implement measures to prevent or treat metabolic acidosis, as ordered.
4. If blood transfusions are necessary, administer fresh-packed red blood cells (RBCs) during dialysis, as ordered.
5. Take measures to decrease catabolism.
6. Encourage compliance with the therapeutic regimen.
7. Implement and evaluate therapy for hyperkalemia.
8. Additional individualized interventions: _____
_____
_____

COLLABORATIVE PROBLEM: *Potential pericarditis, pericardial effusion, and pericardial tamponade related to uremia and/or inadequate dialytic therapy*
Interventions
1. Assess for and report signs and symptoms of pericarditis.
2. Assess dialysis adequacy, and increase frequency as necessary and as ordered.
3. Assess for and report signs and symptoms of pericardial effusion and tamponade.
4. If tamponade develops, prepare the patient for emergency pericardial aspiration.
5. Encourage compliance with the therapeutic regimen.
6. Additional individualized interventions: _____
_____
_____

COLLABORATIVE PROBLEM: *Hypertension related to sodium and water retention and malfunction of the renin-angiotensin-aldosterone system*
Interventions
1. Administer antihypertensive medications, as ordered, and assess for desired and adverse effects.
2. Measure and record blood pressure at various times of day with the patient in supine, sitting, and standing positions.
3. Teach the patient how and why to avoid orthostatic hypotension.
4. Encourage compliance with the therapeutic regimen.

5. Instruct the patient to report any changes in status that may indicate fluid overload.
6. Recognize the significance of funduscopic changes.
7. Additional individualized interventions: _____
_____
_____

COLLABORATIVE PROBLEM: *Anemia related to decreased life span of RBCs in chronic renal failure (CRF), bleeding, decreased production of erythropoietin and RBCs, and blood loss during dialysis*
Interventions
1. Assess for the degree of anemia and its physiologic effects.
2. Administer medications as ordered, and assess for desired and adverse effects.
3. Help the patient develop an activity and exercise schedule to avoid undue fatigue.
4. Avoid unnecessary collection of laboratory specimens.
5. Instruct the patient in measures to prevent bleeding.
6. Administer blood transfusions as indicated and ordered.
7. Additional individualized interventions: _____
_____
_____

COLLABORATIVE PROBLEM: *Potential osteodystrophy and metastatic calcifications related to hyperphosphatemia, hypocalcemia, abnormal vitamin D metabolism, hyperparathyroidism, and elevated aluminum levels*
Interventions
1. Administer, and assess the effects of, phosphate-binding medications, calcium supplements, and vitamin D supplements, as ordered.
2. Weekly, monitor levels of serum calcium, phosphate, alkaline phosphatase, aluminum, and calcium-phosphate product; report abnormal findings.
3. Monitor X-rays for bone fractures and joint deposits.
4. Weekly, palpate joints for enlargement, swelling, and tenderness.
5. Weekly, inspect the patient's gait, joint range of motion, and muscle strength.
6. With the patient, develop an activity and exercise schedule to avoid immobilization.
7. Question the patient daily about hypocalcemia signs and symptoms.
8. Monitor each EKG for prolonged Q-T interval, irritable dysrhythmias, and atrioventricular conduction defects.
9. Assess daily for Chvostek's and Trousseau's signs.
10. Encourage compliance with the therapeutic regimen.
11. Additional individualized interventions: _____
_____
_____

NURSING DIAGNOSIS: *Potential nutritional deficit related to anorexia; nausea; vomiting; diarrhea; restricted dietary intake of nutrients; altered metabolism of proteins, lipids, and carbohydrates; and gastrointestinal inflammation with poor absorption*
Interventions
1. Assess nutritional status on admission.

2. Weigh the patient daily, and compare actual weight with ideal body weight.
3. Encourage the patient to eat the maximum amount of nutrients allowed. Encourage compliance with the dialysis regimen.
4. Encourage foods high in calories (from carbohydrates) and low in protein, potassium, sodium, and water content.
5. Consult with the dietitian to include the patient's preferences in the daily diet.
6. Implement interventions to reduce nausea and vomiting, diarrhea or constipation, and stomatitis.
7. Monitor indicators of dietary adequacy and compliance with diet restrictions.
8. Additional individualized interventions: _____
_____
_____

NURSING DIAGNOSIS: *Potential alteration in oral mucous membrane related to the effects of urea and ammonia*
Interventions
1. Inspect the oral mucous membrane on admission.
2. Teach the patient the appropriate mouth care regimen.
3. Encourage compliance with the therapeutic regimen.
4. Additional individualized interventions: _____
_____
_____

COLLABORATIVE PROBLEM: *Potential peripheral neuropathy related to effects of uremia, fluid and electrolyte imbalances, and acid-base imbalances on the peripheral nervous system*
Interventions
1. On admission, consult a physical therapist for assessment of muscle strength, gait, and degree of neuromuscular impairment.
2. Develop an activity and exercise regimen.
3. Protect the patient from leg and foot trauma.
4. Administer analgesics, as ordered, and monitor effects.
5. Encourage compliance with the therapeutic regimen.
6. Additional individualized interventions: _____
_____
_____

NURSING DIAGNOSIS: *Potential impairment of skin integrity related to decreased activity of oil and sweat glands, scratching, capillary fragility, abnormal blood clotting, anemia, retention of pigments, and deposition of calcium phosphate on the skin*
Interventions
1. Assess the skin for color, turgor, ecchymoses, texture, and edema.
2. Keep the skin clean while relieving dryness and itching; apply lotion, especially while skin is still moist after bathing.
3. Keep the nails trimmed.
4. Monitor serum calcium and phosporus levels weekly.
5. Administer phosphate-binding medications, as ordered.
6. Administer antipruritic medications, as ordered.

7. Encourage compliance with the therapeutic regimen.
8. Additional individualized interventions: _____
_____
_____

NURSING DIAGNOSIS: *Potential alteration in thought processes related to the effects of uremic toxins, acidosis, fluid and electrolyte imbalances, and hypoxia on the central nervous system*
Interventions
1. On admission and daily, assess the patient's thought processes and compare them with premorbid intellectual status.
2. Alter methods of communication with the patient as needed.
3. Minimize environmental stimuli. Alter the environment as needed.
4. Do not administer opiates or barbiturates.
5. Encourage compliance with the therapeutic regimen.
6. Additional individualized interventions: _____
_____
_____

NURSING DIAGNOSIS: *Potential noncompliance related to knowledge deficit; lack of resources; side effects of diet, dialysis, or medications; denial; and poor relationships with health care providers*
Interventions
1. Clarify the patient's understanding of the therapeutic regimen and the consequences of noncompliance.
2. Assess for factors that could contribute to noncompliance. Explore ways to alter the treatment regimen to fit the patient's social and cultural beliefs.
3. Provide instructions about areas of misunderstanding. Allow the patient to make as many decisions and choices, from as many alternatives, as possible.
4. Additional individualized interventions: _____
_____
_____

NURSING DIAGNOSIS: *Potential sexual dysfunction related to the effects of uremia on the endocrine and nervous systems and to the psychosocial impact of CRF and its treatment*
Interventions
1. Discuss with the patient and spouse (or partner) the meaning of sexuality and reproduction to them, ways in which changes in sexual functioning affect masculine and feminine roles, and mutual goals for their sexual functioning.
2. Discuss alternative methods of sexual expression.
3. Emphasize the importance of giving and receiving love and affection as alternatives to performing intercourse.
4. Consider (with the doctor) a penile prosthesis for a male patient.
5. Additional individualized interventions: _____
_____
_____

NURSING DIAGNOSIS: *Potential knowledge deficit related to vascular access care*
Interventions
1. Emphasize the crucial importance of protecting the vascular access.
2. Whether the patient has a shunt or a fistula, instruct him or her to protect the extremity containing the access by avoiding wearing constrictive clothing and jewelry, carrying heavy objects, allowing blood pressure measurements or venous punctures, and lying on the access.
3. In addition to Intervention 2, instruct the patient with an external shunt to:
• check its patency every 4 hours (look at blood, feel for thrill)
• if blood separation is present or thrill is absent, contact a dialysis professional immediately for possible declotting
• perform daily site care
• observe the site for redness, swelling, or drainage
• keep bulldog clamps on the dressing
• do not pull on the tubing
• if the shunt separates, clamp and reconnect it, then notify the doctor
• if the shunt dislodges, apply a tourniquet, and go to the emergency department.
4. In addition to Intervention 2, instruct the patient with a fistula to:
• assess patency daily (feel for pulsations)
• if pulsation is absent, contact a dialysis professional immediately
• if applying a pressure dressing after dialysis, remove the dressing after 4 hours
• check needle insertion sites for bleeding for 24 hours after dialysis.
5. Additional individualized interventions: _____
_____
_____

PATIENT/FAMILY DISCHARGE TEACHING CHECKLIST
___ cause and implications of renal failure
___ purpose of dialysis regimen
___ medications
___ recommended diet and fluid modifications
___ common problems related to CRF and their management
___ care of the shunt and fistula (if patient is receiving hemodialysis) or peritoneal catheter (if patient is receiving peritoneal dialysis)
___ how to obtain and record weight
___ how to measure and record blood pressure and pulse
___ how to maintain an intake and output record
___ problems to report to health care provider
___ financial and community resources to assist with CRF treatment
___ dialysis schedule, location of dialysis facility, and days and times of appointments
___ resources for counseling
___ how to contact doctor or nephrology nurse

DOCUMENTATION CHECKLIST
__ clinical status on admission
__ significant changes in status
__ pertinent laboratory and diagnostic test findings
__ response to medication regimen
__ physical and psychological response to dialysis therapy
__ nutritional intake
__ activity and exercise ability
__ ability to perform self-care measures
__ compliance with the therapeutic regimen
__ patient/family teaching
__ postdischarge referrals and plans for long-term care and follow-up

ASSOCIATED CARE PLANS
Anemia
Death and Dying
Fluid and Electrolyte Imbalances
Grief/Grieving
Ineffective Individual Coping
Knowledge Deficit
Pain
Peritoneal Dialysis

Colostomy

COLLABORATIVE PROBLEM: *Potential stomal necrosis related to the surgical procedure, bowel wall edema, or traction on the mesentery*
Interventions
1. Assess and document stoma color every 8 hours the first 4 postoperative days.
2. If the stoma is ischemic or necrotic, check the proximal bowel's viability.
3. Notify the doctor promptly if necrosis extends to the fascia level.
4. Implement measures to prevent or minimize abdominal distention.
5. Additional individualized interventions: _____

_____

COLLABORATIVE PROBLEM: *Potential stoma retraction related to mucocutaneous separation*
Interventions
1. Assess and document the integrity of the mucocutaneous suture line at each pouch change.
2. Initiate and document nutritional support measures for the patient at risk for nutritional deficiency.
3. Request vitamin A supplements for the patient receiving corticosteroids.
4. For the patient with a loop colostomy stabilized by a rod or bridge, delay removal of the support until the stoma granulates to the abdominal wall.

5. If separation occurs, alter the pouching system to prevent fecal contamination of exposed subcutaneous tissue.
6. Additional individualized interventions: _____

_____

_____

NURSING DIAGNOSIS: *Potential altered skin integrity: peristomal skin breakdown related to contact of fecal material with skin*
Interventions
1. If possible, arrange for preoperative selection of the optimal stoma site.
2. Select a pouching system that matches the patient's abdominal contours.
3. Use pouching principles and products to provide the patient with a secure pouch seal and to protect the skin from stool and tape.
4. Change the pouch every 5 to 7 days and as needed if leakage, burning, or itching occurs.
5. Treat any denudation with absorptive powder and sealant or water.
6. Additional individualized interventions: _____

_____

_____

NURSING DIAGNOSIS: *Knowledge deficit related to management options (applies only to the patient with a descending or sigmoid colostomy)*
Interventions
1. Assess the patient's candidacy for regulation of bowel function by irrigation.
2. If he is a candidate, provide patient teaching about management options.
3. Help the patient explore the options.
4. Establish a teaching plan based on the patient's decision.
5. Additional individualized interventions: _____

_____

_____

NURSING DIAGNOSIS: *Potential altered self-concept: body image related to loss of control of fecal elimination*
Interventions
1. Teach the patient odor-control measures.
2. Teach the patient measures to reduce and control flatus.
3. Teach the patient how to conceal the pouch under clothing.
4. Discuss the normal emotional response to colostomy with the patient and significant others; include helpful coping strategies.
5. Offer United Ostomy Association information; arrange for an "ostomy visitor" if the patient is receptive.
6. Discuss management of the colostomy during occupational, social, and sexual activity. Teach the patient to role-play potentially difficult situations.
7. Additional individualized interventions: _____

_____

_____

NURSING DIAGNOSIS: *Potential sexual dysfunction related to change in body image and/or damage to autonomic nerves (nerve damage applicable only to the patient with a rectal resection, particularly wide resection for cancer)*
Interventions
1. Discuss with patient and spouse (or partner), if possible, the value of openness as well as the fact that both must adapt to the change.
2. Teach measures to secure and conceal the pouch during sexual activity.
3. For a female with a wide rectal resection, discuss the possible need for artificial lubrication.
4. For a male with a wide rectal resection, discuss potential interference with erection and ejaculation but not with sensation or potential for orgasm; discuss alternatives to intercourse (if indicated) and ways to maintain intimacy.
5. Additional individualized interventions: _____
_____
_____

**PATIENT/FAMILY DISCHARGE
TEACHING CHECKLIST**
__ reason for colostomy
__ colostomy impact on bowel function
__ normal stoma characteristics and function
__ pouch-emptying procedure
__ pouch-changing procedure
__ peristomal skin care
__ colostomy irrigation procedure (if applicable)
__ management of mucous fistula or stoma (if applicable)
__ flatus and odor control
__ management of diarrhea and constipation
__ normal adaptation process and postcolostomy feelings
__ community support groups
__ resumption of preoperative life-style
__ potential alteration in sexual function (if applicable)
__ sources of colostomy supplies and reimbursement procedures for them
__ signs and symptoms requiring notification of doctor
__ follow-up care with doctor (and enterostomal therapy nurse, if applicable)
__ how to contact doctor

DOCUMENTATION CHECKLIST
__ clinical status on admission
__ significant changes in clinical status
__ GI tract function
__ stoma color and status of mucocutaneous suture line
__ oral intake and tolerance
__ episodes of abdominal distention, nausea, and vomiting
__ incisional status (any signs of infection)
__ stoma location and abdominal contours
__ management plan, including pouching system selected (and decision about irrigation for patient with descending or sigmoid colostomy)
__ peristomal skin status
__ emotional response to colostomy and discussion of coping strategies

__ patient/family teaching
__ discharge planning

ASSOCIATED CARE PLANS
Fluid and Electrolyte Imbalances
Grief/Grieving
Ineffective Family Coping
Ineffective Individual Coping
Knowledge Deficit
Pain
Surgical Intervention

Congestive Heart Failure

COLLABORATIVE PROBLEM: *Decreased cardiac output related to decreased contractility, altered heart rhythm, fluid volume overload, and/or increased afterload*
Interventions
1. Monitor and document heart rate and rhythm, heart sounds, blood pressure, pulse pressure, and the presence or absence of peripheral pulses.
2. Administer cardiac medications, as ordered, and document the patient's response. Observe for therapeutic and adverse effects.
3. Observe for signs of hypoxemia. Ensure adequate oxygenation with proper positioning and administration of supplemental oxygen, as ordered.
4. Ensure adequate rest.
5. Monitor fluid status: obtain accurate daily weight; maintain accurate intake and output records, assess lung sounds, assess for peripheral edema; and assess for dehydration.
6. Assess the patient's mental status for increasing confusion.
7. Decrease fear and anxiety.
8. Additional individualized interventions: _____
_____
_____

NURSING DIAGNOSIS: *Fluid and electrolyte imbalance related to congestive heart failure (CHF), decreased renal perfusion, and diuretic therapy*
Interventions
1. See the "Fluid and Electrolyte Imbalances" care plan, page 21.
2. Monitor serum creatinine and blood urea nitrogen levels.
3. Monitor serum sodium and potassium levels.
4. Additional individualized interventions: _____
_____
_____

NURSING DIAGNOSIS: *Activity intolerance related to bed rest and decreased cardiac output*
Interventions
1. Determine cardiac stability by evaluating blood pressure, heart rate and rhythm, and indicators of oxygenation.

2. When the patient is stable, institute a graduated activity program according to unit protocol.

3. Evaluate patient tolerance as new activities are introduced.

4. Alternate activity with rest periods.

5. Administer anticoagulants, as ordered.

6. Avoid conditions associated with Valsalva's maneuver.

7. Additional individualized interventions: _____

_____

_____

NURSING DIAGNOSIS: *Nutritional deficit related to decreased appetite and possible dislike of a low-sodium diet*

Interventions

1. Keep a daily record of caloric intake. Consult with the dietitian to identify caloric needs.

2. Assess the patient's dietary preferences, and plan meals to meet treatment requirements and patient needs.

3. Additional individualized interventions: _____

_____

_____

NURSING DIAGNOSIS: *Knowledge deficit related to complex disease process and treatment*

Interventions

1. Once the patient is stable, institute a structured teaching plan.

2. Briefly explain the pathophysiology of CHF.

3. Explain the rationale for dietary restrictions.

4. Explain the rationale for activity restrictions.

5. Teach about medications.

6. Emphasize the importance of self-monitoring for signs and symptoms of increasing CHF.

7. Discuss with the patient and family a plan for emergency care.

8. Review the plan for follow-up care.

9. Additional individualized interventions: _____

_____

_____

NURSING DIAGNOSIS: *Potential noncompliance related to complicated treatment regimen, possible health beliefs, and/or possible negative relationship with caregivers*

Interventions

1. Observe for possible indicators of noncompliance.

2. Evaluate the extent and result of noncompliance.

3. Differentiate true noncompliance from nonadherence to the therapeutic regimen because of other causes.

4. Initiate discussion of the situation with the patient, family, and other caregivers, involving a psychiatric clinician or other care team members as needed.

5. Explicitly express concern for the patient as a person.

6. Emphasize the seriousness of CHF and the importance of self-care.

7. Discuss the following with the patient: life priorities, personal perception of the prognosis, feelings about the length of the illness, the general complexity of treatment, and the degree of confidence in caregivers.

8. Consider the patient's cultural and spiritual background.

9. Ask the patient about his or her level of satisfaction with caregivers.

10. Validate conclusions about reasons for behavior with the patient and significant others.

11. Collaborate with other caregivers to reevaluate the therapeutic plan.

12. Search for alternate solutions.

13. Use creative negotiation strategies to set goals with the patient.

14. If the patient makes an informed choice not to follow the recommendations, and if negotiation is not possible:

• Avoid punitive responses, and accept the decision.

• Keep open the option for future treatment if the patient undergoes a change of mind.

• Respect the patient's readiness to die, if present.

15. Additional individualized interventions: _____

_____

PATIENT/FAMILY DISCHARGE TEACHING CHECKLIST

__ disease process and implications

__ signs and symptoms of increasing CHF

__ all discharge medications' purpose, dosage, administration schedule, and side effects requiring medical attention (usual discharge medications include inotropic agents, diuretics, vasodilators, and anticoagulants)

__ dietary restrictions

__ activity restrictions

__ plan for follow-up care

__ plan for emergency care

__ how to contact doctor

DOCUMENTATION CHECKLIST

__ clinical status on admission

__ significant changes in clinical status

__ pertinent laboratory and diagnostic test findings

__ intake and output

__ nutritional intake

__ response to activity progression

__ response to illness and hospitalization

__ family's response to illness

__ patient/family teaching

__ discharge planning

ASSOCIATED CARE PLANS

Acute Myocardial Infarction

Chronic Renal Failure

Death and Dying

Fluid and Electrolyte Imbalances

Grief/Grieving

Ineffective Individual Coping

Knowledge Deficit

Diabetes Mellitus

COLLABORATIVE PROBLEM: *Hyperglycemia related to inadequate endogenous insulin (Type I) or inadequate endogenous insulin, and insulin resistance (Type II)*
Interventions
1. Administer I.V., I.M., or S.C. insulin, or oral hypoglycemic medications, as ordered, each time checking the glucose level first and giving or withholding the dose accordingly.
2. Establish and maintain an I.V. fluid infusion. Monitor for signs of dehydration. Keep an accurate intake and output record.
3. Monitor fingerstick blood glucose or urine glucose and acetone levels. Document daily weight.
4. Observe for signs of hypoglycemia. If any occur, notify the doctor, obtain blood glucose measurements immediately, and treat immediately with I.V. glucose, glucagon, or oral glucose, depending on hospital protocol and the patient's level of responsiveness.
5. Observe for signs of ketoacidosis. If any occur, notify the doctor immediately, obtain blood glucose measurements immediately, and treat according to hospital protocol.
6. Observe for signs of hyperglycemic hyperosmolar nonketotic coma (HHNK). If suspected, notify the doctor immediately.
7. Additional individualized interventions: _____

_____

_____

NURSING DIAGNOSIS: *Knowledge deficit related to the newly diagnosed complex and chronic disease process*
Interventions
1. See the "Knowledge Deficit" care plan, page 56.
2. Teach management, including the significance of insulin or oral hypoglycemics for disease control. Demonstrate injection techniques. Link medication needs to other factors, such as diet and exercise. Ensure that the patient and family are aware of hypoglycemia signs and treatment and the protocol for managing persistent hyperglycemia, ketoacidosis, or HHNK.
3. Coordinate the patient's, family's, and dietitian's involvement in planning a therapeutic diet for disease control.
4. Teach blood or urine glucose testing methods for home use.
5. Emphasize the importance of regular activity and exercise and of maintaining an approximately equivalent activity level from day to day.
6. Teach the patient to be aware of increased susceptibility to infections; discuss ways to avoid exposure.
7. Discuss vascular complications of the disease process.
• Teach foot care, skin care, leg exercises, and assessment of circulatory status; observe patient demonstration of all techniques. As appropriate, emphasize the importance of quitting smoking. Ensure that the patient and family are sent home with a written foot care protocol.

• Discuss the eye disorders associated with diabetes mellitus (DM). Emphasize the importance of early reporting of vision changes.
• Teach the symptoms of urinary tract infection and renal impairment, and emphasize the importance of prompt treatment.
8. Discuss the implications of diabetic neuropathy.
9. Additional individualized interventions: _____

_____

_____

NURSING DIAGNOSIS: *Health maintenance alteration related to the necessity for disease control*
Interventions
1. Emphasize that control of DM involves coordinating many aspects of daily living with medically prescribed interventions.
2. Assess the patient's resources, including financial management capabilities and the family support system.
3. Involve significant others in all teaching and planning.
4. Arrange appropriate follow-up home health visits before patient discharge.
5. Link the patient and family with community resources and peer groups.
6. Encourage verbalization of feelings, and support healthy coping behaviors.
7. Additional individualized interventions: _____

_____

_____

PATIENT/FAMILY DISCHARGE TEACHING CHECKLIST
___ disease process and implications
___ all discharge medications' purpose, dosage, administration schedule, and side effects requiring medical attention (usual discharge medications include insulin or oral hypoglycemics)
___ blood or urine glucose testing method, and interpretation of results
___ interrelationship of diet, exercise, and other factors in disease management
___ signs of hypoglycemia and appropriate treatment
___ signs of hyperglycemia and appropriate treatment
___ diet management
___ exercise regimen
___ foot care
___ signs of infection and appropriate treatment
___ signs, symptoms, and implications of neuropathy
___ signs and symptoms of retinopathy and need to report them
___ signs and symptoms of urinary or renal complications and need to report them
___ community resources
___ when and how to access emergency medical system
___ date, time, and location of follow-up appointment
___ date and time of follow-up home visit
___ written materials, insulin, and syringes, as provided

DOCUMENTATION CHECKLIST
___ clinical status on admission
___ significant changes in status

___ pertinent laboratory and diagnostic test findings
___ episodes of hyperglycemia or hypoglycemia
___ dietary intake and planning
___ activity and exercise regimen
___ medication therapy
___ I.V. line patency
___ patient/family teaching
___ follow-up arrangements

ASSOCIATED CARE PLANS
Chronic Renal Failure
Fluid and Electrolyte Imbalances
Grief/Grieving
Ineffective Individual Coping
Knowledge Deficit
Retinal Detachment
Thrombophlebitis

Duodenal Ulcer

COLLABORATIVE PROBLEM: *Potential GI hemorrhage related to duodenal ulcer extension into the submucosal layer of the intestinal lining*
Interventions
1. Observe for and report signs of GI hemorrhage.
2. Institute nasogastric intubation if ordered.
3. Institute continuous saline solution lavage if ordered.
4. If the patient is actively bleeding, check vital signs hourly and report a deterioration in status.
5. Treat hypovolemia if it occurs.
6. Prepare the patient for surgery if indicated.
7. Maintain bed rest after the bleeding episode.
8. Additional individualized interventions: _____

_____

_____

NURSING DIAGNOSIS: *Pain related to increased hydrochloric acid secretion and/or increased spasm, intragastric pressure, and upper GI tract motility*
Interventions
1. Administer and document ulcer-healing medications.
2. Provide bed rest and a quiet environment.
3. Teach and reinforce the role of diet in ulcer healing.
4. Encourage intake of adequate calories from basic foods at regular intervals and in frequent, small meals.
5. Teach and reinforce required life-style changes.
6. Discourage smoking.
7. Teach the signs and symptoms of ulcer recurrence and GI bleeding.
8. Additional individualized interventions: _____

_____

_____

PATIENT/FAMILY DISCHARGE TEACHING CHECKLIST
___ nature and implications of disease
___ relationship of ulcer pain and relief modalities
___ all discharge medications' purpose, dosage, admin-

istration schedule, and side effects requiring medical attention (usual discharge medications include antacids, histamine-receptor antagonists, or both)
___ recommended dietary modifications
___ need for smoking cessation program (if applicable)
___ stress-reduction measures
___ signs and symptoms of ulcer recurrence and GI bleeding
___ date, time, and location of follow-up appointment
___ how to contact doctor

DOCUMENTATION CHECKLIST
___ clinical status on admission
___ significant changes in status
___ pertinent diagnostic test findings
___ pain-relief measures
___ nutritional intake and intolerance
___ medication administration
___ patient/family teaching
___ discharge planning

ASSOCIATED CARE PLANS
Esophagitis and Gastroenteritis
Fluid and Electrolyte Imbalances
Ineffective Individual Coping
Knowledge Deficit
Pain

Hysterectomy

COLLABORATIVE PROBLEM: *Potential thromboembolic or hemorrhagic complications related to immobility, venous stasis, pelvic congestion, and/or possible predisposing factors*
Interventions
1. Monitor for signs of bleeding; institute therapy as ordered.
2. Institute measures to prevent and assess for thromboembolic phenomena.
3. Before discharge, teach the patient home care recommendations to prevent bleeding and thromboembolism.
4. Additional individualized interventions: _____

_____

_____

NURSING DIAGNOSIS: *Potential postoperative infection related to abdominal incision, urinary tract proximity, contamination of peritoneal cavity, hypoventilation, anesthesia, and/or preoperative infection*
Interventions
1. Monitor for signs and symptoms of peritonitis.
2. Implement standard postoperative nursing measures to prevent infection.
3. Before discharge, teach the patient about signs and symptoms indicating infection.
4. Additional individualized interventions: _____

_____

_____

NURSING DIAGNOSIS: *Potential urinary retention related to decreased bladder and urethral muscle tone from anesthesia and mechanical trauma*
Interventions
1. Monitor for signs of urinary retention.
2. Implement measures to deal with retention if it occurs.
3. Additional individualized interventions: _____
_____
_____

NURSING DIAGNOSIS: *Pain related to abdominal incision and distention*
Interventions
1. Implement pain-control measures.
2. Offer application of heat to the abdomen.
3. Additional individualized interventions: _____
_____
_____

NURSING DIAGNOSIS: *Potential altered self-concept related to changes in body appearance and function as a result of surgery*
Interventions
1. Assess the patient's level of understanding regarding hysterectomy and the recovery period.
2. Acknowledge the patient's feelings of loss and dependence and her fears of complications.
3. Provide opportunities to discuss concerns.
4. Discuss the patient's plans for recovery at home.
5. Additional individualized interventions: _____
_____
_____

NURSING DIAGNOSIS: *Potential sexual dysfunction: decreased libido and/or dyspareunia related to fatigue, pain, grieving, altered body image, decreased estrogen levels, loss of vaginal sensations, sexual activity restrictions, and/or concerns about acceptance by spouse (or partner)*
Interventions
1. Encourage the patient to explore her perceptions of surgery's effect on her sexual function. Listen sensitively.
2. Discuss the potential impact of surgery on sexuality.
3. Explain that decreased libido and vaginal dryness may result from hormonal loss and that hormonal replacements are available.
4. Suggest ways to ease sexual adjustment during the immediate postoperative period.
5. Provide information and discuss options for conserving the patient's energy and preventing discomfort during her return to sexual functioning.
6. Encourage the patient and spouse (or partner), if present, to share concerns and feelings with each other.
7. Additional individualized interventions: _____
_____
_____

PATIENT/FAMILY DISCHARGE TEACHING CHECKLIST
___ implications of total abdominal hysterectomy
___ all discharge medications' purpose, dosage, administration schedule, and side effects requiring medical attention
___ incision care (aseptic technique, changing the dressing, irrigations, cleansing procedures, hand-washing technique, and proper disposal of soiled dressings)
___ signs and symptoms of possible infection
___ dietary requirements and restrictions, if any
___ activity and exercise restrictions
___ date, time, and location of follow-up appointment
___ how to contact doctor

DOCUMENTATION CHECKLIST
___ clinical status on admission
___ postoperative clinical assessment
___ significant changes in status
___ appearance of incision and wound drainage
___ I.V. line patency and condition of site
___ assessment of pain and relief measures
___ nutritional intake
___ fluid intake and output
___ patient/family teaching
___ discharge planning

ASSOCIATED CARE PLANS
Grief/Grieving
Ineffective Individual Coping
Knowledge Deficit
Pain
Surgical Intervention
Thrombophlebitis

Ileal Conduit Urinary Diversion

NURSING DIAGNOSIS: *Preoperative knowledge deficit related to impending creation of an ileal conduit*
Interventions
1. Assess what the patient already knows about the upcoming cystectomy and creation of an ileal conduit, including experience with anyone who has an ostomy.
2. Assess the patient's ability to learn.
3. Assess the patient's manual dexterity and sensory deficits.
4. Inquire about the patient's previous hydration habits.
5. Describe the construction of the conduit, the rationale for bowel preparation, and normal stomal characteristics.
6. Anticipate problems with pouching, such as tape allergies.
7. Mark the stoma site in the right lower quadrant.
8. If appropriate, discuss the effects cystectomy may have on the male patient's sexual functioning.
9. Additional individualized interventions: _____
_____
_____

COLLABORATIVE PROBLEM: *Potential peritonitis related to gastrointestinal (GI) or genitourinary (GU) anastomosis breakdown or leakage*
Interventions
1. Monitor and document the patency of the nasogastric (NG) tube, NG tube output, abdominal pain and distention, bowel sounds, and appearance and drainage of the abdominal incision.
2. Evaluate for signs of GI anastomosis leakage and peritonitis.
3. Monitor for signs of urine leakage.
4. Additional individualized interventions: _____

_____

_____

COLLABORATIVE PROBLEM: *Potential stomal ischemia and stomal necrosis related to vascular compromise of conduit*
Interventions
1. Apply a disposable transparent urinary pouch, and attach it to a bedside drainage bag.
2. Observe the stoma for color changes every 4 hours.
3. Report stomal color changes immediately.
4. Be prepared to differentiate superficial ischemia from necrosis.
5. Additional individualized interventions: _____

_____

_____

COLLABORATIVE PROBLEM: *Potential stoma retraction and mucocutaneous separation related to peristomal trauma or tension on the intestinal mesentery*
Interventions
1. Apply a pouch with an antireflux valve, as ordered.
2. Always use a skin sealant.
3. If mucocutaneous separation occurs, protect the area and take measures to encourage granulation.
4. Additional individualized interventions: _____

_____

_____

NURSING DIAGNOSIS: *Total urinary incontinence related to creation of an ileal conduit*
Interventions
1. Maintain a good pouch seal.
2. Review the conduit's construction and functioning with the patient.
3. Emphasize and demonstrate normal urine and stoma characteristics.
4. Additional individualized interventions: _____

_____

_____

NURSING DIAGNOSIS: *Disturbed self-concept: body image related to urinary diversion*
Interventions
1. Encourage the patient to express feelings.
2. Allow for privacy when teaching ostomy care.
3. Have the patient empty the pouch in the bathroom.
4. Suggest a visitor from the United Ostomy Association.

5. Show an accepting and tolerant attitude when performing or teaching ostomy care.
6. Additional individualized interventions: _____

_____

_____

NURSING DIAGNOSIS: *Postoperative knowledge deficit related to care of the ileal conduit*
Interventions
1. Instruct the patient in the procedure for emptying the pouch.
2. Demonstrate the use and care of the nighttime bedside drainage bag.
3. Encourage the patient to change the pouch.
4. Teach the patient to treat minor peristomal skin irritations with karaya powder and skin sealant.
5. Explain fluid intake requirements, and demonstrate urine pH tests.
6. List recommended dietary considerations to control urine odor.
7. Define routine follow-up care, and explain the rationale for it.
8. Address any special concerns the patient has about living with an ostomy.
9. Additional individualized interventions: _____

_____

_____

NURSING DIAGNOSIS: *Potential sexual dysfunction: male erectile dysfunction related to cystectomy, possible ejaculatory incompetence if prostate removed*
Interventions
1. Assess the patient's readiness to discuss sexual matters.
2. Describe the separate nerve pathways for sexual excitement, erection, ejaculation, and orgasm; explain which ones may be affected by surgery and why.
3. If indicated, mention sexual alternatives, such as a penile prosthesis or external devices to aid in achieving erections. Provide referral to a urologist or an enterostomal therapy nurse.
4. Additional individualized interventions: _____

_____

_____

PATIENT/FAMILY DISCHARGE TEACHING CHECKLIST
___ extent of tumor and resection
___ nature of urinary diversion performed and its construction
___ incision care (if not healed)
___ procedure for emptying and changing pouch
___ use and cleaning of bedside drainage system
___ treatment of minor peristomal skin irritations
___ written list of supplies and suppliers with doctor's prescription to facilitate insurance payment
___ chemotherapy (if needed) and its expected side effects
___ availability of support groups, such as the United Ostomy Association and American Cancer Society
___ amount and types of fluids preferred, along with any dietary considerations, such as avoiding odor-causing foods

__ signs and symptoms to call doctor about—such as fever, flank pain, and hematuria

__ concerns to call enterostomal therapy nurse about—such as pouch problems and skin or stoma problems

__ signs and symptoms of urinary tract infection

__ considerations in resuming sexual activity

__ date, time, and location of follow-up appointment

__ how to contact doctor

DOCUMENTATION CHECKLIST

__ clinical status on admission

__ significant changes in status

__ pertinent laboratory and diagnostic test findings

__ preoperative marking of stoma site

__ preoperative teaching

__ bowel preparation

__ United Ostomy Association visitor recommendation (if appropriate)

__ stoma viability

__ condition of mucocutaneous border and sutures

__ urine characteristics

__ patient's response to ostomy

__ fluid intake and output

__ presence of stents

__ GI status

__ incision status

__ patient's progress in learning ostomy care

__ patient/family teaching

__ discharge planning

ASSOCIATED CARE PLANS

Fluid and Electrolyte Imbalances
Grief/Grieving
Ineffective Individual Coping
Knowledge Deficit
Surgical Intervention

Ineffective Individual Coping

NURSING DIAGNOSIS: *Ineffective coping related to perception of harmful stimulus*
Interventions
1. Form a positive relationship with the patient.
2. Rule out organic causes for behavioral changes.
3. Provide factual information about the illness and treatment plan.
4. With the patient, identify the source of the threat.
5. Help the patient be specific about the source of the threat and identify modifiable components of the threat.
6. Help the patient identify personal resources.
7. Identify external resources and make appropriate referrals.
8. Keep pain at a tolerable level.
9. Ensure adequate nutrition and sleep.
10. Control environmental stimuli to reduce stressors and promote rest.
11. Offer alternative strategies to counteract the effects of the threat.

12. Give the patient choices related to care.
13. Provide opportunities for loved ones to interact with the patient in meaningful ways.
14. Assess responses to interventions and collaborate with the doctor if medication is necessary.
15. Additional individual interventions: _____
_____
_____

PATIENT/FAMILY DISCHARGE TEACHING CHECKLIST

__ diagnosis, treatment plan, and prognosis

__ expected physiologic responses during recovery

__ expected psychological reactions during recovery

__ community resources appropriate to perceived problem

__ appropriate alternative coping strategies

__ how to contact doctor

DOCUMENTATION CHECKLIST

__ coping status on admission

__ significant changes in appearance, affect, behavior, and perception

__ psychological responses to hospitalization and interventions

__ significant physiologic stress responses

__ sleep patterns

__ nutritional intake

__ response to caregivers

__ response to interventions designed to increase coping skills

__ suicide risk

__ referrals made

__ patient/family teaching

__ discharge planning

ASSOCIATED CARE PLANS

Death and Dying
Grief/Grieving
Ineffective Family Coping
Knowledge Deficit
Pain

Low Back Pain—Conservative Medical Management

NURSING DIAGNOSIS: *Impaired physical mobility related to acute pain and limitations of the therapeutic regimen*
Interventions
1. Maintain strict and complete bed rest for 1 to 6 weeks.
2. Evaluate neurologic function in the lower extremities; report new or increasingly abnormal findings to the doctor.
3. Supervise maintenance of body alignment.
4. Administer medications, as ordered, to control pain, decrease inflammation, and reduce muscle spasm, observing for side effects.

5. Assess lung sounds every 8 hours. Supervise pulmonary hygiene measures.

6. Supervise quadriceps exercises, calf pumping, and circle motions of the ankle, 10 times each, 4 times per day.

7. Apply antiembolism stockings as ordered, removing them twice per day to provide skin care.

8. Supervise position changes every 2 hours, using log-roll turning.

9. Maintain dietary intake high in bulk, fluids, and fiber and reduced in calories while the patient is on bed rest.

10. Coordinate and supervise implementation of a progressive activity schedule.

11. Instruct about movements that may stretch or strain the back.

12. Instruct about the effects of coughing, sneezing, or straining at stool and about appropriate precautionary measures.

13. If ordered, apply pelvic traction properly.

14. If ordered, apply moist heat.

15. If ordered, teach the proper use and application of a brace or corset.

16. Additional individualized interventions: _____

_____

_____

NURSING DIAGNOSIS: *Disturbed self-concept: role performance related to bed rest, effects of medications, prolonged discomfort, and required alterations in activity*

Interventions

1. Allow the patient to participate in care planning and goal setting, letting him or her make as many choices as possible within therapeutic guidelines.

2. Discuss positive and negative feelings associated with recovery phases. Help the patient identify coping resources and refocus negative feelings as appropriate.

3. Avoid authoritarian attitudes.

4. Refer patient to the occupational therapy department as appropriate.

5. Identify, with the patient, strategies to maintain motivation.

6. Additional individualized interventions: _____

_____

_____

NURSING DIAGNOSIS: *Knowledge deficit related to recovery and rehabilitation and long-term management of low back injury*

Interventions

1. Provide information about the anatomy and physiology of the back.

2. Provide information about needed life-style changes related to sitting, driving, standing and walking, lifting, and exercise.

3. Teach correct posture, including assessment technique.

4. Discuss the most common causes of low back pain.

5. Discuss how nerve pressure damage may affect the lower extremities' structure and function. Emphasize the importance of reporting ominous changes.

6. Discuss long-term care issues with the family and significant others.

7. Additional individualized interventions: _____

_____

_____

PATIENT/FAMILY DISCHARGE TEACHING CHECKLIST

___ nature of injury

___ signs and symptoms indicating delayed healing or reinjury

___ recommended daily exercise program

___ common feelings about life-style changes

___ plan for resuming activity

___ resources for support of life-style modifications

___ role of family members and significant others in rehabilitation program

___ proper posture, lifting techniques, and positioning to prevent reinjury

___ all discharge medications' purpose, dosage, administration schedule, and side effects requiring medical attention (usual discharge medications include analgesics and muscle relaxants)

___ dates, times, and location of follow-up appointment

DOCUMENTATION CHECKLIST

___ clinical status on admission

___ significant changes in clinical status

___ pertinent laboratory and diagnostic test findings

___ pain-relief measures

___ nutritional intake

___ elimination status

___ progressive activities schedule and progress

___ immobility complications, if any

___ patient/family teaching

___ discharge planning

ASSOCIATED CARE PLANS

Ineffective Individual Coping
Knowledge Deficit
Laminectomy
Pain

Lung Cancer

COLLABORATIVE PROBLEM: *Hypoxemia related to aberrant cellular growth of lung tissue; bronchial obstruction; increased mucus production; and/or pleurisy*

Interventions

1. Initiate arterial blood gas measurement and monitor for changes in PO_2, as ordered.

2. Administer humidified oxygen, as ordered.

3. Elevate the head of the bed during dyspneic episodes.

4. Evaluate and document breath sounds, respiratory rate, and chest movements. Observe for dyspnea.

5. During episodes of dyspnea, stay with the patient, explain all procedures, and support the patient and family.

6. Encourage the patient to stop or decrease smoking.

7. Teach pursed-lip breathing and relaxation techniques.

8. Additional individualized interventions: _____

_____

_____

COLLABORATIVE PROBLEM: *Potential hemorrhage related to depression of platelet production by chemotherapy*
Interventions

1. Caution the patient to report any bleeding immediately.

2. Initiate and monitor serum platelet counts, as ordered.

3. Caution the patient to use a soft toothbrush or a Waterpik for oral hygiene and to avoid spicy foods.

4. Teach the patient to monitor urine and stools for bleeding signs and to report immediately any that occur.

5. Instruct the patient to use an electric razor for shaving or to grow a beard.

6. Administer medications to suppress menses, as ordered.

7. Teach the patient to report headaches, dizziness, or light-headedness immediately.

8. Avoid intramuscular injections, if possible. If they are unavoidable, apply pressure for at least 5 minutes after the injection.

9. Avoid administering aspirin or aspirin-containing medications.

10. Apply ice packs to bleeding areas.

11. Administer stool softeners.

12. Additional individualized interventions: _____

_____

_____

NURSING DIAGNOSIS: *Pain associated with involvement of peripheral lung structures; metastasis; and/or chemotherapy*
Interventions

1. Instruct the patient to report pain or discomfort immediately.

2. Monitor continuously for signs of pain or discomfort.

3. Involve the patient in pain-control strategies.

4. Administer pain medication, as ordered. Teach the patient or a family member the procedure to use for administering pain medication after discharge.

5. Additional individualized interventions: _____

_____

_____

NURSING DIAGNOSIS: *Potential infection related to immunosuppression from chemotherapy and malnutrition*
Interventions

1. Observe strict medical and surgical asepsis.

2. Monitor and record the patient's temperature every 8 hours. Report even slight temperature variations.

3. Instruct the patient to avoid crowds and persons with infections.

4. Initiate and monitor white blood cell counts.

5. Initiate routine cultures.

6. Additional individualized interventions: _____

_____

_____

NURSING DIAGNOSIS: *Potential sensory-perceptual alteration related to peripheral neuropathies caused by chemotherapy*
Interventions

1. Assess for, document, and report deficits in neurologic functioning, including reports of paresthesia or abnormal deep tendon reflexes.

2. Decrease or discontinue chemotherapy, depending on the severity of neuropathies, as ordered.

3. Explain that changes in sensation are related to chemotherapy, and allow the patient to express fears related to this situation.

4. Protect the area of decreased sensory perception from injury by using a bath thermometer, assessing skin every 8 hours for signs of trauma, applying a dressing to injured areas, using a night-light, and avoiding clutter in activity areas to prevent abrasions, contusions, or falls.

5. Additional individualized interventions: _____

_____

_____

NURSING DIAGNOSIS: *Nutritional deficit related to cachexia associated with tumor growth, anorexia, changes in taste sensation, and/or stomatitis*
Interventions

1. Estimate required protein needs.

2. Develop diet plans based on calculated dietary needs and the patient's food preferences.

3. Increase dietary protein intake.

4. Provide small, frequent feedings.

5. Document weight weekly.

6. Provide antiemetics as ordered.

7. Assess oral mucosa for stomatitis daily and document.

8. Provide a mild mouthwash with viscous lidocaine before meals.

9. Instruct the patient to rinse the mouth with water, diluted hydrogen peroxide, or both, after meals.

10. Instruct the patient to rinse the mouth with yogurt or buttermilk, then swallow it, three times a day.

11. Lubricate lips with a petrolatum product.

12. Assess oral mucosa for infection daily.

13. Administer oral nystatin, as ordered.

14. Additional individualized interventions: _____

_____

_____

NURSING DIAGNOSIS: *Constipation or diarrhea related to chemotherapy*
Interventions

1. Assess and document bowel elimination patterns on admission.

2. Administer antidiarrheal medication, as ordered.

3. Assess for signs of paralytic ileus. Alert the doctor immediately if they are present.

4. Increase dietary fiber intake, provide warm fluids, and promote optimum amounts of exercise.

5. Administer stool softeners as ordered.

6. Additional individualized interventions: _____

_____

_____

NURSING DIAGNOSIS: *Potential altered urinary elimination patterns related to possible development of renal toxicity or hemorrhagic cystitis from chemotherapy*
Interventions
1. Assess and document urinary elimination patterns on admission.
2. Force fluids and administer allopurinol before chemotherapy, as ordered.
3. Alkalinize the patient's urine.
4. Monitor renal function through serum creatinine and 24-hour urine creatinine tests, as ordered.
5. Additional individualized interventions: _____

_____

NURSING DIAGNOSIS: *Activity intolerance related to weakness from cachexia, alteration in protein metabolism, muscle wasting, and/or hypoxemia*
Interventions
1. Determine what activities are tolerated without dyspnea.
2. Instruct the patient to organize activities so that tasks are spaced in manageable units.
3. Teach the use of proper body mechanics, and obtain a consultation with an occupational therapist.
4. Additional individualized interventions: _____

_____

NURSING DIAGNOSIS: *Sleep pattern disturbance related to being awakened by nocturnal cough*
Interventions
1. Assess and document sleep patterns.
2. Provide assistance with pulmonary hygiene during coughing.
3. Instruct the patient to sleep with the head elevated.
4. Exercise caution in administering sedatives and hypnotics.
5. Additional individualized interventions: _____

_____

NURSING DIAGNOSIS: *Disturbed self-concept: body image and self-esteem related to weight loss, cough, sputum production, hair loss, or role changes*
Interventions
1. Approach the patient with an accepting attitude.
2. Assess and document attitudes and responses related to self-concept and role changes.
3. Encourage the patient and family to ventilate feelings.
4. Help the patient accentuate positive features and minimize evidence of weight loss.
5. Encourage use of a portable disposal unit for discarding tissues and sputum.
6. Encourage frequent contact with significant others.
7. Discuss probable hair loss from chemotherapy before chemotherapy is initiated.
8. Remind the patient that hair loss is not permanent.

9. Explain about scalp tourniquets and scalp hypothermia treatments to diminish hair loss.
10. Additional individualized interventions: _____

_____

NURSING DIAGNOSIS: *Altered sexuality patterns related to dyspnea and possible sterility*
Interventions
1. Discuss with the patient changes in patterns of sexual expression that have resulted from diagnosis and treatments.
2. Help the patient and spouse (or partner) discuss desires for sexual expression and intimacy.
3. Discuss options for sexual expression within the patient's physical limitations.
4. Encourage use of supplemental oxygen during intercourse.
5. Provide privacy.
6. Explain that reduced sexual responsiveness may result from fatigue or chemotherapy.
7. Explain that sterility may occur as a result of chemotherapy.
8. Additional individualized interventions: _____

_____

PATIENT/FAMILY DISCHARGE TEACHING CHECKLIST
___ diagnosis
___ chemotherapy effects
___ bleeding prevention, detection, and management
___ use of supplemental oxygen
___ smoking cessation
___ breathing exercises
___ pain-relief measures
___ infection signs and infection-control methods
___ signs of neurologic changes
___ dietary modifications
___ measures to control nausea and vomiting
___ measures to promote normal renal function
___ measures to decrease dyspnea
___ measures to minimize effects of changing body image
___ plans for sexual expression
___ date, time, and location of follow-up appointment
___ how to contact doctor
___ when to seek emergency medical care
___ community resources

DOCUMENTATION CHECKLIST
___ clinical status on admission
___ significant changes in status
___ pertinent laboratory and diagnostic test findings
___ response to chemotherapy
___ episodes of dyspnea
___ oxygen therapy
___ bleeding episodes
___ nutritional status

___ bowel elimination
___ urine elimination
___ activity tolerance
___ sleep patterns
___ patient/family teaching
___ discharge planning

ASSOCIATED CARE PLANS
Death and Dying
Grief/Grieving
Ineffective Family Coping
Ineffective Individual Coping
Knowledge Deficit
Pain

Multiple Sclerosis

NURSING DIAGNOSIS: *Impaired physical mobility related to disease process (demyelinization)*
Interventions
1. Provide rest and prevent fatigue.
2. Institute a physical therapy program, as ordered.
3. Administer and document medication as prescribed for pain, muscle spasm, and inflammation, observing precautions.
4. Assess lung sounds at least every 8 hours.
5. Teach the patient the need for mobility aids.
6. Instruct the patient in safety measures.
7. Assess skin for pressure signs.
8. Assess and counteract the cardiovascular effects of immobility.
9. Medicate with corticosteroids or immunosuppressants, as ordered.
10. Use stress-reduction techniques.
11. Additional individualized interventions: _____

_____

NURSING DIAGNOSIS: *Altered bowel and bladder function related to disease process (demyelinization)*
Interventions
1. Assess and record the patient's present elimination pattern.
2. Evaluate dietary habits.
3. Increase and record fluid intake.
4. Institute and teach a bowel and bladder program.
5. Medicate as ordered to decrease bowel absorption and reduce bowel spasticity.
6. Prevent exposure to infection.
7. Additional individualized interventions: _____

_____

NURSING DIAGNOSIS: *Potential sexual dysfunction related to fatigue, decreased sensation, muscle spasm, and/or urinary incontinence*
Interventions
1. Assess the effects of multiple sclerosis (MS) on sexual function.

2. Encourage the patient and spouse (or partner) to share sexual concerns. Offer to be available as a resource, or refer the couple to another health professional.
3. Offer specific suggestions as indicated by identified problems:
• Initiate sexual activity when energy levels are highest.
• Try different positions.
• Empty the bladder before sexual activity.
• Try oral or manual stimulation.
4. Encourage expressions of mutual affection.
5. Emphasize the importance of discussing birth-control methods and family planning with the doctor.
6. Additional individualized interventions: _____

_____

NURSING DIAGNOSIS: *Disturbed self-concept: body image, self-esteem, and role performance, related to progressive, debilitating effects of disease*
Interventions
1. Encourage the patient to participate in all decisions related to care planning. Discourage dependence on others. Help the patient work toward goals.
2. Facilitate expression of feelings related to losses. See the "Grief/Grieving" and "Ineffective Individual Coping" care plans, pages 41 and 51, respectively.
3. Work with family members to promote patient participation in familiar family roles and rituals and to identify new roles.
4. Encourage the patient to touch affected body parts, perform self-lifting activities as much as possible, and participate in grooming.
5. Provide recognition for goals achieved. Acknowledge evidence of inner strengths and growth as well as external achievement.
6. Additional individualized interventions: _____

_____

NURSING DIAGNOSIS: *Altered family processes related to progressive, debilitating effects of disease on family members and resultant alteration in role-related behavior patterns*
Interventions
1. Assess the family system.
2. Encourage family members to "trade off" in care provision role as necessary.
3. Help the family understand and accept mental changes, if present.
4. Promote healthy habits for family members, such as adequate rest, dietary intake, and relaxation.
5. Assist the family in planning changes in the home environment to facilitate patient care. Provide referral to social services department.
6. Additional individualized interventions: _____

_____

PATIENT/FAMILY DISCHARGE TEACHING CHECKLIST

__ course and nature of multiple sclerosis
__ physical therapy program
__ all discharge medications' purpose, dosage, administration schedule, and side effects requiring medical attention (usual discharge medications include corticosteroids, antispasmodics, and stool softeners)
__ return demonstration of mobility assistance equipment
__ safety instructions for protection from injury related to sensory deficits
__ information regarding problems associated with immobility
__ stress-reduction techniques
__ community resources
__ recommended therapeutic diet
__ bowel and bladder program
__ avoiding exposure to infection
__ date, time and location of follow-up appointment
__ how to contact doctor

DOCUMENTATION CHECKLIST

__ clinical status on admission
__ significant changes in clinical status
__ pertinent laboratory and diagnostic test findings
__ physical therapy program and activity tolerance
__ medication administration
__ nutritional intake
__ fluid intake and output
__ bowel and bladder function
__ patient/family teaching
__ discharge planning

ASSOCIATED CARE PLANS

Grief/Grieving
Ineffective Family Coping
Ineffective Individual Coping

Myasthenia Gravis

COLLABORATIVE PROBLEM: *Muscle weakness related to reduced number of acetylcholine receptors*
Interventions
1. Administer anticholinesterase medications, as ordered.
2. Keep an emergency airway and suctioning and ventilation equipment nearby. Monitor arterial blood gas levels, as ordered.
3. Keep atropine nearby.
4. Periodically assess muscle strength.
5. Keep a daily fatigue and muscle strength log.
6. Contact the doctor if the patient states that more or less medication is needed.
7. Administer succinylcholine and pancuronium, as ordered, with caution.
8. Observe for muscle weakness after aminoglycoside antibiotics or antiarrhythmic medications are administered.
9. Additional individualized interventions: _____
_____
_____

COLLABORATIVE PROBLEM: *Potential aspiration related to impaired swallowing*
Interventions
1. Plan mealtimes to coincide with peak anticholinesterase effects.
2. Ask the patient to evaluate his or her swallowing ability, and order foods of appropriate consistency.
3. Provide rest periods during meals.
4. Keep suctioning equipment at the patient's bedside.
5. Teach the patient and family what to do if choking or aspiration occurs.
6. Additional individualized interventions: _____
_____
_____

NURSING DIAGNOSIS: *Activity intolerance related to muscle fatigue*
Interventions
1. Identify sources of excess energy consumption.
2. Space bathing, grooming, and other activities throughout the day.
3. Rearrange the environment to keep frequently used items close by.
4. Plan a rest period before each meal.
5. Additional individualized interventions: _____
_____
_____

NURSING DIAGNOSIS: *Ineffective airway clearance related to decreased inspiratory force and increased secretion production*
Interventions
1. Demonstrate the cascade cough.
2. Encourage the patient not to suppress coughs.
3. Perform chest physiotherapy and suction as needed.
4. Additional individualized interventions: _____
_____
_____

NURSING DIAGNOSIS: *Ineffective breathing pattern related to muscle fatigue*
Interventions
1. Monitor and document respiratory rate and pattern every 2 hours.
2. Measure vital capacity, tidal volume, and inspiratory force both before and 1 hour after anticholinesterase medication is administered.
3. Additional individualized interventions: _____
_____
_____

NURSING DIAGNOSIS: *Impaired verbal communication related to fatigue of facial and respiratory muscles*
Interventions
1. Minimize frequency and length of patient verbalization.
2. Provide alternate communication methods.
3. Additional individualized interventions: _____
_____
_____

NURSING DIAGNOSIS: *Nutritional deficit related to decreased oral intake*
Interventions
1. Perform a nutritional assessment on admission.
2. Provide a balanced diet.
3. Serve the main meal in the morning.
4. Provide liquids in a cup.
5. Have the patient sit erect during meals.
6. Record all food and nutritional supplements consumed. Evaluate calorie, protein, vitamin, and mineral intake.
7. Consult a dietitian.
8. Additional individualized interventions: _____

_____

NURSING DIAGNOSIS: *Knowledge deficit related to required life-style adjustments*
Interventions
1. Teach the patient and family about the disease process and its implications.
2. Instruct about factors that may precipitate a crisis.
3. Teach the patient and family signs and symptoms of a myasthenic crisis.
4. Teach about medications.
5. Demonstrate how to keep a medication response log.
6. Provide information about how to obtain a medical alert device.
7. Teach ways to cope with decreased activity tolerance.
8. Provide the address of the Myasthenia Gravis Foundation.
9. Additional individualized interventions: _____

_____

PATIENT/FAMILY DISCHARGE TEACHING CHECKLIST
__ nature of disease and implications
__ signs and symptoms of myasthenic and cholinergic crises
__ activity recommendations and limitations
__ airway clearance procedures
__ all discharge medications' purpose, dosage, administration schedule, and side effects requiring medical attention (usual discharge medications include anticholinesterases)
__ community resource and support groups
__ how and where to obtain an emergency identification device
__ emergency medical system access
__ date, time, and location of follow-up appointment
__ how to contact doctor

DOCUMENTATION CHECKLIST
__ clinical status on admission
__ significant changes in status
__ pertinent laboratory and diagnostic test findings
__ responses to medications
__ periods of fatigue or increased weakness
__ swallowing ability

__ respiratory parameters before and after medication administration
__ activity tolerance
__ patient/family teaching
__ discharge planning

ASSOCIATED CARE PLANS
Grief/Grieving
Ineffective Family Coping
Ineffective Individual Coping
Knowledge Deficit
Total Parenteral Nutrition

Prostatectomy

COLLABORATIVE PROBLEM: *Potential hypovolemia related to prostatic or incisional bleeding postoperatively*
Interventions
1. Monitor and document the amount of blood lost from incisional dressings and the urinary drainage system hourly for the first 12 to 24 hours postoperatively, then every 4 hours.
2. Evaluate and document pulse rate, blood pressure, respirations, skin color, and level of consciousness every 4 hours for 24 hours or until stable, then every 8 hours or according to unit protocol.
3. Monitor hemoglobin, hematocrit, platelet, and coagulation values daily. Compare them with preoperative values. Alert the surgeon about abnormal values. Administer blood transfusions as ordered. Consult with the surgeon about applying traction to the catheter or preparing the patient for surgery if bleeding persists.
4. Teach the patient to avoid straining for bowel elimination. Avoid using rectal thermometers or tubes or giving enemas.
5. Administer and document stool softeners and laxatives, as ordered.
6. Teach the patient to avoid lifting heavy objects postoperatively for 6 to 8 weeks.
7. Additional individualized interventions: _____

_____

NURSING DIAGNOSIS: *Potential postoperative infection related to preoperative status, urinary catheter, or drainage placement*
Interventions
1. Monitor and record vital signs, as ordered, typically every 4 hours for 24 hours or until stable, then every 8 hours.
2. Monitor the surgical incision site daily for induration.
3. Monitor drains and catheters for patency, and irrigate as ordered.
4. Provide and document meticulous urinary catheter care at least once daily.
5. Administer I.V. fluids as ordered. Beginning on the first postoperative day, encourage oral fluid intake of 2

to 3 liters daily to maintain urinary output of at least 1,500 ml daily. Record intake and output.

6. Encourage ambulation the day after surgery.

7. Administer and document prophylactic antibiotics, as ordered.

8. Additional individualized interventions: _____

_____

_____

NURSING DIAGNOSIS: *Pain related to urethral stricture, catheter obstruction, bladder spasms, and/or surgical intervention*

Interventions

1. See the "Pain" care plan, page 64.

2. Observe for signs of bladder spasms.

3. Check and irrigate the urinary catheter and tubing for kinks, blood clots, or mucous plugs, as needed.

4. Assess for incisional pain.

5. For severe or persistent pain, administer analgesics or antispasmodics at the onset of pain. Document the medication administration and outcome.

6. Provide alternative pain-relief measures, and teach them to the patient.

7. Additional individualized interventions: _____

_____

_____

NURSING DIAGNOSIS: *Potential urinary retention related to urinary catheter obstruction*

Interventions

1. Monitor and record continuous bladder irrigation, if ordered.

2. If the patient is not on continuous irrigation, irrigate the urinary catheter as needed and ordered.

3. Monitor and document intake and output.

4. Record the patient's weight daily.

5. Observe for suprapubic distention and discomfort every 4 hours while the patient is awake.

6. Additional individualized interventions: _____

_____

_____

NURSING DIAGNOSIS: *Urge incontinence related to urinary catheter removal, trauma to the bladder neck, and/or decrease in detrusor muscle tone, sphincter tone, or both*

Interventions

1. Preoperatively, teach the patient buttock and perineal exercises.

2. Monitor and document the patient's urinary pattern after catheter removal.

3. If a suprapubic catheter is present, measure residual volume after each voiding.

4. Obtain a urine sample with each voiding during the first 24 to 48 hours after catheter removal.

5. Provide absorbent incontinence pads. Keep the perineal area clean and dry.

6. Additional individualized interventions: _____

_____

NURSING DIAGNOSIS: *Potential altered sexuality patterns: decreased libido related to fear of incontinence and decreased self-esteem; infertility related to retrograde ejaculation (from transurethral resection of the prostate or suprapubic prostatectomy); and/or impotence related to parasympathetic nerve damage (from radical prostatectomy)*

Interventions

1. Teach the patient preoperatively, reinforcing postoperatively, the expected effects of prostatectomy with regard to impotence and ejaculation. Include the patient's spouse (or partner) in the discussion.

2. Encourage the patient and spouse (or partner) to verbalize feelings of loss, grief, anxiety, and fear.

3. Encourage discussion between the patient and spouse (or partner) about feelings and expectations in the sexual relationship.

4. Provide information about a penile prosthesis, if appropriate.

5. Provide information and referrals for sexual counseling, as needed, postoperatively.

6. Additional individualized interventions: _____

_____

_____

NURSING DIAGNOSIS: *Disturbed self-concept: self-esteem related to incontinence, potential impotence, and/or sexual alterations*

Interventions

1. Encourage the patient to verbalize feelings about postoperative changes in body functioning and the meaning these changes will have for the patient's life-style.

2. Assist the patient in identifying and using effective coping behaviors.

3. Encourage the patient to continue perineal and buttock exercises to decrease incontinence.

4. Compliment the patient on personal appearance. Instruct the patient's spouse (or partner) and family to provide compliments and positive feedback also.

5. Encourage the patient to participate in activities of daily living and in decisions affecting patient care.

6. Additional individualized interventions: _____

_____

_____

PATIENT/FAMILY DISCHARGE TEACHING CHECKLIST

__ surgical outcome and disease process

__ all discharge medications' purpose, dosage, administration schedule, and side effects requiring medical attention (usual discharge medications include analgesics; antispasmotics, if a urinary catheter is present; and antibiotics)

__ urinary catheter care techniques and supplies

__ signs and symptoms indicating obstruction, bleeding, or infection

__ supplies to manage incontinence

__ exercises to regain urinary control

__ common postoperative feelings

__ appropriate activity level to prevent muscle straining

___ resumption of sexual activity and knowledge of community resources for sexual counseling

___ community and interagency referral

___ need to consult with an oncology specialist (if the diagnosis of cancer is confirmed)

___ availability of cancer support groups

___ date, time, and location of follow-up appointment

___ how to contact doctor

DOCUMENTATION CHECKLIST
___ clinical status on admission

___ significant changes in status

___ pertinent laboratory and diagnostic test findings

___ episodes of hemorrhage

___ transfusion with blood products

___ infection and treatment

___ fluid intake and output

___ urinary obstruction episodes

___ urinary retention

___ urinary incontinence

___ patient/family teaching

___ discharge planning

___ community and interagency referral

ASSOCIATED CARE PLANS
Grief/Grieving
Ineffective Family Coping
Ineffective Individual Coping
Pain
Surgical Intervention
Thrombophlebitis

Surgical Intervention

NURSING DIAGNOSIS: *Knowledge deficit: perioperative routines related to lack of familiarity with hospital procedures*
Interventions
1. See the "Knowledge Deficit" care plan, page 56.
2. Instruct the patient in perioperative routines.
3. Additional individualized interventions: _____

_____

_____

COLLABORATIVE PROBLEM: *Potential shock related to hemorrhage or hypovolemia*
Interventions
1. Monitor and document vital signs on admission to the nursing unit and every 4 hours. Increase the frequency of monitoring as needed. Report abnormalities.
2. Assess the surgical dressing. Record the date and time of any drainage.
3. Assess the amount and character of drainage from wound drainage tubes.
4. Reinforce the surgical dressing as needed.
5. Assess the surgical area for swelling or hematoma.
6. Monitor for changes in mental status.
7. Assess and maintain I.V. patency. Maintain I.V. fluids at the ordered rate.

8. Monitor urine output every hour for 4 hours, then every 4 hours during the immediate postoperative period. Maintain output at >60 ml/hour.
9. Monitor hematocrit and hemoglobin levels, as ordered.
10. Monitor fluid intake and output.
11. Additional individualized interventions: _____

_____

_____

NURSING DIAGNOSIS: *Pain related to surgical tissue trauma and reflex muscle spasm*
Interventions
1. See the "Pain" care plan, page 64.
2. Additional individualized interventions: _____

_____

_____

COLLABORATIVE PROBLEM: *Potential postoperative atelectasis related to immobility and ciliary depression from anesthesia*
Interventions
1. Assess vital signs every 4 hours. Note the characteristics of respirations.
2. Auscultate breath sounds every 4 hours on the first postoperative day, then once per shift.
3. Instruct and coach the patient in diaphragmatic breathing.
4. Assist the patient in using an incentive spirometer.
5. Turn the patient every 2 hours unless contraindicated.
6. Assist the patient to increase ambulation progressively.
7. Encourage adequate fluid intake.
8. Additional individualized interventions: _____

_____

_____

COLLABORATIVE PROBLEM: *Potential postoperative thromboembolic phenomena related to immobility, dehydration, and possible fat particle escape or aggregation*
Interventions
1. Instruct and coach the patient to perform leg exercises hourly.
2. Assess twice daily for signs of thrombophlebitis, pulmonary thromboembolism, and fat embolism. If present, alert the doctor promptly.
3. Encourage early ambulation postoperatively.
4. Avoid using the knee gatch or placing pillows under the patient's knees.
5. Encourage adequate fluid intake.
6. Apply antiembolism stockings, if ordered.
7. Additional individualized interventions: _____

_____

_____

NURSING DIAGNOSIS: *Potential for postoperative injury related to possible changes in mental status due to anesthesia and analgesia*
Interventions
1. Assess the patient's level of consciousness, orientation and ability to follow directions every ½ to 1 hour during the first 8 to 10 hours postoperatively.

2. Position the patient in a side-lying position when drowsy.
3. Keep the bed side rails up until the patient is awake and alert.
4. Keep the call cord within the patient's reach.
5. Keep the bed in the low position.
6. Monitor postural vital signs and assist with initial postoperative activity.
7. Additional individualized interventions: _____
_____

NURSING DIAGNOSIS: *Postoperative impairment of skin integrity related to surgical intervention*
Interventions
1. Assess the surgical wound once per shift for evidence of normal healing or healing problems.
2. Monitor temperature every 4 hours.
3. Maintain a clean, dry incision.
4. Perform wound care, as ordered, using aseptic technique.
5. Instruct the patient and family in recognizing signs and symptoms of infection.
6. Encourage adequate nutritional intake every shift.
7. Additional individualized interventions: _____
_____

NURSING DIAGNOSIS: *Potential postoperative urinary retention related to neuroendocrine response to stress, anesthesia, and recumbent position*
Interventions
1. Assess for signs of urinary retention.
2. Initiate interventions to promote voiding as soon as the patient begins to sense bladder pressure.
3. Provide noninvasive measures to promote voiding.
4. Provide a nonthreatening, supportive atmosphere.
5. Catheterize the patient, if ordered, in response to a complaint of bladder discomfort or an inability to void within 8 hours after surgery.
6. Drain <1,000 ml from the bladder at a time if the patient is catheterized.
7. After catheterization, assess for dysuria, burning, frequency and urgency of urination, and suprapubic discomfort.
8. Additional individualized interventions: _____
_____

COLLABORATIVE PROBLEM: *Potential postoperative paralytic ileus, abdominal pain, or constipation related to immobility, anesthesia, and analgesia*
Interventions
1. Assess the abdomen twice daily.
2. If paralytic ileus occurs, implement treatment, as ordered, and comfort measures.
3. Provide a diet appropriate to peristaltic activity. Ensure that peristalsis has returned before progressing from restricting food and fluids to providing liberal amounts of fluids and solid food.

4. Encourage fluid intake of at least 2 liters/day, unless contraindicated.
5. Encourage frequent position changes and ambulation, as tolerated.
6. Provide privacy during defecation.
7. Consult the doctor concerning the use of laxatives, suppositories, or enemas.
8. Additional individualized interventions: _____
_____

NURSING DIAGNOSIS: *Altered comfort: nausea or vomiting related to GI distention, rapid position changes, and/or cortical stimulation of the vomiting center or chemoreceptor trigger zone*
Interventions
1. Prevent GI overdistention.
2. Limit unpleasant sights, smells, and psychic stimuli.
3. Caution the patient to change position slowly.
4. As soon as possible, advance the patient from narcotics to other analgesics (as ordered) to nonpharmacologic pain-control measures.
5. Administer antiemetics, as ordered.
6. Additional individualized interventions: _____
_____

PATIENT/FAMILY DISCHARGE TEACHING CHECKLIST
___ plan for resuming normal activity
___ wound care
___ signs and symptoms of wound infection or other surgical complications
___ all discharge medications' purpose, dosage, administration, and side effects requiring medical attention (postoperative patients may be discharged with oral analgesics)
___ when and how to contact doctor
___ date, time, and location of follow-up appointment with surgeon
___ community resources appropriate for the surgical intervention performed

DOCUMENTATION CHECKLIST
Preoperatively
___ clinical status on admission
___ significant changes in preoperative status
___ preoperative teaching and its effectiveness
___ preoperative checklist (includes documentation regarding the operative consent, urinalysis, complete blood count, 12-lead EKG, chest X-ray, surgical skin preparation, voiding on call from operating room, and removal of nail polish, jewelry, dentures, glasses, hearing aids, and prostheses)

Postoperatively
___ clinical status on admission from recovery room
___ significant changes in clinical status
___ dressing and wound assessment

___ amount and character of wound drainage (on dressing and through drains)
___ patency of tubes (I.V., nasogastric, Foley, drains)
___ pulmonary hygiene measures
___ pain-relief measures
___ activity tolerance
___ nutritional intake
___ elimination status (urinary and bowel)
___ pertinent laboratory test findings
___ patient/family teaching
___ discharge planning

ASSOCIATED CARE PLANS
Fluid and Electrolyte Imbalances
Grief/Grieving
Ineffective Individual Coping
Knowledge Deficit
Pain

Total Joint Replacement in the Lower Extremity

COLLABORATIVE PROBLEM: *Potential postoperative complications (hypovolemic shock, neurovascular damage, and/or thromboembolic phenomena) related to surgical trauma, bleeding, edema, improper positioning, and/or immobility*
Interventions
Hypovolemic shock
1. See the "Surgical Intervention" care plan, page 71.
2. Maintain patency of the wound drainage device. Monitor the amount of bleeding.
3. Additional individualized interventions: _____

_____

Neurovascular damage
1. Perform neurovascular checks postoperatively every hour for the first 4 hours, then every 2 hours for the next 12 hours, and then every 4 hours until the patient is ambulatory.
2. Alert the doctor immediately if signs of impaired neurovascular function occur.
3. Maintain positioning recommendations.
4. Apply ice packs to the affected joint for 24 to 48 hours postoperatively.
5. Maintain patency of the drainage device as noted.
6. Additional individualized interventions: _____

_____

Thromboembolic phenomena
1. Provide instruction and supervision concerning exercises to prevent thromboembolism.
2. Monitor for signs of thromboembolism. See the "Surgical Intervention" and "Thrombophlebitis" care plans, pages 71 and 229, respectively.

3. Apply antiembolism stockings to both legs (to the affected extremity only after the dressing is removed).
4. Monitor for signs of fat embolism daily.
5. Administer anticoagulants and monitor clotting studies, as ordered.
6. Additional individualized interventions: _____

_____

NURSING DIAGNOSIS: *Impaired physical mobility related to hip or knee surgery*
Interventions
1. Instruct the patient in the correct postoperative positioning of the affected extremity.
2. Instruct the patient in proper postoperative use of a walking device.
3. Ensure that the patient maintains bed rest for 24 to 72 hours postoperatively, as ordered, placing the affected extremity in a neutral position.
4. Observe for dislocation of a hip prosthesis.
5. Supervise the patient in altering position every 2 hours.
6. Implement a planned, progressive ambulation schedule, as ordered.
7. Ensure that unaffected joints are put through full range-of-motion (ROM) exercises three or four times a day.
8. Assist the patient in maintaining preferred routines for rest and sleep.
9. Collaborate with the health care team to design an appropriate rehabilitation plan.
10. Identify, with the patient, specific methods for implementing the plan.
11. Additional individualized interventions: _____

_____

NURSING DIAGNOSIS: *Impaired skin integrity related to surgical intervention*
Interventions
1. Maintain patency and cleanliness of the drainage device.
2. Do not administer injections in the affected extremity.
3. Assess daily for signs of infection.
4. Additional individualized interventions: _____

_____

PATIENT/FAMILY DISCHARGE TEACHING CHECKLIST
___ implications of joint replacement
___ rationale for continued use of antiembolism stockings
___ all discharge medications' purpose, dosage, administration schedule, and side effects requiring medical attention (usual discharge medications include analgesics, antibiotics, anti-inflammatories, and anticoagulants)
___ need for laboratory and medical follow-up if discharged on warfarin
___ schedule for progressive ambulation and weight bearing
___ additional activity restrictions
___ signs and symptoms of infection, bleeding, and dislocation

__ use of self-help devices, such as raised toilet seat
__ appropriate resources for posthospitalization care
__ diet to promote healing
__ wound care
__ date, time, and location of follow-up appointments
__ how to contact doctor

DOCUMENTATION CHECKLIST
__ clinical status on admission
__ significant changes in status
__ preoperative and postoperative teaching
__ position of affected extremity
__ exercises and ROM achieved
__ neurovascular checks
__ calf pain
__ Hemovac drainage
__ progressive ambulation
__ pain-relief measures
__ patient/family teaching
__ discharge planning and referrals
__ presence or absence of disabling fatigue
__ nutritional intake

ASSOCIATED CARE PLANS
Ineffective Individual Coping
Knowledge Deficit
Pain
Surgical Intervention
Thrombophlebitis

Total Parenteral Nutrition

NURSING DIAGNOSIS: *Potential for injury related to complications of total parenteral nutrition (TPN) catheter insertion, displacement, use, or removal*
Interventions
1. Observe for signs and symptoms of respiratory distress or shock during insertion of the central venous catheter (CVC).
2. Maintain the patient in the Trendelenburg position during CVC insertion.
3. Assess for bilateral breath sounds in all lung fields after CVC insertion, and obtain a chest X-ray.
4. Do not begin administering the TPN solution until the position of the catheter tip is confirmed by chest X-ray.
5. Use standardized Luer-Lok connections if attached properly, or tape the connections securely.
6. Before opening the I.V. system to the air, instruct the patient to hold his or her breath and to bear down (the Valsalva's maneuver). If the patient is unable to perform the Valsalva's maneuver, change the tubing only during exhalation.
7. Observe for signs and symptoms of large air emboli. If suspected, position the patient in the Trendelenburg position on the left side, administer oxygen, and notify the doctor immediately.

8. During dressing changes, observe for:
• a suture at the insertion site of a temporary CVC
• a suture at the exit site of a permanent CVC
• increased external catheter length.
9. Observe for inability to withdraw blood, the patient's complaint of chest pain or burning, leaking fluid, and swelling around the insertion site, shoulder, clavicle, or upper extremity.
10. Observe for development of visible collateral circulation on the chest wall.
11. When the catheter is being removed, be sure that
• the patient is supine
• the patient performs Valsalva's maneuver before the catheter is removed
• a completely sealed, airtight dressing is applied over the insertion site after the CVC is discontinued.
12. When the catheter is discontinued, measure its length and observe for jagged edges.
13. Additional individualized interventions: _____

_____

NURSING DIAGNOSIS: *Nutritional deficit related to inability to ingest nutrients orally, inability to digest nutrients optimally, and/or increased metabolic need for nutrients*
Interventions
1. Keep TPN at a constant rate of infusion with an infusion pump.
• Check the bag, flow rate, and patient every half hour.
• Do not interrupt the flow of TPN solution.
• Do not "catch up" if the I.V. is behind or ahead of schedule. Set the I.V. infusion to the ordered rate.
• When discontinuing TPN, decrease the rate to 50 ml/hour for 3 to 4 hours.
2. For sudden stoppage from a clotted catheter or from cardiopulmonary arrest:
• clotted catheter: Hang dextrose 10% in water in another I.V. site to infuse at the same rate the TPN solution was infusing.
• cardiopulmonary arrest: Stop the TPN infusion and provide a bolus of dextrose 50% during cardiopulmonary resuscitation, as ordered.
3. Monitor urine glucose and acetone levels every 6 hours.
4. Monitor serum glucose levels, as ordered.
5. Observe for signs and symptoms of hypoglycemia, hyperglycemia, hyperosmolar overload, electrolyte imbalances, vitamin deficiencies, or trace mineral deficiencies.
6. Infuse I.V. fat emulsion, as ordered, via one of three infusion methods:
• through a separate I.V. line by itself
• connected into the TPN line through a Y-connector added between the TPN catheter and the I.V. tubing
• infused as a 3-in-1 solution.
7. To prevent precipitate formation, ensure that TPN is mixed in a 3-in-1 solution in a ratio of calcium, ≤ 15 mEq/liter; phosphorus, ≤ 30 mEq/liter; and magnesium, ≤ 10 mEq/liter.

8. Evaluate the 3-in-1 solution for correct volume as infused by the infusion pump.

9. Observe for fat separation in the 3-in-1 solution as indicated by a yellow ring around the edges of the solution. Stop TPN if this occurs, and replace the solution bag with a fresh one.

10. Culture the 3-in-1 solution if the patient develops sepsis.

11. Administer a separate fat infusion slowly over the first 15 to 20 minutes (1 ml/minute for a 10% fat infusion or 0.5 ml/minute for a 20% fat infusion). Observe for adverse reactions; if none occur, increase the rate as ordered.

12. If fat emulsion is to be infused in a second I.V. line, infuse it over 4 to 8 hours.

13. Do not use I.V. filters with fat emulsion infusions.

14. Encourage walking or mild exercise to promote nitrogen retention.

15. Weigh the patient at the same time, with the same amount of clothing, and on the same scale daily.

16. When oral intake resumes, initiate a daily count of calories and fat intake.

17. Observe for changes in muscle strength and energy level.

18. Additional individualized interventions: _____

_____

_____

NURSING DIAGNOSIS: *Potential fluid volume excess or deficit related to fluid retention, altered oral intake, or osmotic diuresis*
Interventions

1. See the "Fluid and Electrolyte Imbalances" care plan, page 21.

2. Observe for signs of fluid overload.

3. Observe for signs of fluid deficit.

4. Assess breath sounds every shift.

5. Record intake and output each shift.

6. Weigh the patient daily.

7. Additional individualized interventions: _____

_____

_____

NURSING DIAGNOSIS: *Knowledge deficit related to lack of previous experience with TPN*
Interventions

1. Briefly explain the purpose and method of TPN therapy, including:

• a definition of TPN therapy and the reason for TPN, using terms the patient can understand

• a description of the role of the nutrition support service staff

• a description of the TPN solution

• the procedure for administering TPN solution, including the patient's responsibilities.

2. If the patient is to be discharged on home TPN, collaborate with the nutritional support team to provide appropriate teaching, including complications.

3. See the "Knowledge Deficit" care plan, page 56.

4. Additional individualized interventions: _____

_____

NURSING DIAGNOSIS: *Potential infection related to invasive CVC, leukopenia, or damp dressing*
Interventions

1. Change the catheter dressing, using sterile technique, according to hospital protocol. Apply a completely sealed dressing.

2. Observe the dressing every 8 hours and change it any time it is unsealed or damp.

3. Observe the insertion or exit site every 8 hours for signs of infection. Report any redness, swelling, pain, or purulent drainage.

4. Follow hospital protocol for tubing changes and antibacterial preparation at all connections before changing I.V. tubing.

5. Follow pharmacy or nutrition support services recommendations for I.V. filters.

6. Infuse only TPN solution through the TPN catheter. Do not use the TPN line for injecting medications or withdrawing blood samples.

7. Use only solutions prepared in the pharmacy under a laminar flow hood.

8. Return cloudy or precipitated solution to the pharmacy.

9. Allow each bag or bottle to hang a maximum of 24 hours.

10. Monitor for signs of infection.

11. Additional individualized interventions: _____

_____

_____

PATIENT/FAMILY DISCHARGE TEACHING CHECKLIST

(if the patient is being discharged on home TPN)
___ prevention of home TPN complications
___ actions to take if complications occur
___ where and how to obtain supplies
___ catheter site care
___ procedure for TPN administration
___ community resources
___ date, time, and location of follow-up appointment
___ how to contact doctor

DOCUMENTATION CHECKLIST

___ nutritional status on admission
___ any significant changes in status
___ CVC insertion, including difficulties or complications; length of catheter; position and any change in position: signs of infection, thrombosis, emboli or other postinsertion complication
___ dressing and tubing changes
___ for each bag or bottle of TPN solution and fat emulsion: date, time, name of nurse hanging solution; all ingredients in each bag or bottle; and the rate of infusion
___ patient/family teaching
___ discharge planning

ASSOCIATED CARE PLANS

Fluid and Electrolyte Imbalances
Knowledge Deficit

Appendix

NANDA Nursing Diagnoses Grouped According to Functional Health Patterns·

Health perception–health management pattern
Airway clearance, ineffective
Breathing pattern, ineffective
Gas exchange, impaired

Cardiac output, altered: decreased†
Tissue perfusion, altered†: renal, cerebral,
  cardiopulmonary, gastrointestinal, peripheral

Tissue integrity, impaired†
Skin integrity, impaired

Injury, potential for: poisoning, suffocation, trauma
Infection, potential for

Adjustment, impaired
Growth and development, altered
Health maintenance, altered
Noncompliance (specify)

Nutritional-metabolic pattern
Fluid volume deficit
Fluid volume excess

Body temperature, altered: potential
Hypothermia
Hyperthermia
Thermoregulation, ineffective

Oral mucous membrane, alteration in
Nutrition, altered: less than body requirements
Nutrition, altered: more than body requirements
Swallowing, impaired

Elimination pattern
Bowel elimination, altered: constipation
Bowel elimination, altered: diarrhea
Bowel elimination, altered: incontinence

Incontinence, functional
Incontinence, reflex
Incontinence, stress
Incontinence, urge
Incontinence, total
Urinary elimination, altered patterns
Urinary retention

Activity-exercise pattern
Activity intolerance
Diversional activity deficit
Home maintenance management, impaired

Mobility, impaired physical
Self-care deficit: feeding, bathing/hygiene,
  dressing/grooming, toileting

Sleep-rest pattern
Sleep pattern disturbance

Cognitive-perceptual pattern
Comfort, altered: chronic pain
Comfort, altered: pain

Knowledge deficit (specify)
Thought processes, altered

Sensory-perceptual alterations: visual,
  auditory, kinesthetic, gustatory, tactile, olfactory
Unilateral neglect

Self-perception–self-concept pattern
Hopelessness
Powerlessness
Self-concept, disturbance in: body image
Self-concept, disturbance in: self-esteem
Self-concept, disturbance in: personal identity

Role-relationship pattern
Communication, impaired verbal
Family processes, alteration in
Parenting, altered
Social interaction, impaired
Social isolation
Violence, potential for
Role performance, altered

Sexuality-reproductive pattern
Sexuality, altered patterns
Sexual dysfunction
Rape-trauma syndrome

Coping–stress tolerance pattern
Coping, ineffective individual
Coping, ineffective family: compromised
Coping, ineffective family: disabling
Coping, family: potential for growth
Anxiety
Fear
Grieving, anticipatory
Grieving, dysfunctional
Post-trauma response

Value-belief pattern
Spiritual distress

·The functional health patterns are from Gordon, M. *Nursing Diagnosis:
  Process and Application,* 2nd ed. New York: McGraw-Hill Book Co.,
  1987. The nursing diagnoses are modified from McLane, A.
  *Classification of Nursing Diagnoses: Proceedings of the Seventh
  Conference.* St. Louis: C.V. Mosby Co., 1987.

†The author believes that these diagnoses represent renaming of
  commonly accepted medical terms and recommends that they not be
  used for nursing diagnoses guiding independent nursing care.
  Interdependent nursing care related to these problems is included in
  the list of collaborative problems and labeled with the already familiar
  terms (shock, ischemia, and so forth).

Index

i refers to an illustration; t to a table

i refers to an illustration; t to a table

i refers to an illustration; t to a table

i refers to an illustration; t to a table